The Impact of Our Past

Inquiry and Study Aids
Gerald Hardcastle
Consultants

Dr. John W. Blassingame
Department of History
Yale University

Gerald Hardcastle
Department of Social Studies
Nathan Hale High School, Seattle, Washington

Peter P. Carlin
Acting Supervisor of Social Studies
Cleveland Public Schools

Arthur H. Rumpf
Curriculum Specialist, Secondary Social Studies
Milwaukee Public Schools

The Impact of Our Past

A History of the United States

Bernard A. Weisberger

American Heritage Publishing Co., Inc. New York

Webster Division, McGraw-Hill Book Company
St. Louis, New York, San Francisco, Dallas

Copyright © 1972
by American Heritage Publishing Co., Inc.,
a Subsidiary of McGraw-Hill
All rights reserved.
Reproduction in whole or in part without
permission is prohibited.
Copyright acknowledgments on page 797.
ISBN 07-069052-9

Staff for this book:
John Terry Chase, Creator and Editor
Karen Bowen and Jerome B. Wilke, Art Directors
Rita S. Longabucco, Picture Editor
Ann Moffat, Associate Editor
Madeline M. Marzano, Copy Editor
Francis X. Giordano, Production Supervisor
Maps by Francis & Shaw, Inc.
Drawings by Ronald Bowen

Dr. Bernard A. Weisberger received his PhD in history from the University of Chicago. He has taught at Wayne State, the Universities of Chicago and Rochester, and as a visiting lecturer at Columbia and Stanford. He has been Program Chairman of the American Historical Association, and a holder of fellowships from the American Council of Learned Societies and the Social Science Research Council. His many books include *They Gathered at the River* and *The New Industrial Society*. Dr. Weisberger has also written popular and juvenile histories, and is an Associate Editor of *American Heritage*.

COVER: OKLAHOMA HISTORICAL SOCIETY
At noon on September 16, 1893, some 100,000 "boomers" rushed across the starting line to grab a portion of the recently opened Oklahoma Territory.

TITLE PAGE: PORT OF NEW YORK AUTHORITY
New York City as seen in the 1960's from Brooklyn, across the East River.

Gerald Hardcastle is a graduate of the University of Texas and holds an MA degree in education from Harvard. Since 1956 he has taught history at the junior and senior high school levels in the Seattle Public Schools. In 1963 he was President of the Puget Sound Council for the Social Studies.

CONTENTS

INTRODUCTION
Is America in Crisis? 8

UNIT I
Peopling the Americas

TIMELINE 20

INTERPRETING THE PAST:
Viewpoints on American Civilization 22
1. Early Indian Societies in the Americas 26
2. The Coming of the Europeans 52
3. Slavery Comes to the Americas 78
4. Colonial America 104
ISSUES PAST AND PRESENT:
Is Cultural Conflict Inevitable? 128

UNIT II
The Birth of a Nation

TIMELINE 136

INTERPRETING THE PAST:
The Meaning of the American Revolution 138
5. The Road to Revolution 142
6. Winning the War for Independence 168
7. Forming a Government 192
8. First Steps of the New Nation 218
ISSUES PAST AND PRESENT:
What Are the Limits of Free Speech? 242

UNIT III
The United States Expands to the Pacific

TIMELINE 250

INTERPRETING THE PAST:
The Frontier and the Making of America 252
9. The Pioneer Spirit 256
10. Westward to the Pacific 282
11. The Beginnings of Industrial America 306
ISSUES PAST AND PRESENT:
Is American Expansion a Force for Progress? 330

UNIT IV
A Nation Divided

TIMELINE 338

INTERPRETING THE PAST:
The Causes of the Civil War 340
12. The Coming of the Civil War 344
13. The Civil War 370
14. Reconstruction and the Negro After the Civil War 396
ISSUES PAST AND PRESENT:
Integration or Separation? 422

UNIT V
The United States Becomes an Industrial Giant

TIMELINE	430
INTERPRETING THE PAST:	
Industrialization	432
15. The Making of an Industrial Environment	436
16. A Nation of Cities	464
17. An Age of Reform	488
ISSUES PAST AND PRESENT:	
What Is the Responsibility of the Government for the Welfare of Its Citizens?	512

UNIT VI
The United States Becomes a World Power

TIMELINE	520
INTERPRETING THE PAST:	
The Argument over Empire	522
18. The United States in the Pacific	526
19. The United States and Latin America	550
20. World War I	574
ISSUES PAST AND PRESENT:	
What Should Be America's Role in the World?	598

UNIT VII
The Twenties and Thirties

TIMELINE	606
INTERPRETING THE PAST:	
The Twenties	608
21. The Golden and Not-So-Golden Twenties	612
22. The Great Depression Tests American Democracy	636
23. Between Two World Wars	660
ISSUES PAST AND PRESENT:	
Should Americans Follow the Past?	684

UNIT VIII
A Changing Society in a Changing World

TIMELINE	692
INTERPRETING THE PAST:	
The Significance of Technology	694
24. World War II	698
25. An Age of Challenge and Change	724
26. An Uncertain World	750
ISSUES PAST AND PRESENT:	
How Should We Handle Our Environment?	772

Appendix

The Declaration of Independence	778
The Constitution of the United States	780
The United States Today	794
Presidents and Presidential Administrations	796
Acknowledgments	797
Glossary	798
Index	803

Maps and Graphs

Migration of Indians to the Americas	28
Portugal Sails to the Orient	59
Columbus Discovers a New World	61
New Spain in 1750	65
The Search for a Northwest Passage	66
Early Exploration of North America	74
The Heritage of Africa	81
Colonial America in 1750	104
The Triangular Trade	108
North American Colonies 1689–1763	144
Northeast Campaigns 1775–1778	179
Western Campaign 1778–1779	182
Southern Campaigns 1778–1781	185
The United States in 1783	188
The Northwest Territory	195
Exploring the Louisiana Territory	235
The United States in 1819	238
Trails Across the Alleghenies	262
Southern Agriculture 1850	271
The Exploration of the West 1820–1844	277
Trails to the Pacific 1850	278
The Mexican War 1846–1848	292
The United States in 1853	296
Routes to California	300
Railroads 1860	314
Railroads, Canals, Roads 1850	315
The Missouri Compromise 1820	358
The Compromise of 1850	358
A Nation Divided 1861	367
The Opening Years 1861–1863	372
The Turning Point 1863–1864	387
The South Surrounded 1864–1865	391
The Reconstruction of the South	404
Development of Underground Resources 1860–1910	443
Transcontinental Railroads	445
The Coming of the Indian Reservations 1850–1890	448
Western Cattle Trails	455
Immigration 1860–1935	467
The United States in the Pacific 1784–1917	527
The United States and Latin America 1824–1917	551
World War I	583
Registration of Passenger Cars 1910–1970	617
Income Distribution 1929	640
Tennessee Valley Authority	652
United States Foreign Trade 1910–1970	665
World War II in Europe	711
World War II in the Pacific	716
Distribution of Negro Population	736
Negro Voter Registration in the South	736
The Consumption of Natural Resources 1970	743
Fish Killed by Pollution 1965–1969	743
Income Distribution of Families 1968	744
Europe 1970	752
Asia 1970	757
The United States Today	794
Presidential Administrations	796

BRUCE DAVIDSON, MAGNUM

DON CARL STEFFEN

Is America in Crisis?

The time was December of 1776. A few short months of war against the British had brought little but defeat and desertion. An American army of 20,000 men had been reduced to a few thousand tired, cold, and disheartened men. The glory of the cause which had seemed so worthwhile in July now seemed to be fading as fast as the American soldiers retreating across New Jersey. In how many days or weeks would the end come?

At this low point in the fortunes of the Continental Army, Tom Paine, a one-time London corsetmaker, now a political writer, took pen in hand and wrote, "These are the times that try men's souls. . . ." The title of Paine's stirring pamphlet was *The Crisis*. Today no one doubts that in December of 1776 the United States faced a terrible crisis. It was fighting for its life. Paine's words helped rally Americans to a new sense of purpose, or, as one modern historian has written, *The Crisis* gave Americans "a definition of the issues at stake."

Today, some two hundred years after Paine wrote *The Crisis*, there is much talk of a new crisis in American life. Historians worry about it. Politicians talk about it. The magazines devote much space to it. Television does special programs on it. Students demonstrate about it. People everywhere are concerned.

Their sense, or interpretation, of the crisis varies widely. Some say, "No, America is not in crisis." Others say, "The United States is on the road to disaster." Like Tom Paine, they all try to define the issues at stake. To do so, both pictures and words are used. On the following pages are some of those pictures and words. They do not attempt to give just one answer to the question, "Is America in Crisis?" That will be your job.

Study carefully the pictures and words on the following pages. What do they say about the question? What issues seem to be at stake? When you have finished this introduction, you should be able to give your opinion about whether or not the United States is in crisis. You will also be asked to go one step further: You will be asked for your reasons why America is or is not in crisis. Your answer will be based on a very limited amount of evidence, that is, the pictures and statements in the following ten pages. It will also, of course, be based on what you already know and feel. By the time you have finished all of this book, your answer may well be changed. In fact, it probably will be. By then you will have studied about not only the events that make up American history, but also about some of the questions which have troubled Americans in the past as well as in the present. You may then wish to reread this introduction and once again answer the question it asks to see if your ideas have changed.

Neither white nor Negro Americans have been willing to face, or even to admit, the truth about race relations in the United States. But the truth must be faced—now, while there is still time. It is never too soon for a nation to save itself; it can be too late. For a hundred years, white Americans have clung stubbornly to the false dream that if everyone would just sit still—if "agitators" would just stop agitating—time alone would solve the problem of race. It hasn't, and it never will. For time, as Reverend Martin Luther King, Jr., points out, is neither good nor bad; it is neutral. What matters is how time is used. Time has been used badly in the United States— so badly that not much of it remains before race hatred completely poisons the air we breathe.

"The Negro problem" is no longer hidden on the plantations of the Mississippi Delta nor in the sleepy towns of "the old South." On the contrary, the most serious social problem facing America today is to be found in the heart of the big cities that are the nation's ornaments: New York, Philadelphia, Washington, Chicago, Detroit, Milwaukee, San Francisco, Los Angeles—and in a score of smaller cities like New Haven, Newark, Gary, San Diego. For there is not a city of any importance in the United States that does not now have a large and rapidly growing "Negro problem."

Charles E. Silberman: *Crisis in Black and White*, 1964

We in the United States in the 1960's have reached a new stage in mankind's concern about poverty over the centuries. In this country, for the first time in human history anywhere, massive poverty has now become intolerable because it is no longer *unavoidable*.

All of us must become familiar with the gigantic size of the poverty problem. We have heard too much talk about "pockets" of poverty. The more than 34 million people now living in poverty in the United States are "some pocket."

Nor should we continue to excuse neglect in dealing with poverty on the ground that much of it has been "hidden." It is only a walk of a block or two from some of the most luxurious apartments in New York, our greatest city, to some of the most filthy slums and ghettos.

And with poverty neither "pocketed" nor "hidden," the war against poverty cannot be a limited war. It cannot be isolated from the problem of high unemployment among fully grown people as well as teen-agers, men as well as women, whites as well as Negroes, the skilled as well as the unskilled.

Leon H. Keyserling: *Progress or Poverty*, 1964

DECLAN HAUN, BLACK STAR

BURK UZZLE, MAGNUM

What happens to a dream deferred?

Does it dry up
like a raisin in the sun?
Or fester like a sore—
And then run?
Does it stink like rotten meat?
Or crust and sugar over—
Like a syrupy sweet?
Maybe it just sags
like a heavy load.
Or does it explode?

Langston Hughes

We sputter against The Polluted Environment as if it was invented in the age of the automobile. We compare our smoggy air not with the odors of horse dung and the plague of flies and the smells of garbage and human waste which filled cities in the past, but with the honeysuckle perfumes of some nonexistent City Beautiful. We forget that even if the water in many cities today is not as spring-pure nor as agreeable as we would like, for most of history the water of the cities and of the countryside was undrinkable.

Unless we begin to believe that we won't be dead before morning, we may not be up to the daily tasks of a healthy life.

Daniel J. Boorstin: *A Case of Hypochondria*, 1970

CHARLES HARBUTT, MAGNUM

I will build a motor car so low in price that no man will be unable to own one — and enjoy with his family the blessing of hours of pleasure in God's great open spaces.

Henry Ford: Quoted in *God's Own Junkyard,* by Peter Blake, 1964

BRUCE DAVIDSON, MAGNUM

BURK UZZLE, MAGNUM

In common with most Americans, I recoil from the spreading sight of ruined rivers, foul air, bulldozed suburbs, and neglected cities.

I believe the world faces a crisis of survival which must be fought by the best efforts of men everywhere. In the United States it affects farmers and city dwellers, black men and white men, managers and workers, the well-off and the poor.

By the end of the 1960's, it was recognized that our cities were becoming unlivable, that we were choking on our own wastes, that man himself was an endangered species.

Stewart Udall: *Civilized World Plunging into Computerized Madness,* 1970

The control—and the eventual end—of nuclear armaments is the most urgent of all the problems that face the statesmen of the world. And almost equally urgent is the task of international cooperation to use the limitless possibilities of nuclear energy for the well-being of mankind: for transportation and industrial production, for desalting the seas and harnessing the tides, for the exploration of outer space, and for a hundred other good purposes. For the first time in history, we have the means to create a world that is free of war and free of want.

Henry S. Commager: *Contemporary Civilization*, 1964

LISL STEINER

UPI

The human race today is like a rocket on a launching pad. We have been building up to this moment of takeoff for a long time, and if we can get safely through the takeoff period, we may fly on a new and exciting course for a long time to come. But at this moment, as the powerful new engines are fired, their thrust and roar shakes and stresses every part of the ship and may cause the whole thing to blow up before we can steer it on its way. Our problem today is to harness and direct these tremendous new forces through this dangerous period to the new world instead of to destruction. But unless we can do this, the rapidly increasing strains and crises of the next ten years may kill us all.

John Platt: *What We Must Do*, 1969

Student discontent is widespread—even worldwide—and is now reaching down into secondary schools. Ordinary people, especially young people, are deciding that they are no longer willing to put up with rules and conditions which make life narrower and less satisfying than it could be. In short, they are more concerned with the quality of life, and their relations with people, than with social position and possessions.

Henry Ford II: *The Human Environment and Business*, 1970

If I had a hammer,
I'd hammer in the morning,
I'd hammer in the evening,
All over this land;
I'd hammer out danger,
I'd hammer out a warning,
I'd hammer out love between
All of my brothers,
All over this land.

Lee Hays
Pete Seeger

I am fed up with hippies, Yippies, militants, and nonsense.
Since when have children ruled this country? By virtue of what right or what accomplishment should thousands of teen-agers, wet behind the ears and utterly without the benefit of having lived long enough to have either judgment or wisdom, become the wise men of our time?

Every generation makes mistakes, always has and always will. We have made our share. But my generation has made America the wealthiest country on earth. It has tackled, head-on, a racial problem which no nation on earth in the history of mankind had dared to do. It has declared war on poverty and it has gone to the moon. It has desegregated schools and abolished polio. It has begun what is probably the greatest social and economic revolution in man's history. It has *begun* these things, not finished them.

K. Ross Toole: *An Angry Man Talks Up to Youth*, 1970

BERNIE BOSTON, WASHINGTON *Evening Star*

What was the dream of those who came to America? It was change, rebirth, the eternal desire of men to be born again, the yearning for the second chance. The New World was the second chance. That is what happened in the great flow of people to America. A rebirth occurred, and no place in the world, not Europe itself, has ever been the same. The migration was revolution. Its coat of arms bore and still bears only one word—Freedom. Just freedom, the condition in which a man feels like a human being, like himself. It is "The Dream."

There are those who say the dream is dead or dying. They tell us that America is now only another crowded nation, not even able to keep order.

This is not a "sick society." It is a deeply unsettled and bewildered society, and the reason is not merely the great changes in this last 25 years or so, but the speed of these changes. It is the rate of change that is new. The new problems have piled up more rapidly than our brains and our institutions can cope with. The modern industrial-scientific revolution has jammed us together, polluted much of our air and waters, smeared ugliness over much of our countryside, and increased the tensions of daily living.

But it is absurd to believe that the races of men who turned an empty, forbidding continent into the most efficient engine of production and distribution ever seen, who created the first *mass* democracy with essential order and essential freedom will not solve the problems of crowding, poverty, pollution, and ugliness. Americans are the most natural workers—together in the world. The solutions to our problems will create new problems, after which there will be new solutions, then new problems, and so our life will go on.

We Americans are perfectionists, which simply means that we were not, are not, and never will be satisfied either with the quantities or the qualities in our life.

The kindness and generosity of the American people are still here, and the will for justice is as strong as ever. One day recently, I asked a man who had fled Cuba and had come to this country why most Cubans like himself wanted to come to the United States rather than go to South American countries with the same language and the same general way of life. Was it just the thought of greater economic opportunity?

"No," he said, "many of us would have an easier time, economically, in another country. It's just that we feel better here. We can feel like a human being. There seems to be something universal about this country."

This is from a man who knows the meaning of America in his bones and marrow. Of course, the dream lives on.

Eric Sevareid: *The American Dream*, 1968

ANSEL ADAMS, MAGNUM

When Thomas Paine wrote *The Crisis* some two hundred years ago, news about the War for Independence traveled by messengers on horseback or by letters and newspapers carried on ships or horse-drawn mail coaches. From different sources people got a variety of information—facts, rumors, and opinions. With this information they discussed and debated the meaning of the news, much as we do today. Although there were no marvels of electronic communication such as television or radio, the impact of the news, that is, its force and effect on people's minds and actions, was no less real than today. Did some of the words or pictures in this section make an impact on your thinking? Why?

Now answer the question we began with: Is America in crisis? List the reasons for your answer. Did all of your classmates arrive at the same answer? Why?

Information that helps to prove the truth of an answer is known as *evidence*. What different kinds of evidence were given to you on these twelve pages? Was there enough evidence to arrive at an answer? Did your opinion change? Why? Even if you had more evidence, and even if all of your classmates studied the same evidence, it is still possible that not all of those in your class would answer the question the same way. Some questions have more than one answer. Our senses of taste, sight, touch, smell, and hearing do not always receive information in the same way. Also, our store of experiences and knowledge from the past differ. In short, because we are human, we *interpret* (determine the meaning of) events differently.

In each of the eight units which follow, words, pictures, maps, charts, and graphs will be used to tell you about the discovery and settling of our country, the growth of our government, our conflicts amongst ourselves and with other countries, the inventions of medicine, machines, and weapons, our use and misuse of our soil, trees, minerals, rivers, and lakes, our growth as a world power. In short, you will study those events which have made an impact on the lives of those who lived in the past as well as in the present.

The impact of our past is with us all the time. Only by understanding it can we decide how we might answer some of our nation's most important problems: how to use our resources more wisely, how to balance our desire for personal freedom with our need for law and order, how to best use our country's immense power to bring peace to mankind. Each of the eight units of this book is designed so that you can use your growing knowledge about the impact of our past to decide how to handle the problems as well as the promise of the present and the future.

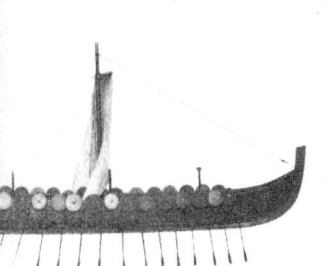
1000 Leif Ericson Lands at Vinland

1324 Kingdom of Mali Flourishes

1418 Prince Henry Opens Academy at Sagres

1519 Cortés Invades Mexico

1099 Jerusalem Captured in First Crusade

1488 Dias Rounds Cape of Good Hope

1492 Columbus Discovers America

UNIT 1
Peopling the Americas

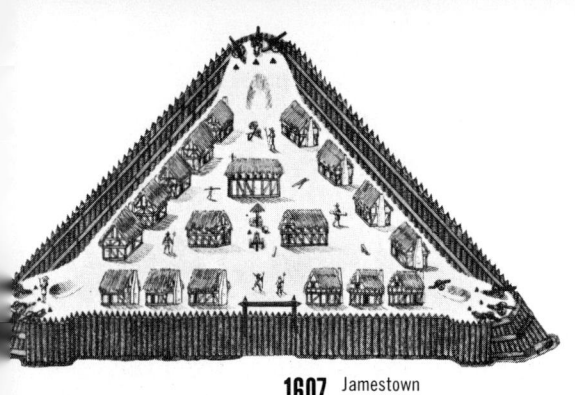

1607 Jamestown Founded

1619 First Negroes Land at Jamestown

1664 English Capture New Amsterdam

1541 De Soto Explores the Mississippi

1613 Tobacco First Sent to England from Virginia

1619 First Meeting of Virginia Burgesses

1723 Benjamin Franklin Arrives in Philadelphia

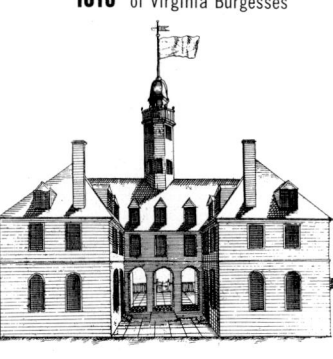

American history is the story of the coming together of many different peoples—sometimes in harmony and sometimes in bloodshed. When Columbus planted Spain's flag on an island in the Caribbean, there were already some 20 million people living in the Americas. These migrants from Asia, whom Columbus incorrectly called Indians, had developed many remarkable societies which we shall study in Chapter 1.

The news Columbus and other early European explorers brought back to Europe began a second period of migration, this time by white Europeans who came in search of riches, freedom, and opportunity and by Africans forcibly brought in chains. Chapter 2 concentrates on the European part of the story, and Chapter 3 on the African. Chapter 4 describes the colonial society that white and black Americans had built along the east coast of North America by around 1750.

The way Americans have viewed their past has been greatly influenced by whichever of these three groups—Indian, African, or European—they are descended from. Thus this unit begins by exploring some of these different "Viewpoints on American Civilization." At the conclusion of the unit there is another special inquiry section called "Is Cultural Conflict Inevitable?" In this final section you will be asked to relate past and present by thinking about how the different peoples of the Americas got along in the past and how they can live in peace and brotherhood today.

TOP, LEFT TO RIGHT:
SMITHSONIAN INSTITUTION
BIBLIOTHEQUE NATIONALE
BIBLIOTHEQUE NATIONALE
VATICAN LIBRARY
A. H. ROBINS COMPANY
STEDMAN, *Narrative*, VOL. II, 1796
COLLECTION OF EDWARD ARNOLD
BOTTOM LEFT TO RIGHT:
UNIVERSITATSBIBLIOTHEK, HEIDELBERG
Journal of Christopher Columbus, 1496
METROPOLITAN MUSEUM OF ART
WISCONSIN STATE HISTORICAL SOCIETY
NEW YORK PUBLIC LIBRARY
COLONIAL WILLIAMSBURG
INSURANCE COMPANY OF NORTH AMERICA

INTERPRETING THE PAST

Viewpoints on American Civilization

On July 4, 1976, the United States will have an important birthday—its 200th. Though many nations in the world are older than the United States, our country is no longer thought of as a "young" nation. It should not be surprising that as the 200th birthday approaches, more and more Americans will be "taking stock" and asking questions about our country's past, present, and future. But Americans have never waited for "important" birthdays to ask such questions. Almost from the very beginning of our history, different people have tried to explain, or interpret, the meaning of the "American experience"—the long record of exploration, settlement, and growth. Interpretations of our history are not made just to satisfy curiosity. They are made to serve as a guide to making decisions about the kind of future that Americans should have, just as you occasionally "interpret" your past (and present) before making important decisions.

Before reading in Unit I about the settlement of America by peoples from Asia, Europe, and Africa, we are going to examine three selections. Each of these is taken from the books of men who, at different periods in our history, have interpreted America's past. As you read each selection, consider these questions:

1. Why does each of the writers view America's history in a different way?
2. Would such different viewpoints tend to help or hurt the United States?

A Churchman's View

When Josiah Strong wrote Our Country, *he was Secretary of the Home Missionary Society of the Congregational Church. He was expressing his own views and not necessarily those of his Church. The Society tried to spread the Christian religion among Americans who were not members of a church. The book was translated into many foreign languages and sold over 170,000 copies, making it something of a best seller in its day.*

JOSIAH STRONG: *OUR COUNTRY*, 1885

It is not necessary to argue to those for whom I write that the two great needs of mankind are first, a pure, spiritual Christianity, and second, freedom. Without doubt, these are the forces which, in the past, have contributed most to the rise of the human race. The Anglo-Saxon, as the great representative of these two ideas, is instructed by God to be his brother's keeper. Add to this sign of God's favor the fact of

An "Anglo-Saxon" is a member of, or descendant from, the groups of people who settled the British Isles in the fifth and sixth centuries.

his rapidly increasing strength in modern times, and we have a demonstration of his destiny.

There can be no reasonable doubt that North America is to be the great home of the Anglo-Saxon and the center of his power, his life, and his influence. We Americans may reasonably expect to develop the highest type of Anglo-Saxon civilization. If there is yet to flower a higher civilization, where is the soil that is to produce it?

The Anglo-Saxon has what may be called a genius for colonizing. His unequaled energy and his personal independence made him a pioneer. He is better than all other peoples in pushing his way into new countries.

"Colonizing" means settling people from a mother country to another land.

In the United States everyone is free to become whatever he can make of himself; free to change himself into the nation's President. Wealth, position, and power are prizes offered for energy. Every farmer's boy, every apprentice and clerk, every friendless and penniless immigrant, is free to enter the contest. In Europe, ranks of society are, like the layers of the earth, fixed and fossilized. There can be no great change without a terrible upheaval, a social earthquake.

An "immigrant" is a person who has settled in a new country.

What is the meaning of such facts? It seems to me that God, with wisdom and skill, is training the Anglo-Saxon race for an hour sure to come in the world's future. Then this race of unequaled energy, with numbers and the might of wealth behind it—the representatives, let us hope, of the largest liberty, the purest Christianity, the highest civilization—will spread itself over the earth. This powerful race will move down upon Mexico, down upon Central and South America, out upon the islands of the sea, over upon Africa and beyond.

1. In 1885 what did Strong believe to be the special mission of Americans in the world? What proofs does he offer that Americans are especially qualified to carry out this mission?
2. According to the author, why had the United States become a powerful nation?
3. Would most Americans today agree with Strong's statements? Why?

Luther Standing Bear, a chief of a tribe of the Sioux Nation, was asked by his friends to write about the history of his people, the Lakotas.

An Indian Chief's View

CHIEF STANDING BEAR:
LAND OF THE SPOTTED EAGLE, 1933

True, the white man brought great change. But the varied fruits of his civilization, though highly colored and inviting,

To "maim" means to mutilate or disable. To "thwart" is to oppose, frustrate, or defeat.

are sickening and deadening. If the result of civilization is to maim, rob, and thwart, then what is progress?

I am going to dare to say that the man who sat on the ground in his tepee thinking about life and its meaning, accepting the kinship of all creatures, and acknowledging unity with the universe of things was pouring into his being the true essence [important characteristics] of civilization. True civilization means being able to rule oneself — not ruling others.

The "civilization" that has been forced upon me has not added one bit to my sense of justice, to my reverence for the rights of life, to my love for truth, honesty, and generosity. Above all, it has not changed my faith in Wakan Tanka — God of the Lakotas. For, after all the great religions have been preached or have been written in books, man — all man — is still faced with the Great Mystery.

So, if today I had a young mind to direct, and I was faced with the duty of choosing between the natural way of my forefathers and that of the white man's present way of civilization, I would immediately set that child's feet in the path of my forefathers. I would raise him to be an Indian!

1. Why does the Chief believe that the white man's idea of progress and civilization is not a good one?
2. Why does the author believe that Indians should be raised as Indians and not as white men?
3. Do many American Indians today agree with Chief Standing Bear's views? Why?

A Black Editor's View

Chuck Stone has been editor of three Negro newspapers: The New York Age, The Washington Afro-American, and the Chicago Defender. He has also served as public information director and vice-chairman of the National Conference on Black Power.

CHUCK STONE:
BLACK POLITICAL POWER IN AMERICA, 1968

The history of the United States is a history of white people, written by white people for white people. Only the accomplishments of white politicians, white statesmen, and white captains of industry have been recorded. If, by chance, some bold black man miraculously crashed through the made-in-America color barriers or even dared to help turn the tide of history, he has been but briefly mentioned among thousands of pages, all hailing the glories that were white.

With the exception of the ten glorious years of Black

Reconstruction, 1867-1877, when black state legislators and public officials laid the foundations for much of today's social legislation, black politicians have been given no prominent place in the making of American politics. American history, written by white historians, has ignored black politicians and black businessmen. Books and stories about "great Negroes" or "famous Negroes" have always described the lives of singers, dancers, professional athletes, ministers, social workers, educators, and "Negro leaders"—never the first Negro U.S. Senator, Congressman, state Supreme Court Justice, distinguished public official, or diplomat.

Whatever key role black politicians and public officials have played in helping to shape American history has been hidden by the lack of recognition by both blacks and whites. It has also been hidden by the lily-white history books in schools and colleges which banished the Negro's importance in American civilization to a bitter, brief period of slavery.

1. According to Stone, which Negroes have been given the most attention in American history books?
2. Why does the author believe that the deeds of black politicians have been left out of American history books?

Perhaps you remember a time when you heard descriptions of an event by two witnesses, but the descriptions were so different that it was hard to believe that the two people had been watching the same event. Sometimes history is like that. One writer emphasizes the contributions of people from one nation or one race and seems to forget the contributions of others. And writers often disagree or are unsure about the meaning of a word, such as *civilized*. Studying history, then, can be a matter of learning to think about what *is not* written as well as what *is*. A writer cannot always tell the "whole story," even when he tries to do so. But sometimes what part of the story he tells, or doesn't tell, explains much about the writer.

For Consideration and Discussion

1. In what ways do the authors of these three selections disagree?
2. What might be some of the results of Americans holding such different viewpoints about the contributions of various races to American civilization?

Summary Questions

1
Early Indian Societies in the Americas

This land of ours, the United States, is made up of people who crowd the subways, airways, and highways, always on the move. Its history begins with human beings in motion, restlessly seeking food, warmth, safety, and a place to rear their young. All animals do that. But man alone, so far as we know, can dream of a better life, and he roams the globe looking for that, too. In the Americas hopeful people from all over the world have been meeting and mingling for thousands of years.

"Thousands of years" may sound like a mistake to you if you think that American history begins with Columbus discovering the New World in 1492. But the Indians who were here to greet him were the first people of "America," and they too were "immigrants."

Think for a moment of the earth as a spaceship voyaging endlessly through space. Many families of mankind live aboard, in "rooms" separated by green forests, wrinkled brown mountains, and blue oceans. If you were in another spaceship, looking through openings in the curtain of cloud, you would see earthlings moving about the icy chambers near the poles as well as the warm gardens at the equator. If you had a time machine that squeezed thousands of years into seconds, you would see streams of humanity migrating over the globe, like columns of ants.

More than 25,000 years ago, such a column began to move from Siberia, in Asia, across a land bridge to Alaska, then on southward. Glaciers still covered much of North America. Later, when the glaciers melted, the level of the ocean rose enough to cover this land bridge. These first migrations took many centuries to spread across North and South America. As they flowed southward, they left their bones, crude tools, weapons, and household utensils in various places, where the earth gradually covered them. Scientists have dug down and found some of this ancient litter. Using special instruments to determine its age, they know that men had reached southern South America about 8,000 years ago.

As you read, think about these questions:
1. Why do groups of people differ so much in the ways they make a living, govern themselves, dress, worship, and express themselves in art?
2. How do the natural surroundings in which a society lives affect the way each society makes a living, governs itself, dresses, worships, and expresses itself in art?
3. Why is art a part of the life of every society?

Portrait of a Cree chief named "Man Who Gives the War Whoop."

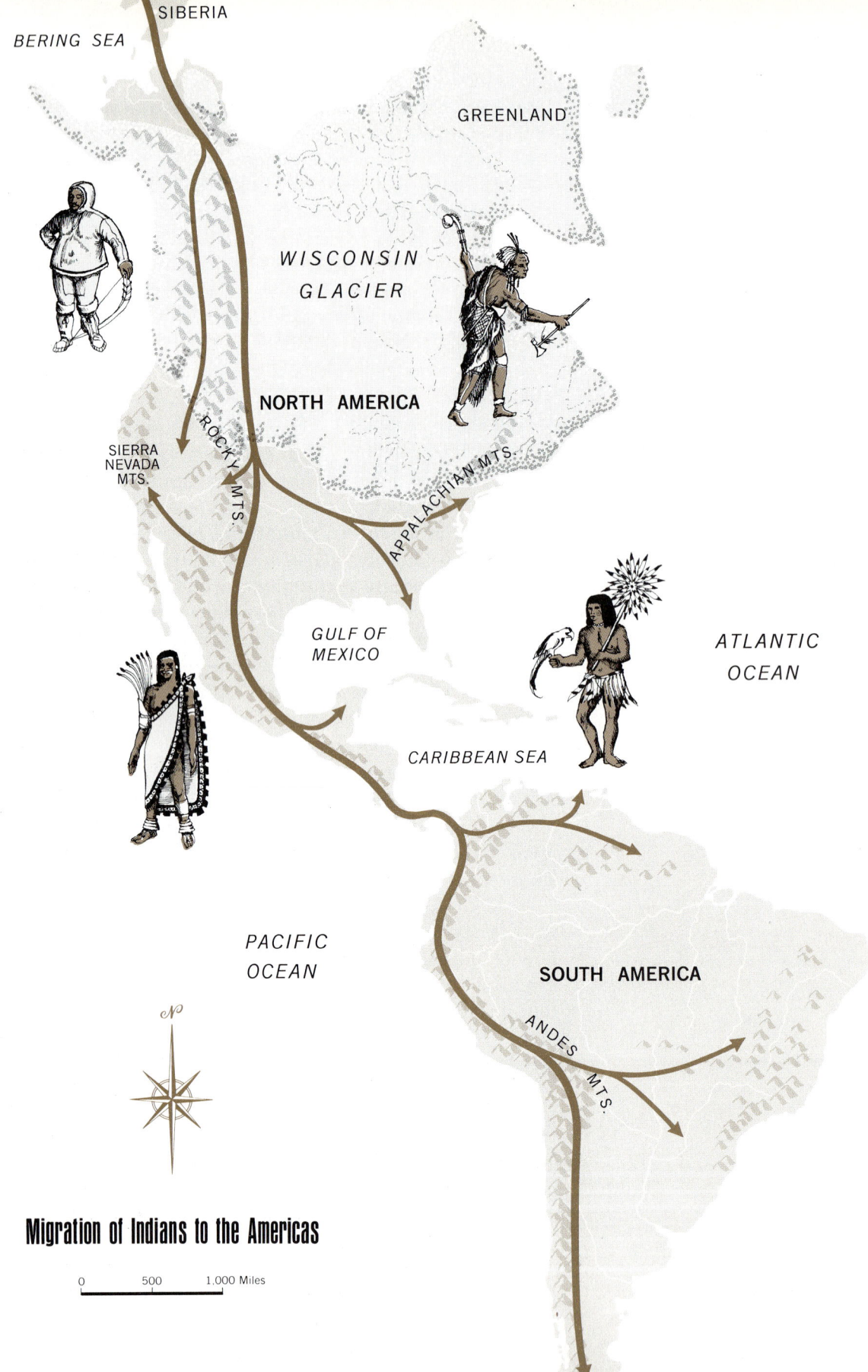

The Continents They Found

The map on the opposite page shows at a glance the migration of these first Americans, but the whole march probably took thousands of years. Compare that to the 200 years since the American Revolution or even the 500 years since Columbus, and you will see that those of us whose ancestors come from Europe or Africa are newcomers in the Western Hemisphere.

The Europeans called all the people whom they found in North and South America "Indians." They were not all alike any more than they lived in "the Indies," that is, East Indies, which Columbus thought he had found. By 1492 there were millions of Indians, divided into hundreds of **societies** (groups of people living together and bound by the same way of life). They were spread over two continents, occupying nearly half the land surface of the earth. Indians, as the map shows, differed as their physical surroundings differed. A fur-bundled Eskimo was called an "Indian." So was a Carib, naked except for a belt of feathers. So were an Iroquois in deerskin leggings in the American forest and an Aztec nobleman who lived in a city high in the mountains of Mexico.

The two continents of North and South America offered many contrasting **environments** (settings or surroundings). Towering mountains run down the entire length of the western parts of these continents. In North America there are great, almost treeless plains that cover the western half of a central plain between the Rockies in the west and the Appalachians in the east. The northeastern part of the continent, however, was once solid forest. Parts of both Americas, shut off from rain-bearing clouds by mountain walls, are deserts. By contrast, in large areas of South and Central America which lie in the low latitudes, jungle foliage multiplies under daily rains.

The many different kinds of natural settings in the Americas can be illustrated by matching some extremes. The Pacific Coast of Colombia, in South America, is one of the world's wettest places, with more than 100 inches of rain a year. Chile's Atacama Desert is one of the driest; rainfall there is barely measurable. The Andes Mountains of Chile harbor some of the world's highest towns more than three miles above sea level; our own Idaho has the deepest gorge, Hells Canyon, which cuts 7,900 feet into the earth. In the town of Churchill, in Canada, the temperature is below freezing six months of the year; in Maracaibo, Venezuela,

LIBRARY OF CONGRESS

AMERICAN MUSEUM OF NATURAL HISTORY

JOSLYN ART MUSEUM

30

the average daily temperature is 90 degrees in January and 94 degrees in August. Indian peoples of the Americas learned to survive in icebound lands and in climates that threatened to bake them. They had to develop tools and skills in order to feed themselves on high, dry plateaus where the air is thin, as well as in steep canyons cut off from the rest of the world.

Indians Created America's First Cultures

It is no wonder, then, that the Indians had so many different **cultures** (ways that members of a society behave). If people live on prairies and depend on the buffalo hunt for food, then the men of the tribe will be good marksmen, and little boys will be taught how to be swift and clever. But if they live in the hot desert (far left), growing corn and beans, then perhaps the greatest respect will go to priests who can bring necessary rain by prayer. The children may then learn that sacred dances are more important than skinning a carcass and be praised for making a good hoe or water pot. Among these first Americans there were many, many different ways of making a living, playing, worshiping, raising families, establishing common rules—and, sad to say, fighting with their neighbors.

But however great the differences among Indians of mountain, desert, and jungle, there were some important likenesses. All Indians, it seems, recognized that they were part of the world of nature. Whether the animals they saw around them were seals or sea gulls or alligators or jaguars, they believed that beasts and men were meant to share the earth. True, they hunted animals for food, as animals hunted each other. They used the skins and bones of animals for their own clothes and dwellings. They cut trees and plants from the earth or dug holes in it to plant crops. But they thought of animals as brothers and the earth as a mother. One Indian, in modern times, said that he would never use a plow because doing so was like plunging a knife into his mother's body!

Indians believed that animals had great powers. Birds, for example, could soar into the skies, where the gods made thunder and lightning. Perhaps they even spoke with the gods. That may be why the mouthpiece of the sacred pipe held by the Cree chief on page 26 is carved in the shape of a bird's head.

Indians were equally impressed by fish, which could live beneath water, unlike men, and by the power of

Indians lived in widely varying climates. Above: South American Indians paddle a canoe down the Amazon River past a steaming jungle. Below: Mandan Indians, aided by sled-pulling dogs, cross the frozen Missouri. Left: Southwest Indians file past giant cacti that flourish in the sun-baked desert.

In 1788 a British officer painted these Algonquins near Quebec, Canada.

NATIONAL GALLERY OF CANADA, OTTAWA

beasts like bears or mountain lions. This is not surprising. We still speak of men as being as sly as a fox, wise as a serpent, fierce as a lion. Indians sometimes thought that by wearing the skins or other parts of such animals or by painting their pictures on houses, robes, or shields they could acquire these qualities.

All Indian cultures shared this belief that men, spirits, and animals were related. This explains another custom common to all the known Indian cultures. They did not believe in the private ownership of land. The sun, air, water, plants, and beasts were made by the gods, or were themselves spirits, so no one person could own them. In the 1800's an American Indian once had a horse which escaped into a white man's pasture. The white man complained to the Indian that the animal had eaten "his" grass. The Indian's reply was, "Did you make the grass grow?"

A tribe or nation might fight another for a hunting ground or a fertile valley. But it was the tribe, not the individual, that made the claim. Moreover, the tribe did not own the land but only used it with the permission of the spirits who ruled the world.

As we shall see, when Europeans first came to America, they believed that most such Indian ideas were "barbarous" and all Indians "savages." But nothing could be further from the truth. Some Indian societies were far from primitive and had highly developed **civilizations**. A civilization arises when a community has gotten beyond the simple battle to stay alive. At this stage of growth, more complicated governments and religions develop with impressive monuments to the civilization's way of life. These monuments take the form of works of art, public buildings and shrines, scientific and engineering feats like highways, and historical records.

Some of the Indian peoples called "savage" by Europeans after 1492 had created remarkable civilizations. They teach us much about how man masters his world.

Questions for Discussion

1. What makes a group of people a society?
2. In what major ways were the Indians of the Americas alike? different?
3. Why did the Indians feel so close to nature?
4. Why did the Indians believe in tribal rights to the land rather than private ownership of it?
5. How do culture and civilization differ?

Early Indian Civilizations of South America

When Peru was conquered by Spaniards in 1532, it was occupied by people who were called by the same name as their ruler, the Inca. Incan civilization had already made enormous strides in man's first task, that of developing an **economy** (the way of making a living). Most people were farmers, not hunters. They had learned to grow various foods which we still eat. These included white potatoes, sweet potatoes, beans, tomatoes, peanuts, and several kinds of corn. They had learned not only to preserve the seeds and plant them each growing season but to breed different varieties of the same plant. This was a tremendous step. A hunting tribe must follow the game animals as they rove for food. But farming people can stay in one place and build a civilization. If they move, they can take their food supply with them and build again.

The Economy and Government of the Incas

The Incas faced the problem of farming on steep Andean mountain slopes. They solved it by cutting terraces, or steps, into the hillsides, which they covered with soil patiently carried up narrow paths in baskets. They laid down grooved stones from which precious rainwater gurgled into irrigation ditches. They enriched the soil by mixing it with carefully collected *guano*, the droppings of birds and bats. With skillfully braided nets they took fish from the seas and lakes (right). Food was shared by all, and extra food was held in storehouses to supply the needy in times of famine.

Above: Incan nobles, using gold-tipped spades, break the earth in a spring planting ceremony. The laborers below, aided by sturdy llamas, bring the harvested grain to a government storage house.

The Incas also learned to breed and tame animals such as the llama, a sure-footed relative of the camel which they used as a pack animal to help them farm large tracts and to carry harvests from field to storehouse (lower left). They domesticated the alpaca, which furnished coarse wool for the common folk. They also hunted wild beasts called the *guanaco* for their meat and *vicuñas* which furnished especially fine wool for the garments of the rich.

Planting and harvesting were important ceremonial acts. Noblemen with golden hoes (upper left) often began the work, just as our governors and mayors sometimes turn the first shovelful of earth on the site of a new dam or tunnel. The Incan people were such fine farmers that a Spanish traveler wrote that whenever they settled a new spot of ground, soon "it caused great happiness to see it."

The Incan **political system** (the way of ruling)

Incan fishermen cast their nets and lines from balsa-log rafts.

The Incan masons above are building a wall. The women hoe a field. Below: Citizens carry the mummified remains of the Lord Inca.

also struck one of the conquering Spaniards with wonder. In 1532 the Incas controlled an **empire** (a large area that includes a number of different territories ruled by a single authority). The Spaniard admired the Incan skill in ruling an empire, "parts of which were rugged and covered with forests, parts mountainous, with snowy peaks and ridges, parts consisting of deserts of sand," and all of it lived in by people with "varying languages, laws, and religions." To hold the empire together peacefully, power in the political system was centered firmly in the Lord Inca.

The Lord Inca divided his empire into four parts. Each was ruled by a nobleman. Under him were other nobles, each responsible for a set number of commoners. The duties of the nobles included yearly visits to villages to make a careful count of their people, animals, and crops. The Lord Inca, therefore, knew quickly how many men he could count on for work in the fields (center left) and for war, and how much grain, gold, and other goods he might expect in tribute. Fine, wide, dry roads with high stone walls (upper left) ran through the empire. Soldiers could move quickly along them to keep order. So could llamas, trotting along with baskets full of tribute to support the government.

The Incan noblemen were men of great power and position. Their high rank was shown by their fine robes and their golden ear plugs, which were disks pushed through holes in the ear lobe. The Spaniards laughed at how the ornaments stretched the flesh, called the Incan noblemen *orejones* ("big ears"), and greedily eyed the gold. The *orejones* were privileged and petted, but they were expected to work hard as officials and soldiers.

Above them all was the Lord Inca himself. He was supposed to be the descendant of Inti, god of the blazing, life-giving sun. When he traveled, as pictured at right, proud noblemen willingly carried his litter. Just as a parasol shielded him from the sun, so his own magnificence was hidden from commoners by gold curtains embroidered with blazing serpents, moons, and other symbols. Only a favored few saw him face to face. His mummified body was preserved and, as the drawing at lower left shows, even the sun and moon gazed at it respectfully.

The Lord Inca's majesty was a tremendous force holding scattered people together. He was like a pope and an emperor combined. The cities where he kept his

Only nobles could carry the golden litter of the Lord Inca.

These gold pieces (right) are typical of Aztec craftsmanship. From left to right are an ear plug, an owl's head, a monkey-head pin, and a lip plug. The elaborate feather shield below once belonged to Montezuma, the ruler of the Aztecs when the Spaniards invaded.

AMERICAN MUSEUM OF NATURAL HISTORY

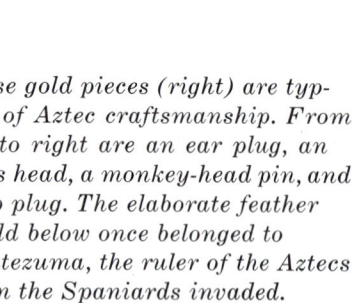

MUSEUM FUR VOLKERKUNDE, VIENNA

palaces and storehouses became centers of public affairs and business. So the Incan political system was one force helping to create an **urban** (city-centered) civilization.

The works of art created by a civilization tell us much about it. First of all, they reveal the state of its **technology** (the ability to apply knowledge to useful purposes). Can its people weave cloth? Can they make dyes? Can they refine metal and file and hammer it into shape? Can they mold and bake clay into pottery? Secondly, a society's art tells what it thinks is beautiful and what it values, or cares most about. Finally, because artists sometimes portray everyday scenes in their sculpture and drawings, they show us what daily life was like in their time. From them we can tell what was carried on a hunt, how women wore their hair, and what kinds of pets children had.

The Art of the Aztecs

The Aztecs were an Indian people who had dominated much of Mexico for nearly a century when the Europeans appeared. Their civilization was intricate and powerful. Their art shows that they could also lavish much care on simple objects and make them beautiful. They were able to dye their jars and their woven cotton garments with brilliant colors made from herbs, berries, and bark. Around the borders of their clothes and around their pottery ran clever designs of repeated lines, zigzags, and squares, just as other patterns repeat themselves in the scales of a fish or a field of grass or a forest of trees.

They were skillful at making small ceremonial objects like breast pins and ear plugs, in gold, in which they reproduced the likenesses of animals such as the owl, monkey, and snake at upper left.

Aztec artists also produced striking effects by weaving feathers into cloth. They thus took advantage of nature's own brilliant plumage. In the Aztec shield at left, decorated with feathers representing a coyote which is also a fire-god, we see this art at its liveliest. The animal itself seems to be made of dancing blue flame, while the feathered rim appears to make a ring of smoke. Artists created objects from wood to which bits of colored stone and shell were fastened.

Through such works of art Aztec craftsmen paid tribute to their heroes, their faith, their world. They all belonged to the artist and he belonged to them.

This turquoise-and-shell ornament represented one of the Aztec gods.

TRUSTEES OF THE BRITISH MUSEUM

PHOTO BY IRMGARD GROTH

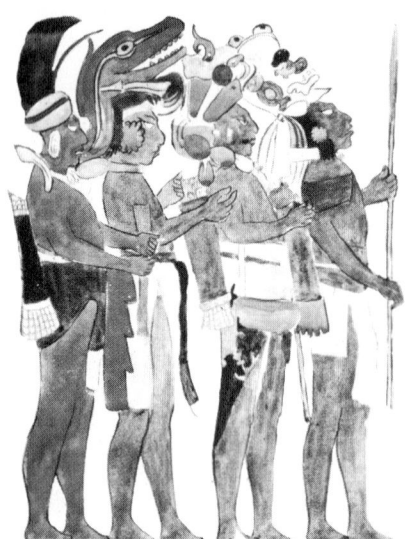

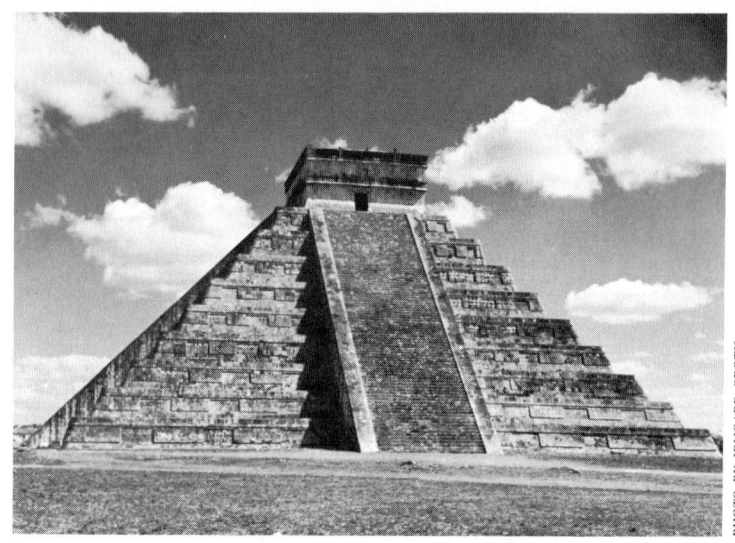

Above: The Mayan temple of Kukulkan in Mexico. At left and right are Mayan warriors. Below: Prisoners of war kneel in terror before priests and spectators in jaguar skins and animal headdresses as their blood is sacrificed to the gods.

PEABODY MUSEUM

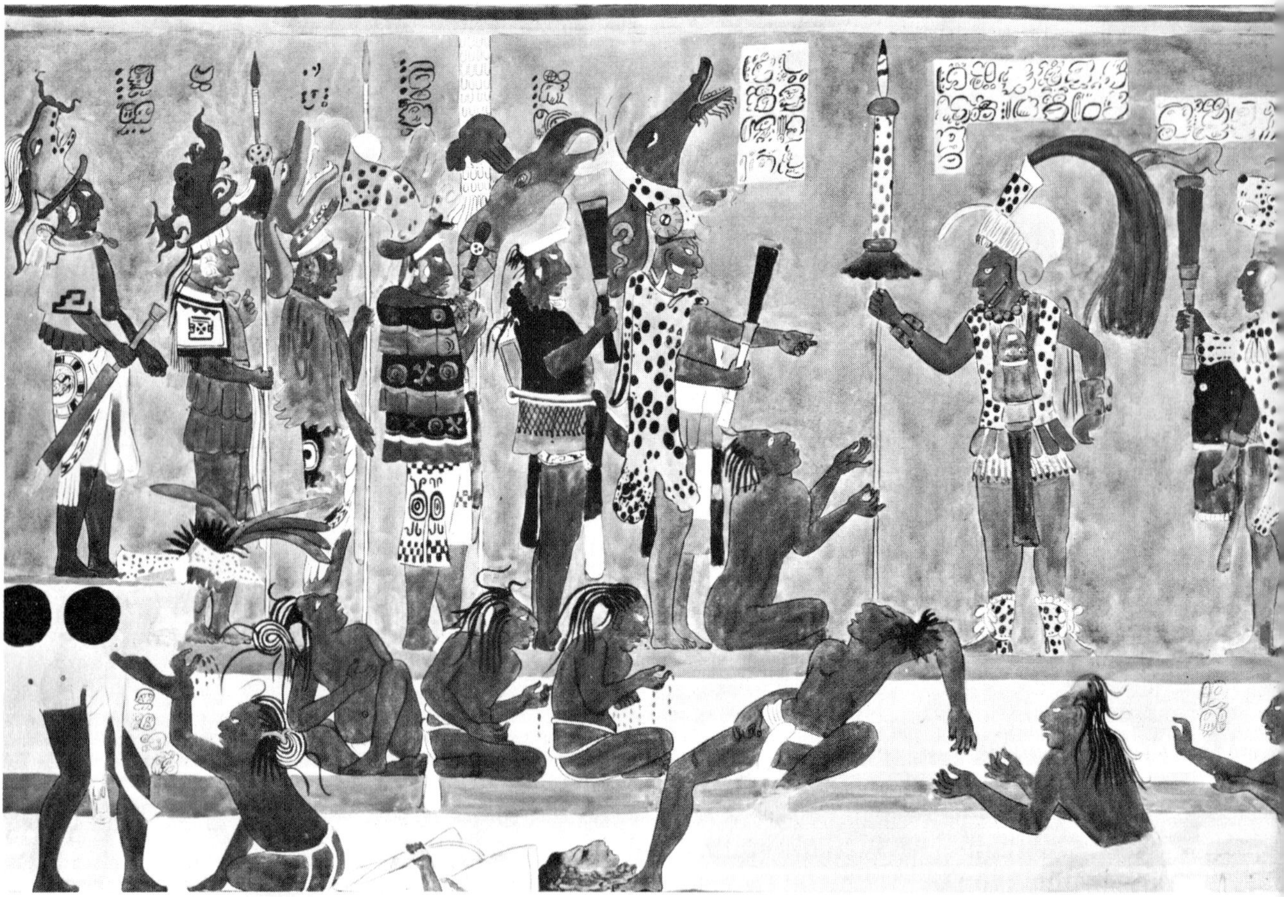

The Mayan Religion

The Mayas were an Indian people who lived in parts of present-day Guatemala, British Honduras, and Mexico. The great age of the Mayan civilization lasted about 600 years and ended around 900 A.D. When Europe was in the so-called Dark Ages, Mayan priests were studying astronomy, Mayan artists were carving fantastic designs in stone, and Mayan workmen were building pyramid-like temples (upper left). Atop these temples Mayan priests performed sacred rites before thousands of devoted followers.

Religion played as large a role in the daily lives of the Mayas as in any other known civilization. The gods, who were both good and bad, controlled life, death, storms, earthquakes, fire, and harvests. The chief Mayan crop was maize, and the plant itself was worshiped as a god. The god associated with the sun was supposed to have a good influence on medicine, books, and writing. The god of death was pictured as a fleshless figure surrounded by animals like an owl or a dog, each of which had an evil significance. In heaven no one worked and it was guaranteed that all good things would be plentiful forever. In Mitnal, the Mayan hell, there was no food, warmth, or end to suffering.

Only the priest-rulers knew the gods' needs, and they told the people what they must do to satisfy the gods. Priests ordered huge religious centers—some as large as a modern city—built in honor of the gods. Only the priests lived in the city, and peasants came, with awe in their hearts, to attend the rituals held there. If the priests forecast bad times, the Mayas cut themselves, collected the blood in bark saucers, and presented it to the gods. If the evil prophecy did not change, sometimes the priests called for a human sacrifice (lower left). During the great age of the Mayas, human sacrifice was not common. As the Mayas became more warlike, the practice increased and reached a peak at Chichen Itza, Mexico, around 1200.

Questions for Discussion

1. How did the Incas use nature to build a civilization?
2. By what means did Incan rulers govern?
3. What does a civilization's art tell us about its technology? its values? its daily life?
4. How was the Aztecs' relationship to nature reflected in ceremonial objects?
5. Why did the Mayas have blood sacrifices?

Indian Societies of North America

To the north of Mexico, no Indian people built a civilization as gorgeous as those of the Incas, Aztecs, or Mayas. Yet the tribes of the United States and Canada developed many remarkable abilities. One of them was to use what nature provided, thoroughly and without waste. When white men first came to live in the wilderness, they learned that they could survive only by imitating the Indians in making nature into a tool chest, medicine cabinet, grocery store, and clothes closet.

The Economy of North American Indians

Tribes differed in their basic ways of providing for themselves. Indians of the Southeast lived in villages (right) and planted their corn and squash in orderly rows (far right). Around the Great Lakes forest Indians hunted deer (far right, above) and small fur-bearing animals. On the Great Plains braves tracked the buffalo. In the Pacific Northwest plentiful supplies of salmon and other fish tempted Indians into their canoes and kept hunger away.

But everywhere there was the same use of natural materials. The bark of trees, stretched over poles, furnished housing for forest dwellers. Fishnets were made of twisted vines or bark strips. A canoe's ribs might be springy saplings; its skin was pieces of birch bark sewed together with strips of animal sinew; it was waterproofed with sticky tree-gum. Spear and arrow shafts were of wood. Points were of sharpened bone or stone. Deerskin furnished leggings and moccasins, which were decorated with porcupine quills or birds' feathers. Dishes were hollowed pieces of wood.

Indians of the treeless plains made remarkable use of the buffalo. Its meat nourished them. Its horns made tools and jewelry. Its hide, cut into strips, provided snowshoes and harness, and in larger pieces, tents and covering for shields. Its teeth made decorations and magic charms. Its shaggy coat provided caps, footwear, and robes. Even the buffalo's stomach was used to store water!

The Indian lived without the convenience of easily replaced manufactured goods. We can scarcely imagine his life in our age of synthetics and throwaway packages. He suffered hunger, cold, and disease in blizzards or droughts; yet so long as nature provided, he needed no outside help. As we shall see, when he came to depend on the white man's guns, blankets, and iron kettles, the Indians' way of life was in serious trouble.

DE BRY, *America*, 1590

This drawing was made about 1590 and shows an East Coast Indian roasting fish on a wooden grill.

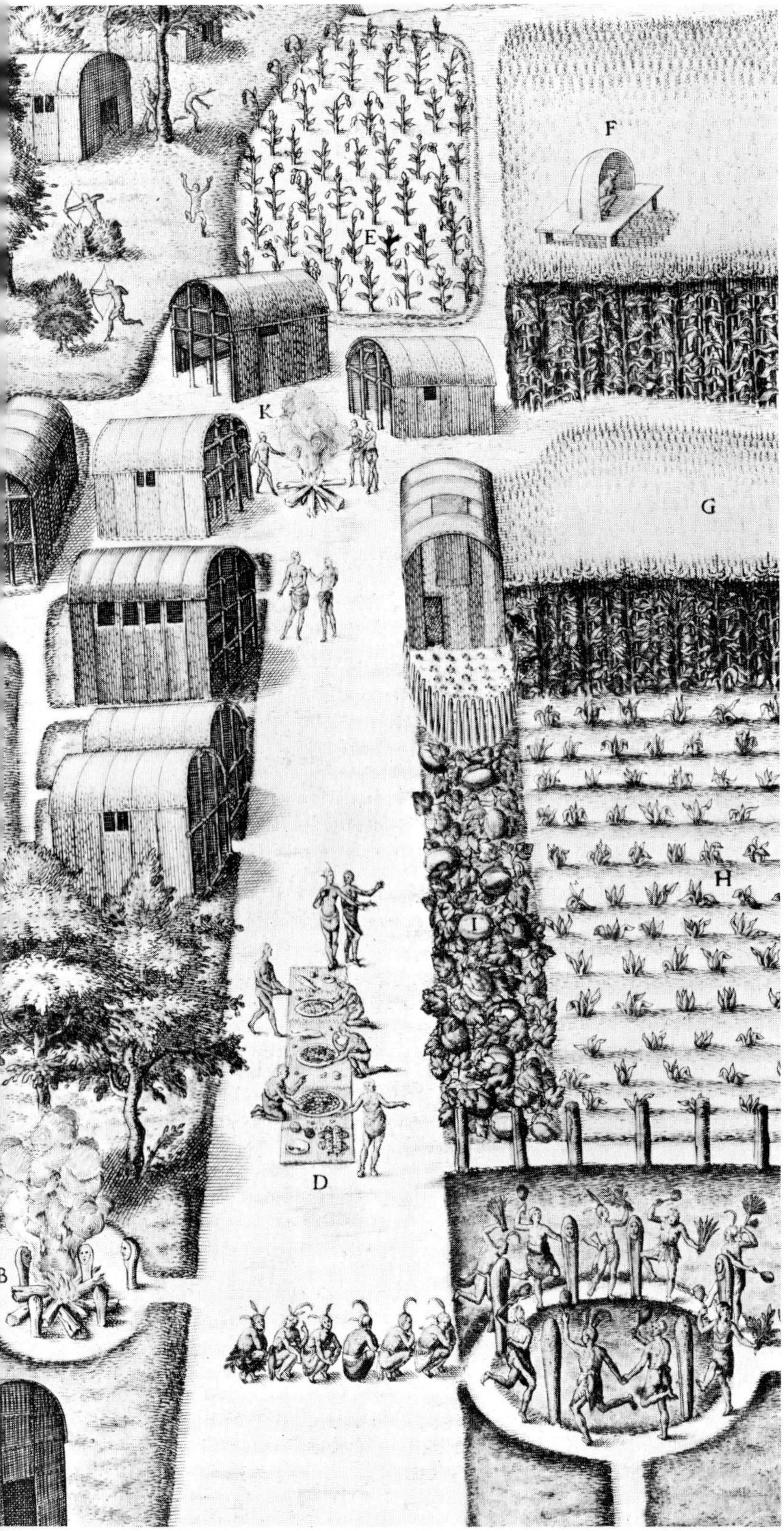

NEW YORK PUBLIC LIBRARY

AMERICAN MUSEUM OF NATURAL HISTORY

LIBRARY OF CONGRESS

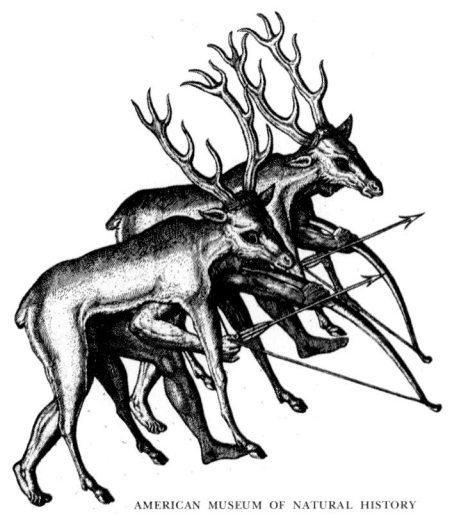

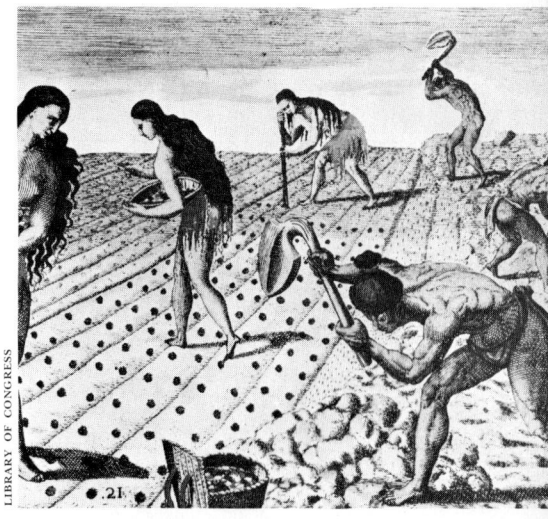

Left: The Indian village of Secotan, North Carolina, as it looked in the 1500's. The two drawings above both show Florida Indians. Hunters often disguised themselves in deerskins, complete with antlers. In the farming scene women plant seed while the men, using fishbone hoes, prepare the ground.

The Government of North American Indians

Political life among the North American Indians was quite varied. The least common political system was a **monarchy** (rule by a single leader). When the nobles of a tribe held the real power, even though there was one recognized leader in nearly every tribe, the political system was an **aristocracy**. Within some tribes a **democracy** (rule by common consent) existed that allowed both men and women to have their say. When Indians from different tribes met, the councils were usually conducted in a democratic manner.

In the drawing (above, left) of a treaty council of Sioux and Iowas, the braves sit in a circle to show that all of them are equal. The leaders were supposedly the bravest as well as the smartest tribal elders. But an ambitious young man could be chosen a leader by fighting well or by performing some clever act such as stealing horses from another tribe.

However the leaders were chosen, an Indian's first loyalty was to his tribe. Villagers lived together and shared the toil of planting and harvesting as a group. Hunting tribes pursued the game together and shared

the kill. If times were lean, all went hungry. If the gods gave many fat bucks or bear, everyone was stuffed full. War parties like the Iowa war party (above, right) marched as a unit, though in battle braves tended to fight for booty and trophies as individuals. Quarrels within the tribe were often settled by councils. If one Cheyenne murdered another, for instance, the elders might exile him or else force him to present gifts to his victim's family to make up for his crime. The Pueblos, who lived literally on top of each other in "apartment houses" of sun-baked brick, dealt with an unruly member by refusing to speak to him until he gave in.

A complex political system was created by the Iroquois. They were actually a **confederacy** (a league) of five nations: the Mohawks, Senecas, Oneidas, Onondagas, and Cayugas. Each nation had its leaders, called "sachems." Some leaders inherited their role and some were chosen by merit. Each year a council of 50 sachems, representing all five nations, met to make war and peace and to settle matters common to all league members. The resemblance to the United States Congress

On the opposite page Sioux and Iowa Plains Indians pass the peace pipe during a treaty council. Above: Plains warriors file off to battle, shields in hand.

45

PORTLAND ART MUSEUM, RASMUSSEN COLLECTION

The objects shown here are the work of Pacific Northwest Indians. Garments like the Tlingit shirt (above) were woven from goat hair over a base of cedar bark. Their complicated designs indicated the wearer's ancestry. The flying frog (below) was once part of a war helmet worn by the Tsimshian tribe.

NATIONAL MUSEUM OF CANADA

may strike you at once. This is perhaps not entirely accidental, for some Americans who wrote our Constitution were familiar with the League of the Iroquois.

Indian Art of the Pacific Northwest

By now you know enough about Indian art to realize its aims were ceremonial, magical, and heraldic, that is, it told something about the owner's ancestors. Of course, the artist also wanted it to be beautiful. You may, therefore, enjoy looking at two of the objects shown here and applying your new knowledge. They are a Kwakiutl sea-monster mask (right) and a Tlingit shirt (upper left). It will be helpful to know that these two tribes lived on the Pacific Coast between Washington and Alaska. Fish and game were plentiful, so the tribes were relatively prosperous. They also developed great skill in using in their artwork colored stones, shells, bits of bone, ivory, bark, and furs.

The mask, first of all, shows skill in woodcarving and in making bright paints. It uses animal elements, of course. You can see the bird's beak. Perhaps the patches of color around the edge are like the mottling on the shell of a turtle. But what animals do you think were the model for those great teeth and huge eyes?

Clearly, something frightening. The mask is grotesque. Perhaps it was meant to frighten people in a religious ritual. What kind of ritual could it be? What would the wearer be trying to impress upon the onlookers—his power? his closeness to spirits? Some of the pleasure of looking at art comes from answering such questions for yourself. Here is one more question: Why are there two faces? If you can find an answer that satisfies you, even if it is not what the artist had in mind, then you and he are partners in a game of mystery and discovery. But you may have to think like an Indian first.

The Tlingit shirt is rather different. Perhaps its many symbols of squares, cones, and ovals represent the lucky signs of different families from whom the wearer was descended. Northwestern Indians were quite interested in descent. Their famous totem poles stood before their houses, carved with the faces of bears, eagles, foxes, and other beasts. The animals were believed to be the founders of the **clans** (groups of related families) to which the owners belonged. Thus Indian art was not only decorative; it also was a way of explaining life.

SMITHSONIAN INSTITUTION

WASHINGTON STATE HISTORICAL SOCIETY

The painting at the top of the page tells a tale much like the Biblical story of Jonah being swallowed by the whale. In this case a salmon has swallowed an Indian. The Tlingit basket above was made of bark and was colored with bright vegetable dyes. At the left is a sea-monster mask used in ceremonies by Kwakiutl Indians of southern Alaska.

MUSEUM OF THE AMERICAN INDIAN, HEYE FOUNDATION

ACADEMY OF NATURAL SCIENCES OF PHILADELPHIA

OKLAHOMA HISTORICAL SOCIETY

Above left: Pueblo Indians of the Southwest perform the Green Corn Dance in front of the pueblo at Jemez near Santa Fe, New Mexico. The buffalo-hide painting at lower left shows an Apache ceremony celebrating the coming of age of young women, who dance arm-in-arm with older women of the tribe around the ceremonial fire.

Religion and the Indians of the Southwest

Religion among the Indians was not something only for Sunday morning. It was mixed with magic and medicine and the daily life of the tribe. It told Indians how to live together and helped them to please the spirits. In the American Southwest the Zuñi and Hopi Indians believed that kindly spirits called kachinas visited the tribe for six months each year as messengers of the gods. During this time priests wearing masks that represented the different kachinas were able to relay the peoples' needs to the gods. The entire tribe took part in these elaborate ceremonies which featured dances, songs, poetry, and beautiful costumes. Hopefully, the gods would be pleased by the ceremony and bring rain or cure a disease. Even though many of the ceremonies lasted for nine days and often one followed another, the worshipers usually remained calm and orderly. Modesty and seriousness were highly valued, and it was believed the spirits would punish anyone involved in conflict or violence.

Folk tales that explained the nature of the universe and its people were an important part of Indian religious ceremonies. All tribes had marvelous legends about this. Some thought that the earth was carried on the back of a great turtle; some that the starry Milky Way was the backbone of the sky; some that certain plants, like prairie grass, were the hair of gods who lived underground. Whatever the legend, it provided an answer to the questions: Where am I? What kind of universe do I live in?

Some southwestern Indian tribes believed that certain individuals, called shamans, were in direct contact with the spiritual world. In some tribes they were medicine men who applied herbs that cured disease. The Navaho shaman presided over curing ceremonies by singing sacred songs, handling holy objects, and making paintings with colored sand, pollen, crushed flowers, and minerals. The purpose of the ceremony was to restore the patient's harmony with nature as well as to cure the disease. Shamans from other tribes conducted ceremonies to guarantee good hunts or plentiful harvests or success in war.

Some ceremonies were individual, but some were tribal. The whole tribe might have a three-day feast when boys reached fighting age or girls became old enough to have children. They were celebrating because the tribe's life would surely go on. Can you imag-

ine a school graduation in a small town, with several days of parties, concerts, dances, dinners, and worship services for everyone? If you can, you are close to understanding an Indian puberty—coming-of-age—ceremony, like the one shown in the Apache skin painting at the bottom of page 48.

Imagination, closeness to nature, strong tribal feeling, and great ingenuity marked the various Indian cultures of the Americas. These first Americans left their names on the land. They placed many foods on our table and many words in our language. They fill our history books and television screens. But in 1492 they were about to lose their position as lords of the Western Hemisphere. The Europeans came and, when their civilization met the Indian world, a tragic story began.

Chapter Review

Questions for Discussion

1. How did the Indians who lived north of Mexico use nature to help them survive?
2. How did the governments of the Indian societies north of Mexico differ?
3. Why did Indians feel such strong loyalty to their tribe? How did they express this loyalty?
4. Why was there such a close relationship between nature and religion in the Indian cultures of the Southwest?

Social Studies Terms

In this chapter you have become acquainted with some new social studies terms: **societies, environments, cultures, civilizations, economy, political system, empire, urban, technology, monarchy, aristocracy, democracy, confederacy, clans.** If you are uncertain about what they mean, look them up in the glossary at the back of the book. Knowing the meaning of these words will help you answer the following questions and learn more in the future.

Summary Questions for Discussion

1. What might be some of the reasons why the Indians moved from Asia to the Americas?
2. Why did Europeans call the native peoples living in the Americas "Indians"? "savages"?
3. Which Indian societies would you call civilized? which savage? Why?
4. How did different groups of American Indians

adapt themselves to the different extremes of the climate and landscape of the Americas?
5. What *values* were most important to the Indians—that is, to what things did they give the greatest importance? How were these values expressed in some of the Indian cultures? in their art? in their religion? in their government?
6. Why is a good system of communications important to the governing of a large territory?
7. What was the relationship among nature, art, and religion in Indian societies?
8. Why did some Indian societies live in and control only a small territory, while other societies controlled vast empires?

Pictures as Historical Evidence

1. If the only pieces of evidence that you had about two different Indian societies were the painting of Northeast Indians on pages 32-33 and the drawing of the Indian village of Secotan on page 43, what could you learn about each society? Do you think both societies are settled? Why? How has each society adapted itself to its environment? How has each society learned to make a living?
2. What does the Aztec art on pages 38 and 39 tell us about the Aztec economy and technology?

Map Study

What land forms might have helped or hindered migration from Siberia to the tip of South America?

For Further Reading

American Heritage Book of Indians. New York: Simon & Schuster, Inc., 1961.

Ancient America, by Jonathan N. Leonard. New York: Time Inc., 1967.

Home of the Red Man, by Robert Silverberg. New York: New York Graphic Society, Ltd., 1963.

The American Indian (Special Edition for Young Readers), by Oliver La Farge. New York: Golden Press, 1960.

The Maya, by Sonia Bleeker. New York: William Morrow & Co., Inc., 1961.

The Sun Kingdom of the Aztecs, by Victor W. Von Hagen. Cleveland: The World Publishing Co., 1958.

2
The Coming of the Europeans

We have seen how, over thousands of years, the Indian peoples of North and South America had built different cultures and impressive civilizations. Now we shall examine how, in a matter of about 250 years, Europeans found and claimed these great continents and began to destroy or subdue the Indian societies in their path. The year 1492 to us is a date of discovery, new beginnings, and promise. To Indians it marks the end of an age of independence. By 1542 the Aztec and Incan empires were overthrown. By 1642 France, Spain, Portugal, England, and Holland had claims to great portions of the Americas and had set up **colonies** (permanent settlements ruled by a geographically separate country, often called a "mother" country) along the coasts. By 1742 one French-Canadian explorer, Pierre de La Vérendrye, had pierced the wilderness of the interior and perhaps reached the Rockies.

Why did the Indian world topple so easily? One reason is suggested by an event that happened in the United States in 1938. A group of radio actors performed a play about an "invasion" of the earth by men from Mars, in spaceships, armed with death-ray guns. Thousands of listeners tuned in late and thought they were hearing a description of real events. Panic-stricken, they jammed highways and fled in automobiles.

If Americans could behave in this way in 1938, imagine the reactions of Indians who had never seen an oceangoing ship, a horse, or a gun. The wonder is that some Indians had the courage to fight back at all.

But there is another reason, too, for the defeat of the Indians by the European invaders. The superior weapons of the Europeans came as a result of a "knowledge explosion" which began around the year 1100. Inside of a few hundred years, this sudden burst of knowledge gave Europeans gunpowder, the printing press, and many scientific discoveries. The new age bred curiosity and appetites for products from strange lands. It sent Europeans out in ships, like the one on the opposite page, to explore the world and to plant European **institutions** (customs and organizations) in the midst of already existing societies.

As you read, think about these questions:
1. Before expeditions can explore unknown lands, what kinds of knowledge and skills are needed?
2. What steps must precede the permanent settlement of newly discovered lands?

European explorers sailed in Spanish galleons, huge three-masted ships.

The scientific studies of the 1500's led to new navigation instruments and improvements in ships. However, little was known about the sea itself, and many sailors still feared it. These horrifying monsters appeared in a history and an atlas published in the mid-sixteenth century.

ALL: TRUSTEES OF THE BRITISH MUSEUM

The Age of Discovery

First, however, Europeans had to conquer their fear of the unknown. For Europeans in about the year 1100, there was no sharp line between real and imaginary places. They thought that the Garden of Eden was somewhere on the map, that the entrance to hell lay in some definite location, that there were countries of men with one eye or no heads. They did know for certain that travel, by either land or sea, was terribly dangerous. On land robbers as well as murderers awaited the luckless traveler. At sea there were pirates, storms, fog, and cruel rocks that could tear the bottom out of a ship.

Ignorance encouraged men to make up legends and tales about the perils that they feared. They believed in seagoing serpents, unicorns, and dragon-like creatures (left) who crunched and swallowed men and ships. It was a brave sailor indeed who would venture out of sight of land when such horrors lay in wait for him, jaws gaping. Before exploration could begin organized, factual knowledge had to replace such nightmares.

Moreover, ships had to be designed which could withstand the buffeting of the open Atlantic and carry enough men and provisions for long voyages. In the generally calm Mediterranean, men could row long, slender galleys. But such vessels would be smashed to bits in rough water, and they needed so many oarsmen and sailors that they were only useful on short journeys. If they had gotten into the open sea, these ships soon would have been lost because little was yet known about navigation. In short, there was no technology for discovery.

Despite this lack of technology, Norsemen, from what is now Norway, built ships which reached Iceland and Greenland in the Atlantic by 1000 A.D. In that year Leif Ericson, a Norseman, landed on the North American coast, probably in northern Newfoundland, which he called "Vinland" because he saw grape vines. But the Norsemen did not explore inland. Nor were they able to maintain **colonists** (permanent settlers from a mother country). In time Ericson's discovery became almost forgotten, even in western Europe.

A Great Change Begins in Europe

But Europe was beginning to change by 1100. Before that time life was tied to the soil and to time-tested, always repeated ways. Working as patiently as their plodding oxen, peasants, like the plowman at

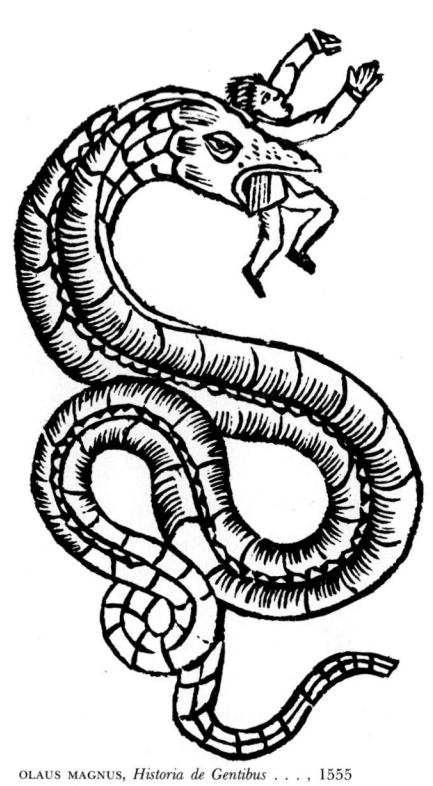

OLAUS MAGNUS, *Historia de Gentibus* . . . , 1555

During the Middle Ages more and more people were able to buy products from distant lands. In this detail from a fifteenth-century French painting, a shopkeeper is doing a good business in gold plate and silverware. He shares the space in this covered market with a cloth dealer and a shoemaker.

lower right, tilled the same plot for generations.

During the Middle Ages there had always been a **barter economy** (an economic system based on the "swapping" of goods for goods): my knife for your coat; my chicken for that pair of shoes you made. But around the year 1100, the longing for more goods encouraged tradesmen to travel longer distances and make more complicated exchanges. Wool cloth from Arras, in northern France, was exchanged for fur from Novgorod, in modern Russia, to make tools and horseshoes. Swords from Toledo, Spain, were exchanged for salted fish from the shores of the Baltic Sea, far to the north. For such enterprises money, loans, and, in time, banks were needed. Thus a **market economy** (an economic system in which men work for wages, and goods are paid for with money) began slowly to take shape.

Adventurous businessmen from many lands began to meet at great fairs to trade. Some of these fairs encouraged developing centers of trade to grow into cities. Along their streets, booths such as the one at left were alive with the sounds of bargaining. Life was still crude, but it was no longer static.

Other forces for change were at work, too. Between 1095 and 1291 there were a number of expeditions by Europeans to Palestine to win back the Holy Land from the Moslems. Although these Crusades failed in the long run to win back the Biblical lands, they helped to turn the Mediterranean Sea into an avenue for European commerce. The Crusaders met with Arab traders whose camels' saddlebags were loaded with spices, silks, gold, and jewels brought thousands of miles by land and sea from Africa and Asia. Soon trade with these lands thrived. Much of it was handled by the merchants of Italian cities, which became bustling and beautiful places. Compare the picture of Naples' busy harbor in 1464 (upper right) with the tranquil medieval farm scene (lower right).

The trade with the Orient and within Europe itself and the increasing knowledge of life in other areas aroused men to demand more of life, to dream ambitiously, and to dare. There is a modern name for what happens in underdeveloped countries when a growing economy begins to provide better food, clothes, and machines that make life easier. It is called a "revolution of rising expectations." Europe underwent such a **revolution** (a sudden, major change), and it provided an important reason for overseas exploration.

Right: A medieval calendar for the month of March shows the activities on a typical farm. Serfs plow the fields, sow the seeds, work the vineyards, and tend the sheep. Above: Italian cities dominated the steadily increasing trade from Africa and Asia, and grew rich distributing the products throughout Europe. European countries sometimes went to war to control these wealthy centers of trade. In this 1464 picture victorious warships tow the defeated fleet into the Bay of Naples.

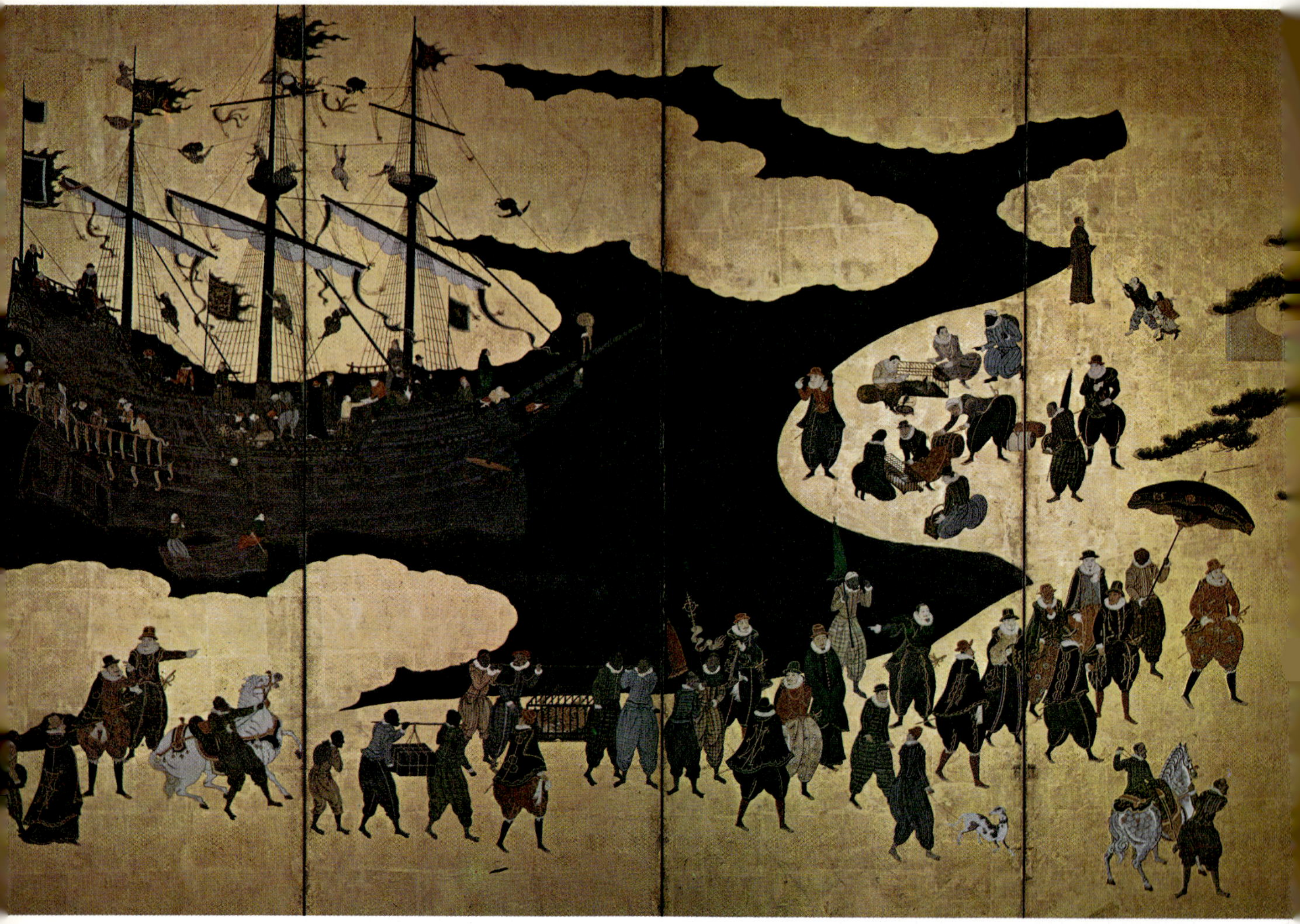

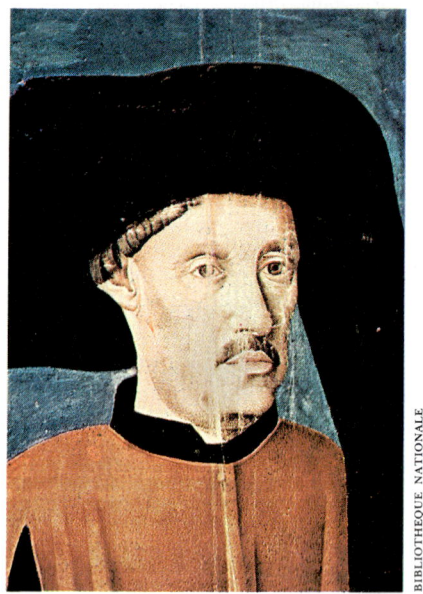

Right: Prince Henry of Portugal never sailed farther than the coast of Morocco, and yet he was known as Henry the Navigator and is sometimes called the "father of the modern world." Henry wanted to explore the unknown coast of Africa and established a school of navigation to which he invited scientists from all over Europe. Despite disappointments and disasters, Henry urged his sailors to "go farther south." By the time of his death in 1460, Portuguese sailors had rounded the shoulder of Africa and returned to tell about it. Above: Portugal went on to establish one of the most far-flung empires and richest overseas trades the world had seen. The Portuguese were the first Westerners to reach the Japanese islands. Here, in the early 1600's, priests and officials greet Portuguese officers wearing pegged pantaloons.

BIBLIOTHEQUE NATIONALE

Portugal Discovers a Route to the East

There was a political change as well. In England, France, Spain, and Portugal—all of them with at least one face turned toward the Atlantic—strong kings came to power between 1100 and 1500. They replaced the old, patchwork rule of quarreling feudal lords with the beginnings of strong, centralized governments. These kings provided money, ships, weapons, and encouragement for the work of exploration.

But in order to explore the world over the horizon, scientific information had to be gathered to replace fears and hunches. One of the fathers of the modern age was a Portuguese prince named Henry the Navigator (lower left). About 1418 Henry established an academy at Sagres, Portugal, overlooking the sea. Portugal was close to Africa, and its leaders were interested in the ivory, gold, pepper, and slaves that might be found there. Henry also believed that following the coastline of Africa might eventually lead to India and its riches. India was to the Portuguese what the moon was to us before the first men landed there. Prince Henry's base at Sagres was their Cape Kennedy.

At Sagres Henry gathered astronomers and geographers and mathematicians who patiently studied scholarly books and "pumped" every sea captain who had voyaged southward for information. This information was turned into charts, improved ships, and instruments of navigation, which Henry gave to captains who then probed down the west coast of Africa toward the equator and beyond (map, right).

Henry died in 1460 but his work went on. In 1488 the Portuguese explorer Bartholomew Dias, blown off course by a storm, found land again to the west instead of the east. He had "turned the corner" of the continent and discovered the Cape of Good Hope. Meanwhile, the Portuguese were prospering on the trade in ivory, gold, and slaves in the Gulf of Guinea.

The road to India was almost open now. In 1497 Vasco da Gama left Lisbon, rounded the Cape, went up the eastern coast of Africa, and then, pointing straight for the rising morning sun, made for Calicut in India.

Da Gama's voyage was not profitable. Yet once he arrived in Asia by water, with his ships and guns, the world had changed. Europe, though composed of small nations, was on its way to five centuries of world domination. For instance, by 1549 Portuguese vessels had sailed as far as Japan (left). By then Portugal owned

Portugal Sails to the Orient

⟵ DaGama
⟵--- Dias

trading posts and territory in Africa, India, and China. Other major European countries wasted no time in seeking equally fine rewards.

Columbus Discovers the New World

The sailors who flew other countries' colors from their mastheads also profited by Portuguese experience and research. One such navigator was Christopher Columbus.

Geographers in his day believed that all of the earth's land was divided among Europe, Asia, and Africa. They simply did not know the Americas were there. Neither did Columbus. What is more, he died in 1506 still believing that he had found a part of Asia. By then a navigator named Amerigo Vespucci knew better and said so. That is why mapmakers agreed to use Vespucci's first name and call the new land mass "America." But to say that Columbus did not know what he had discovered is not to take credit away from him. Columbus began a new era in the history of the world.

Born in 1451 to a weaver in Genoa, Italy, Columbus went to sea as a young man and settled down sometime before 1480 in Lisbon, Portugal. Lisbon was a sailors' and traders' town. There was exciting talk about opening sea routes to the Indies. The more Columbus read and argued, the more certain he became that the direct western course to Asia would be better than continuing the long search for a route around Africa to the east. In 1484 he asked the king of Portugal for ships, guns, crews, and supplies to prove his theory. The king turned the matter over to a committee of experts, who said that Columbus was "a big talker." In a sense he was. He judged the distance to Japan to be about 2,400 miles westward from Europe. It is actually close to 11,000. The Portuguese turned him down. So did King Ferdinand and Queen Isabella of neighboring Spain.

But Columbus was persistent. Finally in 1492, after eight years of pleading, Ferdinand gave in. He was persuaded not only by Queen Isabella but by his own royal treasurer, who thought it was a good gamble.

With his three tiny ships, Columbus sailed from Spain on August 3, 1492. A grim two months followed. The supplies of salted meat, hard bread, dried peas, and wine ran low. The sailors grew mutinous and threatened to make the captain turn back. Finally, in the early morning of October 12, land was sighted. The

DE BRY, *India Occidentalis*, 1590

Théodore de Bry, a well-known Flemish engraver, pictured many of the European explorers of the New World in a book published in 1590. De Bry portrayed frightened and uncivilized Indians greeting Columbus on Hispaniola.

next day at dawn Columbus stepped ashore at a Caribbean island—present-day Watlings Island.

Taino Indians came out in their canoes. They were almost naked. Columbus found them a simple folk, who "invite you to share anything they possess." He observed that "fifty Spaniards could subjugate this entire people." It was a warning of what was to come. By 1548 the Indians were almost all wiped out. The picture at left shows Columbus landing on Hispaniola (map, below), now divided between Haiti and the Dominican Republic. The picture was made in 1590 and beautifully shows how Europeans of that date viewed the Indians and their reception of Columbus.

Questions for Discussion

1. What were the changes that led to the age of discovery and exploration?
2. Why, around 1400, did Europeans have such inexact knowledge about the rest of the world?
3. What were the motives for the discovery of the Americas?
4. In their search for the wealth of Asia, why did the Portuguese sail south, instead of west as Columbus did?
5. Why was the New World named "America"?
6. Why is Columbus one of the great heroes of history?

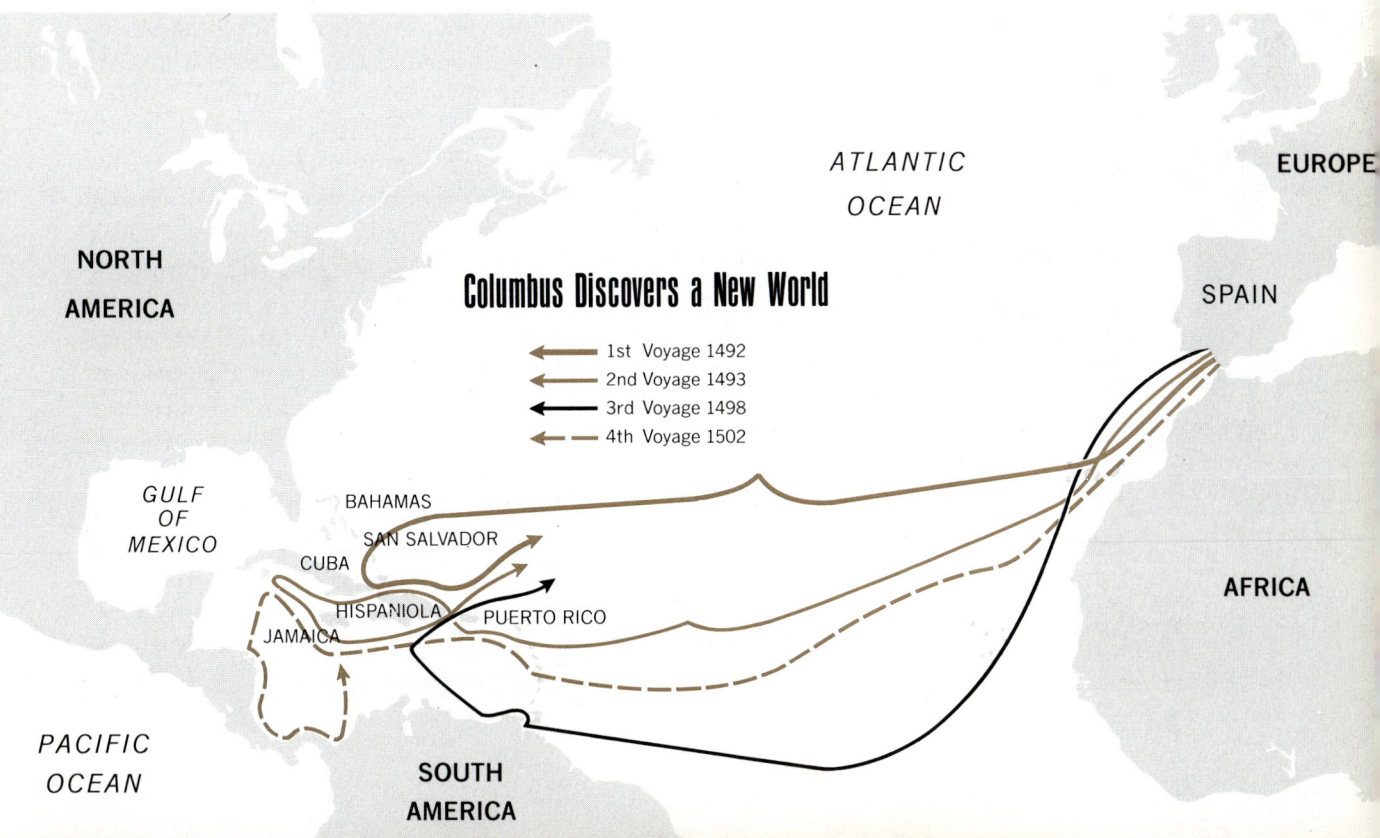

Spain Conquers an Empire in the New World

The world would never be the same again. The discovery of the Americas began a new day in history. The first sign of it was the speed with which the Spaniards rushed to possess what Columbus had found for them. By 1519 Spaniards had conquered parts of Cuba and Hispaniola, Panama and Yucatán, and other tropical regions near the Isthmus of Panama, where the two Americas pinch in and join each other. The magnet that attracted Spain's great explorer-conquerers was gold, which Columbus had seen islanders wearing as jewelry.

The first of these explorers was Vasco de Balboa. In Panama he heard from an Indian about a land to the south where gold was plentiful. Aflame with excitement, Balboa pushed through jungles, swamps, and over mountains. He found not only gold (left) but also the Pacific Ocean, which helped to convince Europeans that they had discovered a new continent and not Asia.

In Cuba another young Spanish soldier, named Hernando Cortés, listened to tales of the fabled empire of the Aztecs. With 11 ships, 600 men, and 16 horses, he landed on the Mexican coast in 1519 and boldly marched his tiny army to the great Aztec city of Tenochtitlán, today's Mexico City. On the way his cavalry and his firearms routed Indian armies. He was helped by the Aztec religious belief, held by even the Emperor Montezuma II, that the Spaniards were gods who had returned to the Aztec people after a long absence. Cortés demanded an audience, a face-to-face talk with Montezuma. When the proud ruler appeared, Cortés had him seized and made a prisoner. The Indians tried to drive the Spanish out but were soundly defeated in battle. Cortés then ordered Montezuma slain. The land of Mexico became New Spain. Cortés had established himself as a **conquistador** (which means "one who conquers" in Spanish).

Mexico fell in 1521. Ten years later the most daring of all the conquistadors, Francisco Pizarro, set out with 180 soldiers, including 27 mounted men, to find the wealth of the Incas. He finally reached Cajamarca, home of the Lord Inca, Atahualpa. Four thousand of the best Incan warriors stood in ranks around Atahualpa's litter. Pizarro and his men were a tiny island of shining armor in a sea of Indian power (right). But his men and their guns lay hidden behind him. A Spanish priest offered the Lord Inca a prayerbook and told him that he must accept Christianity as the true

BOTH: DE BRY, *India Occidentalis*, 1590

This detail from a de Bry engraving shows Balboa accepting tribute in gold from natives of Panama.

faith. Atahualpa, proud and confident, flipped the book into the dust. Then, at a signal from Pizarro, the Spaniards opened fire. Two thousand Indians were slaughtered. Atahualpa was captured and strangled to death, even though he had agreed to become a Christian.

Peru became a part of the Spanish empire in the New World that included large parts of South and Central America and, later, North America. Peru's golden ornaments were melted down into bars and sent in wallowing treasure fleets back to the royal treasury in Madrid. Peru's priests and nobles became simply "Indians," all alike to the Spanish eye. Its peasants and warriors toiled in the fields and the mines for the glory of a faraway foreign ruler. Its temples were plundered and replaced with the churches of the invaders.

The conquistadors believed that their amazing victories were signs of God's approval. They thought of the wealth of the conquered lands as a feast spread for them to enjoy. They saw no reason to respect the customs of the defeated natives. They did not think of themselves as robbers but as among the most civilized people on earth. In this spirit of conquest and plunder, Spain pushed its new empire into the heart of North as well as South and Central America. By 1609 its flag flew over Santa Fe, in today's New Mexico. In the 1700's its explorers and **missionaries** (people sent to do religious or charitable work in a foreign country or territory) carried the flag of Spain and the teachings of the Catholic Church as far north as San Francisco.

How Spain Ruled Its New World Empire

Spanish rulers could not hope to fill great valleys and deserts, some big enough to swallow up all Spain itself, with settlers. Nor could they enforce tight control over Indian tribes scattered over miles of almost impassable mountains. So the political system they developed relied, especially in the territory that later became part of the United States, on the creation of little centers of influence and authority. Especially important were the missions, points of settlement built around a church. The officials of the Catholic Church in Spain took seriously the work of converting the Indians. They insisted that the cruelty of the conquistadors be softened. In the New World different members of religious orders became agents of the empire as

Pizarro conquered Peru easily after his men slaughtered most of the Incan leadership at Cajamarca.

important as soldiers and governors.

These were the first missionaries in the New World. With forced Indian labor they planted gardens and built storehouses, hospitals, chapels, and stately homes. The mission buildings were often grouped around an open plaza or square, as in Spain. Like the mission at upper right, they were built of native materials such as stone and baked clay. These missions were bits of Spain in an American setting. But the bits were changed. The crucifix in the chapel, before which the Indians kneeled, was Spanish. Yet the pottery jugs which held the Communion wine were as Indian as the cornmeal cakes served at the friars' tables. Always the American land put its mark on the Europeans who tried to repeat their own way of life in it.

A few settlers in Spanish North America spread out from these centers to establish ranches. For the owners cattle and grain were the gold and silver of the New World. Guarded by a very few soldiers in *presidios*, military garrisons, and lightly ruled by officials from the *pueblos*, small towns, many Spaniards in America were hardly conscious of being Spanish. If they took Indian wives and had children, as they often did, the youngsters were part of a new breed—Americans.

The center of Spain's sprawling new empire was Mexico City (left). In contrast to a thinly populated place like California, the capital was crowded with the stately homes of bishops, generals, and officials, who were served by the local population. Coaches clattered by. Men in European finery chitchatted. Behind the imposing official buildings were market stalls and ordinary homes. Here was a largely European city where, only 176 years earlier, the Aztecs had worshiped the sun and their feathered emperor.

Questions for Discussion

1. Why were the Aztecs and Incas, whose warriors greatly outnumbered those of Cortés and Pizarro, unable to defend themselves successfully?
2. Why did the Spanish conquistadors believe that their conquests were pleasing to God?
3. How did the work of the missionaries differ from the work of the conquistadors?
4. Why did conquistadors and missionaries, both Christian, differ in their approach to Indians?
5. Why were many Spaniards in America "hardly conscious of being Spanish"?

Exploration du territoire de l'Oregon . . . , 1844

Left: In 1695 the nobles of Mexico City greet a new viceroy. At the time, Mexico City was the largest Spanish city in the world. Above: In 1798 the Spanish founded San Luis Rey de Francia, a mission in southern California.

New Spain in 1750

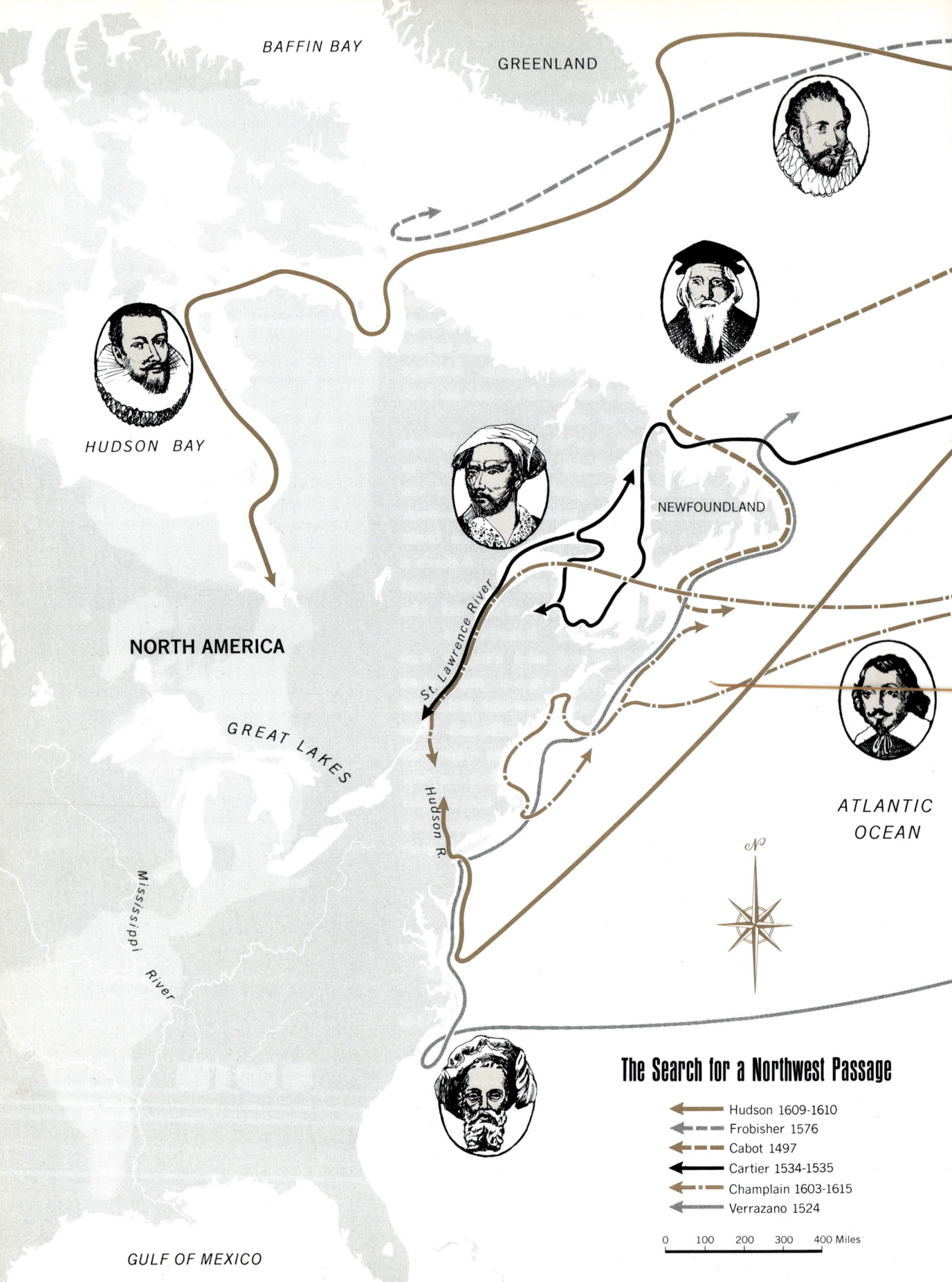

England, France, and Holland Enter the Race for Empire

Spanish success in the New World stirred the envy of other European kings. It was worth sending out expeditions to see if a land like that of the Incas, ready to pillage, lay beyond the sunset. There was another reason, too. No one at first knew the exact shape and size of America. It might be as thin as a serpent. It might be a chain of islands. Somewhere, as Columbus had dreamed, it might have an opening through which vessels could sail westward and stock up on China silk, Calcutta ivory, and Sumatra pepper. The search for the Northwest Passage began. It went on until mapmakers finally realized the full width of the American continent. Many men died in search of the impossible. There *is* a water passage across the top of North America, but it is always closed by ice. Only powerful icebreakers can get through.

First England and then France and Holland joined the race to explore and to establish claims in North America. Each expedition has its own story. But some things that were shared by them all stand out as you look at the map at left.

Exploration was confined mainly to the shorelines of the continent. All the explorers from Cabot to Cartier followed a pattern. They would find an inviting river or bay and sail up it until there was no farther passage. Where the bays cut deeply into the continent, explorers like Hudson went far. The risks were terrible—North Atlantic storms, icebergs, and angry Indians.

But the efforts of the explorers were not wasted. For one thing, they mapped and named most of our coastline, claiming vast areas for the European kings who had sent them. For another, they reported things that made the English, French, and Dutch realize that there were valuable prizes in America other than gold or the Northwest Passage: fish, lumber, furs, land. By 1600 far-sighted statesmen and merchants were brewing a new idea—permanent settlements. The age of exploration was about to give way to the age of colonization.

In 1607, after the failure of an earlier effort, the English established a lasting colony at Jamestown, in Virginia. In 1608, also following unsuccessful attempts to settle Frenchmen elsewhere in the New World, Quebec was founded. It became the capital of French Canada. In 1624 a Dutch post was set up at Fort Orange, now Albany, New York. Within seventeen years three new contestants had entered the North American co-

NOVA BRITANNIA.
OFFRING MOST
Excellent fruites by Planting in
VIRGINIA.
Exciting all such as be well affected
to further the same.

LONDON
Printed for SAMUEL MACHAM, and are to be sold at
his Shop in Pauls Church-yard, at the
Signe of the Bul-head.
1609.

JOHNSON, *Nova Britannia*, 1609

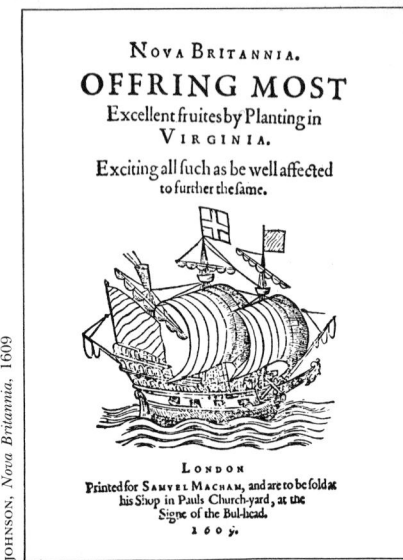

Above: The title page from a 1609 book promoting settlement of Virginia. Below: A drawing of the Jamestown area in 1607. The ships at left—the Discovery, *the* Godspeed, *and the* Susan Constant—*brought colonists from England.*

lonial game. Its prize was a land empire. How did the entrants differ?

The First English Colonies

The English colony at Jamestown began as a company-owned outpost. King James of England gave a group of stockholders called the "Virginia Company" the right to settle and do business on "his" American soil, which he claimed as a result of Cabot's voyage, in return for a share of the profits. As the first stockholders saw it, there would be a fort and storehouse, built by workers brought over in three ships. The colonists would go out to discover gold, trade with native rulers, and even cultivate silkworms. Jewelers, goldsmiths, and weavers would work in the town, preparing the goods to ship home. Food would be grown on company-owned land. You can see this plan all neatly laid out in the picture of Jamestown below.

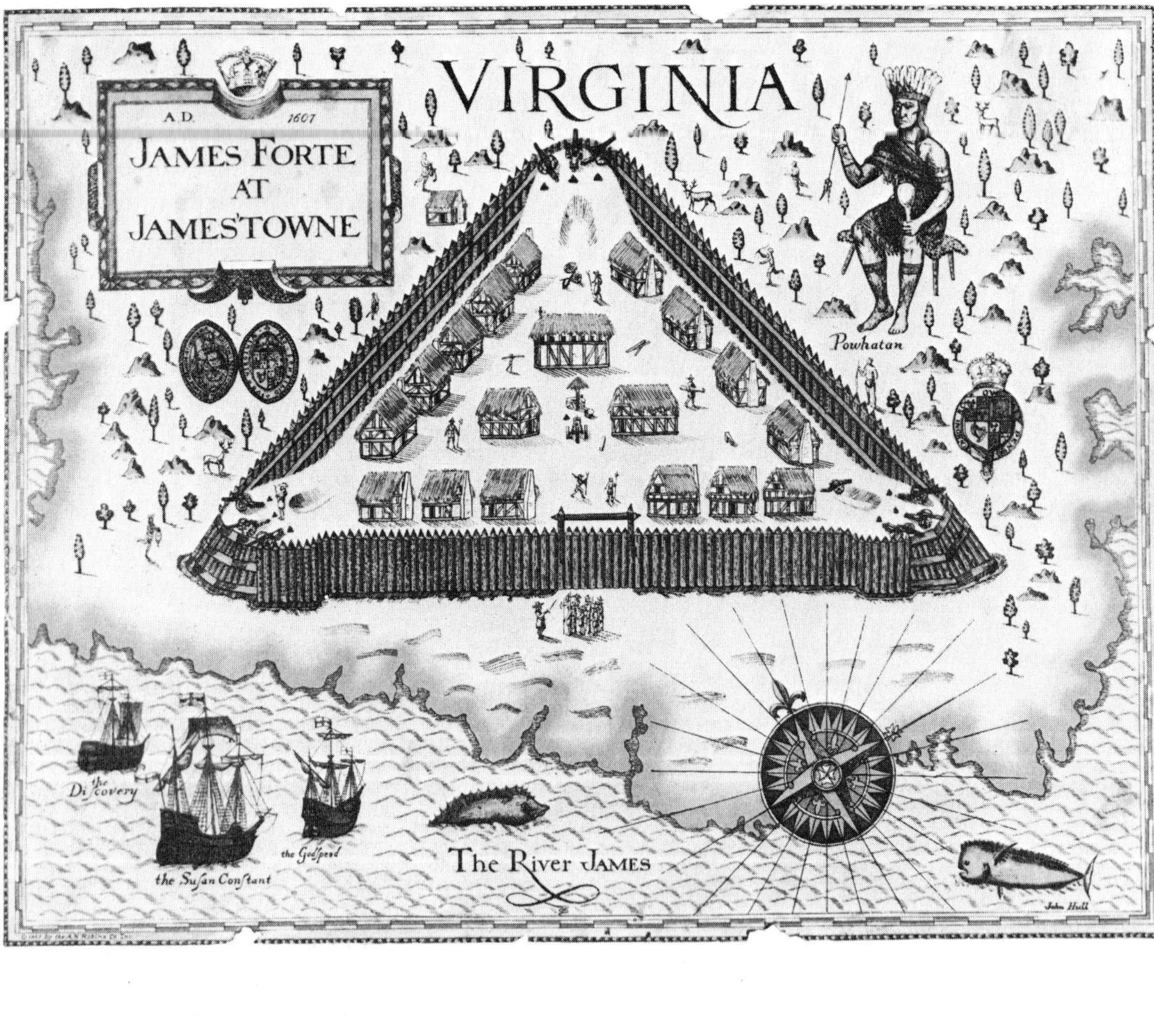

Absolutely none of these dreams worked out. For the first five years, the colonists not only found no gold,

A. H. ROBINS COMPANY

but starved and died of a variety of diseases. Only the strong leadership of John Smith kept them going. Finally, the company decided the way to survive was to divide land among the settlers, who were urged to go out and farm it. Such farming became profitable after 1613 when a shipload of tobacco was sent back to England. King James called it a "stinking weed," but tobacco became very popular in Europe and was the colony's most profitable crop.

That made a great difference in colonizing style. Settlers who are lured to seek "most Excellent fruites by Planting," as in the advertisement at upper left, cannot loot temples and go home the next year. They become permanent residents.

This pattern of settlement existed also in the next English colony, in Massachusetts. The Pilgrims, who landed at Plymouth in 1620, were members of a small, close-knit community, seeking to practice their religion in a way forbidden in England. The picture you see (below, right) was not painted until 1867, and it makes

Above: This picture of Edward Winslow is the only authentic portrait in existence of a Mayflower Pilgrim. He posed for the portrait while visiting England in 1651. His signature appears here above the portrait. Right: A nineteenth-century artist portrayed Pilgrims walking to church, carrying their guns and Bibles.

La Salle and his party, which included friendly Indians and their squaws, cross frozen Lake Michigan. They entered the ice-clogged Mississippi River in February 1682 and reached the river's mouth two months later.

KENNEDY GALLERIES

the Pilgrims look less rugged and work-worn than they actually were. But it does show them doing something customary, going to church as a family. To the Puritans the church was the center of their social life.

France's River Empire

Unlike the town-dwelling New Englanders or the Virginia planters, the French in Canada strung out along a lengthy chain of rivers and lakes. As French explorers moved inland, they found that by using Indian canoes they could move up the St. Lawrence, then into the Great Lakes, then down the rivers flowing into the Mississippi. By 1634 Jean Nicolet had reached present-day Wisconsin. By 1673 two French travelers, Marquette and Joliet, had gotten down the Mississippi as far as modern Arkansas. Nine years later Robert de La Salle, whose men are dragging their canoes across a frozen lake in the picture at left, reached the place where the Mississippi empties into the Gulf of Mexico, near present-day New Orleans.

But France, unlike England, did not allow religious **dissenters** (people who oppose generally accepted practices) to settle freely in North America. Nor did France encourage settlement by promising land and self-rule. French companies were unwilling to do what the Virginia Company had done at first—send more ships and fresh supplies when the first colonies were almost wiped out by disease, hunger, and Indian attack. Frenchmen with a vision of empire, like Champlain and La Salle, pleaded for the king to support them and reap glory, but in vain.

What kept New France going was the profit in the fisheries (right) and, above all, the wealth from trading in the pelt of the little animal shown on the opposite page, the beaver. The characteristic French settler, although there were some farmers, was the trapper (lower right). With snowshoes, rifle, and pouch, he was superb at living in the cold wilderness. He went ever farther in search of new places for his traps and new Indians to give blankets and kettles in exchange for skins. But he was, in ways, like the hunting Indian among whom he dwelt and often married—a nomad.

The Dutch Build New Amsterdam

An important American city was begun in 1626 by the Dutch. They were the last of the four European nations which held colonies that later became part of

MONCEAU, *Traite Général des Pesche,* 1769

PUBLIC ARCHIVES OF CANADA

Above: Fishery workers clean and dry codfish before shipping them to Europe. After being cleaned in the shed at left, the fish were dried on the beach or on the rack at right. Left: The wilderness was home for trappers near Hudson Bay who spent most of the year in search of the beaver (below). A full-grown beaver of 30 to 60 pounds yielded a valuable pelt. Hats made from beaver pelts became very popular in America in the early 1800's.

NEW YORK PUBLIC LIBRARY

After 1621 the Dutch West India Company had a monopoly of all the trade between Holland and the entire coast of North and South America. The company's flag became a familiar sight in many ports in the New World.

the United States. Naturally, we think of New Amsterdam, later New York, as a jewel which the Dutch government should have treasured for its future value. But actually, it was only a minor holding to them. From 1621 the Dutch West India Company had controlled the territory that the Dutch claimed as a result of Henry Hudson's 1609 voyage up the river named for him. As a company it was more interested in the promising sugar trade with Dutch outposts in the Caribbean and South America than in developing a colony in New Amsterdam.

Yet from the start New Amsterdam was an unusual colonial town. It had a fine harbor. Sailing ships came down the Hudson from Albany loaded with furs from the north and with grain from the Dutch farms along the river's banks. At New Amsterdam they transferred their cargoes to seagoing vessels. Wharves and warehouses soon sprang up. Dutch tidiness and orderliness did not permit the town to grow by sloppy chance. It was planned. In the plan (right) you can see the neatly laid-out streets, the rows of houses precisely lined up, the fort at the foot of the island, and the wall built across it to bar the Indians. The wide street you see was called the Broad Way. It later became famous as the theatrical center of New York City and the nation. In the same way the street along the wall became Wall Street, the financial district where much of the country's banking business takes place today.

Because it was such a good port, the city became home to many travelers. It had an international flavor. A visitor in 1643 could claim to hear eighteen languages spoken in the streets. And because the Dutch themselves had just come out of a long religious struggle with Spain in 1624, they adopted a policy of allowing people to be free to practice their own religion.

Though the Dutch did expand into New Jersey, Delaware, and Long Island, New Amsterdam remained the center of their American colony. But during a war between Holland and England in 1664, an English fleet captured the city. Angrily, its last Dutch governor, Peter Stuyvesant, surrendered it and stumped away into history on his peg leg.

Exploration Inland and Claims to a Continent

French, Dutch, and English explorers in the 1500's only touched the edges of the continent. By 1742 Europeans had explored much of the interior, as you can

The city fathers commissioned a drawing of New Amsterdam in 1660 because they were hard pressed to find house sites for new arrivals. After studying the drawing the directors of the Dutch West India Company concluded that "... too great spaces are as yet without buildings ... where the houses ... are surrounded by excessively large plots and gardens." The original drawing has been lost, but this 1670 copy of it survives.

see by looking at the map at left.

The Spanish had begun this work. In 1528 a would-be conquistador named Narvaez was shipwrecked on the Texas coast of the Gulf of Mexico. Cabeza de Vaca, his Negro companion Estevanico, and two other men survived. For eight years they wandered across northern Mexico, living among the Indians. Finally, they came upon a Spanish outpost. The Spaniards were astonished to hear these ragged, bearded "savages" speak their own language. When Cabeza de Vaca and Estevanico finally convinced their listeners that they were Narvaez' men, they were taken to Culiacán, on the Pacific. Thus they were the first explorers to cross the continent north of the Isthmus of Panama.

Gold fever continued to lure Spanish explorers like Hernando de Soto. In 1539 he landed in Florida. For the next three years he pushed northward and westward (getting as far as present-day Oklahoma) in search of legendary cities of gold. Finally, he came to a river as wide as an ocean harbor. The Indians called it the Mississippi. For De Soto it became his grave. When he died of illness and exhaustion, his men were afraid that the Indians would attack if they knew that the Spanish leader was dead, like an ordinary mortal. So they told the Indians that De Soto had gone to heaven to talk with the gods there. Then, in the middle of the night, they rowed out to midstream and threw in the weighted body.

About the same time another Spaniard, Francisco de Coronado, spent several years searching in what became Texas, Kansas, and Colorado for fabled golden cities. He saw buffalo and discovered the Grand Canyons. He also rode over territory which would one day produce oil, wheat, and cattle worth millions of dollars. But his eyes, sweeping the endless prairie grass, could not see the wealth beneath. He gave up in despair.

The French made the greatest strides into the continent's center. Marquette and Joliet went south from Lake Michigan, despite tales of "horrible monsters which devoured men and canoes together." La Salle, following on their trail, reached the Mississippi's mouth, where he claimed all "nations, peoples, provinces, cities, towns, villages, mines, minerals, fisheries, and rivers" in the region drained by the Mississippi for King Louis XIV of France. Since the rivers which finally flow into the Gulf begin as far east as North Carolina and as far west as Montana, he was

making almost two-thirds of the future United States a part of "Louisiana."

Fifty years after La Salle, another French explorer, Pierre de La Vérendrye, headed westward from Lake Superior. In eleven years of searching, he got as far as present-day Montana and probably saw the Rockies. Had he gone only a little farther, he would have found rivers flowing westward to the Pacific Coast. Over a century before, Sir Francis Drake in his round-the-world voyage had cruised along the California coast as far north as present-day San Francisco. In 1741 Vitus Bering explored much of the west coast of Alaska, which he claimed for Russia.

By 1742 the broad outlines of North America were known, and because of these explorations, huge territories had been claimed by England, France, and Spain. The French and Spanish had conquered and were ruling large empires. The English had gone farthest in planting compact, enduring settlements.

But Europeans were not to be the only people to change the history of the Americas. People from another continent were also to become part of the American story. They came from Africa—as prisoners.

Questions for Discussion

1. What is the "Northwest Passage"? Why was the search for it so important to early explorers?
2. What turned the attempt to colonize Virginia from a failure into a success?
3. How did the early efforts of the English, French, and Dutch to colonize North America differ? In what ways were they similar?

Chapter Review

Social Studies Terms

In this chapter you have become acquainted with some social studies and historical terms: **colonies, institutions, colonists, barter economy, market economy, revolution, conquistador, missionaries, dissenters.** Understanding these words will make them a part of your vocabulary and will help you to answer the questions that follow.

Summary Questions for Discussion

1. Compare the problems of getting to the New World by ship in the 1490's with the problems of getting to the moon by spaceship in the 1960's.
2. Why were Europeans able to discover, explore,

and lay a firm claim to so much of the Americas despite the existence of Indian societies?
3. Compare the motives of Spain, England, France, and Holland in establishing claims to the New World.
4. In what ways was religion a factor in European exploration and settlement of the Americas?
5. The culture of the people of modern Mexico is neither all-Spanish nor all-Indian. Why?
6. Why were the English attempts to colonize North America more successful than those of the French?
7. Are we in a new age of discovery and exploration? Will it be as important for man's future as the age of discovery and exploration that began in the 1400's? Why?

Pictures as Historical Evidence

1. How does the artist's view of the Indians in the engraving of Columbus landing on the island of Hispaniola (page 60) differ from the picture on page 63 of the defeat of Atahualpa?
2. Which pictures in this chapter provide evidence for the idea that Europeans conquered the Indians because Europe had a more advanced military technology?

Map Study

1. From the map on page 61 showing Columbus' voyages, can you find a clue as to why Columbus refused to believe that he had not found the Indies?
2. Name some major North American rivers and mountain ranges which European explorers had discovered by 1742.

For Further Reading

Age of Exploration, by John R. Hale. New York: Time Inc., 1966.

Discoverers of the New World, by Josef Berger. New York: American Heritage Publishing Co., Inc., 1960.

Jamestown, First English Colony, by Marshall W. Fishwick. New York: American Heritage Publishing Co., Inc., 1965.

The Pilgrims and Plymouth Colony, by Feenie Ziner. New York: American Heritage Publishing Co., Inc., 1961.

The Voyages of Christopher Columbus, by Sperry Armstrong. New York: Random House, Inc., 1950.

3
Slavery Comes to the Americas

There are some white Americans who proudly trace their ancestors back to Englishmen who helped to found Jamestown. There are also black men and women of today who could claim that honor, if records had been kept of all the children of twenty "negars" dropped off at Jamestown by a Dutch ship in 1619. That was only twelve years after Virginia was founded. Those twenty black men were the pioneers among Americans of African descent. Today they number more than twenty million.

The part that black men and women have played in the making of America is often forgotten. That is largely because they spent most of their first three centuries in the New World in slavery. Africans were enslaved because powerful, armed Europe discovered America and Africa at about the same time. Those who planted colonies in America found that thousands of laborers were needed in the mines and on the plantations that grew sugar, cotton, tobacco, and indigo. European farm workers were slow to settle in a strange, dangerous, demanding new continent. Some Indians were enslaved as laborers, but this practice proved largely unsuccessful. However, the first Portuguese captains who touched on the shores of West Africa during the 1400's found that black slaves were cheap and easy to come by. They became one answer to the labor problem in America.

They did not get into the history books. Yet their work helped to clear the land and grow the crops which were traded for the wealth to build cities. Thus the slave you see being branded is a founding father, too.

The Europeans who owned slaves justified their seizure of Africans, just as they defended their robbery of Indians, by their belief that people with dark skins and strange gods were inferior. They believed it was blessed work for white Christians to bring black "savages" to civilization—even in chains! This sense of superiority was strengthened by European ignorance about Africa. It was described as a dark jungle continent, alive with primitive cannibals. This idea, which lasted until modern times, was wildly wrong.

As you read, think about these questions:
1. Why did the Negro cultures of Africa, like the Indian cultures of America, differ from each other?
2. Why were Africans brought in chains to the New World? Why did they become slaves instead of citizens in the colonies?

An African is branded after being selected as a slave for the New World.

The African Heritage

The map of Africa (opposite page) gives us some idea of the variety and richness of African civilizations. Egypt, which has left us great pyramids, temples, and other works of art, was a powerful state thousands of years before Christianity began. South of Egypt on the Nile River was the kingdom of Kush, with its thriving trade in iron products centering around the capital city of Meroe. In the fourth century A.D., Kush was overcome and largely destroyed by Axum, which became the capital of a new Christian state known as Ethiopia.

These lands are less important to American history, however, than those to the west. Even in the days of the Roman Empire, this southwestern part of Africa was cut off from Europe by the burning sands of the Sahara Desert. Between 640 and 710 A.D., Arabs conquered all of North Africa from Cairo to Fez. The Arab world became yet another barrier between Christian Europe and sub-Saharan (south of the Sahara) Africa.

Europeans, therefore, did not know that this part of Africa was a land of rolling hills, green grasses, and gentle rains. Nor did they learn of its many varied peoples—Kru, Ashanti, Fanti, Ewe, Yoruba, Ibo, and many others. Africans are no more alike than Italians, Swedes, and Irishmen—all Europeans—are alike. Europeans knew nothing of the great kingdoms which united many of these peoples, despite differences of language and culture, long before Europe's own age of growth began around 1100.

In West Africa three great empires—Ghana, Mali, and Songhai—rose and fell along the banks of the Niger River between about 500 and 1600 A.D. Ghana was founded shortly after the Roman Empire began to break up in the fifth century and lasted until the thirteenth century. Its caravans traded with the Arab ports on the Mediterranean coast and with great trading kingdoms of East Africa on the Red Sea.

These kingdoms had powerful armies and treasuries full of gold. An Arab traveler in Ghana in 1076 told how its king could put 200,000 soldiers into the field, and how, when he received his people, he was surrounded by princes with gold plaited into their hair. In 1324 the emperor Mansa Musa of Mali made a pilgrimage to Mecca in Arabia and gave 90 camel-loads of gold to people along the way. In Songhai Timbuktu was an important center of learning and trade.

Along the Gulf of Guinea, south and west of the Niger, were smaller kingdoms such as Benin, Oyo, and

This painting of the emperor of Mali appeared in a fourteenth-century atlas of the known world.

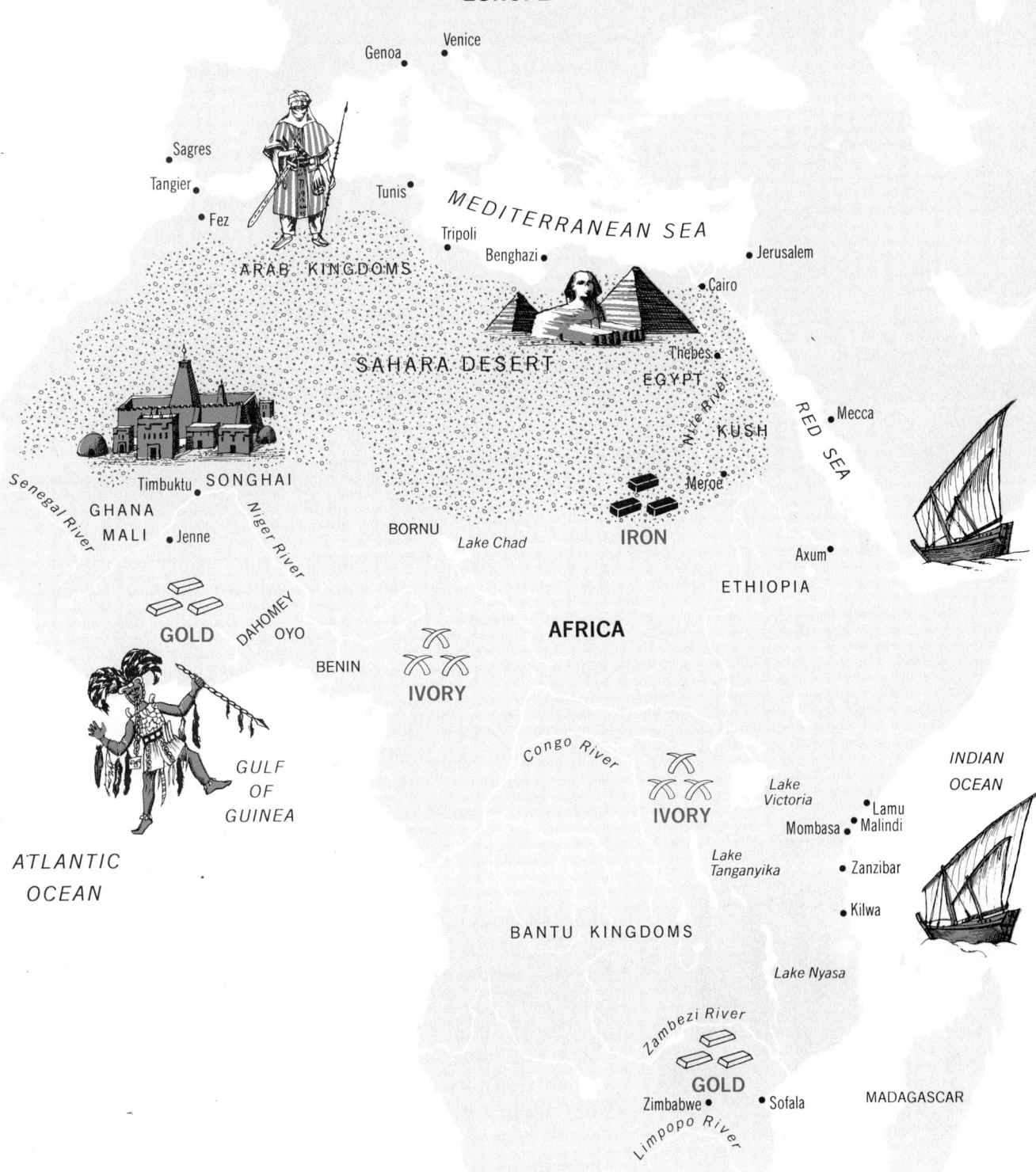

Dahomey. On the east coast of Africa were great trading centers such as Mombasa and Zanzibar, and in the south of Africa, in the area of the Congo, Zambezi, and Limpopo rivers, were powerful Bantu kingdoms.

Economy and Government of West Africa

The peoples of West Africa were farmers who grew millet and other crops and raised cattle in the fields around their villages, as you see in the picture of a Fulani town at right. They also mined and refined gold, manufactured iron farm tools and weapons, and made ceremonial and artistic objects out of bronze, an alloy of copper and tin. One of the few Europeans who visited a West African village reported that he saw men and women "weave cotton, work in leather, and fabricate [make] iron."

The peoples of these states traded their ivory, iron, gold, cattle, and cloth for salt, medicines, books, jewels, and other goods brought in from the north and the ports along the Red Sea and Indian Ocean. In spite of these contacts with outside influences, the desert to the north and the heavy forest along the coast to the south protected them from invasion and discouraged travel. Thus they developed a close-knit pattern of life. Each village was almost a complete little world. Its people were of the same tribe. They lived in groups consisting of **extended families** (grandparents, parents, children, adopted children, grandchildren, some aunts, uncles, and cousins, and servants), usually all in adjoining houses. Many such families formed a clan. Wise men and women of the clans, often after consulting the spirits of dead ancestors, made decisions about sharing work, taking part in ceremonies, getting married, and other events in growing up and growing old. Like feudal Europe, African society did not change greatly from generation to generation.

The political systems of West Africa differed from people to people. Of course, the great rulers of empires were surrounded by officials, generals, treasurers, and other public men of note. Some of the kings of the smaller coastal nations were also strong leaders. For example, the king of Dahomey appointed the headmen of his villages, chose his own heir from among his sons, and named all the royal officers. But other kings had less power. Sometimes their officials could only come from certain aristocratic families and be chosen by the eldest members, including the women, of those

All of the drawings on these two pages first appeared in an early nineteenth-century book by Frederic Shoberl. Above is a goldsmith in a West African village.

ALL: SHOBERL, *The World in Miniature*, 1821

Shoberl pictured many highly skilled West African craftsmen in his book—including the woman spinning cotton at left and the man weaving above. The Fulani town and the plantation at the top of this page were located in the country of Bondu between the Senegal and Gambia rivers.

83

Above: A nineteenth-century artist painted this water color of an elaborate festival he attended in a native village near the Niger River. Left: A king rides his horse through a village on the West African coast, accompanied by servants and followers.

NEW YORK PUBLIC LIBRARY, PICTURE COLLECTION

families. Among some peoples the king was chosen by a council of village chiefs, who shared his power and who could also **depose** (remove) him if they were displeased. For example, if the council of the ruler of Yorubaland sent the "lord" an ostrich egg, it was a sign that he was supposed to kill himself.

Kings had important religious and ceremonial roles, however. They helped to bring good harvests by participating in ceremonies like the festival (upper left) in honor of the Serpent God. They were especially honored when they used their magical powers to please gods and ancestral spirits. But it is important to know that they did not own their peoples or even their lands. They had to divide honors with craftsmen, priests, and village noblemen who owed their **status** (rank or social position in the eyes of others) not to royal favor, but to custom and family.

To outsiders with whom they dealt in trade or fought in war, however, the kings represented their peoples. Like the American Indians, the West Africans had a mixture of monarchy, aristocracy, and democracy in the political arrangements of their differing tribes. The limited powers of the king and the strong influence of religious leaders and well-born families have even led historians to compare West Africa around 1400 with medieval Europe.

If Europe had been invaded in the 1100's by foreigners with super-weapons, who set prince against prince and carried millions of their kidnaped subjects across the sea, as was to happen in West Africa, its history would have been different. West African society, like that of the Indians, was torn apart by an expanding and greedy Europe before it could enter modern times in freedom to grow.

The Heritage of West African Art

Some of our knowledge of West African culture comes from works of art. These works continue to influence craftsmen and to inspire artists the world over. Only certain families could train their children to become craftsmen such as blacksmiths, wood sculptors, or brass casters. Those who had mastered a particular skill made up a privileged group and enjoyed a special position in the society.

The objects created by African artists almost always had a religious meaning. This is true of most so-called "primitive" art. The wooden headdress

Members of the West African Bambara tribe carved the wooden dance mask at left and the wooden dance headdress immediately below. The wooden carving of the horse and rider at the bottom of the page was done by a member of the Dogon tribe in Mali. On the opposite page is a brass sculpture of the head of a young boy.

shown at left center was intended for use in a dance. It mixes grace and humor in its portrayal of an animal with the sweeping horns of an African antelope and the curly tail of a monkey. Perhaps it represented a spirit with a monkey's sense of fun and an antelope's swiftness in pursuit or escape. The dance mask at the far left has an exaggerated nose and lips. You may want to compare it with the Kwakiutl Indian mask shown on page 47. Primitive artists, like modern cartoonists, often twisted things out of their real shape or size to make a point. But African sculptors sometimes chose to portray objects realistically. The dignified head of a young boy at right is clearly such a lifelike portrait. And although West African art had serious purposes, it could also be humorous. The peppery little warrior (lower left) seems to be getting the horse laugh from his mount. Do you think there was once a spear in his hand? Or is he just shaking his fist in rage?

African expression took other forms, too. Olaudah Equiano, a West African boy who was enslaved around 1750 and later learned to write English, said that he came from "a nation of dancers, musicians, and poets." Africans excelled in the use of drums, flutes, horns, xylophones, and other instruments. Music and dance are still part of religious worship for some Americans, who not only sing hymns and listen to choirs but who also perform folk masses and rock 'n' roll plays of Biblical stories. For most West Africans who, like most American Indians, had no written languages songs and dances were an expression of their religion, their traditions, and their history.

Questions for Discussion

1. Why was there so little contact between Europeans and Africans before the middle of the fifteenth century?
2. How did the societies of black Africa differ in the ways they governed themselves?
3. How does a study of the art of black African societies help us to learn about their cultures?
4. What role did music and dance play in the life of West African societies?
5. How do societies without written languages communicate and carry on trade with each other and with outsiders? How do they hand down their customs and traditions from one generation to the next?

ALL OTHERS: PHOTO BY ELIOT ELISOFON

The Slave Trade

The coming of Arab slave caravans and European slave ships blew apart this West African world. Yet, sadly, the fuse which set off this explosion was lit by the Africans themselves. A kind of slavery existed among the tribes, just as some form of compulsory labor existed all over the world from ancient times. The idea of a free labor market in which a workman makes the best bargain he can with an employer is fairly modern.

A West African slave was someone who had to perform work for whomever owned him, who could not leave his owner's service, and who received no payment except food and shelter. His status was below that of a free man. But he often worked no harder and lived no worse than his master. He might well have a family of his own, and he could even be trusted with important responsibilities. He was probably in a better position than a European peasant.

A man became a slave in various ways that did not brand him as a naturally inferior person. He could be a prisoner of war. Or he could have had a period of hard luck which made him unable to pay his debts, so that he might sell himself to pay all he owed. Or he might be a lawbreaker whose punishment was to become a slave to the king, instead of serving a prison sentence as in a

modern nation. Slaves could be sold or given away, and African rulers did give slaves as gifts, in the way that a rich person today might hand over an especially useful power tool or an automobile to a friend.

Beginning around 900 A.D., Arab traders developed a growing trade in slaves whom they carried northward across the desert (above, right) to the Mediterranean coast. That was how some sub-Saharan Africans found their way to Europe before the mid-fifteenth century.

When Europeans first appeared on the Guinea coast, offering iron, firearms, beads, mirrors, cloth, and cowry shells (a kind of seashell used for money in African trade) in exchange for slaves, African chiefs were glad to deal with them. They did not know that the Europeans' demands would be so great, so long-lasting, and would take away millions of men and women. Nor could they know that slavery on a New World plantation was far different from what it was in an African household. For most Africans slavery would be a brutal experience from the first moment of capture.

At first the trade was simple. A captain would land and talk with a local chief or ruler. After some presents were given, the chief would round up a few "natives" who were already slaves and hand them over. It was

Opposite page: An African village is overwhelmed by slave traders who have been supplied with guns by the Europeans. Above: Arab traders drove captured slaves northward across the Sahara Desert. This Sahara sandstorm was drawn by an Englishman who made an attempt to cross the desert in 1818.

Harper's, MARCH 1875

African raiding parties drove their captives from their villages to the waiting slave ships. The slaves were tied together, and those who failed to keep pace were beaten or killed.

almost like trading with the Indians in America for beaver pelts.

Gradually, slavery became more organized. European countries like Portugal, England, and Holland set up special companies to trade in slaves. These companies built permanent bases or forts on the coast. Meanwhile, African chiefs began to send raiding parties into neighboring villages, and perhaps sometimes their own, to round up fresh supplies of slaves. In their greed for profit, these black manhunters made no effort to separate villagers already enslaved from those who were free. Men, women, and children were hustled away from their homes and families in a sudden, devastating surprise attack. Those who resisted were killed. The rest were yoked neck to neck (left) and driven without mercy along the trails southward to the coast. Those falling behind were beaten or murdered.

Once at the fort on the coast, the terrified captives were kept in special pens, called barracoons. Their jailers might be either European or African. Slave-ship crews and captains bargained with these agents (lower right), offering so much cloth or iron or rum for each piece of human merchandise. After much arguing and gulping of rum, an agreement was usually reached. The skipper of the slaver (as ships in the trade were called), perhaps along with his doctor, examined the Africans rounded up for shipment (upper right). Those selected were branded with the buyer's mark and kept in captivity until a full shipload was gathered. The sick or injured who had not been chosen were left to die.

The poor naked African who was prodded and inspected like an animal at an auction was degraded, stripped of all human dignity. So were the Europeans who remained in the forts and drowned their terror of jungle fevers or slave uprisings in liquor. So were the African headmen who earned shells and cloth by selling their own countrymen. The slave trade branded everyone, even those whose flesh was not touched by hot iron.

The Middle Passage to the New World

Then came the worst part, the Middle Passage, as the voyage to the Americas was called. Up to the time of going on board ship, the slaves were at least in familiar territory. Now, chained hand and foot, they were thrown into huge canoes, manned by Kru tribesmen,

Slave-ship doctors examine the Negroes (above) and recommend the healthiest for purchase (below).

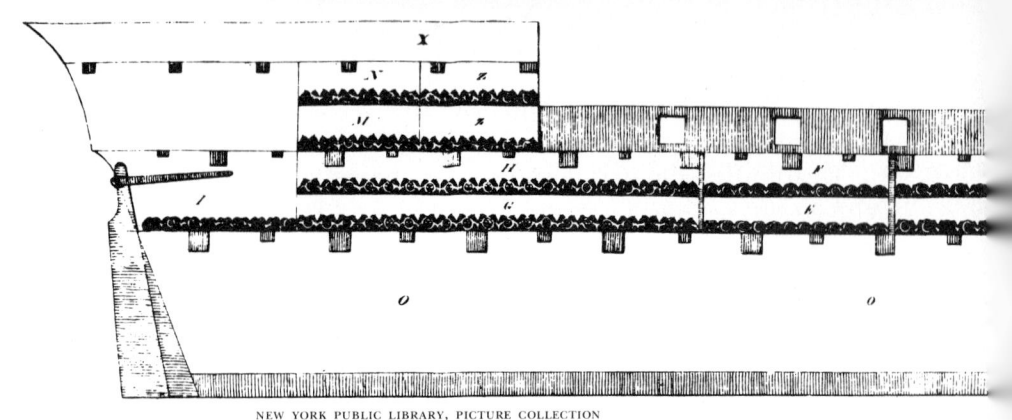

NEW YORK PUBLIC LIBRARY, PICTURE COLLECTION

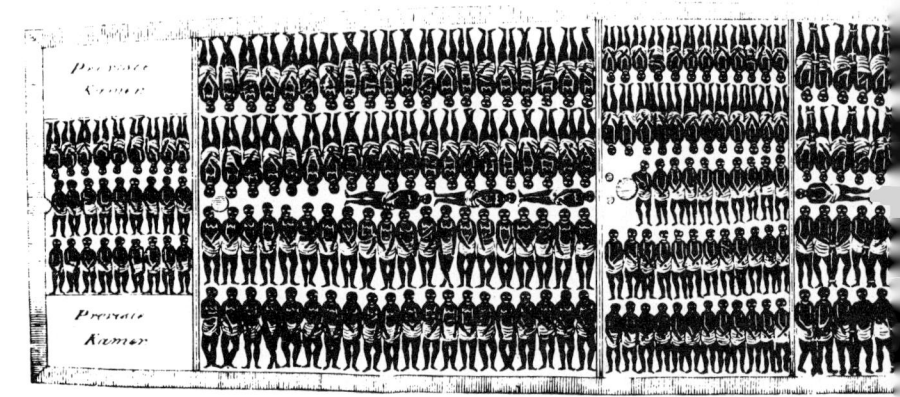

BARBER, *A History of the Amistad Captives*, 1840

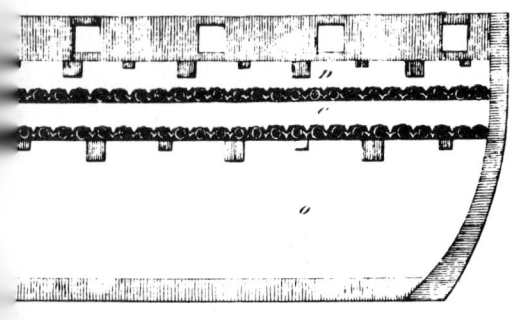

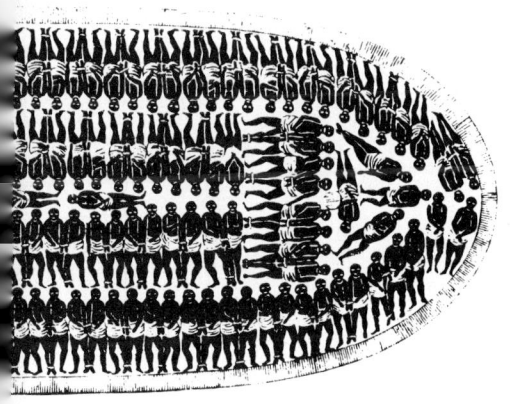

Above: Traders packed their slave cargo as tightly as possible. Men, women, and children were forced to lie with their backs on the deck. The average space allotted to each slave was about 16 inches wide, 5 feet 6 inches long, and 2 feet high. Often, men were chained together to prevent a revolt. Left: In July 1839 a group of 54 Africans seized their Spanish slave ship and killed the captain. Led by an African named Cinque, they sailed the ship to Long Island. There, they were arrested, and the case eventually reached the United States Supreme Court. John Quincy Adams defended them and won their freedom. The Africans raised money for their passage home with public appearances and returned to their native country in 1841.

to be taken out to the ships anchored offshore. Some tried to throw themselves overboard or strangle themselves with their chains. But they were finally forced into the hold of the ship. Since the purpose of the slaver was to pack in as much "cargo" as possible, the blacks were forced to lie on the rough decks crowded next to each other, with no room to sit up. The diagrams of the slave ship at left suggest the terrible jamming involved. In good weather the slaves were brought up on deck during the day, in chains, and fed beans or cooked cereal or sweet potatoes and water. But during storms they lay packed below decks for days on end, wallowing in their own filth. The suffocating stench of a slave ship could be smelled by other vessels miles away. Disease swept through the slave decks, often killing as many as half the "cargo" before the four or five weeks' voyage ended.

The Africans did not take this brutal treatment without resistance. Yet they were always under armed guard, first by their African captors and then by white sailors. The slave Olaudah Equiano believed that these horrible monsters with long hair were going to eat him. In the slave pens ashore and on the ships, there were attempts to murder the guards and to escape. Sometimes they were successful. In 1839 slaves aboard the schooner *Amistad* murdered the officers (lower left) during the voyage from one Cuban port to another. After many adventures the slaves finally got back to Africa. But for the most part, the hardest-battling captives in slave revolts were shot or beaten helpless or killed themselves in despair.

Even with the losses from disease, slave trading was so profitable that it lasted for almost four centuries. The Constitution of the United States outlawed the African slave trade after 1808, but smugglers continued to bring in slaves until slavery was abolished at the end of the Civil War. According to some estimates, 15 million Africans were brought as slaves to the Americas.

Questions for Discussion

1. Describe the slave trade that took place in Africa before and after the white man came.
2. Why was the "Middle Passage" the worst part of the slave trade? Why were so many slaves crowded onto the small slavers?
3. Why was slavery "big business" for so long?

Negroes were often taken from slave ships and then sold to sugar planters in the Caribbean. Slaves harvested the sugar cane (lower right), ground it in the mill (upper right), and then boiled it in vats (below) to make molasses.

Slavery in the Americas

DUTERTRE, *Histoire des Antilles*, 1667

For many of the slaves, New World life began in the West Indies. By 1815 Spanish colonists were importing 10,000 slaves a year to these islands. Thousands were needed on the sugar, indigo, and other plantations owned by French, Dutch, British, and Spanish settlers in the Caribbean islands. Thousands of others were "seasoned" there before being sent to the mainland of North or South America. Seasoning meant accustoming the blacks to plantation work. Slaves often worked from sunup to sundown cutting, hauling, crushing, and then boiling sugar cane, as pictured in this 1667 drawing of a sugar cane plantation in Barbados. Women, even those caring for infants whom they carried on their backs, had the same tasks as men and, like men, were flogged if they did not work fast enough. Food consisted of poor grades of fish, plus a little cornmeal or other grain. No wonder almost a third of the slaves died while being "seasoned."

Slavery was somewhat different under differing colonial powers. In South America, for example, the Negro's fate was softened a little for special reasons. To begin with, the powerful officials of the Spanish church insisted that slaves be baptized as Catholics and allowed lawful marriage. Slave families could not be broken up by sale, as later happened in the English colonies. In addition, women were scarce in early Latin America, and some early white settlers married black or Indian girls. A Latin American population of many strains—European, Indian, African—emerged gradually and hatred among the races lessened. Although most laws for Spanish America were made in Spain, when local government was strong in the New World, it worked against the interests of Indians and blacks. Most New World planters did not marry outside their race and, because their money and racial fears were involved, they tended to be less than fair-minded.

Thus it was not unusual for African slaves to be treated brutally in Portuguese and Spanish mainland colonies. However, they did get a little more recognition of their humanity and suffered a little less because of their race. They often had a good chance of becoming citizens. Although they did revolt now and then, there was not so much bitterness between black servants and white masters as showed itself in other places where slaves were thought of as less than human. The French colony of Haiti provided one example of how much cruelty slavery could breed.

Revolt in Haiti

Haiti was the western half of the island of Hispaniola. Spain gave up that half to France after a war, in 1697. The French sugar planters were especially harsh. They intended not to become permanent residents, but to make money quickly and return home. They had no interest in seeing a thriving island population. Nor did the king in Paris ever think of Haiti's blacks as subjects for whom he had much responsibility. The planters were also gnawed by fear when the slaves came to outnumber them by as many as twenty to one.

All these forces added up to rule by terror. Overseers were allowed to overwork Haitian slaves. Planters found that it was cheaper to replace those who died with new imports from Africa than to take good care of the living. **Black codes** (special laws for blacks) clamped an iron grip on the slaves. They could not meet, carry weapons, strike or insult white men, or move off the plantations without permission. Every means of self-defense was kept from them. Cruel and brutal punishments for lawbreaking were strange ways for "civilized" people to teach correct behavior to "savages." The punishments included whipping, branding, cutting off noses, fingers, and ears, and breaking bones. Thousands of runaways from such bitter rule hid in Haiti's jungles and hills, sometimes leading raids and revolts. A crop of hate was planted well.

Its harvest came in 1791. Led by a slave named Toussaint L'Ouverture, the blacks arose in a bloody revolt, killing their masters and burning the homes of French colonials (upper right). For a time Toussaint allied his forces with the Spanish, who controlled the eastern end of the island, called Santo Domingo. When the British landed in Haiti to support the Spanish, it appeared that France might lose the entire island. Then the government in Paris offered freedom to all blacks who would help it in defeating Spain and England. Toussaint accepted the offer, was made a general, and led the black forces to victory. By 1801 he was the head of a practically independent island.

In 1802 Napoleon sent 20,000 French troops to reestablish his control in Haiti and Santo Domingo. Although Toussaint was captured and imprisoned in France, other Haitian blacks continued to fight. Incidents like the hanging of captured French soldiers (lower right) caused feelings to run high on both

Pierre Toussaint L'Ouverture was the first black man to lead a successful revolt against a colonial power in the New World. By 1801 he had reorganized the government on the island of Hispaniola and had put a new constitution into effect. The next year Napoleon sent troops commanded by General Le Clerc to recapture Haiti and Santo Domingo. Toussaint was betrayed and taken prisoner to France, where he died in prison in 1803. Toussaint's followers defeated the French and proclaimed independence in 1804.

RAINSFORD, Historical Account of the Black Empire of Haiti, 1805

The Haitian blacks vented their rage at the French in many ways. Above, a 1795 engraving shows French homes that have been set afire by the slaves. At left, some French soldiers attempting to put down the revolt are hanged by Negroes. Pictures like these were widely publicized in the United States. What effect do you think the pictures would have upon slave-owners? upon slaves? upon people who did not own slaves?

With the exception of a few private sales, slave-owners purchased their property at public auctions. The poster at right advertises the auction of a cargo of slaves that has just arrived from the Guinea Coast. Slave auctions like the one below in Charleston, South Carolina, were increasingly common as the South adopted plantation agriculture.

sides. Napoleon's troops were finally beaten, and on January 1, 1804, Haitians proclaimed the independence of the New World's first black-ruled nation. This victory of slaves over white masters alarmed slave-owners in America and provided a reason for many of the laws passed to keep slaves in line.

Slavery in Britian's North American Colonies

Slavery in the English colonies was closely tied to racial **prejudice** (an opinion or judgment formed without knowledge of the facts). When the first twenty Africans were landed in Virginia in 1619, it was apparently not certain that they would be slaves. Many white laborers came to the colony as **indentured servants,** that is, servants bound by a legal contract and required to work for one master for a fixed term of years. At first it seemed that Africans would be treated in the same way. After a time they would be given land and freedom. Some won these rewards. But as time went on, the rules for black and white servants became different. Only "Christians" could bear arms, according to a Maryland law of 1648. Africans were not considered Christians at that time. Only whites could meet in groups after dark, said another Maryland law. When a white servant ran away in Virginia, his punishment was to serve a little longer. But when a Negro named John Punch did so in 1640, he was made to serve his master for the rest of his life. In time marriage between blacks and whites was forbidden by law.

By 1700 almost all incoming Africans were sold as slaves at auctions (lower left) after the "cargo" had been advertised in posters such as the one at upper left. Growers of tobacco, rice, and indigo in the southern colonies came to believe they could not do without the labor of Africans. Although blacks were less in demand in the northern settlements, some were brought there as servants and laborers. And northern merchants prospered on the slave trade.

The conditions on the southern plantation in the 1700's depended much on the master. Most slaves were field hands, and most of the time they put in grueling days of hard outdoor work with nothing to look forward to at sunset except another such day. The difference between slavery in Spanish America and the American South was that there was no church or strong central government to protect slaves from their masters. The black slave was a chattel, a piece of movable property,

This detail from a nineteenth-century drawing shows slaves pulling a heavy wagon along a city street.

The American Anti-Slavery Almanac for 1836 *showed a fugitive-slave hunt.*

NEW-YORK HISTORICAL SOCIETY

with no right to a family or anything else of his own. He could not sell his labor for the highest wage as a free laborer could. Nor was he protected by the laws which protected free men. Governments in the English colonies were under strong local influence. In the South that meant letting the planters do what they liked with their slaves.

Yet some planters were learning that the so-called pagan Africans could learn as quickly as any European. A Captain Matthews of Virginia boasted in 1649 of the 40 Negroes who practiced trades in his house. Free Negroes and slaves worked on plantations, and, a century after that, in towns as coachmen, barbers, waiters, cooks, carpenters, blacksmiths, shoemakers, and at many other skilled occupations.

As the number of slaves increased, the white owners took steps to curb the danger of rebellion. Runaways, like the slave shown being hunted down with dogs at left, were severely punished. Black codes not only dealt cruelly with those who resisted white authority but also forbade slaves to gather together. Immigrants to America from other lands could keep many of their customs, worship in the familiar tongue, and gradually grow accustomed to a new style of life as they let go of their past. But the African was forbidden to gather with his kind to share his past. His language, his customs, and often his self-esteem were ripped from him.

A few masters and sincere believers tried to help the Negro by converting him to Christianity. Since religious gatherings were the only kind allowed to blacks, in time churches became important centers of Negro life in America. Black preachers were most likely to be leaders. But colonial governments, especially in the South where slaves were numerous, never were pleased with such efforts. They discouraged kindly masters who tried to educate slaves, especially by teaching them to read. They were not happy with owners who overcame fears and set their slaves free. The reason was that free Negroes, Christian Negroes, and Negroes who could read disproved the white man's argument that Negroes could not take care of themselves and that they needed supervision. Besides, freed slaves would only inspire other blacks to revolt.

That is just what they did. Slavery was always weakened by the good will of some white men and the courage and love of freedom of some blacks. The slaves

were never all happy, as slaveholders liked to believe. From the beginning there was rebellion. In Virginia, as early as 1663, a plan for revolt was uncovered before it could be carried out. South Carolina was the scene of three serious rebellions in 1739. In New York there was a revolt in 1712, in which slaves killed nine whites. These revolts were but a few of many. All were put down. Dozens of blacks were hanged, burned alive, and tortured to frighten others, while the laws hampering free Negroes were made even stricter.

The first United States census in 1790 counted more than 750,000 Negroes in the total population of nearly 4,000,000. Of the Negroes almost 700,000 were slaves. Slavery had become a large part of the new nation's way of life. Its brutality shocked some of the country's best minds. For example, Thomas Jefferson, author of the Declaration of Independence and a slaveholder, was worried. "I tremble for my country," he once wrote, "when I reflect that God is just." He had cause for alarm. Slavery in America would neither live nor die without further bloodshed and brutality.

Questions for Discussion

1. For what kinds of work was slave labor found to be most profitable in the Americas?
2. How were slaves "seasoned" for plantation work in the Americas? Why did so many die in the process?
3. Why did the attitude of the Spanish and Portuguese toward the slaves differ from that of northern Europeans? How was this difference reflected in the ways that slaves were treated?
4. What did L'Ouverture's rebellion against French rule in Haiti prove? Why did it make whites elsewhere more fearful of blacks?
5. In the English colonies in North America, why did the attitude toward, and the treatment of, blacks change between 1619 and 1700?
6. What was the effect of the "black codes" in the English colonies on the culture of slaves?
7. Why did colonial government leaders in the English colonies discourage efforts to educate the blacks?
8. What do the slave rebellions indicate about the Negro's attitude toward his life and treatment?
9. Why did slave revolts fail in the colonies?
10. Why have churches been so important to Negroes in their life in America?

Chapter Review

Social Studies Terms

Before answering the questions which follow, review the meaning of the following terms: **extended families, depose, status, black codes, prejudice, indentured servants.**

Summary Questions for Discussion

1. Why is it important for people to be aware and proud of their history and heritage?
2. Compare the importance of religion to the Negro in his West African homeland and in America.
3. What would be the effect on your personality if you were suddenly captured by a strange people, torn away from your relatives and friends, carried to a land across the sea, and then put in a position of lifelong slavery?
4. Why may blacks as well as whites claim to be founders of American civilization?
5. What scientific and technological advances made it easy for Europeans to dominate both the blacks in Africa and the Indians in America?

Pictures as Historical Evidence

If the pictures in this chapter were the only evidence that was available to you about slavery, what might be a possible hypothesis about the relationship between slavery and violence? Why?

Map Study

Study the map of Africa on page 81. Name three major rivers of Africa. Which one was fairly well-known to Europeans before 1500? Why? In the 1600's which African "product" was more important to Europeans than any of those shown on the map?

For Further Reading

African Kingdoms, by Basil Davidson. New York: Time Inc., 1966.

Amos Fortune, Free Man, by Elizabeth Yates. New York: E. P. Dutton & Co., Inc., 1966.

Glorious Age in Africa, by Daniel Chu and Elliott Skinner. Garden City, New York: Doubleday & Company, Inc., 1965.

Story of the Negro, by Arna Bontemps. New York: Alfred A. Knopf, Inc., 1960.

To Be a Slave, by Lester Julius. New York: The Dial Press, Inc., 1968.

4
Colonial America

Early settlers in America liked to compare themselves to the Biblical Children of Israel in the Promised Land. They took all God's commandments seriously, and especially the one that said, "Be fruitful and multiply." In the first 150 years after England started a colony in Virginia, its colonies did multiply and produce much marvelous "fruit." Little outposts originally facing starvation grew into thriving communities. While the French and Spanish empires spread over millions of empty acres, England's colonists were mostly settled in a compact ribbon of territory, about 50 miles wide, running down the Atlantic Coast (map, opposite). There, in the valleys of the many rivers flowing to the sea, the **pioneers** (people who settle unknown or unclaimed territory) gathered the wealth of the soil and forest. There, they built towns and new ways of life.

We saw, as we looked at Indian and African cultures, the many ways in which men earn a living, get along together, and worship. The bigger and more complicated a society becomes, the more variety it has. A society that has grown bigger than a single tribe or settlement develops many special occupations and **classes** (groups of people who share a role or position in the society). Instead of priests and hunters only, there are, perhaps, bishops and choirboys, generals and riflemen, and hundreds of in-between positions. There are many centers of activity. Towns spring up, full of traders, teachers, workers, lawyers, and other specialists. Many different ways of work and worship make for a colorful pattern.

As the map on the opposite page shows, by 1760 the colonists made a living in many ways. They grew grain, tobacco, and indigo. They combed the forests for furs and for timber to build houses and ships. They fished for the commonplace cod and the mighty whale. They gathered in cities and linked them with the Post Road which cut through the woods and farmlands from what is now Portland, Maine, to St. Augustine, Florida. They built a chain of forts along the edge of the wilderness. Throughout the thirteen colonies men, goods, and ideas mingled in an American setting.

As you read, think about these questions:
1. What natural features of the environment influence the ways in which people make a living?
2. What considerations influenced the choice of leaders in colonial society?

New England: A Shipping Economy

To New England's first settlers, God was everywhere and always watching over His own. Richard Mather, the Puritan minister (lower right), described his stormy voyage from England to Massachusetts in 1635 in his journal. Every fair day was because of "the goodness of our God" and every gale a sign of "His overruling providence." It was important to such faithful believers that a public school system be set up as early in Massachusetts as 1647 so that Satan could not keep man "from the knowledge of the Scriptures." In such classrooms even the littlest Puritans learned their alphabet from a primer, or first reader, that referred to a Bible story or made a religious point with each letter (left). Even before the 1647 law was passed, a "colledge" called Harvard had been founded and a printing press had been set up.

Ministers were natural leaders in a community whose purpose was to work God's will on earth. It was unthinkable at first that anyone should not belong to a church where men could help each other walk the road of holiness. Thus the political system was a **theocracy** (rule by religious leaders).

Christians were meant, in the words of the Puritan leader John Winthrop, to "bear one another's burdens." This meant that "the care of the public must hold sway over all private interests." Individuals did not casually choose their own farms and house lots. Instead, the governments of New England colonies laid out neatly surveyed townships. A central square, on which cattle might browse in the early days, became the "common." Individual plots were marked off and assigned around it. Some lots were reserved for public buildings such as schools. The gridiron pattern, as the 1748 map of New Haven at right shows, became the standard for American towns and cities. In the town meeting all the property owners shared in decision-making, gossip, argument, and the responsibility for such projects as building schools, churches, jails, roads, and bridges.

In early New England church leaders kept tight control over social as well as religious life. Such strict control was hard on dissenters like Roger Williams who openly disagreed with church leaders. He was ordered out of Massachusetts in 1635 for opposing the theocracy, and he fled to what later became Rhode Island. From the start dissent was one of several forces in New England working to bring about growth and different ways of living.

A page from a 1767 New England primer that taught the alphabet.

The layout of New Haven, Connecticut, was typical of most New England towns. The map above includes the names and occupations of the residents. Left: This 1670 woodcut of Richard Mather was the first woodcut made in New England. Mather was a scholarly minister who translated the Psalms in the Puritans' Bay Psalm Book and developed the Puritan system of church government in Massachusetts.

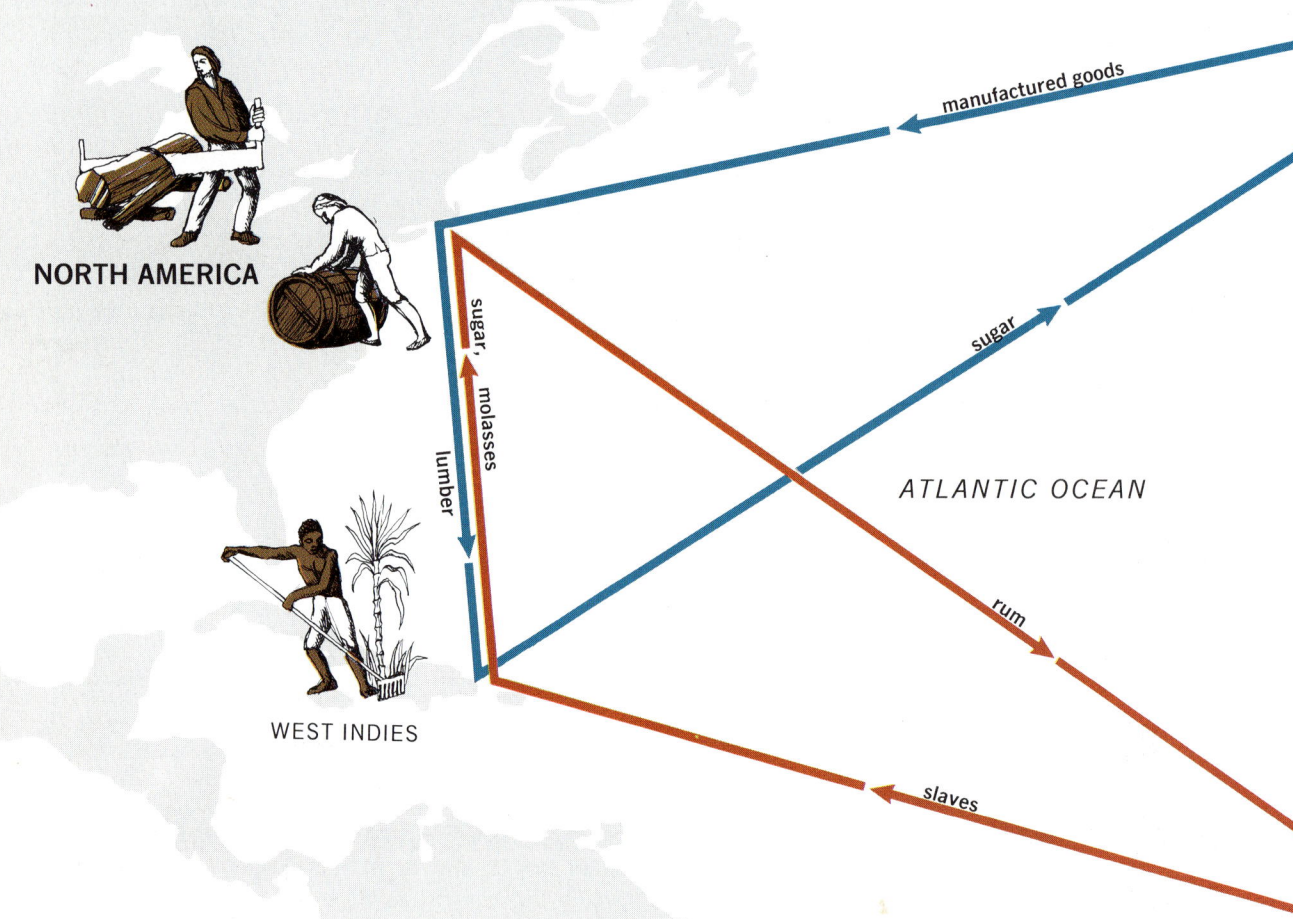

The Triangular Trade

Puritan elders believed that God meant His world to be used and improved. Hard work became a form of worship. So New Englanders, or Yankees, as they came to be called, worked earnestly. They farmed their rocky soil and reaped generous harvests from the forest and sea. The wilderness contained fur, but its trees also furnished fine timbers for ships. As early as 1631 a tiny vessel named *Blessing of the Bay* was launched in Boston. A hundred years later Yankee-built ships, manned by Yankee sailors, were familiar sights in the ports of the West Indies, Europe, and Africa.

New England skippers might clear Boston or Providence with a load of lumber, salted fish, horses, and furs. They would head south, stopping at other colonial ports to take on tobacco and rice. Then they would put in at a West Indian island and unload the horses, the lumber to build the planters' houses and mills, and the fish and rice to feed the slaves. In exchange, the captains would receive sugar and currency. Then they sailed east across the Atlantic, perhaps with a stop in Spain to add wine and lemons to the cargo. Next came London where the furs, sugar, wines, and fruit were sold. Finally, the Yankee vessel would return home, full of furniture, clothing, glass, tools, and ironware.

You will note (map, opposite page) that there was a triangle of trade, its three points being New England, the Caribbean islands, and old England. Another, grimmer triangle existed, too. The New Englanders bought molasses, a by-product of refined sugar cane, from the West Indies. After distilling the molasses in New England, they sailed to the African coast and traded the rum for slaves, then exchanged the slaves for molasses at West Indian ports and brought the syrup back to New England. Later New England became a center of activity against drinking and slavery, but its youthful fortunes rested partly on rum and slave-trading.

As Yankee merchants and sailors gathered in the profits of these trades, things happened. Codfish and pine planks became as important in the once-Puritan world as psalms and farms. Men from Boston and Providence and Salem helped to link three continents lapped by the Atlantic. The isolation of America was broken. The old villages were swelled by newcomers, brightened by imported goods, and stirred by foreign ideas. The new patterns were most clear in Boston.

Above: This 1764 water color of Boston shows the harbor crowded with ships. Right: In 1757 an American artist named John Copley painted this portrait of James Tilley, who was 50 years of age and a very successful New England merchant.

Boston: City of Commerce

By 1760, when it was about 130 years old, Boston had a population of over 15,000. It had come a long way from being a little Puritan holy city in the wilderness. In the picture at upper left, painted in 1764, the four church steeples are the city's tallest structures. Churches were still important in Boston's life, but the masts of the many ships at the wharves also showed what Boston lived by.

Its merchants were honored men. Like James Tilley, whom you see posing proudly (lower left), they dressed well, dined well, and lived in elegant homes. They had the confidence in themselves that Tilley displays as he leans on a ledger that probably shows a fine profit from one of his ships' last trips.

But Boston was not all trade and accounts. Its best citizens included royal officials and the ministers of the handsome brick churches in the heart of town. There was also a middle class of men who made their living by special skills—men like Paul Revere, the son of a French immigrant, who made fine silver bowls, pitchers, tongs, and other objects in his shop. Or like Isaiah Thomas, whose saucy newspaper, the *Massachusetts Spy*, was only one of many items that he turned out on his printing press. Or like the able lawyer named John Adams, who came from "out in the country," went to Harvard, and then came to town to make a career.

There were also Bostonians, including free white men and indentured servants, free blacks and slaves, who got their hands dirty for a living. There were waiters at the inns; grooms for horses; apprentices to tailors, butchers, and shoemakers; men who did odd jobs for grocers, cabinetmakers, stonemasons, and bricklayers; sailors between voyages; workers at the shipyards (right). Boston had that special liveliness that belongs to cities.

This ship's carpenter was one of many employed in the growing New England shipbuilding industries.

Questions for Discussion

1. Why were ministers in colonial New England such highly respected people?
2. How were the religious ideas of the Puritans expressed in their ways of governing themselves and in their attitudes toward dissenters?
3. What was the "triangle of trade?"
4. How did life in colonial Boston differ from life in an early Puritan village?

NEW YORK STATE HISTORICAL ASSOCIATION

The Middle Colonies: America's First Breadbasket

In 1650 a Dutch official wrote of "New Netherland" that it was "the handsomest and pleasantest country that man can behold," with "grass as high as a man's knees" to feed cattle and "all sorts of fresh ponds, brooks, and rivers." Much of the soil of the Middle Colonies—New York, New Jersey, Pennsylvania, Delaware, and parts of Maryland—was level and rich. Once a settler had cleared off the trees, it was easy to grow corn, wheat, rye, oats, and other food crops, as well as flax from which linen is made. In the early stages of settling the land, a pioneer father could feed his family with the plentiful game he shot and with the fish which seemed limitless. Later, when the land was developed, the settlers cultivated orchards and raised pigs and chickens to make up for the wild deer and turkeys which the pioneers had driven away.

The Middle Colonies became America's first farm heartland. Unlike the Old World, land was not hard to get. A farm could be rented from some rich Englishman or Dutchman who had been given a large estate by the government in return for bringing in settlers. Or a poor man could work as an indentured servant for seven years. At the end of that time, some colonies would give him 50 acres for his own. By 1750, however, these opportunities were almost entirely closed to all blacks, except for a handful of free Negroes.

On the generous land the white colonists built a comfortable way of life. On farms like the one above, Europeans who settled in America learned, like Indians, to use everything which nature provided. They ground their own wheat to make flour and baked bread

on their own hearths like the one at lower left. They butchered their own hogs and cattle (right) and salted what meat they did not eat at once for future use. Clothing was made from sheep's wool or from linen. The women of the household prepared the flax fibers, spun them into thread, and wove the cloth. Then they dyed it with bark or berry juices, cut it, and sewed it. The hides of cows, sheep, and pigs were put to good use, too. Once the animal had been skinned, the hides were converted into leather by a local tanner. Then a local craftsman cut, sewed, and glued the leather to make shoes, boots, gloves, leather shirts, and leggings.

Everyone worked hard: the womenfolk at their pots, pans, spinning wheels, and needles and the men in the barns, fields, and stables. Even children had many chores. Can you guess what they would be? The work yielded a reward that landless European peasants could not expect: a chance to be property owners and the opportunity for a better life.

The pioneer settlers needed little from the outside world. Iron and glass had to be bought, although when allowed the Middle Colonies could manufacture them as well as Great Britain. Imported luxuries such as coffee, tea, sugar, books, china dishes, and lace caps also were appreciated by farm folk. Thus these early American communities were, for the most part, **self-sufficient** (able to provide for oneself). This self-sufficiency gave the pioneers a sense of independence which, as we shall see, had a great deal to do with the colonists' beliefs about the role of government and the rights of individuals.

This colonial painting of a New York farm in the early 1700's once hung over the mantel in the house it depicts. The owner and his wife stand in front of the farmhouse, watching the passersby. The Catskill Mountains form the background. The drawings on the opposite page and below were done by an amateur artist from York, Pennsylvania. A York tavern-keeper is seen frying sweet potatoes as a local farm wife deftly slaughters a hog.

HISTORICAL SOCIETY OF YORK COUNTY

Colonial Pennsylvania welcomed a number of religious denominations. The baptism (above) and the Moravian foot-washing ceremony (below) were sketched in the eighteenth century. Right: A Quaker speaks his conscience as others pray silently.

KURZE, *Zuvelassige Nachricht*, 1762

Religious Diversity Welcomed

The Middle Colonies, and especially Pennsylvania, differed from New England in another way than the richness of the farmland. They were not founded by tiny groups of fellow believers who discouraged outsiders, as the first Puritans in Massachusetts did. Instead, they prospered by attracting many newcomers of different faiths. Moreover, William Penn, who founded Pennsylvania in 1681, had a special reason to be friendly to newcomers who were independent-minded in religious matters. Penn himself was a Quaker. The Quakers believed in simplicity of dress, speech, and worship (right). They also believed that each man should be guided by the "inner light" of his conscience. Because they objected to all interference by the government in religious matters, they were terribly persecuted, not only in old England, but in Massachusetts as well.

Europeans were attracted by Pennsylvania—a place of good land, peace, and no whipping posts or gallows for religious minorities. Thousands of Germans from the Rhine Valley, which was torn by wars and church quarrels, emigrated to Penn's paradise. They first came in 1683 and founded a suburb of Philadelphia that is still called Germantown. By 1760 they made up one-third of the colony's population. The "Pennsylvania Dutch" got their name from a mistaken pronunciation of the German word *Deutsch*, meaning "German." They were divided among many religious groups, such as Lutherans, Moravians, Schwenkfelders, Dunkards and Mennonites. After 1700 a number of Presbyterians from northern Ireland came over, too. Some European Jews were attracted by the religious freedom and economic opportunities of New York and Philadelphia. Many English Catholics settled in Maryland, which had been granted in 1632 to Cecilius Calvert, Lord Baltimore, a Catholic Englishman. The Middle Colonies thus welcomed people of many faiths.

Ben Franklin's Philadelphia

Philadelphia was the center of this world where God was thanked for his bounty in many accents. Just as Boston grew beyond a Puritan village, Philadelphia became something bigger than a Quaker reformer's model city. Its special style is shown in the life of its leading citizen, Benjamin Franklin.

Young Ben Franklin, born in 1706, worked for his

brother James, who was a Boston printer. When Ben was sixteen, however, he set out to make his own fortune and headed for Philadelphia. There, he too became a printer, and then the owner of his own paper, *The Pennsylvania Gazette* (top right).

The *Gazette*, like other colonial newspapers, not only printed reports of wars, accidents, disasters, political quarrels, births, and deaths, but through its advertisements told of what was happening in the world of business. The printer who put out the town's "gazette" also set in type laws, sermons, and almanacs, volumes full of information about the weather, tides, and other things useful to sailors and planters. In addition, he sold the latest books imported from Europe. But publishing the *Gazette* was only one of Franklin's activities. Soon he was involved in buying and selling land and goods, and he became wealthy enough to spend most of his time doing the things he liked.

Among his hobbies was science. Franklin's experiment, in which he proved that lightning was electricity by flying a kite on a wire in a storm and drawing a spark from a key at the wire's end, is probably known to you. But he also liked to use his scientific knowledge to develop useful gadgets such as the Franklin stove (right), which heated a room much better than an open fireplace.

He was a great organizer of city services, such as improved street cleaning and a new street-lighting system. He was responsible for setting up a police force, a school that became the University of Pennsylvania, a city hospital, and a circulating library. He served as a deputy postmaster, a member of the colonial lawmaking body, and the colony's agent in London.

Even before the American Revolution, Franklin was showing that the colonies could produce outstanding thinkers. He was a practical American, as eager to be of use in this world as the Puritans were to prepare for the next. This was a new type of man. But Franklin needed a city to challenge his talents, and Philadelphia's diversity and growing urban needs provided this challenge.

Questions for Discussion

1. How did Penn's policies encourage immigration to Pennsylvania?
2. How does Franklin's career illustrate the attractiveness of the colonies for many Europeans?

Benjamin Franklin (below) first published his Pennsylvania Gazette *in 1729. His scientific inventions included the stove (above).*

This engraving shows central Philadelphia in the eighteenth century.

The South: A Plantation Economy

Southward from Pennsylvania was the area of the **staple crops** (crops that people depend upon for trade or food). The most important product was tobacco, with rice running a close second. Both crops required much hard labor by large groups of men. A tobacco plantation was a kind of agricultural factory. Part of the plantation grew food for the work force, but most of it was devoted to producing the leaves which Europeans enjoyed smoking as much as the Indians did.

But these "factories," like the farming communities of the Middle Colonies, were self-sufficient. The plants were grown, cured, put in barrels, and loaded on ships right at the planter's own riverside wharves, as the pictures on the opposite page suggest. In various buildings on the estate, slaves worked as carpenters, blacksmiths, coopers or barrelmakers, shoemakers, tanners, and butchers. One Virginia planter, George Mason, even had Negro spinners, weavers, knitters, and a distiller, who made "every fall a good deal of apple, peach and persimmon brandy" from the plantation orchards.

The planter rarely saw, or needed, much cash. His tobacco was shipped to a factor, or agent, in London who sold it and used the money to buy goods as the planter instructed him—books for the menfolk, ball gowns for the ladies, dolls for the children, hymnbooks for the parson, a coach for the whole family. The plantation owner was often in debt to the factor if tobacco prices fell. Usually, his solution was to borrow more money to buy more land, hoping to grow more tobacco and eventually catch up. Being in debt was often part of a gentleman landowner's way of life.

Like the New England town and the Middle Colony farm, the plantation was a small world of its own. But where the center of authority in the township was the minister, on the plantation it was the master who ruled slaves and whites alike. Of course, not all Southerners owned large estates. Only a very few did, in fact. But the aristocratic holder of many acres set the tone that ambitious young men tried to imitate. It was the planter's social importance that also gave him great political influence. That importance rested partly on his ownership of slaves.

In the world of slavery, both whites and blacks had very definite social ranks. Among southern white men the overseer, who actually supervised slaves at work, had a very low status. Somewhat above him was the

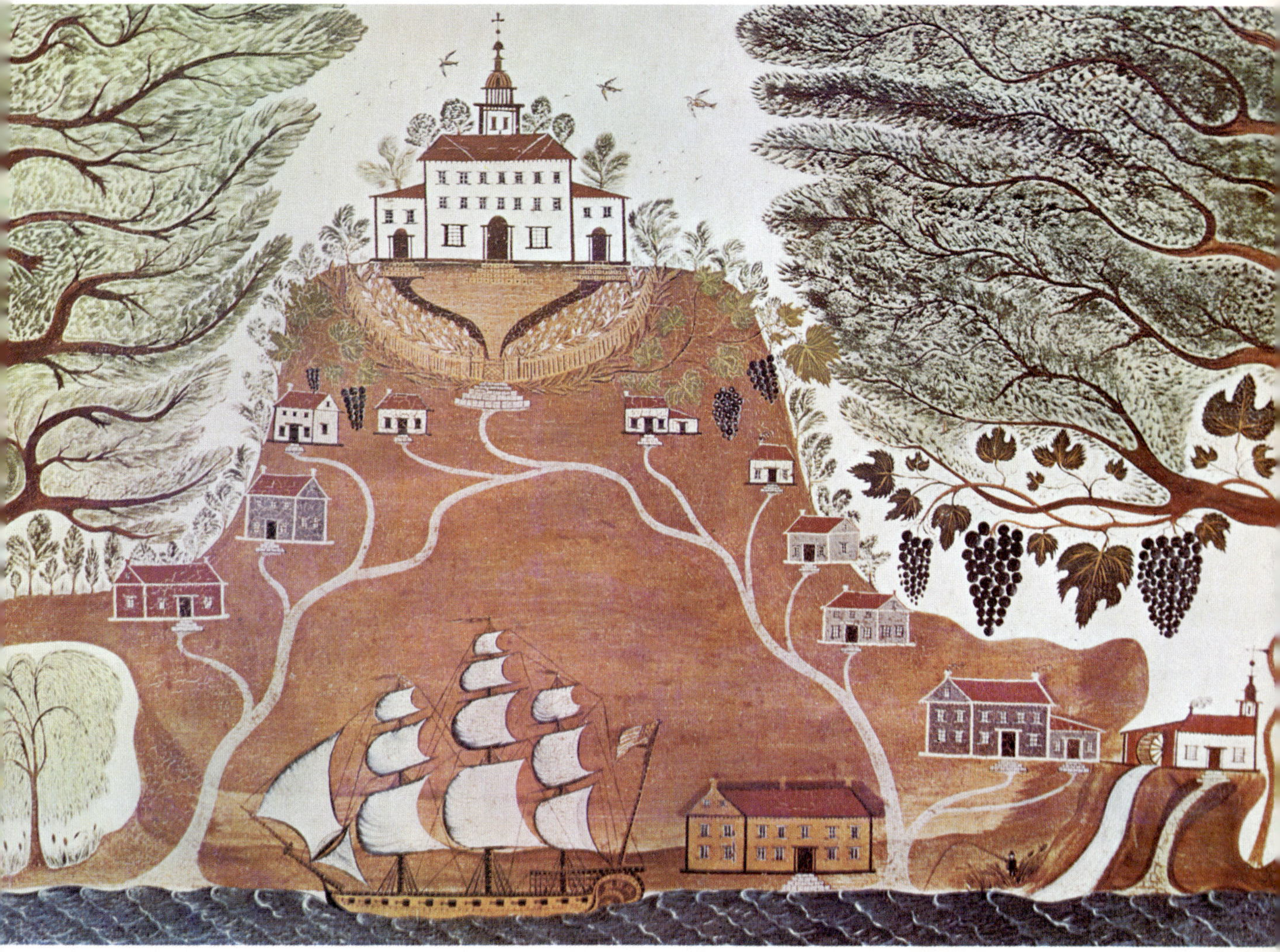

COLONIAL WILLIAMSBURG

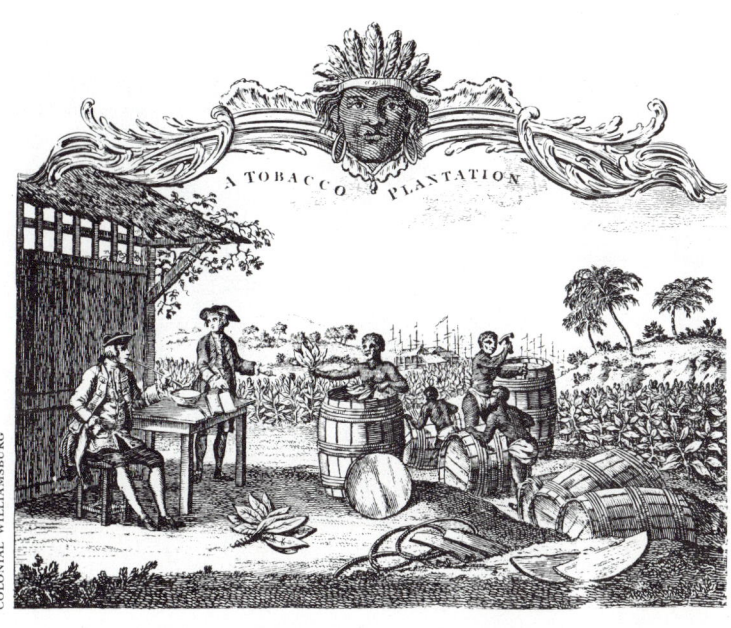

Planters lived well on Virginia plantations that often covered thousands of acres. The plantation pictured above included a great house, slave cabins, barns, warehouses, a water mill, and a dock for ships. Left: Slaves prepare tobacco for shipment on an eighteenth-century plantation.

Left: This water color was sketched near Fredericksburg, Virginia, and is called "An overseer doing his duty." Below: South Carolina slaves enjoy a rare moment of relaxation—possibly preparing for a wedding. Why do you suppose that pictures like this one were popular among the defenders of slavery?

man who owned land but no slaves. The highest rung on the ladder was the class of planters who owned slaves but did not work with them in the fields.

A responsible owner was supposed to be a kind of father to his slaves. He had to settle disputes among them, like a judge. If he chose, he furnished them with religious instruction and led prayer meetings. He was supposed to doctor his sick slaves, with his wife as chief supervisor of nursing. Because he supervised all buildings, roads, and drainage ditches on the plantation, the master also had to be a fairly good architect and engineer. Only a tiny number of plantation owners played all these parts wisely and well. But they were expected to be responsible for many people in a way that almost nobody is in modern life.

As for slaves the closer they got to the owner's family, the more dignity they gained, at least in the eyes of southern whites. The hard-working field hand, in his tattered suit—he was given only two a year—living on cornmeal, fat pork, and molasses in a dirt-floored cabin, was often thought of as a two-legged animal. Skilled workers, especially house servants like the waiter, cook, or nurse (right), led somewhat different lives. These slaves were better dressed and often had a chance to become better educated. They were also more likely to be freed.

Whatever their status, the life of plantation slaves was limited. There was rarely any contact with outside culture. Social life and entertainment were furnished by the slaves themselves. Through songs and dances (lower left), blacks expressed their feelings about their life and work. By so doing, they were creating important kinds of American art which in time would become part of every American's heritage.

One important thing to remember about slavery is that it was a long and brutal episode in our history. It was a terrible system, basically, but many kinds of slaves, from the most oppressed field hand to the talented cabinetmaker, were able to earn money and buy their freedom. There were also many different masters. There were brutes who beat their slaves, but there were also kind men like George Washington who met their responsibilities well and freed their slaves. White and black Southerners built their section together, and the lives of slaves and masters were mingled so that "black" and "white" southern history cannot be separated.

Slaves who worked as house servants usually received better treatment from their masters than the field hands pictured on the opposite page. Here, a black nurse looks after the son of a wealthy Virginian.

Charleston: City of Southern Charm

The South's most important and beautiful city was Charleston, South Carolina, whose waterfront (top right) was lined with fine brick houses. Cities were less important in the South, where there was less commerce and industry than in the northern colonies. But Charleston attracted those who conducted the trade in rice, indigo, and slaves for much of the South.

Charleston's social tone was set by Carolina planters. The growing season on rice plantations was hot and damp. Mosquitoes and fevers were abundant. So the typical Carolina landowner built a town house in Charleston and lived out the unhealthy months there with his family.

Charlestonians tended to imitate French, Spanish, and Dutch West Indian sugar planters as well as English country gentlemen. Elegant clothing, fine furniture, and good food were enjoyed. The Charlestonian of wealth did not give up English styles altogether. He hunted the fox with hound and horn (bottom right) in a costume whose style was borrowed from England. He might send his son to London to study law. In religion he was likely to be a proud member of the government-supported Church of England.

It is a mistake to think that *all* Carolinians lived in this leisurely fashion. In the backwoods there were hard-working new immigrants from northern Ireland who wore homespun clothes, scorned "aristocratic folderol," and believed that only a Methodist, Baptist, or Presbyterian was a true Christian. There were also urban Charlestonians in the business of selling cloth or ships' supplies, who were as sober as Quakers and sometimes were Quakers. But the people looked up to and copied were the landowning gentry, as the ship owners and ministers were in Boston or the grain merchants and bankers were in Philadelphia.

Questions for Discussion

1. How did the South's staple crops promote the growth of plantations?
2. Why did tobacco-plantation owners need little cash to conduct their business?
3. Describe the differences among the classes on a southern plantation.
4. Why were the owners of large plantations in the South politically important, though comparatively few in number?

The small group of plantation owners lived elegantly. Here, an aristocratic couple in Williamsburg, Virginia, dance the quadrille. The quadrille, a square dance of French origin composed of five formal figures and danced by four couples, was popular during colonial times.

Above: An Englishman painted this view of Charleston, South Carolina, from across the Cooper River. Right: A wealthy Charlestonian entertains his friends after dinner. They seem to be enjoying passing a wig around the table. Below: Fox hunting was a favorite sport of colonial Virginia's planters. Here, a hunter and his hounds gather at daybreak for the hunt.

Government in the Colonies

Cecil Calvert, the second Lord Baltimore, posed with his grandson Cecil holding a map of Maryland. Although he was the first proprietor of Maryland and ruled for 43 years, the second Lord Baltimore never visited his colony. Young Cecil was born in Maryland and would have become the fourth Lord Baltimore had he not died at the age of 14.

At the start it was assumed that these little bits of England overseas would be ruled, like England at home, from the top. A mighty proprietor of a colony, such as Maryland's Lord Baltimore who is shown in his impressive finery (left), would give law to his people, like a feudal baron. A business organization like the Virginia Company would manage its "plant" in the New World like any other employer.

But these plans did not take account of some facts. First, with plenty of free land for the taking, New World settlers could easily become "gentlemen landowners." They were not easily made to pay rent to proprietors or obey the orders of English company officials at an ocean's distance—men who shared neither their dangers nor their problems. Soon they demanded—and got—a "say" in affairs. In Virginia in 1619 the company called a meeting of burgesses, representatives of landholders, from around Jamestown. These burgesses did not gather once and go home, as was intended. Instead, they announced that they would meet each year and act as a lawmaking assembly. In Massachusetts in 1634 settlers insisted on choosing delegates to a "General Court" which, like the House of Burgesses in Virginia, also became a **legislature** (lawmaking assembly) and helped to govern the colony. The companies and proprietors had to go along with these demands because they needed newcomers to make their settlements prosper.

It is rather surprising, considering the differences in colonial life that we have seen, that after a century and a half most of the colonies had similar patterns of government. By 1760 every colony had a legislature of some kind, chosen by those white males who owned land or property. All the colonies but one had a governor appointed by the king or the proprietor. The governor was an important figure, to be sure. He was responsible for enforcing royal regulations and controlling foreign trade, manufacturing, and money. He made war, conducted negotiations with the Indians, gave out royal lands, and sat as the colony's chief judge. He selected a council of rich and often well-known colonial leaders, like Virginia's William Byrd (far right), to share his great power.

The governor's power was far from total, for it was the legislatures which raised the tax money to run the government. They voted on how this money should be spent, including how much the governor should be paid.

BOTH: COLONIAL WILLIAMSBURG

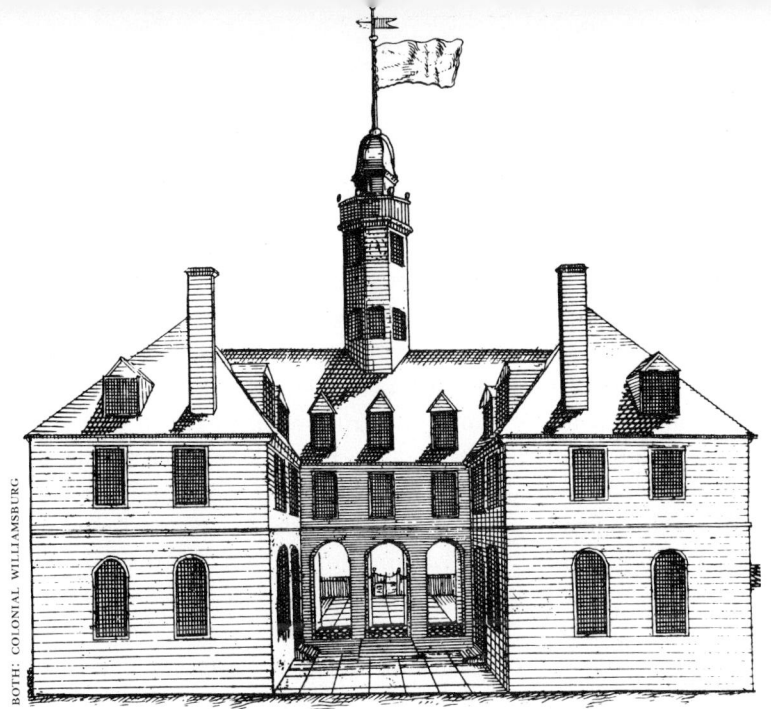

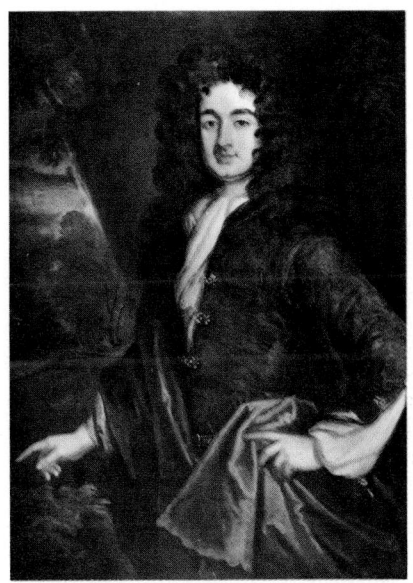

William Byrd II (right), an early eighteenth-century Virginia aristocrat, was a member of the House of Burgesses (above). Below: Patrick Henry argues against England's right to ignore a law passed by the House of Burgesses.

VIRGINIA HISTORICAL SOCIETY

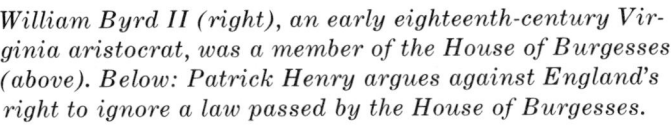

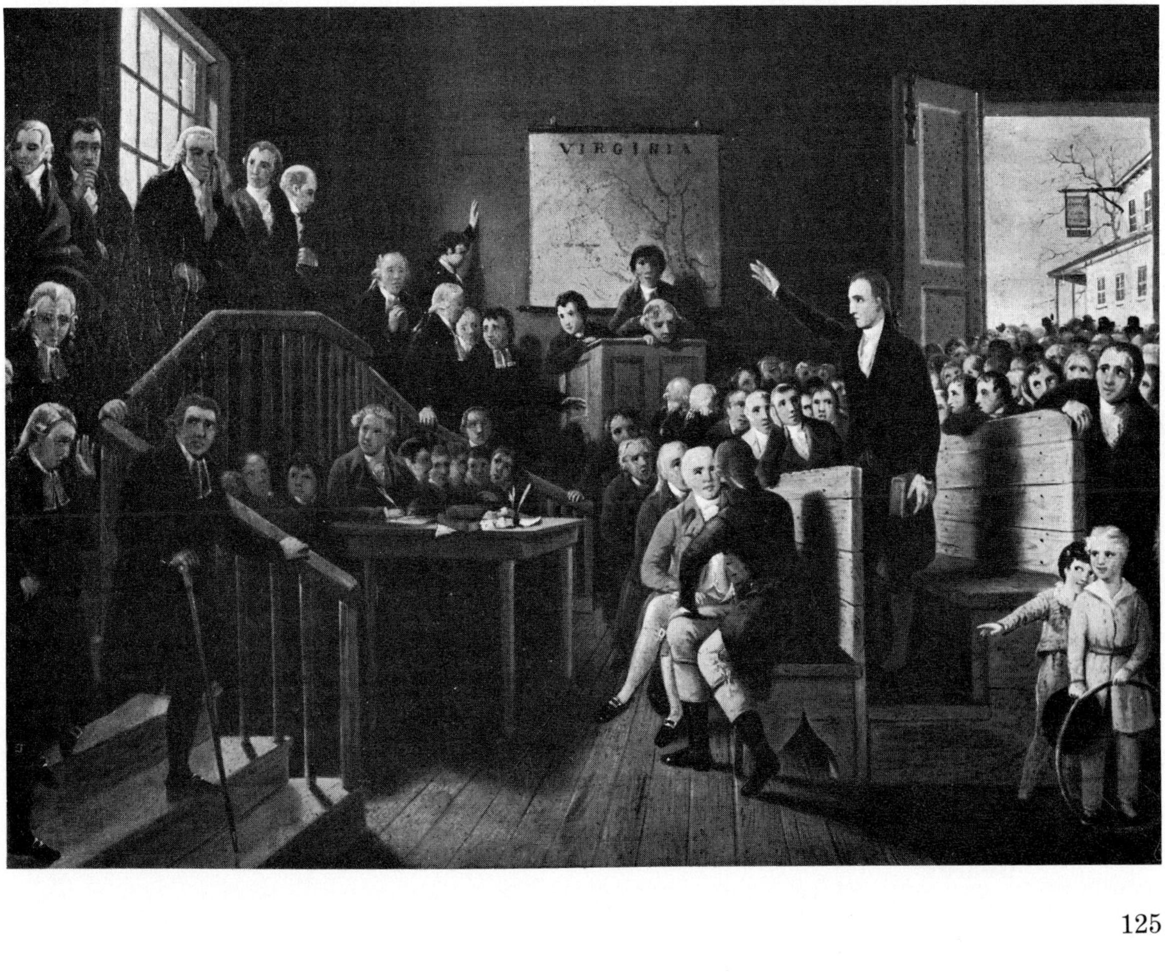

The legislatures also were responsible for schools, roads, criminal laws, and every kind of social regulation from marriage laws to setting curfews, or rules ordering people off the streets after a certain hour.

The men of these legislatures had many arguments among themselves. Planters, merchants, Westerners out on the Indian frontier, city folk, and members of different faiths quarreled at times. Many of their disagreements arose from the uneven and rapid growth of the colonies. Pioneers in the newer, western sections wanted good roads, better defenses, more money for what they produced, cheap land, and freedom of choice in religious matters. Lawmakers from older, settled areas were unwilling to share power or raise taxes to meet such needs. They disliked the rough spokesmen of raw, new districts. But most colonial legislators were from a class of hard-working businessmen and professional men and farmers who felt that they could make their own future by managing their own property. In the painting (page 125, lower right), Patrick Henry, a young Virginian who was one such ambitious middle-class lawyer, addresses a jury. In such plain courthouses and state legislatures as the House of Burgesses (page 125, upper left), American democracy got its start. Long after the Americans rebelled against England, a veteran of the Revolution was asked to give his reason for the rebellion. "Young man," he said, "we had always governed ourselves and we meant to go on doing so. That was all."

Questions for Discussion

1. Why did the pattern of colonial government not follow what was originally planned and expected?
2. How were the people in the English colonies of North America governed?
3. What were the powers of a royal governor of an English colony? In what ways could the legislature limit these powers?
4. What were the powers and duties of a colonial legislature?
5. Which groups in colonial society participated in the government of New England? of the Middle Colonies? of the South?

Chapter Review

Social Studies Terms

Define the following terms: **pioneers, classes, theocracy, self-sufficient, staple crops, legislature.**

Summary Questions for Discussion

1. How important was foreign trade to the economy of New England? the Middle Colonies? the South?
2. Why were the people in some colonies willing to accept the idea of an established church whereas people in other colonies objected strongly to the same idea?
3. Compare the attitude toward the use of land by the early New Englanders with that of the Indians. In what ways was it similar? different?
4. Compare the treatment of dissenters or nonconformists—that is, those who did not follow the rules accepted by a majority of the people—in the societies of the Indians and the Puritans.
5. Why were educational institutions and means of communication—roads, newspapers, messengers—important to those who governed colonies in North America and in the empire of the Incas?
6. How did the class structure that developed in each group of colonies differ? How did these differences affect the way of life in each area?

Pictures as Historical Evidence

What evidence from the pictures on pages 119–123 can you find to support or disprove the following generalization? The social and economic positions of whites and blacks in the South were very similar.

Map Study

By 1750 what five cities had become the largest in the English colonies in America? Why? Check your list against the map on page 104. List the major products you would expect to flow into and out of each of the five cities.

For Further Reading

Everyday Life in Colonial America, by Louis B. Wright. New York: G. P. Putnam's Sons, 1965.

Life in Colonial America, by Elizabeth G. Speare. New York: Random House, Inc., 1963.

Lone Journey: The Life of Roger Williams, by Jeanette Eaton. New York: Harcourt, Brace & World, Inc., 1944.

New Amsterdam Days & Ways: The Dutch Settlers of New York, by Dorothy N. Hults. New York: Harcourt, Brace & World, Inc., 1963.

ISSUES PAST AND PRESENT

Is Cultural Conflict Inevitable?

In the Bible is recorded the story of a group of people who, in an effort to reach heaven, built a high tower, the Tower of Babel. God punished them for their boldness and daring. He destroyed their tower and scattered them "upon the face of the whole earth" (Genesis 11:4). Many people today believe that this story explains the migration of ancient peoples all over the world in search of a better life. Others believe the Biblical version to be a legend. Truth or legend, one fact is clear. As vast as was the earth and as well as man was able to adapt himself to living in lands hot and cold and high and low, there never has been enough space to keep man from bumping into other men. What happens when people of different cultures meet makes up much of the history of the world. Sometimes this contact between cultures took place peacefully, but more often the record of history tells of the tragic conflict that followed. The story of the Europeans in Africa and America is no exception to this rather sad story. You have read in Unit I about some of this conflict between different peoples.

The story of conflict between cultures is not recorded only in history books. You have seen on television or read in newspapers and magazines of such conflicts. Sometimes these stories are fictional and deal with the past or the future (stories of white men fighting the Indians or stories about an invasion from Mars). But often they tell of riots, wars, or other conflicts of the past or present and are very real indeed.

In this last part of Unit I, you will read first some accounts of what happened when peoples of different cultures came into contact with one another. Some of the contacts were peaceful, some violent. Then you will read some words written very recently about ways in which the relations between white people (people whose ancestors came from European cultures) and Negroes and Indians (people whose cultural home was in Africa or America) might be carried on with less conflict than in the past. As you read these selections, consider the following questions:

1. Why are some contacts between cultures peaceful and others violent?
2. Can history teach us any ways to lessen the conflict between cultures? Or is cultural conflict inevitable?

Columbus Meets the Indians

Chapter 2 told you that Christopher Columbus left Spain in August 1492 on his first voyage to the Indies. During the long voyage he kept a secret logbook or diary. This logbook has been lost, but a Spanish missionary and historian, Bartolemé de Las Casas (1474-1566), evidently read it and wrote an account of

Columbus' first voyage. He said that he was using some of Columbus' own words. In the logbook it is recorded that on the night of October 11, over two months after he left Spain, Columbus saw a light. This selection begins with the coming of dawn on the day he landed.

CHRISTOPHER COLUMBUS: *REPORT OF THE FIRST VOYAGE*, 1492

We drifted with sails down, waiting for dawn. Then in the daylight we arrived at an island I called San Salvador. We soon saw naked people. I went on shore in the armed boat, with the captains of the *Niña* and the *Pinta*. I took with me the royal flag, and the captains went with two banners. I called to the two captains, and to the others who had leapt on shore, that we had taken possession of the island for the king and queen.

In order to win the friendship and affection of that people, I presented some of them with red caps and some strings of glass beads which they placed around their necks and with other trifles of no worth which delighted them. They afterwards swam to the boats, bringing us parrots, cotton thread in balls, spears, and many other things, which they bartered for others we gave them. They accepted everything and gave whatever they had with good will. But I thought them to be a very poor people.

They do not carry arms and have no knowledge of them. When I showed them the swords, they took the swords by the edge and, through ignorance, cut themselves. They have no iron. Instead their spears consist of shafts without iron. Some of them have a fish's tooth at the end. I saw some with scars on their bodies. They explained by means of signs that people from neighboring islands tried to capture them, but they had defended themselves.

They must be good servants and very intelligent, because I see that they repeat very quickly what I told them. It is my belief that they would easily become Christians, for they seem not to have any religion.

1. What method did Columbus use to avoid conflict?
2. Why did Columbus say that the natives would easily become Christians?
3. What was his attitude toward the culture of the natives?
4. What was the natives' attitude toward Columbus?
5. What evidence can you find of a cultural gap between Columbus and the Indians?

An African King's Letter

Dom Affonso, King of the Congo, wrote the following letter of complaint to the King of Portugal soon after the Portuguese began to take slaves in Africa.

DOM AFFONSO:
LETTER TO THE KING OF PORTUGAL, 1526

Sir, Your Highness should know how our kingdom is being lost. It would be easy for you to provide for the necessary remedy since it is your merchants and agents who are causing the trouble. They have traded and given away goods in such abundance that many of our vassals, who used to obey us, no longer do so because they are now richer than we ourselves. This is all doing great harm not only to the service of God, but to the security and peace of our kingdom as well.

And we cannot tell you how great the damage is, since these merchants are taking natives, sons of the land, the sons of noblemen and relatives. Thieves and other very evil men grab them and then get paid for them by the merchants. Sir, so great is this evil practice that our country is losing all of its people. Your Highness should not allow this nor accept it. And to avoid it we need from your Kingdom no more than some priests and a few people to teach in schools and no other goods except wine and flour for the holy sacrament.

At our town of Congo, written on the sixth day of July. The King, Dom Affonso.

A "vassal" is one who has placed himself under the protection of another.

The "sacrament" mentioned here is the Eucharist or taking of bread and wine by Christians in remembrance of Christ's Last Supper.

1. How were the Portuguese getting slaves?
2. Who was to blame for the slave trade: the King of Portugal? the Portuguese merchants? the Africans who were capturing other Africans and trading them to the merchants?
3. What contacts with Portugal did Dom Affonso wish to continue?

A French Priest Speaks Out

The priest who wrote this selection around 1770 was trying to sum up the effects of almost 300 years of European exploration and settlement in America.

PIERRE JOSEPH ANDRÉ ROUBAUD:
GENERAL HISTORY OF ASIA, AFRICA, AND AMERICA, 1770–1775

The discovery of America is the most memorable revolution the earth has ever seen by the hand of man. But the

conquest of America is the most shocking disaster mankind has suffered by the hand of man.

These events have changed the face of the universe. Is the earth, because of them, more prosperous? Where is wealth? Where is peace? Where is happiness? And what remains of the former America? Nothing but the sky, the earth, and the memory of nations destroyed.

No, I am mistaken. There still remain slaves and Indians. The slaves are the most badly treated of men. The Indians are constantly attacked, pursued, and destroyed by our arms, our plots, our vices, our diseases, our liquors, etc.

There has been a fearful exchange of evils between Europe and America, and there has not been an exchange of good in return. Americans possessed some secrets; we did not learn them. Europeans possessed many arts; we did not teach them to the Americans. Some corners of the New World have been cultivated. By whom? By Africans and by Americans. For whom? For Europeans. The Old World caught up the New in its whirlpool, but in the collision of these two worlds, the stronger could not crush the weaker without being itself torn and broken.

By "Americans" Roubaud means the Indians in America.

Perhaps more than twenty million Indians perished in America. Many more men were lost to our own continent. It is estimated that Spain spewed eight million Spaniards over the New World. Have Portugal, England, France, Germany, Holland, and other countries lost any less than that, especially if we count the victims of wars and of navigation? Even now, Great Britain is losing men day after day in order to populate this vast wasteland. Africa has already lost nearly twelve million of its own to the New World. It continues to sacrifice, each year, more than sixty thousand.

Gold, either stolen or purchased at the cost of American blood, flowed over Europe in waves, and it scorched a good part of the land. Foolishly it was thought to be the wealth of nations. Vices and errors changed it into a worldwide means for all kinds of disorder.

The treasures of the New World brought Philip II to financial ruin. Spain fell into a most weakened state by drawing these mountains of gold from the mines of Chile, of Mexico, and of Peru. I say mountains of gold because the production of the mines was so huge.

Philip II was King of Spain from 1556 to 1598.

We have sacrificed, and we will continue to sacrifice, the money gotten by our cultivation and our hard work to our love of eating limitless quantities of spices that burn our throats, tea that dries up our mouths, and drugs that poison us. America introduced us to tobacco, which is useless and even dangerous. It increased our supply of coffee, and Europe

satisfied its thirst with a harmful beverage.

To enjoy these products freely we have set up in those colonies two sorts of rule, one over the natives and the other over our transplanted subjects. In short, Europe has based its glory and its power on possessions that were distant and useless. They were gotten at great cost, cultivated at great cost, defended at great cost, and maintained at great cost.

1. What did Roubaud believe to have been the results of contacts between European and non-European cultures?
2. According to Roubaud, why had the contacts caused conflicts both in the Old World and the New World?

A Modern Novelist's View

*In Chapter 1, **cultures** was defined as "ways that members of a society behave." The following selection was written in 1964 by James Oliver Killen, a black novelist and teacher, who discusses the meaning of America having both a black and a white culture. Killen also suggests some of the goals those cultures should work together to achieve.*

JAMES O. KILLEN: EXPLANATION OF THE "BLACK PSYCHE," 1964

"Psyche" means soul or mind.

Just as surely as East is East and West is West, there is a "black" psyche in America and there is a "white" one. The sooner we face up to this fact, the sooner the two shall meet. Most of us Negroes came here in chains and most of you whites came here to escape your chains. Your freedom was our slavery, and that is the reason for the bitter difference in the way we look at life.

In order to justify slavery in a courageous new world which was spouting slogans of freedom and equality and brotherhood, the people who captured and sold slaves created a lie. That lie was that the slaves were subhuman and did not deserve human rights and sympathies. The first job was to convince the outside world of the inborn, natural inferiority of the slaves. The second job was to convince the American people of this. And the third job, which was the cruelest hoax of all, was to convince the slaves themselves that they deserved to be slaves.

When we black folk hear one of our white leaders use the phrase "the free world," even though the same white leader may very well be the governor of the state, we are amazed. Just as the slaves of Washington and Jefferson must have

done — we stare at him and cannot believe our ears. We wonder how this word *freedom* can have such vastly different meanings and such conflicting interpretations.

But the time has come for you [white America] and me [black America] to work this thing out once and for all, to examine the differences inside of us. Time is swiftly running out, and a new dialogue is absolutely necessary. It is so long overdue it is almost half past midnight.

> A "dialogue" is a conversation between people.

This new age has caught our country, yours and mine, asleep, longing for the good old days. Our country slumbers in a world of yesteryears, before Africa and Asia got up off their knees and threw off the black man's burden. That world is gone forever, and black and brown men everywhere are glad, deep in their hearts, but most Western men are upset. This is why the world is becoming much too much for Western men, whoever and wherever you are.

But the world is becoming more and more to my liking. It gladdens my heart to see black and brown men and women come with dignity to the United Nations as a proof of the manhood and the selfhood of the entire human race.

If relationships are to improve between us Americans, black and white and otherwise, if the country is to be saved, we will have to face up to the fact that differences do exist between us.

We are not fighting for the right to be like you. We respect ourselves too much for that. When we fight for freedom, we mean freedom for us to be black, or brown, and you to be white, and yet live together in a free and equal society. This is the only way that integration can mean dignity for both of us.

> "Integration" means the coming together of people of all races without any limits on what a person can or cannot do because of his race.

My fight is not *for* racial sameness but for racial equality, and *against* racial prejudice and discrimination. I work for the day when my people will be free of the racist pressures to be *white like you*. What a tiresome place America would be if freedom meant we all had to think alike and be the same color and wear the same kind of clothes!

You look upon these times as the Atomic Age, the Space Age, the Cold War era. But I believe that when the history of these times is written, it will not be so important who reached the moon first or who made the largest bomb. I believe the great significance will be that this was the century when most of mankind achieved freedom and dignity. For me, this is the Freedom Century.

1. What fact does Killen want Americans to face?
2. What does Killen believe to have been the cause of

conflict between blacks and whites in the United States?
3. Does Killen want to erase or eliminate the differences between black and white cultures in America? Why?
4. What goals does Killen believe that blacks and whites should work together to achieve? In what ways would you expect cultural conflict to change if these goals were achieved?

Distinguishing Between Fact and Opinion

In Columbus' account of his first meeting with the Indians, you read certain conclusions Columbus reached about them. Some of those may be listed as follows:
1. They have no iron.
2. The Indians must be good servants.
3. The Indians must be very intelligent.

He also wrote down some things which he believed to be true but was not sure about:
4. The Indians are a very poor people.
5. The Indians would easily become Christians.

The first three are stated as facts and are in turn based upon Columbus' observations of other facts. Upon what "facts" are each of these conclusions based?

The fourth and fifth are stated as opinions or beliefs. They are also, in turn, based upon Columbus' observations. Upon what "observations" are each of these opinions based?

Making a Generalization

Each of these five statements is a *generalization*. A *generalization* may be defined as a reasonable conclusion based upon a group of facts or observations. The conclusion may be true or false. Often it is difficult to prove one way or the other, though usually the author believes it to be true. Look again at the reading by Pierre Roubaud. Write down on a sheet of paper the heading "Generalizations Made by Roubaud." Then list four generalizations that he made in the article.

Defining Terms

You probably know already that defining a word, or agreeing upon a definition of a word, is not always easy. For instance, you may have been confused when you read one of the conclusions that Columbus wrote in his logbook. It is not listed among the five above, but could be repeated in this way: The Indians do not carry arms and have no knowledge of them.

How does your dictionary define *arms*? According to your dictionary's definition of *arms*, and according to the evidence given in the reading, does it seem that the Indians Columbus met had no knowledge of arms? What did Columbus mean by *arms* when he wrote the statement? Agreement on the definition of a word is sometimes a difficult but very important part

of learning to discuss the truth or lack of truth in a statement. For instance, the truth of some of the five statements of Columbus listed above might depend upon the definition of these words or phrases: *good, very intelligent, very poor, easily,* etc. Did the Indians believe that they were very poor and very intelligent? We do not know, because we do not know what those terms meant to the Indians.

The ability to separate information into facts and opinions is one way of classifying or arranging information. Like the ability to agree upon a definition of a word, it is a skill that is important to the study of history. Read again the article by James O. Killen. Write on a sheet of paper two facts related in the article. Then write two statements of opinion, or belief. Label each set of statements with the correct heading.

What standards should be used to distinguish between a fact and an opinion?

Summary Questions

You have now read a number of sources about cultural conflict. At the beginning of this unit you also read three different opinions about the contributions of different races—white, Indian, and black—to American history. The four chapters in this unit have told you a good deal about the backgrounds of these three races and what happened when they first met. In the light of what you have studied thus far, see what generalizations you can make as answers to the following questions.

1. Why does the contact of people of different cultures often result in conflict?
2. What is the best way to lessen this conflict in our own country? in the world?

1755 Braddock Defeated in Pennsylvania

1765 Parliament Passes the Stamp Act

1776 Independence Declared

1779 Clark Captures Vincennes

1759 Wolfe Takes Quebec

1773 Boston Tea Party

1777 Burgoyne Defeated at Saratoga

UNIT II
The Birth of a Nation

1781 Cornwallis Surrenders at Yorktown

1787 Northwest Ordinance Opens the Way West

1789 Washington Inaugurated First President

1814 The British Burn Washington, D.C.

1786 Shays' Rebellion Begins

1787 Constitutional Convention Meets in Philadelphia

1803 Jefferson Purchases Louisiana

What is the meaning of the American Revolution? This is the question with which our study of Unit II begins. In Chapter 5 we will see that one of the events which hastened the coming of the Revolution was a war between Britain and France, a war in which the colonies played a major role. After this war the colonies began to believe more and more in their ability and right to govern themselves.

Chapter 6 tells how the United States won its independence from Britain in a war that lasted from 1776 to 1783 — the longest war the United States has ever fought. Chapter 7 is an account of how the nation came to grips with the problem of governing itself in a way that was almost as revolutionary as the Revolution itself. This chapter first examines how the Constitution came to be our nation's fundamental law. Then it discusses the basic ideas of the Constitution — ideas by which Americans have ruled themselves for nearly two centuries.

The testing of this infant government's ability to "walk" is the subject of Chapter 8. Serious problems were faced by the nation. Among them was trying to find some balance between the exercise of personal freedoms and the needs of the nation in a time of national danger. *Issues Past and Present*, at the end of the unit, relates this problem to events of the present.

TOP, LEFT TO RIGHT:
NEW YORK PUBLIC LIBRARY
LIBRARY OF CONGRESS
LIBRARY OF CONGRESS
INDIANA HISTORICAL BUREAU
A. S. K. BROWN MILITARY COLLECTION
NEW YORK PUBLIC LIBRARY
NEW YORK PUBLIC LIBRARY
NEW-YORK HISTORICAL SOCIETY
BOTTOM, LEFT TO RIGHT:
NEW-YORK HISTORICAL SOCIETY
COLONIAL WILLIAMSBURG
MANOIR RICHELIEU COLLECTION
CULVER PICTURES
METROPOLITAN MUSEUM OF ART
MCCULLOUGH COLLECTION

INTERPRETING THE PAST

The Meaning of the American Revolution

On July 2, 1776, the Second Continental Congress took the step of declaring the colonies to be "free and independent states." The date, wrote John Adams, was one that ought to be celebrated with "pomp and parade, with shows, games, sports, guns, bells, bonfires and illuminations [fireworks], from one end of this continent to the other, from this time forward forevermore." July 4, the day the Congress officially approved the final wording of the Declaration of Independence, actually became our day of celebration. Because Adams had served with Thomas Jefferson on a committee to write the Declaration, the meaning of the American Revolution was very clear to him. But did it mean the same thing to the thousands of farmers and laborers who bore most of the heavy burden of fighting and suffering? And what does it mean to people today?

As you read the following selections about the American Revolution, keep these questions in mind:

1. What did the authors believe had been gained when the colonies won their independence?
2. Why is the Declaration of Independence still an important historical document?

The Hour Had Come

In the 1800's George Bancroft was the leading historian of the American Revolution. The first volume of his History of the United States *was published in 1834, and the tenth and final volume appeared in 1874. Bancroft believed that when Parliament passed the Intolerable Acts in May of 1774 to punish Massachusetts for the Boston Tea Party, the colonists no longer owed their loyalty to Britain. He believed that during the next two years, until July 4, 1776, the colonists, in fact, were engaged in civil war against Britain.*

GEORGE BANCROFT:
HISTORY OF THE UNITED STATES OF AMERICA, 1874

The hour of the American Revolution had come. The people of the colonies obeyed one general feeling. The resources of the country were so plentiful that their development could neither be guided nor limited by a government beyond the ocean. The colonists were not only able to govern themselves, they alone were able to do so.

When independence came in 1776, it was not an act of sudden passion [feeling]. It had been discussed in every part of the country by farmers and merchants, by mechanics and

planters, by fishermen and backwoodsmen. It had also been discussed in town meetings and from the pulpit; at social gatherings and around the campfires; in newspapers and in pamphlets. The decision had been put off only to make sure of the voice of the people.

The Declaration [of Independence] was not only the announcement of the birth of a people. It was also the establishment of a national government. The war was no longer a civil war. Britain was to become a foreign country. Every former subject of the king in the thirteen colonies now became a citizen of the new republic. Except for this everything remained as before. The colonists were not rebels against the past. They sought no general overthrow of all kings, no worldwide system of republics. George III was cast off not because he was a king, but because he was thought to be a tyrant. The American people did not try to have a social revolution. Every man kept his rights as he had when a colonist.

A "tyrant" is an absolute ruler who uses his power in a cruel manner. A "social revolution" is a sudden, sweeping change in the position of large numbers of people or whole classes within a society.

1. Why does Bancroft think the Americans declared their independence?
2. Why did he believe the colonists had a right to declare their independence?

The author of the following reading is a professor of history at Amherst College.

"Home Rule and Rule at Home"

HENRY STEELE COMMAGER:
OUR BEGINNINGS: A LESSON FOR TODAY, 1941

The Revolution involved two things: home rule and the question of who should rule at home. The British were not able to solve the problem of home rule, and the War of Independence is a monument to their failure. The problem of organizing thirteen independent states into one nation, however, still remained. Could Americans work out a solution to the difficult problem of finding a way to gain national order and unity without sacrificing the freedom and the rights of states? They could and did. The Constitution, under which we are still living today, was a successful solution. That was the greatest contribution of the American Revolution, and its influence has been worldwide.

What of the other basic question—who should rule at home? This question is none other than the question of democracy. Though the question of home rule in the British Empire made the headlines, the question of who was to rule at home

"Home rule" is the principle of self-government of a colony in domestic matters, but not in foreign affairs. Here it means the right of the colonial legislatures to run their own affairs without interference by Parliament.

interested the average man. The fact is that there was quite as much dissatisfaction with the way things were run in the colonies as with the way things were run in Parliament.

Along the Atlantic seaboard—in towns like Boston, New York, Philadelphia, and Charleston or on the banks of the Connecticut, the Hudson, the James—lived the ruling classes. These were the merchants, the large landowners, the shippers, the lawyers, and the government officials. They dominated the colonial assemblies, controlled the courts, owned a large part of the land, worshiped in the proper churches, and were served by slaves or indentured servants. They had long been accustomed to running things their own way—and for their own benefit.

Along the frontier there had come into being a new society. These were the poor people, the small farmers, the former indentured servants, and the apprentices who had run away. They were dissenters for the most part. Their program of action had little to do with the far distant Parliament or George III. They wanted free land, freedom of worship, defense against Indians, and their share of political power.

There was also a small but powerful third group. These were the town dwellers, the seamen, the dockworkers, the carpenters, the laborers, and the apprentices and tradesmen of the rising cities. They were without property, could not vote, and were not represented in the assemblies. By the 1770's the West and the underprivileged townsmen were ripe for revolt. Some outbreaks had already taken place. The War of Independence was their chance to make real many of the democratic ideals and practices favored by the West.

How did they do this? In the first place, the seaboard groups could not carry on war without the support of the back-country peoples. And that support had to be bought by giving in to some of their demands. In the second place, many of the members of the upper classes sided with England and so lost not only their offices and power but their property as well. Great estates were taken from them and sold to small farmers. About 70,000 of the well-to-do fled the country. The ruling classes were greatly weakened by loss of numbers, wealth, and power. As a result, they were not able to resist the demands of the underprivileged. Once this had been achieved, democratic changes followed.

This, then, is the real Revolution. It was not just a war of independence. It was a great creative era in history.

1. How does Commager classify the colonists?
2. According to him how were the two key questions of the Revolution answered?

3. How does Commager's view of "the real Revolution" differ from Bancroft's?

The next selection was written by the same author as the one above. But it was written twenty years later. Events after World War II, which ended in 1945, had caused him to have some more thoughts about the Revolution.

Explosive Principles

HENRY STEELE COMMAGER:
OUR DECLARATION IS STILL A RALLYING CRY, 1961

Members of all the organizations that fear revolution would do well to work to bar the Declaration of Independence from schools and public libraries. Think how explosive are its ideas: All men are created equal. All have a right to life, liberty, and the pursuit of happiness. The purpose of government is to secure *these* rights. Men have a right to overthrow their present governments and to make new governments!

Thoughtful Americans and Europeans realized from the beginning that the experience of America would affect not just a nation but all mankind. The Revolution set an example—first, for the nations of Latin America and, eventually, for the nations and peoples in the Old World and in Asia and Africa. The revolts against colonialism which have swept Asia and Africa in our own time have their historical beginnings in American experience. Americans should have sympathy for those people around the world who are today working to create a nation. We were the first to show that it could be done, and we should be the first to welcome others when they try to repeat our experience.

"Colonialism" is the control of one country by another.

The Declaration of Independence is not simply something to learn in school as we learn so many things that we promptly forget. It is vital and a part of today. It announces principles that are still true. It still calls upon us to pledge our lives, our fortunes, and our honor to their defense.

1. Why does Commager call the principles in the Declaration of Independence "explosive?"
2. Why does he say that it is a document important even to those who do not live in the United States?

1. Read the Declaration of Independence (see Appendix). Does it describe how Americans would like to live or how they really live? Explain your answer.

Summary Question

141

5

The Road to Revolution

One, two, three, heave! — and the statue of the king topples to the ground with a satisfying crash. The people rejoicing at left are New Yorkers on a day in July of 1776. They are celebrating America's Declaration of Independence by acting out the overthrow of England's King George III. More than a statue was toppled during that July. A political revolution was beginning. Thirteen English colonies had proclaimed their freedom. Thus they began a whole modern age of revolution, especially by colonial peoples who lived in a region controlled by a distant nation.

Revolutions do not happen overnight, even though the actual change in government may seem to take place quickly. Before 1776 there were twelve years during which Great Britain and its colonies walked the road to war. Those years saw rising tempers and heard angry voices. They saw legal and peaceful protests turn finally into armed revolt.

Arguments between the colonists and Great Britain appeared to be about small things, such as a few pennies in taxes on a pound of tea or a newspaper. But the roots of conflict ran deeper, to questions such as: Who shall rule? Who shall choose rulers? How do different groups in a nation share the costs and advantages of government fairly? When may an individual or a society resist lawful government? How should local governments, like those of cities or states, share power with a central government that controls a nation or an empire? And finally, when political changes must be made, what methods work best in bringing them about?

Questions like these are not answered all at once or for all time. The leaders who made the American Revolution had to struggle with them long after the last gunshot had echoed away. So long as Americans continue to ask these basic questions and to carry out their ideas of liberty and human rights and justice, the ideas behind the American Revolution are still alive.

As you read, think about these questions:
1. In a war between France and Britain for control of North America, why did the Americans feel that a French victory would threaten their future?
2. Why do people revolt against their government?
3. Why does a dispute sometimes result in violence even though neither side really wants it?

New York rebels topple a gilded statue of George III.

Britain and France Fight for Mastery of North America

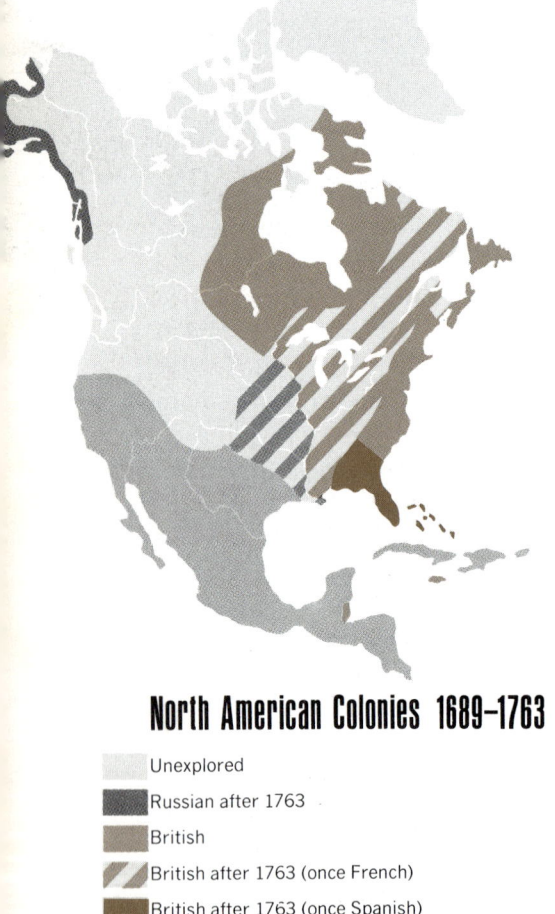

North American Colonies 1689–1763

- Unexplored
- Russian after 1763
- British
- British after 1763 (once French)
- British after 1763 (once Spanish)
- Spanish
- Spanish after 1763 (once French)

The strange thing is that, only fifteen years before the American Revolution began, people of the thirteen colonies were willingly fighting and dying for King George. In 1760 the long battle between France and England to control the eastern half of North America ended. The French were defeated, though the actual peace treaty was not signed until 1763 in Paris. The flag of France had been planted at Quebec at the beginning of the 1600's and the flag of England at Jamestown at about the same time. The rivalry between the two nations broke into war in 1689, and until 1763 they fought with each other for control of North America (map, left). Their conflict was really one long war fought in several episodes.

America Becomes Part of a World War

Each stage of the struggle involved colonists and Europeans thousands of miles from Paris and London. Some of the fighting involved Indians and colonists who were tortured and died in the forests and pioneer settlements of a distant continent. But the battles of France and England grew into a world war involving other powers too, some of which, like France and England, had colonies in Africa and Asia.

What the long war meant to the English colonists is made clear by the scene showing the Deerfield Massacre (upper right). It took place in 1704, during the second round of fighting known as Queen Anne's War. Some 50 Frenchmen and 200 Indians swept into and burned the little town in the Connecticut Valley, killed many of the townspeople, and carried the rest off as prisoners. To the settlers these raids meant tomahawks, scalping knives, screams in the night, and women and children lying mangled in the ashes of their homes. The colonists grew angry and more determined than ever to outstay their French enemies. They also became more loyal to Britain as they became more dependent upon the British army for protection.

Most Indian tribes—the Iroquois being a notable exception—sided with the French. The French colonial system had stressed establishing trading posts rather than permanent settlements. Few Indians were forced from their land, and many benefited from the trade. The English, after initial friendly contact, had begun to push the Indians westward. Many Indians saw the war as a chance to "get back" at the English for 150 years of dishonest and brutal treatment.

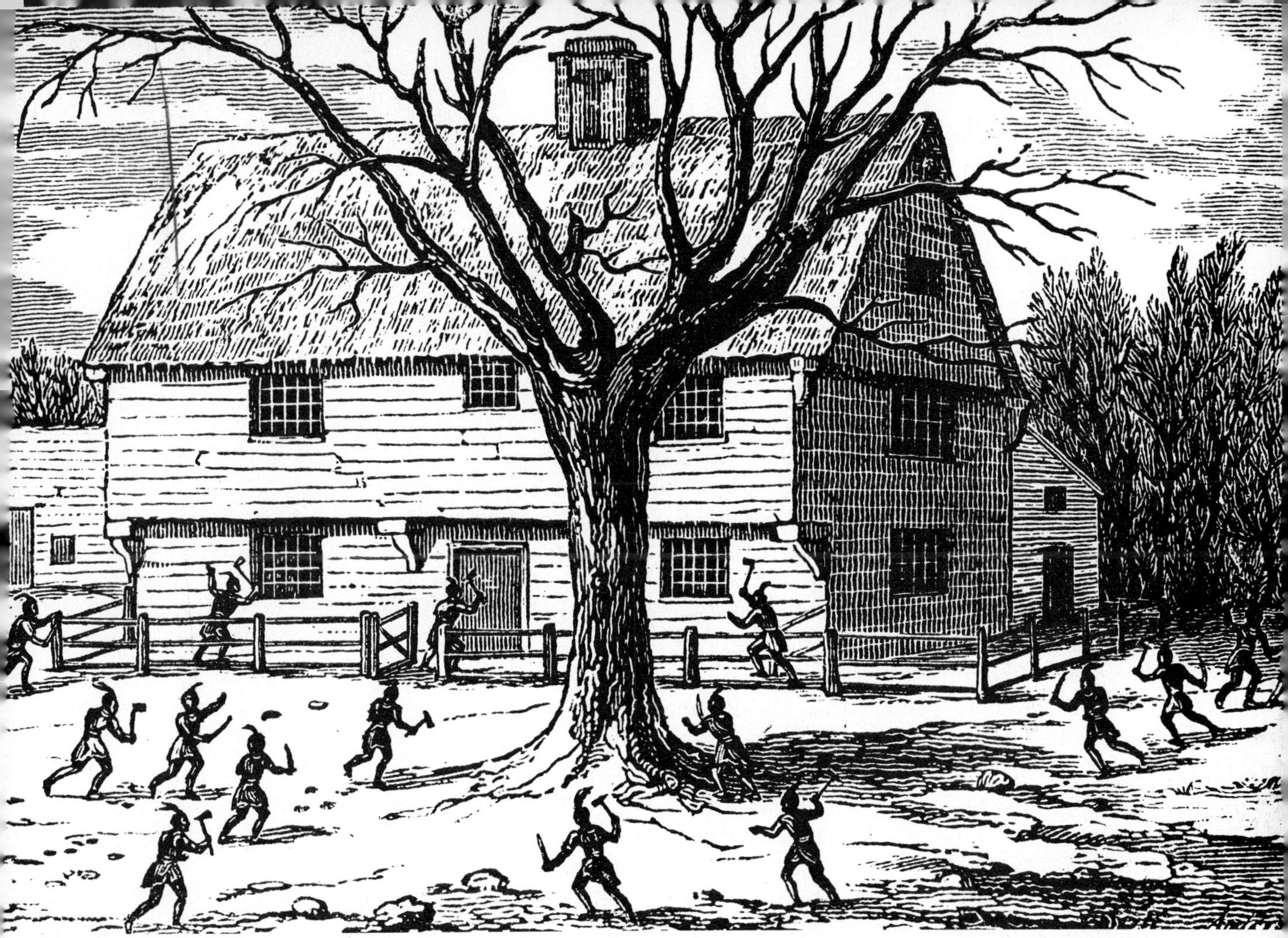

WILLIAMS, *Redeemed Captive Returned to Zion*, 1833

Above: This drawing of the Deerfield Massacre is from a book by a minister who witnessed the raid. Right: An Indian killing a Deerfield resident. Below: Frenchmen and Indians scalp innocent victims in this 1760 English woodcut.

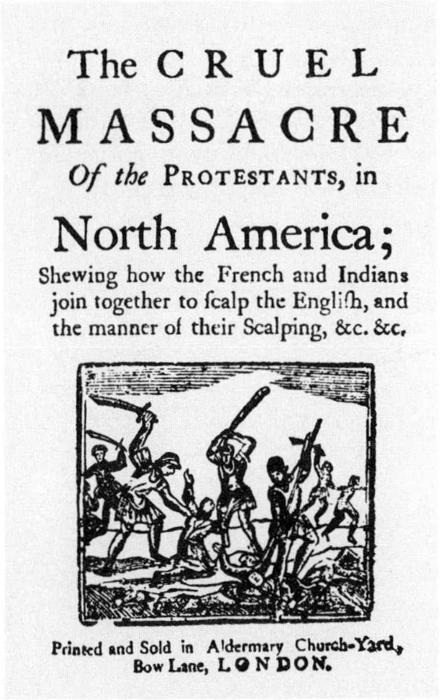

The CRUEL
MASSACRE
Of the PROTESTANTS, in
North America;
Shewing how the French and Indians join together to ſcalp the Engliſh, and the manner of their Scalping, &c. &c.

Printed and Sold in Aldermary Church-Yard, Bow Lane, LONDON.

JOHN CARTER BROWN LIBRARY, BROWN UNIVERSITY

CULVER PICTURES

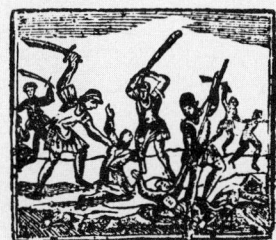

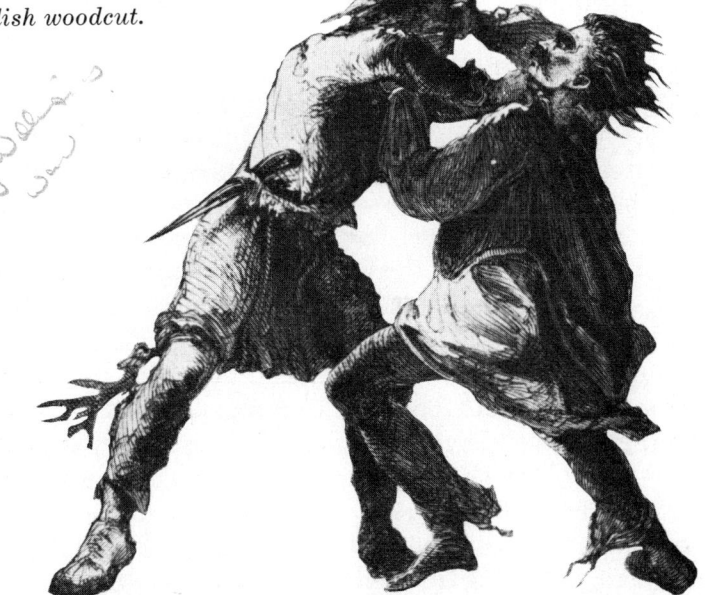

The French and Indian War

After an indecisive third round known as King George's War (1744–1748), France and England headed into a final bloody contest known as the French and Indian War. The fighting began when the French built Fort Duquesne, where Pittsburgh stands today. To do this in 1754, they had to drive off a little force of Virginia **militiamen** (citizens who serve as soldiers in an emergency) commanded by a colonel named George Washington, who in peacetime was a planter.

Why was a Virginia landowner deep in what is now western Pennsylvania, with soldiers? The reason was that Washington and other Virginians believed the future lay in the rich, unsettled lands of the West. Virginia's original charter gave the colony all the territory between the Great Lakes and the Ohio River. So Washington was there to stake a claim for England's king and Virginia's colonists.

The French jumped this claim because they saw what you can see for yourself from the map on page 104. The Ohio River, which begins at Fort Duquesne, is a great water route to the Mississippi Valley. If the French controlled it, they might someday link their settlements on the Gulf of St. Lawrence and the Gulf of Mexico, and dominate the heart of North America. England's colonies would remain cramped along the coast. England decided France must be thrown out.

In 1755 Britain sent an expedition to take Fort Duquesne. The commander, General Edward Braddock, was an honest old fighter trained for European warfare. He was willing to have about a thousand "provincial" troops join his thousand red-coated regulars. After all, England and the provincials had a common interest in taking Fort Duquesne. But he was unwilling to listen to Virginia or Pennsylvania farmers in uniform when they told him how to fight in the wilderness.

Braddock marched his men in close ranks (upper right) to the beat of fife and drum, along the trail cut through the dark tangle of forest. A few miles from the fort, French and Indian soldiers swooped down on his great, slow, snakelike column and began to fire on it from the cover of trees. Washington and other colonial officers begged permission to let the British fight like the Indians or the experienced backwoodsmen—that is, to fight as individuals or in small groups and take full advantage of the protection of trees and rocks. Instead, Braddock insisted that they remain in column,

Above: General Braddock and his troops march in stiff formation toward Fort Duquesne. Right: Hidden by rocks and trees, the French and Indians ambush the British. General Braddock, mortally wounded, is falling from his horse. The man on the horse next to Braddock may be his aide-de-camp, George Washington.

NEW YORK PUBLIC LIBRARY, PICTURE COLLECTION

STATE HISTORICAL SOCIETY OF WISCONSIN

firing away blindly while bullets from unseen enemies cut them down. In the end Braddock was killed, more than half of his troops became casualties, and the shattered task force retreated.

For the next four years the war went badly for the English, but in 1759 the tide turned. William Pitt, the energetic English Prime Minister, sent a slender, red-haired general named James Wolfe to take Quebec. It was a big assignment for a man of 32—only about 10 years older than a modern college senior. Quebec was the heart and brain of the long French river "empire." If that city were taken, New France would be finished.

Quebec seemed invincible, perched on high cliffs overlooking the St. Lawrence. But Wolfe had himself rowed along the bank, and his keen eye picked out a tiny, unguarded path crooking its way to the top. On the night of September 12, 1759, whaleboats drifted ashore and unloaded troops who struggled up the trail amid whispered commands and curses. By dawn some 3,000 English soldiers were drawn up on level ground outside the city. The able but surprised French commander, Marquis de Montcalm, had to fight. The battle was fought European-style, long rows of infantrymen crashing out volleys through the smoke, then reloading and advancing in a line. When the smoke cleared both Generals Wolfe and Montcalm had been killed, but the British had won. Quebec surrendered. The next year saw the fall of all remaining French strongholds in Canada. By the treaty signed in 1763, France gave Canada to Great Britain. At the same time France gave Louisiana to Spain.

There were many meanings to the end of France's Canadian adventure. First, the British had become masters of North America, but at a huge financial cost. Secondly, American colonists had gained valuable experience in fighting with and against professional European troops. Finally, the fear of France that had driven the English colonists closer to Britain for many years was gone. These three facts would now combine in a pattern of trouble for England.

British troops under the command of General James Wolfe land at a lightly guarded cove near Quebec. The landing surprised the French who did not believe the British could sail up the St. Lawrence River from Louisburg to Quebec. The British troops moved up the ravine, overpowered the pickets, and defeated the main French force on the Plains of Abraham.

Questions for Discussion

1. What common interest did the Americans and the British have in driving the French out of North America?
2. Why did the British want to capture Fort Duquesne and Quebec?

The Making of a Revolution

The government in London quickly moved to clean up the wreckage of the war and pay its huge costs. Among the first steps was a 1763 ruling to forbid settlement west of a "Proclamation Line" running down the Alleghenies (map, page 104). The proclamation would hold back pioneers until an Indian **policy** (plan of action) could be worked out. This seemed especially necessary after a gifted Indian named Pontiac united many tribes in a rebellion in 1763 that took a year to subdue. But the measure angered the colonists.

Next, London tightened up the machinery for collecting **duties** (import taxes). But worst of all was an act proposed in 1765 by Britain's Prime Minister, George Grenville, for raising **revenue** (government income) by requiring that newspapers, legal documents, licenses, and business forms could only be printed on paper with special stamps attached. The colonists would have to buy these stamps. In Grenville's eyes this would only be fair. The colonies would only be paying for their own past and future defense.

But the Stamp Act looked vastly different across 3,000 miles of ocean. The colonists grumblingly recognized London's right to regulate boundary affairs by proclamation lines and foreign trade by molasses duties. But the Stamp Act was a direct tax. And, as Virginians and Pennsylvanians and New Yorkers saw it, such a tax could be levied only by their assemblies, to which they themselves sent elected delegates, not by faraway Parliament. As a simple slogan put it, "No taxation without representation." Colonial legislatures protested the new law bitterly and claimed, as loyal Englishmen, the rights for which the English themselves had fought against tyrannical kings.

But protest did not stop there. The year 1765 saw the beginning of new forms of colonial resistance. There was cooperation among the colonies as delegates met in a Stamp Act Congress, which passed resolutions of protest. There was economic pressure because hundreds of merchants agreed to **boycott** (not to buy) British goods until the hated law was rejected. There was **propaganda** (the circulation of information aimed to arouse strong emotions for one side of a case) like the cartoon shown at left. Finally, there was violence (right). Mobs broke into warehouses and burned the stamps stored there. Faced by this upsurge, the British Parliament promptly **repealed** (withdrew) the Stamp Act.

Colonists reacted sharply to the Stamp Act. A 1765 magazine carried the propaganda above. Right: A 1784 engraving shows irate Bostonians burning the stamps.

> AMERICANS!
> BEAR IN REMEMBRANCE
> The HORRID MASSACRE!
> Perpetrated in King-ftreet, BOSTON,
> New-England,
> On the Evening of March the Fifth, 1770.
> When FIVE of your fellow countrymen,
> GRAY, MAVERICK, CALDWELL, ATTUCKS,
> and CARR,
> Lay wallowing in their Gore!
> Being *bafely*, and moſt *inhumanly*
> MURDERED!

Two years after the Boston Massacre, colonial leaders were still using the event to stir up anti-British feelings. Here, Americans are asked to remember the horrid Massacre and the five men who were murdered. Crispus Attucks, a former slave who had run away from his master, was one of the five and possibly the leader of the mob.

The Boston Massacre

Parliament ended the Stamp Act because it could not be enforced. But some members of Parliament made sure that the colonists understood that London was still boss. A Declaratory Act was passed in 1766, saying that Parliament had a right to make laws for the whole empire, "in all cases whatsoever." The next year Britain's chief financial minister, Charles Townshend, a witty, high-living aristocrat called "Champagne Charlie," had new taxes placed on imported paint, glass, paper, and tea.

Once more boycott agreements and protest meetings and newspaper editorials cried in outrage against this "tyranny." Once more, too, government officials — and pro-British "loyal" colonists who believed that even unpopular laws ought to be obeyed — were threatened with mob action. In Boston the threats seemed disturbing enough for Britain to bring in troops. The British argued that the life of no one — rich or poor, pro-Yankee or pro-British — was safe without law and order. But Bostonians felt as some residents of poor or nonwhite neighborhoods do today. The "police" — the red-coated soldiers — were the enemy, no matter what they did or did not do.

This feeling led to a number of street brawls between the troops and Bostonian sailors and workers. Usually after some spitting, shoving, name-calling, and a few arrests, these fights were broken up. But on the night of March 5, 1770, a squad of British soldiers was faced with a crowd that was hooting and throwing snowballs and rocks. A British captain trying to cool things down said something that sounded like "Fire!" The furious "lobsterbacks" blasted shots (upper right) directly into the crowd. Five Boston men died.

No matter who had started the fight, this was a dreadful moment. Angry talk had been replaced by bullets. Men had died. The colonists had martyrs, people who suffer for a cause, and could claim that "unarm'd, defenceless and innocent citizens" had been slaughtered in what they called the "Boston Massacre."

Makers of a Revolution

Many colonists who had been lukewarm in support of the Patriot, anti-British, side were now shocked into joining the protesters. But this process did not happen accidentally. It was encouraged by careful planning and hard work.

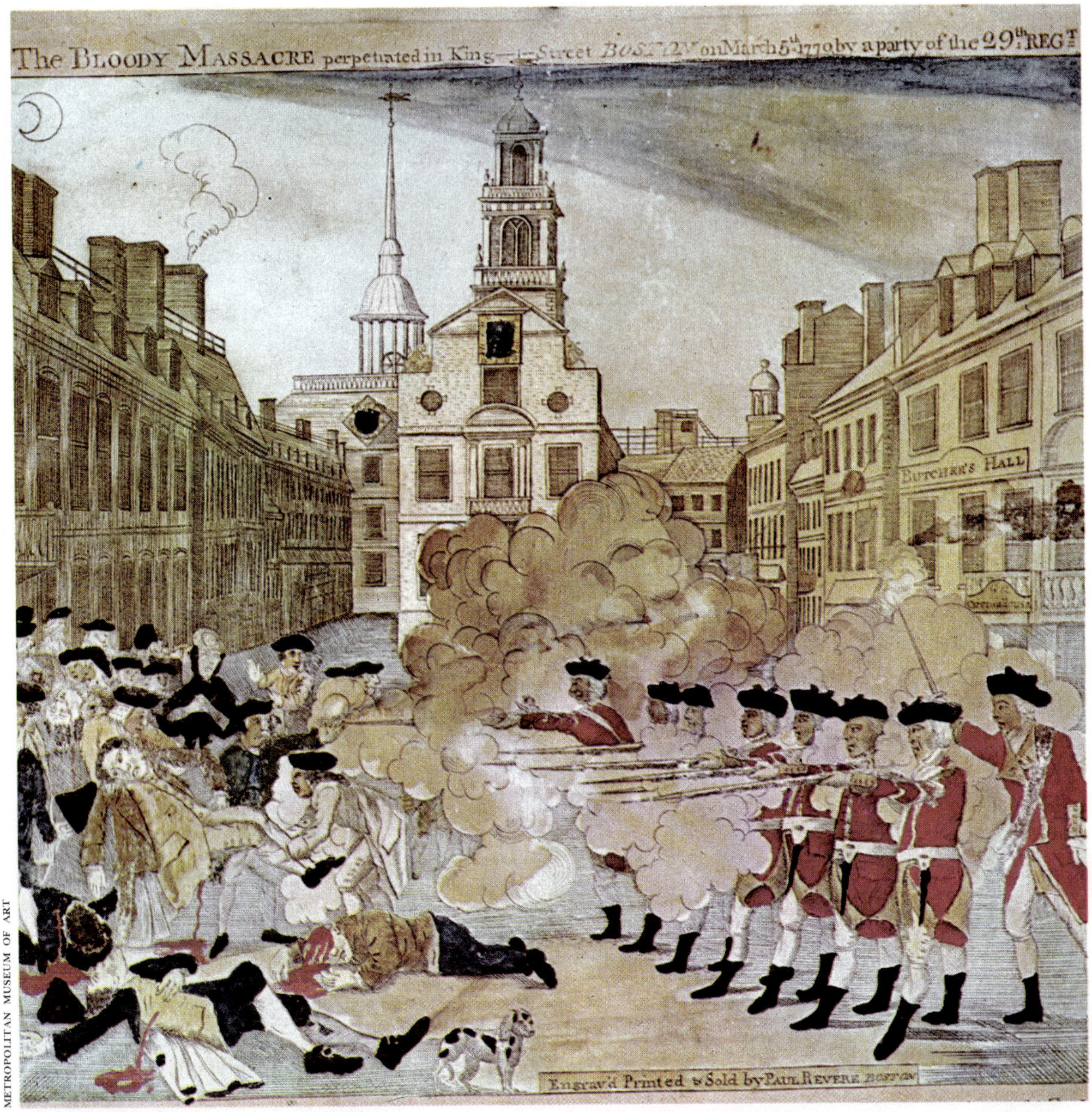

METROPOLITAN MUSEUM OF ART

LIBRARY OF CONGRESS

Paul Revere's engravings show the Massacre (above) and the coffins of the five men who had died (left). Why do you think Revere did not show that the mob in Boston was rioting when the British opened fire?

To arouse people to armed action takes organization and skill in appealing to emotion. In the thirteen colonies were some exceptionally able **radicals** (those who believe in and work for revolutionary changes). Some of them are pictured here. For example, Patrick Henry (bottom, right), whom we saw in the last chapter arguing a case in Virginia, had a gift for great phrases. In Virginia's assembly he made a speech against the Stamp Act of 1765, comparing George III to past tyrants. When some other member gasped "Treason!" Henry snapped, "If this be treason, make the most of it!" Ten years later, when urging the Virginians to raise a militia and prepare to fight Britain if need be, he said, "Give me liberty—or give me death!" Long after men had forgotten exactly what the rest of his speech was about, Henry's battle cries made men's blood boil.

Boston's Samuel Adams (left) was no spellbinder with words. He was not an especially good lawyer, but he was a fine organizer. He was a guiding spirit of the Boston chapter of the Sons of Liberty, a group of Patriots in various colonies who organized parades and rallies to condemn the Stamp Act, the Townshend taxes, and other British "villainies." Adams also founded a political discussion club in Boston—where most of the discussion was anti-British. He founded a newspaper to tell readers how wicked it was for the House of Commons "at 3,000 miles distance" to rule American colonists who would soon outnumber Britain's population. And Adams was also a founder of the Massachusetts Committee of Correspondence. Each colony's committee exchanged information and plans with the committees in other colonies. They drew the colonies together and kept the pot of resistance boiling everywhere.

Another radical, Thomas Paine (top, right), did not arrive in America until the eve of war in 1774. He had been unable to earn a living in England as a government worker, corset maker, grocer, or teacher. But in America he was the man to put the argument for independence in the hard-hitting language of *Common Sense*.

Debate in England

Radicals like Sam Adams and Patrick Henry were always opposed in the colonies by **moderates** (those who believe in and work for slow, orderly change) who

Radicals, like Samuel Adams (left), Thomas Paine (above), and Patrick Henry (below), spoke out against British colonial rule and then demanded revolution.

believed that peace could be worked out within the system of British rule, which had lasted for more than a century and a half. Moderates believed that there was no need for a **confrontation** (head-on meeting) involving force between both parties. Only radicals who called themselves Patriots desired that. The colonies had thrived under Britain's flag. True, they were not represented in Parliament. But most Englishmen were not either, since only wealthy property owners could vote. Better to let nonviolent boycotts and appeals to the king's generosity do their work. Wild talk about rights and resistance only stirred up trouble.

Some Englishmen in Parliament took the same moderate view. A number of them spoke for the British merchants who were badly hurt by the loss of their colonial buyers of cloth, hardware, shoes, and other manufactured goods. Some friends of the American colonists agreed with their American "cousins" in places like Philadelphia that governments ought to have very little power over men's lives and property.

In 1775 one other line of pro-American argument was put forward by Edmund Burke, a famous British writer of the day, in a long speech in Parliament. He called for **conciliation** (an effort to bring about good will) with the colonists. They had prospered for many years without much attention from Parliament, he said. Their prosperity enabled them to enrich the whole empire with their trade. They took care of their local affairs, including taxation, ably. "Obedience is what makes government," said Burke, and the colonists obeyed their assemblies. If the royal ministers were foolish enough to force the colonists to obey London, they would only breed hatred. The British would be killing the American goose that laid golden eggs, as a British cartoon (left) expressed it.

Calls for conciliation did not win out. The king and the men he chose for top jobs believed that they had unlimited power over the colonies or none at all. This "either-or" attitude resulted in a **polarization** (movement away from moderate positions to two conflicting extreme positions) of opinion. "Blows must decide," said George III.

In 1770 the British repealed the Townshend Acts, but kept the tax on tea to prove they still had the right of taxation. Then in 1773 they proposed that only the British East India Company be allowed to sell tea in America. Such an act would ruin American importers.

Some men in England saw the struggle with the colonies as harmful to the Empire. A cartoon that appeared early in 1776 shows the government ministers killing the American goose that laid the Empire's golden eggs.

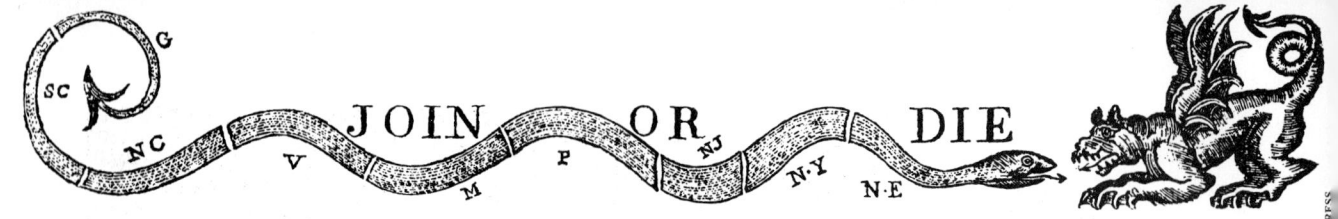

Above: Ben Franklin's famous cartoon first appeared in a 1754 edition of his Pennsylvania Gazette. *Twenty years later Paul Revere engraved this version for the* Massachusetts Spy. *Right: In Boston a British tax collector who has been tarred and feathered is given a dose of boiling tea by followers of Samuel Adams.*

As Patriot pamphlets pointed out, this was proof of Parliament's bad intentions. Stern measures were needed. New boycott agreements were signed. The spirit of violence was at work, too (right).

Ships loaded with the hated tea were turned back at New York and Philadelphia but were allowed by the royal governor to tie up at Boston wharves. The Sons of Liberty had an answer to that. On the night of December 16, 1773, a group of men disguised as Indians with tomahawks marched boldly aboard the three tea ships. They hauled out the chests of tea, smashed them open, and poured the contents into the harbor. The "Boston Tea Party" was open defiance.

London recognized the challenge. This was not peaceful dissent but lawless destruction of property. So Parliament passed a set of laws designed to punish Massachusetts. The colonists often referred to them as the "Intolerable Acts." Massachusetts was deprived of self-government. And after June 1, 1774, the port of Boston was to be closed to all ships until the tea was paid for. Submission or starvation was the choice.

The other colonies suddenly found themselves united in Boston's defense. If one colonial "child" could be punished, so could all the children. The message seemed to be "Join or Die," as Ben Franklin's slogan (above) put it. Shipments of food were sent into Boston by land. What was more, a call went out for a meeting of delegates from all the colonies to meet in Philadelphia in September to discuss ways of resistance.

This First Continental Congress moved the colonies closer to war. The delegates adopted a new boycott agreement, urged the colonies to raise militia to protect themselves, and insisted that they would never submit to what they called the "unlawful" taxes of Parliament. Virginia's Patrick Henry expressed the delegates' feelings: "I am not a Virginian," he said, "but an American." The Congress was not yet a government, but an American nation was emerging.

Question for Discussion

1. In the disputes between England and the colonies, why did the voices urging moderation lose out to those in favor of more radical action?

Right: Paul Revere rides toward Lexington to warn of the British advance. Revere was captured before he reached Concord, but Dr. Samuel Prescott made it through to warn the minutemen there. Below: In this engraving by militiaman Amos Doolittle, the redcoats open fire on retreating minutemen at Lexington. Major Pitcairn is on horseback.

CULVER PICTURES

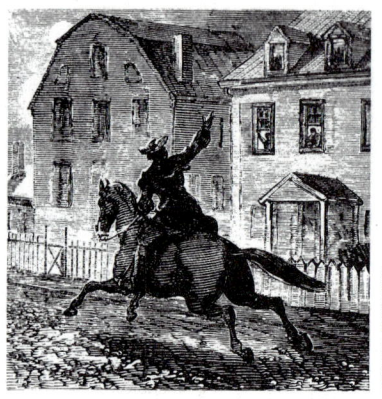

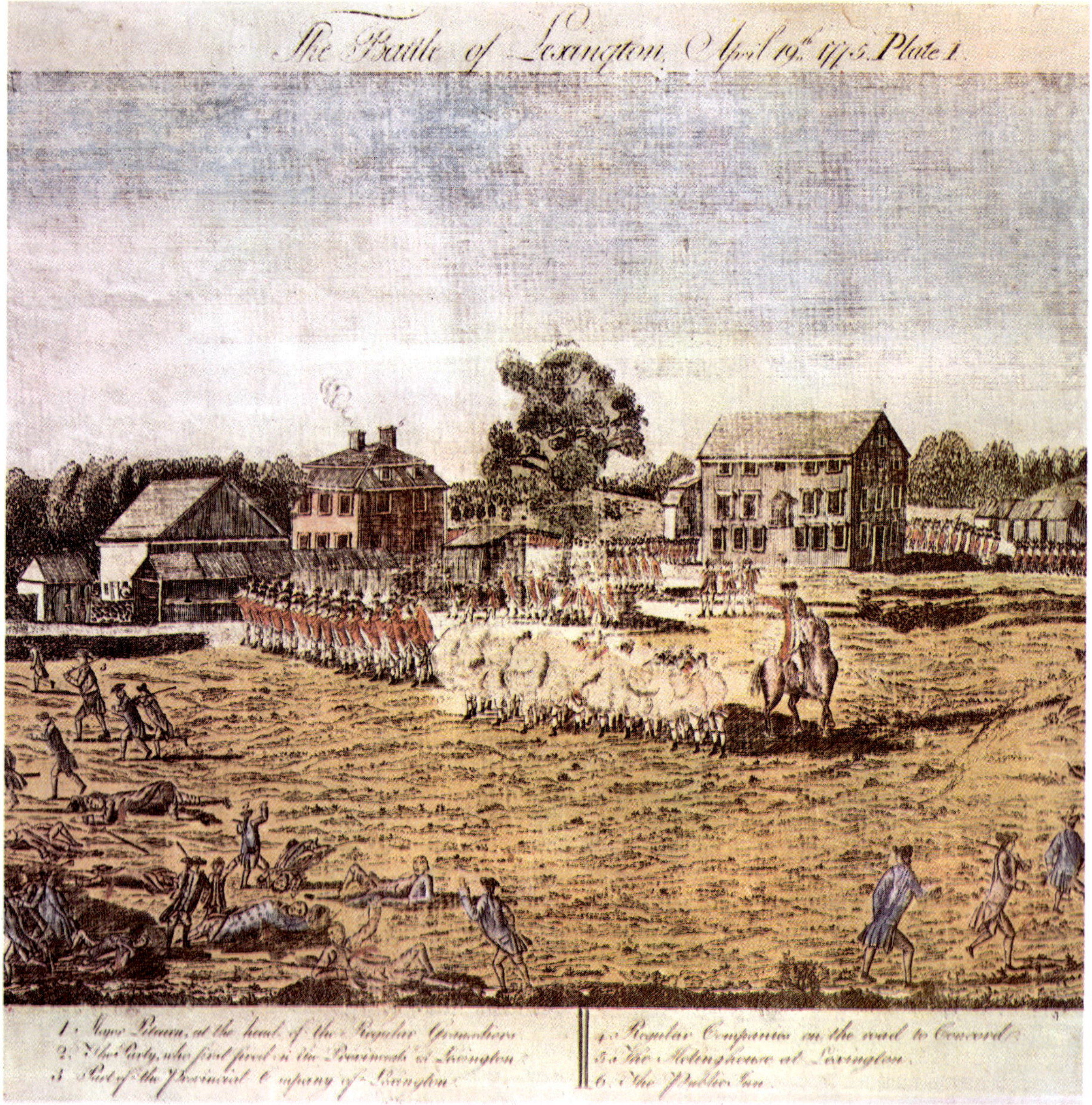

ALBANY INSTITUTE OF HISTORY AND ART

The Shot Heard Round the World

Radical tactics in America and stiff-necked policies in England had turned a movement for **home rule** (self-government) within the British Empire into a drive toward separation. As late as the spring of 1775, few colonies were talking of independence. But each week brought events which left little room for compromise. Men were becoming captives of their own actions.

General Thomas Gage, commanding British troops in Boston, was keeping an eye on the little groups of colonial militia who were drilling in nearby towns and were ready for action at a minute's notice. In April he planned an unpleasant surprise for these "minutemen." He would march a body of troops into Concord, seventeen miles away. The "provincials" were supposed to have some arms stored there. In a quick, surprise move, he would seize these arms. It would not be war; it would be like a police raid to pick up illegal guns. It would put the colonists off balance and warn them that the British would allow no more rebellious acts.

Gage did not count on the excellent ability of the Bostonians to get wind of his plans. When his raiding party gathered in the chilly predawn darkness of April 19, Paul Revere and William Dawes had already slipped out of town and were riding the roads to Concord and nearby Lexington to warn the minutemen.

When the advance guard of the 700-man task force of redcoats got to Lexington on the way to Concord, they found about 40 minutemen lined up. No one is quite sure what happened next. The American captain, John Parker, was a veteran soldier who did not want to fight against such odds. The British commander, Major John Pitcairn, was under orders to avoid a fight if possible. But as the British line moved forward and the Yankees, though nervous, refused to fall back, someone fired a shot. The redcoats were edgy, too. A volley crashed out from their ranks and probably from the Americans at the same moment. But when the smoke had cleared, the minutemen were falling back—and eight of them lay dead on the ground.

This was the real thing. Death, now an umpire in the dispute between mother country and colonies, had a profitable April day. The British pushed on to Concord but after a sharp skirmish discovered that they were now opposed by hundreds of Americans. Word had spread fast, and companies of militia were pouring in from every village within a few hours' march. The British officers decided to pull back to Boston. But their

To arouse sympathy for the Revolution after the Battle of Concord, propaganda was circulated like the cartoon (right) of a British retreat and the broadside (below) of the wounded and killed. The list indicates that, despite a general policy of exclusion from the militia, Negroes like Prince Easterbrooks fought in these first battles.

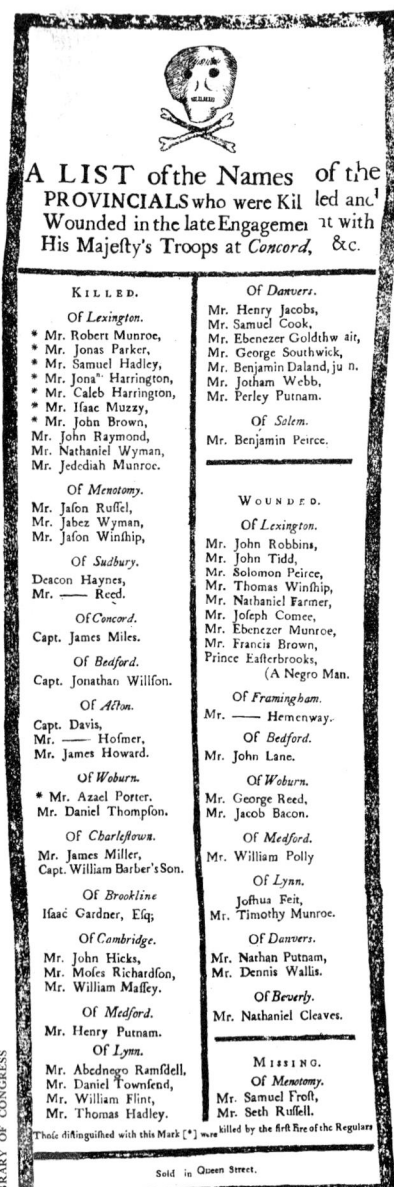

orderly retreat turned into a disaster when the "country bumpkins" from Massachusetts farms, firing from behind houses, stone walls, and haystacks, attacked the retreating British. In a "Furnass of Musquetry" the British almost fled back to base. Seventy-three were killed, and nearly three times as many wounded.

The importance of the day was enormous. Messengers galloped down post roads with the news that the British had shot down Americans once more, at Lexington and Concord. Yet there was good news too, for the Americans had shown themselves able to punish the British savagely. The cartoon (above) picturing the British as donkeys, braying in flight, shows a second result of the Battles of Lexington and Concord. These victories, and the cartoons they inspired, encouraged Americans to feel that they could handle British troops.

Soon companies from all over New England poured

into the area around Boston. In May one American outfit even captured the great northern fort at Ticonderoga on Lake Champlain from a small, surprised British garrison. Massachusetts began to try to feed, equip, and drill the country boys who were coming into camp. They were becoming an army instead of a collection of part-time fighters.

By the time the Second Continental Congress met in May, it had a war to deal with. Moderates still urged, and eventually got, a final petition to the king. But the members also went about planning for a Continental Army to support New England's forces. The job was made harder because Congress had no idea of how much authority it had. The delegates were representatives of communities that were rapidly becoming ex-colonies, but were not yet states. The one certain fact was that the door to peace was nearly closed.

The Battle of Bunker Hill Brings War Closer

War became inevitable on June 17, 1775, at the Battle of Bunker Hill. This was a high point near Charlestown, a village just across the bay from Boston. The Americans had moved out the night before to fortify it. If they could get cannon up its slopes, they could easily bombard the British ships and soldiers below. The British knew this, too. They could not allow it. So, that morning, more than 2,000 British troops were rowed across the bay and lined up in neat scarlet ranks for a charge against a little fortification that the Americans had built, not on Bunker Hill but on Breed's Hill, next to it. While this took place the British fleet bombarded Charlestown and destroyed it (far right).

In midafternoon the British lines advanced up the slope, drums thundering, bayonets glinting in the sun. They came within a few yards of the breastworks behind which were the Americans, mostly dressed in their everyday homespun and carrying weapons of every kind and size—old captured French muskets, hunting guns, pistols, even weapons made in local blacksmiths' shops. At a word of command, a crashing fire leaped from the muzzles. The British were mowed down by hundreds. Some companies were cut to eight or nine men. The British straggled down the hill to lick their wounds. Gamely, they tried again, and another assault was shattered. Finally, a third attack was successful. Out of ammunition, the Yankees retreated and "lost" the battle. But, once again, the provincials had shown themselves able to stand up to England's best-trained and bravest soldiers. Among those making their stand on the hill was Salem Poor, a Negro whose bravery was commended by his officers. Some 5,000 black Americans served in the first American army during the Revolutionary War.

Bunker Hill was a full-fledged battle between organized forces, including ships of war. A town had been leveled. There was no longer any doubt on either side that a long, costly struggle was ahead. In preparation Congress had given command of the American army to the respected, experienced Virginia soldier, George Washington. Two weeks earlier, after hearing the news of Lexington, Washington had written to a friend a few sentences summing up the feelings of a man who had never been a radical. "Unhappy it is . . . that the once happy and peaceful plains of America are either to be drenched with Blood, or Inhabited by Slaves.

Above: A number of Negroes distinguished themselves in the fighting on Breed's Hill. The black man in this detail from a John Trumbull painting may be Salem Poor, who was commended by fourteen officers for his bravery. Another Negro, Peter Salem, is often credited with killing Major Pitcairn. Right: The British burn nearby Charlestown during the Battle of Bunker Hill.

NATIONAL GALLERY OF ART, COLLECTION OF EDGAR WILLIAM AND BERNICE CHRYSLER GARBISCH

Sad alternative! But can a virtuous Man hesitate in his choice?"

Questions for Discussion

1. Why was General Gage watching the militia in the towns outside Boston?
2. Who were the minutemen? How did they get that name?
3. Why did Gage send an expedition to Concord?
4. Was Gage's action wise? Why?
5. What was the significance of the fighting at Lexington and Concord? How did the radicals use the event to win support for their cause?
6. At what point did an all-out war between Britain and its American colonies become inevitable? Be prepared to defend your answer.
7. What steps did the Second Continental Congress take to prepare the colonies for war?

Chapter Review

Social Studies Terms

militiamen, policy, duties, revenue, boycott, propaganda, repealed, radicals, moderates, confrontation, conciliation, polarization, home rule

Summary Questions for Discussion

1. What is a revolution? In the conflict in values which led to the Revolution, to which values did the king and his advisers give the greatest importance? Which values did the colonists feel were most important?
2. How could the ties between Britain and the colonies have been peacefully maintained?
3. Is the use of violence as a means of protest ever justified? If so, when?
4. What did Edmund Burke mean when he said, "Obedience is what makes government"? Do you agree? Why?
5. In what ways did the British use of force against the colonists at Lexington and Concord have a result opposite from the purpose for which it was intended?
6. Did the government in London "overreact" to the Boston Tea Party? Why?
7. Cite some examples from recent history to prove that the boycott is still used as a weapon of protest. Why do some boycotts succeed and others fail?

8. It was about six years between the Boston Massacre and the Declaration of Independence. Why did the colonists wait so long to declare their independence?
9. How could the British government have prevented the street brawls between the troops stationed in Boston and some of the local citizens?
10. What part did propaganda play in arousing the colonists to rebel against their lawful government, the British?

Pictures as Historical Evidence

Compare some modern political cartoons with those in this chapter. How does modern cartoon style differ from that of the earlier age? In what ways is it similar? How do cartoonists use pictures instead of words to put across a message? How do modern magazine advertisements or political posters put their messages across without using words?

Map Study

From a study of the map on page 144, tell why the territory lost by France in 1763 was considered by the colonists on the Atlantic seacoast to be of great importance for their future.

For Further Reading

America's Ethan Allen, by Stewart Holbrook. Boston: Houghton Mifflin Company, 1949.

Battle for the Rock: The Story of Wolfe and Montcalm, by Joseph Schull. Toronto: The Macmillan Company, 1961.

Battle in the Wilderness, by Konrad Kellen. New York: Walker & Company, 1961.

Lexington, Concord and Bunker Hill, by Francis Russell and R. M. Ketchum. New York: American Heritage Publishing Co., Inc., 1963.

Sun of Thunder: Patrick Henry, by Julia M. Carson. New York: Longmans, Green & Co., 1945.

The Boston Massacre, by Alice Dickinson. New York: Franklin Watts, Inc., 1968.

The French and Indian Wars, by Francis Russell and L. H. Gipsom. New York: American Heritage Publishing Co., Inc., 1962.

The Many Worlds of Benjamin Franklin, by Frank R. Donovan and Whitfield J. Bell. New York: American Heritage Publishing Co., Inc., 1964.

6
Winning the War for Independence

The six-foot-two, very masculine figure on the opposite page is the "virtuous man" who could not hesitate to choose America's side after the Battle of Lexington. As commander of the Revolutionary forces, George Washington gave the rebellious colonies one of the first things a revolution needs—exceptional **leadership**.

Washington was not superhuman. In peacetime he loved hunts and dancing parties as much as any other Virginia gentleman. In war he was no genius. He made many battlefield mistakes, some of which nearly cost him his army. He did not win so much respect from his generals that they always obeyed him, nor did he always keep his temper with officers who fumbled their tasks. Also he quarreled with Congress when it refused his requests.

But Washington had two qualities which blazed out like lighthouses of hope in the war's darkest days. He was unselfish and steady. Everyone knew that he would never use his position to seek power, praise, wealth, or the other prizes that tempt even the best of men. When the British seemed unbeatable, Washington never thought of surrendering or resigning. He was in the war to win independence for his country.

In any society one job of a leader is to demonstrate the qualities which the society most admires. In self-governing, hard-working, eighteenth-century America, this ideal figure was a man of property, common sense, and dedication to public service. Washington was neither a sage nor a saint, but he was a courageous, levelheaded leader of men. His countrymen knew this, and they were willing to follow him.

Fortunately, the colonies had many gifted leaders. In the Continental Congress sat two future Presidents, John Adams and Thomas Jefferson, as well as Benjamin Franklin and dozens of others who would one day be governors, senators, judges, and makers of constitutions. America had one basic ingredient for success in a revolution: leadership.

As you read, think about these questions:
1. In addition to good leadership, what are some other ingredients for a successful revolution?
2. In war what are some of the advantages and disadvantages of being on the defensive? of being on the offensive?
3. Why did the United States need help from foreign countries to win the Revolution?

George Washington surveys the battlefield at Trenton, New Jersey.

Independence and War

Revolutions often begin with enthusiasm like that shown by the people raising the liberty pole and recruiting troops for the Revolutionary army in the picture at right. But in time all revolutionary struggle brings wounds, pain, hunger, and death. To give them the strength to endure such suffering, men need a cause greater than quarrels over a tax on tea or stamps. By January of 1776 some men were urging that Congress give the Patriots a cause worth dying for by taking the giant step of declaring the colonies independent.

So said Thomas Paine in the pamphlet *Common Sense*. Paine told the Americans that they owed nothing to the king of England or to any king. An honest man was worth more than all the "crowned ruffians of Europe." America was a vast continent. It could no longer be ruled by a small island. Furthermore, America's cause was, in Paine's words, the cause of all "ye that love mankind." When *Common Sense* sold several hundred thousand copies, Congress felt that **public opinion** (the common beliefs of the members of a society on public issues) favored independence. In addition, Congress knew that the colonies must become independent in order to seek foreign support. In June of 1776 a resolution of independence was proposed in Congress, and a committee was chosen to write a "declaration" explaining the step. The resolution was adopted on July 2. The declaration was approved on July 4 and signed by the members in August.

Redheaded, 33-year-old Thomas Jefferson, a Virginia lawyer, planter, and gifted thinker, actually wrote the Declaration of Independence. He was chosen for the job by his fellow committee members because they knew he was a first-rate writer, and they wanted the Declaration to make a convincing appeal to people's emotions as well as to present a sound legal argument. Jefferson did both brilliantly. He appealed to the "opinions of mankind." He argued that whenever a government anywhere denied men their rights to life, liberty, and the pursuit of happiness, they had a right to overthrow and replace it. These statements helped give the Revolution an **ideology** (a political faith).

Some have noted a certain contradiction in the fact that Jefferson held slaves while he wrote of liberty. But men can and do describe a perfect world worth struggling for without being perfect themselves. In time Jefferson's words would inspire those who wished to end slavery.

In 1776 Patriots hold a rally to encourage volunteer enlistment.

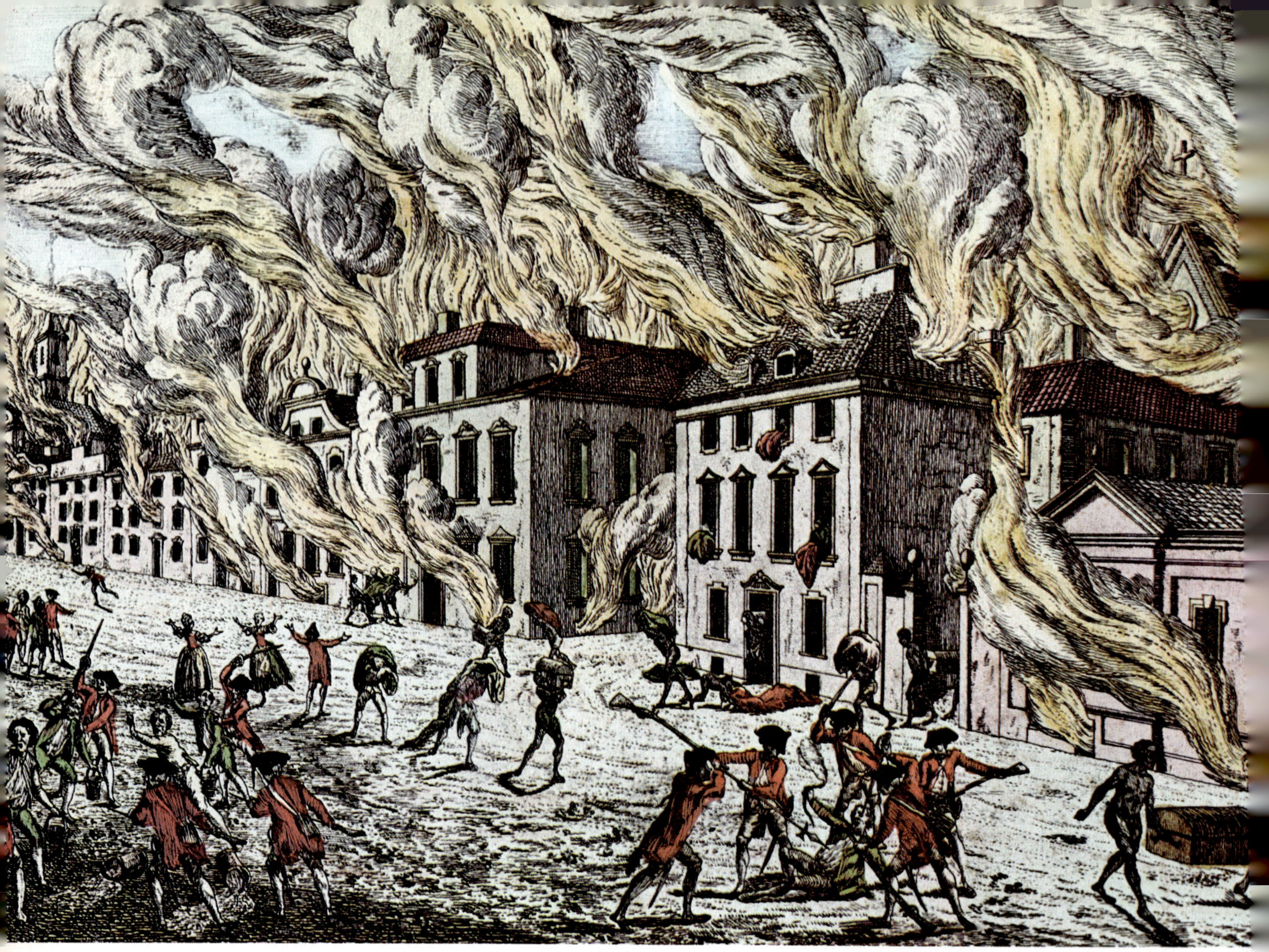

MORRISTOWN NATIONAL HISTORICAL PARK

Above: On September 21, 1776, a fire raged through New York City and destroyed over 1,000 buildings. The British accused Americans of starting it and captured some suspects, who were strung up by their heels or bayoneted and thrown into the flames. Nathan Hale was caught trying to flee the city, and General William Howe ordered him hanged without a trial. The fire greatly inconvenienced the British who had counted on housing their troops in the city. George Washington said of the fire, "Providence, or some good honest fellow, has done more for us than we were disposed to do for ourselves."

METROPOLITAN MUSEUM OF ART

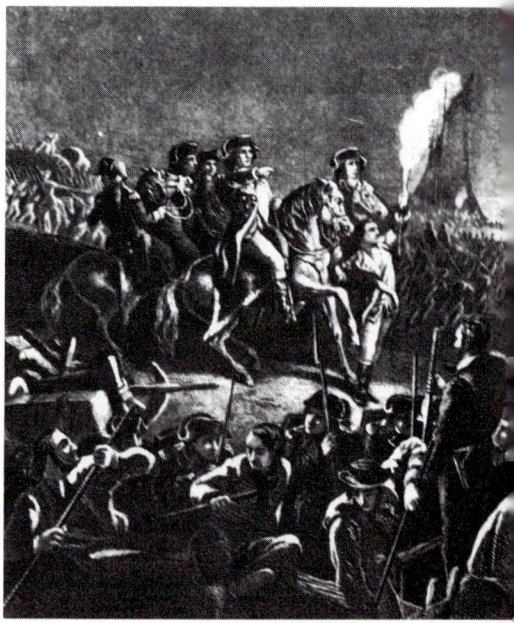

Howe Drives Washington Out of New York

While the war of words was being waged, the war with guns went on. In the summer of 1776 the Americans were doing better in propaganda than in battles. In June the war shifted southward when the British left Boston by sea and moved against New York City. This city was not easy to defend because it was on Manhattan Island. Also the British fleet controlled the surrounding waters. Still Washington could not give it up without a fight. Late in August, while British ships massed in the harbor, Washington, under the cover of bad weather, moved part of his troops across the East River to modern-day Brooklyn.

It proved to be a big mistake. Britain's General William Howe landed 15,000 troops and attacked at once. The Americans still lacked the experience and skill to stand up to waves of red-coated British troops and their green-clad, German-speaking, Hessian **mercenaries** (professional soldiers hired by a country other than their own), who advanced in machinelike ranks. By August 28 Washington's forces were battered and weak. Facing them was a powerful enemy. The Americans badly needed new supplies and men, but reinforcements were stranded on the other side of the river—and enemy warships could blast anything that moved.

But sometimes an army of amateurs has advantages. Among Washington's men were two regiments from the fishing towns of Salem and Marblehead in Massachusetts. On a pitch-dark, rainy night, these salty "soldiers" laid down their muskets and manned the oars of a collection of small boats gathered from wharves along the river. Working through the night, they shuttled back and forth (lower left), bringing the army to safety on the Manhattan shore.

Still the American forces were far from safe. Between September and November Washington fought several battles as he retreated northward. Each bought a little time. But the British were driving on. They soon had all of New York City, shown here (upper left) during a fire that may have been set by the retreating Americans to rob the British of the prize. As the British advanced they captured carelessly guarded American forts full of men and supplies. By December they were chasing what Washington called "the wretched remains of a broken army" westward across New Jersey. Washington saw 5,000 of his men taken prisoner. Morale, the will to win, was nearly shattered.

Below: In August 1776 between 10,000 and 12,000 American troops were secretly evacuated from Long Island across the East River to New York City.

Washington Counterattacks at Trenton

Now came a time when the man Tom Paine called a "sunshine patriot"—the man who only supports a winner—gave up. The American soldiers shivered around the campfires, without shoes, blankets, or winter uniforms, while Washington wrote that the "cry of want [lack] of Provisions" came to him from everywhere. Sickness struck down hundreds. The enlistments of many militiamen were due to expire. Deserters were slipping away at an alarming rate.

Then George Washington showed his great side. He knew he was in danger. Like a hunted fox, he was almost in the jaws of the hounds. But what if the fox suddenly startled everyone by turning around and tearing the throat out of the closest pursuer? On the snowstorm-lashed night of December 25, Washington ferried his men across the ice-choked Delaware River and marched them along the New Jersey shore to Trenton. There, three Hessian regiments were sleeping off a Christmas drunk, convinced that neither man nor beast would stir in such bitter weather. Out of the sleety dawn the ragged but game Americans suddenly burst (below). Within two hours the Hessian commander was killed, 900 of his men were prisoners, and the Americans were hauling captured supplies back to the boats. A week later Washington crossed the Delaware again and beat the British at Princeton. Then

ANNE S. K. BROWN MILITARY COLLECTION, BROWN UNIVERSITY

both armies went into winter quarters, for in those days guns and wagons could move on the rough dirt roads only after winter snows and spring thaws were over.

This brilliant counterattack when things were darkest forced the British to plan a third year of effort to crush the rebels. It also gave the colonists courage and so restored their morale.

Division on the Home Front

Success was by no means certain in early 1777. All through the colonies the Patriots, who favored independence, and the Tories, who were pro-British, were bitterly opposed. The debate split townships, congregations, and even families.

Men were Tories for many reasons, both honorable and selfish. Some were connected with great families that had been honored by the king. Some were making a good profit supplying the British armies. Some doubted that the Patriots would ever be able to control the radicals who had burned stamps and dumped tea. Some, like the Scottish backwoods settlers in North Carolina, simply disliked the Revolutionary leaders and went Tory in order to settle old scores with the coastal landowners who supported Congress. And some felt that loyalty to the Crown should not be given only as a reward for good behavior: "My king, right or wrong."

On the morning of December 26, 1776, American troops led by George Washington surprise Hessian mercenaries guarding the village of Trenton, New Jersey. The battle was fought with artillery, bayonet, and sword because bad weather had made most muskets useless.

Many colonists remained loyal to England. During the Stamp Act crisis a town meeting (right) dissolved into an armed clash and a Tory was strung up (below). Above is a recruiting poster for a Tory regiment formed in 1776.

The Patriots, too, rebelled for a variety of reasons. But many colonists—perhaps one in three—never really took one side or the other and, like most silent bystanders, simply waited out events.

So unity came slowly. Congress was trying to create a new political **consensus** (general agreement). This struggle for a peaceable way to unite different groups under a single system of rule was to go on at least until the year 1800.

Unity is always hard to achieve, but in wartime it is almost impossible without violence. Because men get killed in battle, others feel ready to kill anyone they think disloyal. Young Tory men enlisted with British-led units and killed fellow colonists. Tory and Patriot militiamen burned the homes of neighbors who supported the other side. Patriot courts seized Tory property, and Tories in occupied areas betrayed Patriots to the British. War is not a business for saints. It would take time—until people were tired enough of violence—to find nonviolent methods of dissent and disagreement.

The Crucial Year

Then came a decisive year—mid-1777 to mid-1778. Late in July of 1777 the British moved an expedition by water and land against Philadelphia. In hot summer and hazy autumn, they beat Washington's men in several battles, occupied Philadelphia, and chased the Continental Congress to York, Pennsylvania. In December the "rebel" army went into winter camp at nearby Valley Forge.

Despite hunger and subzero weather, Washington continued to drill his hard-pressed, unfortunate troops. Washington's army was ill-fed not because Pennsylvania's farms produced no beef and cider, but because there was a shortage of wagons for delivery. Also state governments lagged in furnishing their assigned shares of medicine, clothes, and blankets, and many merchants refused to accept the paper money issued by Congress. But the third straight winter of American survival proved that the rebels could not be starved out. Besides, at Valley Forge Washington already had news of a stunning American victory the autumn before that would soon turn the tide.

In June of 1777 a British army was gathered in Canada under "Gentleman Johnny" Burgoyne, a poetry-writing, party-loving British general who had a

TRUMBULL, M'Fingal, 1795

VALLEY FORGE HISTORICAL SOCIETY

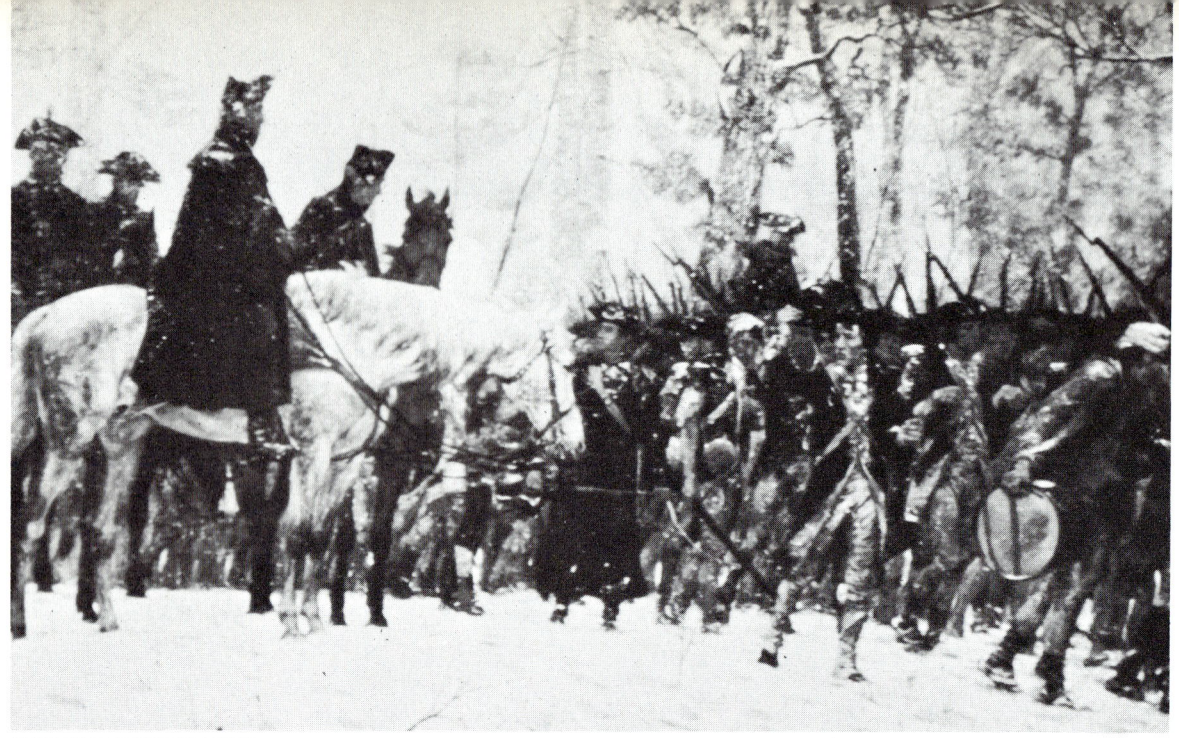

Above: Washington reviews his ragged army at Valley Forge. Below: In October 1777 Benedict Arnold, riding the white horse, leads a charge during the crucial battle at Saratoga.

FORT TICONDEROGA MUSEUM

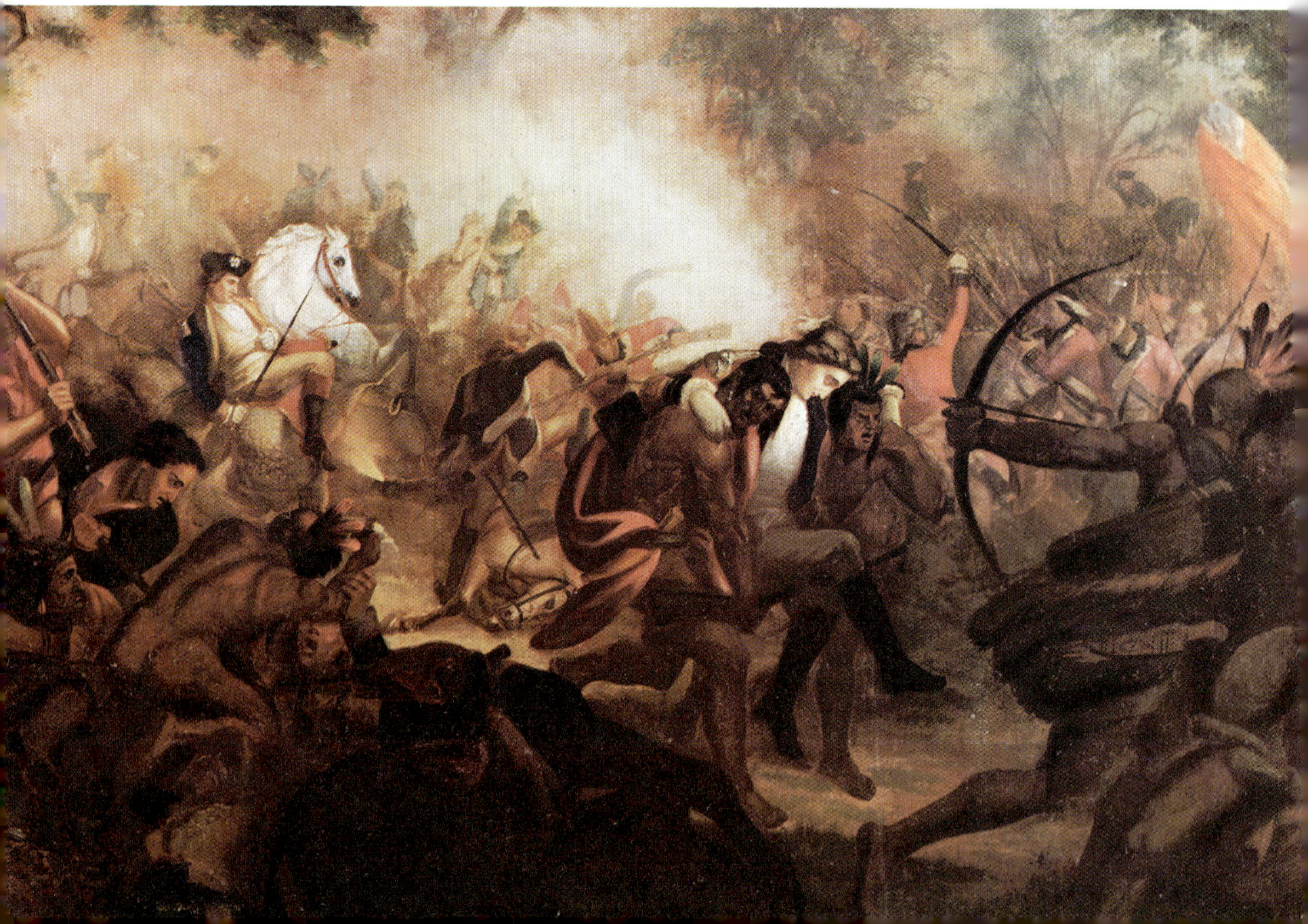

great **strategy** (an overall plan) to end the war. He would move down from Canada, as shown in the map at right, along Lake George and Lake Champlain to the Hudson River. At Albany he would meet redcoats sent north from New York by General Howe. A wall of British bayonets would split the colonies.

But Burgoyne was fighting inland, where geography worked for the Americans. Like Braddock's men 22 years before, Burgoyne's columns of British and Hessians thrashed through the upstate New York wilderness in the hot weather, slowed to a crawl by their heavy guns and wagons. New England, anxious not to be cut off, sent militiamen who swarmed around Burgoyne like "birds of prey," as one of his men said. Burgoyne's Indian partners, against orders, killed settlers and roused the countryside further against him. Worse, General Howe never sent the promised help from New York City, but instead had decided to leave there to take Philadelphia.

By October, after suffering two stunning defeats against generals like Benedict Arnold, Burgoyne's army was surrounded at Saratoga (lower left). Four days later Burgoyne surrendered his entire force. The Americans had not only thwarted a third British campaign but captured a whole royal army. Only a year later one of America's heroes at Saratoga, General Arnold, turned traitor and aided the British.

A third phase of the war now began. By 1778 the British had shown that they could capture almost any American port city. They could win battles in the open field. Their control of the sea—like control of the air today—gave them power to move freely. But they could not move far inland to destroy American farms and break popular resistance. After 1778, therefore, it became clear that the war would not be won only on the settled strip of coastline, where British armies could win European-style battles.

Questions for Discussion

1. What arguments were used by radical leaders in support of American independence from Britain?
2. Why was Thomas Jefferson chosen for the job of writing the Declaration of Independence?
3. Discuss the feelings that a modern "sunshine patriot" would have toward his country.
4. Why did the Continental Congress have difficulty unifying the country behind the Patriot cause?

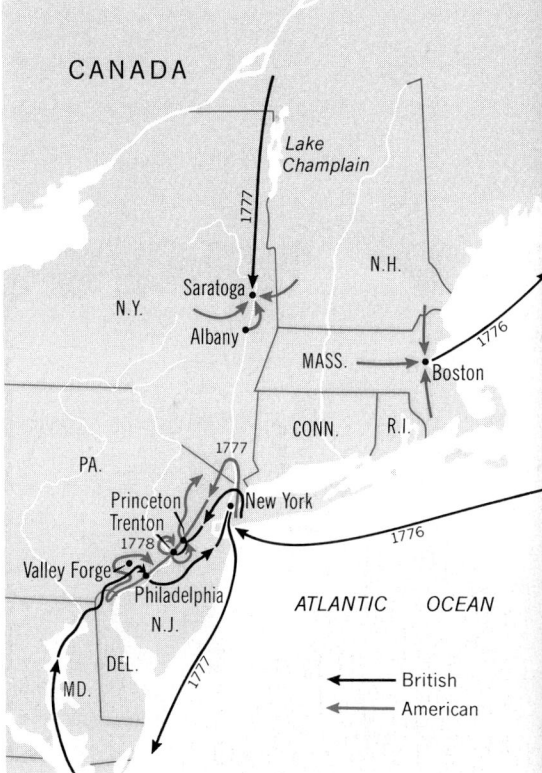

Northeast Campaigns 1775-1778

The Tide Turns

The first great sign of change came as a result of the victory at Saratoga, when France and the United States signed a treaty of **alliance** (a formal agreement to give each other help). In February 1778 the Americans gained the support of mighty France.

King Louis XVI of France did not join the fight because he loved liberty or the Americans, even though many of his subjects deeply admired Benjamin Franklin, one of the ambassadors Congress had sent to France to **negotiate** (arrange) the treaty (upper right). What King Louis wanted was simply to get back at England for France's losses in the French and Indian War.

But to the Americans France's entry into combat was a godsend. As the ally of a great power, Congress could now borrow money more easily. In addition, Washington would soon get trained French troops and, of even greater importance, the French navy to help him. Spain and the Netherlands were soon drawn into the fight against Britain. Now, England could no longer give full attention to America.

Besides the troops sent by France, individual Europeans volunteered to fight on the American side. Two of them were Thaddeus Kosciusko of Poland (left) and France's Marquis de Lafayette (far right). They believed that young men everywhere could share in man's endless struggle for liberty by joining the colonists' rebellion. The words of Thomas Jefferson were beginning to have their worldwide appeal.

For a lifelong officer like the Prussian Baron Friedrich von Steuben (right), opportunity was probably as important as democratic ideals. At Valley Forge he began to teach Washington's officers and men the many things he knew about military hygiene, or cleanliness and disease prevention, as well as drill, organization, and discipline. He contributed another vital element of revolutionary success—training.

The War in the West and at Sea

The scene of battle now shifted toward Britain's enemies at points thousands of miles apart—deep in the heart of North America and out at sea.

In June of 1778 a band of about 200 western riflemen crowded onto rafts in the Ohio River. They were starting one of the most important expeditions of the war. Virginia claimed all the land west and north of her boundaries. One of her militia officers, Colonel George Rogers Clark, believed he could enforce that claim by

Poland's Thaddeus Kosciusko gave the Patriot army invaluable instruction in military engineering.

Above: Ben Franklin is received at Versailles Palace. Below: France's Marquis de Lafayette in 1781.

Prussia's Friedrich von Steuben, who spoke very little English, trained the American army during the winter at Valley Forge.

Western Campaign 1778–1779

⟵ American

A modern painting shows British Lieutenant Colonel Henry Hamilton surrendering Fort Sackville at Vincennes to George Rogers Clark in February 1779.

capturing British posts in the old Ohio country.

Clark performed his mission brilliantly. He floated and marched to the Mississippi and captured some settlements in Illinois. Then he doubled back toward a British fort at Vincennes (map, upper left), in present-day Indiana. By then it was February of 1779. Melting snows had turned the whole area into a swamp. After slogging the last few miles through water that sometimes reached shoulder-height, Clark boldly attacked and forced the surrender of the British commander (left).

This astonishing feat had broken the British hold on the area between the Alleghenies and the Mississippi. When the time came for the peace treaty, American negotiators claimed that territory and set the new nation's flag one-third of the way to the Pacific.

No less important to the war's outcome were American and French victories at sea. There was a tiny American navy that played no real part in the winning of the war. But Americans did outfit privateers, or lightly armed, fast, privately owned ships, which destroyed millions of dollars' worth of British shipping.

At sea the French navy bore the brunt of the fighting, most of which took place far from the colonial coastline. These sea fights were formal, savage affairs in which long lines of rocking wooden ships, yardarm to yardarm, pounded each other to splinters (lower right). Although many of these grisly slaughtering matches ended in a draw, French naval power proved to be decisive in the final American victory.

The War in the South

In 1779 the British decided to shift the war into the South. There, the last acts were played. During 1780 and 1781 war swept cruelly through backwoods communities. Those years made the reputation of commanders specializing in hit-and-run tactics.

The British strategy of cutting away the southern half of the new nation—just as Burgoyne's campaign was supposed to slice off New England—seemed to work at first. By early 1779 the British controlled Georgia. The redcoats swept deep into Virginia in 1779, then easily captured Charleston in 1780. At Camden, South Carolina, they routed an American army. The British believed that the region was full of people who would be moved by these triumphs to aid the Loyalist, or pro-British, side. But the great Tory

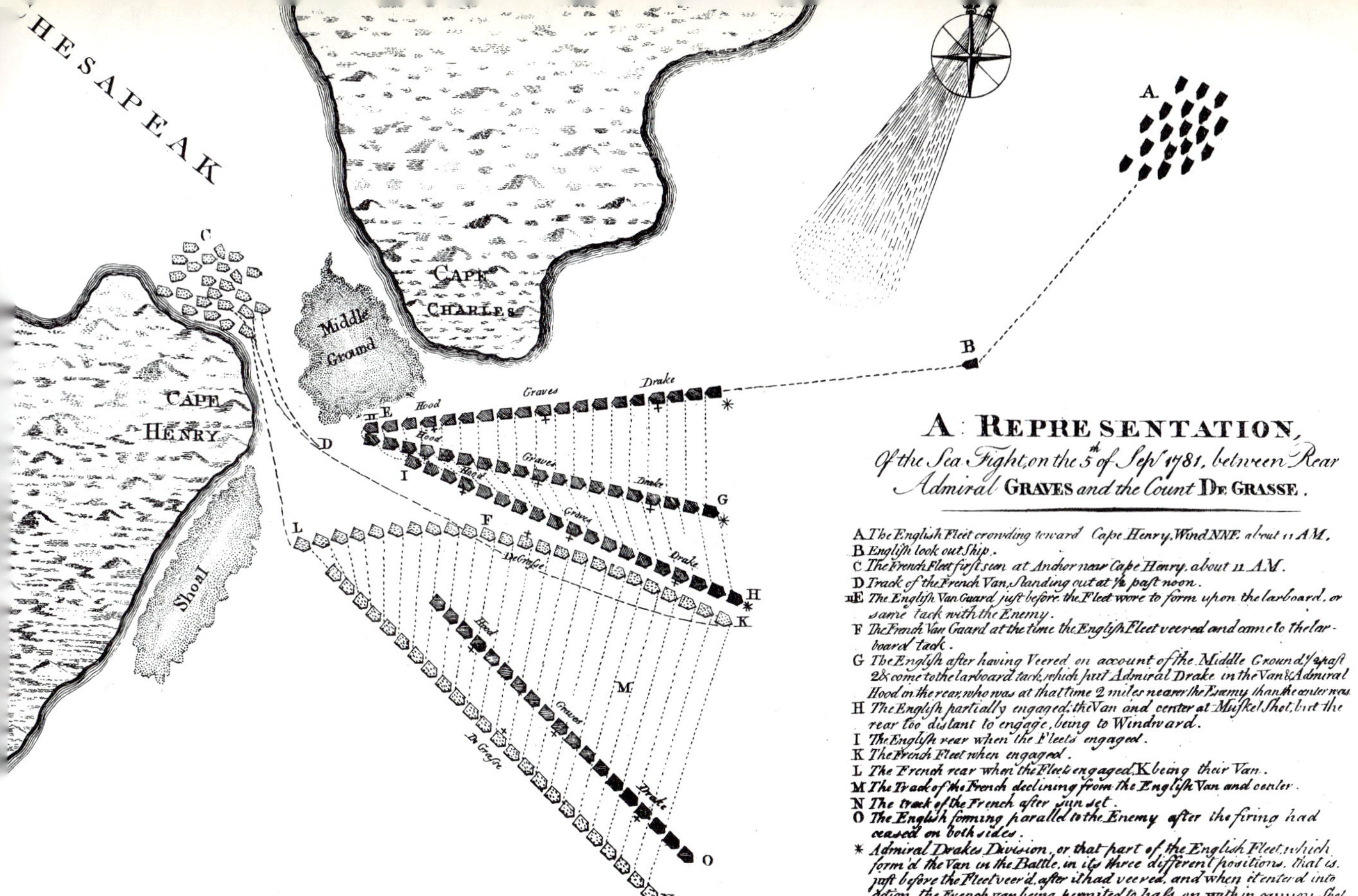
CHESAPEAK
CAPE CHARLES
Middle Ground
CAPE HENRY
Shoal
A
B
C
D
E
F
G
H
I
K
L
M
N
O
Hood
Graves
Drake
De Grasse
A: REPRESENTATION,
Of the Sea Fight, on the 5th of Sepr 1781, between Rear Admiral GRAVES and the Count DE GRASSE.
A The English Fleet crowding toward Cape Henry, Wind NNE about 11 AM.
B English look out Ship.
C The French Fleet first seen at Anchor near Cape Henry, about 11 AM.
D Track of the French Van, Standing out at ½ past noon.
E The English Van Guard just before the Fleet wore to form upon the larboard, or same tack with the Enemy.
F The French Van Gaard at the time the English Fleet veered and came to the larboard tack.
G The English after having Veered on account of the Middle Ground ½ past 2 & come to the larboard tack, which put Admiral Drake in the Van & Admiral Hood on the rear, who was at that time 2 miles nearer the Enemy than the center was.
H The English partially engaged; the Van and center at Muskel Shot, but the rear too distant to engage, being to Windward.
I The English rear when the Fleets engaged.
K The French Fleet when engaged.
L The French rear when the Fleets engaged, K being their Van.
M The Track of the French declining from the English Van and center.
N The track of the French after sun set.
O The English forming parallel to the Enemy after the firing had ceased on both sides.
* Admiral Drakes Division, or that part of the English Fleet which form'd the Van in the Battle, in its three different positions, that is, just before the Fleet veer'd, after it had veered, and when it enter'd into action, the French van being permited to pass on with in cannon Shot from our center to our van, or nearly so, before the Signal was made to engage.
French 24 Ships 1822 Guns 18.200 Men
English 19 Ships 1408 Guns 11.311 Men
The French Superior by 5. Ships 414 Guns 6889 Men
NB: Neither Fleet had at this time any land Forces aboard or in Transports.

Below: British and French ships battle in March 1781. Later, in the war's most crucial sea battle (map, above), England failed to break the French blockade of the Chesapeake Bay, and Cornwallis was stranded in Yorktown.

GRAVES, *Two Letters . . .*, 1783

MARINERS MUSEUM, NEWPORT NEWS

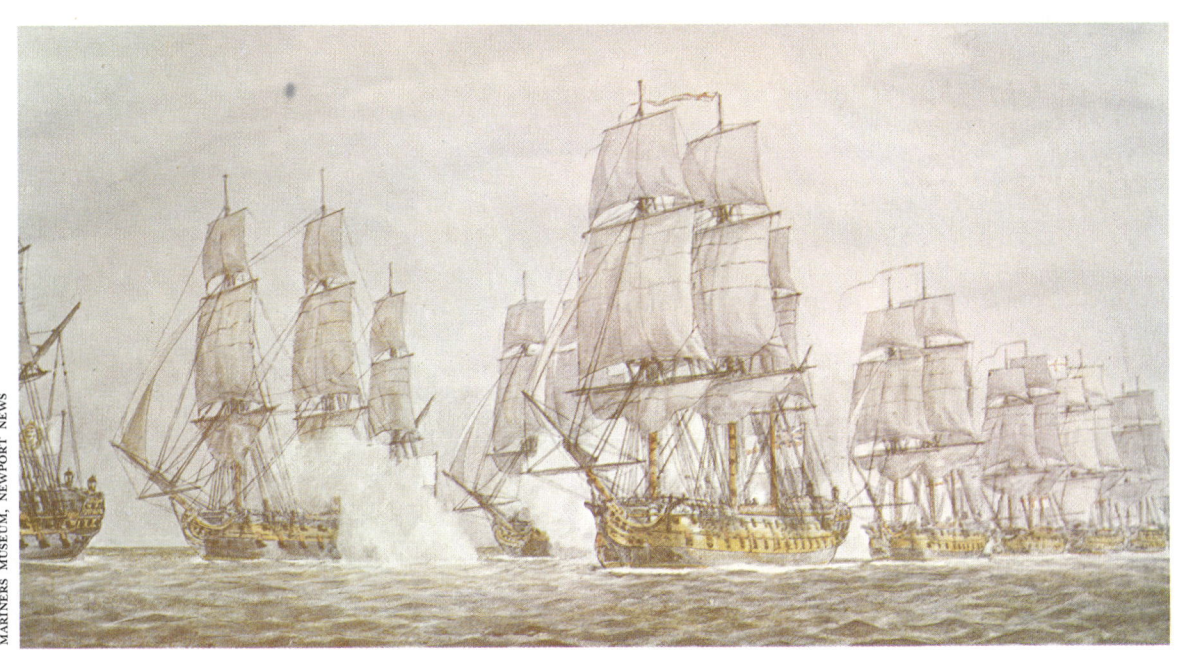

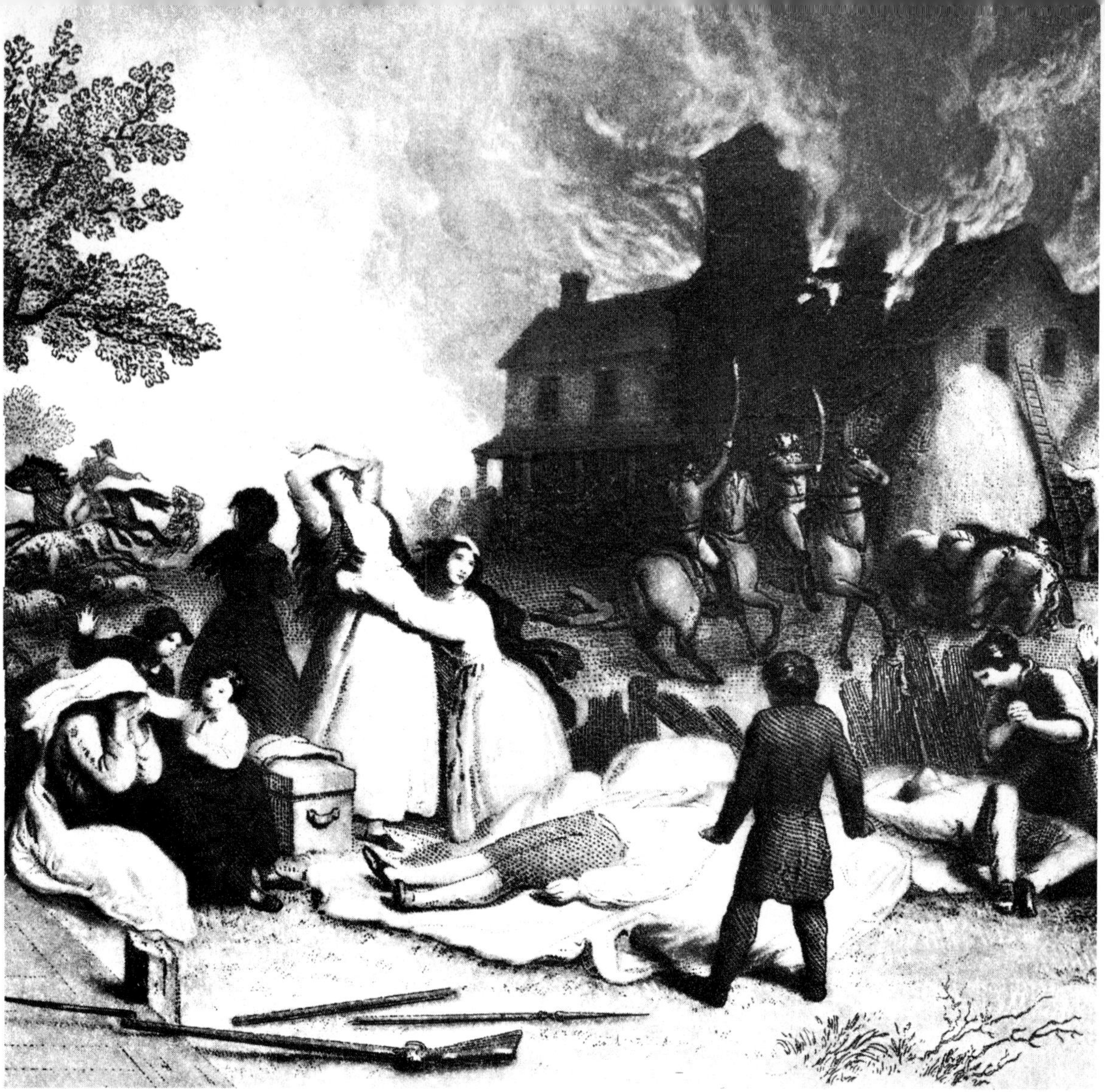

LIBRARY OF CONGRESS

Above: In May 1780 British troops led by Colonel Banastre Tarleton swept through the Waxhaws, a wooded frontier region on the border of North and South Carolina. Shortly after witnessing the massacre, thirteen-year-old Andrew Jackson (center, foreground) joined the Patriot army. Right: "Swamp Fox" Marion (on horseback, second from left) and some of his highly successful guerrilla troops take a raft across the Pee Dee River in South Carolina.

PRESTON DAVIE COLLECTION

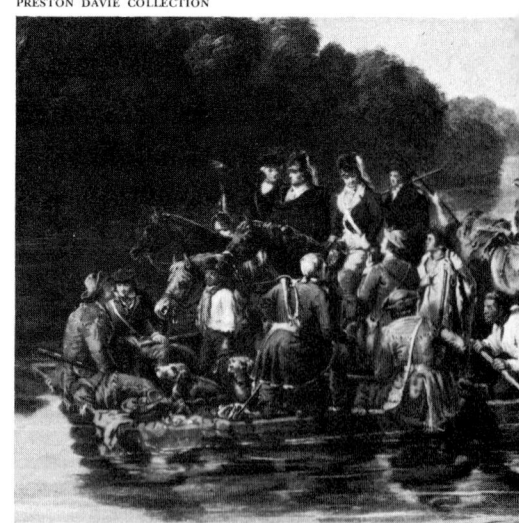

uprising never took place. Instead, a new American force was brought together under General Nathanael Greene, who described his tactics in these words: "We fight, get beat, rise, and fight again."

Besides Greene's uniformed Americans, General Francis Marion, known as the "Swamp Fox," led a ragtag group of Patriots who used **guerrilla warfare** with devastating effectiveness. They would appear suddenly, hit hard at a British wagon train or supply post, then run and hide while the flames lit the sky. Stealthily moving through the swamp, Marion's guerrillas (lower left) kept a far larger British force off balance. Hit-and-run tactics enable a small and weak force to outfight superior numbers. Rebels, from ancient Hebrews fighting Roman garrisons in Palestine to Vietcong, have used them.

Guerrilla warfare, however, made any American a suspicious character to British officers, and any Tory a potential threat to the American force. Houses were set aflame, young boys dragged to prison, crops destroyed, farm animals and slaves carried away. Starvation, disease, massacre, and grief were the fate of many innocent Southerners, as the picture of a British raid on an American plantation vividly shows (upper left).

The war in the South brought the Negro's part in the Revolution into focus. The British reminded blacks that their masters, though fighting for "liberty," still were slave-owners. In 1779 the British promised freedom to Negroes who would join their side. An unknown number of slaves ran away from their masters to do so.

The Americans themselves turned gradually to enlisting slaves and free blacks. Congress discouraged it at first, anxious to keep guns out of black hands. But by the middle of the war, manpower was scarce. So several states, on their own, enrolled blacks, free and slave, in the ranks.

Of the 5,000 blacks who served, some were freed as a reward for service, others because their Tory owners fled. So the Revolution, though not planned that way, was a small step toward ending slavery.

Questions for Discussion

1. What help did the Patriot cause receive from foreign countries?
2. Under what conditions is guerrilla warfare likely to be most effective?

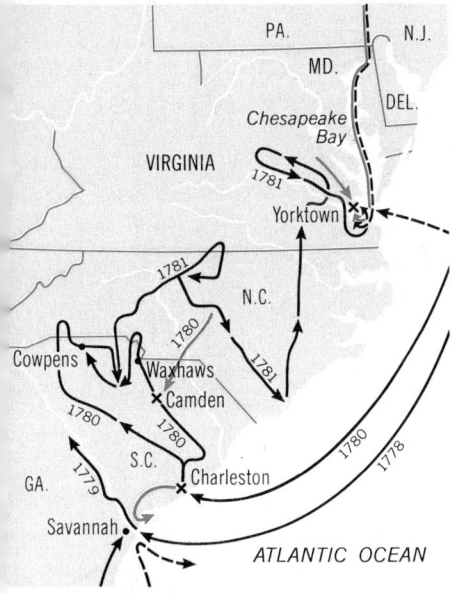

Southern Campaigns 1778–1781

← British
← American
←--- French

Victory at Yorktown and the Treaty of Peace

In the summer of 1781, drums rattled across New York and New England. Washington's forces had long been keeping an eye on the British in New York. His veterans were now joined by many French regiments under Count Jean Rochambeau. Exciting news came from the South. Lord Charles Cornwallis and his army were in Virginia, at Yorktown, with a river on either side and the Chesapeake Bay at their back. A French admiral, François de Grasse, was in the West Indies with a large fleet. If he could come up into the bay, he might be able to defeat Cornwallis and free the South.

The plan depended on the French and Americans getting down to the coast of Virginia quickly. So knapsacks were packed, sweethearts kissed, and good-bys said both in French and English. By land and water Washington's and Rochambeau's men hurried southward to destiny.

The climax actually came at sea on September 5, 1781. It was then that France's Admiral Comte de Grasse beat off a British fleet under Admiral Thomas Lord Graves. Sea power did its work. For a few weeks the French and Americans could close in on an English general whose lines of supply and retreat were cut off by French warships.

On October 18, 1781, defeated redcoats march between lines of French (rear) and Americans at Yorktown. Louis Van Blarenberghe, a Frenchman who was at Yorktown for the surrender, completed this oil painting in 1785.

On October 17, as more than 15,000 French and American besiegers moved steadily closer, Lord Cornwallis asked for terms of surrender. Two days later, for the second time in four years, a whole British army marched out to lay down its arms (above). It passed between ranks of smiling Frenchmen, some remembering Quebec, and Americans, many with recollections of the bad autumn of 1776.

Yorktown did much more than free the South. It was the end of the war. England had fought for almost seven years to subdue its angry colonists and make them help pay the cost of driving France from Canada. Now England was deeper in debt than ever, bogged down in a world war, and pushed part way out of the Ohio country. It was time to face facts, swallow pride, and admit defeat. That, too, takes a kind of national strength. Treaty-making dragged on for two more years, in leisurely eighteenth-century fashion, until 1783. But there were no more campaigns. The British musicians had chosen an appropriate tune to play as their men paraded out at Yorktown—"The World Turned Upside Down."

Wars do not end exactly when the guns stop firing. A humorist once said peace was "an interval of cheat-

ing between two periods of fighting." That is a bit harsh. But a famous German general once put it another way when he wrote that war was an extension or continuation of **diplomacy** (the art of conducting relations between nations). Diplomacy exists because independent nations have interests which are sometimes in conflict, just as people living in a crowded, busy house have arguments over space, quiet, and the use of strategic places like bathrooms and kitchens. Nations try to solve their disputes by political and economic pressures and by bargaining, as individuals do. A war is a confession that these peaceful means have failed.

The American Revolution did not end in 1783. Attempts to start a new political system and to unify the thirteen colonies went on in the making of the Constitution, as we shall see. The quarrels between Americans and the British over territories and other economic matters such as trade went on, too. But now Americans were a separate nation and could use the full diplomatic and military power of the nation to gain important goals. Some of the lingering issues are shown in the map on the opposite page.

The American flag flew over the Allegheny Mountains and up to the banks of the Mississippi River, but the British remained in forts at Niagara, Detroit, and other places. Their agents still offered blankets, rum, and hopes of restored power to the Indians in return for furs. Yankee skippers still were entangled with British regulations governing trade with the West Indies. Yankee fishermen still needed to know where the boundaries between the fishing waters off Maine and Canada lay. Patriots and Tories had each suffered property losses, and the American and British governments each tried to win payments for war damages.

Not all the trouble spots involved England. Spain was to become a problem on the United States' southern border. The British had given Florida to Spain in the 1783 treaty. As the owner of Louisiana since 1763, the Spanish also held New Orleans which was the natural port connecting the Mississippi with the Atlantic. Clearly, as Americans moved westward they would use the Mississippi as their outlet to the world and would not let another nation control the river's mouth. Settling disputes that arose from expansion made difficult the tasks of American diplomats. But for nations, like men, trouble is a sign of life.

Chapter Review

Questions for Discussion

1. In the Revolution why was sea power important to both sides?
2. When did the Revolution end? Explain.
3. What issues between the British and the Americans were left unresolved by the Revolution? Why were they likely to be diplomatic sore-spots?
4. Why was control of the mouth of the Mississippi so important to the United States?

Social Studies Terms

leadership, public opinion, ideology, mercenaries, consensus, strategy, alliance, negotiate, guerrilla warfare, diplomacy

Summary Questions for Discussion

1. What were the qualities that made George Washington a great commanding general of the Continental Army?
2. In the Revolution how did both free and slave Negroes make a contribution to the Patriot cause?
3. How would you describe the American ideology of 1776? of today?
4. Why did the Americans issue a Declaration of Independence instead of a Declaration of War?
5. During the Revolution how did the British generals turn the rule of "divide and conquer" into strategy? Why did the strategy fail to work?
6. In what ways did warfare in the American Revolution differ from warfare today? In what ways was it similar?
7. How did some of the values of the American Tories differ from those of the Patriots?
8. In the war against Britain, why would the United States and France be natural allies?
9. In the Declaration of Independence, what arguments did Jefferson use to convince his fellow Americans that independence was a just and legal step? Why did he appeal to the "opinions of mankind" rather than simply to the opinions of Americans?
10. What was the purpose of George Rogers Clark's expedition into the interior of the United States? What were the results, both military and nonmilitary, of his victory?
11. What do you think is the most important ingredient for diplomatic success?

Pictures as Historical Evidence

What pictures, if any, in this chapter would provide evidence against the following generalization? The Americans won the Revolutionary War with little difficulty and with no significant help from foreigners or from foreign countries.

Map Study

Look again at the map with the title *Northeast Campaigns 1775-1778* on page 179. Why, in 1776, were the British troops pulled out of Boston? What was the general strategy in Howe's move against New York in the same year? What was General Burgoyne's strategy in pushing south from Canada in 1777? Why in each case did the strategy fail to work?

Now, refer to the map of *Southern Campaigns 1778-1781* on page 185. Why did the British shift the war to the South in 1778? What did Cornwallis believe to be the strategic advantage of his position at Yorktown in 1781? Why did his position turn out to be a disadvantage, rather than an advantage?

For Further Reading

Benedict Arnold, by Jeannette C. Nolan. New York: Julian Messner, 1956.

Free Men Must Stand, by Eric W. Barnes. New York: McGraw-Hill Book Company, 1962.

George Washington, by Marcus Cunliffe. New York: American Heritage Publishing Co., Inc., 1966.

The American Revolution: A British View, by Clorida Clarke. New York: McGraw-Hill Book Company, 1967.

The Battle of Saratoga, by John R. Cuneo. New York: The Macmillan Co., 1967.

The Battle of Yorktown, by Thomas J. Fleming. New York: American Heritage Publishing Co., Inc., 1968.

The Declaration of Independence, by Cornel A. Lengyel. New York: Grosset & Dunlap, Inc., 1968.

The Revolutionary War, by B. McDowell. New York: National Geographic Society, 1967.

Thomas Jefferson and His World, by Henry Moscow. New York: American Heritage Publishing Co., Inc., 1960.

7
Forming a Government

In romantic stories the hero always manages to slay the dragon and win the lovely girl. The American who painted the scene on the opposite page portrayed a very romantic view of the results of the Revolutionary War. The gallant sailor represents the United States. He has beaten the wicked British. Now he is being honored by the fair Miss Liberty. Together, they will live happily ever after.

History has a less fanciful tale to tell of the new nation's first years. When the war was over in 1783, there was no agreement among Americans to form a single nation, nor was there an agreement about the kind of government such a nation should have.

In a sense cooperating to win the war had been easy. Also the Patriots knew the truth of Ben Franklin's famous statement that if they did not all hang together, they would all hang separately.

In peacetime cooperation did not come so easily. Without war's threats it was harder to smooth over the differences between big states and small ones, states with many slaves and states with few, states with western lands and states without them, states whose people lived mostly by the profits of seafaring and states whose wealth came largely from plantations.

The First Continental Congress of 1774 was a gathering of delegates from widely separated colonies which thought of themselves practically as independent little nations. The next year they formed a temporary wartime government. In 1776 they declared their independence of Britain. By 1781 all of the states had adopted an agreement, the Articles of Confederation, which put this wartime government on a permanent footing.

Though the Articles of Confederation created a "United States of America," each state kept its "sovereignty, freedom and independence," much like a member of today's United Nations. Six years later what we now know as the Constitutional Convention was held, but it began only as a meeting of men sent by their states to undo some troublesome kinks in the Articles. In those thirteen years between 1774 and 1787, a span about equal to your present age, Americans advanced toward national government, step by uncertain step.

As you read, think about these questions:
1. Why is establishing a new government difficult?
2. Why is compromise so necessary in a democratic government?

This romantic view of Liberty crowning America was painted in the 1830's.

NEW-YORK HISTORICAL SOCIETY

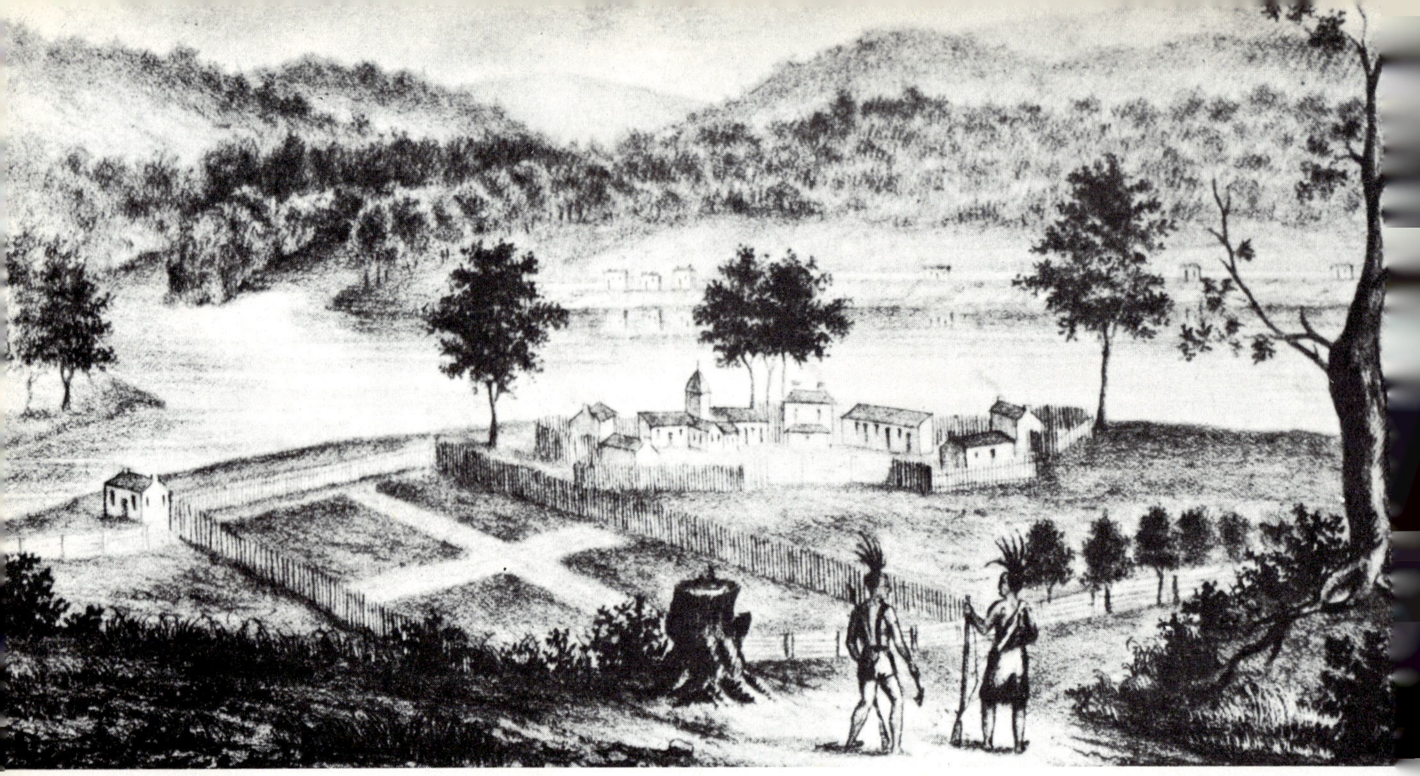

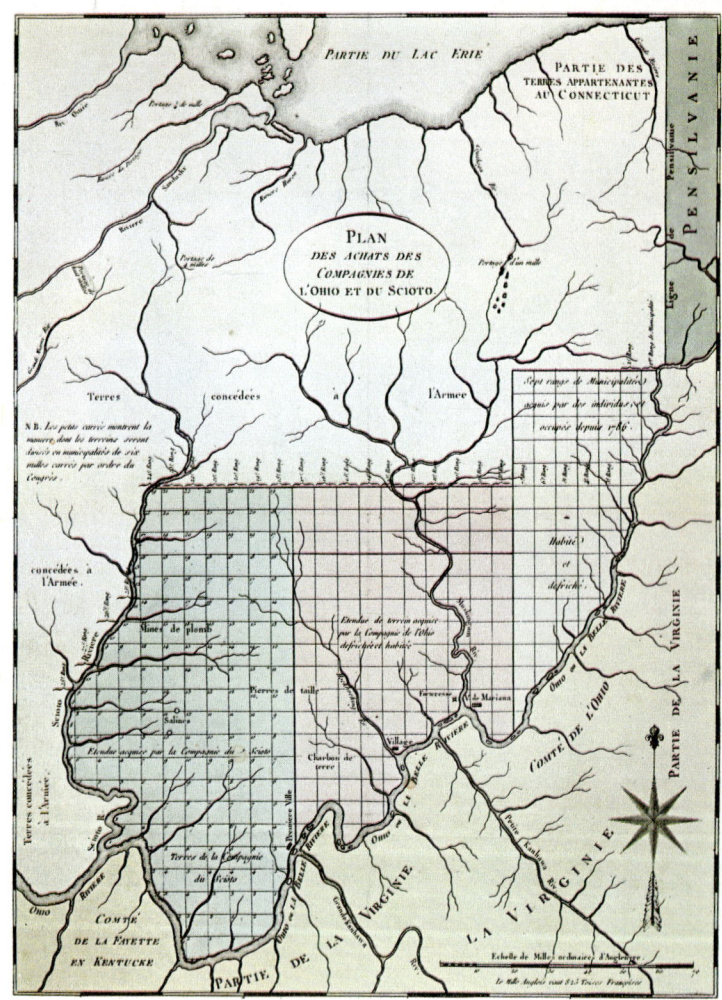

Right: This map shows land areas in the Northwest Territory that were purchased by the Ohio and Scioto Companies. The writing is French because the Scioto Company tried to attract settlers from France but never succeeded in establishing a lasting settlement. Above: The Ohio Company built the village of Marietta, across the Muskingham River from Fort Harmar. This lithograph shows the fort and village as they appeared in 1790.

LIBRARY OF CONGRESS

Government Under the Articles of Confederation

The troubled times gave Americans one advantage. Many members of assemblies which drew up and **ratified** (gave approval to) state and national constitutions had served in colonial legislatures and in the various revolutionary governments. Their ideas of government were tempered by experience. The handling of western lands is an example of how the new nation benefited from such experience.

The signing of the Articles of Confederation only became possible when the states which had land claims running deep into the West agreed to give them up and have them become part of the **public domain** (land owned by all the states together). How should this land be given to settlers? Under the colonial system individuals had been allowed to carve out choice portions wherever they liked, provided they had the royal governor's permission. Such a system made for a wild scramble to get permission and to grab the best plots.

The Great Land Ordinances of the Confederation

By an **ordinance** (law) of 1785, Congress set up a new plan for the Northwest Territory. The public domain was to be surveyed and divided into six-mile-square townships (map, far left). These townships were further divided into mile-square sections. Neatly mapped and numbered, such sections were to be sold by the government, at conveniently located offices, to all customers who could pay. The idea was to have a fair and orderly procession westward that the United States could control by deciding when to open certain areas for sale. The money from land sales would add greatly to the treasury. The revenue from one section in every township would be for public schools.

How would settlers in the new lands be governed? After their own unpleasant experience with British attempts to rule them from London, the members of the Confederation Congress knew how hard it would be for them to manage "colonists" deep in the western wilds. In 1787 they passed another ordinance for the Northwest Territory, which consisted of the public domain north of the Ohio River (map, left). Under this ordinance early settlers would at first be ruled by Congress, followed by a period of limited home rule. When a part of the territory had a population of at least 60,000 free inhabitants, it could become a state and be admitted to the United States. Eventually, five states—Ohio, Illinois, Indiana, Michigan, and Wiscon-

The Northwest Territory

195

sin—were made out of this area. This system of gaining statehood was used later for other territories taken or bought by the United States, right up through 1959 when Alaska and Hawaii were admitted as the 49th and 50th states.

The Northwest Ordinance was remarkably generous. It told the inhabitants of America's inland "empire" that, as their population grew, they would become equals of the "mother country" on the Atlantic Coast. It guaranteed the basic rights of citizens of the United States to the territorial residents who were temporarily voteless. It even prohibited slavery in the area. Experience was paying off. It was almost as if the former subjects of George III were saying, "This is how you should have treated us!"

The Articles of Confederation were only an agreement of association among the thirteen ex-colonies. Each one, now that it was a **sovereign** (fully independent and self-governing) state, furiously guarded its own freedom. Each state had one vote in Congress, regardless of its size or population. Nothing could be done without the consent of two-thirds, or nine, of the states. Furthermore, the Articles could not be changed without the consent of every single state. Above all, Congress could not tax the states. It could ask the states to share the common expenses in proportion to each state's population. But the state itself had to collect the funds from its citizens and forward the money, if it chose, to Congress. The people of a state never paid a cent in taxes directly to the United States. There was no single **executive** (chief officer) to enforce the laws that Congress made.

The arrangement was perfect for preventing the central government from destroying the freedom of the states, but it left the United States without power to do many things in need of doing. For example, the British remained in their old fur posts in the Northwest, despite the provisions of the peace treaty. They barred American ships from their West Indian ports, thus crippling New England's commerce. They sold manufactured goods at low prices in American markets, driving American manufacturers out of business. At the same time the Spanish often prevented the export of American goods through New Orleans, and the Indians were causing trouble.

The United States had the authority, under the Articles, to raise armies and make treaties to deal with

BOTH: CULVER PICTURES

In September 1786 armed protesters led by Daniel Shays appeared at a courthouse in Springfield, Massachusetts. They were hoping to prevent the court from taking actions against debtors. A violent confrontation was avoided when Shays' men and the local militia agreed to disperse, and the court adjourned.

these problems. It could not, however, force the states to obey these treaties, nor could it make the states pay such expenses. The states soon fell behind in payments. Without money or strong control over its member states, the Confederation did not have diplomatic, military, and financial muscle.

Shays' Rebellion Shows the Confederation's Weakness

But in many men's minds, that was not the fatal weakness. After all, the country had managed to win a war under the Articles. The great fear of many men was that unless the states were really united, they would go their separate ways or be picked off, one by one, by foreign enemies.

Opponents of the Articles were deeply disturbed by an episode in Massachusetts in 1786. Times were very hard there, and a number of people could not pay their debts or taxes. Under law that meant their farms would be taken and sold. But under the leadership of a war veteran, Daniel Shays, numbers of them blocked the steps of courthouses (opposite page) and prevented the judges from deciding their cases. Later Shays' men attacked a government arsenal, or weapons storage center, in Springfield (right) but were driven away by Massachusetts militia. Then the uprising collapsed.

Shays' Rebellion was a serious matter. Forcible defiance of the law could lead to **anarchy** (a condition in which there is no government at all). Then life might become a free-for-all, with neither law nor order. Some fathers of the Revolution began to see things as the British had in 1774. Where would resistance end? "Are your people mad?" wrote George Washington to a Massachusetts friend. A British paper crowed that the Yankees, "having overturned the government under which they were born and bred are unwilling to submit to any kind of government."

In January 1787 Shays and his men returned to Springfield to attack the state arsenal. This time Massachusetts' troops drove them off, and shortly afterward the rebellion collapsed. However, most of the reforms sought by the protesters soon became law.

Questions for Discussion

1. In adopting policies for the distribution of land and for governing settlers in the public domain, how did the Congress of the Confederation profit from experience under British rule?
2. How did the Articles of Confederation reflect the American distrust of strong government?
3. What problems revealed some of the weaknesses of the Articles of Confederation?

Making and Ratifying the Constitution

Given time, the Confederation might have been able to solve some of its problems when prosperity returned to the land. But by 1786 thoughtful men in all the states were becoming convinced that basic changes were needed. It was not enough to get the states to pay their requisitions or to stop levying taxes on each other's products or to agree as a group to honor treaties with foreign powers. Therefore, a proposal was made to Congress that a gathering of delegates be held in Philadelphia the next year to consider "defects" in the Articles of Confederation.

So in May of 1787 a group of men chosen by their states met once more in the Quaker city where the First Continental Congress had proclaimed America's independence eleven summers before. Almost at once they reached an important agreement: that their real mission was to begin at the beginning and rewrite the Articles entirely. They agreed, too, to keep the proceedings secret so that they could finish the job free from public pressure. Through four hot summer months, they worked six days a week under the familiar and trusted leadership of George Washington, one of Virginia's delegates, seen here presiding over the Convention. Not all of the delegates stayed the whole time, nor signed the final draft on September 17, nor were pleased with the results. Little Rhode Island did not send any delegates at all.

The finished Constitution was a set of compromises, and compromises always anger some people. However, compromise was needed, for every delegate was determined to defend the interests of his own state as well as those of the nation. The large states wanted a national legislature based on population. They reasoned that those states with the most taxpayers should have the loudest voice. But the small states feared that they would be permanent losers in a lawmaking body that made decisions by counting noses. In the end they agreed to have a legislature consisting of two chambers: a Senate in which each state was equally represented, and a House of Representatives based on population. (See Article I, Sections 2 and 3 at the back of the book.) Slaveholding states wanted their blacks counted toward representation in the House, but not counted if Congress collected a tax from each state in proportion to its population. The compromise was to count each slave as three-fifths of a man (Article I, Section 2).

So it went, down the line, issue after issue—the

In this detail from a painting by Thomas Prichard Rossiter, George Washington (seated, upper right) presides over the Constitutional Convention of 1787, as delegates sign the Constitution.

slave trade might be prohibited, but not before 1808 (Article I, Section 9). Duties might be placed on imports (Article I, Section 8) to protect northern manufacturers from foreign competitors, but not on exports (Article I, Section 9), which were most important to the southern states. There were hot tempers in the hot meeting rooms. But problems were settled by debate. After years of trouble the era of violence was ending. The experienced politicians knew that there is a time to pull down and a time to build. The time to build had come.

The Struggle over Ratification

As the delegates rode homeward from Philadelphia, the brilliant autumn countryside that they saw from their coach windows was the scene of lively debate. The delegates had provided that the Constitution should be ratified by conventions in the states. Approval must come from the people, the source of power. In meetinghouses, taverns, and parlors in cities and in country towns, the people read hastily printed copies of the Constitution and got ready to choose delegates to the ratifying conventions. The Federalists, those who supported the Constitution, were soon exchanging verbal shots with the anti-Federalists, who opposed the Constitution.

The anti-Federalists were generally those who saw no benefit and much possible harm in a stong central government. They pointed out that the Constitution as drafted did not protect individual liberties. It put no limit on the taxing powers of Congress. The President, as commander in chief of the armies, might use them to make himself a **dictator** (a ruler who has total authority without any limits or checks by others). Also the lifetime appointments of Supreme Court justices would make for a judicial aristocracy of men who would not have to answer to the people.

Above all, the states which had proudly resisted England's tyranny were reduced to what some thought was second-class status. The Preamble to the Constitution spoke of "We the people" and made no mention of states. States could no longer protect themselves with armies and navies, make their own treaties with Indians or friendly powers, or coin money if they needed it (Article I, Section 8). Article VI clearly said that the Constitution was the "supreme Law of the Land" and that even state judges should obey it, what-

The Declaration of Independence, the Articles of Confederation, and the United States Constitution were all signed at Independence Hall, Philadelphia, seen here as it appeared in 1778.

ever their own state constitutions or laws might say.

To answer all these objections, the Federalists, led by Alexander Hamilton, James Madison, and John Jay, pointed out the urgent need of union. They also stressed the limits and checks on the national government's powers. They agreed that if the Constitution were ratified they would immediately support constitutional **amendments** (changes) to guarantee individual liberties. These first ten amendments, known as the Bill of Rights, were ratified in 1791. They appealed to all those who had something to gain from a government that could stand up to foreign powers and promote commerce and prosperity. It was worth taking some risks with a strong government, they said, to gain these ends. All government was a calculated risk in which people traded some liberty in return for protection from disorder.

The Federalists convinced a majority. One after another, beginning with Delaware, the states ratified the Constitution. By June of 1788 nine states had joined—enough to start the new government (Article VII). New York and Virginia, two big, key states whose absence would have been crippling, came along that summer of 1788, after hot debate. North Carolina and Rhode Island held out until after the new government was in office. The picture at the right shows the celebration of ratification in New York, a scene repeated in all the states whenever ratification took place.

There were hard feelings, of course. In Pennsylvania, for example, where the vote was close, Federalist crowds lit a bonfire to celebrate, but enraged anti-Federalists drove them away and "converted the intended joy into mourning" by burning a copy of the Constitution in the fire. But the attitude of most anti-Federalists was that of Patrick Henry of Virginia, who said he would "patiently wait in expectation of seeing that government changed." The people's willingness to wait and see what the new government actually did was what saved the nation from further turmoil. Trust was the real miracle of Philadelphia.

Questions for Discussion

1. What were some of the important compromises which were written into the Constitution?
2. Summarize the arguments of the Federalists for acceptance of the Constitution and the arguments of the anti-Federalists for its rejection.

BROWN BROTHERS

After a desperate struggle New York ratified the Constitution on July 26, 1788, by the slim margin of 30 to 27. Above, supporters of the Constitution celebrate with a thirteen-gun salute.

The Basic Principles of the Constitution

As the pen-scratched draft (right) indicates, the Constitution underwent many changes before it was ready for ratification. Even after the Constitution was ratified, it continued to change. First came changes by amendment—the passage of the Bill of Rights. Decisions of the Supreme Court have also changed the Constitution. In the case of *Marbury v. Madison* in 1803, the Supreme Court decided that a law passed by Congress was in conflict with the Constitution, and was therefore null and void. This power of **judicial review** (the right of the Supreme Court to determine if a law is constitutional) has made the Supreme Court a most important part of the American political system. Finally, although the Constitution did not provide for certain practices such as political parties, custom has made them a part of American political life.

The Constitution has changed with the times, but its basic principles have remained the same. The first of these is the principle of **federalism** which works as follows. The Federal government has certain **exclusive powers** (powers held by only one level of government) spelled out in Article I, Section 8. For example, it alone may coin money and make treaties. But the Tenth Amendment plainly says that any power not clearly given to the Federal government remains with the states or with the people. Therefore, the states also have exclusive powers, such as the right to regulate education and marriage. There are also some **concurrent powers** (powers shared by two governments). Both governments may collect taxes. Both have courts to interpret the laws. In short, the answer of the Constitution to the question of whether there should be a single central government or many state governments is "both!"

Conflicts between the Federal and state governments began to spring up at once. But a second principle of the Constitution is that the courts, rather than the armed forces, settle these disputes. All judges in all courts, state and Federal, recognize the Constitution, and laws or treaties made under its authority, as the supreme law of the land. And all officials, in the long run, bow to the rulings of the courts. Only on rare occasions has it been necessary for force to be used to carry a court decision into effect. One such exception was the use of Federal troops to bring about the court-ordered integration of Central High School in Little Rock, Arkansas, in 1957. And only once, during our

[6]

this clause post ? peachments of Officers of the United States; to all cases of Admiralty and Maritime Jurisdiction; to Controversies between two or more States, ~~(between citizens of the same State claiming lands under grants of different States)~~ between a State and citizens of another State, between citizens of different States, and between a State or the citizens thereof and foreign States, citizens or subjects. (In cases of Impeachment, cases affecting Ambassadors, other Public Ministers and Consuls, and those in which a State shall be party, ~~this jurisdiction shall be original~~. *The Supreme Court shall have original jurisdiction* In all the other cases beforementioned ~~judicial appeal~~, with such exceptions and under such regulations as the Legislature shall make. ~~The Legislature may assign any part of the jurisdiction abovementioned (except the trial of the President of the United States) in the manner and under the limitations which it shall think proper, to such Inferior Courts as it shall constitute from time to time.~~

Sect. 4. The trial of all crimes (except in cases of impeachment) shall be by jury — and such trial shall be held in the State where the said crimes shall have been committed; but when not committed within any State, then the trial shall be at such place or places as the legislature may direct — The privilege of the writ of Habeas Corpus shall not be suspended: unless where in cases of rebellion or invasion the public safety may require it.

Agreed.

~~Sect. 4. The trial of all criminal offences (except in cases of impeachments) shall be in the State where they shall be committed; and shall be by jury.~~

Sect. 5. Judgment, in cases of Impeachment, shall not extend further than to removal from office, and disqualification to hold and enjoy any office of honour, trust or profit under the United States. But the party convicted shall nevertheless be liable and subject to indictment, trial, judgment and punishment, according to law.

agreed

XII

No State shall coin money; nor grant letters of marque and reprisal; nor enter into any treaty, alliance, or confederation; nor grant any title of nobility.

agreed.

XIII

No State, without the consent of the Legislature of the United States, shall lay imposts or duties on imports; nor keep troops or ships of war in time of peace; nor enter into any agreement or compact with another State, or with any foreign power; nor engage in any war, unless it shall be actually invaded by enemies, or the danger of invasion be so imminent, as not to admit of a delay, until the Legislature of the United States can be consulted.

agreed. —

XIIII

The citizens of each State shall be entitled to all privileges and immunities of citizens in the several States.

agreed.

XIV.

Any person charged with treason, felony, or ~~high misdemeanor~~ *other crime* in any State, who shall flee from justice, and shall be found in any other State, shall, on demand of the Executive Power of the State from which he fled, be delivered up and removed to the State having jurisdiction of the offence.

Any person bound to service or labor in any of the United States shall escape into another State, he or she shall not be discharged from such service or labor in consequence of any regulations subsisting in the State to which they escape; but shall be delivered up to the Person justly claiming their services or labor

referred to the Com of five — inserted Sep 23

XVI

Full faith shall be given in each State to the *public* acts ~~of the Legislatures, and~~ to ~~the~~ records and judicial proceedings of ~~the courts and magistrates of~~ every other State: *and the Legislature may by general laws prescribe the manner in which such acts, records, and proceedings shall be proved and the effect thereof.*

XVII

New States may be admitted by the legislature into this Union: but no new State shall be hereafter formed or erected within the jurisdiction of any of the present States without the consent of the legislature of such State as well as of the General legislature. Nor shall any State be formed by the junction of two or more States, or parts thereof without the consent of the Legislatures of such States as well as of the Legislature of the United States.

XVII

Civil War, did the system break down to the point where bayonets and guns replaced judges' opinions in deciding a contest between the nation and the states.

Finally, the powers of the Federal government are carefully limited by the Bill of Rights which specifically forbids the Federal government to do some things — such as establishing an official religion (First Amendment). In addition, as we shall see, the powers of each branch — executive, legislative, and judicial — of the Federal government are limited by a system of checks and balances.

The Constitution's makers were always struggling for a balance between a government strong enough to get things done but not strong enough to take away the liberties of its people. One of the reasons they managed so well was that their opinions reflected certain attitudes that Americans held.

The Powers of the Presidency

The men who met in Philadelphia wanted a vigorous executive who could and would see that the nation's intentions were carried out. They wanted a leader. They gave the President command of the armed forces and the diplomatic service and the right to choose many Federal officials as well as the heads of executive departments (Article II, Section 2). These people would all be responsible to the President.

At the same time the checks and balances of the Constitution put many restrictions on the President. But equally as important as the Constitution's limits were people's feelings that the President should be someone like themselves and not a grandiose, pompous figure who ruled from on high like George III, shown in his royal ermine robes at the left. Even so, one anti-Federalist grumbled that the chief executive would be an "elective king."

The very first Congress decided not to address the President by any elegant titles such as "His Elective Highness," a name suggested by Vice President John Adams. Since Adams was rather roly-poly, one congressman made fun of his idea by suggesting that the Vice President be called "His Rotundity." A simple title suited President George Washington (right). He was a very dignified man, but he cared neither for fancy clothing nor for fancy names. The tradition he set was carried even further by the third President, Thomas Jefferson, who walked to his own inauguration

George III, crowned King of Great Britain at the age of 22, is shown here in his coronation robes.

and, in his slippers, entertained a startled British ambassador in the White House.

The ideal of the President as an ordinary man who puts aside his own business to serve the people has lasted to this day. Even though the President today is one of the most powerful men on earth, he still exercises his leadership by winning people's loyalty as an individual. That is why he still takes part in such public ceremonies as tossing out the first ball at the season's opening baseball game. Compare this practice with that of the Incan nobles on page 34 of Chapter 1 who turned the first shovelful of earth for planting the year's crop.

The Extent of Democracy in the Constitution

The Constitution also reflects the competing viewpoints of its makers on the question: How aristocratic or democratic should the new government be? As lawyers and propertied men, many of the founding fathers distrusted what they called the "passions" of the "mob" or those who might have nothing to lose from a sudden overthrow of the government. Because the Federal government was limited in its power, the power of any voting majority would also be limited.

Furthermore, parts of the national government were, and some still are, removed from popular control. Until the Seventeenth Amendment was passed in 1913, Senators were chosen by the state legislatures instead of directly by the people (Article I, Section 3). The President was not, and still is not, directly chosen by the people (Article II, Section 1). He is formally chosen by Presidential electors from each state who are themselves chosen by the people of each state.

On the other hand, the Constitution had some surprisingly democratic provisions at a time when monarchy and aristocracy were the common thing throughout the world. Representatives had to appeal to the voters for re-election every two years (Article I, Section 2). No property qualifications were required for holding any Federal office. No religious test, such as one to determine if a person believes in God, might be imposed for the holders of any such office (Article VI). Persons eligible to vote for members of the lower houses of state legislatures had to be allowed the right to vote for members of the House of Representatives (Article I, Section 2). Some defenders of the Constitution expected that representatives would be chosen

WHITE HOUSE HISTORICAL ASSOCIATION

This portrait shows George Washington around the time of his inauguration as President in 1789.

not just by the rich, the educated, and the powerful, but also by people from ordinary walks of life.

There was a movement toward democracy throughout the country in the 1780's. It could be seen in the action of states like Virginia in establishing freedom of religion and in forbidding practices which had tended to restrict ownership of the land to the rich. People talked, even in the South, of a day when slavery might vanish. Many states considered relaxing laws which imposed harsh punishments for small crimes or threw men in jail for debts.

This current of democracy was to continue as the young country grew. The feeling of the people was different from other societies, where a hereditary aristocracy or a crowned king governed. Rather, Americans believed what Thomas Jefferson had said—men might not be angels, but there were no angels in human form fit to govern them. Unlike English aristocrats (above), the power of American politicians, who had to seek votes from the people (left), was not a matter of privilege.

Both the ideal of a President who leads by example and that of the democratic politician taking his case to his "bosses," the people, have been lasting elements in American life. They were embodied in the Constitution as a reaction to what the colonists had experienced under British rule. The hard-working people of young

Above: An English artist painted this water color to poke fun at the "best families" in England on their way to greet the King at his palace. Left: An American politician presents his point of view to the people.

S. SEYER, *Memoirs Historical and Topical of Bristol, 1823*

Many of the do's and don'ts in the Bill of Rights resulted from previous British experience. Opposite: These eighteenth-century English Quakers were free to hold religious meetings. The First Amendment guarantees freedom of religion. Above: The punishment for this seventeenth-century Englishman is a tongue-branding. The Eighth Amendment forbids cruel and unusual punishments.

America resented it when tracts of land or public office and honor went to the friends and favorites of royal governors and titled proprietors. They were moving toward the belief that life is a race in which everyone ought to get a fair chance.

Government as the Servant of the People

Yet one thing the Americans got directly from the English experience was the idea that the individual enjoys certain rights that the government was forbidden to take away. This differed from the view of some ancient societies that the king or chieftain was a god personified who therefore had a god's total power over all of his subjects. Dictatorships also think that the individual is far less important than society or its political form, the government.

But eighteenth-century Americans thought of the government as a servant and not as a master of the people. They knew that it had great powers, with its armies and policemen. They therefore made a list of things that the government was firmly forbidden to do with that power. The first ten amendments, known as the Bill of Rights, are quite clear. Congress may make *no* law limiting the freedom of speech, press, or religion; excessive bail shall not be imposed; no person shall be compelled to be a witness against himself in a criminal case. The Bill of Rights guarantees absolutely the rights of petition and of freedom from unreasonable search and arbitrary arrest. It also assures speedy jury trials and raises other barriers against a government that might try to break the spirit of its people by cruel punishments like that being inflicted on the English Quaker at the left. And the Ninth and Tenth Amendments say that this list of prohibitions is not complete. The states and the people keep all rights not expressly given to the central authorities by the Constitution.

As we shall see, there have been many challenges to the Bill of Rights, especially in times of war. One came as early as 1798, when Congress passed the Alien and Sedition Acts, severely limiting freedom of speech. But such laws have always been fought and eventually repealed.

Checks and Balances Provided by the Constitution

The Constitution was a kind of written contract between the people and the government they created,

among the people themselves, and even among the states. As such it was something rather new in history. Another novelty was the ingenious way in which it divided the power of the Federal government among various branches and made it possible for each to block or slow down the others. The Constitution was a carefully thought-out answer to the ever present problem: how to trust government enough not to cripple it and so deprive people of its advantages, yet not trust it too much and so perhaps enslave the people.

The system of checks and balances helped with the answer. Congress may pass laws, but if a President thinks them hasty or unwise, he can **veto** (reject) them. Yet if two-thirds of the members of each house of Congress still support the law, they can override the veto (Article I, Section 7).

The President can appoint men to high offices. But if the Senate thinks these men poorly qualified, it can refuse to **confirm** (approve) them (Article II, Section 2), as it has done on many occasions. The President can order the army and the navy into military action without waiting for Congress to approve. But only Congress has the power to declare war and to provide money for the armed services.

The Constitution also provides that the House of Representatives may **impeach** (order a trial of) the President if the House decides he is guilty of serious illegal acts. If the Senate, which would be the jury, votes to convict the President by a two-thirds majority, he is removed from office. This provision has been used only once when in 1868 President Andrew Johnson was impeached and came within one vote of being removed.

The life-appointed justices of the Supreme Court seem to be independent of Congress. Yet Congress can change the number of the judges. The President appoints judges, but his choices can be accepted or rejected by the Senate. In addition, Congress has the power to impeach justices. Finally, though the Court may declare acts of Congress or of state legislatures unconstitutional, it, unlike the executive branch, has no power to carry out its decisions. In a famous case of 1832, *Worcester v. Georgia*, the Court ruled that Georgia had violated the Constitution in chasing certain Indians from reservation lands in the state. President Andrew Jackson, who sympathized with Georgia, declared, "[Chief Justice] John Marshall has made his decision. Now let him enforce it." Marshall found he

The Constitution provides a system of checks to balance the power among the three branches of government. Right: In April 1882 President Chester A. Arthur vetoed a bill that would have kept Chinese laborers out of the United States for twenty years. This contemporary cartoon praises Arthur's action. Below right: In February 1868 the House of Representatives voted 126 to 47 to impeach President Andrew Johnson. Here, Thaddeus Stevens urges his fellow Representatives to vote for impeachment. Below left: In June 1952 the Supreme Court ruled that President Harry S. Truman's seizure of the steel mills was unconstitutional. The Court's decision inspired this cartoon.

could not. The Indians never got back their land.

But on the whole, the system of checks and balances works, as the three examples from our history shown at the left indicate. The Constitution the framers wrote was not perfect, but as the aged Benjamin Franklin, a delegate to the Convention, put it, he was astonished to find it "approaching so near to perfection as it does." The new government, Franklin thought, could be "a blessing to the people if well administered." He asked his fellow delegates who were dissatisfied with certain notions of the Constitution to sign it anyway and give it a chance to operate. By and large, the whole country has done the same thing for 200 years, changing this or that provision from time to time. Thus the government the Constitution created is always in the process of changing.

By July of 1788, twelve years after the colonies had resolved to be independent, Congress was notified that nine states had ratified the Constitution. The United States was at last to be really united. The machinery we are familiar with now would be put together and operating for the first time.

Questions for Discussion

1. In addition to change by formal amendment, what other methods have been used to alter the Constitution to meet the needs of changing times?
2. Why did federalism become one of the basic principles of the Constitution?
3. What are some of the powers that may be exercised only by the national government? only by state governments? both by the national and by state governments?
4. Why were the Ninth and Tenth Amendments included in the Bill of Rights? How did they protect the people? the states?
5. What do we mean when we say that the Constitution, Federal law, and treaties together make up "the supreme Law of the Land"?
6. In what ways did the Constitution reflect experiences of the Americans under British rule?
7. What methods of control over the government do the people have?
8. Which amendment to the Constitution was violated by the Alien and Sedition Acts?
9. Why was the Constitution a rather unique document?

JOHN CARTER BROWN LIBRARY, BROWN UNIVERSITY

The Nation Elects its First President

A 1789 display expresses America's confidence in George Washington. He is surrounded by the coats of arms of the thirteen original states and the Federal government.

The work began in the states. They would have to choose senators, representatives, and Presidential electors. There were few **precedents** (examples from the past) to serve as models in choosing the President. But choosing senators and representatives was not much of a problem. The states had plenty of experience in choosing their own assemblymen and delegates to the many conventions and congresses that had met since the fires of protest were first lit in 1765. The voting was usually done in meetings in townships and county seats. There was no one election day. The eleven states in the Union by March of 1789 were to choose their senators, representatives, and electors at various times between October 1788 and the following January. In every state but Pennsylvania it was necessary to own some property to vote. In Pennsylvania a voter only had to be a taxpayer.

Each state had its own idea of how to pick Presidential electors. In five states people voted directly for them. In Massachusetts the voters chose twice as many as were allowed (that is, twice as many as the state's number of representatives and senators), and the legislature cut the list by half. In Georgia, Connecticut, and South Carolina, the legislature did the choosing. New York never agreed on how it should be done and so cast no votes in the first Presidential election.

The election was a little disorganized. It was as if some carpenters, using familiar tools, were trying to put up a building according to a new plan, of which no one had an absolutely clear picture.

One thing was quite certain, however. The one man in the new nation on whom Southerners, Yankees, Quakers, backwoodsmen, city men, the wealthy, and those who hoped to be wealthy looked with respect was George Washington. He gave the country its first essential unifying force. The Presidential electors met in their various state capitals. Each voted for two men. The name with the highest total of votes was to become President, and the runner-up Vice President. When the votes were opened and counted by the newly assembled Senate, meeting in New York, the nation's first capital, George Washington had received the vote of every one of the 69 electors. New England's John Adams had 34. Washington (center left) was truly the hub around which the states were linked. Because of him, federalism became a practice and not just a theory.

213

Right: A thirteen-gun salute welcomes the gaily decorated barge bearing President-elect George Washington to New York Bay. Above: Robert R. Livingston of New York administers the oath of office to Washington. This detail is from an Amos Doolittle engraving of the inauguration made from a drawing by an eyewitness.

Washington's Inauguration

Once more, George Washington was called from his plantation at Mount Vernon to serve his country. He thought of himself as a modern version of the Roman General Cincinnatus, who left farming for public duty. Washington had little enthusiasm for more years of working hard for others while his own affairs were neglected. He wrote a friend that he felt like "a culprit going to the place of his execution." But duty was duty, and early in April he set out for New York.

It was a triumphal procession. Crowds turned out at every crossroads town. The bigger cities competed in honoring him. At Baltimore there was a grand banquet. At Philadelphia an arch of laurel boughs was put up under which the national hero might ride. New York outdid itself. Washington was rowed across the harbor from the New Jersey shore to Manhattan Island in a splendid barge manned by thirteen smartly dressed sailors (right). Foreign warships at anchor fired salutes. Flags decorated the rigging of merchant ships. Cheers filled the air.

That was April 23. One week later, as cannon shots boomed and church bells rang, Washington took the oath of office on the balcony of Federal Hall in Manhattan (left). Washington always had good sense about how to play the part. He accepted the crowd's cheers, rode in a handsome coach, and was as dignified as any crowned prince when he received callers. But he also wore, for his inauguration, a plain brown suit of cloth made in Connecticut. He wished to encourage American manufacturing, and setting a personal example seemed a fine way to do it.

Behind him stood Vice President John Adams, who had once defended the soldiers accused of the Boston Massacre and had ten years later helped write the Declaration of Independence. There, too, stood the first Speaker of the House of Representatives, Frederick Muhlenberg, the son of a German immigrant. Together, the three men stood for much in the history of the very young nation. They were making a beginning, and much remained to be done. But the world would be watching and learning. "The preservation of the sacred fire of liberty," said Washington in his inaugural speech, was deeply, perhaps finally, "staked on the experiment intrusted in the hands of the American people." They would have to prove whether a nation could be both self-governing and successful.

Chapter Review

Questions for Discussion

1. What is a Presidential elector?
2. How does the present method of selecting a President differ from the method used in 1789?
3. In what ways was George Washington important in getting the principle of federalism put into practice?
4. What events, people, or political institutions tended to give Americans a sense of unity by 1790?

Social Studies Terms

ratified, public domain, ordinance, sovereign, executive, anarchy, dictator, amendments, judicial review, federalism, exclusive powers, concurrent powers, veto, confirm, impeach, precedents

Summary Questions for Discussion

1. Why are the problems of peacetime sometimes harder to solve than the problems of wartime?
2. How did the Constitution give the government of the United States more diplomatic power? more military power? more financial power?
3. Would it be better if lawmakers met behind closed doors today, as the Founding Fathers did in Philadelphia? Why?
4. Why are Supreme Court justices and Federal judges appointed rather than elected? What are the advantages and disadvantages of lifetime appointments?
5. Should the President be elected for life? Why? Should he be elected directly by the people? Why did the Founding Fathers want it otherwise?
6. How does the system of checks and balances and separation of powers among the three branches of government affect the running of our government? Is this system an advantage or a disadvantage? Why?
7. What are some of the values most clearly expressed in the Bill of Rights? Do they give the individual too much or too little freedom?
8. Why is it usually unnecessary to use the power of the President to enforce the decisions of the Supreme Court?
9. Name some of the ways in which the Constitution favored a democratic approach toward the governing of the new nation.
10. Think of your family as a small society. Does this

society have the same goals for its members as the United States government has for its "family" of citizens? Is the family society governed democratically? Who has financial, law-making, and law-enforcement power? Can all groups in our society—schools, clubs, street gangs, churches—be governed by democratic rules? Why?

11. Thomas Jefferson wrote in the Declaration of Independence of "certain unalienable Rights." How was a guarantee of these rights made a part of the Constitution?
12. Does the Constitution reserve certain rights to the government which are not given to individuals? Why? What rights did the states give up in order to have a national government with the power to protect lives and property?
13. How does the Constitution protect the power of the smaller states?
14. Make a hypothesis to explain why members of the House of Representatives are elected every two years and members of the Senate every six years.

Map Study

Which natural features shown on the map on page 195 were important for the economic development of the Northwest Territory? Why? What man-made features would be necessary to provide fairly rapid transportation to the states on the Atlantic Coast?

For Further Reading

Equal Justice Under Law, by The Foundation of the Federal Bar Association. New York: Grosset & Dunlap, Inc., 1965.

Father of the Constitution: James Madison, by Katharine E. Wilkie and Elizabeth R. Moseley. New York: Julian Messner, 1963.

Freedom of the Press in America, by David J. Goldman. Minneapolis: Lerner Publications Co., 1967.

Our Constitution and What It Means, by William A. Kottmeyer. New York: McGraw-Hill Book Company, 1965.

Shays' Rebellion, by Monroe Stearns. New York: Franklin Watts, Inc., 1968.

The U.S. Constitution and the Men Who Wrote It, by Leroy Hayman. New York: Four Winds Press, 1966.

Your Freedoms: The Bill of Rights, by Frank K. Kelly. New York: G. P. Putnam's Sons, 1964.

8
First Steps of the New Nation

It took only four months for the Constitutional Convention to draw up a plan of government. But the making of a nation takes longer. A nation is a body of people who usually share a territory, a language, an independent political system, and many common beliefs and traditions. The government is only the machinery that carries out a nation's will. National feeling is often so strong that a nation can be defeated in war and occupied for years, but will survive in the hearts of the people and become free again.

The United States became a nation in the middle of an age of **nationalism** (intense loyalty to, and feeling for, one's own nation). Struggles for national independence erupted throughout Europe and the Americas in the nineteenth century, and in Asia, Africa, and the Middle East in the twentieth century.

The building of an American nation began long before independence was declared in 1776. The use of the English language and the heritage of English traditions acted as a unifying force. The post roads that connected colonial towns helped to make a nation. Every problem shared by all the colonies, such as frontier defense, was a force for nationhood. Soldiers and sailors from different colonies, fighting side by side against the French, were creating a nation. Colonial editors protesting in chorus against Parliament also were creating a nation.

By 1789 there was a United States of America, under the Constitution. But it was, as Washington said, an experiment whose success was not certain. Then came 30 years during which the new American nation passed a number of difficult tests. It held free elections in which two clashing parties exchanged power peaceably. Its first leaders, the Federalists, built a sound financial system, gained some respect abroad, and forced a few angry citizens at home to obey the nation's laws. The Federalists' successors, the Democratic-Republicans, doubled the nation's territory and fought and won a second war with Great Britain. By 1819 Americans were able to celebrate Independence Day (right), certain that the young nation could stand on its own.

As you read, think about the following questions:
1. What were some of the developments that helped to keep the United States united?
2. How did young America win international respect?
3. What role did political parties play in this period?

Philadelphians celebrate the Fourth of July in 1819.

Washington's First Administration

A variety of coins and paper money was in use in eighteenth-century America. Right: The head and tail of a 1793 copper half-cent piece and a 1789 small change bank note. Below: The head and tail of a 1795 ten-dollar gold piece and a 1782 bank check—the oldest known check in the United States.

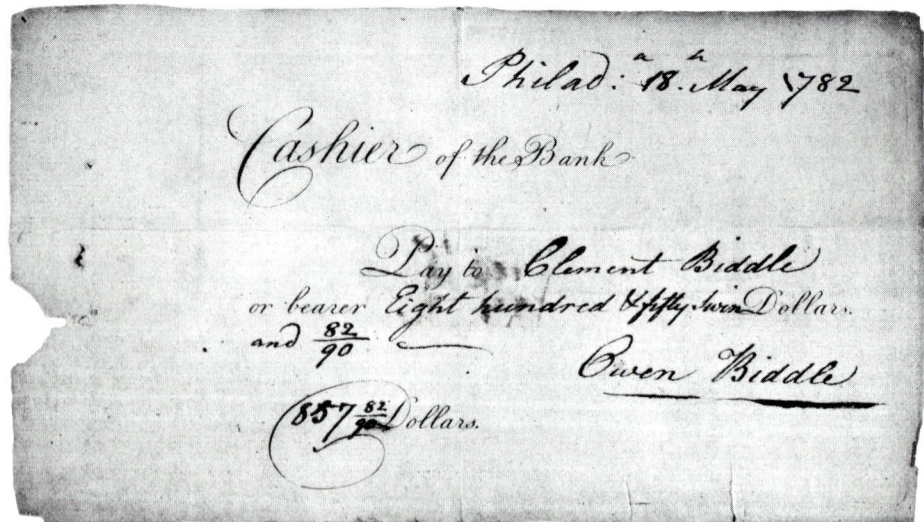

Alexander Hamilton and the Treasury

A new nation is full of opportunities for bright young men. For the critically important job of Secretary of the Treasury, Washington chose 34-year-old Alexander Hamilton. Born in the West Indies, by the age of 14 he was the right-hand man of a West Indian merchant. At 19 he was a student at what is now Columbia College, in New York City, and was involved in radical politics as the author of anti-British pamphlets. At 20 he was an officer in the army and then later became military secretary to General Washington. At 30 he was a brilliant lawyer and a New York delegate to the Constitutional Convention. At 34 Hamilton was a tested political warrior and financial expert.

But radical as he might have been when it came to American independence, Hamilton did not favor total democracy. He distrusted unchecked rule by the "mass of people" and favored a government run by "the rich and well-born." His main desire, however, was an energetic government. He hoped for a partnership between elected officials and forward-looking, wealthy merchants and manufacturers. Hamilton believed that trade and manufacturing increased employment, encouraged immigration, and so helped farmers by providing a market for farm products.

Hamilton used his role as national money-manager to promote these ideas. First, he proposed that the national government pay all its wartime debts with new loans. Hamilton insisted that the United States must pay its debts to other nations in order to have its currency accepted. He also wanted the central government to pay the war debts of the states. Hamilton believed that these policies would benefit the whole nation and also increase the states' respect for the central government.

Next, Hamilton asked Congress to create a special bank to keep the government's money and to control the amount of money local banks could lend. Opponents argued that Congress was not granted this power in the Constitution. But Hamilton saw no problem. Article I, Section 8 said that Congress could make all laws necessary and proper for carrying out its powers. This has been called the "elastic clause." Congress had the power to coin money, collect taxes, and borrow money. If creating a bank was necessary to perform these tasks, then, said Hamilton, the bank was constitutional. If Congress was directed to do a job, it could also make

The first Secretary of the Treasury, Alexander Hamilton (above), urged Congress to create a national banking system. In 1791 the First Bank of the United States was established in Philadelphia (opposite page, top).

the tools for the job. This use of the elastic clause of Article I, Section 8 gave former anti-Federalists nightmares. They suspected the central government of being too powerful already and feared that the elastic clause would turn into a cord twisted around the necks of the states.

Hamilton skillfully used his political experience to persuade Congress to adopt his program, including the First Bank of the United States. As trade and commerce revived after 1789, confidence in Hamilton's policies grew. United States coins and paper currency like some of those illustrated of page 220 were good anywhere. In a man's pocket they were a very solid reminder of his nationality.

Thomas Jefferson—First Secretary of State

The first Secretary of State was Thomas Jefferson. As author of the Declaration of Independence, he had told the world why Americans planned to free themselves from Britain. Now he was the President's chief spokesman of the new nation's foreign policy. He had his hands full almost at once.

Shortly after Washington was inaugurated, a revolution broke out in France. In 1789 the French overthrew the monarchy, and four years later they beheaded their king, Louis XVI. To Europe's other monarchs the French Revolution was as welcome as a case of smallpox. They moved to stamp out the disease before it spread. Austria, England, Spain, and other European nations were soon at war with the French. The fighting lasted, with only a few interruptions, for 22 years and laid many problems on the United States' doorstep.

The first of these problems was what to do about our 1778 alliance with France. Did the alliance require us to go to war on France's side? Washington was in a spot. It was important to keep the word of the United States—as important as paying debts. But a war would be a disaster for a young nation just getting on its feet. The President asked the advice of his Cabinet. Hamilton argued for tearing up the treaty now that the king who had approved it was dead. Jefferson said that the treaty was not with the king but with the French nation, which was still very much alive. But he advised that we proclaim our **neutrality** (a policy of not taking sides). In 1793 Washington did issue a Proclamation of Neutrality.

Chief Justice John Jay is burned in effigy by citizens angry over the terms of the treaty he negotiated with England in 1794.

This problem was only the beginning of trouble. Both French and British warships attacked American vessels trading with the other side and seized the cargoes. Being neutral was dangerous. At any time between 1793 and 1812, America might reasonably have gone to war with either the French or the British, but there were special reasons for a fight with the British. They still held the western forts which they were supposed to have given up in 1783. They refused to allow Yankee vessels to trade with the British West Indies. In turn, the British were angered because some states interfered with the collection of pre-Revolutionary War debts owed by Americans to British merchants.

Tension rose so high that Washington decided to send John Jay, first Chief Justice of the Supreme Court, to negotiate a treaty with Britain. The agreement Jay reached was hardly satisfactory. The British agreed once more to leave the Northwest, but they did not retreat an inch on their "right" to seize American ships headed for French harbors. They allowed only a tiny trade with their West Indian islands. And Jay had to promise in return that his government would levy no special taxes on British imports and would pay the prewar debts.

There was a roar of protest at the treaty. Among those attacking the treaty was Jefferson, who had resigned as Secretary of State in 1794. Jay was burned in effigy (left). Washington, however, used his prestige to support the pact, and it was confirmed by the Senate in 1795. If the infant nation had gone to war with Britain, it might have been overwhelmed—or perhaps have had to beg help from the French and risk becoming a French puppet. In any case Washington was eager to keep the nation free of foreign entanglements.

The Whiskey Rebellion

Foreign affairs furnished thorny problems for the Washington **administration** (the name given to a President and his chief policy-makers, as well as to their term in office). But they had an easier time dealing with a challenge on the home front known as the Whiskey Rebellion.

One of Hamilton's new taxes was an **excise tax** (a tax levied on the production, sale, or consumption of a product within a country) on liquor. This tax was especially hated on the frontier of western Pennsyl-

In January 1794 Thomas Jefferson, the first Secretary of State, resigned from office and temporarily retired to private life.

Pennsylvania farmers, outraged by the new Federal excise tax on liquor, tar and feather a Federal tax collector. The violence continued, and in 1794 President Washington called out the militia to enforce the Federal law.

vania. The settlers there faced a brutal struggle transporting their corn, rye, and wheat by wagon. Roads were swampy in wet weather, dusty in dry weather, and rocky in all seasons. But 24 bushels of grain could be distilled into 2 kegs of whiskey. One on each side was a perfect load for a pack horse. The corn walked to market, as the farmers said. Besides, the farmers themselves used the whiskey as both currency and medicine, as well as to celebrate great occasions and cheer up a hard life.

All over western Pennsylvania men not only denounced the excise tax collectors but tarred and feathered them as shown at the left. They believed they were doing just what colonial crowds had done to Stamp Act officials, and with as good reason. In August of 1794 protesters marched into Pittsburgh.

To the Federalists this was Shays' Rebellion once more. They were determined to prove that the United States was ruled by its laws. So Washington ordered 15,000 militia into service.

But as the army moved westward, the rebellion fizzled out. The rebels were dispersed, and eventually agreed to the tax and signed loyalty oaths to the government (lower right). Washington had shown that Federal authority would be used when needed.

The suppression of the Whiskey Rebellion was an important symbol of the new nation's firmness. On a little point of land between two branches of the Potomac River, another, more lasting national symbol was being created.

Washington, D. C., Becomes the Nation's Capital

The Constitution gave Congress power to create a district which would become the "seat of Government." In 1790 the lawmakers chose the location for this District of Columbia and looked for an expert to design the new capital city, to be called Washington. The President recommended Major Pierre Charles L'Enfant.

L'Enfant was a French-born architect and engineer who believed that the capital should express the spirit of America—wide open like the future, but still anchored to the wisdom of the past. His plan called for a Capitol building on a hill and a "presidential palace" facing it at the opposite end of a wide mall, or promenade. There would be wide avenues cutting through the regular checkerboard pattern of streets as the plan

METROPOLITAN MUSEUM OF ART, COLLECTION OF EDGAR WILLIAM AND BERNICE CHRYSLER GARBISCH

Above: An eyewitness painted Commander in Chief George Washington at Fort Cumberland, Maryland, reviewing some of the troops called out to suppress the Whiskey Rebellion. Left: Some of the rebels who were caught by the Federal army were allowed to go free after signing this oath. Only two men were put in jail, and they were later pardoned by Washington.

LIBRARY OF CONGRESS

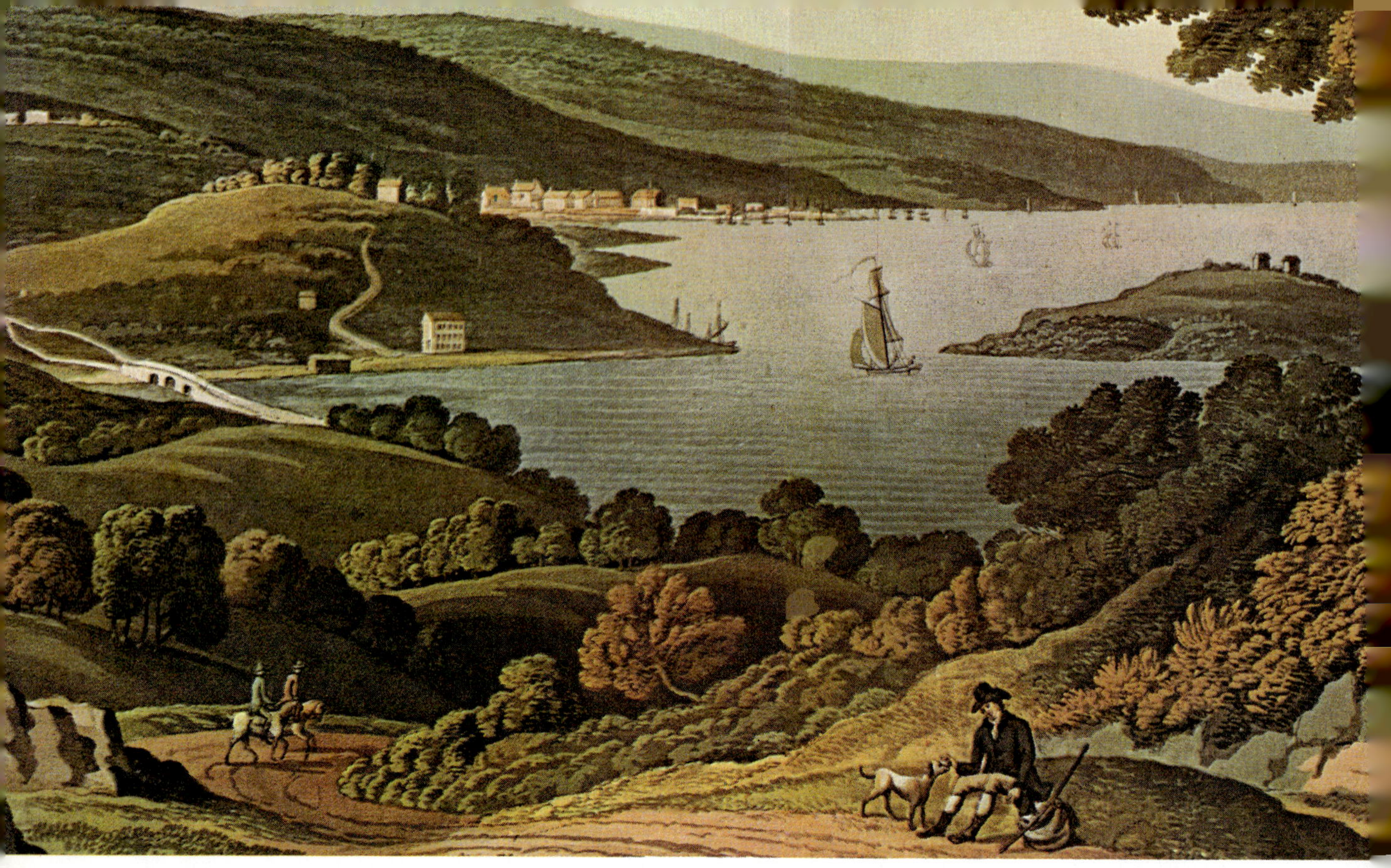

Right: A 1792 official engraving of the plans for the proposed city of Washington. Above: A rustic view of Georgetown, the Potomac River, and Washington, D.C., in 1801. Below: Benjamin Latrobe's design for the hall in the south wing of the Capitol.

LIBRARY OF CONGRESS

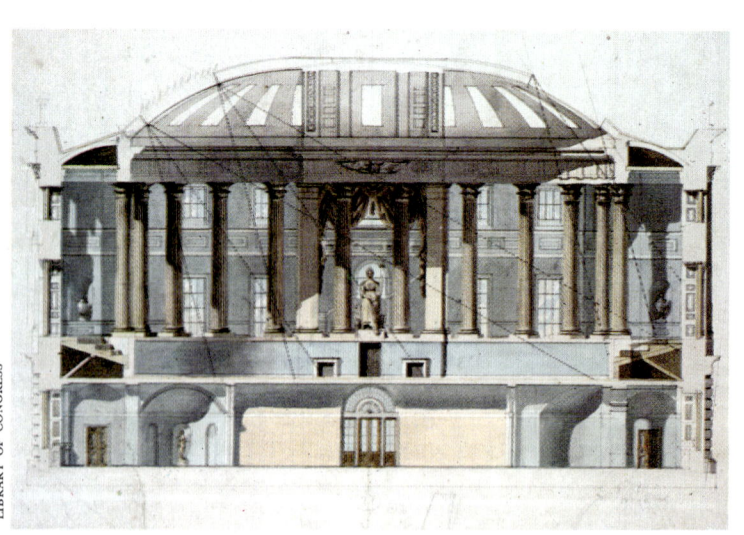

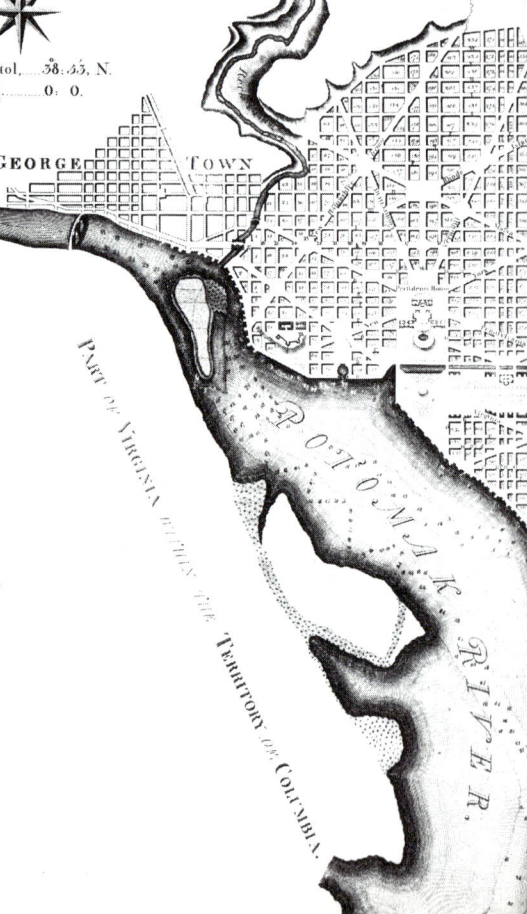

Pierre L'Enfant designed Washington, D.C. Benjamin Banneker surveyed the District of Columbia.

(lower left) shows. Where these diagonal avenues crisscrossed, there would be open spaces. These would be saved for fountains, gardens, statues, and noble buildings in the style of ancient Greece and Rome.

L'Enfant was ahead of his time as a city planner. He was also hot-tempered and demanded more money and more obedience than Congress would stand for. After many quarrels Congress fired him.

The job of continuing his work fell to a Marylander named Andrew Ellicott, one of three men appointed as surveyors of the District. Ellicott's co-worker was a friend and neighbor named Benjamin Banneker, a highly talented black man. Banneker was thus the first Negro to receive a Presidential appointment.

Banneker's father was a slave who was later able to buy his freedom and send his son to a private school. Benjamin's keen mind soon led him beyond the school's program. He taught himself mathematics and astronomy as well as surveying. After helping to design Washington, he, like Benjamin Franklin, wrote and published almanacs. He sent one to Thomas Jefferson with a note saying he hoped the almanac would prove that any "narrow prejudices" about blacks being "brutish" were false.

Slowly, Washington, D.C., came into existence. Its buildings were the work of some gifted immigrants. The Capitol was designed by William Thornton, born in the West Indies, and Benjamin Latrobe, from England. The President's "palace," the White House, got its basic design from Irish-born James Hoban. Black, white, native-born, and foreign-born, all had a hand in creating the finished product. The United States was a "nation of nations" from the start.

Questions for Discussion

1. Why is it important for a government to have a good financial rating? What policies did Hamilton favor to give the nation a good financial rating?
2. What is the "elastic clause" of the Constitution? Why is it so called? How did Hamilton use the clause to strengthen the national government? Why were anti-Federalists fearful of his use of the clause?
3. Why did the Federalists compare the Whiskey Rebellion to Shays' Rebellion? Why was the crushing of the Whiskey Rebellion a victory for the national government?

A 1798 political cartoon shows Federalists and Democratic-Republicans "debating" at Congress Hall in Philadelphia.

The Growth of Political Parties

Each year the country moved toward greater unity. Yet one development seemed to be tearing the United States apart faster than the new government could bring the country together—political parties. Differences of opinion are bound to occur in a free society. The country had divided once on whether to support the Constitution. Soon after 1789 a new split opened between followers of Jefferson and those of Hamilton.

We have already seen what Hamilton favored. Jefferson, who opposed Hamilton, believed in strong local, but not strong Federal, government. He distrusted government efforts to encourage manufacturing and urban growth. In his view only a man living on the fruits of his own land could be truly free. Farmers, he said, were "the chosen people of God." Cities added only as much strength to a nation "as sores do to the human body." If Americans were crowded into cities they would soon "go to eating one another." Jefferson also welcomed the French Revolution. "A little rebellion, now and then," he wrote in 1787, was a "good thing for any country." To Hamilton such thoughts were horrifying.

Gradually, pro-Hamilton and pro-Jefferson groups formed, first in Congress, then in the country. The Hamiltonians called themselves Federalists. The Jefferson followers took the name of Democratic-Republicans. When Washington retired at the end of his second term, he was alarmed. New England was mostly Federalist. The South and West were generally Democratic-Republican. Would the sections be torn apart? In his Farewell Address Washington asked Americans to shield themselves from "the jealousies and heartburnings" of party argument. He also urged them not to take sides in foreign wars. Otherwise there would be "frequent collisions" and even "bloody contests."

Nevertheless, party spirit still flared after the hotly contested Presidential election of 1796, won by John Adams and the Federalists. The picture of a fight in Congress (left) is clearly meant to be humorous; yet the angry feelings of the day almost destroyed the Bill of Rights.

In 1798 the Federalist Congress passed a set of Alien and Sedition Acts. Three alien laws were aimed at foreigners who sympathized with Republican, pro-French ideas. One allowed the President, without trial, to jail or **deport** (send out of the country) "dangerous" immigrants who had not yet been **naturalized**

> **REPUBLICANS**
> Turn out, turn out and save your Country from ruin!
>
> From an *Emperor*—from a *King*—from the iron grasp of a *British Tory Faction*—an unprincipled banditti of British speculators. The hireling tools and emissaries of his majesty king George the 3d have thronged our city and diffused the poison of principles among us.
>
> **DOWN WITH THE TORIES, DOWN WITH THE BRITISH FACTION,**
>
> Before they have it in their power to enslave you, and reduce your families to distress by heavy taxation. Republicans want no Tribute-liars—they want no ship Ocean-liars—they want no Rufus King's for Lords—they want no Varick to lord it over them—they want no Jones for senator, who fought with the British against the Americans in time of the war.—But they want in their places such men as
>
> *Jefferson & Clinton,*
> who fought their Country's Battles in the year '76

The Federalist cartoon on the opposite page claims that President Thomas Jefferson is destroying the Federal government. However, Jefferson won re-election in 1804. The poster above is from his re-election campaign.

(legally made citizens). The Sedition Act allowed the Federal government to arrest and try those who uttered "false, scandalous and malicious" criticism of public officials.

The Alien and Sedition Acts were short-lived. Republican state legislatures in Virginia and Kentucky passed resolutions saying that such unconstitutional acts were null and void within those states. This doctrine of **nullification** could destroy the unity created by the Constitution. If nullification were allowed, the states could ignore Federal law. Both the Alien and Sedition Acts and the Virginia and Kentucky Resolutions seemed to prove that Washington's fears about the country's being torn apart by party hatred were well founded.

Things were not so bad as they seemed, however. To begin with, parties began to be a unifying force. A Virginia planter might vote Republican because he liked Jefferson's agrarian, pro-farm ideas. But so might an Irish immigrant who only cared that the Republicans were opposed to England, Ireland's old enemy. A Rhode Island maker of cotton cloth was likely to vote Federalist because he approved of Hamilton's idea of a protective tariff, or tax, against foreign textiles. But so would a Charleston ship carpenter who believed that the Federalists encouraged commerce, which meant more ships, and so more work for him.

Party loyalties, therefore, united sections and classes. In a system of two great parties, each one had to unite many groups into a **coalition** (temporary alliance) in order to win elections. Jefferson, who ran for President in 1800, recognized the danger of disunity. However, the outspokenness of the great Virginian frightened many people. He was brilliant; he loved the good things of life; and he was hospitable to all kinds of radical ideas. The cartoon at the right highlights the deep feelings of many Hamiltonians that such a man was a tool of the devil. Federalists believed that, if Jefferson were elected, he would sink the navy, dismiss the Senate and the Supreme Court, and perhaps even attack religion and the family.

Power Changes Hands

In the close election of 1800, Jefferson was chosen President. The Federalists waited for doomsday. But Jefferson chose to soothe rather than punish his enemies. In his inaugural address he called for "har-

mony and affection." Like Washington, he urged an end to "political intolerance." He declared, "We are all Republicans, we are all Federalists." To this he added a statement of belief that really explained his apparent radicalism. If any citizens wished to dissolve the Union or change the form of government, he said, "Let them stand undisturbed as monuments of the safety with which error of opinion can be tolerated when reason is left free to combat it."

"Mad Tom," as Jefferson was called in cartoons like the one at the right, did not always believe in radical schemes. But he was always willing to listen. Whereas the Sedition Act seemed to say that too much free speech pulls a society apart, Jefferson argued that only the free discussion of ideas can persuade people to change their laws and rulers peaceably. The peaceful takeover by the Republicans was well named "the revolution of 1800." It proved that power could change hands in the United States with no angrier sound than that of pens scratching voters' choices on ballots.

It was just as well that Jefferson was open-minded. As President he soon found that men in power must sometimes change their ideas to keep up with events. Jefferson believed in a simple, inexpensive government with "a few plain duties to be performed by a few servants." But in his two terms, the "plain duties" of the administration came to include the fighting of an undeclared foreign war and the making of a treaty that doubled the nation's size.

MAD TOM in A RAGE

Questions for Discussion

1. In a democratic society why is it almost inevitable that people will divide into political parties?
2. In what ways did Jefferson's political ideas differ from those of Hamilton? Why did Jefferson's political ideas frighten some Americans in 1800?
3. Which of the two men do you think would be best qualified to be President of the United States today? Why?
4. How did the Alien and Sedition Acts lead to the passage of the Virginia and Kentucky Resolutions? What doctrine was announced in the Resolutions?
5. In what ways did political parties both divide and unite people in the early days of our country?
6. Why was Jefferson a firm believer in allowing those who disagreed with the government to speak out?

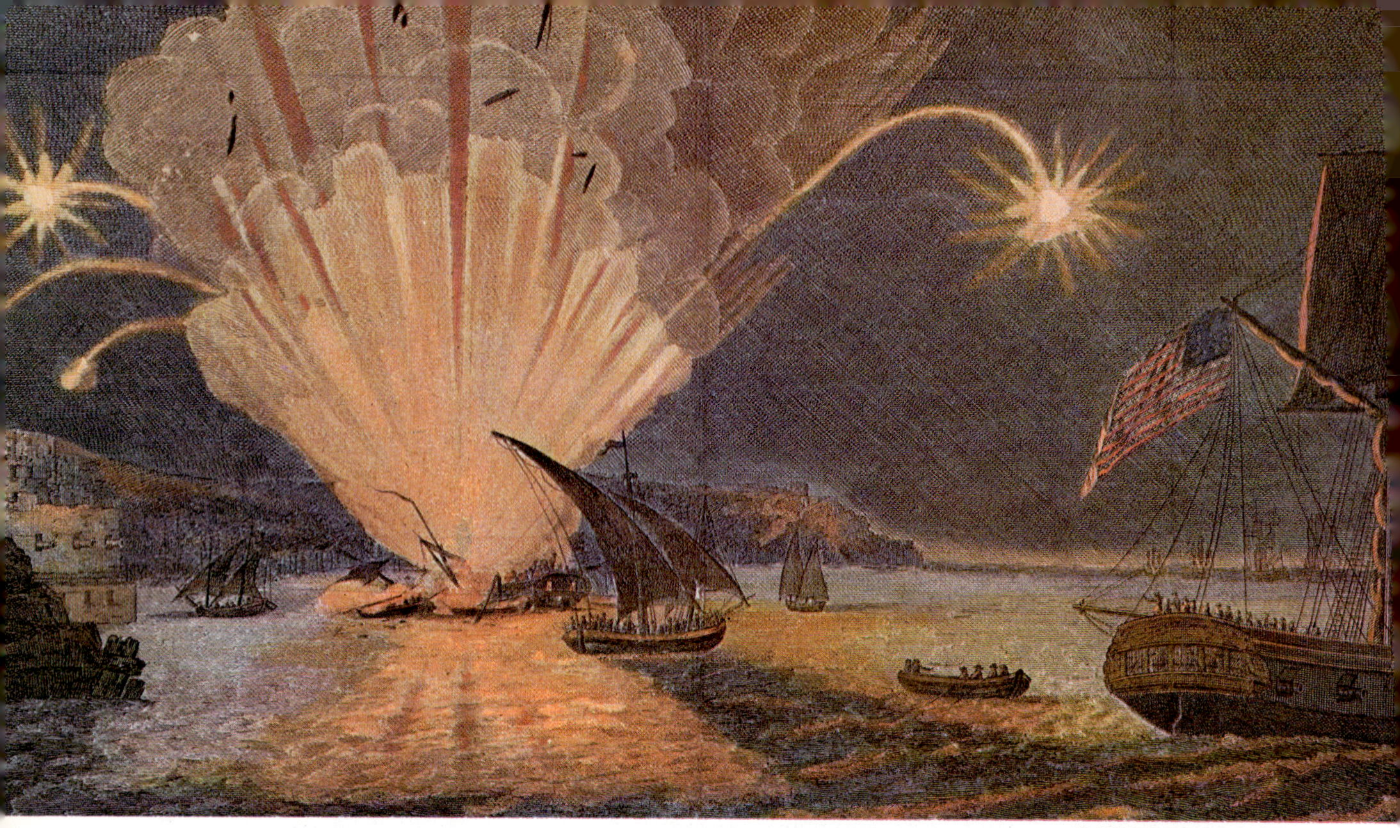

FRANKLIN D. ROOSEVELT LIBRARY

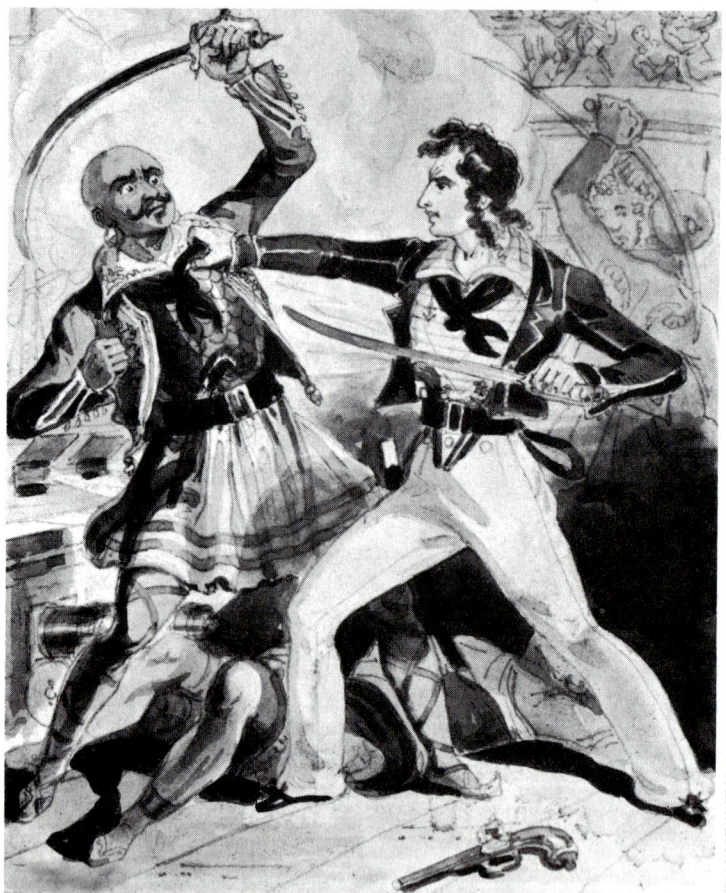

From 1801 until 1805 the United States fought an undeclared war against Tripoli. Right: An American sailor fights off a pirate trying to board a United States ship. Above: In September 1804 Captain Richard Somers loaded his ship—the Intrepid*—with gunpowder and sailed into a harbor in Tripoli, hoping to destroy the Tripolitan fleet. Before he could accomplish his mission, the* Intrepid *blew up, killing Somers and his entire crew.*

NEW-YORK HISTORICAL SOCIETY, OLDS COLLECTION

The Administrations of Thomas Jefferson

Jefferson was barely settled in the White House when Tripoli, a small North African state, stirred up trouble. Like other little countries along the Mediterranean coast of Africa, Tripoli permitted its armed ships to capture defenseless foreign merchant ships. The only way for European nations and the United States to escape such piracy was to pay **tribute** (protection money).

In the spring of 1801, Tripoli demanded more money. Jefferson angrily refused. Tripoli declared war. The United States sent its tiny young navy into action and fought a series of sharp battles with the enemy. In 1805 Tripoli asked for peace. It is only fair to say that European nations had often winked at piracy — when the victims were their enemies. As an emerging power the United States gained prestige by battling Tripoli and encouraging freedom of the seas.

To Jefferson a still more serious problem was the seizing of American cargoes by the British and the French. Still worse was the British practice of **impressment** (the forcible drafting of American citizens into the Royal Navy). British warships would stop American vessels and search them for deserters from the British fleet. Sailors who could not prove American citizenship were impressed. It was as humiliating as it would be, for example, if Soviet soldiers came aboard American passenger planes at European airports and dragged off people whom they accused of being Soviet citizens trying to escape to the West.

Yet Jefferson could not afford to fight the British or the French. He tried various ways of bringing pressure on them. One of his plans was an **embargo** (suspension of all trade) with other nations. Seagoing New Englanders suffered severely from the embargo. Yankee newspaper cartoonists spelled the word backwards and raged against the O GRAB ME and its creator, Jefferson. The embargo was ended in 1809 against all nations except Britain and France.

Presidents Thomas Jefferson and James Madison hoped to avoid war with England by enforcing embargoes. This 1809 broadside credits them with success.

The Louisiana Purchase

Jefferson's greatest contribution to the young nation was not made on the shores of Tripoli. His master stroke as President was the Louisiana Purchase.

In 1800 Napoleon Bonaparte, the powerful dictator of France, forced Spain to give him the Louisiana Territory. Jefferson was worried about having New Orleans in the hands of a strong power. It was vital to

Shortly after he returned from his expedition, Meriwether Lewis posed for this portrait. The ermine-tailed cape he is wearing is probably the one that was presented to him by a chief of the Shoshoni tribe.

keep the Mississippi open for western trade. So in 1803 Jefferson sent agents to try to buy New Orleans from France. When they reached Paris, Napoleon had decided—in part because of the successful Haitian revolt led by Toussaint L'Ouverture—to sell the Louisiana Territory. He stunned the American envoys by offering them the entire territory for $15 million. They accepted.

When the news reached Jefferson, weeks later by ship, he was in a spot. Though Congress had authorized Jefferson to buy New Orleans, neither Congress nor the Constitution had given him the right to buy the entire territory. Jefferson had less excuse to buy the Louisiana Territory than Hamilton had had to create a national bank to handle the government's finances. Yet Jefferson's wish to increase the size, power, and security of the new country he had helped to create was so strong that he put aside his principles and accepted Napoleon's offer.

In doing so he won a rich prize. The Louisiana Territory included parts of a dozen future states and doubled the size of the country. It contained what would one day be portions of the gold and silver mines of the Rockies, the oil and natural gas wells and the ranch lands of the Southwest, and the wheat-growing farms of the Great Plains.

In 1804 Jefferson sent two army officers, Meriwether Lewis (left) and William Clark, to explore the Louisiana Territory (map, right) and go beyond it to the Pacific. They were to learn everything possible about the land, the Indians, the animals, and the climate. They were to collect specimens, as our lunar explorers have been doing.

The two captains set out from St. Louis in May of 1804. The expedition was a breathtaking, two-and-one-half-year adventure. After months of terrible perils—hailstorms, attacks by grizzlies, snakebites, overturned canoes, swarms of mosquitoes, and fevers—they came down the Columbia River to its mouth. On November 7, 1805, Clark, whose spelling did not compare with his abilities as an explorer, wrote in his journal: "Ocian in view! O! The joy!"

Questions for Discussion

1. Why did so many New Englanders object to Jefferson's embargo?
2. Why was the Lewis and Clark expedition so important to the future of the nation?

MISSOURI HISTORICAL SOCIETY

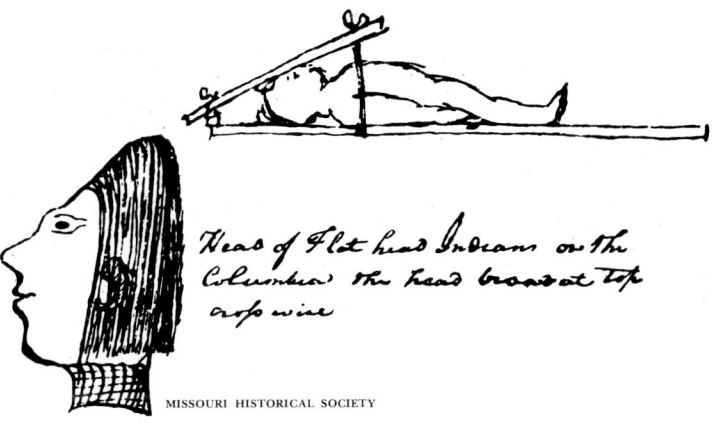

William Clark made some rough sketches in the notebook he kept during the expedition with Meriwether Lewis. This excerpt shows how the Chinook Indians flattened their infants' heads by binding them between boards.

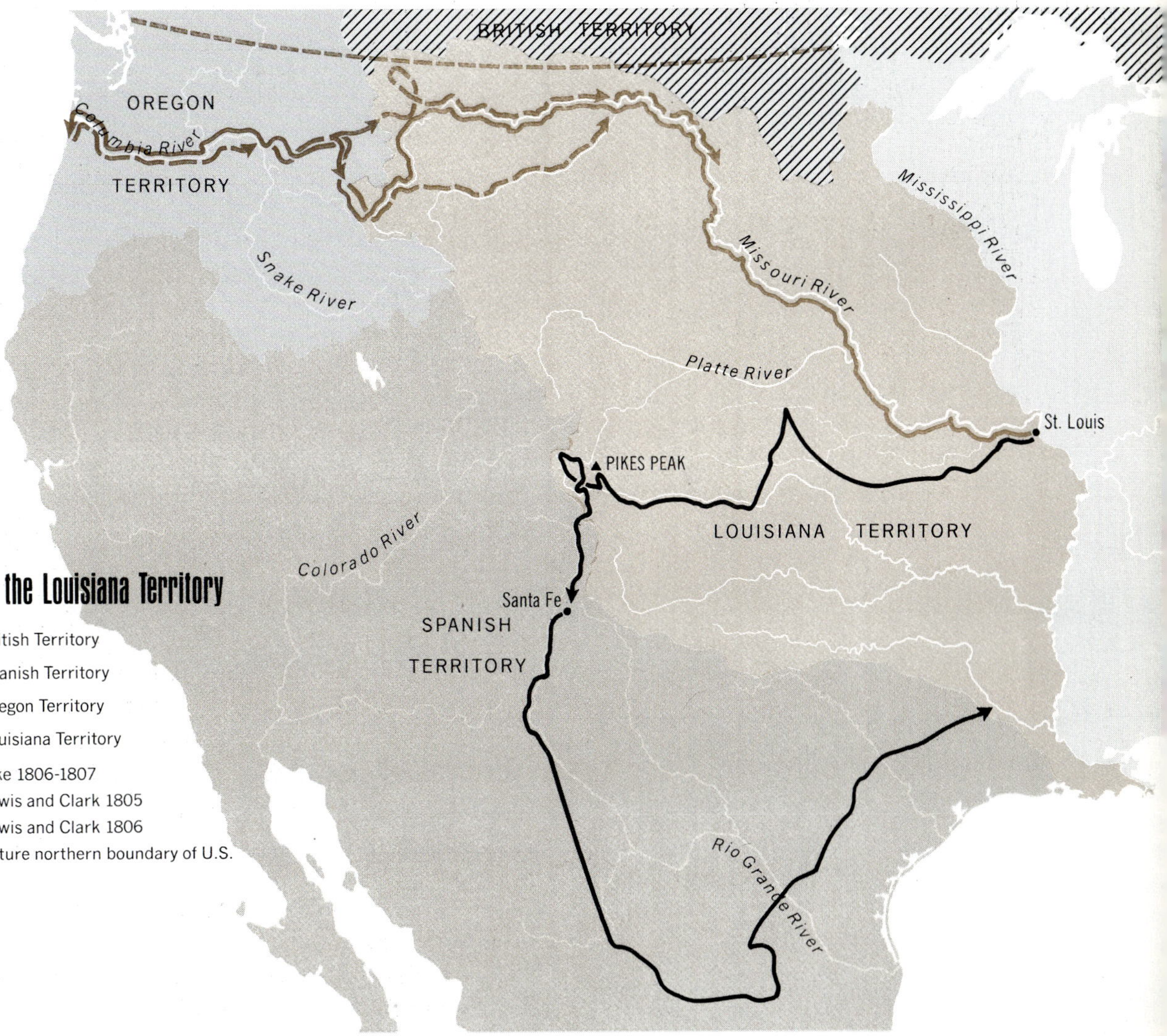

The drawing below is supposed to show the British advance on Washington, D.C., just before they occupied and burned parts of the city on August 24, 1814. In fact, they faced little opposition, and their advance was not that formal.

NEW-YORK HISTORICAL SOCIETY

The War of 1812

By 1812, thanks to Jefferson's bold purchase, the United States was a nation whose boundaries stretched from the Atlantic to the Rocky Mountains. This was a great change for a former "confederation" of thirteen states. But at sea America still suffered as a weak neutral caught between strong warring powers. Gradually, pressure built up for a war to save the nation's "honor." Great Britain was the logical target. The war fever was strongest in the West. There, settlers still believed that British bribes egged on every hostile Indian. There, too, cocky American politicians cast an eye at lightly defended Canada. Fresh from victories against the Indians, some western "War Hawks" believed that Canada would be easy pickings.

War was declared in June of 1812. Yet only a few days earlier, Parliament had voted to give up the policy of interfering with American shipping. Many British merchants did not want to lose their profitable trade with the United States. This time British politicians, who did not want to kill the goose that laid golden eggs, won. But it was too late. War had started.

For a time the war threatened to destroy everything that had been built up by the United States since the end of the Revolution. The War Hawks had foolishly overestimated American power. The little navy fought gallantly, and against great odds won several remarkable victories at sea. But British naval power was overwhelming, and the American navy was soon destroyed or bottled up in port. In one combat between the British *Shannon* and the American *Chesapeake*, the Americans lost the battle but gained a slogan. The American captain, James Lawrence, was mortally wounded. As he was carried below, he gasped, "Don't give up the ship!" In other combat on Lake Erie, Captain Oliver Hazard Perry successfully defeated a British squadron near Put-in-Bay on Lake Erie and added another famous saying when he reported, "We have met the enemy and they are ours."

On the Canadian frontier militiamen from New York and New England, where the war was unpopular, often refused to go beyond the borders of their own states to fight. Tax collections were poor, and the Federal government was nearly bankrupt. The crowning blow came on August 24, 1814, when a British force sailed up Chesapeake Bay, landed in Maryland, marched on Washington, and burned the nation's new capital (left). President Madison had just escaped.

The British suffered their worst defeat in the War of 1812 at the Battle of New Orleans. Here, British Major General Sir Edward Pakenham lies dying in the midst of the battle.

The United States in 1819

The "battle" was less formal than the contemporary drawing on page 236 suggests. The only American soldiers nearby were Maryland and Virginia militiamen who had run away the day before, after a brief fight. British soldiers amused themselves by sitting in the hall of the House of Representatives, voting to burn the "nest of Yankee democracy," and then doing so. The White House also went up in flames. It seemed that an army of militiamen could not save the country. A point as low as the dismal days of December 1776 had apparently been reached.

Victory and Triumph at the Peace Table

Yet things improved steadily after that dark summer week in 1814. A few weeks later the British moved northward to attack Baltimore. From the Patapsco River their fleet pounded Fort McHenry, the key to the city. Despite an all-night bombardment, the Americans held out. Dawn saw their flag still flying. The British abandoned the attempt, and their northward drive collapsed.

Almost at the same time as the British failure at Baltimore, another British force invading from Canada was stopped on Lake Champlain. The British, who had little interest in the war to begin with, now moved to end it. They sent envoys to a meeting with American peacemakers at Ghent, in Belgium. On Christmas Eve in 1814, both sides signed a treaty that more or less called the war a draw. It said nothing about the issues of free trade and sailors' rights, and left the American boundary with Canada where it had been before the war. Both sides agreed to negotiate the other issues between them at later dates.

But the news that peace had been declared arrived too late to prevent a major battle and an American victory. Before the Treaty of Ghent was signed, the British had sent a 7,500-man expedition from Jamaica to New Orleans to seize the mouth of the Mississippi. The British landing force of crack troops left their ships below New Orleans and marched westward toward the city. Waiting for them was an American army commanded by a militia general named Andrew Jackson. Jackson's 6,000-man force was made up of several elements. He had frontiersmen from Tennessee and Kentucky, all dead shots. He had French-speaking planters from New Orleans, a detachment commanded by the pirate Jean Lafitte, and two battalions of free

A British fleet bombards Fort McHenry in Baltimore harbor during the night of September 13–14, 1814. At dawn the American flag still flew over the fort. The battle inspired Francis Scott Key to write a poem which he set to the tune of a then popular drinking song. "The Star-Spangled Banner" became the unofficial national anthem and, in 1931, Congress made it official.

blacks from New Orleans.

On the misty morning of January 8, 1815, the British troops advanced against the Americans, who were lined up behind a breastwork of cotton bales. Deadly accurate fire killed or wounded 2,100 British soldiers. The Americans had only 71 casualties. The nation was jubilant. Thereafter, Americans remembered the victories of the war and forgot the defeats. Some even called the conflict "The Second War of Independence."

In the four years immediately after the war, a series of treaties reflected the growing power of the nation (map, page 238). In 1817 the British agreed to a treaty, known as the Rush-Bagot Treaty, that **demilitarized** (made the establishment of forts and military forces illegal) the boundary with Canada. By the Convention of 1818, the British and the Americans also agreed that the boundary between the United States and Canada would be at the 49th parallel from Lake of the Woods to the Rockies. In addition, the United States and Great Britain agreed to share the Oregon County north of the 42nd parallel.

In 1819 Secretary of State John Quincy Adams negotiated another treaty, this one with Spain. One part of this Adams-Oñis Treaty sold Florida to the United States. The more important part traced out the boundary between Mexico and the Louisiana Territory. Spain gave up its claims to the Oregon Country and agreed to a western boundary of the Louisiana Territory south of the 42nd parallel. These two treaties gave the United States a boundary that ran all the way to the Pacific Ocean. The treaties also marked the end of American involvement in European wars for the next 100 years. The nation was free to turn away from the Atlantic and concentrate on its vast new lands to the west. The United States had finally emerged from Europe's shadow.

Questions for Discussion

1. Why did the War Hawks receive their greatest support in the West?
2. Who commanded the American forces at the Battle of New Orleans? Why is the battle sometimes described as an "accidental battle in an accidental war"?
3. What were the provisions of the Rush-Bagot Treaty of 1818? How did it help to strengthen friendship between the United States and Canada?

Chapter Review

Social Studies Terms

nationalism, neutrality, administration, excise tax, deport, naturalized, nullification, coalition, tribute, impressment, embargo, demilitarized

Summary Questions for Discussion

1. Discuss the generalization: Events from 1789 to 1819 prove that the Constitution was a major improvement over the Articles of Confederation.
2. What values made some people follow Hamilton rather than Jefferson? What are some of the values that were shared by the followers of both men?
3. Why did both the Alien and Sedition Acts and the Virginia and Kentucky Resolutions represent a threat to the young United States?
4. How did the experience of actually being President change some of Jefferson's views?
5. What means does the President have to enforce Federal law? Why does he rarely have to use force to do it?
6. How was the new capital of Washington a mirror of the progress and promise of the new nation?
7. In a democracy how can needed changes take place without violence?
8. How did the Louisiana Purchase increase the security and the size of the United States?

Map Study

Study the map *Exploring the Louisiana Territory* on page 235. Why did Lewis and Clark begin their journey at St. Louis? Why did they follow the Missouri and Columbia rather than the Platte and Snake rivers? Why was it important that they go beyond United States territory?

For Further Reading

The Amazing Alexander Hamilton, by Arthur Orrmont. New York: Julian Messner, 1964.

The War of 1812, by Don Lawson. New York: Abelard-Schuman, Limited, 1966.

The Whiskey Rebellion, by David C. Knight. New York: Franklin Watts, Inc., 1968.

The Wide World of Aaron Burr, by Helen Orlob. Philadelphia: The Westminster Press, 1968.

To the Pacific with Lewis and Clark, by Ralph K. Andrist. New York: American Heritage Publishing Co., Inc., 1967.

ISSUES PAST AND PRESENT

What Are the Limits of Free Speech?

Throughout Unit II you have read of ways in which governments, first in the colonies and then in the United States, tried to meet the problem of governing their people with unity and order while allowing as much individual freedom as possible.

List some examples from Unit II in which governments have had problems with the way that people expressed disagreement with leaders and policies. In some of these examples was there a danger to persons or property? At those times were there any limits to freedom of expression? Was force used to check any forms of protest, as it was in the Whiskey Rebellion, for instance? Why? Were there times when order and unity were more important than freedom of expression? Why?

In 1796 a writer in Philadelphia bragged about "the happy privilege of an American, that he may prattle [chatter] and print in what way he pleases and without anyone to make him afraid." Just two years later the "happy privilege" of free speech guaranteed Americans by the First Amendment to the Constitution was to have a setback. As you have read in Chapter 8, in 1798 a Federalist-dominated Congress passed the Alien and Sedition Acts. The Sedition Act made it a crime to publish or say anything "false, scandalous, and malicious" about high government officials. The capture of many American ships had led to an undeclared naval war with France. Did not the conditions of near-war against such a dangerous enemy justify some limitations of the right of free speech?

Protecting the nation was only one of two purposes which the sponsors of the Sedition Act had in mind. The other was to help the Federalists win the elections of 1800 by making it difficult for the Republicans to publish or say anything very critical of the Federalists. Many Republicans, especially newspaper editors, took the act as a personal challenge and deliberately printed or said things to bring about their arrest. They wanted to see if the act was constitutional, but they also wanted to make the Federalists look like enemies of free speech. In the language of today, they deliberately sought a confrontation. Arguments, charges, and countercharges were a common part of the daily news and were incredibly vicious.

Freedom of speech was not something discovered at the time the Bill of Rights was written. When the colonies were young, free speech simply meant that one could talk to another person and say what he wanted to say without having to fear that he would be arrested. Slowly it became the right to speak one's mind, without fear of arrest and punishment, to a group of people in a tavern, in a church, or at a town meeting. With the growth of cities and the settlement of towns on the fron-

tier, the right was extended to the publication of newspapers and books.

In August 1735 John Peter Zenger was tried for printing criticism of the royal governor of New York in his newspaper. Zenger's lawyer based his defense on the fact that what Zenger had published was true. Even if his criticism had been true, he was still guilty of criminal libel under the law of that time. Nevertheless, the jury found Zenger not guilty. The case helped to establish the principle of freedom of the press.

"Freedom of speech" is a very broad term that includes at least a part of the other rights in the First Amendment: freedom of the press, of assembly, of petition, and of religion. These rights are in fact so closely related that they are wrapped up in a single amendment—the First.

Many times since 1798 the United States has found itself in wars—officially declared wars, such as World War I and the War of 1812, or undeclared wars, such as the naval war with France or the war in Vietnam. In either case the President has thought it necessary to take steps, including the use of military force, to protect the security of the nation. It is in times like these that disputes about freedom of speech are probably hardest to settle. In times of national danger what are the limits of free speech? Is national unity, or the appearance of national unity, more important than freedom to express disagreement with government, its leaders, and its policies?

In Defense of the Sedition Act

This selection was written in 1798 by Secretary of State Timothy Pickering, who was also a leading Federalist.

TIMOTHY PICKERING:
DEFENSE OF THE SEDITION ACT, 1798

The Sedition Act has been shamefully misrepresented as an attack upon the freedom of speech and of the press. On the contrary, we find that it punishes only pests of society and disturbers of order and tranquillity [quiet]. What honest man can justly be alarmed at such a law or can wish unlimited permission to be given for the publication of malicious lies? Because we have the right to speak and publish our opinions, it does not necessarily follow that we may exercise it in saying false and malicious slanders against our neighbor or our government any more than, under cover of freedom of action, we may knock down the first man we meet and exempt [remove] ourselves from punishment by pleading that we are free to

"Malicious" means with evil intentions.

"Slanders" are statements which damage a person's reputation.

do so. We may indeed use our tongues or our pens and carry our clubs or our muskets whenever we please. But, at the same time, we must be responsible and punishable for making such "improper use of either [tongues or muskets] as to injure others in their characters, their persons, or their property."

> Pickering's quote here is from the Sedition Act.

1. What arguments were used by Pickering to defend the Sedition Act?
2. Would you agree with his position? Why?

A Supreme Court Majority Opinion

> "Espionage" means spying.
> "Scurrilous" means indecent.
> "Abusive" means damaging.

During World War I laws were again passed to limit free speech. The Espionage Act of 1917 made it a crime to help the enemy or hinder the recruiting of men into the armed forces. The Sedition Act of May 1918 made it a crime for anyone to try to persuade others not to buy war bonds or to "utter [say], print, write, or publish any disloyal, scurrilous, or abusive language" about the government, the Constitution, or military uniforms.

On August 28, 1917, Charles Schenck was arrested in New York City and accused of passing out leaflets to encourage military men to disobey their officers. Because copies of the leaflet had been mailed to some men who had been drafted, Schenck was also accused of hindering the recruitment of men into the armed forces.

On one side of each leaflet, it said that a draftee is little better than a convict. In heated language it said, "Do not submit to intimidation." The other side of the sheet was headed, "Assert Your Rights." It stated, "If you do not assert [stand up for] your rights, you are helping to deny rights which it is the solemn duty of all citizens and residents of the United States to keep." It denied the power of the government to send United States citizens to foreign shores to shoot the people of other lands. It also said that words could not express the condemnation such cold-blooded cruelty deserved. It ended with the words, "You must do your share to maintain, support, and uphold the rights of the people of this country."

> "Intimidation" means frightening by threats.

Schenck was tried and found guilty of violating the Espionage Act. He appealed to the Supreme Court. Part of the opinion of the majority of the judges follows. It was written by Justice Oliver Wendell Holmes. It has become one of the most famous and important Supreme Court opinions ever written.

OLIVER WENDELL HOLMES:
MAJORITY OPINION, Schenck v. U.S., 1919

The leaflet could have only one effect upon persons subject to the draft: to try to influence them to block carrying it out.

But, it is said, suppose that this leaflet tended to influence men that way. Isn't this a right protected by the First Amendment? In many places and in ordinary times, Schenck would have been within his rights. But whether a deed is right or wrong depends upon the circumstances in which it is done. The strongest protection of free speech would not protect a man in falsely shouting fire in a theater and causing a panic. In every case we must ask this question: Are the words of such kind, or used in such circumstances, as to create a clear and present danger that they will bring about important evils which Congress has a right to prevent? When a nation is at war, many things that might be said in time of peace hinder the war effort, so much so that saying them will not be tolerated [put up with] as long as there are men fighting. No court could regard them as protected by any constitutional right.

The judgment against Schenck is confirmed [upheld].

1. What did Schenck want the people who received his leaflets to do?
2. Why did Justice Holmes believe that Schenck's conviction should be upheld?
3. Would you agree? Why?

A Supreme Court Dissenting Opinion

Another case from World War I involved Russian immigrants all in their twenties. In 1917 a revolution in Russia had overthrown the ruling czarist government. This government and those of the United States, England, Japan, and France had been allies in World War I against Germany and Austria-Hungary. In the summer of 1918, a few months before World War I ended, England, Japan, and the United States sent troops to Russia. The reason given was to guard military supplies which had been shipped to that country to help the Russians fight the Germans. The young Russian immigrants objected to this action, feeling that the Allied troops in Russia were a threat to the Russian Revolution. They printed 9,000 leaflets, each ending with these words:

"The Russian Revolution cries: 'Workers of the World! Awake! Rise! Put down your enemy and mine!' Yes friends, there is only one enemy of the workers of the world and that is Capitalism. It is a crime that workers of America, workers of Germany, workers of Japan, and workers of other countries fight the Workers' Republic of Russia. Awake! Awake, You Workers of the World!"

A second leaflet said that the money of American workers was paying for bullets to be used against Russians. It called for a general strike to show "that not only the Russian Worker

"Capitalism" is an economic system in which the means of producing goods are owned by individuals and not by the government.

A "general strike" is a refusal to work by all employees of all the industries in a nation.

fights for freedom, but also here in America lives the spirit of revolution." Those who distributed the leaflets in the United States were arrested. One of them was Jacob Abrams.

Abrams was convicted of a conspiracy [plot] to bring the form of the government of the United States into contempt [disrespect] and scorn, of intending to stir up and encourage resistance to the United States in the war, and of a plot to hinder production essential to the war effort.

This opinion is the dissenting opinion of the two judges who disagreed with the majority opinion in this case. It was also written by Justice Holmes, and like the majority opinion in the Schenck *case, became very famous. Today judges often use the ideas expressed by Holmes in both the* Schenck *and* Abrams *case to decide some of the limits of free speech.*

> A "dissenting opinion" is an opinion given by one or more judges against the majority opinion.

OLIVER WENDELL HOLMES:
DISSENTING OPINION, Abrams v. U.S., 1919

What was said in the two leaflets in no way attacks the form of government of the United States. The suggestion to workers in the ammunition factories that they are producing bullets to murder Russians and the further call for a general strike do urge curtailment [slowing down] of production of things necessary for the war. But to make the action criminal, the Act of May 16, 1918, requires that it should be "with intent by such curtailment to cripple or hinder the United States in the prosecution [carrying on] of the war." I do not see how anyone can find the intent required by the Act in any of Abrams' words. Abrams' only purpose is to help Russia and stop American interference there against the popular government — not to hinder the United States in the war that it was carrying on.

> By "popular government" Holmes meant the communist government set up to replace the czarist government.

Men should realize that the passage of time has upset many of the faiths that men have fought to defend. If they realize this, they may come to believe that the final good desired can be reached better by a free exchange of ideas. The best test of truth is the power of the thought to get itself accepted in competition with other thoughts. That, at any rate, is the theory of our Constitution. We should always be on guard against attempts to stop the expression of opinions that we hate and believe to be deadly, unless they so directly threaten the lawful and urgent purposes of the law that stopping them right now is necessary to save the country. Of course I am speaking only of expressions of opinions and advice, which were all that were in the leaflets distributed by Abrams. I believe that Abrams was deprived of his rights.

1. What did Abrams want the workers who read his leaflets to do? What effect was this supposed to have on the United States government?
2. What does Holmes mean by "free exchange of ideas?"
3. Why did Holmes believe that the conviction of Schenck should have been upheld but the conviction of Abrams should not?
4. Would you agree? Why?

The Views of a Magazine Editor of Today

In the 1960's the United States found itself more and more involved in an undeclared war between Communist and non-Communist forces in Southeast Asia. The reasons the United States became involved, and what we were trying to do in Southeast Asia, seemed to be clear to some Americans but not to others. The "war" became the subject of much debate. Some felt that the war effort was causing problems within the United States. Others argued that money which we should be spending to solve problems at home was being wasted on a foreign war. Once again, many people began to ask about—and test—the limits of free speech. There was open ridicule of military leaders and the President. Sometimes young men were encouraged to resist the draft. "Sit-downs" in front of trains carrying military supplies took place. Other forms of protest included such acts as burning draft cards or United States flags and the flying of United States flags upside-down. A few people began actively to call for a revolution to overthrow the system of government. These words appeared in 1968 in the national magazine Saturday Review *as one writer's response to the growing debate.*

RICHARD L. TOBIN:
RESPONSIBLE FOR THE ABUSE OF THAT LIBERTY,
1968

"Abuse" means to use in the wrong way.

In the winter of 1791–1792, the First Amendment was brought into force. This Amendment has been essential to the American way and it has been a blueprint for democracies everywhere. Rights guaranteed in the First Amendment are the first rights to be swept away in any dictatorship.

Supreme Court Justice Hugo Black wrote in 1941 that the First Amendment "does not speak in uncertain language." It clearly prohibits any law "abridging [restricting] freedom of speech or of the press." As Justice Felix Frankfurter wrote in 1946, "Without a free press there can be no free society. That is self-evident." However, freedom of the press is not an end [goal] in itself but a means to an end—a free society.

"Censorship" means cutting out the parts thought to be dangerous or offensive.

How much freedom of the press we have, and how we use it, should be looked at that way.

Censorship of the press is not only dangerous but absurd. But we have always liked the words, written in 1818, in the Constitution of the State of Connecticut that clearly state that every citizen may freely speak, write, and publish his feelings on all subjects, "being responsible for the abuse of that liberty." In other words, for the privilege of freedom there is a price tag and that price tag is a common-sense judgment of what news and information may or may not actually damage or destroy the free society in which one operates.

We are always hearing nowadays about the rights of free speech, press, and assembly; however, the price tag of responsibility does not always show. Freedom of speech, press, or assembly will exist only so long as those lucky few granted this privilege exercise it while "being responsible for the abuse of that liberty." It is as simply logical as that.

1. Why does Tobin say that a dictator first sweeps away the rights of free speech, press, religion, and assembly?
2. What kinds of free speech do you believe Tobin thinks an abuse of the privilege? Why?
3. What kinds of limitations, if any, do you think there should be on "free speech?"

Freedom, Order, and Free Speech Today

Families, clubs, neighborhood gangs, churches, schools, cities, and states must also make and enforce written or unwritten rules to handle the problem of permitting freedom while maintaining order. Are rules in these societies made in the same way that rules are made at the national level? Do they allow dissent and freedom of speech? Why?

Personal Freedom and Responsibility

With how many organizations or groups are you involved? Write down:

1. Some of the ways that you may express yourself as a member of those groups;
2. Some of the ways the organization or group checks the methods of expression you may use;
3. The kinds of punishment you might expect if you violate those checks; and, finally,
4. How you would change the rules in your club, school, team, church, etc., to allow more freedom of expression without losing the desired amount of order and unity.

Study carefully the cartoon. Who are the two people in the lower right-hand corner? Write your own caption [heading] for this cartoon. Now write a short paragraph about what the cartoonist is trying to say about freedom of speech.

How did you find the man who is making the speech? Who are the people carrying the signs? In how many ways does the cartoonist indicate disapproval of the speaker or of what he is saying? Are both the speaker and the members of his audience in the cartoon getting a chance to exercise their freedom of speech? Why?

Would Timothy Pickering, if he were alive today, defend the behavior of the members of the audience? Would Oliver Wendell Holmes? Would Richard L. Tobin? Why?

Interpreting a Cartoon

© 1968 HERBLOCK, NEW YORK *Post*

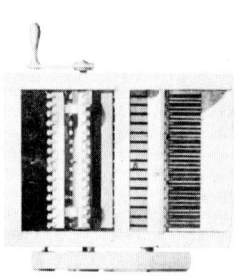
1793 Whitney Invents Cotton Gin

1807 Fulton's Clermont Steams Along the Hudson

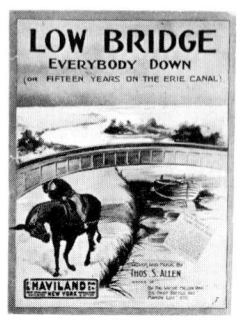
1817 Erie Canal Begun

1775 Boone Leads Settlers into Kentucky

1794 Indians Defeated at Fallen Timbers

1813 Boston Manufacturing Company Founded

1824 Marshall Hands Down Gibbons v. Ogden Dec

UNIT III
The United States Expands to the Pacific

1827 Baltimore and Ohio Railroad Founded

1836 Texas Wins Independence

1846 Oregon Territory Acquired by Treaty

1832 Jackson Vetoes Bank Recharter

1837 Panic and Depression

1848 First Women's Rights Convention

1849 Gold Rush in California

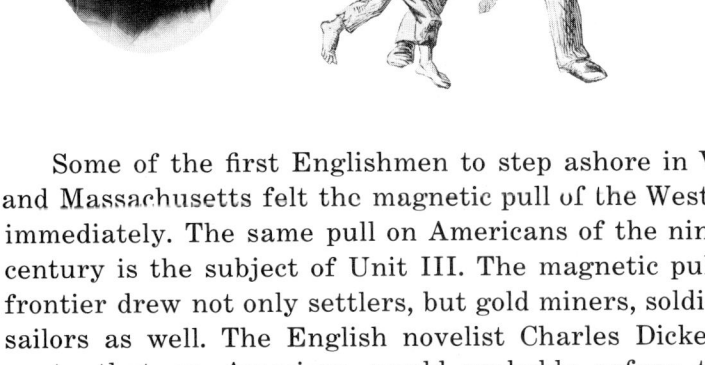

Some of the first Englishmen to step ashore in Virginia and Massachusetts felt the magnetic pull of the West almost immediately. The same pull on Americans of the nineteenth century is the subject of Unit III. The magnetic pull of the frontier drew not only settlers, but gold miners, soldiers, and sailors as well. The English novelist Charles Dickens once wrote that an American would probably refuse to enter heaven unless assured that he would be allowed to move farther west. What has the frontier meant to Americans? This is the historical question with which the unit begins.

The unit's three chapters describe different phases of American expansion in the 1800's. Chapter 9 is about the kind of life led by settlers on the frontier, the growth of new states in the Old Northwest and the Old Southwest, and the invasion of white men into Indian lands in the Far West. Chapter 10 tells the story of the carving of new states and territories in the Far West out of lands that were either claimed or owned by other countries. Chapter 11 describes the rapid changes in transportation and industry that went along with, and sometimes speeded up, the movement westward. The political and social effects of this first period of American industrial growth are also examined.

Was this burst of expansion a force for progress? This is the question asked in the final part of the unit.

TOP, LEFT TO RIGHT:
NATIONAL ARCHIVES
DETROIT INSTITUTE OF ARTS
NEW YORK STATE LIBRARY
ASSOCIATION AMERICAN RAILROADS
SAN JACINTO MUSEUM OF HISTORY
OREGON STATE HIGHWAY DEPARTMENT
BOTTOM, LEFT TO RIGHT:
WASHINGTON UNIVERSITY, ST. LOUIS
CHICAGO HISTORICAL SOCIETY
LIBRARY OF CONGRESS
SUPREME COURT OF THE UNITED STATES
LIBRARY OF CONGRESS
LIBRARY OF CONGRESS
NEW-YORK HISTORICAL SOCIETY
LOS ANGELES COUNTY MUSEUM

INTERPRETING THE PAST

The Frontier and the Making of America

At one time or another every part of the United States has been a frontier in which settlers struggled to make a living from the wilderness. Observers soon noticed that while men could change the frontier with axes, plows, and guns, the frontier could also change the men who went there. In 1728 the humorous aristocrat, William Byrd II of Virginia, described a journey he made to the frontier along the Virginia-North Carolina border. The backwoodsmen, he said, were lazy and accustomed to soft living because they made their women do all the hard work! Since then other Americans and foreign visitors have tried to answer questions about what role the frontier has played in the making of America and of the American people. As you read the following selections, keep these questions in mind:

1. Did having a frontier for such a long time make the United States different from other countries? If so, in what ways?
2. Did the frontier change those who went West? Why?
3. Do Americans still have a "frontier" attitude? If so, is that a good or a bad thing? Why?

A Mississippi Valley Preacher

About 1830 a preacher wrote a kind of guidebook for people who were planning to travel or settle in the frontier region west of the Allegheny Mountains. In his guidebook Reverend Robert Baird tried to sum up the difference between the frontiersmen of the West and well-established Easterners.

REVEREND ROBERT BAIRD:
VIEW OF THE VALLEY OF THE MISSISSIPPI, 1832

The differences of character of the people of the West are all created by the different circumstances in which the people have been placed in that new world. The differences of character are:

1. *A spirit of adventure,* a willingness to go through any hardship or danger to do what they want to do. The western people think nothing of making a long journey and of suffering every kind of hardship.

2. *Independence of thought and action.* They have felt this from their childhood. Men who can endure anything, who have lived as free as the mountain air or as the deer and the buffalo, will act independently during all of their life.

3. *An apparent roughness,* which seems to some to be *rudeness of manners.*

These things are especially true of the agricultural parts and also in some ways of the new towns and villages. It is not that the people are ignorant and barbaric, as some think. The characteristics [qualities] are the result of people being thrown together in unsettled areas where there are so few other people. Also there is perfect equality on the frontier. People know little about each other's background. Each man is lord of the soil which he cultivates. A log cabin is all that the best of families can expect to have for years. Few can possess those things which create differences in rank [status] in society. Frontier living has laid the foundation for the equality, simple manners, great readiness to make friends, and freedom of speech one sees among the people of the West.

1. In what ways did Baird believe Westerners to be different from other Americans?
2. What circumstances did Baird think explained their character?

Was the West responsible for that which was best or that which was worst in American society? American writers still debate the question. In the 1880's the Englishman Lord James Bryce offered his answer after taking a long and careful look at the United States, its people, and its institutions.

An English Traveler

LORD JAMES BRYCE:
THE AMERICAN COMMONWEALTH, 1888

The West is the most American part of America. It is the part of the country where those features which distinguish America from Europe can be seen most clearly. In the West all is bustle, motion, and struggle. Even immigrants from Europe learn the ways of the West almost as quickly as they learn the language of the country.

When hardworking and unsettled Americans go West, they leave their old homes determined to get wealth and success. They throw themselves into work feverishly. They get up early; they work all day; they have few pleasures and few chances for relaxation. No one has any fixed occupation. He is a storekeeper today, a ranchman tomorrow, a miner next week. In the West you must be able to do anything. The risky and shifting life of Westerners strengthens the reckless habits of the people.

This haste and excitement, this concentration on the development of the natural resources of the country, are

"Scum" is impure material that often forms on the surface of liquids.

"Speculation" means the engagement in risky business dealings on the chance of making a big or quick profit.

unfortunate. Just as a town built in a hurry is seldom well built, so a society would be healthier if it does not grow too swiftly. Doubtless much of the scum will be cleared away from the surface when the liquid settles and cools down. Lawlessness and lynch-law will disappear. Saloons and gambling houses will not succeed in a well-behaved population. Schools will improve and universities will grow out of the raw colleges which one already finds even in the new territories. Nevertheless, some of the bad political habits that one sees on the Atlantic Coast may also be seen in western towns. The restlessness, the love of speculation, and the feverish eagerness for quick and showy profits may soak into the minds of the western people for centuries to come. These are some of the shadows which the traveler can see falling across the glowing landscape of the Great West.

1. Which qualities of Westerners does Bryce admire? Which does he criticize?
2. What did Bryce expect to happen as the West was settled? Was he right? Give examples.

A Young Historian

In Chicago in 1893 a young historian from the University of Wisconsin, Frederick Jackson Turner, made a speech at a meeting of American historians. "The true point of view in the history of this nation is not the Atlantic Coast," he said. "It is the Great West." Until then no historian had defined what the frontier meant to America quite as thoroughly as he. His speech was inspired by the census report for 1890. The report stated that there was no longer a line running through the West which could be called "the frontier." There were only pockets of unsettled territory in the midst of other areas which were too well settled to be called frontier territory any longer. In short, the frontier was no more. The following selection is adapted from Turner's famous speech.

FREDERICK JACKSON TURNER:
THE SIGNIFICANCE OF THE FRONTIER IN AMERICAN HISTORY, 1893

Up to our own day [1893] American history has been mostly the history of the settlement of the Great West. The existence of an area of free land which grew smaller as American settlement advanced westward explains American development.

At first the frontier was the Atlantic Coast. It was then the frontier of Europe. Moving westward, the frontier became

more and more American. Thus the advance of the frontier westward has meant a steady movement away from the influence of Europe and a steady growth of independence in American ways.

The frontier encouraged the formation of a special national character even though Americans came from different lands. The coast was mainly English. Later, tides of immigration from other countries flowed across the West. On the frontier the immigrants were Americanized and melted into a mixed race—English in neither nationality nor characteristics. This process of Americanization has gone on until now.

"Americanized" means to become American in spirit, methods, and customs.

The middle region of the colonies was less English than New England or the South. It had a wide mixture of nationalities. Thus it became the typically American region. This region, entered by New York harbor, was an open door to all Europe. The men of the frontier were more like the men in the middle region than like those of the other sections.

But the most important effect of the frontier has been in pushing forward democracy here and in Europe. The frontier produces individualism. It produces a dislike for control. Frontier conditions that existed in the colonies are important causes of the American Revolution.

"Individualism" means living the way one wants to live, without too much thought for the opinions of others in society.

The frontier states that came into the Union in the first 25 years of its existence came in with very democratic rules for voting. The democracy of western states had effects of the highest importance upon the older eastern states. It was *western* New York that forced an extension [widening] of the right to vote in that state in 1821. It was *western* Virginia that forced the Tidewater region to lower the barriers to voting in 1830.

"Tidewater" is the area of low land along the Atlantic Coast.

Since the days of Columbus, America has been another name for opportunity. Each frontier furnished a new field of opportunity, a gate of escape from the limitations of the past. Freshness, confidence, scorn of an older society, and impatience with its ideas were part of the frontier. And now, four centuries after the discovery of America and at the end of 100 years of life under the Constitution, the frontier has gone. With its going the first period of American history has closed.

Summary Questions

1. In what respects do Baird, Bryce, and Turner agree? disagree?
2. To remain "American" do we have to have a frontier? Are there any new frontiers to take the place of the one that disappeared in 1890?
3. Why have so many Americans thought of *frontier*, *democracy*, and *equality* as having nearly the same meaning?

9
The Pioneer Spirit

Henry David Thoreau, an American writer in Concord, Massachusetts, used to take walks for exercise. He noticed that whenever he started out without any destination in mind he always found himself heading westward. "I must walk toward Oregon," he wrote in 1845, "and not toward Europe." In saying that he felt drawn westward, Thoreau expressed a feeling shared by many of his fellow Americans.

Most nations have legendary heroes who become the subjects of popular tales and pictures. American movies and television shows frequently have a forest hunter like Daniel Boone or a Rocky Mountain fur trapper like Jedediah Smith (left) as the hero. Each seems to be alone, free, and unafraid of danger. Each is a Westerner.

The westward movement began with colonial settlements such as Deerfield, Massachusetts. By 1775 the **frontier,** the area of farthest westward settlement, was in Kentucky and Tennessee. By 1850 enough Americans were settled in California to demand, and get, statehood. It took 150 years to reach the Alleghenies, but only 75 years more to reach the Pacific.

In this great migration across a continent, American life took on patterns of thinking that still exist. One was the belief that growth was a good thing and that the future would always be an improvement upon the past. Another was the willingness to use up land, grass, timber, and game with little thought that there might be a limit to such abundance. Still another pattern was the respect given to an individual who, without social position or wealth, made his own way by hard work and ability.

Expansion westward was only part of the story of national growth. Growing cities and factories opened the way to wealth, as did the abundant land. The builder of railroads or the developer of mines was as much a pioneer as the mountain trailblazer. But it was the westward march that symbolized the adventurous spirit of young America. Some of our greatest strength as a free people comes from this frontier experience. But so do some of our problems, as we struggle to save the land from pollution and overcrowding.

As you read, think about these questions:
1. Why have Americans, despite the hardships involved, been drawn to the West?
2. Why are the pioneer, the mountain man, and the cowboy American folk heroes?

Harvey Dunn's painting captures the spirit of explorer Jedediah Smith.

Right: Advertisements promised a great future in the West. This 1836 poster promotes a new town site in Illinois. Below: As this 1839 cartoon illustrates, many of those who went West returned a good deal less enthusiastically than they had set out.

The Lure of the West

The most powerful magnet pulling Americans westward was cheap, undeveloped land. In a nation of farmers, landownership made any man his own master. A move to new land meant the opportunity to raise bigger and better crops and a chance to climb in the world. No one who knew how to plow and plant and was willing to "pull up stakes" had to feel trapped by past failures.

The land, however, was never completely free. The Federal government sold land at auctions, like the one advertised at the upper left, but always in plots of a minimum size and at a minimum price. In 1785 a settler needed at least $640 in cash to buy the smallest sized farm that the government sold. By 1820, after several changes in land laws, as little as $100 in cash could put a family on its own farm of 80 acres. Even that sum represented the savings of a year or two of hard work.

Many pioneers, called "squatters," tried to get free land by clearing a farm without owning it, in the hopes that in time possession would give them **title** (legal ownership). There was a great risk that, after years of bitter effort, some rightful owner would appear to claim it.

Both the squatters and those who bought their land needed some **capital** (money, tools, and other things necessary for production). Pioneers needed axes, plows, seeds, wagons, horses, oxen, chickens, guns, and ammunition. With no crop to sell for at least a year, the pioneer almost always needed some cash, too. It is in this sense that the pioneer was, like others who own their own businesses and sell their products for profit, a **capitalist.**

Often he bought his land from a private company of **land speculators** who bought thousands or millions of acres from the government not to farm but to sell for a profit. Though speculators often sold pioneers bad land at high prices, some companies honestly worked to improve their holdings and attract customers by building roads, mills, bridges, and other aids to settlement.

In spite of the problems of getting a frontier farm started, millions of Americans found the means to move westward. Often the same family made many such moves. Most land gave generous harvests, and more land always seemed to be available farther west. To many pioneers it did not seem necessary to care for the soil or to save trees and protect game animals for the future.

Government and Pioneering

Moving westward was an adventure into the unknown. The first few families to move to a new frontier were intruders in a strange and sometimes harsh world. They had to survive sickness without doctors and hospitals and disasters without policemen. If vital tools broke or food supplies were destroyed, there rarely were lifesaving replacements available. Only after a number of families had settled a new frontier did the beginnings of organized community life appear.

Because he had to depend upon himself, the early Westerner became a strong individualist. When he needed help he rarely looked beyond his few neighbors. He was apt to be impatient with the government, which seemed far away, hard to reach, and run by men who did not understand his problems.

Yet in certain key ways, such as transportation and defense, the western pioneer relied on government more than most Americans. When the early settler had finally harvested his first crop of corn or fattened his hogs, he still faced the problem of getting his produce to market. A nearby river was helpful as it was easy to float goods downstream on rafts or in flatboats. Land transportation, however, was unbelievably poor. The

260

picture (above, left) shows a coach going through a stump-filled country road. Rain turned such "back-country" roads into mudholes in which men, animals, and wagons sank with a helpless squish. New settlers badly needed level, well-drained highways. They had to have bridges and canals. The demand for such "internal improvements," as they were then called, was basic in western life. Only government had the capital to undertake these **public works** (construction paid for by taxes and beneficial to an entire community).

Likewise, the Federal government's army was sorely needed for defense against what settlers considered the Indian menace. From colonial days on Westerners demanded that lawmaking bodies located in the East spend money on forts and troops in Indian country. Each westward step of the frontier was accomplished not only by self-reliance, but also by the efforts of an active Federal government.

Pioneers faced miserable road conditions and sometimes hostile Indians. Above left: This "road" into the West is cleared of trees, but stumps remain as dangers to horses, coaches, and passengers. Travel was halted so often that the expression "to be stumped" became part of the American language. Above: In 1835 Seminole Indians attacked this blockhouse in Florida.

Questions for Discussion

1. What were the essentials for starting a farm on a tract of frontier land?
2. In what ways did the pioneer depend upon the Federal government? Why?

Across the Alleghenies

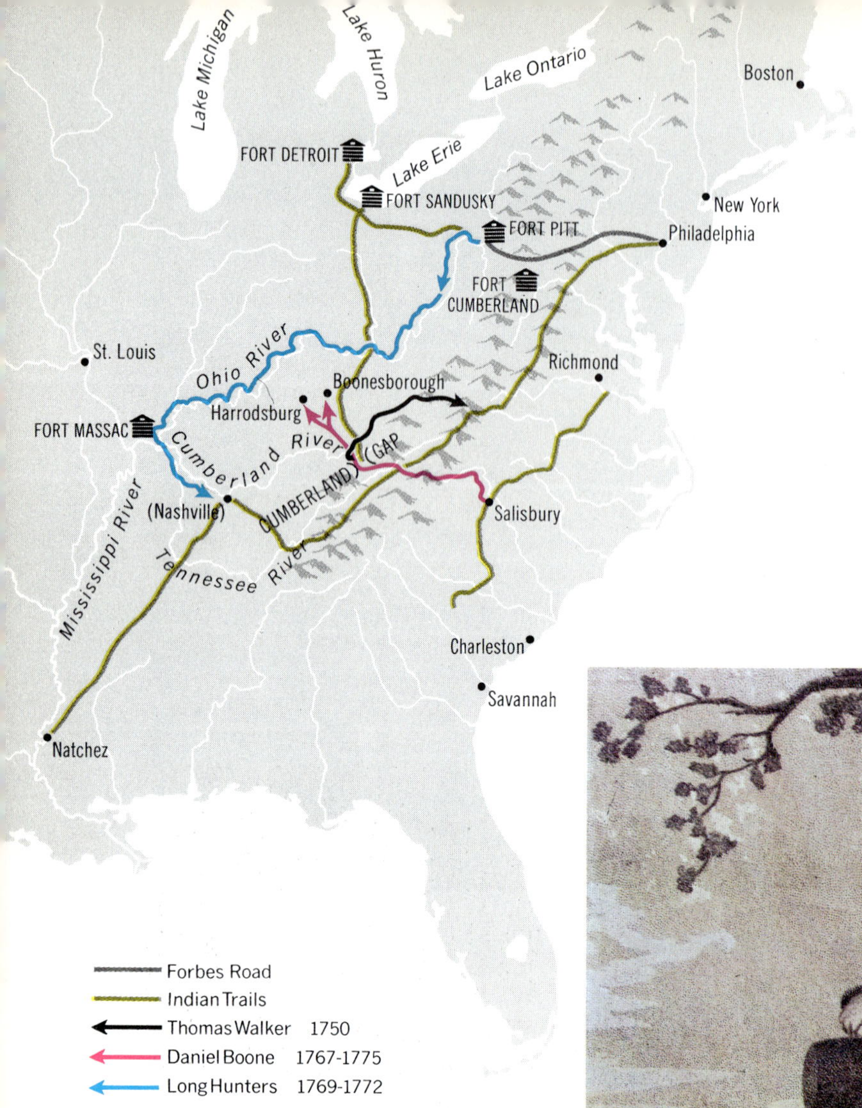

Trails Across the Alleghenies

- Forbes Road
- Indian Trails
- Thomas Walker 1750
- Daniel Boone 1767-1775
- Long Hunters 1769-1772

Daniel Boone's love of the frontier became legendary. This engraving was made from a portrait painted when Boone was 85.

The first push of westward migration broke through the barrier of the Allegheny Mountains about 1760. After 1765 settlers on their way West could get as far as Pittsburgh on roads that had been cut by the British armies during the French and Indian War. From Pittsburgh they could float down the Ohio. An inviting gateway through the southern part of the Alleghenies was Cumberland Gap, shown on the map at the left. Through it passed the people of the future state of Kentucky. Many of them were led by the remarkable Daniel Boone (left).

Boone was born near Reading, Pennsylvania, in 1734. He did not have much formal schooling, but at the age of twelve, he was an experienced hunter and traveler in the wilderness. When he was in his teens, his family moved to North Carolina. Soon afterward he went along on Braddock's ill-fated expedition. Then Boone settled down in North Carolina to farm, but each winter he was off with traps and gun to spend months in the lonely forests where he felt most at home.

In 1775 a group of land speculators, the Transylvania Company, hired Boone to lead a party of settlers into Kentucky. Boone led the families who would be the company's future customers through Cumberland Gap, and directed them in building a fort (right).

Indian attacks in defense of their invaded hunting grounds were frequent. Kentucky soon became known as "the dark and bloody ground." Along with other leaders Boone held the settlements together. His admiring neighbors elected him to posts such as legislator, sheriff, and colonel of militia. But he had a longing to move on. In 1788 he pushed northward into modern West Virginia, and then to Missouri where, in 1820, he died.

Boone was glorified later because he was a new type of national hero. A good, brave, uneducated man, he won respect for his courage and his skill in leading "civilized" Easterners into the wilds of the West.

By the end of the Revolution, settlements had been planted in Kentucky and Tennessee. In both places the pioneers met, elected officials, and challenged the authority of Virginia and North Carolina to govern them. The "colonists" of the Alleghenies were successful in getting Kentucky admitted as a state in 1792, and Tennessee in 1796.

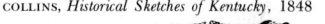
COLLINS, *Historical Sketches of Kentucky*, 1848

In March 1775 Daniel Boone led the first large party of settlers through the Cumberland Gap and then northwest to the Kentucky River. There, at Boonesborough, Kentucky, they built this small but important frontier outpost.

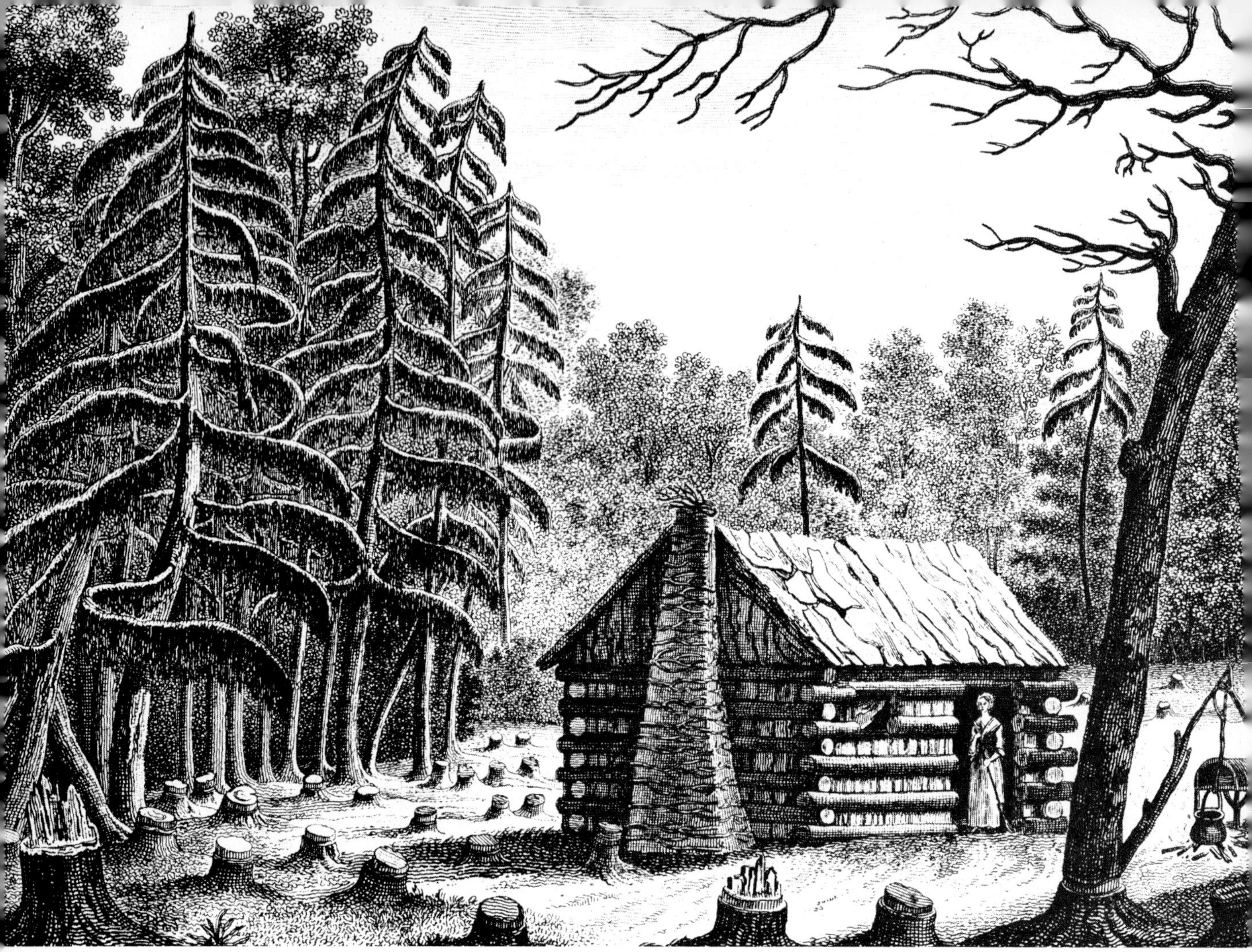

Voyage dans l'Amerique Septentrionale, 1826

Above: A French artist made this engraving of a log cabin to show his countrymen America's typical frontier setting. Right: A frontier trapper returns laden with pelts to his family's log cabin.

NEW-YORK HISTORICAL SOCIETY

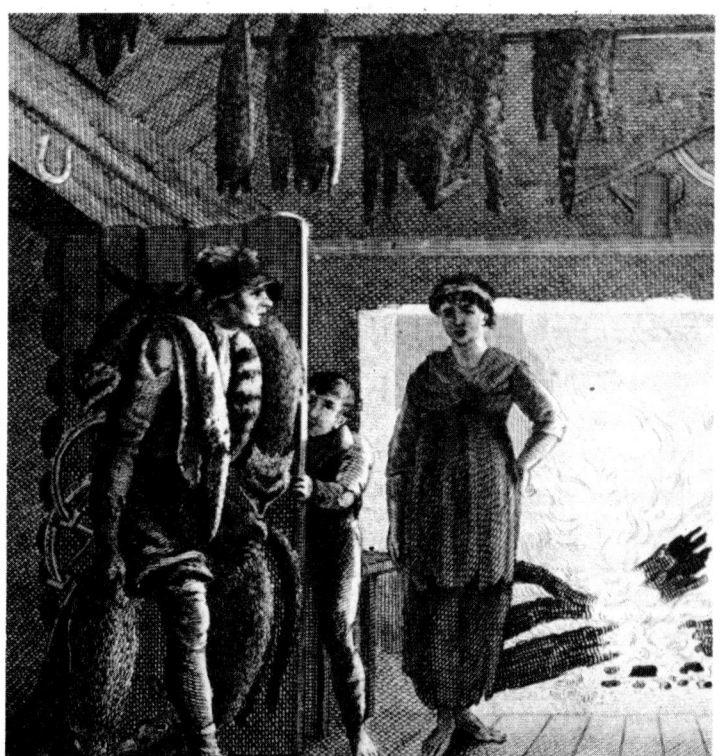

The Log-Cabin Frontier

This earliest national frontier showed the important role of natural surroundings in shaping the settlers' way of life. Theirs was the woodman's world. Thick, uncut forest, which was both enemy and friend, covered the land. The forest might hide a hungry bear or a stalking Indian. Yet it also supplied life's essential needs. In a land of abundant trees, the log cabin came to symbolize this frontier.

It was not a comfortable home. Usually, its single room had a dirt floor, which might later be covered with planks as in the cabin at the lower left. In winter the blaze in the fireplace never was allowed to die out because it was the only source of light and heat for comfort and cooking. Openings for windows often were not cut because glass was too expensive, so the cabin was likely to be hot and smoky. Large families shared such one-room homes, complete with bugs, mice, dirt, and odors. Life on the frontier was often far more drab than life in the East. But there was a difference. Log-cabin families believed that their condition was temporary. When the farm was finally producing, they would build a better home. Nothing but bad luck could stop them.

In addition to lumber for log cabins, the forest also furnished the wood for farm tools, stocks for guns, parts for traps, and rails for fences. Clothing, such as buckskin shirts and raccoonskin caps, came from forest animals.

Along with the gun the basic tool of log-cabin civilization was the ax. An experienced backwoodsman could bring down a heavy tree with a few strokes. Grown sons helped their fathers clear the forest and turn it into farmland.

Like Daniel Boone, pioneer settlers were often thought of by Easterners as being especially noble because they worked so hard, were so independent, and lived so far from the "corrupting" influences of the cities, as Jefferson might have put it. Yet their efforts were aimed at having someday all the luxuries and comforts of civilization.

Questions for Discussion

1. In what ways was the forest both a friend and an enemy to the Allegheny pioneer?
2. How did those who went West to escape civilization actually prepare the way for its coming?

Settling the Old Northwest and Southwest

The next big thrust of westward migration, from about 1800 to 1850, settled the region of rolling hills and prairie (right) between the Alleghenies and the Mississippi. This was the West contained in the original boundaries of 1783. Each advance of the white man meant the loss of the Indians' land and freedom.

In the summer of 1789, war with the Indians broke out in the Northwest Territory. There were two reasons. First, there were many "border incidents" between Indian and white hunting parties. In addition, the British were encouraging the Indians to form a confederacy of tribes north of the Ohio River and to resist the American advance. At first it seemed that the Indians might actually be successful. In 1790 they ambushed and defeated a small party led by General Josiah Harmar. A year later they badly defeated a force led by General Arthur St. Clair and killed some 630 Americans.

Washington now called on another wartime general to subdue the Northwest. Like most American generals of his time, "Mad Anthony" Wayne was a successful civilian-turned-soldier. He had been a tanner and then a surveyor in Pennsylvania before the Revolution, and a Congressman and a southern planter afterward. After spending a year carefully drilling his recruits, he marched into Indian country and let word spread that he would attack on a certain day in August of 1794. It was a clever trick. Wayne knew that the braves fasted before a battle. He sat for three days, waiting while the Indians grew hungrier each hour. Finally, when many of them had given up and left their camp in search of food, he attacked. In a few hours the Indians were defeated.

This Battle of Fallen Timbers had a powerful impact on people's minds. The British, who were supposed to be neutral, no longer dared to aid the Indians openly. The chiefs therefore realized that they could not hope to stop the Americans, who would raise new armies and keep coming. So in 1795 they signed, at Wayne's dictation (left), the Treaty of Greenville, giving up their hunting lands in present-day southeastern Indiana and southern Ohio. Would-be-settlers were heartened to realize that the new national government could and would open the way into the Northwest for them. The Treaty of Greenville thus gave real meaning to the Ordinances of 1785 and 1787. Self-government and cheap land would have meant little without protection.

CHICAGO HISTORICAL SOCIETY

An Indian approaches two American army officers at the signing of the Treaty of Greenville.

JOSLYN ART MUSEUM, NATURAL GAS COMPANY COLLECTION

Carl Bodmer, a Swiss artist who toured the United States from 1832 to 1834, painted this view of a farm on the Illinois prairie during the winter.

NATIONAL GALLERY OF ART, GIFT OF EDGAR WILLIAM AND BERNICE CHRYSLER GARBISCH

WHALING MUSEUM, NEW BEDFORD

268

Community Living on the Frontier

Now, thousands of settlers flocked into the Northwest. There were enough to make Ohio a state in 1803, Indiana in 1816, and Illinois in 1818. For each pioneer family the westward move meant the individual experience of pulling up roots. Yet there was always a group aspect to frontier living.

The log-cabin settler was isolated from civilization. But for exactly that reason, he had to depend heavily on other nearby pioneers for help in emergencies. Besides, the basic human need for companionship was bound to bring people together. Many tasks were shared. When it was time to put up a cabin, for example, neighbors might unite to roll and lift the heavy logs and eat the food prepared by the women and refresh themselves with cider and whiskey. At such community gatherings as the "Scutching Bee" (upper left), flax plants were prepared for weaving into linen.

Another unifying event was the camp meeting. Thousands of frontiersmen believed in a genuine, burning hell to which they would go if they did not get God's help in repenting of their wickedness and changing their ways. At outdoor gatherings, like that at lower left, preachers in buckskin, who were themselves pioneers with no formal education, shouted at sinners to turn away from evil. The listeners often twisted and squirmed in fear or leaped and sang for joy.

A strange combination of frontier forces worked to form the American character. There was a democratic spirit evident in the plain speech and dress of everyone. Any attempt to put on airs was certain to be resented. Yet in this classless society an individual who did not share the common outlook on any subject was viewed with suspicion. A young man who did not want to fight Indians or become prosperous, or a young woman who doubted the authority of preachers or thought that girls should be well-educated, was not likely to be popular. The individualistic pioneer was very much influenced by majority opinion because the need for community closeness was overpowering.

The Southwestern Cotton Frontier

So many wagons crowded the roads into the old Northwest after 1815 that a foreigner wrote, "The old America seems to be breaking up and moving westward." The same movement was going on south of the Ohio River. Its driving force was cheap land, but it

Above: Pennsylvania settlers hold a community "Flax-Scutching Bee." Frontier folk made an enjoyable social event out of the dull chore of beating flax to separate the valuable linen fibers from the woody pulp. Left: Religious camp meetings, full of shouting preachers and groaning sinners, provided a sure-fire remedy for frontier loneliness.

received much help from the invention of a Yankee.

Eli Whitney was born in 1765 to a well-off Massachusetts farmer. Since his boyhood he had loved to tinker, and before he was out of his teens he had run a successful nail-manufacturing business. At the late age of 23 he entered Yale College as a freshman, even though he was older than most seniors. Upon graduating in 1792 he went South. While he was a guest on a Georgia plantation, he heard local landowners say that England's growing textile industry needed raw cotton so badly that cotton could become a more profitable crop for the South than tobacco, rice, or indigo. But the only kind of cotton that grew easily in the South had stubborn, clinging seeds in it. A hard-working slave could clean only a pound or so a day. If someone could design a machine to do the job more quickly, the South would have another important cash crop.

Within ten days Whitney designed a model and by April 1793 had perfected the device shown at left. Now a slave could grind out 50 pounds of cotton fiber a day. Soon water-powered cotton gins cleaned millions of pounds and made cotton king of southern crops.

Southerners swarmed across the southern Appalachians in search of good cotton lands (map, upper right). A North Carolina planter wrote, "The Alabama fever rages here with great violence and has carried off vast numbers of our citizens." Enough were "carried off" to make Mississippi a state in 1817, and Alabama in 1819.

The Southwest, too, was a frontier. Its large planters were not old, settled, aristocratic families, but newcomers on their way up in the world. The best lands and biggest plantations were in river valleys, but in the hills dwelt thousands of hard-working small farmers, eager for cheap land and internal improvements.

But this cotton frontier differed in one all-important way. It gave slavery a new lease on life and greatly extended the area in which slave labor could be used. By 1820 the South was booming. King cotton was no more ready to give up slavery than New England would have been to give up seafaring.

A New Indian Policy

The usual way of dealing with Indian tribes was to sign treaties with them at meetings. Indians would gather for several days of pipe-smoking, exchanging of gifts, and drinking of whiskey, which American

YALE UNIVERSITY ART GALLERY

NATIONAL ARCHIVES

Eli Whitney as painted by Samuel F. B. Morse and one of Whitney's drawings for the first cotton gin.

Southern Agriculture 1850

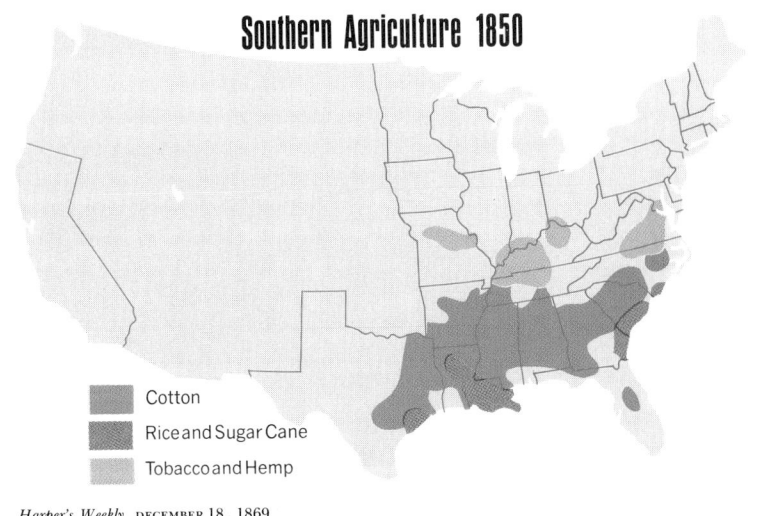

- Cotton
- Rice and Sugar Cane
- Tobacco and Hemp

This picture from Harper's Weekly *shows Whitney's cotton gin in operation. Although his gin revolutionized cotton production in the South, Whitney himself received little money from his invention.*

Harper's Weekly, DECEMBER 18, 1869

officials encouraged to confuse the Indians' judgment. Then the Indians would trade more of their hunting lands for money and supplies. Surrounded by soldiers, as shown at lower right, the chiefs had little choice. If such "diplomatic" tactics failed, there was always the army or the militia (lower left).

As the line of settlement swept toward the Mississippi, the government devised a new Indian policy. All the nation's Indians should give up their old lands and move west of the Mississippi to the Great Plains. Their new lands would be guaranteed to them forever. Once a "permanent Indian frontier" was set up, clashes between whites and Indians would end.

This seemingly generous offer had drawbacks. On the Great Plains, which extended to the Rockies, there were almost no trees and little rainfall. Almost all Americans believed, in 1825, that white men could not survive on what was then called the "Great American Desert." But Congress assumed that because some Indians survived on the plains, all Indians could.

The eastern Indians themselves knew better and resisted resettlement as long as possible. The process was most cruel for southern Indians of the Five Civilized Tribes—Choctaw, Creek, Chickasaw, Chero-

Below right: In March 1814 troops led by Andrew Jackson defeated the Creek Indians at the Battle of Horseshoe Bend. Shortly afterward Jackson accepted the surrender of a Creek chief. Below: In about 1837 the Georgia militia attacked this Creek Indian village.

272

kee, and Seminole—who had long been adapted to white ways. The Cherokees, for example, had become farmers in North Carolina and Georgia and owned thousands of cattle, slaves, gristmills, sawmills, cotton gins, and looms. They had a written language, a school system, and a newspaper. They even organized, in 1827, a self-governing state, the Cherokee Republic.

But Georgia speculators and settlers were eager to get their hands on the Cherokee lands. The United States refused to protect them. Eventually, the Cherokees were forced to sign agreements to give up their lands and then were driven mercilessly west to the new Indian Territory, with great loss of life, along the "Trail of Tears." In 1889 even the Indian Territory was taken by the white man and renamed Oklahoma.

Questions for Discussion

1. Why did frontier communities have many group activities? Are such activities still part of the American way of life?
2. How did the cotton gin promote western settlement?
3. Why were the Indians unable to stop the pioneers' invasion of Indian lands?

Below: In August 1825 a number of Indian tribes and representatives of the United States government attended this Grand Council at Prairie du Chien, Wisconsin. Within 25 years nearly all of the tribes represented there had ceded their hunting lands to the United States government.

SIGMUND SAMUEL CANADIANA GALLERY

Above: In 1847 H. G. Hine painted this view of the untamed prairie before it disappeared. Right: For Plains Indians killing buffalo was far more than a sport. A successful hunt meant survival. Jacob Alfred Miller's "Yell of Triumph" captures the spirit of a buffalo hunt. Far right: George Catlin made this sketch of the Comanche method of loosing arrows at an enemy while still using one's horse as a shield.

WALTERS ART GALLERY (© 1951 UNIVERSITY OF OKLAHOMA PRESS)

Discovering the Far West

Many pioneers had settled on the grassy prairies in Illinois and Indiana, east of the Mississippi. But these lands were well-watered, easy to farm, and not far from wooded areas. When white settlers moved beyond the Mississippi to the edge of the Great Plains, they halted before the challenge of a new environment. Distances were huge. Streams to travel on were rare. The farther one moved toward the Rocky Mountains, the drier the soil became. Mounted Indians (left) were a new and difficult "enemy."

Yet beyond those mountains and the deserts of the Southwest lay a fertile Pacific Coast region. Beginning around 1840 some settlers began to find ways across plain and mountain to this new promised land. On these journeys they met the Plains Indians—Sioux, Blackfeet, Cheyennes, Arapahos, Apaches, Comanches, and others, dwellers in the last area of the United States to be overrun by whites.

The Plains Indians whom you see hunting (upper left) and celebrating (lower left) depended upon the buffalo for their existence. We saw in the opening chapter how the hides, horns, and bones of the buffalo enabled Plains Indians to flourish in a treeless world.

Curiously, the white man had something to do with aiding temporarily the Plains Indians. The Spaniards introduced the horse into North America. Some of their mounts escaped and multiplied into magnificent herds of wild horses. Sometime after 1720 Indians learned to capture and ride them. They then were able to hunt the buffalo with far more ease and success than on foot. When some Indians were able to replace bows and arrows with firearms, hunting was even easier.

The Kiowa, Sioux, Cheyenne, Arapaho, and other Plains tribes became mounted, nomadic Indians instead of settled villagers raising corn and beans. A splendid, buffalo-based Plains Indian culture grew up. It left behind it fine bone ornaments and tepees and shields of buffalo hide decorated with paintings of mounted hunters and warriors. The combining of the white man's horse and gun with the Indians' skill in pursuing and using the buffalo produced a new kind of Indian culture. It flourished only 150 years before "civilized" whites moved in and destroyed it.

Mountain Men Explore the Far West

The first white probings into the Plains and mountain world, however, were made by men who were

CATLIN, *Souvenir of the North American Indians*, 1850

275

themselves ill at ease in settled surroundings. These were the mountain men who worked for the fur-trapping companies. By the 1820's they were pursuing the beaver and other fur-bearing animals all the way to the Rockies.

Trappers like Jedediah Smith or Jim Beckwourth (left) or Jim Bridger (right) were men who could live alone in a wilderness different from the one Daniel Boone had known. They could wander over thousands of square miles of mountain and desert and find their way from place to place as easily as a city man finds his way from his home to his office. They disappeared alone into mountain country each fall and spent the winter trapping and living with the Indians. They could read animal tracks and other hunting clues with the skill of the Indians. They lived with Indian women, decorated their clothing with feathers and shells, sometimes painted their faces, and used Indian charms, spells, and herbs to "make medicine" when they were sick. They survived terrible mishaps—blizzards, near-starvation, and ghastly wounds from hostile Indians or wild animals.

In springtime they appeared at trappers' rendezvous, or meeting points, where fur buyers and sellers met, unloaded their peltry, ate and drank themselves contented, and then were off again. They were truly free, as civilized men find it almost impossible to be.

Yet, like Daniel Boone, they opened the way for organized parties of men attempting to conquer the wilderness. In 1824 Jedediah Smith pioneered a route through South Pass in Wyoming, which became a key gateway to the Oregon Trail. Three years later he made the first overland trip to California. Peter Skene Ogden, a Canadian competing with American fur trappers in the disputed Oregon Territory, explored the north side of the Great Salt Lake. In 1828 Sylvester Pattie and his son James found their way from Santa Fe to San Diego, only to be thrown into jail by the Mexican governor there. In July 1833 Joe Walker left Fort Bonneville, followed the Humboldt River, crossed the Sierra Nevadas, and arrived in San Francisco.

Soon mountain men's trails were crisscrossing the Far West (map, right). In 1842 the Federal government showed its increasing interest in the West by sending an expedition under Lieutenant John C. Frémont and his trapper-guide Kit Carson to explore the central Rockies.

James Beckwourth was among the first trappers and explorers in the West. For a while Beckwourth—who was part Negro—served as the chief of a Crow Indian tribe.

Below: James Bridger was the first white man known to have visited Great Salt Lake. Right: Kit Carson won nationwide fame as the guide for three highly publicized expeditions to the West led by John C. Frémont.

STATE HISTORICAL SOCIETY OF COLORADO

KANSAS STATE HISTORICAL SOCIETY

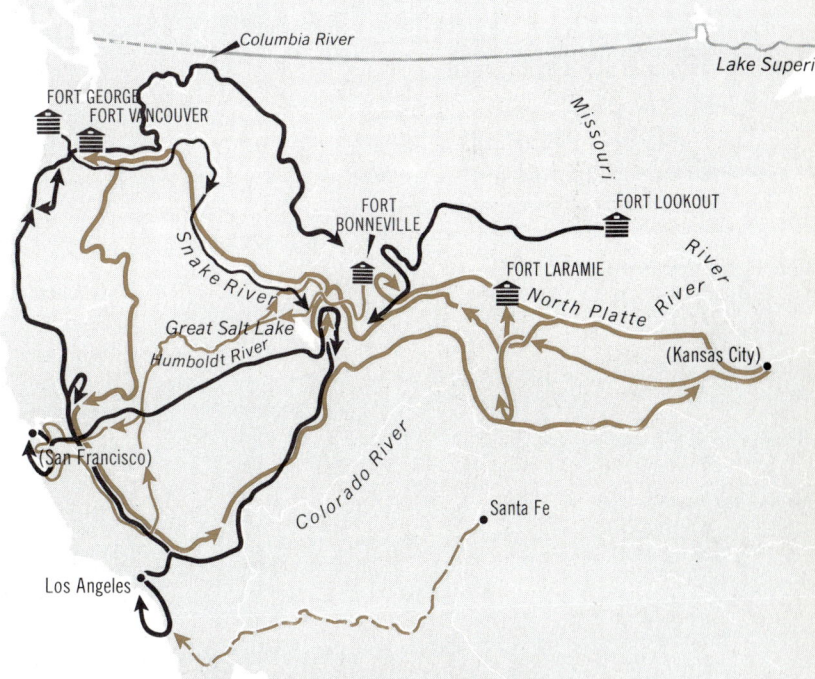

The Exploration of the West 1820–1844

- Jedediah S. Smith 1823–1829
- Peter Skene Ogden 1824–1825
- James and Sylvester Pattie 1825–1828
- Joe Walker 1833–1834
- John C. Frémont and Kit Carson 1842–1844

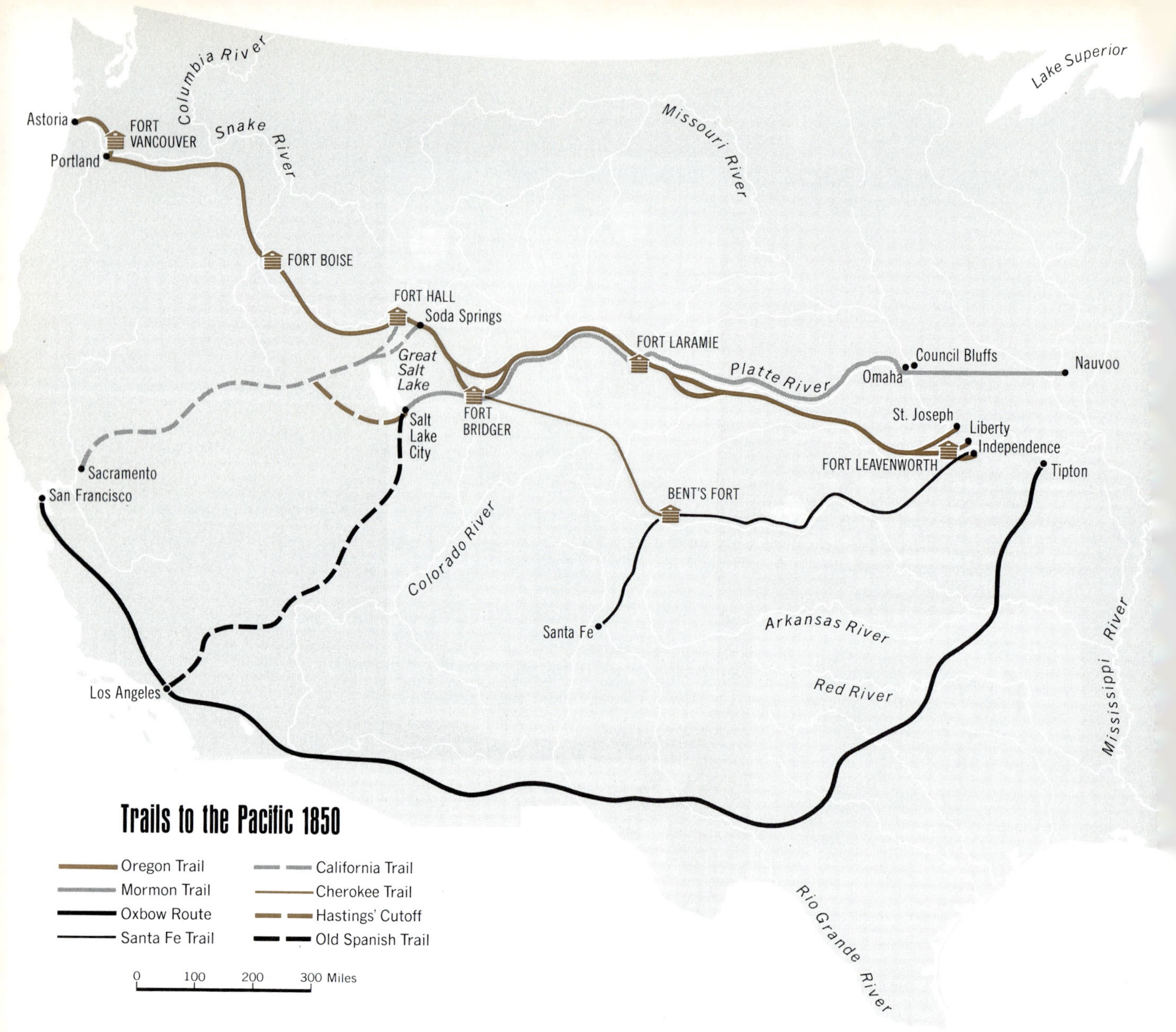

Trails to the Pacific 1850

— Oregon Trail
--- California Trail
— Mormon Trail
— Cherokee Trail
— Oxbow Route
--- Hastings' Cutoff
— Santa Fe Trail
— Old Spanish Trail

0 100 200 300 Miles

278

The Settling of the Far West

The trails found by the mountain men were soon put to use by traders and immigrants. In 1824 businessmen in Missouri began to send yearly caravans to Santa Fe, then part of Mexico. The long strings of wagons brought textiles and tools and hardware from the United States. In exchange, they got silver, mules, and furs from Mexico. By 1846 bawling oxen and teamsters cursing in fluent American were common sounds in the southern Rockies.

Other American pioneers headed for Oregon. They included fur trappers, businessmen, and missionaries like Marcus Whitman, who went to Oregon in 1836 to bring the benefits of his medical training and his religious zeal to the native Indians. Soon news of the rich soil, timberlands, flashing streams, and abundant furs inspired thousands of Easterners to head West.

Americans were also heading for California in ships. Merchant ships from New England were sailing around Cape Horn, at South America's southern tip, and beating their way northward to the California coast. There they swapped manufactured goods for cowhides which they took back to shoemaking factories in New England. Visitors to California aboard these ships brought back glowing reports of the climate and fertile soil of this Mexican province.

It did not matter much to them that California was a province of Mexico and that the United States still shared Oregon with the British. As Americans they were coming to believe that it was their right to go anywhere on the continent if opportunity beckoned.

By the summer of 1846 wagon trains were beginning to cross the great western expanses. Whole parties of families, with wagons loaded with household goods, left Independence, Missouri, in the spring. With luck they would have crossed the plains and mountains and would be grazing their animals on the banks of western rivers before the autumn snows flew. The overland trail was long and dangerous. Yet women and children were now making the trek that only a few mountain trappers had braved five and ten years earlier. In 1846 the Mormons, members of a religious community, were driven from Illinois by neighbors who did not share their beliefs. Nearly a year and a half later they settled near the shores of the Great Salt Lake. The Puritan migration of 1630 to Massachusetts was enacted all over again on Far Western soil.

Settlers moving west camp along the Laramie River in Wyoming.

In 1850, when American citizens were living within earshot of Pacific breakers, other Americans, born before the Revolution's end, were still alive. The rapid expansion of the nation westward was certain to have important results. The most immediate result was a loud outcry for American possession of the Far West. That demand led to a bitterly debated war on Mexico. That war, in turn, brought a civil war over slavery closer.

Questions for Discussion

1. Why were the Indians of the northern Plains not farmers? Why did they not travel extensively in canoes? What do the answers to these two questions show about the relationship between environment and a people's way of life?
2. Who were the mountain men? How did they prepare the way for the coming of American civilization to the Far West?
3. Why was the Pacific Coast settled before the Great Plains?
4. What was the most important political impact of rapid expansion into the West?

Chapter Review

Social Studies Terms

frontier, title, capital, capitalist, land speculators, public works

Summary Questions for Discussion

1. In what way was the demand for home rule by settlers of Tennessee and Kentucky a continuation of an old American tradition? Cite examples.
2. What factors combined to make the extension of the nation's boundaries to the Pacific a fairly swift movement? What problems caused by this movement are we still trying to solve?
3. Why did the pioneers tend to band together in very close-knit communities?
4. Was environment as important in shaping the pioneers' way of life as it was in shaping the Indians' way of life? Explain.
5. Could the conflict between westering pioneers and Indians have been avoided? How?
6. You have read in this chapter that Americans had a mental image of the ideal frontier hero. What picture did they have of the Indian, and how did this idea differ from that of the frontier hero?

7. Compare the reasons why each of these men has been a type of national hero: Daniel Boone, George Washington, Benjamin Franklin. Do Americans have the same admiration and respect for "pioneers" in space travel as Americans of the nineteenth century had for Daniel Boone? Why?
8. What things about the westward movement do you find most admirable? least admirable?
9. Are Americans today making better use of the continent's natural resources than the pioneers? Why?

Pictures as Historical Evidence

What pictorial evidence can you find to support the following generalization? The challenges of living on the frontier demanded community closeness.

Map Study

Compare the map on page 277, *The Exploration of the West 1820–1844*, with that on page 278, *Trails to the Pacific 1850*. What does the comparison reveal about the relationship between exploration and settlement? Why did so many of the trails converge [come together] in the area around the Great Salt Lake?

For Further Reading

Daniel Boone, by James Daugherty. New York: The Viking Press, Inc., 1966.
Famous Pioneers, by Franklin Folsom. Irvington-on-Hudson, N.Y.: Harvey House, Inc., 1963.
Frontier Living, by Edwin Tunis. New York: The World Publishing Company, 1961.
Indians of the Plains, by Eugene Rachlis. New York: American Heritage Publishing Co., Inc., 1960.
Kit Carson and the Wild Frontier, by Ralph Moody. New York: Random House, Inc., 1955.
My Antonia, by Willa Cather. Boston: Houghton Mifflin Company, 1918.
Trappers and Mountain Men, by Evan Jones. New York: American Heritage Publishing Co., Inc., 1961.
Where the Wind Blew Free, by Gene Jones. New York: W. W. Norton & Company, Inc., 1967.

10
Westward to the Pacific

On a May day in 1846, Senator Thomas Hart Benton, of Missouri, gave a speech on the subject of Oregon. In those days people came to the visitors' gallery in the Senate to listen to good speakers. Senator Benton did not disappoint them. He said that Oregon, then not part of the United States, must become American. "The van of the Caucasian race now top the Rocky Mountains," he said, "and spread down to the shores of the Pacific. In a few years a great population will grow up there." Benton thought that, in time, such growth would improve the condition of Asia. American civilization would surge westward across the sea and change the entire world for the better. Therefore, the settling of American farmers in the Columbia River valley was, he said, "the most momentous human event in the history of man."

Senator Benton expressed a feeling that gripped millions of Americans. It was a feeling, in the words of a magazine editor, of "our manifest destiny to overspread the continent." The same feeling that America's expansion was part of God's plan for a better world was expressed by a young poet, Walt Whitman, when he wrote that from "Democracy, with its manly heart and its lion strength," would spring "the great FUTURE of this Western World!" Likewise, the spirit of **Manifest Destiny** was clearly shown in the 1872 painting at left. The farmer and miner, the covered wagon and stagecoach, the locomotive and telegraph line are all pictured as agents of American progress. They sweep westward as part of a divine plan.

This booming confidence that the American eagle should stretch its wings from the Atlantic to the Pacific Ocean was exciting. It was also rather hard on other people who stood in the way, like the "inferior" Indians or "backward" Mexicans or people from "worn-out" England, who manned the outposts of the British Empire in Canada and Oregon. It was a natural result of the optimism created in Americans by events up to 1845: invention, economic growth, success in diplomacy, and especially expansion westward.

As you read, think about these questions:
1. Why did the movement of Americans to the West so often lead to conflict with other peoples?
2. What part did the army play in the nation's expansion westward?
3. What opportunities did expansion offer to a person with money to invest?

John Gast pictured Manifest Destiny as a goddess guiding expansion.

The Lone Star State

Stephen Austin, seen in this 1833 painting, tried desperately to find a peaceful solution for the problems between Texas and Mexico.

Westward expansion was not a process that stopped at boundary lines. The first large overflow of Americans into foreign territory after 1820 surged into the Mexican province of Texas. By this time Mexico had won its independence after a long struggle. The first large group of American settlers in Texas was led by Stephen F. Austin (left), the son of a restless Connecticut Yankee. In 1796 his father, Moses Austin, moved to the Far West and operated a lead mine in modern Missouri, then under the Spanish flag. In 1820 he asked Mexican authorities for permission to settle 300 American families in the northeastern province of Texas. But before he was given approval, Moses died. It was Stephen, rather than his pioneer father, who led the settlers into the promised land.

The Mexican government thought it had made a good bargain. It wanted additional settlers in Texas for the same reasons that colonial promoters in Virginia or Pennsylvania had wanted to find new settlers for their lands: The settlers would cultivate the soil, pay taxes, and keep the Indians in check.

What Texas offered to men like Austin is suggested in part by the scenes at right. Cattle-ranching could be highly profitable on the grasslands of the rich plains. Those who succeeded became great landowners, living in comfortable *ranchos* (upper right). In time the booming cotton frontier was perhaps an even more assured way to quick wealth.

Austin's little colony prospered. The Mexicans were encouraged to invite other Americans to become land agents or *empresarios*, who received large grants of land and were responsible for colonizing them. By 1830 Texas presented a strange picture. Its Spanish-speaking settlers had given it a Hispanic flavor, as the costume of the Mexican cowboy at the lower right shows. But some 20,000 American "immigrants" made Texas a typical southwestern frontier, full of land speculators and pioneers with ambitious plans.

Could the Mexicans govern these hardy, adventurous, aggressive newcomers? It seemed so at first. One Texan wrote to a friend, praising the liberty which the Mexican constitution of 1824 promised them. But trouble was brewing.

Texans Fight at the Alamo

At heart the American settlers did not think of themselves as bound by Mexican laws. For example,

Right: This impressive home belonged to the owner of a large ranch in Mexico. Below: A cowboy throws a young bull during a roundup in Mexico.

KENNEDY GALLERIES

SOUTHWEST MUSEUM OF LOS ANGELES, CARL DENTZEL COLLECTION

285

COLLECTION OF MRS. BILL ARTHUR AND MRS. AL WARNER, DALLAS

Defending the Alamo, Davy Crockett clubs Mexicans with his rifle.

although most of them were Protestants, they were supposed to adopt the Catholic faith. Few of them did. As one Texan wrote, "There is no such thing as attending church, since no religion except the Roman Catholic is tolerated, and we have no priests among us." Although Mexico outlawed slavery, under pressure from American settlers, it was allowed to exist in Texas.

Even though Austin sincerely urged all Texans to respect Mexican laws, few had much respect for the government in Mexico City. They thought Mexico was inexperienced in self-government. Only its generals and rich men had much power, and they were jealous of each other. Revolutions brought frequent changes of rulers, leading the Texans to the harsh judgment expressed by one of them in a letter: "The Mexicans are never long at peace with each other; ignorant and degraded as many of them are, they are not capable of ruling, nor yet of being ruled."

MUSEO DE HISTORIA, CHAPULTEPEC

The First Company of New Orleans Volunteers carried this flag at the Alamo. Now torn and faded, it is the only surviving flag of the Alamo's defenders. In the center was an eagle and the inscription "God and Liberty."

In 1833 the Texas settlers asked for a constitutional change to give their province more **autonomy** (right of self-government). The Mexicans did not like this any better than the American government would have liked a request by some states of the Union to go back to the Articles of Confederation. They refused. In 1835 the Mexican president, Antonio de Santa Anna, withdrew many of the rights Texans enjoyed and sent troops to frighten them. The struggle had now grown to the point where fighting broke out. In October of 1835 the Texans and Mexican troops clashed.

A convention of settlers was scheduled to meet on March 1, 1836. Five days earlier Santa Anna, marching into Texas with about 6,000 troops, surrounded some 187 Americans in the Alamo, a former mission in San Antonio. On March 2 Texas declared itself independent. On March 6 the Mexicans blasted their way through the Alamo's walls (left) and killed every one of the overwhelmed, but still battling, defenders, including Jim Bowie, Davy Crockett, and the commanding officer, Colonel William Travis. The Texans now had a battle cry in their struggle for independence—"Remember the Alamo!"

Texas Wins Its Independence

By 1835 many American volunteers had come to Texas to help the settlers fight Mexico. One of them, Sam Houston, was to become the George Washington of Texas. He was an unusual American. As a young

man he entered the army and fought against the Creek Indians under Andrew Jackson. Like his good friend Jackson, he settled in Tennessee. There, he became a landowner, a congressman, and finally the governor. But, unlike Jackson, Houston was not an Indian hater. In 1829, after suddenly resigning his office for mysterious personal reasons, he went to live among the Cherokees, and was actually adopted into the tribe.

In 1835 Houston arrived in Texas. Because of his military experience, he was given command of its tiny army. After the Alamo fell—and he had been against making a stand there—he took a position on the western bank of the San Jacinto River, near Galveston Bay, in April 1836. The pursuing Mexicans were overconfident, and encamped without proper guards. Like the Hessians at Trenton, they were astonished when their "beaten" foes suddenly attacked them, shouting like demons and shooting cannon loaded with bits of broken horseshoes—the only ammunition they had. In a few hours it was all over. Though wounded, Houston personally took Santa Anna's surrender (right).

The Mexican government did not officially recognize Texas' independence, but after the Battle of San Jacinto, it gave up any serious efforts to reconquer its lost province. For nine years Texas was an independent nation under a new flag with a single star. The "Lone Star Republic" received diplomatic recognition from the United States, France, and England. Thousands of new settlers from the United States helped to swell the prosperity of growing little towns like Austin, the nation's capital (lower right). Here, merchants trading in cotton and cattle began to develop those urban institutions that in time would give the southwestern frontier its own thriving cities.

Despite the new nation's successful start, Sam Houston, the Republic's first president, wanted and expected a union with the United States. But until 1845 American political problems delayed the marriage of the two republics.

Questions for Discussion

1. What were the natural resources which attracted the first American settlers to Texas?
2. Why did Texans begin to demand more autonomy?
3. Compare Sam Houston and George Washington.
4. How did American settlement in Texas promote the development of urban centers?

STATE CAPITOL, AUSTIN, TEXAS

LIBRARY OF CONGRESS

Above: After the Battle of San Jacinto in April 1836, Sam Houston, lying wounded, accepts the surrender of Santa Anna. The Mexican commander also signed a treaty with Houston recognizing the Republic of Texas. Although the Mexican government rejected the treaty, Texas functioned as an independent nation for nine years. Left: Austin, seen here as it appeared in 1840, served as the capital of Texas.

War with Mexico

In 1844 the feelings of expansionists began to be expressed in politics. So did another kind of feeling. A growing number of Americans were opposed to the further spread of slavery. When it came to the Texas question, antislavery and expansionist attitudes clashed. **Annexing** that "nation" would add a huge new slave state to the Union—perhaps more if Texas chose to be cut up into several states. Some antislavery leaders even charged that in 1835 President Andrew Jackson, a Southerner and a slaveholder, had encouraged Southerner Sam Houston to revolt, steal Texas from Mexico, and then bring Texas into the United States as a slave state.

The 1844 Presidential election offered a test of public opinion on the matter. By 1844 the old Federalist and Republican parties had disappeared. The two major parties were now the Whigs and the Democrats. The most likely candidates were Henry Clay (right) of Kentucky for the Whigs and New York's Martin Van Buren for the Democrats. Both were eager to avoid battles over slavery which would tend to split the nation. So both opposed annexing Texas.

The result was dramatic. The nominating convention of Van Buren's own party refused to select him. Instead, it chose James K. Polk (far left), a determined expansionist, who favored taking Texas. He also wanted the United States to get California and to take over the rich Oregon country.

In the election itself patriotic feelings ran high. Polk won in a close vote over Clay. He believed, rightly, that his victory at the polls meant that the nation supported his views on expansion. But public opinion in a democracy is not always entirely clear. Was the vote for Polk a vote for more slave territory? Did Americans want new lands without caring much whether acquiring such lands would complicate the slavery question? Americans were for expansion, but were they neutral, or even opposed, to slavery?

Polk Settles the Oregon Question

Actually, Polk's earliest expansionist move, which concerned Oregon, did not affect slave territory at all. In 1845 he announced to Great Britain that the United States would not renew the joint occupation agreement of 1818. This might mean that the United States would insist on taking all of Oregon. At that time Oregon's boundaries ran from the 42nd parallel

This 1844 Democratic Party banner shows candidates Polk and Dallas.

290

of latitude, the northern boundary of California, to beyond the 54th parallel, along the southern tip of Alaska. Oregon then extended from the Rockies to the Pacific Ocean. While the British thought the situation over, Polk let it be known that he would compromise on a boundary at the 49th parallel. That would give the United States the area already settled by several thousand American families. Since the British knew that they could hardly defend far-away Oregon in a war with these Yankees, they quickly took this way out. By June of 1846 Polk had bluffed his way into getting Oregon without a fight.

Polk Reaches for California

Polk meanwhile was making a bid for California. First, he sent an agent to offer to buy the province, but the Mexicans refused even to listen to what they believed was an insulting offer to trade their soil for money. Polk then sent John C. Frémont and a party of explorers to California. Frémont later claimed that he had secret orders from Polk to aid Americans there should they decide to rebel, as the Texans had done.

But it took events in Texas to give the United States a chance to take California by force. In March of 1845, even before Polk's inauguration, Congress voted to annex the Republic of Texas and make it the Lone Star State. Mexico believed this to be a hostile act. In addition, Mexico argued that Texas was smaller than the Americans claimed and that its southern boundary was not the Rio Grande River, but the Nueces River farther north.

War with Mexico Begins

In answer, Polk ordered United States troops in Texas to advance as far as the Rio Grande and seize the disputed region. On April 25, 1846, Mexican soldiers and a party of American cavalrymen clashed. Several Americans were killed. When this news reached Washington, it gave Polk an excuse for a fight. War "exists by the act of Mexico," he told Congress. Congress promptly declared war. Now Manifest Destiny marched in uniform, with bugles blowing.

War with Mexico—The First Phase

The Mexican War was a strange conflict. It was the nation's first war fought entirely on foreign soil. Its prizes were territories that were hundreds of miles

This Whig Party banner of 1844 features candidate Henry Clay.

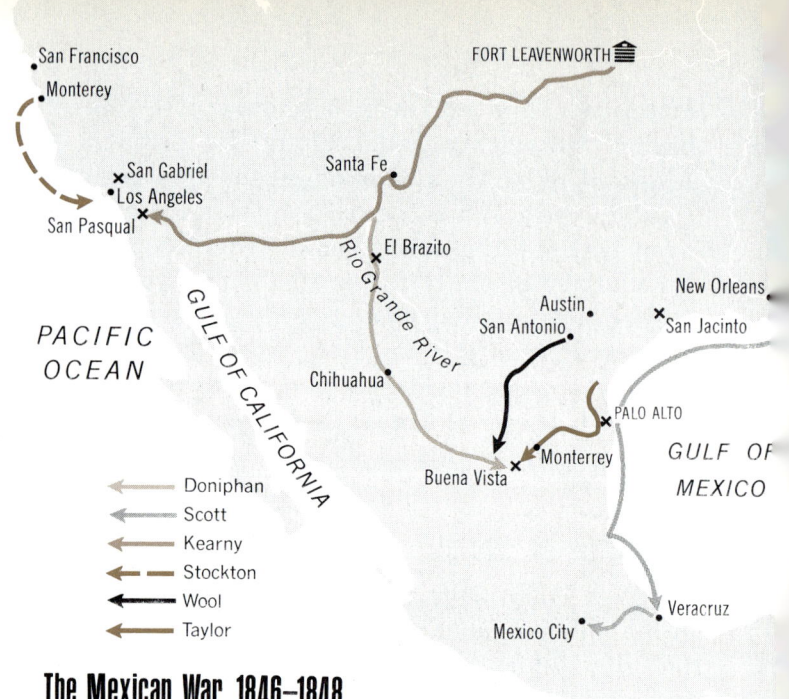

The Mexican War 1846–1848

FRANKLIN D. ROOSEVELT LIBRARY

292

away from settled America. To capture them whole armies would have to move over empty country where even mountain men had sometimes gone hungry. It would be like fighting in the Arctic today—without cargo planes to help. The tiny American army of 1846 had to enroll thousands of untrained volunteers and depend on them to do these challenging tasks.

Yet these things were actually accomplished. The first planned step of the war would be the occupation of northern Mexico. General Zachary Taylor (right) was chosen to lead a force westward from the Rio Grande. Known to his men as "Old Rough and Ready," Taylor was a veteran of frontier service. He usually wore an unkempt uniform and a straw hat and slouched in the saddle on his horse, "Old Whitey." But there was nothing slovenly about the way his soldiers fought. In May of 1846 they met the Mexicans in two sharp fights at Palo Alto and Resaca de la Palma (map, upper left). In both battles American sharpshooting skill and use of artillery proved too much for the Mexicans. Taylor pushed onward, occupied Monterrey, and then Saltillo. By the end of 1846 his force was deep in Mexico.

Meanwhile, an expedition of some 1,600 men, under General Stephen W. Kearny, left Fort Leavenworth, Kansas, bound west. Day after day, they rolled through the Southwest, battling thirst, heat, and dust, and keeping their eyes open for hostile Indians and Mexican armies. In six weeks Kearny reached Santa Fe, where the Mexicans surrendered without a fight. Then he pushed on to the Pacific, where he overcame the Mexican forces at San Pasqual in southern California (lower left). By January of 1847 his forces were in command of Los Angeles. Together with Marines and soldiers led by Commodore Robert Stockton and by Frémont, they won control of California for the United States.

Above: General Zachary Taylor was first mentioned as a Presidential candidate after he won a number of battles early in the Mexican War. Left: On December 6, 1846, troops led by General Stephen W. Kearny defeated a larger force of Californians at San Pasqual, near San Diego.

In February of 1847 the Mexicans tried to turn the tide with a furious attack on Taylor's outnumbered forces at Buena Vista. But on Washington's Birthday the Americans beat them off in a bloody engagement. The war's opening phase was now over.

War with Mexico—The Second Phase

The second part of the war was a six-month campaign, in 1847, to force Mexico to sue for peace by capturing Mexico City, its capital. Only with Ameri-

cans in "the halls of Montezuma" would the Mexicans sign a treaty formally giving up the provinces which they had lost to the United States army. General Winfield Scott, an able but vain officer nicknamed "Old Fuss and Feathers," commanded this operation. "Old Rough and Ready" General Taylor was ordered to stay on the defensive while Scott won this final glory. Both generals were Whigs, and President Polk did not want either one to shine too brightly in contrast to the Democrats. It was a lost cause, however. Both did run for the Presidency as Whigs, Taylor winning in 1848 and Scott losing four years later.

With about 10,000 men Scott sailed south to Veracruz on the Gulf of Mexico. By the end of March 1847, his troops had taken the city. Now, step by step, they began to march inland on a long, upward climb. The little army included many young officers trained at West Point, the national military academy. They were proving the value of their training and getting experience that they would use on both sides in the Civil War a few years later. Among them were Ulysses S. Grant and Robert E. Lee. Mile after mile, they and their regiments of American farm boys marched and prodded horses and mules over the twisting mountain roads to conquer lands once known to Cortés' Spaniards.

In September they reached Mexico City. The Mexicans fought back gallantly. The savagery of the final battles is shown in the picture at the right. It depicts the successful storming of Chapultepec, a key defensive point, on September 13. One week later the Stars and Stripes flew over Mexico City. Santa Anna gathered his forces for one last attack, only to be finally defeated in October. Both sides now waited for the negotiations that would end the war.

At home the war had been bitterly opposed. An Ohio congressman had said that, if he were a Mexican, he would welcome the Americans "with bloody hands to hospitable graves," meaning he would happily kill the invaders and then bury them. An Illinois congressman named Abraham Lincoln called, unsuccessfully, for an investigation to see if President Polk had lied about the Mexican attack of April 1846 that started the fighting.

The Treaty of Guadalupe Hidalgo

The Treaty of Guadalupe Hidalgo, signed in February of 1848, was a triumph for the United States. It gave the nation the Mexican provinces of Upper Cali-

NEW-YORK HISTORICAL SOCIETY

Americans storm Chapultepec Castle, bravely defended by young cadets.

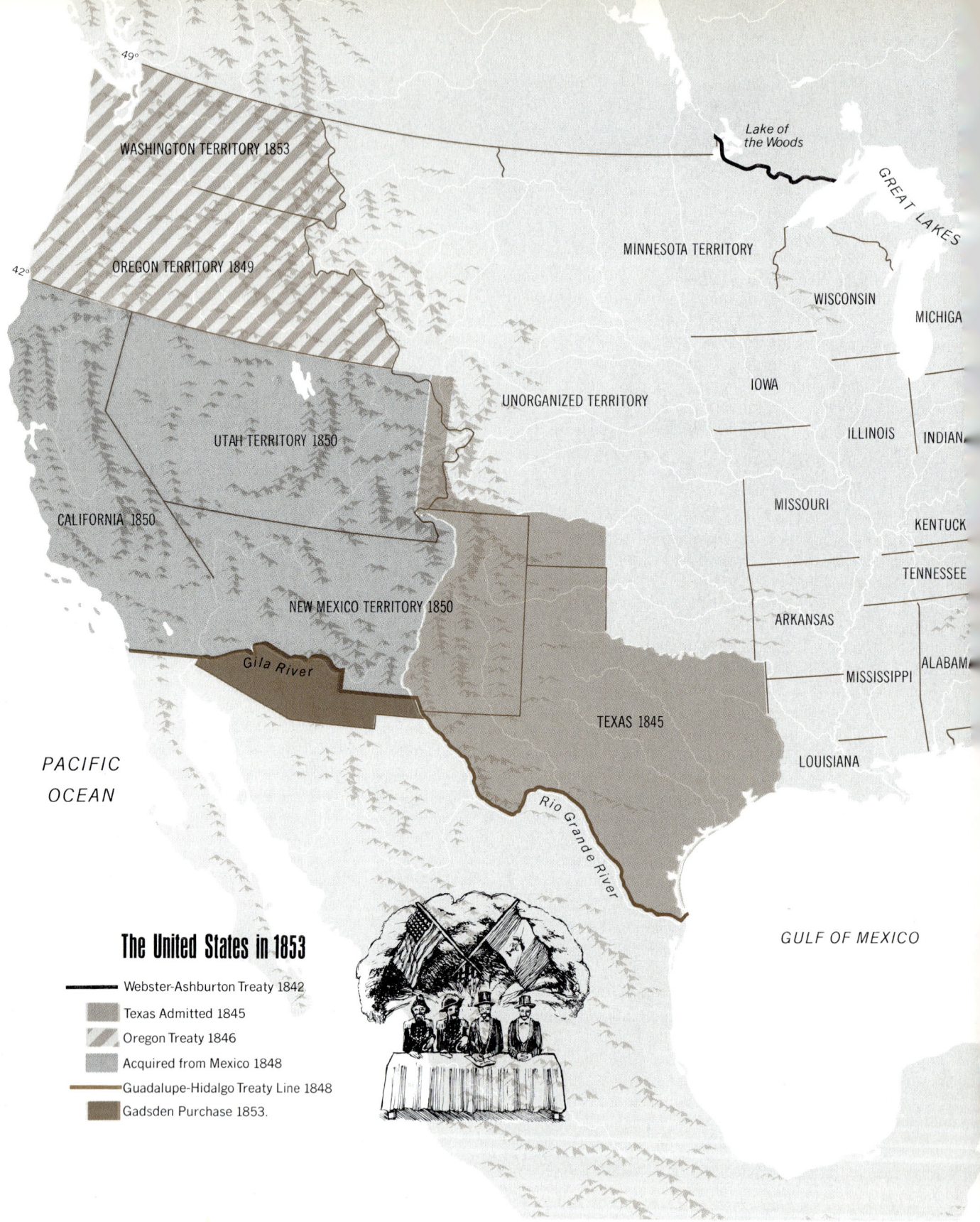

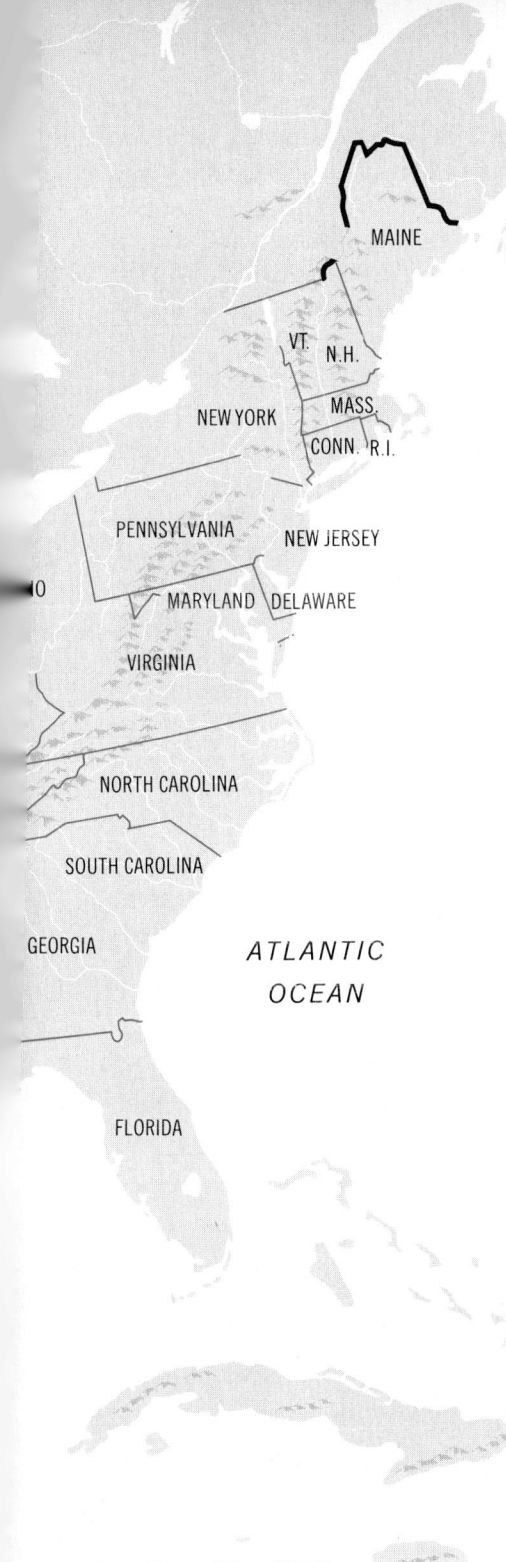

fornia and New Mexico, as the map at left shows. These embraced four future southwestern states. For these lands the United States paid Mexico $15 million. To this day some Americans consider this payment to be "conscience money" for a bad deed. Others believed such expansion was both right and part of the nation's Manifest Destiny.

By taking the Oregon Territory and California, and by clearing up the dispute over Texas by war, the incredible Polk gained vast parts of the West in his one term of office. Only a little territory remained to be added. In 1853 the government was planning to build one or more railroads to the Pacific. One possible route was along the south bank of the Gila River, the boundary set by the 1848 treaty. James Gadsden was sent to Mexico to purchase the little strip that bears his name, for another $10 million. The Gadsden Purchase completed United States expansion into North American territory that was contiguous—that is, touching its existing boundaries. The next steps of expansion would lead into the Pacific Ocean and the Caribbean Sea.

Only 60 years separated the ratification of the Constitution from the Treaty of Guadalupe Hidalgo. Most Americans thought that this speedy expansion was a sign of God's pleasure with the United States. They were given further reasons for this view by an amazing coincidence. Nine days before the treaty was signed, gold was discovered in California's American River valley.

This meant that California and some parts of the other newly won territories would be settled almost overnight. Soon gold-hungry pioneers swarmed westward in droves. As a result, many problems, especially the future of slavery, had to be faced before the country had much time to think about them. Such sudden growth was exciting, but it also proved deeply upsetting.

Questions for Discussion

1. Why was the annexation of Texas a controversial national issue?
2. How did President Polk get Oregon without causing a war with Great Britain?
3. How did events in Texas give the United States a chance to take California by force?
4. Why was there opposition in the United States to the Mexican War?

The Fulfillment of Manifest Destiny

It was James Marshall, an American, who on January 24, 1848, discovered bright nuggets of gold at the bottom of a California stream and thereby changed the history of the West. At the time he was building a sawmill for John A. Sutter. A Swiss citizen, Sutter was an immigrant to California. His ranch, in modern Sacramento, was a welcome resting place for American overland travelers arriving in California after six hard months on the trail. Although Marshall and Sutter both tried to keep the news of the gold-strike secret, it rapidly leaked out to the world. By December of 1848 President Polk was mentioning California gold discoveries in his annual message to Congress. As 1849 dawned men began to pour into the region. In that year alone perhaps 40,000 arrived. Gold was as great a magnet to them as it had been to the Spaniards three centuries earlier. It seemed as if Coronado's fabled cities had been found at last.

What made the gold fields especially enticing was that many people believed it took little organized effort or capital to become rich. The basic tool could be as simple as a washbasin. The individual prospector, like the one shown at left, scooped up some earth, poured water over it, and sloshed it around to wash dissolved soil away from the heavy particles of gold, which sank to the bottom. Soon men began to use the same method on a larger scale by shoveling earth into wooden boxes (right). This washing, or placer mining process, could make a man rich very quickly, even when he started empty-handed. Many Americans came to believe that it was the Manifest Destiny of the United States to shower wealth on its citizens.

From every American county and from many foreign lands, men flocked to California. Soon ships lay deserted and rotting in San Francisco Bay as their crews fled into the hills to hunt for gold. The gold seekers gathered in camps where, like the frontiersmen before them, they set up informal governments which made their own rules. Among the rules were strict provisions for honoring a man's claim to exclusive mining rights on a piece of gold-bearing ground that he found first. Yet no one ever honored poor John Sutter's claim. The camps dealt out quick, harsh punishments, including **lynching** (executing without a trial). Government by **vigilantes** (unofficial policemen who also often act as self-appointed judges and jurors) was a part of the gold-rush experience.

The lone prospector above and the men at the right are hoping to find gold loosely mixed with the sand and gravel at the bottom of a California stream.

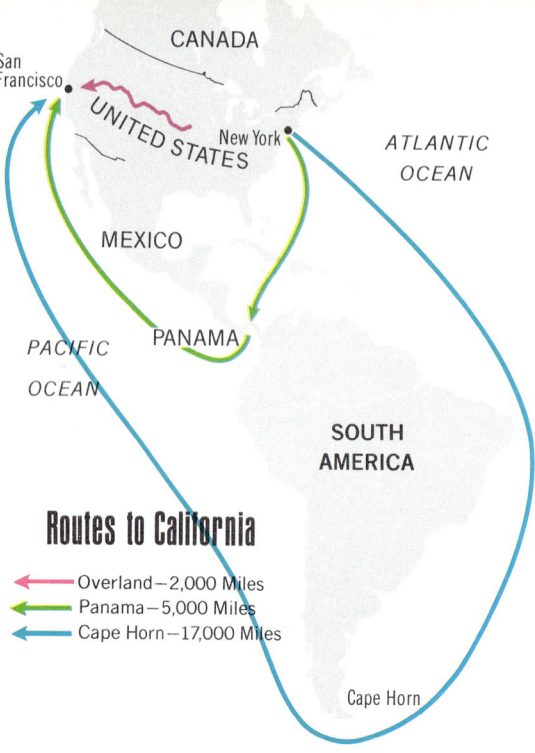

CANADA
San Francisco
UNITED STATES
New York
ATLANTIC OCEAN
MEXICO
PANAMA
PACIFIC OCEAN
SOUTH AMERICA
Cape Horn
Routes to California
Overland—2,000 Miles
Panama—5,000 Miles
Cape Horn—17,000 Miles

Right: Advertisements like this one were common at the height of the clipper-ship boom in the 1850's. Below: The storm-tossed clipper ship in this painting is probably the Young America.

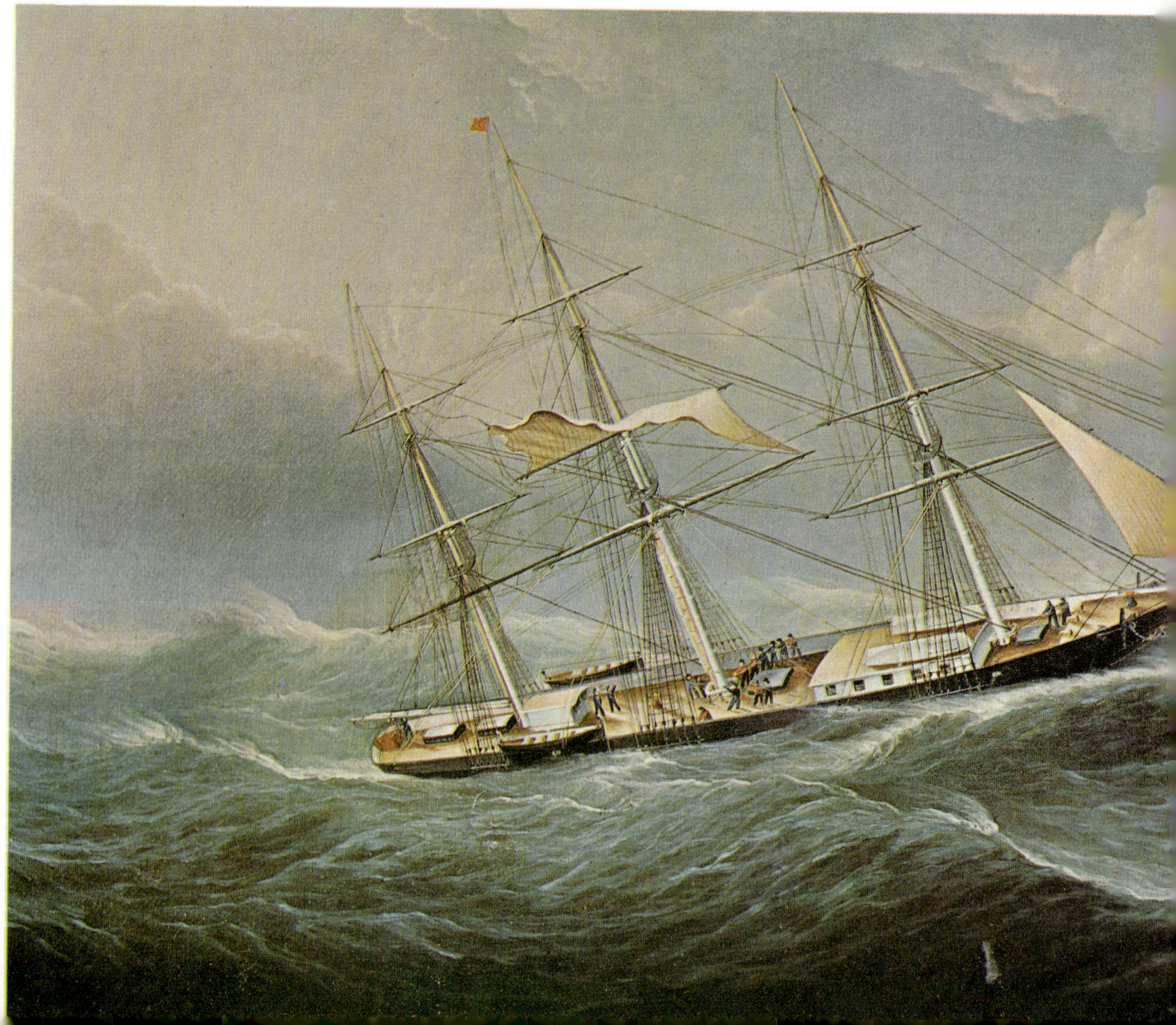

MARINE HISTORICAL ASSOCIATION, MYSTIC

The Great Days of the Clipper Ship

The gold rush had some other economic results besides adding millions to the nation's wealth. It helped to stimulate the growth of the American shipping industry and American business involvement in Central America.

The map at left shows three ways of reaching California. The most popular one was the rugged, six-month overland trip. A second way was to take a fast clipper ship (lower left) around South America's lower tip, storm-swept Cape Horn. That 17,000-mile adventure took 5 to 8 months, though the record-setting *Flying Cloud* did it in 89 days. In 1849 over 700 ships left East Coast ports for California.

The high fares and freight rates of the California run encouraged American shipbuilders to turn out more of the swift, beautiful greyhounds of the sea. These vessels made Americans challengers of the British and other maritime nations on the world's sea lanes. Many of these clippers, originally built for the California trade, went to China for cargoes of tea and silk and to Australia for wheat and gold. So the American presence in the Pacific was strengthened. Maritime expansion went hand in hand with continental growth.

A third route to California was by sea to Nicaragua or Panama. There, travelers took canoes, mules, and sometimes lake and river steamboats, through the Central American jungles, to the Pacific. Then they went north by sea once more. By 1850 this expensive trip was only six to eight weeks long but, like the overland route, full of dangers from fever, bandits, snakes, and insects.

Enough Americans took it, however, to make it profitable for New York businessmen like Cornelius Vanderbilt to set up companies that arranged the entire trip. American dollars, machinery, and engineers began to reach this little-known region of Central America. The United States government became involved as well. Once the nation had an Atlantic and a Pacific coastline, it was clear that the American navy would have to be able to move quickly from one to the other. The likeliest way was by a canal across some part of Central America. In 1850 the United States signed the Clayton-Bulwer Treaty with Great Britain, whose powerful navy made it mistress of the seas. Each nation agreed not to build or fortify such a canal without the consent of the other.

301

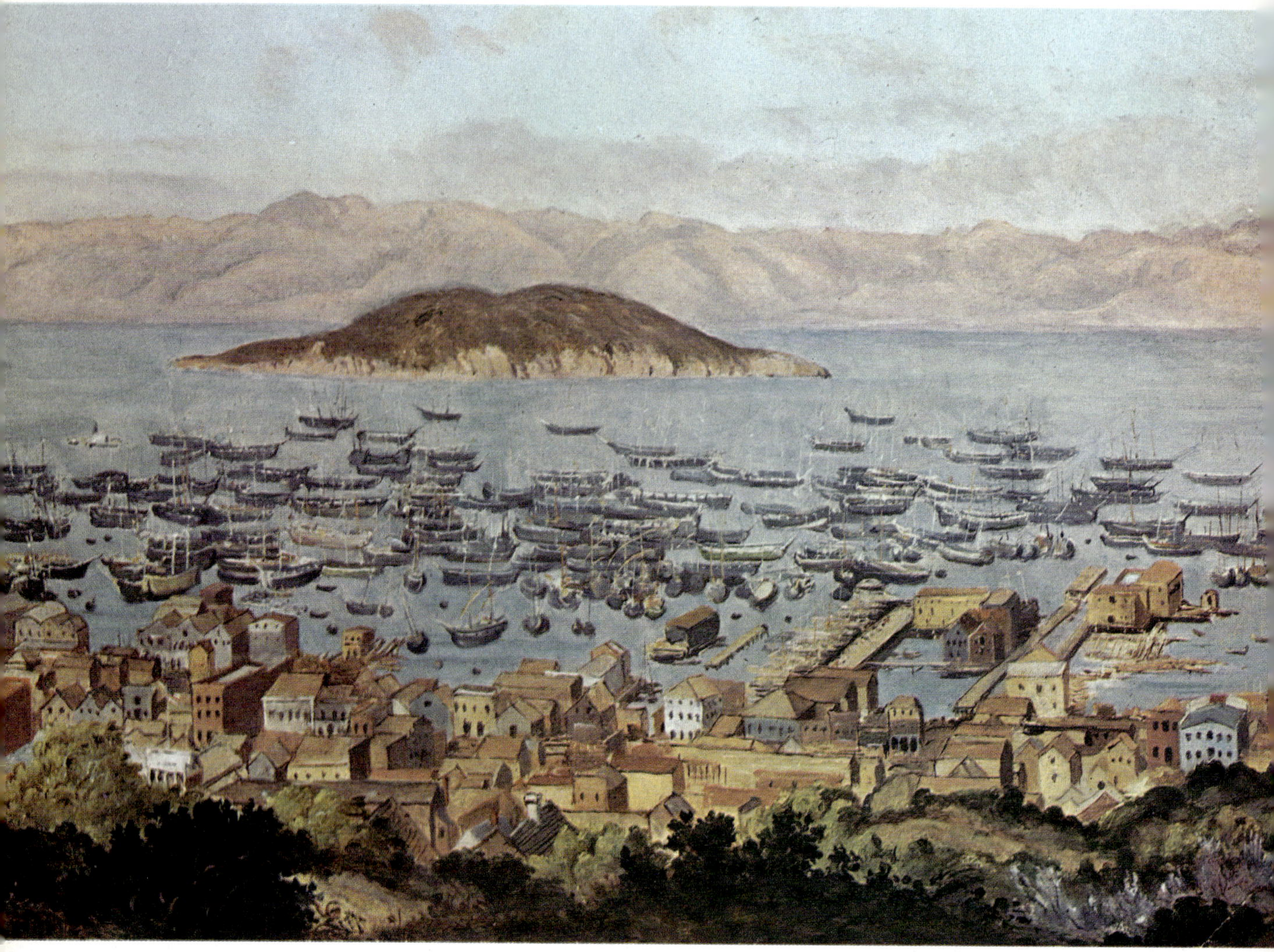

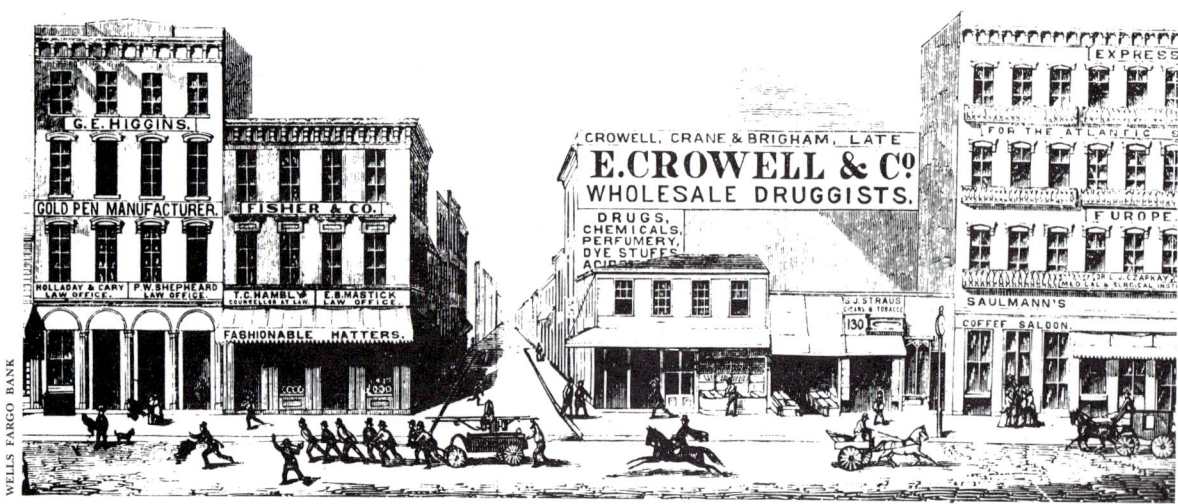

MRS. CELIA TOBIN CLARK, SAN MATEO

In the 1850's San Francisco's harbor (above) and Montgomery Street (below) bustled with activity.

WELLS FARGO BANK

San Francisco—Center of the Booming West

Expansion, then, seemed to mean that the United States government would support the efforts of American pioneers wherever they went. It also meant that American businessmen found new opportunities. The growth of San Francisco illustrates how new opportunities stimulated rapid urban growth in the Far West.

Not all of California's wealth was dug from the earth by prospectors and miners. The sudden rise of San Francisco's population created new problems. Thousands of newcomers needed food and shelter. Banks and express companies were needed to keep and move the gold. Warehouses had to be built to store cargoes for ships. Some pioneers discovered that selling tools, groceries, and liquor to the miners at high prices was more profitable and less dangerous than prospecting. They could charge such high prices at first because goods were extremely scarce. The profits these businessmen made were then reinvested in still larger businesses.

This rapid growth also increased the variety of occupations needed to keep the community running. The pictures at left illustrate this change. The ships crowding the harbor made opportunities of many kinds. Merchants thrived by selling the ships' cargoes. Lawyers prospered by arranging contracts for sales and new businesses. Shopkeepers made money selling shoes, clothing, and medicines to sailors and arriving prospectors, weary after months at sea. As the drawings at the left and the right show, by 1858 San Francisco was a growing center of commerce and trade.

The wealth from the gold fields found its way not only into the pockets of San Franciscans, but also into homes, schools, and churches. Some of it was turned into stocks and bonds—representing shares in new mines, railroads to the East, shipping lines, and factories. Such rapid economic growth meant that mining camps soon gave way to a modern state, with cities. These cities offered more of the comforts of life and a more complicated pattern of living. Thus the gold rush, once again like other frontiers, was one of the forces creating urban America.

The era of Manifest Destiny closed in a frenzy of business activity. "Hurry, work, sweat, run" seemed the national motto. In time Americans even came to believe that the man who got rich was helping his country as much as the soldier or explorer.

This 1858 drawing shows the New World Market in San Francisco.

Chapter Review

Questions for Discussion

1. Why did so many Americans believe that the gold fields of California offered a quick and easy way to become wealthy?
2. What were the effects of the gold rush on the United States?
3. Why did maritime expansion and westward expansion occur at the same time?
4. What was the reason for the early interest of the United States in Nicaragua and the Isthmus of Panama as routes for a canal connecting the Atlantic and Pacific?
5. What was the main provision of the Clayton-Bulwer Treaty? Why was Great Britain the other party to the treaty?
6. How did the discovery of gold influence the growth of urban areas such as San Francisco?

Social Studies Terms

Manifest Destiny, autonomy, annexing, lynching, vigilantes

Summary Questions for Discussion

1. Why were Westerners, who seemed to have plenty of land around them for settlement, very often the most enthusiastic expansionists?
2. What role did capitalism play in the early settlement of the West?
3. How was the Texans' demand for autonomy a continuation of an American tradition that had begun long before? Cite examples.
4. How was the United States able to benefit from political troubles in Mexico?
5. What gave many Americans confidence in the "rightness" of Manifest Destiny?
6. What conflict in values caused the delay over the annexation of Texas?
7. After the Gadsden Purchase why did American settlement not expand farther—into Canada or present-day northern Mexico?
8. Why does a shortage of goods drive prices up? Does a surplus of goods have the opposite effect? Why? Make a generalization about the relationship between prices and supply of goods. Illustrate it with examples from your own experience.
9. Is "vigilante justice" really justice? What is the danger of this form of justice?

10. When groups of citizens in the West "took the law into their own hands," what value were they placing ahead of strict obedience to the law?

Map Study

Study the map, *The United States in 1853,* on pages 296 and 297 and then answer these questions:
1. Why were territories organized in the Far West before they were organized in the Midwest? What were the obstacles to settlement in the area labeled "Unorganized Territory?"
2. What states were eventually formed from the land acquired from Mexico as a result of the Mexican War? What states were formed from Washington and Oregon Territories?
3. Why was the Gadsden Purchase made?

For Further Reading

Clipper Ships and Captains, by Jane D. Lyon. New York: American Heritage Publishing Co., Inc., 1962.

Donald Mackay and the Clipper Ships, by Mary Ellen Chase. Boston: Houghton Mifflin Company, 1959.

James Knox Polk, by Edwin P. Hoyt. Chicago: Reilly & Lee Books, 1965.

Texas and the War with Mexico, by Fairfax Downey. New York: American Heritage Publishing Co., Inc., 1961.

The California Gold Rush, by Ralph K. Andrist. New York: American Heritage Publishing Co., Inc., 1961.

The Story of the Mexican War, by Red Reeder. New York: Meredith Press, 1967.

The Sweep Westward, by Margaret L. Coit. New York: Time, Inc., 1963.

The War with Mexico, by Irving Werstein. New York: W. W. Norton & Company, Inc., 1965.

Westward on the Oregon Trail, by Marian T. Place. New York: American Heritage Publishing Co., Inc., 1962.

11
The Beginnings of Industrial America

Part of Mark Twain's novel *Huckleberry Finn* tells of how Huck and Jim, a runaway slave, float down the Mississippi on a raft, searching for freedom. The time is the 1840's. One very dark night they hear the pounding of a steamboat engine. At first the steamboat looks like "a black cloud with rows of glow-worms around it," but then "all of a sudden," says Huck, "she bulged out, big and scary, with a long row of wide-open furnace doors shining like red-hot teeth and her monstrous bows and guards hanging right over us." As one historian has noted, the age of steam-powered machines burst upon the United States like that steamboat: suddenly, powerfully, and sometimes destructively.

By 1800 technology had begun to change American life. The cotton gin, created in 1793, furnished a model of how one invention could change the life of a whole region. It strengthened slavery, increased the pressure to move the Indians westward, and quickly brought new southern states into the Union. After 1800 a whole group of inventions began to redirect the energies of the entire country.

Steam power, which had first been developed for industrial purposes in England in the late 1700's, was applied to transportation. It soon began to conquer the problems of long-distance travel in the rugged interior of the continent. Steamboats (left) and locomotives helped to build an American nation in which Texas Rangers mowed down Indians with Connecticut-made revolvers, and the bacon on a New Yorker's table came all the way from Cincinnati.

In addition, other steam-powered machines began to turn out huge quantities of goods and to pit new classes of people against each other. The capitalists who owned these machines and the laborers who worked them had neither past experience nor clear rules to guide them in getting along with each other.

In countless ways the machine age began to pose problems for Americans, even as it was creating abundance never before seen in the history of the world.

As you read, think about these questions:
1. How did changes in transportation affect the settlement of the West and the development of the West's resources?
2. How might a worker benefit by a change from handwork to factory work? What might he lose?
3. Why does the introduction of industry in an agricultural economy bring major changes?

Steamboats belching smoke crowd a New Orleans levee in 1853.

Right: The toughest engineering problem on the Erie Canal was how to get the canal over a rocky cliff at present-day Lockport. A double set of 5 locks solved the problem. Each one was cut out of solid rock and had a lift of 12 feet. At one point the horse and driver were 60 feet above the bottom lock. Below: As soon as the Erie Canal opened, it was jammed with traffic. Some families spent their entire lives on the canal in boats that were little more than shanties on a raft. When tolls were abolished in 1882, the canal had more than paid for itself. Today part of the New York State Barge Canal System follows the original Erie Canal route.

CANAL MUSEUM, SYRACUSE

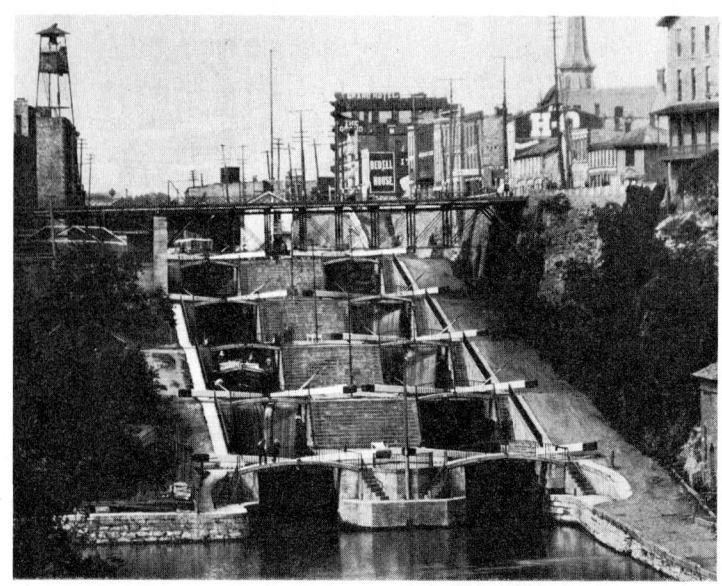

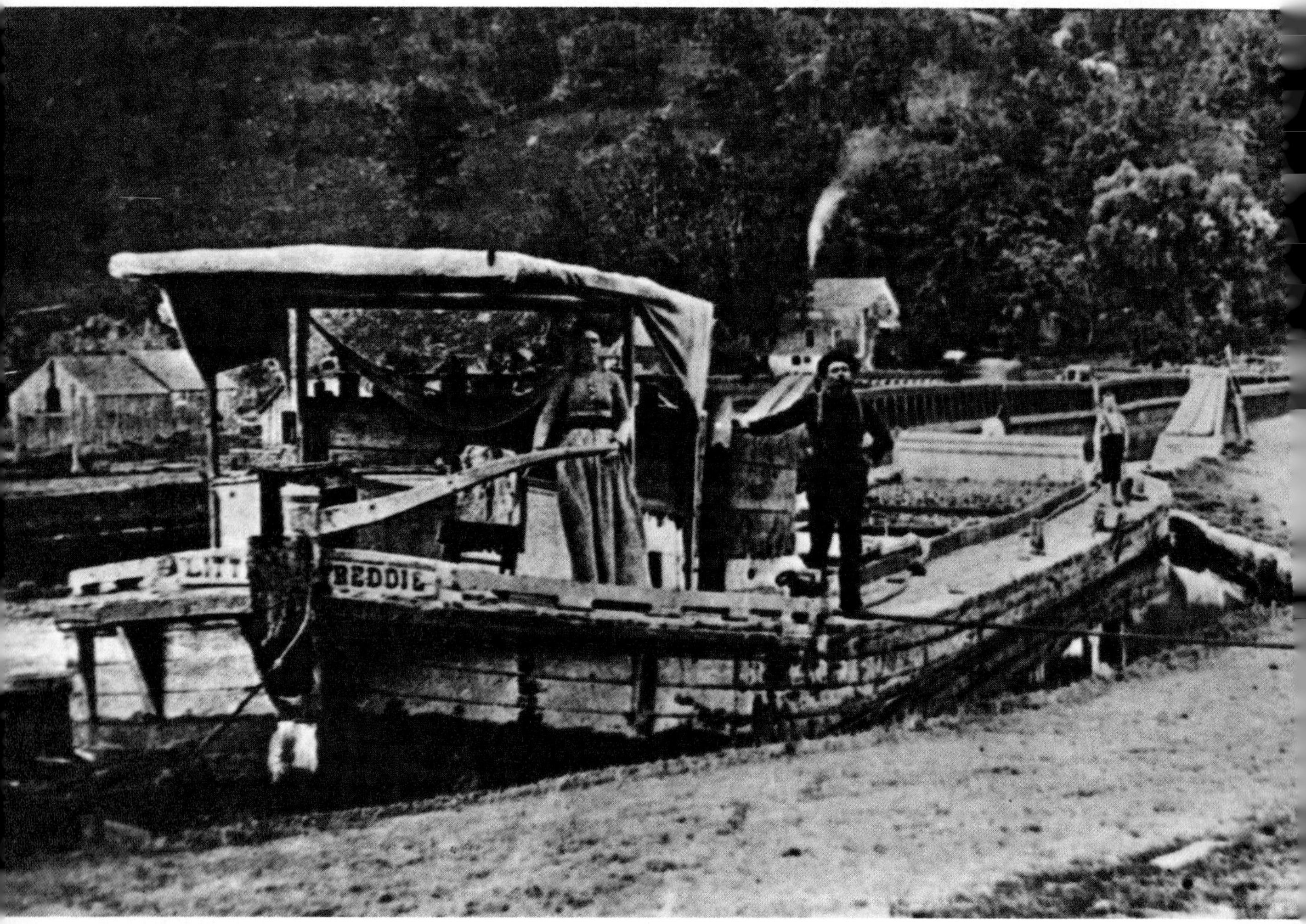

An Expanding Transportation System

The coming of the canal was the first major step in the development of a national transportation system. A canal is nothing more than a man-made ditch, full of water, connecting two bodies of water. It looks unexciting, but that is its great advantage. It has no storms like the sea, no rapids like a river, and no rocks, potholes, sharp turns, and steep hills like a road. In the nineteenth century patient horses or mules could tow a clumsy-looking, heavily loaded towboat at a steady five miles an hour for hundreds of miles without danger or great expense (lower left).

A few canals were built in the United States as early as the 1790's. But in 1817 work was begun on the best-known of them all, New York's Erie Canal. It was built to connect the Hudson River at Albany with Lake Erie at Buffalo. Such a canal would provide a water "highway" through the mountain barrier between East and West.

The father of the Erie Canal was De Witt Clinton, the governor of New York State. Clinton was an early booster, or a vigorous promoter, of the existing glories and future greatness of his state. He tirelessly tried to influence lawmakers, a process known as **lobbying**, to vote money for building the canal. His opponents scoffed at "Clinton's Ditch" as an impractical idea. It would have to run for more than 350 miles through country which was still mostly wilderness. Opponents claimed that the cost of construction would be huge and that the canal would never earn much in return. But Clinton fought hard for his project and won public opinion to his side. New York State then gave Clinton the money he needed.

The canal took eight years to build. Hundreds of men felled trees, hauled away stumps, and blasted through solid rock to build the canal and its towpath and bridges. Locks (upper left) were constructed to raise and lower boats over steep hills. Many laborers, including a large number of Irish immigrants, died from disease and accidents on the job. But in October 1825 a triumphant Clinton boarded a canal boat at Buffalo. He cruised down to New York City where he poured a barrel of Lake Erie water into the ocean. The Great Lakes and the Atlantic were now joined. Thousands of families took this safe water route westward to new homes. And millions of tons of freight moved along the Erie. So much money came pouring in from tolls that a canal-building boom swept the country.

The Steamboat and the River Town

Many men had thought about using steam to propel vessels from the time that workable, movable steam engines first appeared. Yet an invention can only succeed when the time for it is ripe. In 1787 a forgotten American named John Fitch built an awkward-looking steamboat and ran it on the Delaware River. But Fitch could not find the other men whose talents he needed. These included engineers to help him build more and better boats, promoters to interest people in their use, investors to put up money and organize steamboat lines, and politicians who would get state governments to help. Lacking these supporters, Fitch eventually had to give up the idea of being a steamboat operator.

By 1807 things had changed. A New York businessman and political leader, Robert Livingston, believed that a steamboat line on the Hudson River would prove profitable. He turned to his friend Robert Fulton to build a vessel for him. Like his fellow Pennsylvanian, Benjamin Franklin, Fulton was an all-around inventor who had even built a submarine with a crude periscope (far right). Fulton designed a small ship called the *Clermont* (lower right). In 1807 it thrashed from New York upriver to Albany, then back to New York, at a speed of five miles an hour.

Businessmen were now ready to take advantage of a boat that traveled upstream independently of wind conditions. Livingston and Fulton created a corporation to run steamboats on the Hudson and got the state of New York to grant them a **monopoly** (the exclusive right to sell a product or run a particular business). Soon Livingston and Fulton were prospering.

Livingston and Fulton also encouraged an engineer named Nicholas Roosevelt to build a steamboat at Pittsburgh, which, in 1811, traveled down to New Orleans. By the 1830's hundreds of riverboats were cruising the Ohio and Mississippi and their tributaries. Their decks were packed with barrels of pork, bales of cotton, crates of liquor, textiles, machinery, and other items of commerce, as well as with passengers. River cities like Pittsburgh, Cincinnati, Louisville, St. Louis, and New Orleans began to grow and prosper. Trade made river towns like Cincinnati (upper right) into thriving cities just as surely as ocean trade had enriched colonial Boston. Cincinnati soon became known as the "Queen of the West."

Above right: Robert Fulton drew this self-portrait on his plans for the Nautilus, *a submarine he designed for the French in 1801. When completed the submarine could go down 25 feet and stay under water for more than 4 hours, but Fulton was unable to persuade the French, the British, or the Americans to order one. Right: In 1807 Fulton's* Clermont *steams up the Hudson River from New York City to Albany. Although many people called his new vessel "Fulton's Folly," steamboats soon became the major form of river transportation. Above: In 1848 steamboats traveling the Ohio River often stopped at Cincinnati.*

CINCINNATI PUBLIC LIBRARY

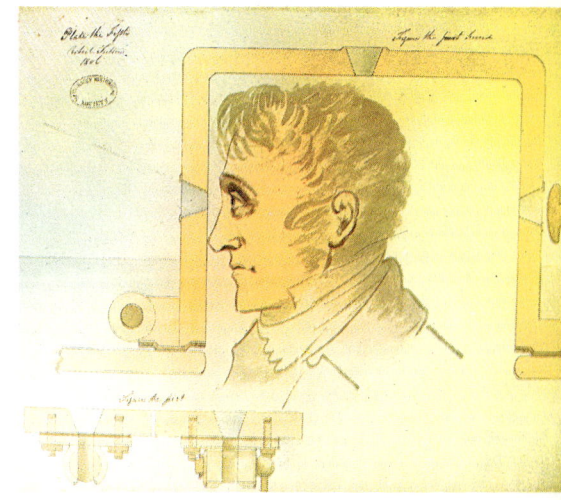

NEW JERSEY HISTORICAL SOCIETY

NEW YORK PUBLIC LIBRARY, PRINTS DIVISION

311

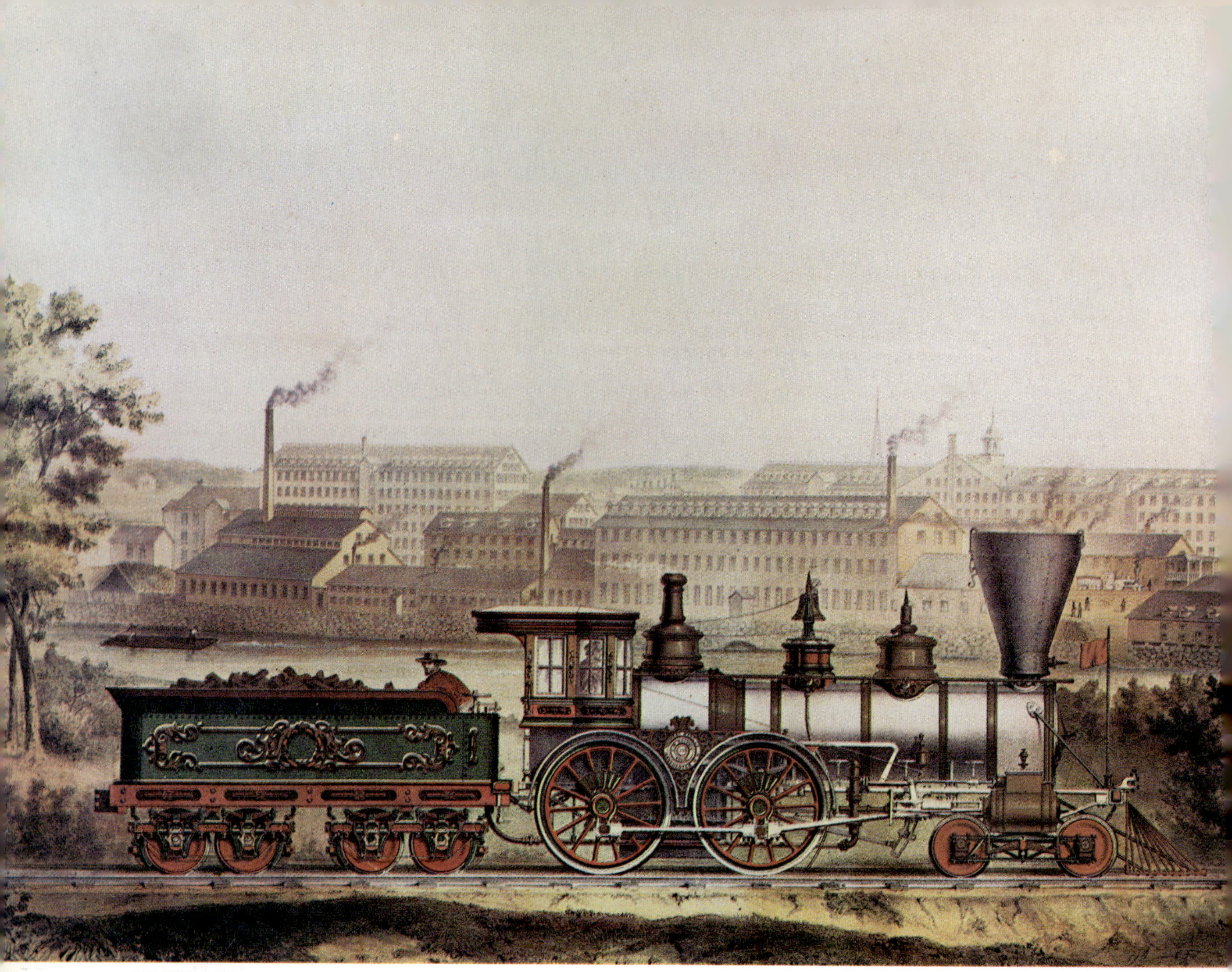

OLD PRINT SHOP

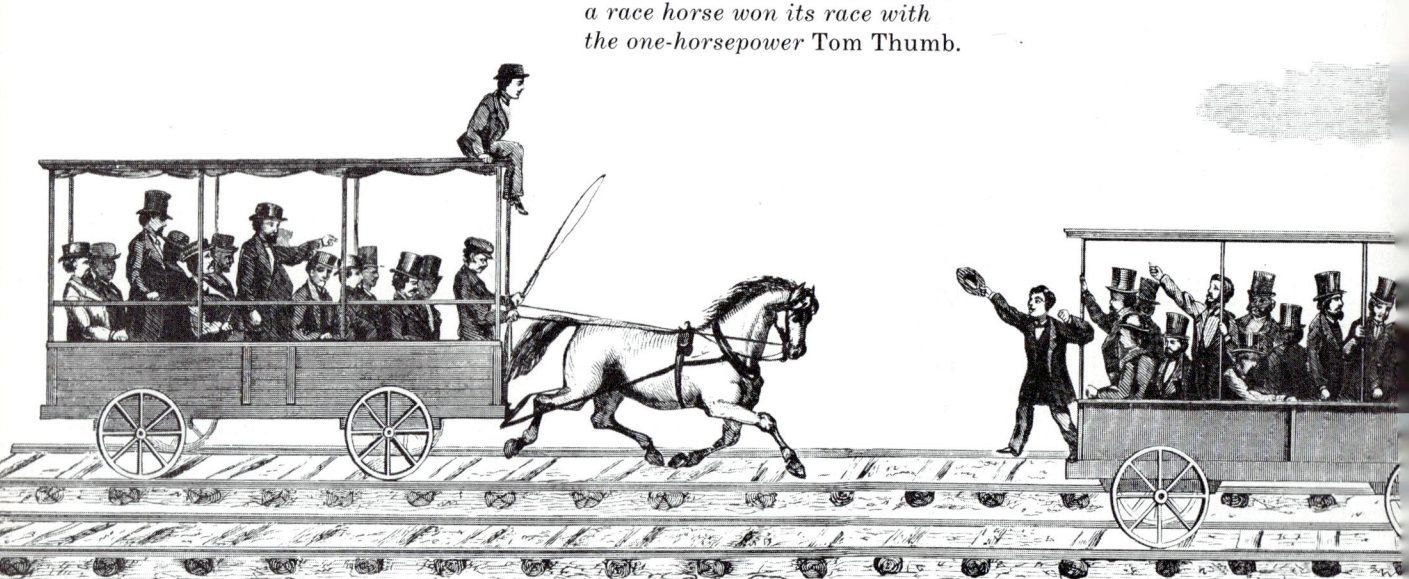

Below: In 1830 a tram pulled by a race horse won its race with the one-horsepower Tom Thumb.

ASSOCIATION AMERICAN RAILROADS

The Early Days of Railroading

The iron horse now came puffing and snorting onto the scene. Both English and American inventors had developed workable locomotives by 1825. In the United States the first railroad promoters were the businessmen of the growing cities. They wanted a transportation system that would bring farm produce from the nearby countryside to their warehouses, and then carry the manufactured goods they sold back to the farmers. Between 1828 and 1835 the merchants of Baltimore, Boston, Charleston, New York, and Philadelphia had sponsored short rail lines.

Between 1830 and 1850 the railroad-building boom overtook the canal boom. In 1830 there were 1,277 miles of canals and only 73 miles of railroad tracks. By 1850 there were 3,698 miles of canals and 8,879 miles of rails. The next 10 years saw a huge growth of railroads marking the end of the canal-building boom (see maps, pages 314–315).

Early locomotives were clumsy-looking things. But *Tom Thumb* (lower left), built in 1830 for the Baltimore and Ohio, excited the top-hatted gentlemen who were taken on a trial run. When *Tom Thumb* was tearing along at better than ten miles an hour, some of them took out pens and notebooks and wrote their names just to prove that "even at that great velocity [speed] it was possible to do so."

Engines grew in size and power. The 1856 model (upper left) is to the *Tom Thumb* what a big modern jet is to a one-engine propeller plane of wood and canvas. In those early days of railroading, locomotives were painted and decorated like Indian religious objects. The locomotives were like gods to the Americans: stronger than any animal, swifter than the wind, and never tired.

Not everyone was delighted, however, as the poster at the immediate left shows. The early locomotives filled the air with smoke, set fires with showers of sparks, frightened horses, and killed people in accidents. Some Americans believed that the progress they represented had too high a cost in dirt, noise, and danger.

A Transportation Network for the Nation

Although progress was fought by some Americans, gradually the canals, steamboat lines, and railroads formed a network which unified the country.

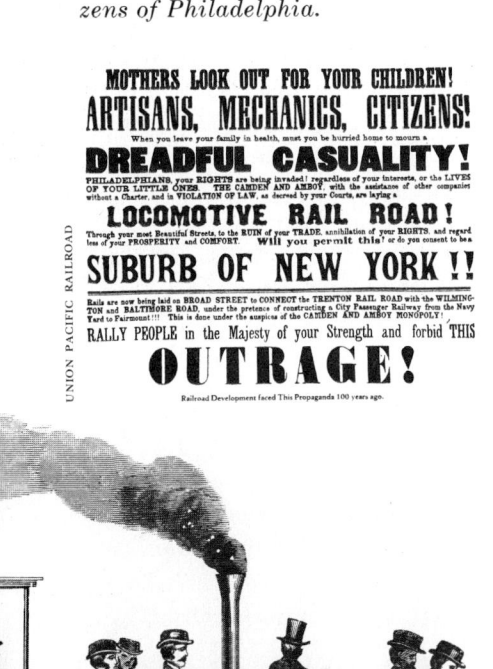

Left: Just as the railroad promoted industrialization, factories sometimes financed new rail lines and the development of new engines. In 1856 a New Hampshire manufacturing company, seen in the background of this painting, built this large wood-burning engine. Below: Many Americans were horrified by creeping industrialism and warned of future disasters. This poster attacks railroads as an outrage and a threat to the health of the citizens of Philadelphia.

The Constitution had joined these areas in a common political system. That meant that a passenger or a load of freight from a point inland, such as Cincinnati, could go about a thousand miles to New Orleans or to New York without making change of currency or hitting a language barrier. But as late as 1815 the trip from Cincinnati to New York took nearly two months.

By 1852, however, the Cincinnati–New York time, by rail, was a week or even less, and steamboats made the river journey from Cincinnati to New Orleans in about the same time. Between 1815 and 1860 railroads had reduced by 95 per cent the cost of sending freight overland.

High-speed transportation gave the United States east of the Mississippi the kind of economic unity that the Constitution provided politically. The linking of numerous short rail lines by 1860 (map, left) created a single, national market. Now the crops of the South and the West fed and clothed the industrial Northeast, while, in exchange, manufactured goods sped to the farms, ranches, and plantations of the West and the South. Each section of the country was becoming increasingly specialized in what it produced and increasingly dependent on other parts of the country for those goods it did not produce. The net result was a national economy of interdependent parts.

This national transportation system opened up new opportunities for everyone. Thousands of people were encouraged to move West and start new farms while others were encouraged to go into the manufacturing or trading of goods. Young America was moving faster and getting bigger, richer, and busier.

Questions for Discussion

1. How did the Erie Canal promote western settlement? What other benefits did it bring to the State of New York and the nation?
2. Why did Robert Fulton succeed in doing what John Fitch had failed to do?
3. For river and ocean-going transportation, what were the advantages of steam power over sail?
4. How did the steamboat help to open up the interior of the United States?
5. Why did businessmen become interested in railroad development?
6. Why did the railroad replace the canal as the most important means of internal transportation?

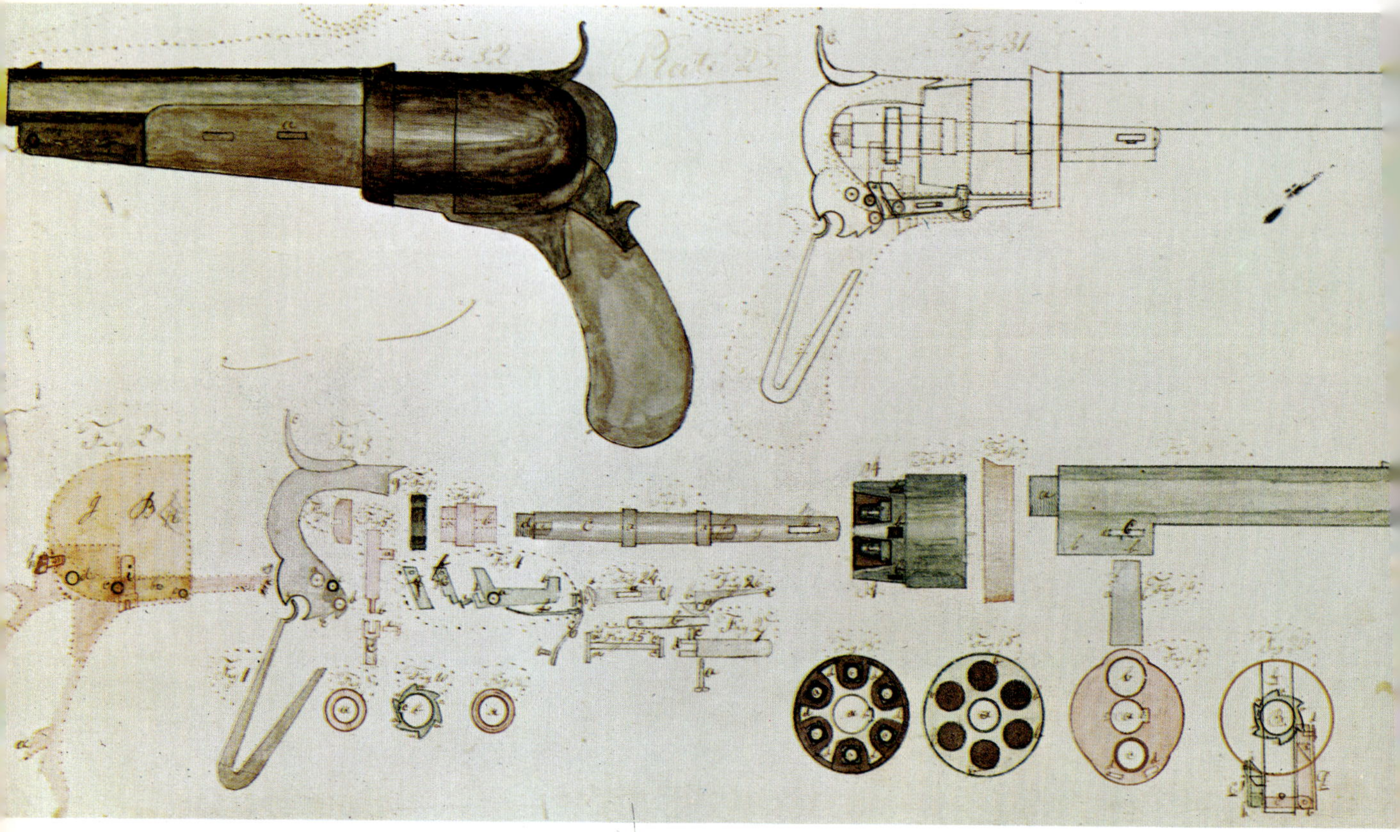

CONNECTICUT STATE LIBRARY, COLT COLLECTION

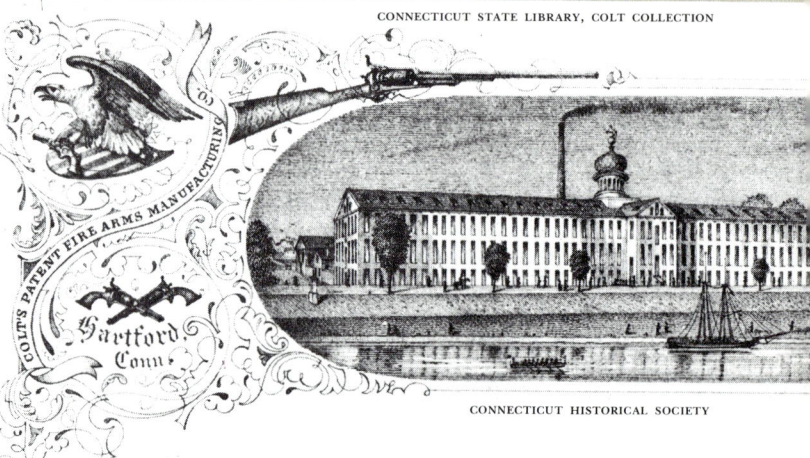

CONNECTICUT HISTORICAL SOCIETY

WADSWORTH ATHENEUM

At the time of his death in 1862, Samuel Colt (left) was America's best-known and wealthiest inventor. His drawing at the top of this page was made for a British patent on a multishot pistol. A picture of Colt's firearms factory appeared on the company letterhead seen directly above.

The Rise of Industry

The transportation revolution was only one part of an **industrial revolution** (a sweeping change in the way men manufacture goods and make a living). At the beginning of this great change, a French visitor to the United States wrote of how man, turning "each drop of water into a reservoir of steam," could change the world. He predicted that one day "a small part of the human race" could "produce all the material comforts" needed by mankind.

At the heart of the industrial revolution was the new technique of **mass production.** First, inventors created machines with tireless iron arms and fingers that multiplied human effort—sewing machines, power looms, and countless others. Many such machines were then placed in a single location, the factory. The factory's final product was made one part at a time, each part by a different machine. And these machines were so precise that the completed article—whether it was a locomotive or a pocket watch—could be assembled from or repaired with these interchangeable parts. Lastly, the machines could be set up so that the product would be put together as it moved from one man to the next in an assembly line.

The United States began to develop the elements of mass production in the 1790's when spinning and weaving machines were introduced in Rhode Island. At first these machines were run by water power, but by the 1820's the steam engine was rapidly replacing the paddle wheel as the source of power for industry. Shortly before the War of 1812, Eli Whitney, inventor of the cotton gin, began to make rifles with interchangeable parts. Inspectors for his biggest customer, the United States government, were amazed when workmen put together finished guns from piles of barrels, locks, triggers, and guards. Later the first assembly lines were set up.

One of the pioneers of this method of production was Samuel Colt (lower left). In the 1840's Colt sold his fast-firing revolvers to the Texas Rangers. They found Colt's invention to be a deadly weapon in fighting the Comanches. By 1848 Colt had his own gun factory (left) in Hartford, Connecticut.

The Factory Workers—A New Class

When factories first began to appear in New England, their owners faced a shortage of workers. It was hard to find men willing to trade the sea or the

WHITE, *Memoir of Samuel Slater*, 1836

Young women, supervised by a man, operate power looms in a New England textile factory.

farm for factory labor. Besides, many rural Yankees agreed with Virginia's Thomas Jefferson that industrial workers were bound to be overworked and underpaid, and that they would quickly become paupers and criminals. Some New England manufacturers came up with a clever plan to disprove these gloomy predictions.

When the Boston Manufacturing Company opened a textile factory at Waltham, Massachusetts, in 1813, its workers were mostly young women (right), daughters of farmers in the area around Boston. The girls were expected to live in boarding houses which the company built near the factory. In these boarding houses the girls were supervised by older women, and they had regular hours for rising, eating, visiting, and churchgoing. This routine would keep them from evil habits.

At first factory work was welcome to the girls. It allowed some freedom even when the work lasted fourteen hours a day, six days a week. The reason was simple. Hard work and strict rules were a familiar part of life on the farms from which the girls came. In the factory and boarding house, the country girls had company. More important, on payday they could jingle their own money—even after paying for their board. From the manufacturers' point of view, hiring women made sense because there was a shortage of men willing to leave their farms for factory work at low wages.

In an age when women had not worked outside the home and had few legal rights to property of their own, this was a great stride toward independence. The girl who earned three dollars a week in wages was learning, as one of them said, "to think for herself." She expected to marry and leave the factory with a bit of money with which to begin family life in a home of her own. So the factory actually began to change the pattern of family life and the roles of the sexes.

The boarding-house system was only an experiment, and it did not last forever.

Questions for Discussion

1. Why was the development of interchangeable parts and the assembly line an important step in the industrialization of the United States?
2. Why did New England textile-factory owners hire mostly young women instead of men? How did factory work give women more independence?

In this detail from a woodcut by Winslow Homer, women workers are leaving a New England factory.

Harper's Weekly, JULY 25, 1868

An Age of Reform

The tremendous changes made by the industrial revolution caused many citizens to think about how to **reform** (improve) American society. The Constitution promised everyone—except Negroes—the "Blessings of Liberty." The machine age promised abundance. The many different reformers between 1820 to 1850 hoped to make both these dreams come true.

First, there were those who wanted political reforms. In 1820 almost every state had some kind of property requirement for **suffrage** (the right to vote). Unions and other reform associations fought hard to get universal manhood suffrage, which then meant the right for white males over 21 to vote. By 1840 this battle had been won in many states.

A second kind of reform was economic. In the 1830's and 1840's some workers began to join trade **unions.** These were associations which united workingmen to improve their wages and working conditions. The unions led **strikes** (work stoppages) to force employers to grant their demands. They also lobbied for laws to reach these goals. For example, a drive to limit the workday to ten hours, without reductions in pay, was successful by 1860 in some states.

Still another kind of reform aimed at improving institutions, such as schools, insane asylums, and prisons. In the 1840's many states had laws establishing public schools. But these schools did not meet the needs of an increasingly industrial society. In the 1830's a young lawyer named Horace Mann argued that every state should provide the best possible cost-free schooling for all its children. "If we do not prepare children to become good citizens," he wrote, "our republic must go down to destruction." By 1837 Mann had won his battle for public education and was appointed secretary of the newly created Massachusetts State Board of Education.

Humanitarianism, the belief that all mankind should have a better life, underlay a fourth kind of reform. It aimed to improve the position of large groups of people who were the victims of unfairness. A drive to abolish slavery, which will be studied later, was the most powerful such movement. Another was the effort to better the condition of women. In free America women could not vote, hold certain jobs, or own property. Even wealthy women were confined to the home and to a limited education in "polite" accomplishments like drawing and piano-playing.

This drawing was the architect's grand design for New Harmony. In fact, the utopian community never got beyond the log-cabin stage.

In 1830 a few bold **feminists** (women who fight for women's rights) attacked these injustices. Amelia Bloomer designed "bloomers" (lower right) to free a woman from heavy, trailing skirts and to let her move around actively in the world. In 1848 another feminist, Elizabeth Cady Stanton (upper right), helped to call a women's rights convention in upstate New York. The convention issued a document that quoted the opening of the Declaration of Independence word for word, except to say that "all men and women are created equal." Mrs. Stanton, joined by co-workers such as Susan B. Anthony, fought for women's suffrage. This action won them the name of "suffragettes." Despite their efforts, it was not until 1920 that all American women over 21 years of age were guaranteed the right to vote.

A fifth type of reform was aimed at raising the moral tone of all society by getting people to change habits that the reformers thought were bad. The move for **temperance** (prohibition or strict control over the drinking of liquor) was one of these.

Finally, there were reformers who withdrew to live apart in little communities where like-minded people could show others how to live the good life. These tiny **utopias** (a name for an imaginary land with a perfect society) generally did not last long. In 1825 Robert Owen, an English reformer, started a colony in New Harmony, Indiana. Owen aimed to replace capitalistic competition with planned cooperation. Other utopias worked on different plans. One of the most famous was Brook Farm, begun in 1841 near Boston, Massachusetts. There, some of the brainiest men and women of New England ran a farm where landownership and work were shared by all. In 1848 in Oneida, New York, John Humphrey Noyes founded the most radical utopia. Oneida Colony replaced family life with a system in which each member considered himself married to all the other members. Though the Oneida Colony was very successful, it dropped its more radical ideas 30 years later.

Questions for Discussion

1. What one objective was shared by all of the reform movements?
2. What labor problems did the workers try to solve by joining trade unions?
3. What would be your idea of a modern utopia?

LIBRARY OF CONGRESS

Elizabeth Cady Stanton (top) campaigned for women's rights. Feminists wearing "daring" bloomers (above) received much publicity.

The Age of Jackson

The 1830's are sometimes called the Age of Jackson because Andrew Jackson (left), President from 1829 to 1837, seemed to embody the individualistic, tough, get-ahead spirit of the nation. In years when steamboat and factory whistles shrieked, "Hurry up! Succeed!" he showed, by example, how to do it.

Jackson, born fairly poor in the Carolina backwoods, had no formal schooling. Yet in frontier Tennessee natural ability made him a landowner and a business success. His only legal training was in "reading law"—a kind of on-the-job training—in the office of a lawyer. Yet, when his neighbors elected him a judge, he never doubted his ability to decide cases justly. His only training for combat was in the duels brought on by his hot temper. Yet, as a general, he trounced both Creek Indians and British troops.

Plain people admired this powerhouse, this self-made man. They wanted him for President, as the poster (opposite page, upper right) makes clear. In 1828 the "common man" finally elected the uncommon "Old Hickory" to the White House. He was the first President since Washington without a college education, Cabinet experience, or diplomatic service.

In office Jackson was all bold action. He approved of a house-cleaning of the Federal government, and he replaced many old-time holders of government jobs with his followers. Jackson thought that this **spoils system** (so named from a Jackson man's remark, "to the victor belong the spoils") was democracy in action. He called it "rotation in office." Everyone, said Jackson, could perform the few, simple duties of government; therefore, as many as possible should have a chance. This would give the people control over the **bureaucracy** (all the departments and the non-elected officials who carry out the laws passed by legislatures).

Jackson also used the veto power freely when he thought that a measure was not in the public interest. He did not restrict himself, as some thought he should, to the veto of bills which he thought unconstitutional.

In 1832 South Carolina threatened to refuse to collect within its borders the Federal **tariff** (a tax on goods imported from other countries). Most Carolinians thought this tax was too high. Jackson was stern and quick in his counterthreat to use troops against the state for daring to nullify a Federal law.

A showdown was prevented by a lowering of the tariff. To Jackson's admirers this forceful use of

This portrait of Andrew Jackson was admired by his followers, and copies of it often were carried in campaign parades.

the power of the Federal government was a sign of strength. They pictured him as a dashing hero on a prancing horse (right), while his enemies pictured him as "King Andrew." By 1836 Jacksonians had organized a new national party that called itself Democratic. In 1836 anti-Jacksonians also formed a party and named it after those Englishmen who had battled against royal power. So the Whig party was born.

Jackson's War Against the Bank

But the outstanding event of Jackson's Presidency was his war on the Second Bank of the United States. The industrial revolution had created some difficult political questions. Should the government play an even larger part in making economic decisions than it already did? Some believed that a democratic government must, for example, help make decisions about wages and the number of hours a man could be asked to work by his employer. Others insisted that any such enlargement of government's power was a threat to freedom. They wanted the economy to run without government intervention. This policy is known by its French name, laissez faire for "let it alone."

One special area of economic life that affected all the others was **credit** (the power to borrow money). In the growing nation farmers and businessmen alike borrowed regularly to buy land or to start a shop, a factory, or a railroad. Banks lent them this money and charged a price for it, called **interest.** The money lent was not gold or silver, but paper "bank notes," carrying the bank's promise to pay the borrower on demand. Anything that prevented men from getting credit meant that they could not start new enterprises unless they were very rich.

In 1816 Congress had chartered the Second Bank of the United States. Like Hamilton's First Bank of the United States, it was a private bank, but was allowed to collect and hold the money of the government. Like all banks, it made loans from its **deposits** (money the bank held in its vaults). The Second Bank of the United States was the country's biggest financial agent. Throughout the country smaller banks often turned to it for loans. By granting or refusing such requests, the Second Bank had strong control over credit. Some men said that such a restraining hand was useful. Too much easy borrowing would make trouble if people were unable to pay their debts.

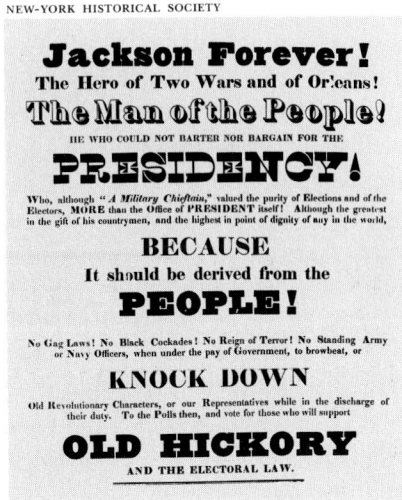

The hero of the Battle of New Orleans (below) is featured on an 1828 campaign poster (above).

But only 5 of the bank's 25 directors were chosen by the President. Jackson believed that it was wrong for a few powerful bankers from the East to have a death grip on the nation's economic growth. It angered Jackson that Nicholas Biddle, the bank's very wealthy director, could reward friendly bankers with loans and deny them to outsiders. So when a bill to renew the charter came to him in 1832, he vetoed it in a message that blasted the bank's power. Biddle struck back with a bitter propaganda campaign to defeat Jackson for re-election. But Jackson's power struck like the thunderbolt in the cartoon (right). The old Indian fighter, who thought of the bank as a "monster," loved nothing more than such a battle. "The Bank," he said, "is trying to kill me, but I will kill it." The people re-elected Jackson, and the Second Bank of the United States was dead.

After the Bank War many laboring men admired Old Hickory for his victory over big business. But because the bank could no longer limit credit, many businessmen, too, approved of what Jackson had done. They now believed he stood for equal opportunity for all investors, not merely rich businessmen.

John Marshall—The Law and Business

While Jackson had reduced Federal control over business, Chief Justice John Marshall (lower right) was further extending the freedom of business. Marshall, a Virginian and a Federalist, sat as Chief Justice of the Supreme Court from 1801 to 1835. In a series of decisions, he declared unconstitutional the laws which many states had made for regulating corporations. Since there was almost no Federal regulation of business at this time, the result was to leave business free to do almost anything it wanted.

Boom and Bust

During the 1830's business took advantage of its freedom and grew at a rapid pace. After Jackson vetoed the charter of the Second Bank of the United States in 1832, smaller banks began to lend money freely. When Jackson started depositing the Federal government's revenues in state-chartered banks, they too made generous loans. Optimism swept the country. Thousands of people bought land as prices rose in a fever of **speculation** (risky investment in the hope of quick or large profits). Trouble lay ahead.

LIBRARY OF CONGRESS

Above: In 1833 Andrew Jackson began removing Federal deposits from the Second Bank of the United States. In this contemporary cartoon the bank's power crumbles before the President's thunderbolt. *Right:* Although he had no prior judicial experience, John Marshall was a most influential Chief Justice. During his 34 years in office, he established that the Supreme Court had the power to determine whether or not a law was constitutional. Other Court decisions expanded the power of the Federal government, restricted the powers of the states, and established protections for private property.

VIRGINIA STATE LIBRARY, SAINT-MEMIN COLLECTION

LIBRARY OF CONGRESS

NEW-YORK HISTORICAL SOCIETY

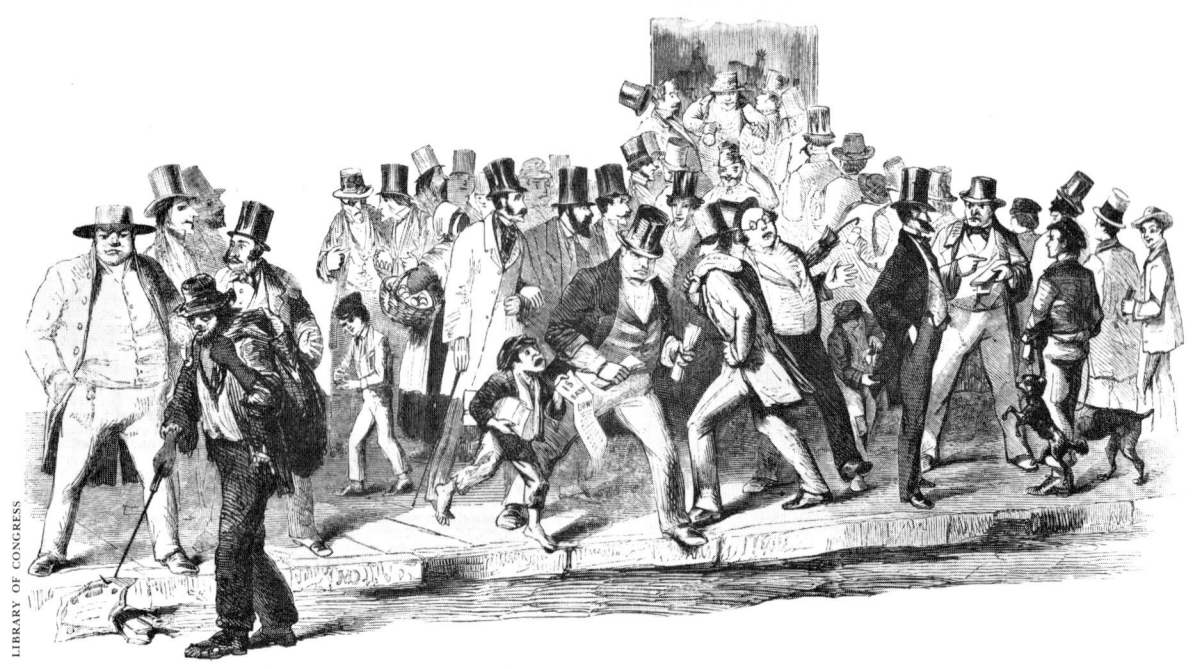

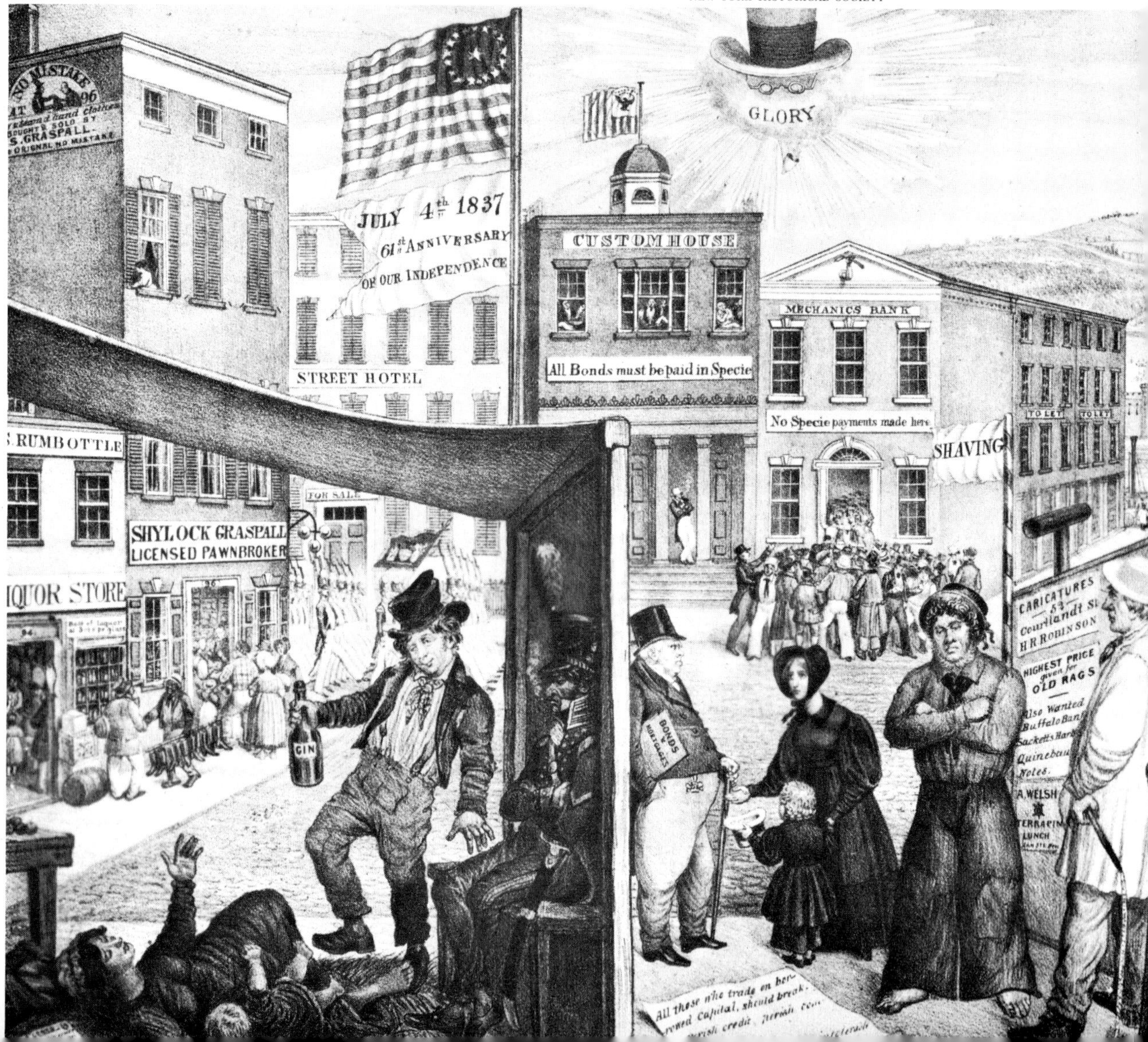

Below: A Whig cartoonist's version of the panic of 1837 has Andrew Jackson overlooking idle ships and workmen and worried bank depositors. Hard times have handed the pawnbroker and the liquor dealer at the left a booming business. Left: During the panic of 1857, a Harper's Weekly *cartoon showed New Yorkers desperately trying to withdraw their money from a savings bank.*

In the election of 1836, the voters chose Martin Van Buren of New York, then Vice-President, to succeed Jackson. Though he was a clever politician, Van Buren walked straight into unavoidable disaster. He was like a man who inherits a house whose roof immediately falls in. The Bank War, whatever political arguments might be made in its favor, had created a dangerous economic situation. What then happened shows how a boom that has gone too far too fast brings trouble.

Because the banks had loaned too much money, they began to fear that they could not possibly get it back from their borrowers in a reasonable length of time. So they asked for immediate repayment of some of their loans. But the borrowers did not yet have any money—just hopes of future profits. To make matters worse, in 1836 the Federal government said that it would accept only gold or silver as payment for the vast amounts of public land it had sold.

Businessmen who owed the government money for this land demanded gold and silver instead of banknotes from their banks. But the banks did not have enough gold or silver to meet these requests. In 1837 a panic, or wave of fear, spread across the country, and all banks were forced to close. Because the banks were closed, bank notes suddenly became worthless pieces of paper. Businessmen then found themselves with vaults full of bank notes that no one would accept.

Soon corporations were going **bankrupt** (out of business because of their inability to pay their creditors). Land sales fell off by half. Factories closed their doors. Public works stood idle. Thousands of workingmen were jobless. They had never borrowed a cent; nor had they created the panic or the **depression** (a period of drastic economic decline during which business activity decreases, prices fall, and unemployment rises) which followed. Yet they and their families suffered by it, as did all Americans. The cartoon at lower left pictures the angry feelings of much of the nation.

The price of leaving economic growth unregulated let the country in for periods of runaway prosperity followed by panic and depression. In 1857 there was another panic (above, left), followed in time by a boom. In 1873, 1893, and 1929 there were other panics. Since 1837 everyone has been affected by a huge, impersonal economic system that has showered wealth during boom periods and has left thousands jobless and

327

hungry during depressions. Once again expansion proved to be a mixed blessing.

Questions for Discussion

1. How did Jackson defend the spoils system?
2. Why was the Whig Party formed?
3. What was the disagreement between those who favored laissez faire and those who favored a larger role for government in making economic decisions?
4. Why did westerners generally favor a policy of easy credit?
5. How did the Second Bank of the United States have control over credit in the West and South?
6. Why did many businessmen, as well as farmers and laborers, approve of Jackson's veto of the bill renewing the bank's charter?
7. How did some of those who had not borrowed money suffer in the depression that followed the panic of 1837?

Chapter Review

Social Studies Terms

lobbying, monopoly, industrial revolution, mass production, reform, suffrage, unions, strikes, feminists, temperance, utopias, spoils system, bureaucracy, tariff, credit, interest, deposits, speculation, bankrupt, depression

Summary Questions for Discussion

1. In what ways did industrialization before the Civil War change the lives of men and women?
2. This chapter describes the effect of the steamboat on Huck and Jim as sudden, powerful, and sometimes destructive. Have some modern inventions had a similar effect on the lives of Americans? Why?
3. Why did the era of canal building end at approximately the same time that the age of railroads began?
4. How were improvements in transportation both a cause and a result of the rapid settlement of the West?
5. What invention in transportation has had the most far-reaching effect on American life? Defend your answer.
6. In the first half of the nineteenth century, what industries made the greatest use of mass production, interchangeable parts, and assembly lines?

What kinds of production could not be adapted to these developments in industry? Why?
7. In the nineteenth century why did most people see nothing undemocratic about not allowing women to vote?
8. Compare some of the nineteenth century efforts to create utopian societies with similar efforts today. What similarities are there? What differences?
9. Why does a rapid expansion of credit sometimes create economic problems?
10. Did Jackson use Presidential power wisely? Explain.

Pictures as Historical Evidence

How would you use the pictures and maps in this chapter to disprove the following generalization? Between 1800 and 1860 life in America underwent no important changes.

Map Study

Compare the two maps on pages 314–315. Why are there so many more roads, highways, canals, and railroads in the North than in the South? What do the maps show about railroad construction between 1850 and 1860? Would possession of New Orleans have been as important to farmers in the Old Northwest in 1860 as it was in 1803? Why?

Which of the cities shown on these maps were important because of their location on the ocean or some inland waterway before the eras of canal and railroad building? Which were canal terminals by 1850?

For Further Reading

Adventures of Huckleberry Finn, by Mark Twain. New York: The Macmillan Company, 1962.

Andrew Jackson, by Ralph K. Andrist. New York: American Heritage Publishing Co., Inc., 1963.

Following the Frontier: American Transportation in the Nineteenth Century, by Leonard F. James. New York: Harcourt, Brace & World, Inc., 1968.

Men of Science and Invention, by Michael Blow. New York: American Heritage Publishing Co., Inc., 1960.

Railroads in the Days of Steam, by Albert L. McCready. New York: American Heritage Publishing Co., Inc., 1960.

The Erie Canal, by Ralph K. Andrist. New York: American Heritage Publishing Co., Inc., 1964.

ISSUES PAST AND PRESENT

Is American Expansion a Force for Progress?

Americans have always been great believers in progress. There are many reasons for this. One, of course, is that the first people who came to Virginia and Massachusetts, and many of the millions who followed them, started with next-to-nothing, except perhaps their religious faith and optimism. Many suffered terrible hardships, but most of them actually made progress. They dreamed of great things for themselves and then set to work to make the dreams come true.

Another reason that Americans came to be such strong believers in progress is that in coming to America they gladly left behind them a past. The past, they felt, had been generally unkind to them and so they welcomed the future.

Words such as *America, new, frontier, expansion,* and *progress* were all tied together in their minds. In 1839 Captain Frederick Marryat, an English visitor to the United States, wrote, "*Go ahead* is the real motto of the country."

Most Americans have never thought progress meant just accumulating more and better things. If asked to define *progress*, an American might tell about such things as expanding industries, new states and territories, and improved living conditions. But Americans did not consider that kind of progress to be an end in itself. It was a means of reaching higher ends. The final goals were always lofty: freedom, equality, justice, democracy, and "the pursuit of happiness."

To many Americans territorial expansion seemed to go right along with progress in reaching these higher goals. But Americans never ceased to ask questions about the relationship between expansion and progress. Think about these questions as you read the following selections:

1. What is progress? How can it be measured?
2. Has expansion been a force for progress? How?

"The Country Made the City"

John Dean Caton was a Chicago lawyer who, in 1893, wrote about the settlement of the area around his hometown some 60 years earlier. This passage is typical of many nineteenth-century descriptions of the way expansion brought civilization to the West.

JOHN DEAN CATON: *'TIS SIXTY YEARS SINCE IN CHICAGO,* 1893

After 1834 settlers began to edge their way onto the prairies, miles away from the timber. There they built their little huts or shanties. It was astonishing how men, even

those starting very poorly, got along, and finally prospered. When, in 1838 and 1839, operations on the Illinois and Michigan Canal were halted, the laborers on that canal each bought a sack of cornmeal which they placed in their wheelbarrows. Followed by their wives and little ones, they started out into the broad prairies, selected places which suited them, and with their spades cut up sods to build little shanties. They dug holes in nearby low places to get water and spaded a place for a garden. There they planted a variety of vegetables, which grew in the same season, in order to add something to their cornmeal diet. In this way was a large portion of La Salle County first settled by hundreds of men. Some of today's most wealthy and respected citizens of that county had been the little boys who, led by their mothers on foot, followed their fathers into the unbroken prairie.

> The canal workers had been required to own their own tools and wheelbarrows.

> La Salle County is about 40 miles west of Chicago.

Twenty years later he who traveled through that country where those sod huts were first built would find a great change. Now there were neat farmhouses painted white and surrounded by flower gardens, fine barns, herds of cattle and horses in the pastures, and great crops of grain in the fields or being harvested with reapers drawn by horses. He would find roads laid out, bridges across the streams, and white schoolhouses nearby.

The first settlers were somewhat clannish. The separate localities were known as the Norwegian settlement, the Irish settlement, the French settlement, or the Yankee settlement. But succeeding generations became so intermingled that these names meant only geographical locations. Now all have become Americans. They speak only the English language, and are devoted to the principles of our institutions.

> "Clannish" means tending to stick close to one's own kind.

In the absence of modern means of transportation, it was impossible for the land right around Chicago to furnish enough business to build up a great city. Railroads and canals came along and extended the area which could reach Chicago and contribute to its trade. As these railroads and canals spread far and wide, the commerce of the city increased to the same extent. The city has grown in the same proportion. The country around the city has made the city, and not the city the country.

1. How does Caton measure progress?
2. According to Caton what kinds of progress did settlement bring to the prairies?
3. What evidence in the selection shows that the settlers valued forms of progress other than just making a living?
4. Did expansion make for Americanization? How?

"The God of Armies Is with Us"

The following speech is by the same Commodore Robert F. Stockton who, in the Mexican War, assisted in the conquest of California. On December 30, 1847, the citizens of Philadelphia gave a dinner in his honor. At this time the fighting was all over, but the peace treaty had not been signed, and Stockton strongly favored continuing the war.

ROBERT F. STOCKTON:
SPEECH ON THE WAR WITH MEXICO, 1847

Wherever our soldiers have carried our arms, victory has awaited them. We see them rushing against walls bristling with bayonets and artillery and lined with legions of armed men. We see our youthful heroes charging from fort to fort, and, in the middle of the smoke and thunder of the battle, we see the flag of our country waving. [At this point cheering burst forth from Stockton's audience.]

Gentlemen, how has all this been done? Is it only because of the wisdom of the President's cabinet and the skill of our armies? These are all well, very well. But we must look beyond all this for the secret of our successes and the source of our remarkable prosperity. It is because the spirit of our pilgrim fathers is with us. It is because the God of armies and the Lord of hosts is with us. [Tremendous applause.] And how is it with poor, unfortunate, wretched Mexico? Ever since the days of the last of the Montezumas, quarrels within that country have disturbed its peace. Its territory has been drenched with the blood of its own children. Within the last 25 years, revolution has followed revolution. Now, in the fight with us Mexico has been beaten in every field.

High responsibilities and noble goals stand before us, and to reach them we must increase our armies in Mexico, *cost what it may*. [Great applause.] Fifty thousand men must go to Mexico. Let me state the reasons why this increase in the size of our forces in Mexico is required.

Mexico is poor and wretched. Why? Misgovernment, greed, unceasing wrong, merciless cruelty, and pride—these have been a curse on the unhappy country and made it what it is. Let us hope that a better and happier day is now about to dawn upon unfortunate Mexico. We must now forgive it all its trespasses, and, returning good for evil, make it free and happy!

If I were the President, I would prosecute [carry on] this war for the sole purpose of saving Mexicans from misrule and fighting among themselves. The war might be stretched out for 50 years. It might cost enough money to demand from us

"Trespasses" here means sins or errors.

each year half of all that we own. I would still insist that the blessings of civil and religious liberty should be guaranteed to Mexico. We dare not shrink from this solemn duty.

1. From this speech can you tell what kind of progress Stockton believed had been made by American expansion into land once owned by Mexico? How did he propose to bring about the same kind of progress in Mexico itself?
2. Why was Stockton so convinced of the rightness of his method of spreading the influence of the United States?

"A Model for All Other Governments"

Albert Gallatin was born in Switzerland in 1761 but moved to the United States in 1780, partly because of his belief in the high ideals of the American Revolution. He was Secretary of the Treasury under Jefferson and Madison. When the war with Mexico began, he was 85 years old.

ALBERT GALLATIN: *PEACE WITH MEXICO*, 1847

Before this unfortunate war, the United States always had acted strictly according to the rules of justice. It never had injured another nation voluntarily. Every addition of territory from foreign powers was honestly made as the result of treaties, not forced upon, but freely agreed to by the other countries. Keeping the peace was always a primary goal. Taking up arms was always in self-defense.

The United States' mission was to be a model for all other governments, and for all other nations less fortunate than it, to hold fast to the highest principles of political morality. Now, an appeal has been made to your worst passions: to greed, to the thirst of an unjust increase in power by brutal force, to the love of military fame and of false glory.

To justify the war in which we are now involved, a most extraordinary statement has been made. It is said that the people of the United States are a superior race of people to those in Mexico. It is said this gives the United States the right to conquer and keep in bondage the other nation. This, it is also said, will be the way to enlighten the degraded [corrupt] Mexicans, to improve their social state, and to increase the happiness of the masses.

Is it agreeable with the principle of democracy to say that one race is superior to another? This claim and other claims about improving Mexico are just excuses justifying an unjust seizure of power. These claims are full of unbounded greed and

ambition. Truth never was or can be spread by fire and sword or by any means other than purely moral ones.

1. What did Gallatin believe the United States had lost by going to war with Mexico?
2. Did he believe that the expansion which would result from the war would be a force for progress or a danger to our future? Why?

Welding the Lands Together

On May 10, 1869, two years before this poem was published in Leaves of Grass, *the transcontinental railroad was completed. The Suez Canal was also completed in 1869. In 1858 the first message had been sent over the transatlantic cable. Walt Whitman celebrated all three accomplishments in "Passage to India."*

WALT WHITMAN: *PASSAGE TO INDIA,* 1871

Singing my days,
Singing the great achievements of the present,
Singing the strong light works of engineers . . .

Passage to India!
Lo, soul, seest thou not God's purpose from the first?
The earth to be spann'd, connected by network,
The races, neighbors, to marry and be given in marriage,
The oceans to be cross'd, the distant brought near,
The lands to be welded together.

A worship new I sing,
You captains, voyagers, explorers, yours,
You, not for trade or transportation only,
But in God's name, and for thy sake O soul.

"Surmounting" means overcoming.

I see over my own continent the Pacific railroad surmounting every barrier,

The Platte River is in Nebraska.

I see continual trains of cars winding along the Platte carrying freight and passengers,
I hear the locomotives rushing and roaring, and the shrill steam-whistle . . .

"Eastern" and "Western" seas here mean the Atlantic and Pacific oceans.

Bridging the three or four thousand miles of land travel,
Tying the Eastern to the Western sea,
The road between Europe and Asia.

1. According to the poet what kinds of progress were made when the transcontinental railroad was completed?
2. Did Whitman view American expansion as contributing to the world's progress? Explain.

Today, the center of population in the United States is still shifting to the West. But the expansion of what some believe to be progress does not always take place in a westward direction, as the next selection indicates.

The Vanishing McCalls

WAYNE KERNODLE:
THE LAST OF THE RUGGED INDIVIDUALISTS, 1960

That fierce individualist, the southern mountaineer, has long been one of America's favorite characters. He has given us a whole series of folk heroes, from Andrew Jackson and Davy Crockett to Li'l Abner. His songs have become a national fad. He has inspired a great amount of literature, ranging from serious fiction to the hillbilly cartoon.

And now he is about to vanish, without hope of rescue. As the new highways push into dozens of once-hidden coves, they are destroying that isolation which, over the course of the years, molded the character of the southern highlander. What he is really like can well be seen in the McCalls of Pin Hook Gap.

Pin Hook Gap lies in the westernmost end of North Carolina. Its total population is five McCalls plus an assortment of bears, panthers, rattlesnakes, and wild pigs. Only two of the McCalls have ever been more than 50 miles from Pin Hook during their entire lives. What they do and how they do it is entirely up to them. They are independent but will share a real offer of friendship. Their wishes are simple but include the great wish not to be "a-dickertated to" [dictated to] by anyone or anything.

Everything about the McCall cabin expresses an independent way of life. Their father had built the cabin when he first came to Pin Hook. The furniture was all made by hand from cherry or walnut trees. It had the simple, true lines of great workmanship and was both comfortable and as sturdy as the rocks which surrounded the cove. All of their belongings were made with tools which they had hammered out themselves. The long rifle which stands across the entrance to the house has a barrel made by Charlie McCall.

"Progress" is on its way to Pin Hook Gap. The people at the country store were talking about the engineers who had been making surveys for paving the road and connecting it with the Blue Ridge Parkway at Wagon Road Gap and from there to Routes 19 and 23. This will connect with Highway 441.

It is evident that this way of life is already doomed. Twenty-one years ago, when I made my first close contact with the people of this region, the individualistic spirit was

---

A "rugged individualist" is a person who stubbornly defends his right to do things in his way, by himself, and for himself.

Here, "coves" means small valleys in the sides of mountains.

the first thing you noticed about the people you met. They were not special people. They were most everybody who lived there, and they simply did what was to them right and natural. As pioneers, their ancestors had pushed into these wilderness areas, staked out their claims, and settled for good. Until after World War II, they escaped much of the change which was occurring elsewhere. Because opportunities for making money were not abundant, education and "refinement" were neglected.

Many thoughtful people in this region are watching the present changes with regret. Radio, television, movies, industry, labor unions, paved roads, parkways, and tourists have invaded their backcountry. In different ways such urban influences have begun to standardize [make alike] the lives of all mountaineers. Working hours, types of work, wages, clothes, speech, and manners that once were highly individualized are becoming standardized.

There were some in the region who welcomed "progress." They joined hands with those who offered new opportunities. And they finally got progress in the shape of two big mills which now threaten to pollute the clear waters of the rivers.

Becoming tied to the city and to the urban way of life seems to have become the overriding urge of the present population. The informal way of life has given way to formal organization. The social and civic activities are carried on by clubs which promote civic improvement—such as bigger and better highways into the towns and larger attractions for tourists.

Recreational activities of the old type like berry-picking, mountain fox hunting, and folk dancing have also been disappearing under the onslaught of spectator sports. High-school football games on lighted fields and folk festivals with imported rock-and-roll guitar players have crowded out many of the old-time street dances, informal hoedowns, and singing conventions. Now kids sport long haircuts, talk slang, and dress "sharp." Their mothers belong to women's clubs.

The cabins are being replaced by rows of little white houses. A sameness about everything is developing, including the manicured camping sites for tourists, with neat piles of wood cut to the proper length for the outdoor grills. A few pure specimens like the McCalls remain. In another generation their type will disappear forever. Such men already are strangers in their own land.

1. What does the author believe "progress" is bringing into the mountain coves?
2. Are other peoples in the United States losing an

individualistic way of life to progress? Who? Why?
3. How is progress affecting the way of life in your community? Why?

Making Generalizations

You have seen in these readings and in other parts of Unit III that in the United States expansion has occurred in different ways. It has happened sometimes quietly, as when the settlers went out onto the prairies on foot, and sometimes noisily, with a roar of cannon. Though territorial expansion is no longer one of our national goals, the reading about the McCalls indicates that many Americans still think of progress as some kind of expansion. Before making a generalization about the main question of this section—Is American expansion a force for progress?—you may want to consider these questions again. What is progress? How can it be measured? Then state your generalization simply: American expansion is (or is not) a force for progress. Write a paragraph explaining your answer.

Primary and Secondary Sources

The reasons for your answer can be taken from the five documents in this section or from Chapters 9, 10, and 11. The documents in this section are called *primary sources* because they are written or spoken by people who had first-hand experiences with what they wrote or spoke about. But monuments, pottery fragments, letters, photographs, diaries, stamps, Roman ruins, weapons, coins, and tools are primary sources, too. They tell us about the way different peoples lived and what they thought about and valued.

Written accounts of interpretations, like textbooks and historical novels, based on primary sources, are called *secondary accounts*. Chapters 9, 10, and 11 are secondary accounts on such subjects as pioneering, industrialism, and the war with Mexico. The topic we considered at the beginning of Unit III—the meaning of the frontier—is closely related to the question you are considering now. For example, how did Lord Bryce and Frederick Jackson Turner seem to answer our question about expansion and progress? If you go to the school or public library for other information about the frontier, expansion, and progress, classify the sources you find as primary or secondary.

1831 Garrison Founds the Liberator

1850 Compromise of 1850

1857 Dred Scott Decision

1820 Missouri Compromise

1832 Nullification Crisis

1855 Kansas-Nebraska Act Leads to Violence

1859 John Brown's Harpers Ferry Raid

UNIT IV
A Nation Divided

1863 Emancipation Proclamation
1867 Military Reconstruction Begins
1896 Plessy v. Ferguson Decision Supports Segregation

1861 Fort Sumter Falls
1865 Lee Surrenders at Appomattox
1877 Troops Withdrawn from South
1909 Du Bois Helps Found NAACP

The uniting of thirteen separate governments into one nation in 1776 was one of the most important and happiest turning points in the history of our country. The splitting of the nation into two parts from 1861 to 1865 was no less important, but was marked by great bitterness and destruction. Now, more than 100 years after the Civil War, its tragic effects are still felt throughout our nation.

Interpreting the Past, which opens Unit IV, presents documents both from the years before 1861 and from the years closer to our own time for a look into the causes of the Civil War. Chapter 12 describes some of the differences and disputes which tended to drive the northern, southern, and western sections of the country apart, even as other forces were tending to unite them.

The main subject of Chapter 13 is the fighting which scarred farms and forests and stained the land with the blood of young men. Attention is also given to the economic and political struggles that took place behind the lines.

The attempts of a wounded nation to heal itself and of Negroes to gain a life of dignity as United States citizens are the subjects of Chapter 14. The story of this period is full of a new kind of conflict—a conflict too often between races, a conflict not yet resolved. This most troublesome problem is the subject of *Issues Past and Present*.

TOP, LEFT TO RIGHT:
FREDERICK MESERVE COLLECTION
CULVER PICTURES
MISSOURI HISTORICAL SOCIETY
LIBRARY OF CONGRESS
Harper's Weekly, JULY 25, 1868
LIBRARY OF CONGRESS
BOTTOM, LEFT TO RIGHT:
NEW YORK CITY ART COMMITTEE
GEORGE EASTMAN HOUSE
YALE UNIVERSITY ART GALLERY
STATE HOUSE, TOPEKA
NEW YORK PUBLIC LIBRARY
LIBRARY OF CONGRESS
NEW YORK PUBLIC LIBRARY
NAACP

INTERPRETING THE PAST

The Causes of the Civil War

Firemen seldom leave the ruins of a fire without probing among the charred timbers or the blackened walls to find out what started the blaze. Historians probe among the ruins and the records of wars in order to determine their causes and to prevent renewed destruction.

Civil wars often seem more senseless and destructive than other wars because they are like a fight between the members of a family. Peaceful ways of settling differences are forgotten and give way to violence between those who a short time before were united in achieving truly worthwhile goals.

American historians have given our Civil War, one of the most destructive in history, special attention. As you read the primary and secondary sources presented here, consider these questions:

1. Why do some wars have their roots in events that took place long before the actual fighting began?
2. What caused the Civil War?

Two Views on Race

George Fitzhugh was a Virginia lawyer who, in the 1850's, wrote two books and many articles on slavery. They were widely read in the South. His ideas about blacks and slavery were popular among southern whites.

William Lloyd Garrison, one of the most famous of the northern whites who wanted to abolish slavery, wrote the words quoted below for a Baltimore newspaper.

GEORGE FITZHUGH: *SOUTHERN THOUGHT*, 1857

Men in general have made inferior [lower] races and individuals slaves to their superiors. How fortunate for the South that it has this inferior race, the blacks. It lets it make the whites a privileged class. It frees the whites from all the lower types of work done by servants.

A "privileged class" is a group of people who enjoy rights or advantages denied to others in the same society.

WILLIAM LLOYD GARRISON: *GENIUS OF UNIVERSAL EMANCIPATION*, 1830

I deny the idea that God has made one portion of the human race superior to another. No matter how many races are joined together—no matter how many different shades of color there are between tribes or nations—give them the same chances to improve and a fair start at the same time. The result will be equally brilliant, equally productive, equally grand.

1. What is the main point of disagreement between Fitzhugh and Garrison?
2. Is there a reason for the Civil War indicated in these quotes? Explain your answer.

All One Thing or All the Other

The speech from which these words are taken was made by Abraham Lincoln on June 17, 1858. He had just been nominated by the Republican state convention, meeting in Springfield, Illinois, to run for the United States Senate.

ABRAHAM LINCOLN: *THE HOUSE DIVIDED*, 1858

Agitation [deep concern] about slavery will not cease until a crisis shall have been reached and passed. "A house divided against itself cannot stand." I believe this government cannot endure permanently half slave and half free. I do not expect the Union to be dissolved — I do not expect the house to fall — but I do expect it will cease to be divided. It will become all one thing, or all the other. Either the opponents of slavery will stop the further spread of it or its defenders will push it forward till it shall become lawful in all the States, old as well as new, North as well as South.

The quotation which Lincoln gives here is from the New Testament (Matthew 12:25).

The "Union" is the nation acting as a whole.

1. Did Lincoln say in this speech that he was in favor of abolishing slavery? Explain your answer.
2. What possible cause for the Civil War is indicated in this speech?

The South Will Never Submit

Like Lincoln, Otho Singleton was born in Kentucky and became a successful lawyer and politician. After moving to Mississippi he was elected to Congress in 1858.

OTHO ROBARDS SINGLETON: *SPEECH IN CONGRESS*, 1860

What will be the future of the southern slaveholder? If slavery is limited to the places where it exists now, it will necessarily be overthrown. It is only a question of time. We now have 4 million slaves in the 15 southern States. That population doubles itself, according to the census returns, every 25 years, by natural increase. Fifty years from now we will have 16 million slaves. Do you think that we will ever agree to have our 4 million Negroes made equal with ourselves, our wives, and our children? The South will never

submit [give in] to that. It does not matter what evils come upon those of us in the South. It does not matter how deep we may have to wade through blood. We must keep our slaves in their present position as slaves. If we are not allowed to do this inside of the Union, I tell you that it will be done outside of it. We do not intend to be kept within our present limits. There are not enough men in all the North to keep 3 million armed Southerners from going into the surrounding territories. You ask me if we can preserve this institution of slavery if we leave the Union? I believe we can. You ask me when will the time come, when will the South be united? It will come; it will be united when you elect a Black Republican as President of the United States. Can we stand by and permit such a man to be President? What would we have to hope for? We can never quietly stand by and permit the control of the army and navy to go into the hands of a Black Republican President.

Many Southerners spoke of all Republicans as "Black Republicans," mostly because Republicans wanted to limit the spread of slavery.

1. In what way is this speech a reply, or not a reply, to Lincoln's *The House Divided* speech?
2. What reasons for the Civil War not mentioned by Fitzhugh, Garrison, or Lincoln are indicated in this speech?

The Question Dividing the Nation

The next selection was written by a historian many years after the Civil War. After completing his studies at Columbia University, Charles Ramsdell returned to his native state of Texas where he taught for many years at the university. The selection was part of an article in a special magazine for historians.

CHARLES W. RAMSDELL: *THE NATURAL LIMITS OF SLAVERY'S EXPANSION*, 1929

The question dividing the nation before 1861 was whether the Federal government should permit and protect the expansion of slavery into the western territories. This was not always the main cause of dispute between the sections, but no other question was the subject of such continuous and widespread interest or of such bitter debate. It was this question that caused so much agitation and excitement in so many political contests between 1843 and 1860. It seems safe to say that if this question had been eliminated or settled peacefully, there would have been no secession and no Civil War.

"Secession" means withdrawal from the Union.

1. If Ramsdell's interpretation of the main cause is correct, how might the Civil War have been prevented?

While the contemporary historian Bruce Catton was a reporter and newspaper writer, he began to study the Civil War as a hobby. Since World War II he has written many books and articles on the war.

Change and Fear of Change

BRUCE CATTON: *THE COMING FURY*, 1961

A deep change was taking place in the world in the years before the Civil War. The invention of the steam engine, the development of semi-automatic machinery, the growth of worldwide systems of cheap transportation, and the opening of limitless markets that had never existed before—all these made it possible for some nations to become industrialized.

In the United States industrialization took place mostly in the northern States. Yet the South was also directly involved in the wave of industrialization. The vast cotton fields of the Gulf States were the base for the great world textile industry. Cotton was a necessary factor in the growth and progress of the economic revolution that was taking place.

This put the South in an extremely difficult position. It was contributing to the very thing that was certain to change its own society. But for a great number of reasons the South tried to stay just as it was in a time when everything men lived by was changing from top to bottom. The Industrial Revolution was underway and it could not be stopped.

Many decisions, made at different times and places, North and South, brought about the Civil War. None of these decisions can be fully explained. Some people would just not admit that things were changing. Many, who liked things as they were, feared and even hated change. Both fear and change, especially fear *of* change, were important factors in bringing on the war. The change was inevitable; the fear of change led to conflict instead of compromise.

1. Why was the South affected by the changes that the Industrial Revolution was bringing to the North?
2. Has Catton suggested any as yet unmentioned cause or causes of the Civil War? Explain your answer.

Summary Questions

Some people are again predicting that issues dividing Americans will result in civil war. Consider again the possible causes of the Civil War. Which, if any, of these problems continues today? Do you feel that there are any causes or combination of causes which could possibly lead to civil war in your lifetime? Why or why not?

12

The Coming of the Civil War

> Mine eyes have seen the glory of the coming of the Lord;
> He is trampling out the vintage where the grapes of wrath are stored.

That is how the "Battle Hymn of the Republic," a song of the Civil War, begins. The blazing eyes of John Brown (right) reflect the bloodshed and hatred of the scene of war which surrounds him. In 1861 darkness overtook the American success story. Until then good things seemed to be guaranteed to the young nation. Despite some hard times, like the depression of 1837, there had been steady growth, prosperity, and unity until the 1850's. But in 1861 war between the North and the South tore the nation apart. It took 4 years and 600,000 young men's lives to reunite the nation—and end slavery.

Why did the war come? The generation that fought it had simple answers. To some Northerners it was God's just judgment on the land for the sin of slavery. Yet many other Northerners would have denied such an idea. The war to them was only to save the **Union** (the nation acting as a whole) from the efforts of "traitors" to destroy it. Southerners believed that the war grew out of northern violations of the South's constitutional rights. In their eyes they were resisting in 1861 a wrongful government much as their forefathers had done in 1776.

Later generations had other answers. Some historians say the war was inevitable because of different social outlooks between North and South that went back to the differences between colonial Massachusetts and colonial Virginia. Other historians believe that the root causes were in economic conflict between the industrial North and the agricultural South. Some lay the blame on impatience: Neither the North nor the South wanted to wait for time to settle their quarrels.

We do not know *the* answer. In history there are many causes for an event. The explanation of an event by more than one cause may seem less satisfying than simple answers that promise to end all doubts. Yet the easy answer is not always the right one. Because people believed in simple answers, the fiery spirit of Bible-and-rifle-carrying John Brown marched on.

As you read, think about these questions:
1. What differences between the North, South, and West led to civil war?
2. Why is compromise often a part of making laws?

A gigantic figure of John Brown dominates this modern painting.

Below: New York has long been a crowded center of trade and commerce. In the 1850's the boundaries of New York City were limited to Manhattan Island (center). Brooklyn (lower right) was a separate city and Queens (upper right) a growing village across the East River. Across the Hudson River in New Jersey, Hoboken (left center) and Jersey City (lower left) were thriving. Right: New York's population grew each day with the arrival of immigrants like this Irish family.

CULVER PICTURES

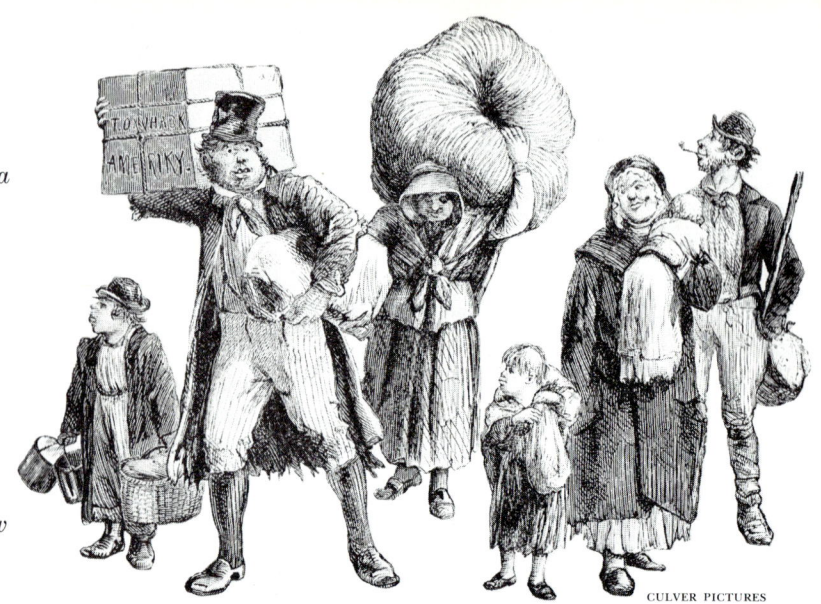

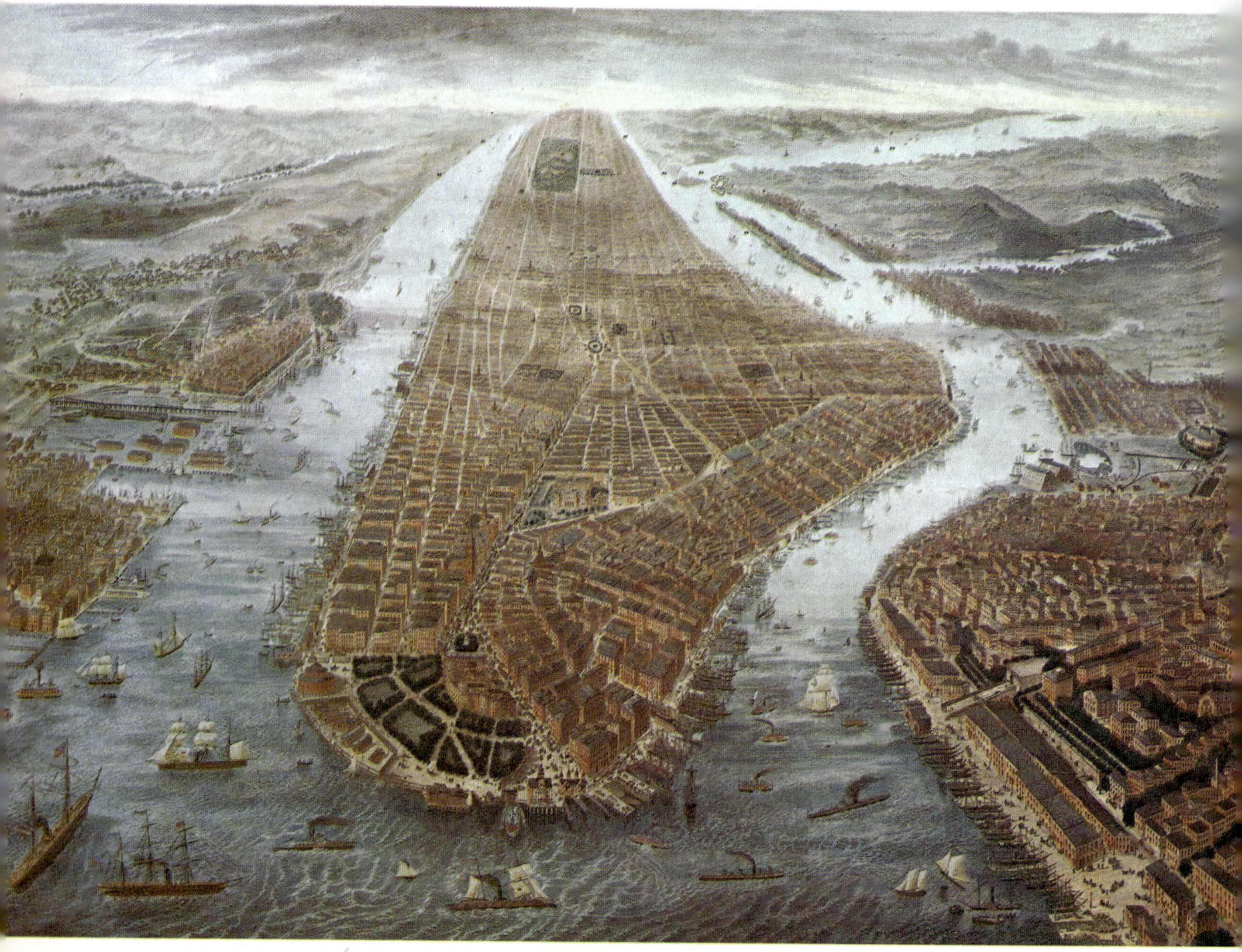

NEW YORK PUBLIC LIBRARY, PRINTS DIVISION

Sectional Patterns

Sometimes the same forces which seemed to knit the nation together were also helping to divide it. Rapid growth was common to the entire nation, but changed different sections of it in different ways. By 1830 each of the three sections of the United States—Northeast, South, and West—had a different basic economy. As a result, each also had a widely different style of social and cultural life. In population and area these sections were as large as most European countries. Americans often felt more devoted to the section than to the nation in which they lived. So the United States, from 1830 to 1860, became more of a federation of sections—a federation not foreseen in the Constitution.

The Northeast Becomes More Urban and Industrial

The first such great section was the Northeast. It included New England, New York, New Jersey, and Pennsylvania. In 1830 the Northeast had a population of about 5.5 million. In 1860, after 30 years of industrial boom, the figure had risen to over 10.5 million. Hundreds of thousands of Northeasterners worked in the factories which turned out boots, shoes, textiles, clocks, guns, sewing machines, and other manufactured goods.

The Northeast still had a large farm population, but the section's flavor was becoming more and more urban and industrial. Its booming factories attracted a large part of a growing number of immigrants. Between 1820 and 1860 over 5 million foreign newcomers arrived. Like the family at the upper left, most of them were from Ireland or other northern European nations such as Scotland, England, Germany, or the Scandinavian countries. Though many went westward to grow with frontier communities, thousands settled in factory towns and big cities.

To the ports of Boston, New York, and Philadelphia came ships loaded with cotton, silk, tea, gold, and grain. The view of busy New York at the left is the kind that young Walt Whitman saw daily in "mast-stemm'd Manhattan." "Thrive, cities," he wrote. "Bring your freight."

The South Falls Behind

The South presented a strikingly different picture. Although the South grew sugar, rice, and tobacco as well as cotton, and although the upper southern states of Missouri, Kentucky, Delaware, and Maryland produced more mules, horses, corn, and hemp than cotton,

people thought of the South in terms of the large cotton plantation. They pictured the plantation as being worked by hundreds of slaves in spite of the fact that in 1860 fewer than 50,000 white Southerners out of 8 million owned more than 20 slaves. Nevertheless, Southerners themselves liked to act as if the typical pattern of the section was life on a great plantation. The painting (upper right) shows a world of grace and charm, free from the problems and pressures of city life. According to this ideal view of the old South's ways, kindly masters took care of slaves who were never thrown out of work by industrial panics such as the one in 1837.

The reality was not much like the plantation ideal. A large class of Southerners owned small farms which they worked with the aid of their families and perhaps a few slaves. Their "plantation houses" were slightly improved log cabins. They themselves were plain and poorly educated men. Often they envied their great slave-owning neighbors whom they generally voted into office.

The slaves themselves were far from carefree. Most of them were shabbily dressed field workers like those at right. Their usual diet of corn bread and fat meat did not give them much strength for hard, dawn-to-dusk outdoor work. In their windowless and over-crowded huts, sickness was common but good medical care rare.

The whole South paid a price for the cotton boom. Most of the money saved out of profits went into land and slaves. Also the slave labor force consumed very few goods. So southern merchants had little reason to stock up on low-cost clothes and goods for a large market. The South, therefore, had little industry, few large cities, and few jobs to attract immigrants. As a result, governments of southern states had few tax dollars to spend on schools and other improvements. The South fed raw cotton to the mills of a fast-growing modern world but reaped few benefits.

The Booming West Grows Closer to the Northeast

The West was a kind of "balance wheel" between the other, older sections. Like the South, it was mostly agricultural, and profitably so. In 1859 western states of the old Northwest Territory, plus newer states like Iowa and Minnesota, grew a good part of the 830 million bushels of corn and 172 million bushels of

LOUISIANA STATE MUSEUM

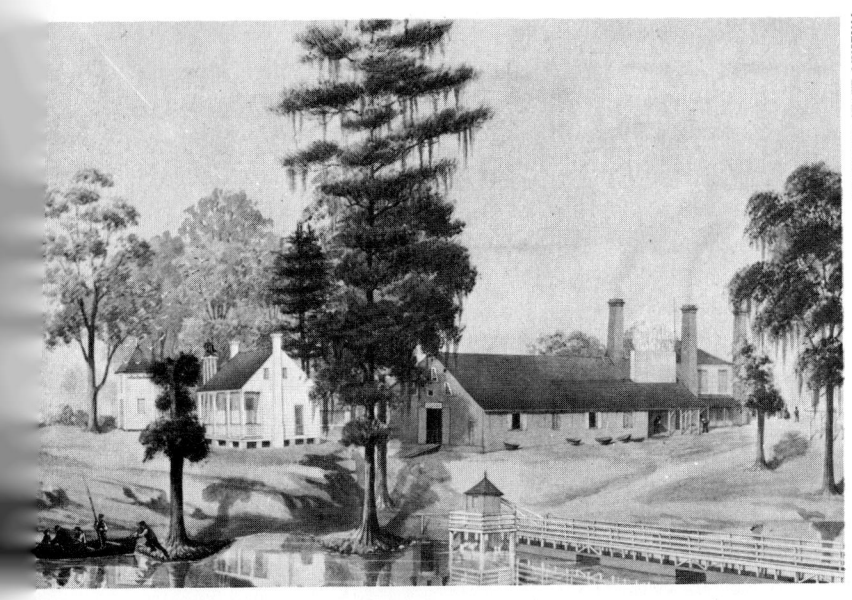

The grandeur of this Louisiana sugar plantation (left) contrasts sharply with the miserable quarters of this old slave and his great-grandchildren (below).

WILFRID DELLQUEST COLLECTION, LA JOLLA

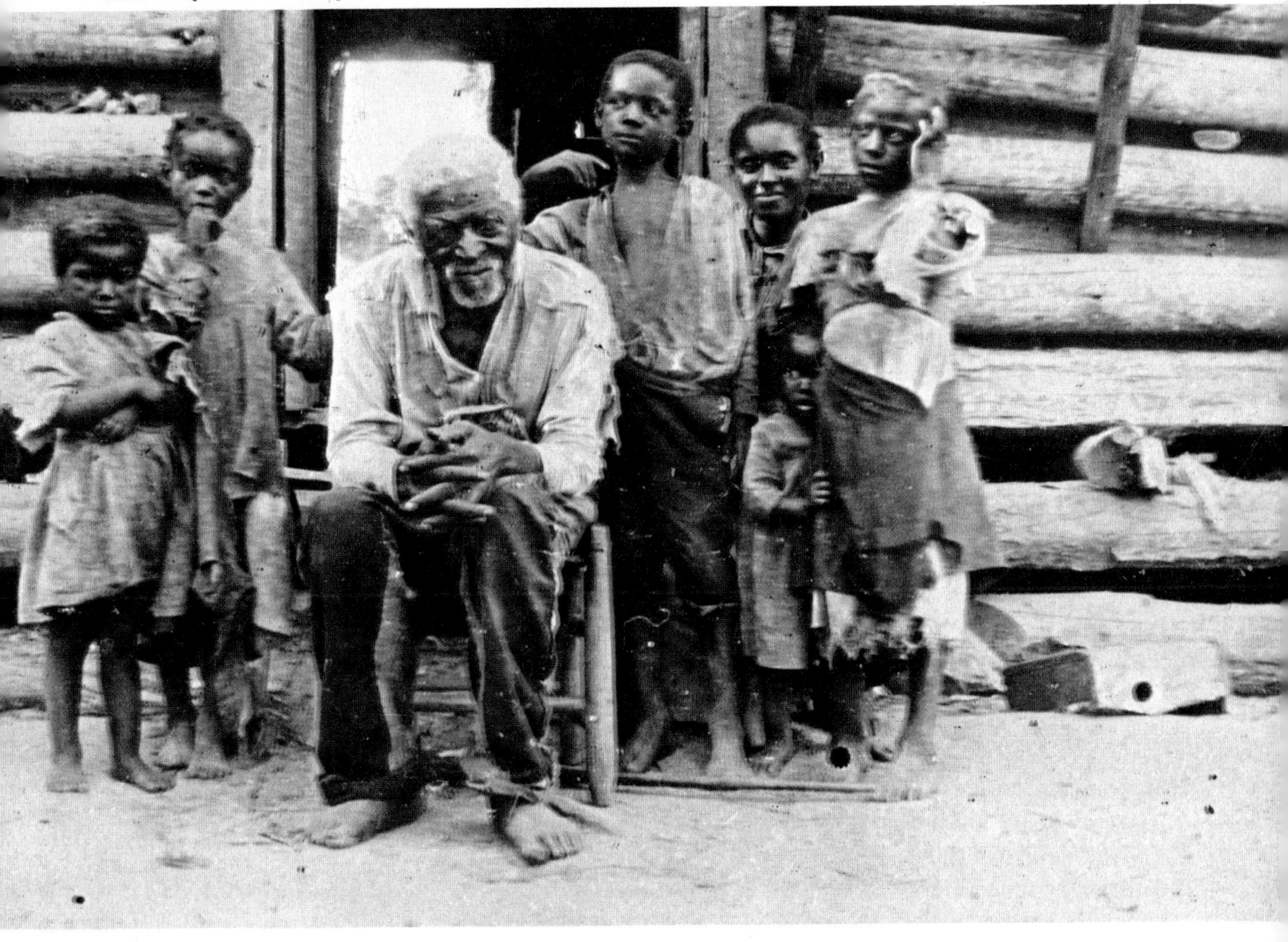

wheat harvested in the United States. With the help of new inventions like the mechanical reaper (lower right), the West was becoming the nation's breadbasket. It was also the nation's butcher shop, raising many of the 32 million hogs and 15 million cattle on American farms and ranches.

Like the Northeast, the West became home to many different peoples. The Ohio Valley was settled in good part by the same kind of Southerners who brought their axes and their camp meetings to the mountains of Kentucky. But after the Erie Canal opened, the area around the Great Lakes filled with New Englanders and New Yorkers. Immigrants from Europe also moved toward the untouched, cheap lands of the new states. By 1860 Missouri, Illinois, and Wisconsin had very large German populations. Wisconsin and Minnesota attracted many newcomers from Scandinavia to farm and to work in the lumber industry. So many loggers were Swedish that a saw was called a "Swedish fiddle."

Unlike the South, the West did not depend only on farming for its wealth. Industry moved westward, too. In cities on the banks of the great western rivers, factories rose to pack meat, distill whiskey, make rope from locally grown hemp, and build steamboats and farm machinery. By 1860 St. Louis (upper right) was a well-developed city with newspapers, lecture halls, theaters, and handsome buildings. So was Cincinnati. Even "upstart" Chicago, not chartered until the mid-1830's, was humming with activity by 1860. The city's lakeside wharves and rail depots were already beginning to make it what the famous poet Carl Sandburg much later called hog butcher, stacker of wheat, and freight handler to the world.

In 1860 a large part of the West's produce was still going downriver to New Orleans. But more and more shipments went by railroad to eastern cities. On the eve of the Civil War, this growing link between the West and the Northeast created an important change in the political line-up of the nation's sections.

The Politics of Sectionalism

The main job of politicians from 1830 onward was to arrange peaceful bargains among these three sections, so that the growing country might remain one nation. Each section had many **pressure groups** (people united by a common desire to get something from the government by applying pressure). But in each the

Above: St. Louis grew in size as traffic along the Mississippi River increased. However, a railroad on the far river bank was to tie St. Louis to the North rather than to the South via the Mississippi—and shatter the South's hopes for a strong link to markets in the West. Right: western factories supplied farmers with much of the latest equipment. Here, a factory in Springfield, Ohio, advertises its farm machinery for 1859.

CHICAGO HISTORICAL SOCIETY

LIBRARY OF CONGRESS

351

basic economic pattern made one such group dominant.

In the Northeast, after 1815, manufacturers spoke with the loudest voice. Successful northeastern politicians had to pay close attention to the needs of investors in industry, since the well-being of the entire area depended on busy factories. The strongest demand of the manufacturers was for a tariff on imports to protect the items that they made. Such a tax on imported goods was deliberately high. Its aim was not to raise revenue but to make it unprofitable for foreigners to sell products in the United States which would compete with American manufactures.

In the South the cotton-growing slaveholders were the pillars of politics. The tariff outraged them. As they saw it, the southern cotton crop when sold abroad earned money to spend on low-cost British and European manufactures. But the tariff forced Southerners and other farming Americans to buy Yankee goods with higher price tags. Southern spokesmen claimed that the tariff compelled the South to **subsidize** (give financial help to) northern industry.

In the West the most outstanding needs were for cheap land and government help in improving transportation. Politicians who hoped to win the West, therefore, tried to include these demands in a legislative package, or group of laws, which would also appeal to other sections. The political leaders who aimed at national victory for their parties then had to win Congressional adoption of their combined proposals for laws to benefit each section. Great debates rang out in Congress, like that shown at left, between South Carolina's Senator Robert Hayne and Massachusetts' silver-tongued Daniel Webster in 1830.

This sectional debate started as a competition between the South and the North for western votes. A Connecticut Senator introduced a resolution to cut down on public land sales in order to discourage factory workers from going West. Hayne attacked this idea, hoping to win popularity with Westerners who wanted to see the population of their section keep on growing.

But Hayne took the argument beyond that. He said that the national government had no right whatever to harm the interests of one section for the benefit of another. When it did so Hayne claimed that the Union, the Federal government, threatened liberty. The states must check a too-powerful Federal government from taking away their sovereignty. The Constitution

FANEUIL HALL, BOSTON

In the Senate on January 26, 1830, Daniel Webster delivers his celebrated reply to Robert Hayne. The speech was not a logical reply to the points raised by Hayne. It is famous because it stirred up a tremendous emotional reaction on behalf of the Union.

did not create one nation, he insisted. It was a compact, or agreement, among states, to be observed only when it served their best interests. Hayne's speech was a strong defense of **states' rights.**

Webster replied eloquently. He strongly defended American nationalism. The American people were one. The nation as a whole was their creation. Its success was the best way of winning freedom for all. The Union had made growth and prosperity possible. It should not be destroyed by local jealousies and roadblocks. He closed with a famous passage. He prayed that, when he looked at the sun for the last time in his life, he would not see it "shining on the broken and dishonored fragments of a once glorious Union," but on an American flag with "not a stripe erased or polluted, nor a single star obscured." That flag should carry the sentiment "dear to every true American heart—Liberty *and* Union, now and forever, one and inseparable."

So long as the sections stayed roughly equal in wealth and population, and the differences between them were economic, government by "horse-swapping" could go on. Compromise was possible on the basis of sharing the wealth of an expanding economy—some for you, some for me.

But through the 1830's and 1840's, dangerous things were happening. The Northeast and the West were outracing the South in growth and population. As a result, Southerners were losing the sense of security that comes from dealing as an equal. Also slavery was becoming a political issue. Unlike other sectional issues, slavery was not just a dollars-and-cents matter. It dealt with black and white, right and wrong, and the values by which men live. When slavery became a battleground between sections, the "game" of sectional bargaining was played for blood.

Questions for Discussion

1. How did rapid economic growth tend to unite the country in some ways and divide it in others?
2. How did the Industrial Revolution change the economy of the North?
3. Why did the cotton boom not result in widespread southern industrial and urban development?
4. After 1830 what pressure group became the dominant political voice in the Northeast? the South? the West? What conflicts were bound to emerge among the three sections?

United States Telegraph, OCTOBER 19, 1832

The tariff question was the subject of bitter sectional debate for a number of years. The southern viewpoint—that the North was growing rich while the South suffered the consequences—was presented in this 1832 cartoon.

Slavery Divides the Nation

In 1820 there were a number of antislavery societies in both the North and the South. Their members believed that slavery was an evil that would pass away slowly as the world grew wiser and right-thinking masters freed their "servants." Some knew that even **emancipated** (freed) blacks suffered greatly from discrimination in the United States. They thought they could solve the problem by raising money to settle freed slaves in their "homeland" of Africa.

Abolitionists Seek an End to Slavery

Around 1830 a new spirit took hold of those who were against slavery. It rejected gradualism, the idea that slow change is best. Gradualism, the new antislavery leaders felt, was failing. Besides, slavery was a *sin*—and sin must be cut out of national life immediately. As time went on this spirit grew, aided by such best-selling antislavery novels as Harriet Beecher Stowe's *Uncle Tom's Cabin* (left). Its hero, Uncle Tom, a slave, is a sincere Christian with no bad habits and no angry feelings. He is almost too good to be true. Yet *Uncle Tom's Cabin* was powerful propaganda in the 1850's. Many of its readers came to see every slaveholder as a cruel bully and every slave as a black saint. Such unthinking judgment about the behavior of an entire group of people added to the likelihood of bitter conflict.

In addition to emotion becoming more important in antislavery circles after 1830, there was a new **militancy** (willingness to fight) among whites in the movement. The best known white antislavery militant was William Lloyd Garrison (upper right). In 1831 he began publication of an antislavery newspaper, *The Liberator*. Concerning slavery, he said, "I will not excuse—I will not retreat a single inch—AND I WILL BE HEARD."

There was a third force behind the new movement for immediate **abolition** (the ending of slavery and the slave trade) after 1830. It was a stirring among black Americans—both the approximately 320,000 Negroes who were free and the 2 million slaves. A black small-business man in Boston named David Walker spoke for many free Negroes in 1829 when he published a little volume known as *Walker's Appeal*. To white Americans he cried out, "We must and shall be free, I say, in spite of you." To enslaved blacks he urged resistance and escape, and an end to fear because "the

NEW-YORK HISTORICAL SOCIETY

The cover of the children's version of Uncle Tom's Cabin, *1853.*

PRIVATE COLLECTION

LIBRARY OF CONGRESS

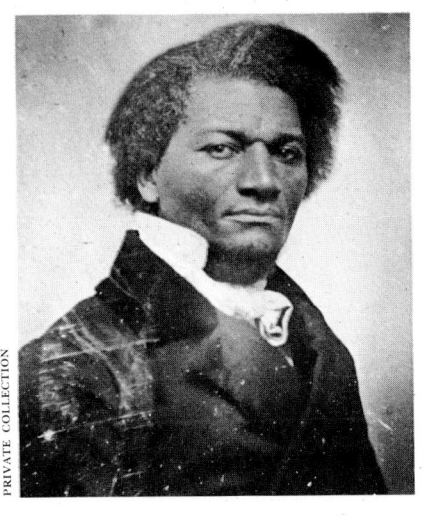

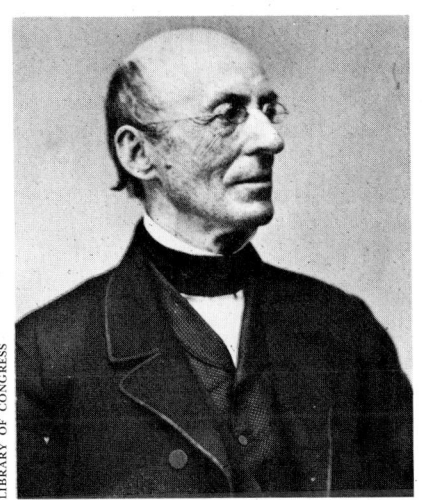

Above: Speeches by ex-slave Frederick Douglass aroused abolitionist support. William Lloyd Garrison protested slavery by burning a copy of the Constitution at a Fourth of July celebration. Below: Outsiders break up an 1860 meeting of Boston abolitionists.

Harper's Weekly, DECEMBER 15, 1860

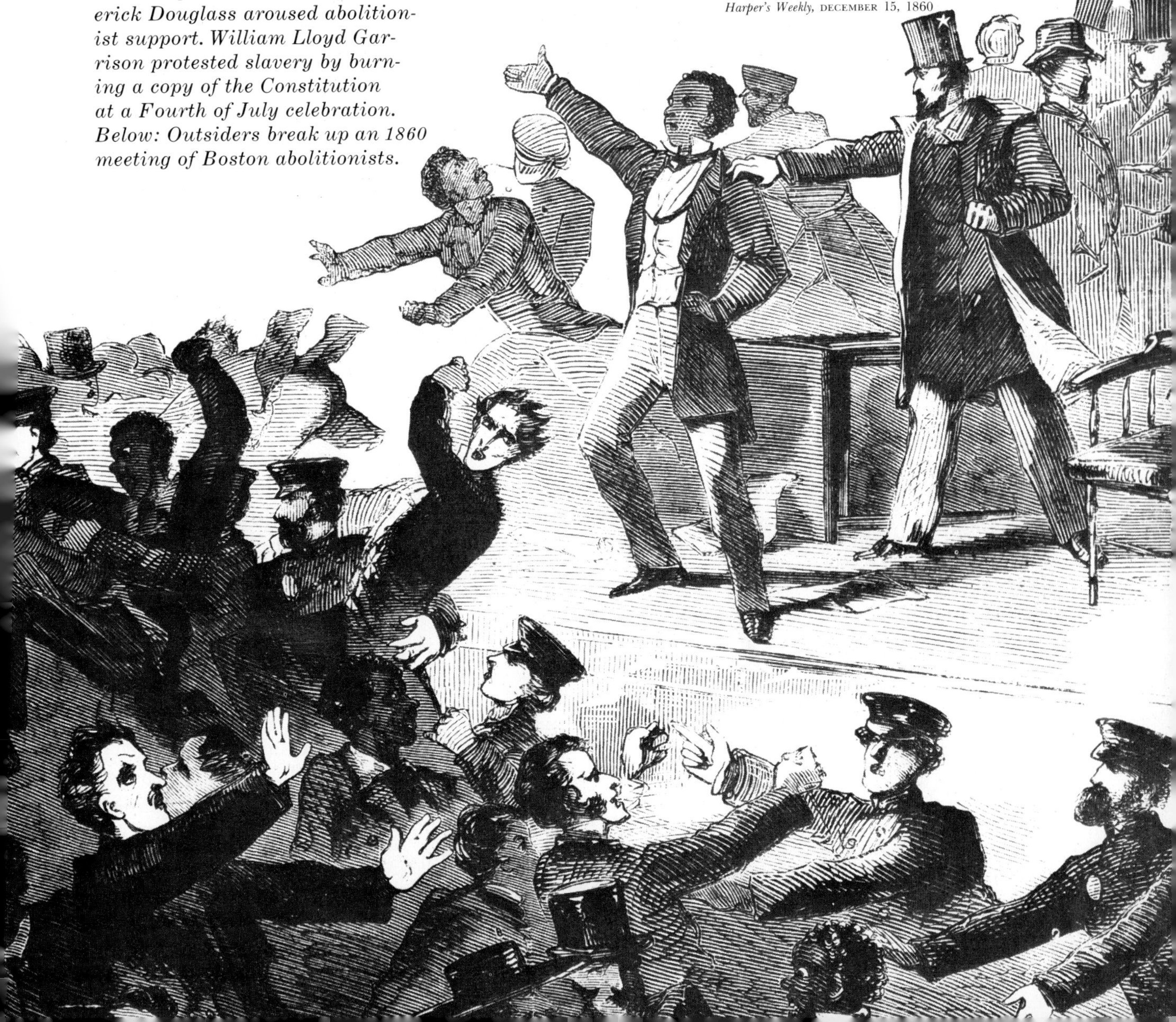

Above and opposite page: A common defense of slavery appears in these 1841 cartoons. The slaves are well-clothed and happy, and the owners are willing to do anything to increase the comfort of their slaves. Factory workers are ill-clothed and starving during hard times, and the factory owner cruelly ignores their plight.

God of justice and of armies will surely go before you." About a thousand slaves a year did "protest" against slavery by running away. Later some who were educated became speakers and writers in the antislavery cause. Others, like Harriet Tubman, helped southern slaves escape to freedom. The most famous ex-slave abolitionist was Frederick Douglass (preceding page). Born in 1817, he managed to learn to read and write even though he was a slave. In 1838 he escaped. After bitter months of supporting himself by doing odd jobs, he joined the antislavery movement. He was a powerful speaker and writer, and in Rochester, New York, he established a newspaper, the *North Star*, which was a kind of black readers' *Liberator*. Douglass' pen and speeches soon made him famous.

As the antislavery argument gained in fierceness, violence flamed. In 1831 in Southampton, Virginia, Nat Turner, a slave preacher, led a revolt which he said was the result of a direct commandment to him by God. Some 50 white persons were killed before Turner and his followers were captured and hanged.

While the rage against slavery mounted, so did the feelings of its defenders. Even in the North, whites who feared and hated both black and white opponents of slavery broke up abolitionist meetings, tarred and feathered abolitionist speakers, and burned the offices of abolitionist newspapers.

The South Defends Slavery

Southerners were hurt and bewildered by all of this. Most of them were respectable, hard-working, Bible-reading Americans and, as we saw, most of them did not own slaves. Abolitionist papers painted them as being lazy — a terrible sin in that day and age — living, or hoping to live, off the labor of others. They were branded as enemies of progress and accused of sins that ran from drunkenness to the sale of children — born to them by black women.

Southerners defended slavery in several ways. One was a simple constitutional argument. The Constitution permitted slavery. Those states which allowed it ought not to be criticized, since the Constitution was an agreement among states with different customs.

Southerners also insisted that blacks were unable to govern themselves without white help. Yet if set free and given the privileges of whites, including the vote, the blacks would then be in a majority in some

southern communities and rule their white neighbors. Almost no Northerner would accept such a fate himself!

A third southern argument was simply that slaves were needed to grow cotton profitably. Besides, Southerners also pointed out that they had made a huge investment in slaves. Southerners even argued that slavery was a good thing for slaves, as illustrated in the margins of these pages. The slaves, they said, did not suffer from the uncertainty of the industrial, capitalistic system. White workers were hired at the lowest possible wages, then fired, and allowed to starve in hard times (right). A competitive society was only war between capital and labor, with labor usually losing. In the agricultural South, on the other hand, capital owned labor and looked after it in return for service (left). Kindness replaced social warfare.

But in defending slavery and their belief in **white supremacy** (the control of political, social, and economic life by whites only), white Southerners were driven further and further from democratic ways. Southern postmasters opened the mails and burned abolitionist newspapers. Southern Congressmen tried to "gag" Congress by blocking debate on antislavery petitions. Such actions tended to prove abolitionist charges that slavery was a threat to freedom in the entire nation. The South stood alone in challenging the official national belief in liberty for all. A few abolitionists, equally alone, argued in favor of ending a union with slaveholders.

The Search for a Compromise

The job of the politician was to arrange agreements by compromise among groups and sections. The aim of the reformer was to create a just, perhaps a perfect, society. Slavery brought politicians and reformers onto a collision course. Yet the Federal government was not able to deal directly with slavery. Under the Constitution it had no control over the institution. However, whenever the question of slavery in the territories arose, the national government became involved. There, its power was clear. The first great clash in Congress on the subject came in 1820. It had the alarming urgency, to the aging Thomas Jefferson, of "a firebell in the night."

When Missouri asked Congress for statehood, New York Representative James Tallmadge, Jr., proposed that before being admitted, the would-be state should

bar the entry of any new slaves and gradually free those already there. A bitter debate followed throughout much of 1819. Could Congress ban the creation of future slave states, so that, as the nation grew, the South would eventually become a minority in the Senate? Could Congress tell a southern slaveholder, "If you want to settle in Missouri, you must give up your slaves. You cannot move freely in this country with your special 'property.'"

Opponents of the Tallmadge plan answered all such questions with a ringing "No!" Tallmadge supporters urged Southerners to think twice. Many Southerners agreed that slavery was a curse and a burden. Let them "plant not its seeds in this uncorrupt soil."

The Missouri Compromise of 1820

A compromise was reached. Its chief arranger was the popular, persuasive Henry Clay (upper right). Clay won votes to admit Missouri as a slave state. But at the same time Maine, New England's last frontier, would be admitted as a free state to keep balance in the Senate. A line was drawn across the Louisiana Purchase territory at 36° 30′ north latitude. Though Missouri, which lay north of the line, might keep slavery, it should be banned "forever" in all the rest of the area north of 36° 30′ (map, center left).

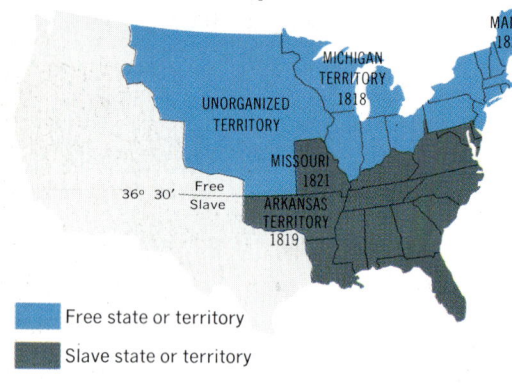

Clay's argument was that compromise was the price of Union. "All government," he said, "is founded upon the principle of mutual concession [giving in]. Let him who elevates [raises] himself above humanity ... say ... I never will compromise." But haters of slavery only saw that the evil had been given a green light to spread westward. "We had it in our power to stop the progress of slavery," said one sadly, "*and we chose to let it go on.*"

Through twenty years of national growth and debate over slavery, the Missouri Compromise of 1820 stood firm. But the Mexican War forced the nation to face the question once more in the new territories taken from Mexico (see map, left). In 1848 a national Free-Soil Party was formed. It wanted both to have the government give pioneers free land and to keep slavery out of any new United States territory. Slaveholders prepared to defend their rights. When California in 1849 asked to enter the Union with a constitution barring slavery, some Southerners threatened to leave the Union.

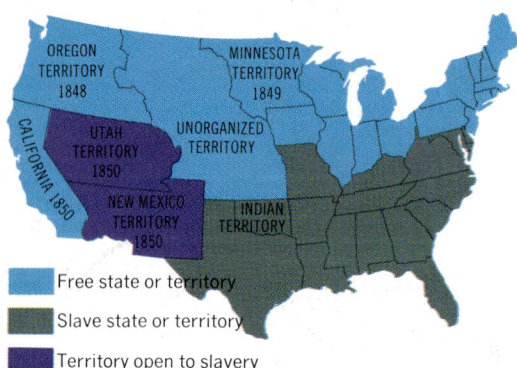

The Compromise of 1850

Three aging political veterans opened the Congressional debate. John C. Calhoun (lower right), near death, listened while a younger Senator read his speech. The South, it said, was a minority in the Union now. The Constitution had not created a nation in which a majority had unlimited power. Minority rights were supposed to be recognized. The North must give the South its due and stop stirring up the slavery question, or the Union was as good as ended.

Clay offered a new compromise. California would be a free state. Territorial governments would be organized for Utah and New Mexico with nothing said about slavery one way or the other. That would postpone the question until they were ready for statehood. Slaves could be kept, but not bought or sold, in the District of Columbia. But Northerners must agree to a very strict Fugitive Slave Act which would force officials of the Federal and of all state governments to make vigorous efforts to catch runaway slaves.

On March 7, 1850, Daniel Webster (upper left, opposite page) rose in Congress to defend Clay's plan. Geography would doom slavery, Webster boomed. Cotton could never grow in the desolate deserts and craggy mountains of the Far West, and slavery would not go where it was not profitable. Let nature, not battlefields, make the final judgment.

After many weeks the compromise measures, as suggested by Clay, were passed. Talk of southern **secession** (withdrawal from the Union) quieted. The firebell had rung a second time, and the alarm had been answered. But the coals were still smoldering.

Compromise Fails—The Kansas-Nebraska Act

Four years after the Compromise of 1850, the nation began a sudden rush away from the spirit of compromise. Illinois' Democratic Senator Stephen A. Douglas introduced a bill to organize territorial governments for Kansas and Nebraska. As a believer in western growth, he hoped to encourage settlement there. But to get votes for his measure from southern Senators, Douglas agreed to a section repealing the Missouri Compromise. There should be no rules against slavery. The territorial legislatures, elected by the settlers to govern until statehood, should decide whether or not to admit slaves.

Douglas believed that this idea of **popular sover-**

Daniel Webster (opposite), Henry Clay (above), and John C. Calhoun (below) dominated debate in the Senate prior to the Civil War.

eignty (letting the local people decide) was fair. But hundreds of thousands of Northerners raged that the South had gone back on its word. The Whig Party had been beaten so badly in 1852 that it almost disappeared. But ex-Whigs, Free-Soilers, and angry northern Democrats joined in "anti-Nebraska" organizations which soon merged into a new party that took the name Republican and strongly opposed the extension of slavery.

After the Kansas-Nebraska Act was passed, Kansas itself became the scene of a conflict between proslavery and "free state" antislavery pioneers. In the elections for a territorial legislature, thousands of proslavery men from neighboring Missouri crossed the border and voted illegally. Free-state settlers boycotted this body and formed a government of their own. Armed parties from both sides began raiding each other's homes and settlements. Troops attempted to preserve order (right), but the situation was still tense when James Buchanan (upper right) was inaugurated President on March 4, 1857.

Two days later came a staggering blow to the antislavery forces. The Supreme Court's Chief Justice Roger B. Taney (upper left) announced a seven-to-two majority decision in the case of *Dred Scott v. Sandford*. Scott (lower left) was a Missouri slave. His former owner had once taken him into Minnesota, north of the 36° 30' line. Later Scott became the property of an abolitionist, who let him sue for his freedom on the grounds that his stay on free soil ended his slave status. The test case backfired. The Court held that Congress could not deny any white American his property rights anywhere under the flag. Taney added that Scott was not and could not be a citizen of his state or of the United States. When the Constitution was adopted, Taney said, Negroes "had no rights which the white man was bound [by law] to respect." The Missouri Compromise was dead.

Supreme Court Chief Justice Roger B. Taney (above) ruled that as a slave Dred Scott (below) had no rights as an American citizen.

Questions for Discussion

1. Why did abolitionists reject gradualism as a solution to the slavery problem?
2. What arguments were used by Southerners to defend slavery?
3. Why did the admission of both Missouri and California to the Union cause conflicts between Northerners and Southerners? How were they settled?

Below: In 1855 antislavery forces in Kansas ran this ad attacking the proslavery legislature. The slavery issue provoked both sides to violence. John Brown led one gang that killed five proslavery advocates. Free-staters formed a separate legislature, but troops dispersed it to prevent further violence. Right: When James Buchanan became President, "Bleeding Kansas" was still a problem. His inept leadership added to the crisis, and it was not until 1861 that Kansas became a state.

LIBRARY OF CONGRESS

Now we DO ASSERT and we declare, despite all the bolts and bars of the iniquitous Legislature of Kansas, that

"PERSONS HAVE NOT THE RIGHT TO HOLD SLAVES IN THIS TERRITORY."

BOTH: KANSAS STATE HISTORICAL SOCIETY

The Rush to War

In the last few years of peace, certain great questions of human rights and governmental power were raised. The first of these was whether or not the United States should remain neutral on the moral question of slavery. The issue was put clearly in the fall of 1858, in Illinois, in a series of debates between Abraham Lincoln and Stephen A. Douglas. Each was his party's choice for Senator.

The Lincoln-Douglas Debates

Both Douglas, the Democrat, and Lincoln, the Republican, were products of the frontier. Douglas had migrated from Vermont to Illinois and had become a lawyer. Lincoln had come from Kentucky and had followed the same calling. Both men were popular with their neighbors.

Both believed that friends of liberty all over the world looked to the Union as a model of democratic government. Both believed in national expansion and in progress through hard work. Both believed in the politics of compromise. But where these two middle-aged, middle-class, white, western lawyers differed was on what America should do about slavery.

Imagine that you are attending their last debate in Alton, Illinois, on October 15, 1858. Both men are tired and their clothes rumpled from travel. Four or five thousand spectators have come by boat and rail from as far away as Springfield and St. Louis. There are banners, bands, and picnic lunches. In Illinois in 1858 politics is a form of recreation.

Douglas speaks first. He follows a line of thinking he has used in earlier debates. First, he argues that each community must decide its institutions for itself. ". . . In my opinion this government can endure forever, divided into free and slave States as our fathers made it,—each State having the right to prohibit, abolish, or sustain slavery just as it pleases." Then he goes on to a theme popular in this southern Illinois community—white supremacy. It is true, says Douglas, that the whole nation claims to believe in the Declaration of Independence, which holds all men to be created equal and thus seems to bar slavery. But, he adds, the Declaration "had no reference to negroes at all. . . ." Its sponsors "did not mean negro, nor the savage Indians, nor the Fejee Islanders, nor any other barbarous race. They were speaking of white men." "Humanity" requires giving blacks some "privileges,"

but what they must be, each state and territory should answer itself. Then, amid cheers, he sits down.

Lincoln rises and begins speaking in his high-pitched voice. He must speak carefully. Douglas has insisted that Lincoln is at heart an abolitionist and a believer in Negro equality. This charge will lose him votes. So Lincoln repeats, in different words, what he has said in earlier speeches. At Springfield he has said, "The negro is not our equal in color—perhaps not in many other respects; still, in the right to put into his mouth the bread that his own hands have earned, he is the equal of every other man, white or black." At Charleston, Illinois, he has gone as far as he will go to appeal to prejudice: "I am not nor ever have been in favor of making voters or jurors of negroes, nor of qualifying them to hold office, nor to intermarry with white people." But, he goes on, he can feel this way and still hate slavery.

Lincoln denies that the founders of the nation expected the United States to remain half slave and half free. They thought that slavery was dying. They provided for ending the slave trade in 1808. They even avoided the use of the word *slave* in the Constitution. They voted to make the Northwest Territory free. All that the Republicans want, the tall man goes on, is to keep slavery from growing. Then it will die, as it did in the North just after the Revolution.

The nation, Lincoln says, cannot simply let the future of slavery be left to the choice of white communities in the territories. The issue must be faced by the whole nation, he concludes. On one hand are the rights of humanity, on the other "the spirit that says 'You work and toil and earn bread and I'll eat it.'" Whether such a statement comes from a tyrannical king or "from one race of men as an apology for [defense of] enslaving another, it is the same tyrannical principle." Lincoln sits down to cheers and music.

Lincoln lost the election, but he made a reputation which led to the Republican Presidential nomination two years later. The question he raised still lives: Can a society survive unless all its members are treated as equals?

John Brown's Raid at Harpers Ferry

In 1859 an even more agonizing question arose. Can a society be purified by violent means? True, the American Revolution had been violent. But its leaders

Douglas (left), the "Little Giant," beat Lincoln in their Senate race.

Harper's Weekly, NOVEMBER 5, 1859

BOSTON ATHENEUM

A photograph of John Brown (right) about three years before the Harpers Ferry Raid where he was wounded (above) and then executed in December 1859 (below).

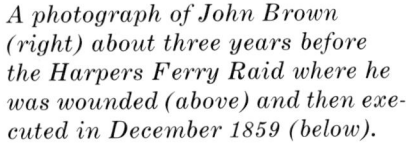

LIBRARY OF CONGRESS

did not hate all Englishmen—only certain rulers and their acts. Nor did they believe that they were directly following God's orders. But in 1859 John Brown (upper left) did think of himself as God's officer, with power and duty to punish sinners. And he also believed that the crimes of his guilty land had to be washed away with blood.

By October of 1859 Brown had hit on a plan. He would gather a small troop, descend on a border region, and free a few slaves by force. Then they would retreat to a mountain hideout and form a free state. Black and white haters of slavery would realize that the time was ripe to strike for freedom. One push would trigger an uprising and bring slavery crashing down in ruins.

On October 16, 1859, Brown and some twenty men, including five free Negroes, moved into Harpers Ferry, Virginia (now West Virginia), and seized the government arsenal there from a few surprised workers. They went out into the countryside, gathered a few slaves and some white prisoners, then went back to the arsenal and—did nothing! Hoping for a slave revolt, Brown waited while Federal and state troops poured into the town. He was wounded and captured with eleven of his followers. Ten were killed—including Brown's two sons. After a speedy trial for treason, Brown was hanged by the state of Virginia in a public ceremony (left).

The raid was a total failure. But the deepest fears of southern whites had been touched. Had Brown not tried to raise the blacks to murder them in bed? Southerners demanded to know if the North supported Brown. Few actually did so. Few would have agreed with spokesmen like Henry David Thoreau, who called Brown "the bravest and humanest man in all the country." Most Americans in the North felt that slavery was lawful, if not just, and law must be respected.

But Southerners panicked. In 1860 hundreds of thousands of them believed that all Republicans—"black Republicans," they called them—were secretly in favor of deeds like Brown's. If the Republicans won the election, the South would no longer be safe in the Union. It must secede. That is what happened. In the spring of 1860 the Democratic Party, one of the last institutions to have both northern and southern supporters, split into two parts. One followed Douglas and nominated him for President. The other, more

actively proslavery, chose John C. Breckenridge. The Republicans nominated Lincoln, and a fourth party of neutralists, the Constitutional Union Party, was also formed. When the four-way contest was over, Abraham Lincoln led with just under 40 per cent of the popular vote and a majority in the Electoral College.

The South Secedes

Promptly, South Carolina seceded, followed within four months by six other deep-South states. They took over most Federal forts and other properties within their boundaries without any fighting. But in South Carolina's Charleston Harbor, Fort Sumter remained in government hands. It became the fuse that led to the gunpowder.

One final, basic issue was now presented. The seceded states organized themselves as the Confederate States of America, with their capital in Montgomery, Alabama, and elected former Mississippi Senator Jefferson Davis (left) as their President. What should Abraham Lincoln do about the secession of seven states when he took office on March 4, 1861?

His problem was a difficult one. If he simply left the Confederate States alone, he would be admitting that the Union was dissolved. But his argument against secession was that the Union was not just an agreement among sovereign states but also an agreement among the people. The people could dissolve the Union but the states could not. Yet Lincoln could not easily force the Confederates back into loyalty. The slaveholding states which had not seceded as of March 4, 1861, declared that the Union must be voluntary. They, too, would secede if their sister states were invaded.

In his inaugural address Lincoln tried to steer a middle course between threats and surrender. He said he would try to hold on to Federal property in the seceded states. But he would not try to deliver the mails or collect customs duties by force. He appealed to the secessionists to return voluntarily to the Union. If they felt threatened as a minority, he declared, they should stay in the Union and convince others of the rightness of their cause, and thus become a majority.

If they forced their views on other states, that would lead to tyranny. If they broke up the Union, that was a step toward anarchy. To both the secessionists and the abolitionists, Lincoln's message was

Top: The Charleston Mercury *announces the secession of South Carolina. Above: Jefferson Davis was an officer in the Mexican War, a Senator, and Secretary of War from 1853 to 1857. He opposed immediate secession in 1860; when it came he wanted to command the Confederate army. Instead, he was elected President of the Confederate States of America.*

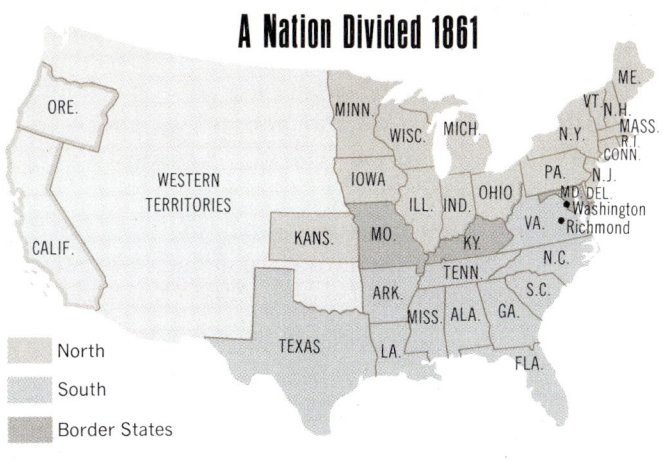

A Nation Divided 1861

- North
- South
- Border States

On April 14, 1860, the rebel flag flies over Fort Sumter as troops begin the cleanup after their successful bombardment.

"Wait!" "Why should there not be a patient confidence in the ultimate justice of the people? Is there any better or equal hope in the world?" Lincoln wanted neither anarchy nor tyranny.

But to many Americans the time was past for listening to reason. South Carolinians continued to resent the Federal force at Fort Sumter. They felt that the national flag flying within sight of Charleston belonged to a "foreign power." South Carolina said that any attempt to bring fresh men or supplies into the fort would be resisted.

Finally, food began to run low. Lincoln had to give up the fort or send provisions to its men. He chose the latter course, informing the South Carolina authorities that he was sending only bread, not bullets. But it was too late. On April 12 at 4:30 A.M., Confederate cannon around the harbor opened non-stop bombardment that lasted 34 hours. The garrison had to surrender. The Confederates had captured Fort Sumter. They had fired on the national flag. Lincoln believed that there was no choice but to meet force with force, and he called for 75,000 volunteers. Civil war had come, and God had "loosed the fateful lightning of His terrible, swift sword."

Questions for Discussion

1. What were the views of both Lincoln and Douglas on the question of white supremacy?
2. What did Lincoln say was the attitude of the Republican Party toward slavery? Why was the Republican Party opposed to abolitionism?
3. How did John Brown's raid help to move the nation toward the Civil War?
4. In his inaugural address how did Lincoln attempt to bring the South back into the Union?

Chapter Review

Social Studies Terms

Union, pressure groups, subsidize, states' rights, emancipated, militancy, abolition, white supremacy, secession, popular sovereignty

Summary Questions for Discussion

1. In the South how did the ideal picture of plantation life differ from the reality?
2. Why did transportation developments affect the economies of the West and North more than the South?

3. What effect did the abolitionists' movement have on the search for a compromise? Why?
4. How did southern and northern politicians differ in their interpretation of the Constitution?
5. List the values most important to a southern slaveholder. List those most important to a northern abolitionist. Why do conflicts in values often lead to violence? Is there a way to prevent violence that arises from a conflict in values?
6. Would slavery have spread to the Far West if it had been legal there? Why?
7. What upset the balance between the sections and broke down the system of compromise that until 1850 had settled disputes between the North and South?
8. Why was the Dred Scott decision so important? How did the case backfire on its sponsors?

Pictures as Historical Evidence

Which pictures in this chapter might tell why most western states did not secede? Explain.

Map Study

Compare the two maps, *The Compromise of 1850* (page 358) and *A Nation Divided* (page 367). What states were added to the Union between the time of the Compromise of 1850 and the outbreak of the Civil War? Were any of these states slave states? Why? Which northern states would it have been easier for the South to invade if Missouri, Kentucky, Delaware, and Maryland had seceded and joined the southern states?

For Further Reading

Abraham Lincoln in Peace and War, by Earl Schenck Miers. New York: American Heritage Publishing Co., Inc., 1964.

Four Took Freedom: The Lives of Harriet Tubman, Frederick Douglass, Robert Smalls, and Blanche K. Bruce, by Philip Sterling and Rayford Logan. Garden City: Doubleday & Company, Inc., 1967.

Slavery in the United States, by Leonard W. Ingraham. New York: Franklin Watts, Inc., 1968.

The Dred Scott Decision, by Frank Latham. New York: Franklin Watts, Inc., 1968.

The Fight for Union, by Margaret L. Coit. Boston: Houghton Mifflin Company, 1961.

13
The Civil War

It was July 4, 1861, the first Independence Day of the Civil War. Celebrations of the Glorious Fourth were missing some of their usual enthusiasm because everyone knew that both the North and the South were completing their preparations for the fighting that would begin within a few weeks. Lincoln tried to brace Americans by telling them, in a message to Congress, why their fathers and husbands and sons were going to war against their own countrymen. His message can be summarized in six words that were read to the Congress: "This is essentially a people's contest."

Later, at Gettysburg in November of 1863, he said that the soldiers buried in the national cemetery there had died so that "government of the people, by the people, for the people, shall not perish from the earth."

The Confederates were equally convinced that their cause was just and of worldwide importance. In explaining the war to the Confederate Congress, President Jefferson Davis said that it stemmed from unjust northern attacks on slavery, which had raised Negroes "from brutal savagery into docile [tame], intelligent, and civilized agricultural laborers." The southern people had to secede, said Davis, to "avoid the dangers with which they were openly menaced." It was a matter of free men defending their rights.

Black Americans did not believe that the coming war was only a white man's quarrel. Their own futures were at stake. Many free Negroes felt like Levin Tilmon of New York, who wrote Lincoln four days before Fort Sumter was fired upon: "If your Honor wishes colored volunteers, you have only to signify [say so]." As for the slaves, they could not speak out. But a Charleston lady noticed that when war talk crackled at Charleston dinner tables, the black servants "make no sign. Are they . . . stupid, or wiser than we are: silent, and strong, biding their time?"

Northerners and Southerners, whites and blacks, prepared to fight and die for their beliefs. People from all walks of life, of all ages and both sexes would suffer. But most of the dying would be done by young men like the recruits at left, some of whom were not much older than you. The "people's war" was mainly their war.

As you read, think about these questions:
1. Why is the Civil War often called the first truly modern war?
2. What factors determine victory in war?
3. Why is there often dissent during war?

Young Confederates posed proudly before the first Battle of Bull Run.

Trial by Arms

The Opening Years 1861–1863

The first year was one of arming, organizing, and finding out how big a struggle the war would be. All over the North and South recruits joined volunteer companies raised in their home towns. The new civilian soldiers elected local community leaders as their lieutenants and captains and marched alongside their neighbors and friends. At first discipline was slack. War seemed like a big camp-out, and many companies had their own uniforms, designed to look dashing.

But time quickly changed all that. The companies were brought together in regiments of about a thousand men, and the regiments were attached to corps, divisions, and armies. The recruits marched or rode to training camps far from home. There, tough new colonels and generals taught them that army life meant drill, camp cleanups, marches, and guard duty. Soon the volunteers learned that war also meant loneliness and sickness. Finally, came combat, wounds, and sometimes death.

In July 1861 about 35,000 raw Union recruits, who had gathered around Washington, bravely started out to seize Richmond, the Confederate capital, about 90 miles away. On July 21 at Bull Run, Virginia, a short distance from Washington, they met a somewhat smaller and equally untrained Confederate force. After a long day of bitter fighting (right), the sudden arrival of Confederate reinforcements turned the tide. The Union forces broke into panic and almost ran back to the shadow of the Capitol. The Congressmen and others who had ridden out with picnic baskets to watch the "show" were caught in the rout. Hopes of ending the rebellion before autumn were left on the battlefield along with the dead.

In the East each side maneuvered to capture the other side's capital city. These campaigns in Virginia attracted the greatest share of the public's attention. But the Civil War's more important theater was probably in the West, the heartland from which most southern supplies had to come. From the start the Federal armies did well in this region. In June of 1861 the area which is now West Virginia was occupied by Federal troops. In February of 1862 one Union spearhead stabbed deep into central Tennessee. In April a joint land and sea expedition seized New Orleans and moved up the Mississippi to a point just below Vicksburg (map, left). Another moved down the Mississippi and captured Memphis in June.

The first major Civil War battle was a confused and bloody fight between two green armies at Bull Run, Virginia, on July 21, 1861. However, this 1889 romantic painting features dashing, gallant cavalrymen and soldiers dying bravely and painlessly.

NEW-YORK HISTORICAL SOCIETY

Lee Attacks the North

In the East the rebels seemed to be winning all the opening rounds. General George B. McClellan (far right) took charge of the Army of the Potomac, the Union force based in and around Washington. McClellan was fond of military pomp and ceremony. Yet his real talent was not in combat but planning campaigns, training troops, and building a smoothly working system of **logistics** (the bringing of men, weapons, and supplies together at the right time and place).

In March of 1862 McClellan put most of his army on transports and sailed them down to a peninsula between two Virginia rivers, the York and the James. With this safe seaborne supply line behind him, he began a cautious advance toward Richmond. His opponent, General Robert E. Lee (top right), was a Virginian, a professional soldier, and an enemy of secession. When Virginia seceded he resigned from the United States Army, saying that he was unwilling to fight against "my relatives, my children, my home."

Lee was as daring as McClellan was cautious. In late June, when McClellan was at last on the outskirts of Richmond, Lee attacked him in a series of actions known as the Seven Days' Battles. The Union army was so badly mauled that it had to be withdrawn all the way to the Washington area. So the war entered a second full year. Not only was victory for the North not in sight, but Lee was attacking boldly.

Aided by his brilliant second-in-command, General Thomas J. ("Stonewall") Jackson, Lee staged an invasion of the North. His Army of Northern Virginia beat the Union troops a second time on the field of Bull Run, then swung into Maryland. The war-weary troops enjoyed the corn, fruit, and poultry of fertile farms in harvest season. But death gathered the biggest crop on September 17 when the two armies met in the Battle of Antietam. After a day of short-range blazing away at each other in orchards and cornfields, about 11,000 were killed or wounded on each side. Lee's losses (right) were almost a quarter of his force. He had to give up his attack and retire into Virginia. This Union victory ended the first Confederate drive northward. But the price was tragically high.

Questions for Discussion

1. What was the strategy of the North? the South?
2. How did Bull Run change the war?

General George B. McClellan (far right) commanded Union forces until Lincoln removed him in November 1862. Two years later McClellan was the Democratic nominee for President. Robert E. Lee, astride his horse Traveller (right), is regarded as the most brilliant Civil War general. More Americans died in the Civil War than in any war in the nation's history. A young private from Georgia (below right) was killed at Malvern Hill during the Peninsula campaign. Directly below, Southerners lay dead in a cornfield after the Battle of Antietam in September 1862.

The Economics and Politics of War

At the war's opening everyone thought that one side would be beaten in a great battle or two, and then surrender. But the Civil War would be won by steady pressure, by overpowering material superiority, by a slow breaking-down of the enemy's will and strength. The South, the weaker side, might win battlefield victories. But the North could survive defeat and come back with more men and guns. Each month war brought greater reliance on new inventions such as ironclad warships, the railroad, and the military telegraph. The North could make more of these.

The Booming North

Lincoln's half of the nation entered the war with tremendous advantages: about 22 million people to 5 million southern whites, over 20,000 of the country's 30,000 miles of railroad, and most of its ships, banks, and factories. These advantages grew greater each year of the war.

The West was in a tremendous spurt of growth. In one day in the 1860's, a judge in Nebraska counted 400 westward-bound wagons at a river crossing. Encouraged by the demands of war, agricultural production soared. The gold mines of California and the silver mines of Nevada were breaking records for output. In Michigan and Minnesota lumberjacks cut down stately trees by the thousands. Around Oil Creek, Pennsylvania, where profitable wells were first drilled in 1859, the war years were prosperous.

In the East factories busily turned out the equipment needed for Union armed forces—rifles, pistols, cannon, gunpowder, telegraph wire, pontoon bridges, uniforms, shoes, canned foods, ships, locomotives, rails, engines, and spare parts. The agricultural South could not match the power so evident in the huge piles of Union army supplies like those shown at a base in Virginia (left).

The Blockaded South

The war was bringing the North into the modern world with giant steps. At the same time it drove the South deeper into poverty. Each month of the war southern bridges, steamboats, and railroad lines were destroyed. Moreover, the Union occupation of the upper South early in the war took from the Confederacy valuable areas that produced horses, cattle, and foodstuffs. Prices soon began to climb. Farmers

During the Peninsula campaign in 1862, Union troops captured the supply depot in Yorktown, Virginia. This photograph shows some of the vast number of weapons stored there by the Union army.

refused to accept payment for their crops in Confederate paper money. Food dealers began **hoarding** (piling up stocks far beyond immediate needs) and **profiteering** (charging outrageous prices for items that are scarce). In cities proud sons and daughters of the South, famed before the war for their hospitality, stood in line to buy precious flour and meat.

The South had counted on the sale of its cotton to European nations to earn enough gold to carry on the war and prop up the Confederate economy. But each month the northern **blockade** of warships shutting off southern ports grew tighter. Soon bales of unsold cotton piled up on southern wharves (upper right). King Cotton could not save the Confederacy. A few fast blockade-running vessels got out with some cotton and brought back small cargoes of munitions, medicines, and other vital supplies. But they were like an eyedropper of water to a man dying of thirst.

Southerners grew ever more desperate. After a family's crops had been taken by either army, its slaves had run away, and its able-bodied men had all gone, there was little to do except move to some new place where friends or relatives might help. Thousands, like the miserable **refugees** (people who flee from invasion or persecution) at lower right, did so. White Southerners now tasted something few Americans had known: frustration and defeat. Being human, they tended to blame the Yankees and overlook the part that southern leadership had played in bringing on the war. A future harvest of sectional hate was planted as the war ground on.

Lincoln Issues the Emancipation Proclamation

The war aim of most Northerners was only to restore the Union. Therefore, Lincoln did not want to advance very far in front of public opinion by emancipating, or setting free, the slaves, particularly when he was trying to keep the four slaveholding states of Kentucky, Maryland, Delaware, and Missouri in the Union. "My paramount [main] object in this struggle is to save the Union," he wrote, "and is not either to save or to destroy slavery."

Yet the war itself doomed slavery. When southern men left for the front, slave-catching patrols stopped operating. When Union troops took over a region, local courts no longer sat to enforce the laws controlling "human property." Most important, thousands of

Left: As a result of the Union blockade, the harbor in Charleston, South Carolina, is crowded with stranded ships and rotting cotton. Below: Driven by fear of the advancing Union armies, these Southerners abandoned their farms and gathered a few cherished belongings in the hope of finding a safer place to live.

SOUTH CAROLINA HISTORICAL SOCIETY

NATIONAL ARCHIVES

METROPOLITAN MUSEUM OF ART

BOTH: LIBRARY OF CONGRESS

Left: In 1862 a refugee family flees from slavery across the Rappahannock River in Virginia into northern lines. Far left: A vicious anti-Lincoln engraving shows him stepping on the Constitution as he signs the Emancipation Proclamation with ink from a devil's pot. Below: This photograph of soldiers of the 107th U.S. Colored Infantry was taken near Washington, D.C.

slaves themselves ran away to Union lines, where they found work cooking, washing, driving wagons, and being useful in other ways.

Lincoln was aware that slaves performing non-combat jobs were a great help to the southern war effort and that freed slaves could be equally useful to the North. It was this line of reasoning—slavery should be ended as a military measure—that finally moved him to act.

Using his power as commander-in-chief of the armed forces, Lincoln issued the Emancipation Proclamation on January 1, 1863. It stated that from that date on, all slaves in areas of rebellion would be forever free. Of course, the slaves in those areas were not really freed until Union armies gained control of the invaded South. After the war the Thirteenth Amendment to the Constitution was adopted to free the slaves in the Union states. Lincoln's opponents raged that he had illegally punished individual Southerners, whether guilty of rebellion or not, by taking away their property. Southerners, and some conservative Northerners, felt like the pro-Confederate artist who showed Lincoln (upper left) signing the Emancipation Proclamation at the devil's bidding. But throughout the North and South, blacks and sympathetic whites rejoiced at the end of more than 200 years of slavery. War had finally cut a bloody path through the tangled legal problem of emancipation.

Meanwhile, blacks did not sit with folded hands while whites argued about them. From the start of the war, freeborn Negroes and ex-slaves asked for the right to be enrolled in the Union army. Many Northerners objected. They believed either that the Negroes would not fight or that, if they went South with guns in hand, they would take revenge on the whites in John Brown's fashion. Both beliefs were false. The proof came when the needs of manpower finally overcame prejudice in 1862, and black regiments were formed and sent into action.

From their first exposure to combat in October of 1862, blacks earned the admiration of many white officers, like one who wrote that they fought "with a coolness and bravery that would have done credit to veteran soldiers." Those in the picture at lower left were among 186,000 black troops—about one-tenth of the whole Union army—who shared the hardships of war.

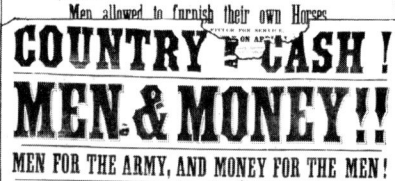

Recruitment, Resistance, and Riot

Not all Northerners flocked to the colors. Many families, especially in the border areas of Maryland, Missouri, southern Ohio, Indiana, and Illinois, resented the war. Some had relatives in the Confederate armies. Almost all of them disliked Negroes and "black Republicans." Coming from poorer and less urbanized parts of their states, they were not influenced by the Republican argument that slavery stood in the way of progress. Progress seemed to have passed them by. These northern war resisters, sometimes called "Copperheads," were often arrested for having acted or spoken against the war and were attacked by neighbors who supported it.

The most bitter outburst of antiwar feeling came in 1863 when the Union began to enforce a **conscription** (draft) law. The South drafted men almost from the start. But the North, as shown in the recruiting posters at left, tried to fill the ranks by making patriotic appeals and offering **bounties** (payments for joining the service). Finally, however, a conscription act was passed. It had a deeply unfair provision which allowed a man to escape service by paying $300, which would be given as a bounty to a substitute. Though many wealthy young men had enlisted, others were willing to buy their way out of duty and danger.

In New York City this especially enraged the poorer people, among whom were many Irish immigrants. Though thousands of Irish were fighting in Union armies, those who stayed at home to work were bitter. High wartime prices ate into their wages. Shabby living conditions sharpened their anger. Many came to feel that the war was being fought to free Negroes, who would then compete with white laborers for jobs and status. So, when the draft calls were announced, savage rioting (right) broke out. Blacks were special targets of mob rage. A Negro orphanage was burned, and dozens of blacks were lynched. Troops finally had to be called in to restore order. All the war-resistance movements took root among people who felt that the war gave them nothing, but took their lives and taxes for remote purposes.

Questions for Discussion

1. What advantages did the North have in fighting a modern war which the South lacked?
2. How did Negroes contribute to a Union victory?

NEW-YORK HISTORICAL SOCIETY

MUSEUM OF THE CITY OF NEW YORK, J. CLARENCE DAVIES COLLECTION

Above: In July 1863 mobs in New York City rioting against the draft looted and burned homes and even tried to kill the children living in a Negro orphanage they had burned. Below: Police broke up another mob trying to destroy the offices of the New York Tribune. Opposite: Ads calling for volunteers to the Union army.

Right: Robert E. Lee confers with Stonewall Jackson at Chancellorsville, unaware that it was to be their last meeting. Below: At the climax of the fighting at Gettysburg, General Pickett's troops overrun an artillery battery. However, their heroic charge was doomed for there were no reinforcements to take advantage of the break in the Union lines.

LIBRARY OF CONGRESS

GETTYSBURG NATIONAL MILITARY PARK

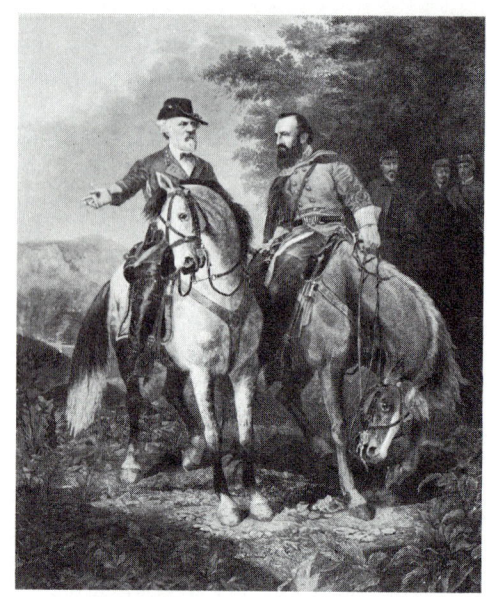

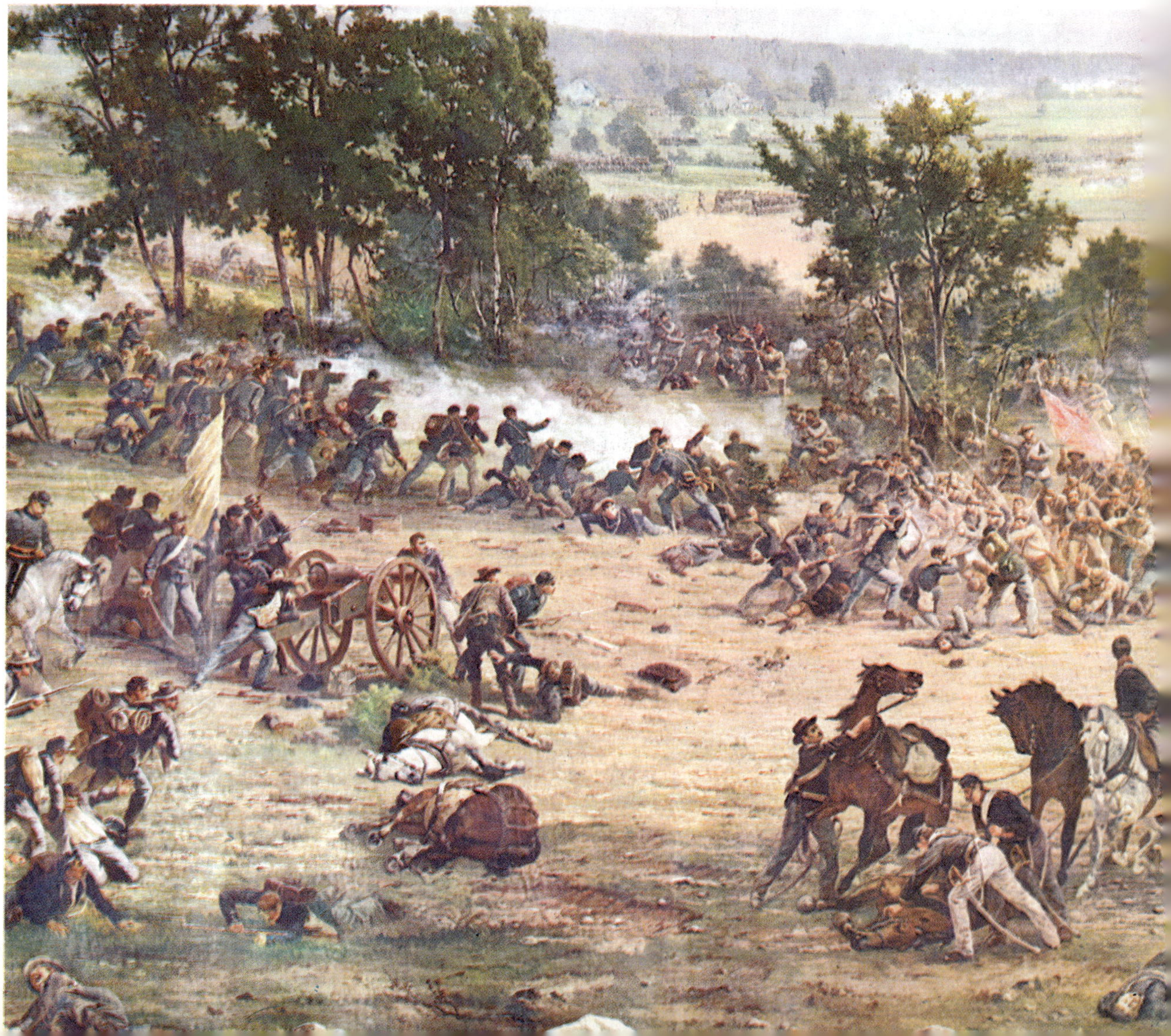

"War Is Hell"

The war was a great tidal wave, sweeping everything before it. But the verdict of victory or defeat had to be given on the battlefield. Halfway through the war, in the spring of 1863, General Robert E. Lee readied a new effort to swing that verdict in favor of the South.

In May Lee threw back a Union advance on Richmond at the Battle of Chancellorsville. The North's Army of the Potomac was temporarily disorganized and demoralized. Lee also had suffered a loss when Stonewall Jackson was killed, accidentally shot by his own men. But Lee decided to take advantage of the situation and move 80,000 men into Maryland and Pennsylvania. Perhaps that would convince the North that a military victory was impossible and force northern leaders to ask for peace. So, late in June, the Army of Northern Virginia tramped along the roads running northward, and the Army of the Potomac moved alongside, keeping between the Confederates and Washington. On July 1, at the little crossroads town of Gettysburg, Pennsylvania, patrols of both armies met. Soon nearly 200,000 men were in full battle.

The Union forces were pushed out of Gettysburg onto ridges and hills south and east of town. On July 2 Lee hurled attack after attack at their lines, waiting each time to see the Yankees reel back toward Philadelphia or Baltimore. But each thrust was beaten back in desperate fighting that cost some regiments up to 80 per cent in casualties. On July 3 came the last all-out effort. A thunderous cannonade filled the hot sky with smoke puffs. Then General George Pickett's division stepped out to attack the center of the Union line. As the southern troops charged across the several hundred yards of open ground between the armies, volley after volley ripped through their ranks. A handful reached the Union lines (below, left). There was fierce hand-to-hand fighting; then the Southerners not yet dead or wounded straggled back to their starting point. It was all over. Lee had no strength to attack again. He stayed in position briefly while rescue parties went over the field, picking up groaning, wounded men. Then he retreated. The high tide of Confederate advance had been reached. By historical coincidence, just one day after Pickett's charge—Independence Day, 1863—the back of the Confederacy was broken in the West, at Vicksburg on the Mississippi River, by the North's General Ulysses S. Grant. The capture of

LIBRARY OF CONGRESS

MRS. BYRON DEXTER COLLECTION

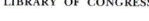

MARINERS MUSEUM, NEWPORT NEWS

Below left: Admiral David Porter's fleet runs the rebel blockade of the Mississippi River near Vicksburg. General Ulysses S. Grant directed the Union victory at Vicksburg in July 1863. Left: President Lincoln, seen here in an 1863 Brady photograph, ended his long search for a general who could defeat Lee when he gave command of the Union armies to Grant in March 1864. Grant was to succeed where five previous generals had failed. Here, he meets with his chief of staff, General John Rawlins, in Cold Harbor, Virginia, in June 1864.

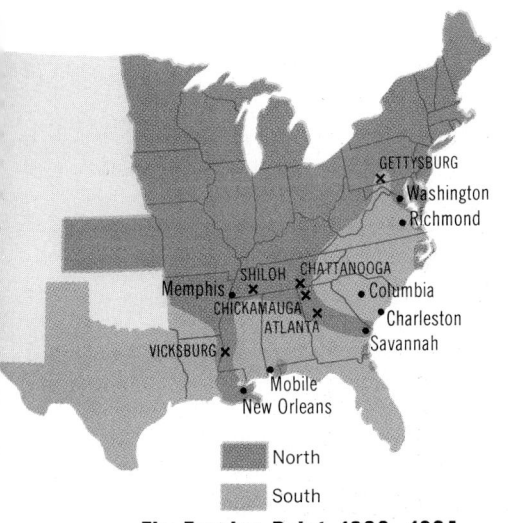

The Turning Point 1863–1864

this key point ended a bitter and important campaign that had lasted nearly a year.

Grant Takes Vicksburg

In the autumn of 1862, Union forces seemed to have been stopped cold at Vicksburg. Cannons on high bluffs along the Mississippi blasted any ships moving past. They also protected the town from land assault from the north. The capture of Vicksburg would allow the Union forces to go downriver and cut the Confederacy in two. But as long as the town remained in Confederate hands, it was an important symbol of resistance that built southern morale.

After several fruitless attacks General Ulysses S. Grant (seated at left) thought of a plan. Unlike McClellan who enjoyed the spit-and-polish of army life, Grant—though he was a West Point graduate—disliked soldiering. He had gone to the Point mainly to get a college education at government expense and repay it with time in the army. He had resigned in the 1850's, unable to support his family on army pay. At the outbreak of war, he had returned to service.

Grant came from an Ohio farm. He had no fancy ways but much common sense. He could give commands but he did not strut. He usually appeared in a rumpled private's uniform with his starred shoulder straps of rank pinned to it. Yet this plain-looking "country cousin" had a mind for large-scale strategic thinking. He would take chances when necessary but he saw the military problem of the North clearly: how to make its superior power count.

In the spring of 1863, Grant knew that Union armies were attacking Vicksburg from the north side, because that position allowed them to protect their supply line to Memphis. Why not break that pattern and march the army down the west bank of the river, out of range of Vicksburg's guns? Let the Union's gunboats and transports dash past the sleeping city by night. Then let them ferry the troops across the Mississippi to swing around south and east of Vicksburg and come at it from its unprotected side facing away from the river. As for the supply line, forget it. All the ammunition needed for a short campaign could be carried and food could come from the countryside.

This bold plan worked perfectly. Grant made his move past Vicksburg on May 4 (lower left). Three weeks later he had won three battles and clamped a siege

line all around the town. The defending Confederate garrison and townspeople held out for a month and a half, huddling in caves along the riverside to escape shelling and eating mule meat when they were desperately hungry. Then they surrendered. Grant became a new hero of the advancing North.

Sherman Marches to the Atlantic

Now Grant was called East to take over the Army of the Potomac, as well as the overall command of the war. He left General William Tecumseh Sherman (left), another Ohioan, in charge in the West. Sherman was also a former "regular" officer who had rejoined the army in 1861. He, too, saw that victory would come only as the North overpowered the South. Sherman did not see any romance in combat. "War is hell," he said bluntly. What he meant was that war was a brutal contest. To win meant not just battlefield victories but also the destruction of the enemy's resources and will to fight, including hurting civilians.

In May of 1864 Sherman moved with more than 100,000 men out of southern Tennessee and into Georgia. Mile by mile, he used his superiority in numbers to outflank the Confederate army and force it to retreat toward Atlanta, the railroad hub of the South. The city fell in September. After resting his troops Sherman began the war's most devastating operation. Like Grant, he would abandon his base of supplies and feed his armies off the land. But he would do more. He would have scouting parties pick up every chicken, turkey, cow, ox, and horse in their path. They would burn every wagon, corncrib, barn, mill, warehouse, and shop that might be useful to any Confederates who followed them. They would pull up railroad tracks, heat them red hot, and twist them around telegraph poles (lower right). They would, in Sherman's words, "make Georgia howl." Sherman did not hate southern civilians, but if their sufferings caused a quicker collapse of the Confederacy, the misery of the war would be over that much sooner. A few more hungry women and children would mean fewer dead heroes.

On December 22, 1864, Sherman's columns reached Savannah, leaving a 50-mile-wide swath of destruction behind them. In February of 1865 he turned northward into the Carolinas. At Columbia, South Carolina's capital, a fire swept the town (right). It is still not known whether the fire was set by Sherman's men or

BOTH: LIBRARY OF CONGRESS

A grim and determined General William Tecumseh Sherman posed for this photograph dressed in his typical careless fashion.

KEAN ARCHIVES

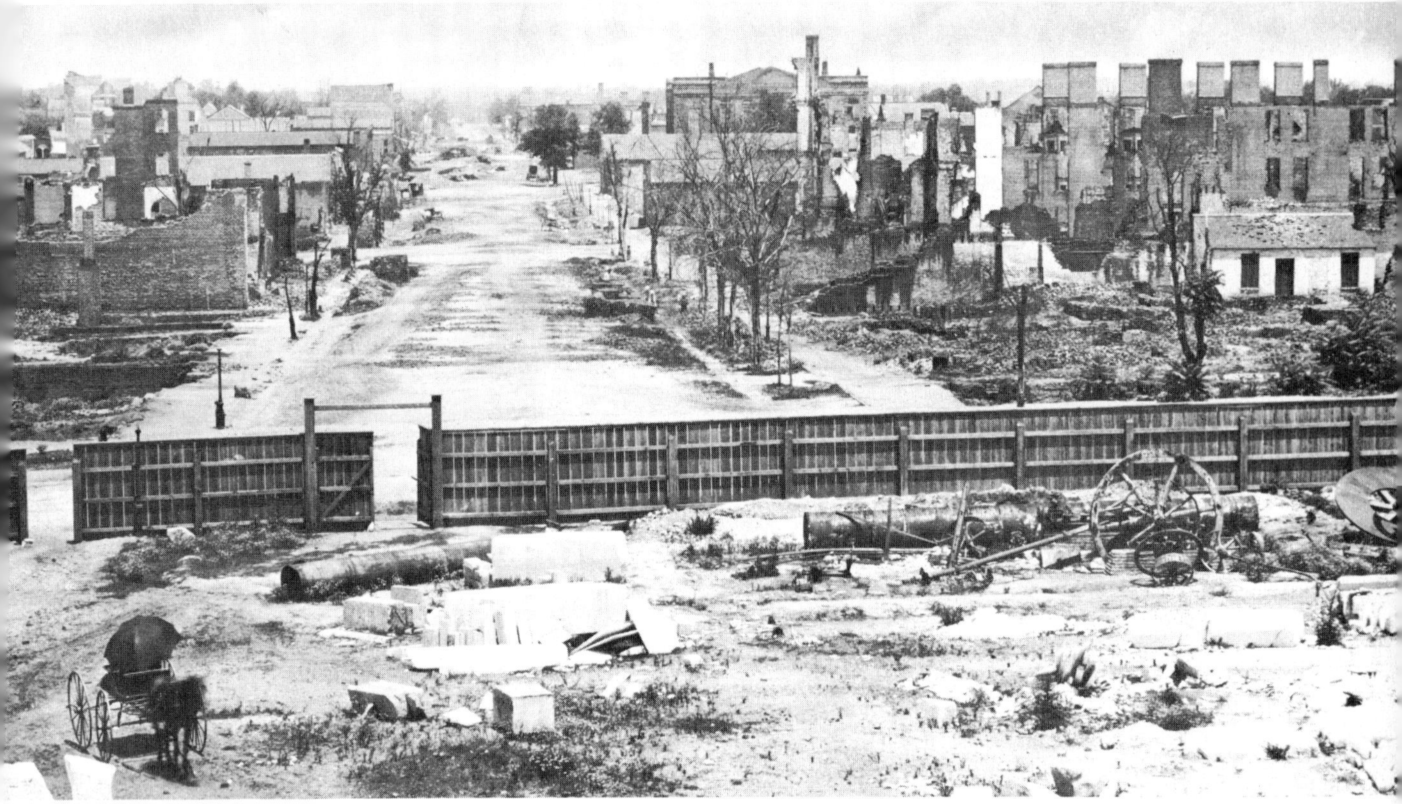

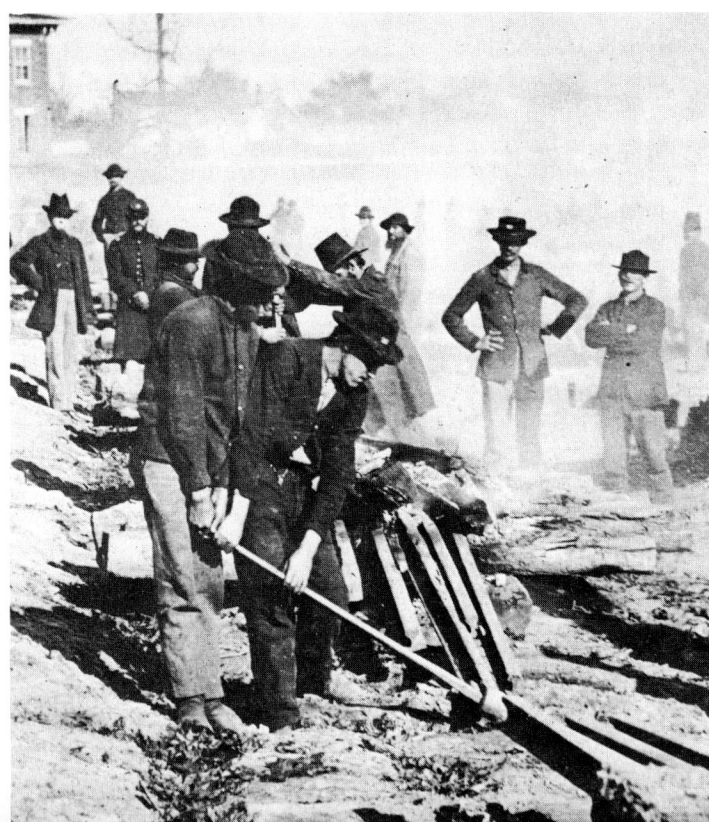

Left: Sherman's men in Georgia pry loose some railroad tracks which were then heated, twisted into "Sherman hairpins," and used to decorate tree trunks all the way to the sea. Above: In 1865 a fire in Union-occupied Columbia, South Carolina, destroyed two-thirds of the town.

the retreating "rebs." But those gutted buildings showed why Sherman's name was hated in the white South long after Grant was forgiven.

Grant Pursues Lee

Meantime, in Virginia, Grant mapped out a final strategy. Up to 1864 the Army of the Potomac advanced, fought a battle, and then, if it did not win, went back into quarters to wait for the next effort, as eighteenth-century armies had done. Grant had a different idea. On May 4, 1864, he moved south (map, right) from a position near the old battlefield of Chancellorsville. Lee met him head-on in the three-day-long Battle of the Wilderness. At its end both sides were battered and bloody. But Lee's army was unbroken, and Grant's casualties had been heavier. Yet instead of retiring to rest and refit, Grant again moved his men forward, around Lee's right flank. Lee dropped back and again met Grant; once more the woods echoed with the thunder and shouting of combat. Still a third time Grant circled to Lee's right, and Lee turned with him, keeping his back to Richmond. And then Grant's plan became clear. He would force Lee into constant action. Lee could not replace lost men and equipment as readily as the Union armies. Ceaseless fighting would wear him down. Lincoln understood the idea. He telegraphed Grant: "Hold on with a bulldog grip, and chew and choke as much as possible." But the Union "bulldog" was chewed, too. Heavy casualties were the cost of Grant's plan. Yet it was working.

The Siege of Petersburg

By July Lee and Grant had circled around Richmond, and Grant had Lee pinned down at Petersburg, south of the Confederate capital. Lee could not move without leaving the city open to capture. And with Grant's army blocking his path, Lee could not receive supplies from the deep South. As Grant's men steadily attacked Lee's lines, the Confederates responded by digging trenches and building "bombproof" forts like those at right. Union troops protected themselves from counterattack in the same way. The war became a dreary business. Men crouched in holes in the earth, battling heat, mud, insects, and sickness. Each day brought small engagements and mounting casualties. Tragedies, like the death of the young soldier at far right, multiplied daily, week after bloody week. War

Above: Confident Union troops await orders for the Petersburg spring offensive. Right: This young Confederate died in one of the final assaults. Below: Abandoned trenches scarred the countryside after the nine-month siege.

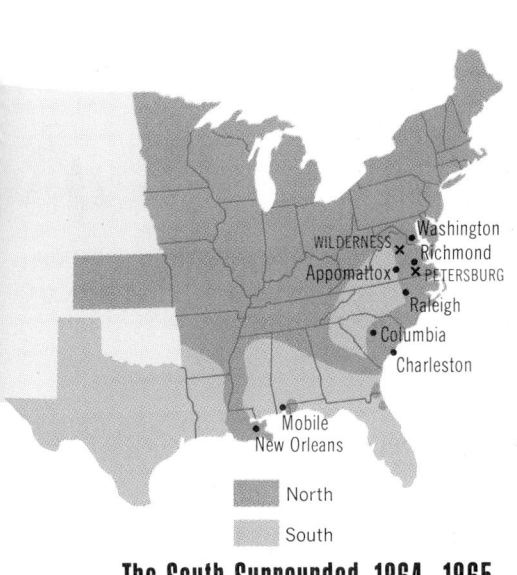

The South Surrounded 1864–1865

SURRENDER OF GEN. LEE!

"The Year of Jubilee has come! Let all the People Rejoice!"

Below: Thomas Nast made this rough sketch of General Lee at Appomattox Courthouse and called it "Peace, the sole object of all." Right: The former capitol of the Confederacy can be seen rising in the background of fire-gutted Richmond. Above: This is a detail from a broadside that appeared in Detroit on April 10, 1865, and called for every man, woman, and child to join in patriotic singing and rejoicing at 3 P.M.

in 1864 was moments of pain and terror between long stretches of boredom. Modern warfare is, in fact, much like modern industry: huge in scale and blindly impersonal.

Richmond Falls

The end was inevitable. As spring thaws warmed the earth in March of 1865, Grant renewed his attacks and kept lengthening his front line by adding troops to its wings. Lee extended his line to meet these threats but his much smaller force was being stretched thin, and he knew one good blow would wipe him out. He could no longer save Richmond. The best he could do was try to slip away and save the army. On April 2, 1865, he gave notice to the Confederate government that the city must be abandoned. Fires lit the sky as the retreating army burned its remaining stores and supplies to keep them out of Yankee hands. Carriages full of worried officials with precious records jammed the streets. In the firelight mobs of looters raced about with arms full of stolen food and clothing. Confederate Richmond died in fire and brimstone. Soon Union troops—blacks included—marched triumphantly down the streets, between ruins like those at the left. The end was near.

Lee Surrenders at Appomattox Courthouse

It came on April 9. Lee had tried to move westward to the safety of the mountains. But Union troops overtook and surrounded his tired survivors. To avoid further bloodshed he sent a flag of **truce** (an agreement by opposing forces to cease fire temporarily) to Grant to ask for terms of surrender. In a private house at Appomattox, he and Grant signed the surrender agreement. The Confederates were to be paroled—that is, allowed to go home in return for a promise not to take up arms again. They were given rations and were allowed to take their horses and mules with them for farmwork.

Grant, the man who had been made into a giant by the war, acted like someone who knew how to bring real peace. Within a few weeks all the other Confederate forces in the field surrendered. The dream of a slaveholding republic, supplying the world with cotton and an example of aristocratic virtue, was over. The Union was saved. The personal anguish and joy of each American who fought on either side could never be

recorded. "The real war," wrote the great poet Walt Whitman, "will never get in the books."

But if the human side of the war was hard to record, the results were not. The argument for secession died forever on the battlefield. Democracy and the Union survived the war, proving their inner strength to the world that watched. Above all, the Civil War ended one era of race relations and began another. Slavery was gone. If blacks were no longer slaves, they must be men, and as men they were entitled to a full and equal share in the nation. The war and emancipation were first steps on the road to that share. But many hard journeys lay ahead.

Questions for Discussion

1. What was Lee's purpose in making the 1863 invasion of Pennsylvania and Maryland? Why was the battle at Gettysburg a turning point in the war?
2. What was the strategic importance of Grant's capture of Vicksburg?
3. What qualities made Lee a great general? Grant a great general?
4. What was Sherman's strategy in his famous march through Georgia? What tactics did he use?
5. Why were Grant's tactics in forcing Lee to surrender criticized by many Northerners?

Chapter Review

Social Studies Terms

logistics, hoarding, profiteering, blockade, refugees, conscription, bounties, truce

Summary Questions for Discussion

1. Why did Lincoln call the Civil War "a people's contest?"
2. What different interpretations of the purpose of fighting the war were made by Lincoln and Davis?
3. Why was it almost inevitable that the navy as well as the army would play a decisive role in the Civil War?
4. In what ways was the Civil War different from previous wars in which the United States had fought? Why did it last much longer than most people on both sides expected in 1861?
5. What advantages did each side have in the Civil War? What disadvantages?
6. Why did Lincoln not abolish slavery at the beginning of the war instead of on January 1, 1863?

7. How did Lincoln justify the issuance of the Emancipation Proclamation? To what parts of the United States did it apply? How was slavery finally abolished in all of the United States?
8. Why did the free Negroes of the North feel that they had a heavy stake in a Union victory? Why was the decision not to use blacks in the Union army reversed?
9. Did the Civil War have the same economic effect in the South as it had in the North? Why?
10. What did Sherman mean when he said that "War is hell?" How did he justify his tactics on humanitarian grounds?
11. How did the Civil War contribute to sectional hatred even after the war ended?

Pictures as Historical Evidence

Look at the painting of the first Battle of Bull Run on page 373 and the photograph of the after-effects of the Battle of Antietam on page 375. Compare the attitude towards war expressed by the painting and the photograph.

Map Study

1. Why did geography generally favor the North in the Civil War?
2. Why was the West such an important theatre?
3. Why were the Confederate losses shown on the map *The Opening Years 1861-1863* (page 372) a hard blow to the war economy of the South?

For Further Reading

Embattled Confederates, by Bell Irvin Wiley. New York: Harper & Row, 1964.

Jefferson Davis, by Allen Tate. New York: G. P. Putnam's Sons, 1969.

Robert E. Lee, by Jonathan Daniels. Boston: Houghton Mifflin Company, 1960.

Swords, Stars and Bars, by Lee McGiffin. New York: E. P. Dutton & Co., Inc., 1960.

The Battle of Gettysburg, by Bruce Catton. New York: American Heritage Publishing Co., Inc., 1963.

Ulysses S. Grant, by Henry Thomas. New York: G. P. Putnam's Sons, 1961.

Worth Fighting For, by Agnes McCarthy and Lawrence Reddick. Garden City: Doubleday & Company, Inc., 1965.

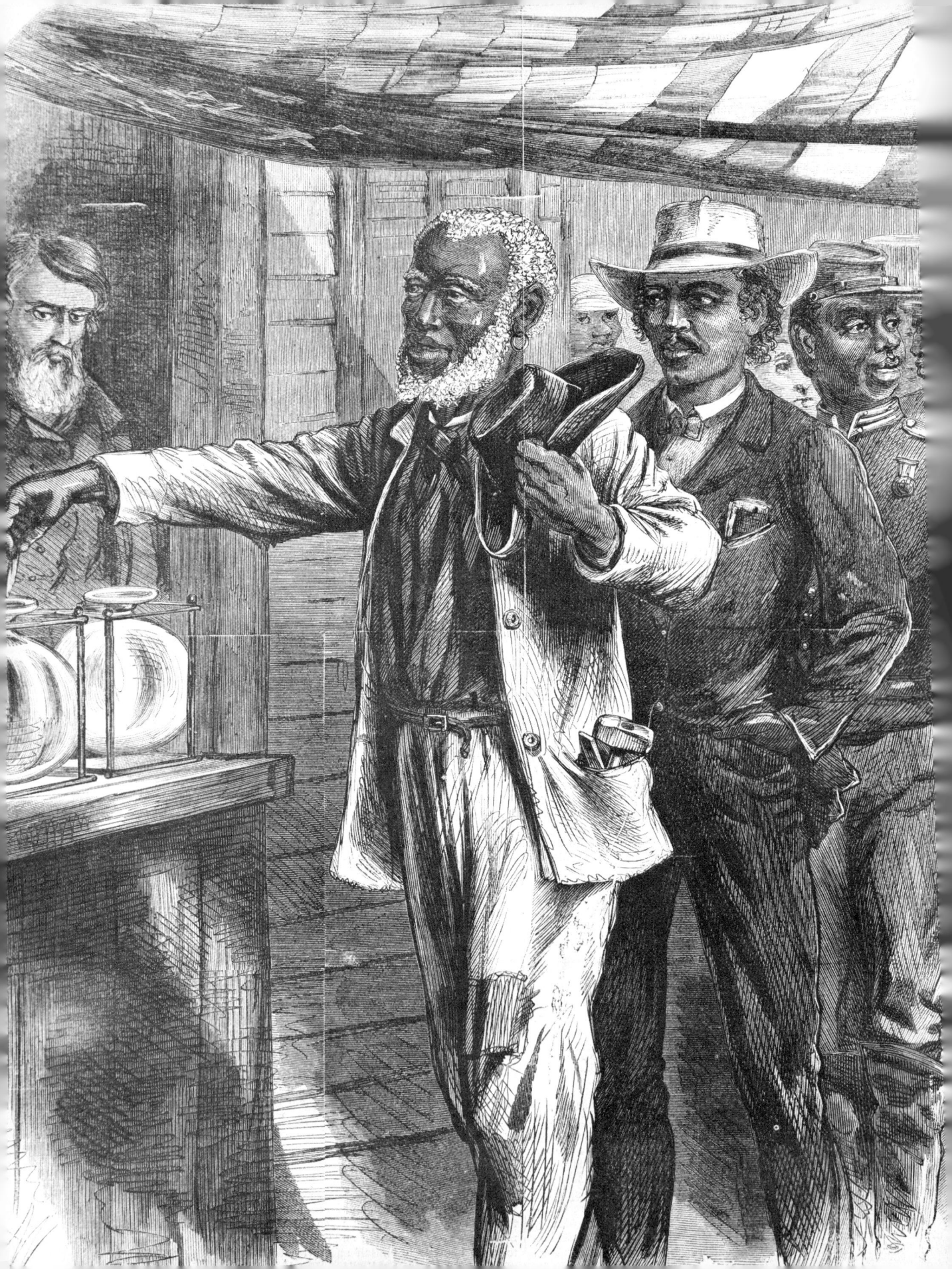

14
Reconstruction and the Negro After the Civil War

Booker T. Washington was only nine years old in 1865, but he never forgot the day when he and the other slaves on James Burroughs' Virginia plantation were asked to gather at the master's house. There, they were told, "You are all free. You can go where you please." The tears of joy shed by Booker's mother were among his sharpest memories of the Emancipation Proclamation.

Not all slave-owners made a ceremony of freeing their "property." Many held on to the slaves until Union armies occupied their lands. But sooner or later freedom came. When it did there was cheering in the slave quarters, but also some fear. For freedom is a great thing, but when it is new, it can be a frightening experience.

And for some 4 million ex-slaves, freedom was brand new. Little in American history before 1865 gave them any example to follow. Though the ex-slaves made up about one-tenth of the whole nation's population and nearly half of the South's, they belonged to a race that almost every white American considered inferior. To improve their status they would need education, prosperity, and able leadership. Yet almost no ex-slave in 1865 had even the skills, tools, or land needed just to support himself.

Black Americans, therefore, did not walk an easy road. At first the North tried to help by forcing a change in southern patterns of race relations. The Fourteenth Amendment to the Constitution, ratified in 1868, recognized Negroes as citizens. The Fifteenth, ratified in 1870, gave them the vote, as the drawing at the left shows. But in time the white South, with northern consent, went back to the practice of keeping Negroes helpless and exploited.

Southern blacks, meanwhile, sometimes bent with the wind and sometimes fought back. But they never gave up their own drive for genuine equality. In theory, equality was now theirs by constitutional amendment. In practice, the actual behavior of the North and the South showed that both sections believed in white supremacy.

As you read, think about these questions:
1. What new problems did emancipation bring to ex-slaves in the South?
2. Why have blacks in the United States been unable to obtain equality with whites?
3. Why is social change so hard to achieve?

"The First Vote" appeared in the Harper's Weekly *of November 16, 1867.*

Reconstruction in the South

Reconstruction (the process of bringing the ex-Confederate states back into the Union) went through several phases. As the war came to an end, Lincoln planned to restore civilian government to the occupied southern states by permitting them to have free elections as soon as a small minority of their white voters took an oath of loyalty to the Union. But five days after Lee's surrender, an assassin's bullet cut down Lincoln. Andrew Johnson, his successor, freely pardoned highly placed former rebels, restoring their **civil rights** (rights as citizens of the United States). By the end of 1865, nearly all of the seceded states had organized new governments. Their officials were often ex-Confederates.

These first Reconstruction state governments quickly passed new laws to replace the old slave codes. Ex-slaves were recognized as individuals in a legal sense. This meant that their marriages (upper right) were legalized, and they were given certain new rights, such as to make contracts, to testify in court, and to hold and transfer property. But southern whites firmly believed that Negroes would not work unless they were forced to. So the new black codes provided severe punishments for a black who left his job for any reason without first getting a white's permission. Nor was there any hint in the new southern state constitutions that Negroes would ever be allowed to vote.

Meanwhile, the North was trying to prepare southern blacks for life outside of slavery. In 1865 a special organization, the Freedmen's Bureau, was set up by the Federal government for this task. It was one of the nation's first **welfare agencies** (special organizations of the government which act to improve the living conditions of people, especially those who are unfortunate or are handicapped). Freedmen's Bureau officials operated as health inspectors, judges, and school superintendents. They also supervised the reopening of plantations and businesses, opened schools that were taught by volunteer teachers (left) from the North, and gave food, clothing, and medical supplies to both black and white refugees from the war's destruction. The Bureau made arrangements for landowners without workers to make contracts with ex-slaves. Such contracts usually provided for one year's wages.

White Southerners resented this "outside interference," especially when some Bureau officers expressed the feeling that the Negro should immediately

Harriet W. Murray, a teacher working for the Freedmen's Bureau, instructs two of her young pupils.

be put in possession of all his rights as a man. When the white employer and the black farm hand—formerly master and slave—disagreed about their bargain, the black could appeal to the Freedmen's Bureau for judgment. The work of the Bureau ran head-on into the spirit behind the black codes. Though the Bureau did not always take the Negroes' side, many blacks believed that without it they would be, as one Negro group said, "sheep in the midst of wolves."

The Constitution Is Amended

Sheep among wolves need protection. A group of Republicans in Congress known as Radical Republicans had watched the Johnson policies with dismay. They believed that the remaking of southern society must be entrusted to loyal Union men in the South—which generally meant blacks. These Radical Republicans were not radical enough to take land outright from the ex-slaveholders and divide it among the freedmen. In 1866 it was considered an outrage to seize private property even from ex-rebels. Emancipation itself was as far as the North would go in the widespread taking of "property."

Between 1867 and 1870 the process of "radicalizing" the former Confederate states took place as the Radical Republicans moved against the black codes and other threats to Negro rights. They got Congress to pass the Fourteenth Amendment and send it to the states to be ratified. This amendment provided that every person born or naturalized in the United States was automatically a citizen of the United States and of the state in which he lived. No state might limit the legal rights of any of its citizens or deny them the equal protection of the laws. A Civil Rights Act of 1875—later declared unconstitutional—enforced the Fourteenth Amendment by setting penalties for denying any citizen equal treatment in public eating places, hotels, theaters, streetcars, and railroads.

The Fourteenth Amendment did not specifically give the Negro the vote. Many northern Republicans were at first unwilling to give the Negro the vote either in their own states or in the South. But finally, the urge to create a black-based Republican party in the South overcame the prejudices of northern Republicans who were not Radicals. They agreed to the Fifteenth Amendment, ratified in 1870, which specifically forbade any state to refuse suffrage to a

Harper's Weekly, JUNE 30, 1866

Harper's Weekly, JULY 25, 1868

Top: A chaplain from the Freedmen's Bureau presides over the marriage of a Negro soldier in Vicksburg, Mississippi. Above: This 1868 cartoon gave support to the belief that Federal troops were necessary to protect Negroes from vicious southern whites.

United States citizen because of his color. Congress put teeth into this amendment with two laws of 1871 which made it an offense to interfere with any citizen's right to vote.

The Radical Republicans acted from mixed motives. Some were genuinely interested in the rights of Negroes. Others were probably more interested in using black voters to defeat political enemies, North and South. Yet, in the Fourteenth and Fifteenth Amendments, they had written into the Constitution itself an attack on **racism** (the belief that some races are naturally inferior to others) and a promise of equality. The question thereafter was whether the nation as a whole would live up to the promise of equality, or only try to make the South obey it, or ignore it.

In the 1866 elections for Congress, the Radicals in the Republican ranks won a heavy majority in both houses. The next year they moved to force the South toward equality. They passed acts which overthrew the Lincoln-Johnson state governments and put the South back under military occupation. Army commanders were ordered to enroll voters for new state constitutional conventions. Blacks were to be allowed both to vote for the members at these conventions and to be members themselves. But most southern white leaders were banned from voting and officeholding. After new state constitutions were written, this same new **electorate** (body of voters) would elect state legislatures. When these lawmaking bodies ratified the Fourteenth, and later the Fifteenth, Amendments, the state would be readmitted to the Union.

Negroes in Politics

The Southern Republican state governments gave Americans of African descent their first real chance at a share in political power. While hundreds of blacks sat in state legislatures, they were in a majority only in the lower houses of South Carolina and Mississippi, and then just for a short while. They always worked with elected whites—either with Southerners who had taken no part in public life in Confederate days or with Northerners who had not come South until after the war. Nor did black legislators object to restoring suffrage to ex-Confederates rapidly. Black officeholders included both ex-slaves and educated men who had never been enslaved. They performed their tasks of state government the way any group of white officials

*Below right: In this 1868 drawing southern blacks campaign for public office for the first time.
Right: These men were the first Negroes elected to Congress after the Civil War. Hiram R. Revels, seated at the far left, was the first black Senator. Revels, who had never been a slave and who had served as a chaplain for a Negro regiment during the Civil War, was elected from Mississippi to serve the final year of an unexpired term. In 1875 Blanche K. Bruce was elected to the Senate from Mississippi and became the only Negro in the nineteenth century to serve a full six-year term. Below: This cartoon expresses high hopes for the Civil Rights Act of 1875. However, the Supreme Court declared the act unconstitutional in a series of decisions handed down in 1883.*

Harper's Weekly, APRIL 24, 1875

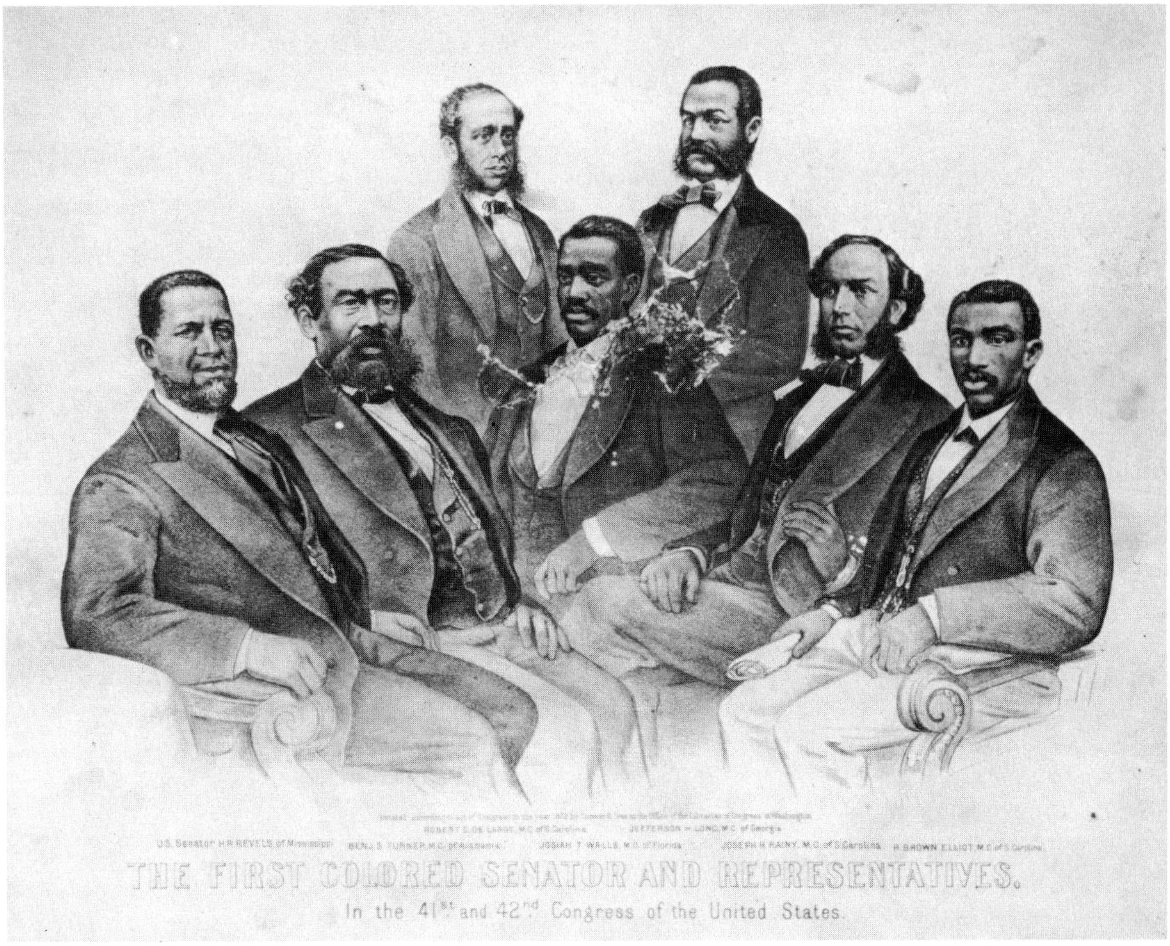

MISSISSIPPI DEPARTMENT OF ARCHIVES AND HISTORY

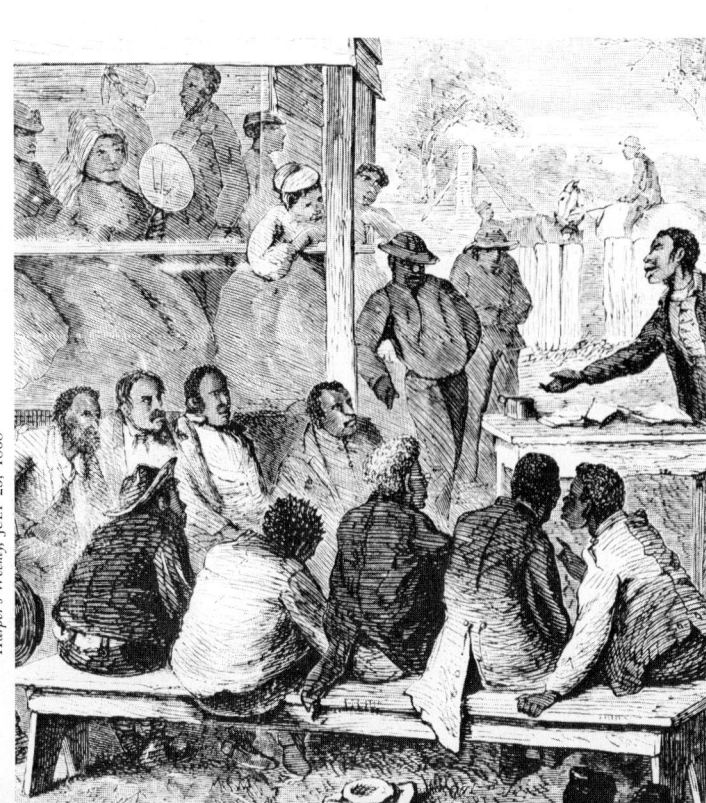

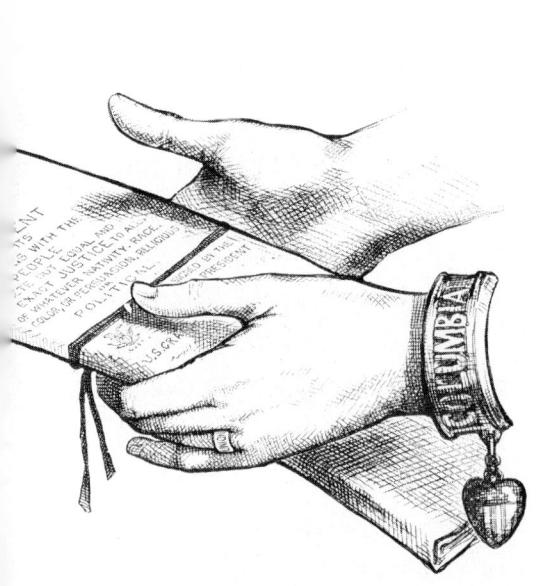

Harper's Weekly, JULY 25, 1868

The Ku Klux Klan organized as the "Invisible Empire of the South" and set out to restore social and political white supremacy. Members wore hoods and robes, like those in the 1868 photograph at the left, to keep their identities secret and to terrorize Negroes. An 1868 pro-Klan Alabama weekly printed the flag above, with snakes for stripes and black faces for the stars representing southern states. In 1870 and 1871 the Federal government passed laws designed to reduce the power of the Klan. Very few influential white Southerners were ever members of the Klan, and its power gradually faded away.

did—some well and a few badly. A few black candidates were elected and served in both houses of Congress.

Southerners Oppose Reconstruction

The very sight of black men in seats of power was a sign that a social revolution was taking place in the South. White Southerners who were accustomed to dominating the region's life simply would not accept this. Almost at once they began to fight back.

One way whites resisted was by campaigning for Democrats pledged to restore "home rule." That meant white control of the states, though not necessarily barring all blacks from government. When they could not persuade enough voters, some southern whites went outside the law. White election officials found ways to cheat Negroes of the vote. On Election Day polling places were moved to new locations—revealed only to whites. Or white votes were counted twice and black votes not at all.

And when cheating failed there was force. Many organizations of whites took fanciful names and set out to frighten blacks away from the polls. The best known was the Ku Klux Klan, founded in Tennessee in 1865. Its officials had weird titles like "kleagles" and "wizards." Its members dressed in grotesque robes and hoods (left). These costumes were supposed to frighten the superstitious "darkies." They also made the white wearers feel self-important, just as the ritual paint and feathers did that were worn by Indian braves. But the Klan was not just a harmless, secret club with passwords and special costumes. It was a **terrorist** group, whose purpose was to frighten Negroes by whipping, burning, and shooting blacks bold enough to claim their constitutional rights.

The Klan's hate-filled propaganda dimmed chances of cooperation between blacks and whites in rebuilding the South. Southern white moderates regretted, but did not break up, the Klan. The blacks themselves fought back as best they could through organizations and defense associations of their own. But gradually, the blacks began to lose ground, just as they had at the time of the black codes in 1865. But this time the North did not come to their aid.

Reconstruction Comes to an End

One by one, the southern states again elected governments based on the principle of white supremacy.

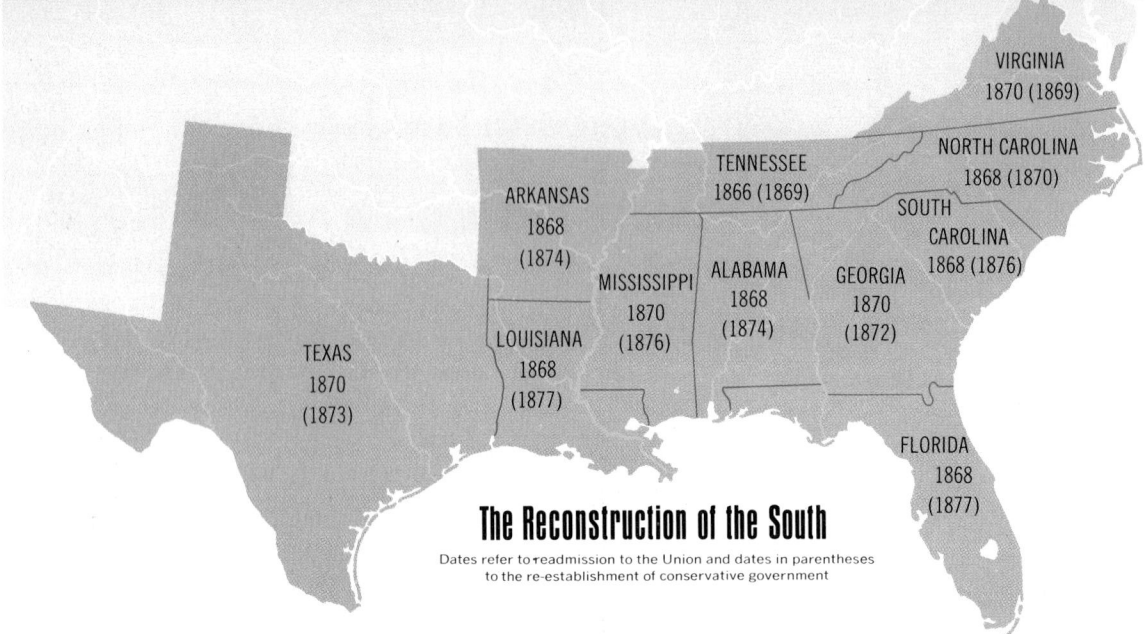

The Reconstruction of the South

Dates refer to readmission to the Union and dates in parentheses to the re-establishment of conservative government

After a severe depression claimed the nation's attention in 1873, Republicans lost ground both in the North and in the South. Finally, in 1876, only three states—Louisiana, Florida, and South Carolina—still had Republican governments in which blacks took part (map, above). The northern public was losing its interest in changing the South.

In the Presidential race of 1876, the Democrat, Samuel J. Tilden, won the popular vote. But before the Democrats could celebrate their victory, disturbing news came from Louisiana, Florida, and South Carolina. Republican officials there claimed that those states had voted in favor of the Republican candidate, Rutherford B. Hayes (far right). Their electoral votes would put Hayes in the White House.

"Fraud!" cried the Democrats. They argued that a fair count would give the three states to Tilden. Republicans answered that any really fair southern election—one in which blacks were not afraid to vote—would yield a Republican victory.

Early in 1877 a special committee appointed by Congress with an eight-to-seven Republican majority began to investigate who had actually won the election in the three states. By a straight party-line vote, they awarded all the disputed electoral votes to Hayes. Inauguration Day approached. Would the whole of Congress accept this report? Or would enraged Democrats refuse to recognize President Hayes? Would the election system break down? The country seemed to be headed for serious trouble.

Then a behind-the-scenes deal was arranged. Congress awarded the disputed election to the Republicans. But Hayes, in turn, agreed to withdraw the last Federal troops (above) from the South. Without the support of these troops, the last southern Radical governments were soon defeated.

But there was more to the Compromise of 1877 than troop withdrawal. Republicans in Congress also secretly promised to vote for Federal gifts of land, loans, and appropriations, grants of public money, to help the South build post offices, lighthouses, and railroads, to improve rivers and harbors, and to develop local mining and lumbering industries. This was in line with a Republican policy of encouraging economic growth by public aid to businessmen. Unlike the prewar planter aristocracy, Democratic Party leaders of the new South also approved of this policy. The southern social revolution ended by mutual agreement between northern and southern politicians to help capitalists in both sections with their business enterprises. The whole nation was in a mood for industrial and commercial expansion. In the public mind protection of the rights of nonwhite minorities, whether Negro, Indian, or Oriental, took a low rank in the list of important tasks.

Below: President Rutherford B. Hayes kept his agreement to end military reconstruction. Above: On April 24, 1877, Federal troops leave New Orleans amidst cheers from local residents.

Questions for Discussion

1. What was Reconstruction? How long did it last?
2. How did the Freedmen's Bureau try to prepare the ex-slaves for life as free men?

The Birth of Jim Crow

Now it was the turn of white Southerners to call the tune in race relations. The return of the Democrats to full power did not throw all Negroes out of politics immediately. Some southern leaders, usually educated and responsible men, believed that there was room for capable people of both races in honest government. Besides, there was always a chance that too much **repression** (denial of rights) would give a few Republicans an excuse to take action which would lead back to the pre-1877 political pattern. Therefore, small numbers of Negroes were allowed to vote and sit in state legislatures. Some were even appointed by Democrats to offices in the state governments. But those blacks who "bucked the system" were kept in line by force and other means, as illustrated in the cartoon at left. They might be arrested by the police for very small offenses. Or they might lose their jobs. Such repression was possible because both political and economic power was firmly in white hands.

After the Civil War most landless blacks became **sharecroppers**. A black family would live on a portion of a former plantation, raise cotton, and give a large share of the harvested crop to the landowner as rent for the land and in return for tools, seeds, and work animals which the landowner usually provided. A single owner might have many such families working for him. The "cropper" also got food and clothing, on credit, at a white-owned store. He was supposed to pay for these by selling his share of the crop. But at the year's end, the money he got was usually not enough to pay what he owed. So he began each new season deeper in debt to the storekeeper.

There were some white sharecroppers too, but for most black farmers this was the only way of making a living. The black sharecropper tilled another man's soil with another man's tools. He rarely saw cash. His diet of fat meat and corn bread kept him in the grip of illness. His children received almost no education in the inferior, **segregated** (racially separated) schools provided for blacks. His wife and daughters had no future except as servants to white families. If he protested politically the planter might throw him off his land and the merchant refuse him credit. Being without dollars, he was without power. His condition seemed little improved over slavery times. In some ways it may have been worse, for though free, the sharecropper was still enslaved by poverty.

MILTON MELTZER COLLECTION

White Southerners, armed with guns, prevent Negroes from voting in this cartoon called, "Everything Points to a Democratic Victory this Fall."

Although they were no longer slaves, many Negroes were forced to take jobs that were not much different from their chores as slaves. The sharecroppers at the left worked long hours on land owned by white men. The black woman above worked as a nurse for a wealthy southern family.

An Age of Violence

Violence has often been a means of settling arguments among poor, uneducated men. Moreover, in the pre-Civil War South, even gentlemen fought duels, though they were in violation of the law. But in the years after 1877, anti-black violence had a special meaning. It enforced the unwritten law that Negroes must live as underlings. Unwritten laws or customs can often be as powerful in regulating social behavior as official legal codes.

Violence also remained a basic method of enforcing white supremacy. In times of stress, when legal authorities are far away or slow to act, it is all too common for people to take the law into their own hands.

Lynching was not a southern invention. But in the postwar South, it was used primarily against blacks. Such violence was based on the false idea that Africans were "savages." Since the African Negro, according to one book of the period, had achieved nothing "of the least service to mankind," the American Negro must—through fear—be made to behave. Armed with this view of the past and a genuine fear of black retaliation for years of enslavement, "civilized" white men lynched thousands of blacks accused of "crimes" from insulting a white person to murder.

In 1893 a black man named Henry Smith was accused of the murder of a three-year-old white girl in Paris, Texas. A posse was deputized to bring him in. Captured far from Paris, Smith confessed after his first night with the posse. Over 10,000 people, shouting for revenge (left), "sentenced" him to burn at the stake. Across the country between 1890 and 1920, 2,523 Negroes were executed without a trial. Despite the efforts of reformers, anti-lynching bills repeatedly failed to pass in Congress, but lynching slowly became a rarity.

Negroes, and some poor whites, were subjected to other cruelties as well. Even when legally tried, those accused of crimes faced a bitter experience if convicted. Often they were sent to chain gangs (lower right) or to work on roads or in state-owned lumber camps, quarries, or farms. Sometimes the state leased convicted criminals out to private employers; that is, the employers paid so much per day and could work the convicts as they pleased. In both cases the conditions were inhuman. Bad food, brutal punishment, and outright killings were common.

Harper's Weekly, OCTOBER 18, 1879

Left: In 1893 a Negro is lynched for the murder of a three-year-old girl in Texas. Above: An 1879 Nast cartoon on the death of Negro voting. Below: A chain gang of Negro prisoners at work.

WILFRID DELLQUEST COLLECTION, LA JOLLA

Segregation by Law

The South also turned to written laws to enforce the racial **caste system** which it shared with the rest of the nation. In a caste system entire groups of people have an unchangeable status based on birth. In the South a person's race largely determined his social status. No matter what an individual Negro did or did not do, he could not change his skin color. And this condemned him to second-class status. Between 1877 and 1910 southern lawmakers passed codes that required segregation in schools, restaurants, streetcars, railroads, and all other public gathering places. The unstated but clear purpose of these laws was to enforce the idea of Negro inferiority. The all-Negro facilities were always poorer and shabbier than those for whites. The segregation laws received the unofficial name of "Jim Crow," after a minstrel show based on a slave of that name. The Negro thus was linked in the public eye with a grotesque comic character. He was a clown or a savage, but never a man. Although northern states did not formally pass segregation laws, most hotels, restaurants, and other such places either discouraged or actually shut out black customers. Jim Crow did not live only in "Dixie."

Segregation laws were not enacted without arguments. Blacks reminded white lawmakers that during Reconstruction they had shared public facilities without creating problems. In 1867 black protests had forced the city of New Orleans to give up Jim Crow streetcars. New Orleans even had integrated schools until 1877. This was unusual, though the national Civil Rights Act of 1875 did not require desegregated education. In 1877 a group of Negroes told a northern magazine writer, "We want to be treated like men... regardless of color." Some southern whites agreed. One southern editor wrote that there was no need to "browbeat and spit upon the colored man." Another editor declared that the South needed separate cars for "rowdy or drunken white passengers" more than Jim Crow cars for black ones.

But by 1910 the segregationists had won out. Soon white Southerners forgot how new these laws were. They came to believe—wrongly—that Jim Crow was part of an old southern tradition instead of a practice that grew up after Reconstruction.

Late in the 1880's white Southerners also moved to bury the Fifteenth Amendment. In the 1890's a new po-

ALL: LIBRARY OF CONGRESS

Ben Tillman was nicknamed "Pitchfork Ben" because of his strong support from poor farmers and his belief that force should be used to keep the Negro down.

litical party arose which challenged the Democrats nationwide for about ten years. It was called the People's Party, or the **Populists.** Populists were mostly poor white farmers who, like the Negro, needed better schools, fair wages for labor, higher prices for crops, and limits on high interest rates and freight charges. At first it seemed that black and white victims of poverty might work together as Populists. But after a time that hope failed. Whites in both parties realized that black voters might be able to bargain with both sides for support. This prospect of black influence disturbed whites of all classes. The aftermath of the Populist revolt, therefore, was a host of new state laws that almost entirely eliminated Negroes from the polls. Led by men such as South Carolina's one-eyed "Pitchfork Ben" Tillman (left), southern states devised special **poll taxes** (taxes on voting) and **literacy tests** (tests of a person's ability to read and write). These were used to bar blacks from voting, but not whites. "We have scratched our heads to find out how we could eliminate the last one of them," said Tillman. "We stuffed ballot boxes. We shot them. We are not ashamed of it." Soon the last black state legislators were gone.

Northern public opinion did not challenge these actions. So the last hope for the blacks lay in the Supreme Court. But in the 1880's and 1890's, it too accepted **disfranchisement** (removal of the right to vote) and segregation. In the civil rights cases of 1883, the Court decided that discrimination by individuals, such as restaurant owners, did not violate the Fourteenth Amendment. And in 1896, in *Plessy v. Ferguson*, it held that a Louisiana law requiring "separate but equal" accommodations on railroads did not deny blacks the equal protection of the laws. The decision was used to justify "separate but equal" facilities from schools to graveyards. In fact, such accommodations were never equal. Moreover, as Justice John Marshall Harlan (lower right) angrily declared in his **dissent** (an opinion delivered in opposition to the majority opinion of a court), "Our Constitution is color-blind." But it would be years before a majority of the Court took this view.

Questions for Discussion

1. Why was a sharecropper nearly always in debt?
2. Why did black and white poor farmers fail to unite in the Populist cause?

"Daddy" Rice based a minstrel act (top) on the antics of a slave named Jim Crow. As a Justice, former slave-owner John Harlan (above) voted for Negro rights.

After the Civil War many Negroes migrated from the rural South to homesteads in the West, like the one below near Guthrie, Oklahoma. Opportunities for migration appeared frequently in ads such as the one at right which promises low-cost transportation from Kentucky to Kansas. Other Negroes chose to move to large cities. The black population of Harlem, a section of New York City, increased by 51 per cent between 1900 and 1910. Many of the new arrivals came from the South and sought apartments like those shown at left.

BROWN BROTHERS

The Search for New Answers

All Colored People THAT WANT TO **GO TO KANSAS,** On September 5th, 1877, Can do so for $5.00

Northern white men and a few Southerners had tried to remake the South's social pattern. Then southern white men had torn up their work. During all this time blacks themselves were not mere bystanders. They were trying to build their own futures. The limited number of educated black leaders explored and discussed several choices with their hard-pressed people. One choice was simply to leave the scene of distress. Many southern rural churches encouraged members of their congregations to move to the West. For example, in 1879 alone some 40,000 black Americans treked westward, settling mainly in Kansas and Indiana. They did not find a land of easy pickings. Farmwork was dull and difficult. The cabin at left was probably not furnished much better than a sharecropper's shack. But like white Americans who moved to new frontiers, this cabin's black owners could hope for better things to come.

Other blacks took part in the westward movement. They became cowpunchers or cavalrymen in the Indian wars. After their trail-riding and bugle-call days were over, they settled on the Great Plains.

Like whites, blacks also tried to escape to the city. A growing number migrated to the upper northern cities (upper left). During World War I the number increased sharply as Negroes took jobs in defense industries. But long before then black country boys and girls began to leave home to make their fortunes in southern towns. They cooked, waited on tables, practiced trades, and drove wagons in Atlanta, Birmingham, St. Louis, New Orleans, and Memphis. A few got factory jobs. A few became members of a growing black middle class. They were doctors, lawyers, teachers, and owners of grocery stores, funeral parlors, barbershops, saloons, insurance companies, and other businesses serving the black community.

In 1900 over 72 American cities each had more than 5,000 Negro residents. Washington, Baltimore, and New Orleans each had more than 75,000. Like other poor immigrants from Europe who were new to city life, many poor blacks had a hard time finding jobs and decent housing, staying healthy and out of trouble with the law. In 1910 concerned blacks founded the National Urban League to help such Negro newcomers with the problems of city living that they faced in common with other Americans. A new age in black leadership was beginning.

BROWN BROTHERS

Booker T. Washington, who chose the name "Washington" on his first day of school, is well known for his work on behalf of improved vocational education and business conditions for blacks. Privately, he also fought railroad segregation and raised money to bring test cases to the Supreme Court on the Negro's right to vote in all elections.

The Rise of Negro Leaders

Leaders of the black community needed education badly. In order to get fair treatment from the white world, they would have to use the same means as whites who had complaints. They would need to publish newspapers, influence lawmakers, take legal action, and raise funds. Only schooled blacks could do such work. After 1865 such Afro-American leaders came from two places: the black churches and the black colleges.

Negro members of American churches organized separately in far greater numbers than they had before the Civil War. Their purpose was to be independent of white control and to avoid the humiliation of being segregated within the churches by white fellow Christians. Hundreds of thousands of Colored Baptists, African Methodists, and members of other religious bodies gave the rituals of white Christianity a black style. More important, black ministers became experienced in organizing their members for common action.

Booker T. Washington as Educator

Negro colleges such as Howard, Fisk, and Atlanta were founded during Reconstruction with funds from the Freedmen's Bureau and private donations. To blacks they were what Harvard was to the little Massachusetts colony in 1636 — a place to train future leaders. One such school, Virginia's Hampton Institute, produced one of the best-known of all black Americans.

One day in the early 1870's a dusty, teen-aged boy showed up there and asked for admission. He was the small boy at the beginning of this chapter — Booker T. Washington (left). After emancipation he had gone with his family to West Virginia. There, he worked in a coal mine and at odd jobs. After graduating from Hampton he was inspired by the idea that rural southern Negroes should stay in the South and strive for economic independence instead of moving north to the cities. The black path up from slavery lay through learning trades and modern farming methods.

In 1881 Washington, who had become a teacher, had a chance to try out his idea. He was put in charge of a new Negro college in Alabama, Tuskegee Institute. In fifteen years of driving work, Washington made it a model industrial and agricultural school.

In 1881, with just 4 run-down buildings and only 30 students, Booker T. Washington founded Tuskegee Institute for Negroes. By 1906 there were 1,600 students and over 100 buildings, many built by students like those seen above from the Class of 1903. Room, board, and tuition for a year was $146. A student unable to pay could work during the day and go to class at night. Most of the classroom time was spent learning trades like bricklaying and carpentry, but academic courses were available. The school baseball team for the 1903 season is pictured at right.

BOTH: LIBRARY OF CONGRESS

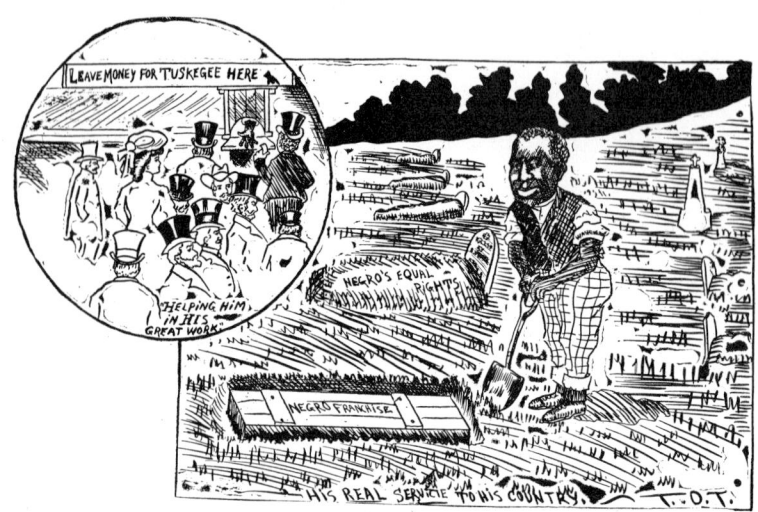

The Guardian, DECEMBER 13, 1902

TUSKEGEE INSTITUTE

Washington's long-range hope was the Negro's complete integration into American life. His announced goal of educating Negroes demanded that he obtain funds and public support. As the cartoon (left) suggests, Washington sought contributions from the wealthy. Also, as seen in the photograph of an anniversary celebration at Tuskegee (below), he maintained close relationships with such public leaders as President Theodore Roosevelt.

Proud of its young graduates, like those shown on page 415, Washington next planned an attack on the entire Negro problem in the South.

Booker T. Washington as Politician

In September of 1895 Washington was invited to speak at the Atlanta Cotton States Exposition, a fair held to show off southern industrial progress. He used his remarks about black businessmen to make an offer to white Southerners. The principal of Tuskegee reasoned that the South needed a productive black labor force, and blacks needed economic power. He would therefore urge whites to help with his programs of agricultural and vocational education. In return, he would urge blacks to spend less time seeking social equality and political advancement and more time studying carpentry, bookkeeping, stock-breeding, and other practical subjects.

To black listeners in Atlanta Washington said that they should "dignify and glorify common labor" and learn that "it is at the bottom of life we must begin and not at the top." Dignity and acceptance would eventually come to blacks, as it would to any race with "anything to contribute to the markets of the world." To whites Washington said that blacks, then one-third of the southern populace, could be one-third of the South's prosperity instead of one-third of its ignorance and poverty. He added, "In all things that are purely social we can be as separate as the fingers, yet one as the hand in all things essential to mutual progress." To both races he promised that his plan would bring a new heaven "into our beloved South."

Many blacks, in 1895 and afterward, sharply criticized this so-called "Atlanta Compromise." But the white world was eager to hear and believe what Washington said. He became known among them as a leader of his race. Rich whites asked his opinion before donating to black schools or charities. Republican Presidents sought his views on selecting Negroes to be named to the few Federal jobs that still went to blacks. Theodore Roosevelt, seen at lower left with Washington at Tuskegee, made national headlines when he invited Washington to the White House to discuss such matters and sat down to the family meal with him. Southerners raged at the breach of their racial "etiquette," though in fact Roosevelt did not intend to change things basically in the South.

Washington was a devoted early promoter of black capitalism. He held frequent meetings to encourage Negro farmers to buy and improve more land. He also was a leader in forming the National Negro Business League, which helped black businessmen get loans and information vital to success.

Black Leadership Becomes More Militant

White leaders listened to Booker T. Washington on racial matters in part because they liked his soft-spoken, peaceful approach. Actually, Washington was indirectly working against disfranchisement and segregation laws. But he wanted those white people who dominated national life to support his program of upgrading the Negro's economic status—in his view, the best long-run method to end Jim Crow. It was easier to get that support by avoiding anger or resentment.

But this style offended some young blacks. They saw Washington as a man who seemed to flatter whites and ignore injustices in order to build up his own power. Their anger was sharpened by the increasing number of segregation laws and by a series of race riots in both the South and the North. In 1906 a race riot rocked Atlanta. Two years later another exploded in Springfield, Illinois—Lincoln's home town!

A number of youthful Negro thinkers challenged Washington publicly. One of the best known was William Edward Burghardt Du Bois (left). Born in 1868 in Massachusetts, Du Bois attended Fisk University, then did advanced studies at Harvard and in Europe. He became a pioneer in the field of **sociology** (the scientific study of social behavior).

Du Bois thought that Washington was too concerned with moneymaking. In a book called *The Souls of Black Folk*, published in 1903, Du Bois argued that blacks had gifts of what would now be called "soul" which could not be measured in dollars. Later he wrote that the Negro race, like all races, would be "saved by its exceptional men," such as philosophers, poets, and scientists. Black education should train thinkers, not just vegetable-growers and bricklayers.

Du Bois and a number of other black opponents of Washington's views met in 1905 on the Canadian side of Niagara Falls, where they were sure of fair treatment in hotels and restaurants. They posed solemnly and with determination (right) for a camera. Later they planned a public demand for "every single right

NAACP

William Du Bois (above) opposed Washington's emphasis on vocational rather than academic training and his apparent willingness to wait for equal rights. Du Bois felt that Negroes must speak out constantly against discrimination and oppression. Supporters of Du Bois' views met in Niagara Falls, Canada, in 1905 (right) to organize a program of public action for the constitutional rights of America's blacks.

that belongs to a freeborn American—political, civil, and social."

Many members of the black "Niagara Movement" helped to found the National Association for the Advancement of Colored People (NAACP) in 1909. They were joined by a number of white men and women who felt that in this way they were helping the whole United States. American democracy could not work unless all races shared its promises. The NAACP promised to work for change through lobbying and lawsuits. Because it did not take the outwardly soothing tone of Booker T. Washington, the NAACP was considered radical at the time of its birth.

Fifty years after John Brown's raid, blacks had made many strides forward. But much remained to be done to improve the quality of American democracy.

Questions for Discussion

1. What problems were faced by the Negroes who migrated to the cities of the South and North? What organization was founded to help them?
2. What institutions were the sources of Negro community leadership after 1865?
3. How did Booker T. Washington's ideas about Negro advancement differ from those of W. E. B. Du Bois?
4. What was the so-called "Atlanta Compromise" favored and announced by Booker T. Washington? Why did some blacks denounce it?

Chapter Review

Social Studies Terms

Reconstruction, civil rights, welfare agencies, racism, electorate, terrorist, repression, sharecroppers, segregated, caste system, Populists, poll taxes, literacy tests, disfranchisement, dissent, sociology

Summary Questions for Discussion

1. Why did the Civil War and the amendments immediately following it fail to place blacks on an equal footing with whites?
2. In the period after Reconstruction, why did both white Northerners and Southerners favor policies which would ensure white supremacy?
3. Are the civil rights of Negroes more or less secure today than they were after *Plessy v. Ferguson*?
4. To correct injustices in the South, why were Negroes unable to obtain relief in the local and Federal courts?

5. What did Justice Harlan mean when he said that "Our Constitution is color-blind?"
6. Why do unwritten laws or customs sometimes have the same effect as written laws? What are some unwritten laws or customs that govern relations in your school or in the community where you live?
7. What might be a hypothesis to explain why some whites have used terror and violence in their relationships with blacks since the Civil War?
8. Why did migration to the cities often not change the Negroes' status as second-class citizens?
9. Why have Negro ministers often been both church and community leaders?
10. Contrast the educations of Booker T. Washington and W. E. B. Du Bois. How would the type of education received by each man influence his views about the best path for Negro advancement?
11. In the Negroes' struggle for equality, was gaining economic power more important than gaining political power? Why?

Pictures as Historical Evidence

"Despite a great many difficulties, black Americans enjoyed more political and economic opportunity after the Civil War than before." Make a list of those pictures in this chapter which would tend to support such a statement and a list which would contradict such a statement. Then, in your own words, tell why you think the statement is basically true or false.

Map Study

What four southern states were the last to re-establish conservative governments? How did this affect the outcome of the election of 1876?

For Further Reading

Lift Every Voice: The Lives of Booker T. Washington, W. E. B. Du Bois, Mary Church Terrell and James Weldon Johnson, by Dorothy Sterling. Garden City: Doubleday & Company, Inc., 1965.

100 Years of Negro Freedom, by Arna Bontemps. New York: Dodd, Mead & Co., 1961.

Rifles and War Bonnets: Negro Cavalry in the West, by Marian T. Place. New York: Ives Washburn, Inc., 1968.

Thaddeus Stevens and the Fight for Negro Rights, by Milton Meltzer. New York: Thomas Y. Crowell Company, 1967.

ISSUES PAST AND PRESENT

Integration or Separation?

"Separatism" is the policy and belief that blacks and whites should live and work in separate neighborhoods, towns, counties, or states. A separatist society is one in which blacks and whites live and work apart from each other.

The awful gulf that still divides many blacks and whites in this country was described before the Civil War by a Frenchman, Gustave de Beaumont, visiting in this country. In 1830 he wrote, "Slave or free, the Negroes everywhere form a people apart from the whites." The relationship between blacks and whites has been the longest lasting of the problems left unsolved by that war. For many years it was popular in American schools to refer to this gulf as "the Negro problem" or to think of it as a problem of the South. Now, many thoughtful Americans of all races realize that it is a "white problem" too, and that it is a national or even international, not just a southern or American, problem.

At the time Beaumont was in the United States, what to do with the blacks was a question that was debated mainly among whites. It is still debated among whites, but blacks themselves now want to have the main voice in deciding their own future. In this unit's *Issues Past and Present*, we will read the words of black authors who, since the Civil War, have written about the future of black people in this country. Much of this writing in recent times has been about the question of whether blacks should favor a policy and program for the integration of black and white Americans or a policy and program of separatism. As you will see, black leaders do not have a single point of view, but we may note that none of these authors favors segregation, a word which implies a *forced* separation of blacks and whites. As you read, think about these questions:

1. Should blacks and whites live in their own neighborhoods, towns, or states and on their own farms with only other people of the same race for friends, neighbors, and fellow workers? Why?
2. What do blacks gain by integration with whites? What do they lose? What would they gain and lose by separation?
3. Have Negroes gained equality since the Civil War?

Frederick Douglass' View

Although most of the new state constitutions written for reconstructed southern states provided for systems of public education, only two, those of South Carolina and Louisiana, specifically provided for integrated schooling. The rest said nothing about integration. But even in South Carolina and Louisiana, nothing but segregated schools were to be found by 1870. In 1872 United States Senator Charles Sumner, a Radical Republican from Massachusetts, introduced a bill in Congress to provide integrated public schools in the District of Columbia. These words supporting the bill are from an article by Frederick Douglass in Douglass' own newspaper, The New National Era.

FREDERICK DOUGLASS:
WE WANT MIXED SCHOOLS, 1872

We hope for the speedy passage of the bill to establish mixed schools in the District of Columbia in order that the mad current of prejudice against the Negro may be stopped. Also separation of the colored children from the whites teaches the colored children that the whites are superior to them. We want to destroy the terrible influence this idea has upon them.

Throughout the South all the schools should be mixed. We are convinced that the interests of the poor whites and the colored people are the same. Both are ignorant, and both are the tools of scheming white men. The poor whites are used especially in ways that are not in their own best interests. In the South everything that will bring the poor white man and the colored man closer together should be done. They should both be taught to make common cause [work together] against the rich landholders of the South who never thought a poor white man to be of as much importance as slaves. Educate the poor white children and the colored children together. Let them grow up to know that color makes no difference as to the rights of a man. Let them know that both the black man and the white man are at home in the United States. Let them know that the country is as much the country of one as of the other, and that both together must make it a valuable country.

We want mixed schools not because our colored schools are inferior to white schools, not because colored instructors are inferior to white instructors. We want mixed schools in order to do away with a system that raises one class of people and lowers another. We believe that in mixed schools colored as well as white teachers should be employed, but neither unless they are competent. We look to mixed schools to teach that worth and ability should determine manhood and not race and color.

"Competent" means able to do a job well.

1. What does Douglass want? Why? Do you agree? Why?
2. How does Douglass describe the class structure of the South? In his view what were its effects?
3. Would Chapter 14 tend to support his view or not? Explain.

When Douglass wrote during Reconstruction (1865–1877), many black leaders, full of hope, believed that in a reconstructed, integrated South there would be no limit to the progress toward equality made by blacks. But for many the end of Reconstruction, the passage of Jim Crow laws, and a policy of

Elijah Muhammad's Message

white supremacy shattered those hopes. Some began to look for a new road to equality. One of these was Elijah Muhammad, founder of the Nation of Islam, one of the first organizations to reject the idea of the integration of blacks and whites. Malcolm X became a member of the movement while in prison, and upon release in 1952 soon became the chief spokesman for Elijah Muhammad. Malcolm X was assassinated in 1965, not long after he broke away from the Black Muslim movement. Here he recalls in his Autobiography *some words spoken by Elijah Muhammad at a Muslim mass rally in 1960.*

Malcolm Little and many other Black Muslims adopted the last name of "X" to symbolize their rejection of a last name given to their families by former slaveholders.

"Sitting-in" refers to the occupation of restaurants and other places by blacks and whites to force store owners or public officials to treat blacks the same as whites.

MALCOLM LITTLE:
THE AUTOBIOGRAPHY OF MALCOLM X, 1965

"The *ignorance* we of the black race here in America have, and the *self-hatred* we have, they are fine examples of what the white slavemaster has seen fit to teach to us. Do we show the plain common sense, like every other people on this planet Earth, to unite among ourselves? No! We are humbling ourselves, sitting-in, and begging-in, trying to *unite* with the slavemaster! I don't seem able to imagine any more ridiculous sight. A thousand ways every day, the white man is telling you 'You can't live here, you can't enter here, you can't eat here, drink here, walk here, work here, you can't ride here, you can't play here, you can't study here.' Haven't we yet seen enough to see that he has no plan to *unite* with you?...

"You have sweated blood to help him build a country so rich that he can today afford to give away millions—even to his *enemies!* And when those enemies have gotten enough from him to then be able to attack him, you have been his brave soldiers, *dying* for him. And you have been always his most faithful servant during the so-called 'peaceful' times—

"And, *still*, this Christian American white man has not got it in him to find the human *decency*, and enough sense of *justice*, to recognize us, and accept us, the black people who have done so much for him, as fellow human beings!"

[Members of the audience respond]

"YAH, Man!"..."Um-huh!" "Teach, Messenger!"..."Yah!" ..."Tell 'em!"..."You right!"..."Take your *time* up there, little Messenger!"..."Oh, *yes!*"

[Elijah Muhammad continues]

"So let us, the black people, *separate* ourselves from this white man slavemaster, who despises us so much!...

"Why *shouldn't* this white man who likes to think and call himself so good, and so generous, this white man who finances even his enemies—why *shouldn't* he subsidize a separate state,

a separate territory, for we black people who have been such faithful slaves and servants? A separate territory on which we can lift *ourselves* out of these white man's *slums* for us, and his *breadlines* for us. And even for *those* he is complaining that we cost him too much! We can then do something for *ourselves!* We never have done what we *could*—because we have been brainwashed so well by the slavemaster white man that we must come to him, begging him for everything we want, and need—....

"We black people don't *know* what we can do. You never can know what *anything* can do—until it is set *free*, to act by itself! If you have a cat in your house that you pamper and pet, you have to free that cat, set it on its *own*, in the woods, before you can see that the cat had it *in* him to shelter and feed itself!

"We, the black people here in America, we never have been *free* to find *out* what we really can *do!* We have knowledge and experience to pool to do for ourselves! All of our lives we have farmed—we can grow our own food. We can set up factories to manufacture our own necessities! We can build other kinds of businesses, to establish trade, and commerce—and become independent, as other civilized people are—....

"We can *throw off* our brainwashing, and our self-hate, and live as *brothers* together...."

1. What does Elijah Muhammad want blacks to do?
2. What does he want the whites to do for blacks? How does he justify this demand?
3. Do you agree? Why?

Whitney Young's Viewpoint

Whitney M. Young, Jr., was the Executive Director of the National Urban League from 1961 until his death in March of 1971. The Urban League was founded in New York City in 1910 to help Negro migrants from the South adjust to urban living in northern cities. As it has grown, it has concentrated its efforts on helping blacks living in cities throughout the country get better housing, jobs, education, and health services. Whitney Young wrote the following selection for the August 1970 issue of Ebony *magazine.*

WHITNEY M. YOUNG, JR.:
SEPARATISM? WE ARE SEPARATED—AND THAT'S THE CAUSE OF ALL OUR WOES, 1970

There are no virtues [good things] to be found in segregation, whether forced upon us by white racists or sought out by ourselves.

A "ghetto" is a section of a city in which the members of one race, religion, or nationality are forced to live.

The black man was segregated on Southern plantations. He is segregated now in urban ghettos. Separatism is not some goal we ought to strive for. We already have a separatist society. It's here. Now. We are separate in every real sense — and the result has been *powerlessness*, not power; *poverty*, not riches; *discrimination*, not equality.

The black ghetto is proof of this. The schools, the hospitals, the police protection, and even the quality of food and goods available are not as good as those found in white neighborhoods. The evils so widespread in the ghetto are allowed to exist because only black people live there. If whites sent their children to schools in the black ghetto, those schools would improve. White society would not tolerate decaying school buildings and shortages of textbooks for their kids the way they accept it for blacks. Hospitals in white neighborhoods don't stick beds in hallways the way ghetto hospitals do. They know the whites who run hospitals for whites won't allow it. Supermarkets don't overcharge for spoiled food in white neighborhoods, either. Their managers know that white people, not blacks, would be victims.

It's all well and good to say that black power and control in the black community would end these evils. In some ways they would. But no neighborhood is an island unto itself. The black ghetto, like any white neighborhood, would be dependent upon money and services provided by the city, by the state, and by the Federal government. And unless the 88 per cent of the population of this country which is white packs up and moves elsewhere, those governments will be dominated by white people. And there has never been any sign, in our whole history, that white institutions will treat separate black neighborhoods as well as they treat whites.

Separatism as a strategy for equality has never worked and it never will. The South is dotted with all-black towns. They've got all the symbols and organizations of power — black mayors, black police, black schools. But they don't have sidewalks, money, or jobs.

I believe in the need for an integrated society, not because being with whites is, of itself, a good thing, but because it is only through being a part of the mainstream of American life that full equality can be won.

Integration does not mean that black values will be rejected or that we desire to imitate white society. The black man's best hope lies in an Open Society. Belief in an Open Society says "Yes!" to a belief that black people can compete on an equal basis with whites. Whenever blacks have had the chance, we have shown that we can compete successfully, whether it's been on the Supreme Court or on the basketball court.

The Open Society toward which we must strive is a society in which black people have their fair share of the power, the wealth, and the comforts of the whole society. It is a society in which blacks have the choice to live in a black neighborhood or to live in an integrated one, in which blacks have control over decisions affecting their lives in the same way that other groups have. It is a society based on respect for each other and complete equality. There isn't a reason in the world why we should settle for anything less. The struggle may be long and difficult, but nothing worthwhile has ever been achieved without a struggle.

1. On what points are Elijah Muhammad and Whitney Young in agreement? in disagreement?
2. What does Young mean by an "Open Society?"
3. Do you agree with Young? Why?

Using Statistics

You have just finished comparing a number of opinions by different Negroes about what black Americans ought to do to improve their economic position, their social status, and their sense of human dignity. In some degree each author's viewpoint depended on how much he thought Negroes had shared in the benefits of American development. Some of the benefits that concerned the authors were education, employment, and housing.

Below are three statistical tables which will tell you something about what share white Americans and black Americans have had of the benefits of our society. *Statistics* are collections of information. The statistics in the tables below were gathered by the United States Bureau of the Census and other government agencies. Every ten years a census is taken to see how many Americans there are, how much they earn, how much education they have, and so on. The government studies or analyzes the data it has collected and then prepares tables like the ones below which summarize its findings.

Such statistics are very useful, for they provide the best means we have of finding out what is actually happening in our huge country which now has more than 200 million people. However, statistics need to be studied carefully in order to understand their full meaning. After you have looked at each table, write a sentence or two in your own words telling what each table means to you. After you have done that, tell whether the statements which follow each table are true or false and why. You will find that these questions require some careful study or analysis of the information in the tables.

TABLE I

School Enrollment Whites and Nonwhites*
1860–1960

Year	White	Nonwhite
1960	84.8	81.3
1940	75.6	68.4
1920	65.7	53.5
1900	53.6	31.1
1880	62.0	33.8
1860	59.6	1.9

* Figures are given in percentages of those attending school from the ages of 5 to 19.

1. During Reconstruction a much larger percentage of Negroes went to school than had gone before slavery was abolished.
2. The over-all trend in school enrollment is for the percentage of whites and nonwhites to become increasingly the same.
3. Probably the most discouraging years for Negroes as far as school enrollment is concerned were:
   (a) the period from 1940 to 1960,
   (b) the period from 1900 to 1920,
   (c) the period from 1880 to 1900.

TABLE II

Median Family Income 1967

	Negro	White
United States	$4,939	$8,318
Northeast	5,764	8,746
North Central	6,540	8,414
South	3,992	7,448
West	6,590	8,901

1. In 1967 Negroes and whites shared equally in American prosperity.
2. Where a black family lives makes no difference in its income compared to the incomes of white families in the same region.

TABLE III

Persons Below the Poverty Level*
1959–1967

	Per Cent		Number in Millions	
	*Nonwhite***	*White*	*Nonwhite***	*White*
1959	55%	18%	10.7	28.2
1960	55%	18%	11.4	28.7
1961	55%	17%	11.6	26.5
1962	54%	16%	11.6	25.4
1963	51%	15%	11.2	24.1
1964	49%	14%	10.9	23.4
1965	46%	13%	10.5	21.4
1966	40%	12%	9.3	19.5
1967	35%	10%	8.3	17.6

* The poverty definition is based on the minimum food and other needs of families. As applied to 1967 incomes, the poverty threshold for a nonfarm family of four was $3,330.
** Includes all nonwhite, not just Negroes.

1. The table provides good evidence for the hypothesis that economic equality between white and nonwhite Americans was growing between 1959 and 1967.

Summary Questions

In Unit IV you have studied a variety of materials about America's racial problems between blacks and whites. Now see what answers or generalizations you can give to the questions asked at the beginning of this inquiry section.

1. Should blacks and whites live separately in their own neighborhoods, towns, or states and on their own farms, working in their own factories, with only people of the same race for friends, neighbors, and fellow workers? Why?
2. What do blacks gain by integration with whites? What do they lose? What would they gain or lose by separation?
3. Have Negroes gained greater equality with white Americans since the Civil War? Explain your answer.
4. What further information would help answer these questions? Why?

1856 Bessemer Develops Steel Process

1862 Homestead Act Passed

1876 Bell Invents Telephone

1859 First Oil Well Drilled

1869 Stephens Organizes Knights of Labor

1879 Edison Develops Incandescent Lamp

UNIT V
The United States Becomes an Industrial Giant

1886 Gompers Heads A.F. of L.

1892 Homestead Steelworkers Strike

1903 Wright Brothers Airplane

1920 Urban Population Excedes Rural

1890 Sherman Antitrust Act Passed

1901 Teddy Roosevelt Becomes President

1909 Mass Production of Ford "Model T"

The United States Census Report for 1970 stated that only one out of every twenty Americans lives on a farm any longer. In 1870, even as farmers' sons and daughters were leaving the plains and prairies for jobs in the cities, such a figure would scarcely have been thought possible. Surely, as Thomas Jefferson had hoped, America would always be mostly a nation of small farmers. Few people could forecast the tremendous impact of industrialization.

The starting point for our study of Unit V, *Interpreting the Past*, presents contrasting views of the results of industrialization in the United States. Chapter 15 describes the forces that were turning the country into an industrial giant. Chapter 16 pictures the new kind of industrial city which became the home of an increasing number of Americans. Industrialization and urbanization brought major changes in the way Americans lived. These changes, and the era of reform which sought to meet the challenge of change, are the subject of Chapter 17.

Problems like low farm prices, festering slums, dirty politics, and unsafe mines and mills demanded new solutions. "What is the responsibility of the government for the welfare of its citizens?" asked the reformers. Both the reformers and the opponents of reform had answers to this question, as we will see in *Issues Past and Present* which closes this unit.

TOP, LEFT TO RIGHT:
Scientific American
NEW-YORK HISTORICAL SOCIETY
SMITHSONIAN INSTITUTION
NATIONAL ARCHIVES
LIBRARY OF CONGRESS
SMITHSONIAN INSTITUTION
HAZELTON PUBLIC LIBRARY
BOTTOM, LEFT TO RIGHT:
DRAKE MEMORIAL MUSEUM
CULVER PICTURES
SMITHSONIAN INSTITUTION
NEW-YORK HISTORICAL SOCIETY
BROWN BROTHERS
HENRY FORD MUSEUM

INTERPRETING THE PAST

Industrialization

Life in a Factory Town

Before the Civil War the cotton gin and the steam engine had shown Americans how machines could bring far-reaching changes in their daily lives. And while the country expanded to the Pacific, the census reports told of rapid increases in population caused both by high birth rates and large-scale immigration from Europe. Large numbers of those who were added to the population figures stayed on farms or moved to farms. But many others found the cities more attractive places to live. After the Civil War cities and factories grew at a dizzying pace. Many writers praised the growing national strength and wealth represented by industrialization and urbanization. Some writers, however, noted that if industrialization and urbanization achieved some goals of American society, they also threatened others.

Between 1869 and 1900 many states investigated the living and working conditions of factory workers and their families. This report prepared for the Massachusetts legislature in 1875 was typical of many of these reports.

SIXTH ANNUAL REPORT OF THE BUREAU OF STATISTICS OF LABOR, STATE OF MASSACHUSETTS, 1875

A "tenement" is a low-rental apartment building.

Holyoke, Massachusetts, has more and worse large tenement houses than any manufacturing town of textile fabrics in the state. These houses are built in such a manner that there is almost no way to escape in case of fire. Sewage arrangements are very poor. In many cases there is no way to carry the garbage from the sinks. Instead, it is allowed to run wherever it can make its way. Parts of yards are covered with filth and green slime. Only 20 feet away people are living in basements of houses 3 feet below the level of the yard. On one large block there are 18 tenements, 4 stories high, each with 90 rooms and frequently with more than 3 people to a room. The tenement has only 2 three-feet doorways on the front and none on the back. There is a dark alley only 6 feet wide. Our investigators visited some tenements having bedrooms into which neither light nor air could enter, since there were no windows and no means of ventilation. It is no wonder that in 1872 the death rate was greater in Holyoke than in any large town in Massachusetts, except Fall River. If an epidemic [disease] should come to them now, in the condition they are in, its effects would be great.

1. Why do you think tenements like those in Holyoke were built?

2. What effects would the living conditions described above have on the people who lived there?
3. How do the conditions described by the report compare with conditions in modern industrial areas?

An Industrialist's View

The following selection is by America's most famous steelmaker and one of the richest men of the nineteenth century.

ANDREW CARNEGIE: *WEALTH*, 1889

Human life has not only been changed within the past few hundred years, it has been revolutionized. In primitive days there was little difference between the houses, dress, food, and environment of those who were chiefs and those who were their servants. There was, to a large degree, social equality. The contrast today between the palaces of the millionaires and the cottages of the laborers shows us the change which has come with civilization.

This change, however, is not to be regretted, but welcomed as highly beneficial [helpful]. For progress there must be homes of great wealth to preserve the best things of civilization. Therefore, it is much better to have this great difference between rich and poor than to have general poverty. Neither master nor servant was as well off in the "good old times" as today. Whether change be for good or bad, it has come and is beyond our power to reverse. Therefore, it should be accepted and made the best of. It is a waste of time to criticize what must happen.

By today's methods of manufacturing the world gets goods of excellent quality at prices which even the people of 25 years ago would have thought unbelievable. The poor enjoy what once the rich could not afford. What were luxuries then have become necessities now. The laborer now has more comforts than the farmer had a few generations ago. The farmer has more luxuries than the landlord had. The farmer is more richly clothed and better housed. The landlord has more rare books and pictures and more artistic furnishings than the king could have in olden times.

1. Why did Carnegie believe that the contrast between the living conditions of the workers and those of the rich was not a bad thing?
2. According to Carnegie how had industrialization affected both "masters" and "servants?"
3. Would the previous reading agree with or contradict Carnegie's view of the industrial laborer? Why?

A Poet's View

The author of the short poem which follows was born in 1876 in Norfolk, Virginia.

SARAH N. CLEGHORN: *THE GOLF LINKS*, 1917

*The golf links lie so near the mill
That almost every day
The laboring children can look out
And see the men at play.*

1. Why do you believe children were hired to work in mills?
2. Do you think Sarah Cleghorn and Andrew Carnegie had the same opinion about the condition of industrial laborers? Why?

A Modern Historian's View

Louis Hacker was educated at Columbia University and began to teach there in 1935. His special field of study has been the economic history of the United States.

LOUIS M. HACKER: *INDUSTRIAL CAPITALISM*, 1957

"Real income" means the value of the goods and services a person can buy with his wages.

The country's national income rose from $2.38 billion in 1850 to $19.36 billion in 1900. At the same time, the real income for the average working person almost doubled, that is, increased from $787 to $1,388 per year.

This was the good work done by America's first industrial capitalists. They owned and managed their businesses, took risks, made enormous profits, and reinvested most of those profits in factories and machines that would create more business and more jobs. Great steps forward in technology were possible only because they were willing to take risks. There is no doubt they took part in cut-throat and unfair means of competition. On the other hand, those same capitalists lowered costs, reduced prices, and kept wages high.

It is true that there were low standards of living among certain groups of workers. In part, this was due to the crowding of great urban centers just springing up. In part, it was due to very low wages which workers, starting as unskilled laborers, were receiving. However, many of the leaders of business were themselves workers at one time.

1. How does Hacker's view of industrialism compare with Carnegie's? with the report to Massachusetts?
2. What evidence does Hacker give to support his view?

A Second Historian's View

The following piece was written by a high school teacher who is also a writer and an editor in New York City.

JOHN ANTHONY SCOTT: *THE GILDED AGE*, 1969

The Civil War was the beginning of the age of tycoons. The rise of large-scale industry centralized power and control in the hands of leading industrialists and financiers. Hundreds of these people, as a result, piled up great fortunes. Often they were brilliant organizers, wise and talented businessmen. They beat down their own workers, swindled the general public, and fought each other without mercy. By 1900 the highest places in steel, railroad, oil, meatpacking, milling, banking, and other industries were in the hands of men such as these.

"Tycoons" are wealthy and powerful businessmen.

"Financiers" are experts in large-scale money matters.

"Swindled" means cheated.

There was a sharp, wide division between these enormously wealthy rulers of industry on one side and the masses living in poverty on the other. The majority of the people, whether in the industrial cities or on the farms, lived a life of hard labor that too often went along with deep poverty. Side by side with this was a parade of luxury, as the wealthy competed with each other in elegant display. They built luxury yachts in which they entertained kings and queens. They ransacked Europe for its art treasures, and then hid them away in private mansions. They built palaces which stood as monuments to their vanity [self-love] and waste.

1. How does Scott's interpretation of the "Gilded Age" compare with Carnegie's? with Hacker's?

Determining the Question

One of the most difficult parts of making an inquiry is to identify what ought to be studied. You have just finished reading a series of viewpoints on industrialization. What is the question raised by these readings? To identify the question you may want to make a list of what each author said about the effects of industrialization. Write a sentence or two saying what you think the question to be studied further is.

15 The Making of an Industrial Environment

In 1876 the Declaration of Independence was 100 years old. The United States gave itself a centennial birthday party with a mighty industrial fair in Philadelphia. In the city where the little united colonies had proclaimed their freedom, great buildings rose. One of them, the Hall of Machinery, contained a gigantic steam engine. It powered thirteen acres of other machines for combing wool, spinning cotton, printing newspapers, sewing cloth, and doing many other kinds of work. Walt Whitman wrote of these inventions: "This, this and these, America, shall be *your* pyramids." Americans took such marvels as signs of their greatness as a people.

Yet 1876 was only one milestone on a long road. The streams of manufactured goods that began to flow from American factories around 1820 soon became torrents. By 1900 the United States was a leading world producer of steel, oil, and coal. All these were basic to modern industry. In addition, American-made clothing, machinery, foodstuffs, and other products traveled the world over. Africans and Asians wore garments of American cloth; Argentine farmers plowed with American plows; and Japanese soldiers, after a victorious war over China, were given American-made watches as rewards for bravery.

Although the early factory system had made some changes in the way Americans lived, it was the huge industrial growth after the Civil War that changed their surroundings almost completely. In 1860 Americans were largely a nation of farmers. Sixty years later the majority of them lived in cities. In 1860 the United States was inhabited almost entirely by English-speaking peoples. But by 1910 hundreds of thousands of strangers from places as far away as China and Russia were familiar sights in eastern and western cities.

In Lincoln's day Americans lived in a land of open skies, untouched forests, and clear streams. Half a century after Lincoln's death, large areas of the American landscape were lit by blast furnaces and iron foundries at night, like the one at left, and made smoky by factory chimneys in daytime. America had become a powerful — and different — land.

As you read, think about these questions:
1. What are the elements of industrialization?
2. How did industrialization change the United States and the way Americans lived?

John Weir painted this busy northern iron foundry in the 1860's.

The Elements of Industrialization

BOTH: BROWN BROTHERS

Many elements went into this change from a frontier America to a world workshop. History, culture, and geography gave the United States a head start in three key areas: leadership, labor, and resources.

A new breed of strong, self-made men, that is, men who did not inherit wealth or social position but earned success anyway, led America's march to industrial might. In a fast-growing country that preached equality, a clever, hard-working young man could succeed in business even without a family fortune to give him a start. He would receive society's encouragement because of the nation's tradition of hard work and thrift and frontier America's long practice of admiring material growth and progress.

Industrial leaders like oil refiner John D. Rockefeller (right) or steel king Andrew Carnegie (left) were not just ordinary businessmen. They were unusually energetic and decisive. They were able to think big. They planned huge business operations, certain that a growing nation would buy all they made. They worshiped efficiency. They bought expensive machinery and paid high salaries to expert engineers to cut only a few cents off the cost of refining a barrel of oil or making a ton of steel. But those pennies, multiplied by millions of tons or barrels, added up to huge savings in the costs of manufacture. These lower costs meant lower prices. Lower prices attracted more customers, and this meant bigger sales and therefore more profits.

The new captains of industry were often ruthless competitors—but only until they had eliminated competition. They believed it was wasteful for many small makers of the same product to fight each other for raw materials, workers, and customers. Their ideal was to achieve monopoly, or near-monopoly, with one company, or a few, dominating each industry.

These qualities and attitudes are shown best in the career of Rockefeller. Rockefeller began as a Cleveland bookkeeper with a salary of $3.50 a week. Of this he saved enough to enter the grocery business. In 1863 he turned to oil refining. It was a risky enterprise. Prices rose and fell overnight. Rockefeller decided to lead in making the industry more efficient. First, he made his Standard Oil Company an outstanding refinery. One way to do so was to control all the ingredients of the finished product. Standard made its own oil barrels from Rockefeller-owned timber. It delivered

oil products in Rockefeller-purchased wagons.

In 1870 Standard was refining 3,000 barrels of oil a day. Now Rockefeller met with other Cleveland refiners. He pointed out to them that as rivals they competed in buying crude oil, refining machinery, and providing transportation, thus driving their costs higher. Then they competed in selling the refined oil, driving down the prices they received. But if they combined they could dictate their own terms to both their suppliers and customers. If they did not combine Standard alone would undersell them and drive them out of business. Faced with such a choice, 32 independent refineries sold out to Rockefeller.

During the 1880's Standard built or bought oil fields, tanks, pipelines, and warehouses all over the country. In 1886 its annual output was over 10 million barrels of refined oil. Standard, composed of many united companies, controlled each step in refining. Yet while Rockefeller managed this huge empire, he would write to superintendents asking them to account for a few barrel stoppers worth less than a penny each. These practices were part of what he called "better business principles."

The steelman Andrew Carnegie illustrates the attitude many captains of industry held toward wealth and power. Carnegie was a frequent writer for magazines. One of his articles was entitled "The Gospel of Wealth." A gospel is a statement of faith believed to be absolutely true. Carnegie's gospel said that the very rich had a duty to use their wealth for the public good, rather than leaving it to their children. They should donate freely to such good works as libraries, hospitals, and universities. Thus the fortunes made by the captains of industry would advance the whole human race.

Numbers of American millionaires who shared this idea gave away remarkable sums of money. Their skills and generosity benefited the nation. Yet the gospel of wealth really said that a few great firms should rule the economy and a few rich men improve society by gifts. These ideas were a long way from the older American ideal of equal chances for all.

Labor for Hire

Another requirement for a massive increase in industrial production is a steady supply of labor. A great deal of rugged muscle power was needed to dig

Left: Andrew Carnegie invested early in the steel industry. He described his policy as "put all good eggs in one basket and then watch the basket." Below: John D. Rockefeller donated a tenth of his huge income to the public.

coal and iron ore from the earth, cut down trees for lumber, hammer steel rails into place, and dig foundation trenches for factories and city buildings. Once machines were in place in a factory, they needed hands to run them. However, those hands could belong to women and children (lower right) as well as men.

The United States had two sources of labor. One was its own countryside. From mountain and prairie country boys and girls followed the lure of the city. They found jobs in heavy industry and in the offices, stores, and city services, such as police, fire, and sanitation departments, of the growing urban world.

Secondly, there was immigration. America's reputation as a land of freedom and opportunity paid off in economic terms because it attracted a mighty labor force. Between 1860 and 1920 nearly 30 million migrated here from Europe and Asia. That number almost equaled the whole United States population in the year of Lincoln's election. Vast numbers of these newcomers became industrial workers. The western section of the first transcontinental railroad, for example, was built by Chinese laborers (upper right).

Most immigrants before 1900 came from Northern Europe: England, Ireland, Scotland, Germany, and Scandinavia. Thereafter, the majority were Italians, Poles, Russians, Hungarians, and other eastern and southern European people. Many of them ended up working in mines (left) or steel mills. The textile and garment industries attracted many Russian Jewish immigrants, French Canadians, and people of Mediterranean origin. In the textile mills of Lawrence, Massachusetts, in 1912, it was said that more than twenty languages were spoken.

This labor was both plentiful and cheap. So many people wanted jobs that they were willing to work long hours for low wages. Women and children of poor families did much of the work in the "light" industries that required little hauling and lifting.

Resources for Industry

A major advantage possessed by the United States in becoming an industrial giant was geographical: the abundance of resources of North America. The mountain ranges were great storehouses of gold, silver, lead, copper, coal, and other mineral treasures. The forests seemed limitless. Petroleum lay in huge natural underground reservoirs, waiting to gush forth their

Left: Pennsylvania coal miners prepare to descend for a day's work. Above: In the 1880's Chinese workers on the Northern Pacific Railroad pause for a photograph. Below: Women and children clean oysters and shrimp in a Gulf Coast cannery.

CULVER PICTURES

black gold like the gusher at left.

Coal and oil are essential to modern industry. They furnish its work-energy. As they are burned either in gasoline engines or in furnaces, they make steam that drives the generators that, in turn, make electricity. Steel is the basic building material of modern times. Thus the graph of oil, coal, and steel production at the lower right illustrates the forward surge of the United States.

Petroleum products were almost unknown in 1860. By 1910 production in all forms had soared from a few thousand to billions of gallons. This growth came even before widespread use of the gasoline, or internal-combustion, engine. Most petroleum was refined into lubricants, which prevent moving machine parts from wearing each other out by friction, and into kerosene for heating and lighting purposes.

Before 1858 steel was costly and little was produced, although men knew that it was tougher and longer-lasting than iron. In the 1850's an Englishman and an American separately discovered processes for burning impurities out of molten iron by forcing a blast of air through it. The adding of other minerals completed the process. The resulting steel was both extremely strong and cheap to produce. Thereafter, American blast furnaces worked steadily. Huge new deposits like the Mesabi Range were discovered and then mined by powerful steam shovels (right). As late as 1867 fewer than 23,000 tons were produced. But by 1910 the United States led the world in millions of tons produced. The steel went into rails, railroad cars, ships, armor plate, machinery, bridges, wire cables, and skyscrapers.

Revolution in Communications and Transportation

In the industrial environment raw materials and finished goods moved back and forth over vast distances under the commands of the great managers. This movement would have been impossible without a huge transportation network. Andrew Carnegie explained the situation in 1901. A ton of steel, he wrote, cost about fifteen dollars to produce. To make each pound in that ton took two pounds of iron ore moved 1,000 miles by water, one pound of coke made from coal transported 50 miles, and one-third of a pound of limestone carried 140 miles.

The growth of railroads was the main development

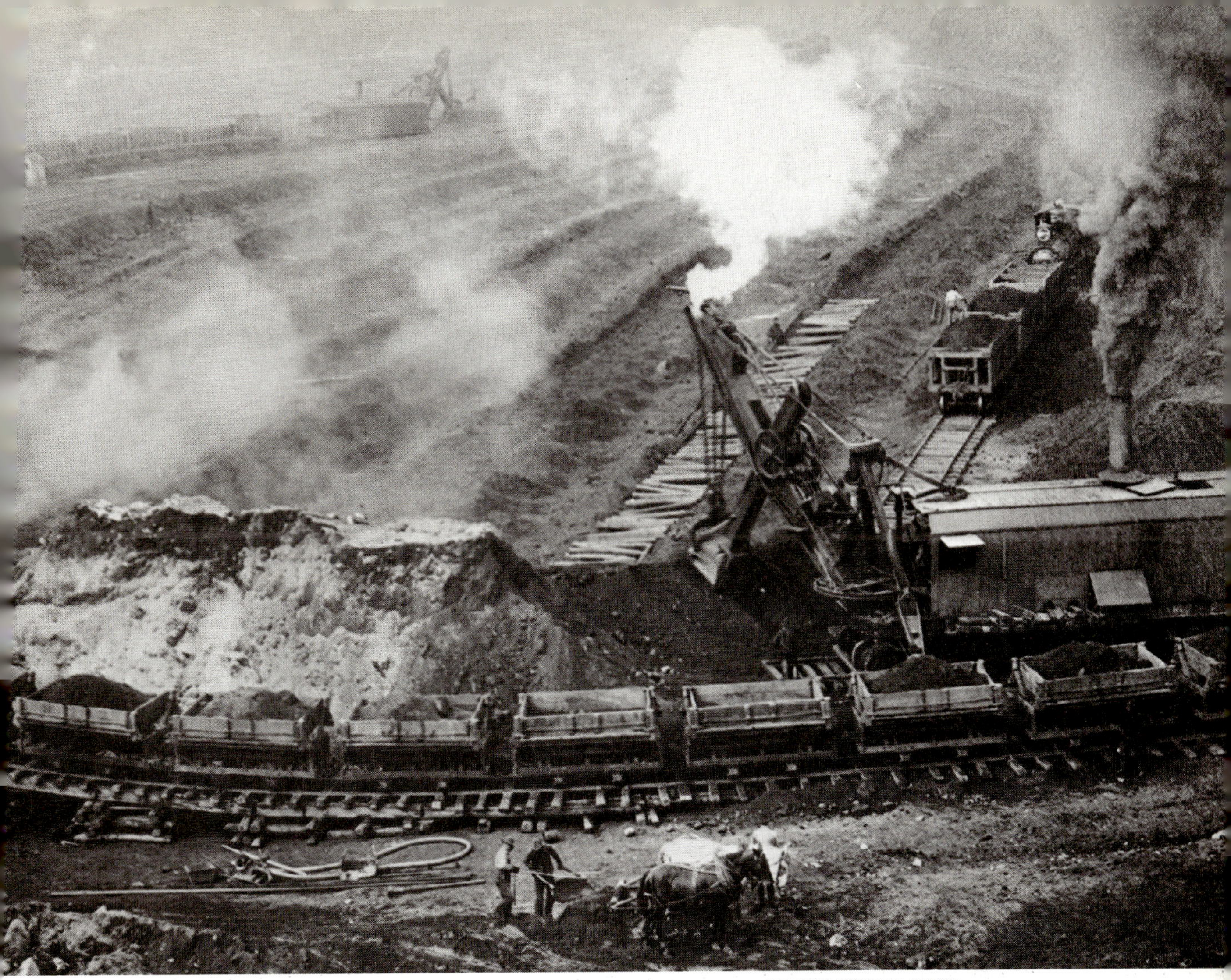

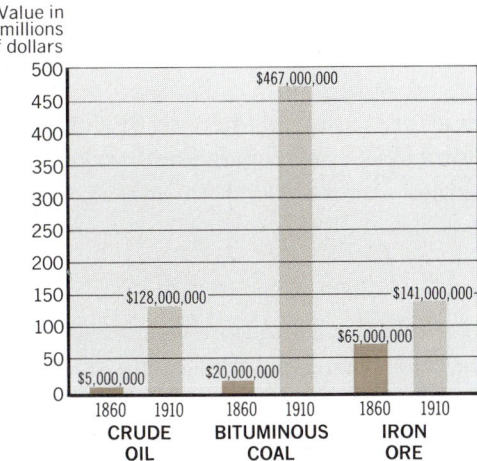

MINNESOTA HISTORICAL SOCIETY

Development of Underground Resources 1860–1910

Resource	1860	1910
Crude Oil	$5,000,000	$128,000,000
Bituminous Coal	$20,000,000	$467,000,000
Iron Ore	$65,000,000	$141,000,000

Above: In 1890 rich deposits of workable iron ore were discovered at the Mesabi Range in Minnesota. Developed largely with Rockefeller money, the range became the chief source of iron ore for steelmaking in the United States. Rockefeller later sold his interest to Andrew Carnegie. The Mahoning mine in this 1899 photograph became the largest open-pit mine in the world. Far left: These Texas oil prospectors have struck it rich. Although oil was discovered in Texas as early as 1867, the first big strike was made at Beaumont, Texas, in 1901. By 1928 Texas led the nation in oil production.

making such industrial miracles possible. The nation's railroad mileage grew from some 30,000 in 1860 to over 350,000 in 1910. In this half-century of furious railroad construction, the attention-catching "spectaculars" were the five transcontinental lines (map, lower right) completed between 1869 and 1893. Each of these lines had to be pushed through thousands of miles of barren or mountainous country (upper right). They were superb achievements of organization and engineering skill, like today's globe-girdling airlines.

The real railroad revolution was in building the smaller lines in the East and South. These lines carried the everyday necessities produced by farm and factory to even the tiniest villages and towns, thus making them a part of the nation's rapidly expanding economic system.

Communications also underwent a revolution. The telegraph dated from 1844, but after the Civil War a set of new inventions greatly increased its speed and power of operation. In 1866 a telegraph cable was laid on the floor of the Atlantic. After that Europe and America could communicate with each other at the speed of electricity. By 1910 early experiments in sending messages by radio waves instead of wires had been successful also.

Many electrical inventions of this period were developed by the practical genius of Thomas Edison (upper left). In 1876 another genius, Alexander Graham Bell (lower left), worked out a device for changing voice sounds into electric currents and transmitting, or sending, them by wire. You know his invention as the telephone. As early as 1900 more than a million were in use in the United States.

Speedy communications allowed men to organize industries with nationwide and worldwide markets. The globe was shrinking, and as it did so human behavior was changing.

Mass Production Comes of Age

As we saw earlier, rapid production of goods by assembly-line methods was taking place as early as the 1840's. But the quantity of goods produced increased enormously in the last half of the 1800's. The principles remained the same. Machine-work replaced handwork as much as possible. Many identical, interchangeable parts were produced. These were put together to make a finished object on an assembly line. Yet, compared

Thomas Alva Edison after 72 hours of continuous work improving his wax-cylinder phonograph in 1888.

Alexander Graham Bell at the New York end of the first telephone connection to Chicago in 1892.

DENVER PUBLIC LIBRARY, WESTERN COLLECTION

The Denver and Rio Grande Railroad connected mining towns by pushing tracks across these rugged Colorado mountains.

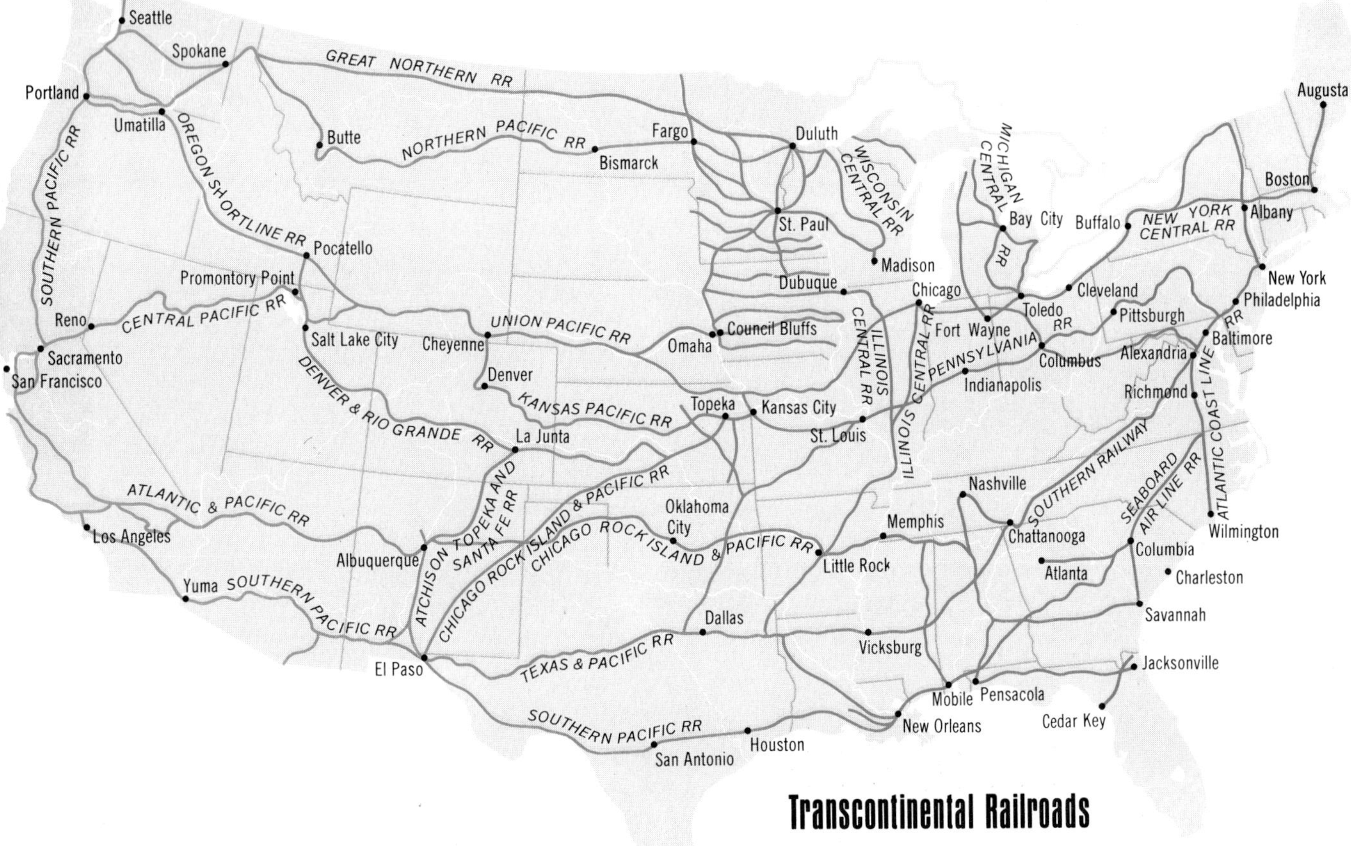

Transcontinental Railroads

BROWN BROTHERS

VALENTINE MUSEUM, COOK COLLECTION

Left: Negroes remove the stems from tobacco in a mechanized cigarette factory. Above: This 1913 photograph shows one day's output of chassis for the Model T at the Highland Park Ford plant in Michigan. Largely as a result of Ford's efficient assembly line, the basic price of the finished Model T dropped from $950 in 1909 to $550 in 1913 to $290 in 1926.

to the earlier models, the machines of the new age were like giants matched against pygmies.

For example, a cotton mill worker in 1840, working about 14 hours a day, could make about 10,000 yards of cloth a year. In 1886, working 10 hours a day, he could make 30,000 yards each year. In 1845 a Massachusetts bootmaker put out about one and a half pairs of boots each day; by 1885 in many factories the number was up to 7 pairs. A new kind of furnace for melting glass came into general use in 1885. It allowed 4 men to produce a million square feet of glass in 18 days. The old furnace had needed 28 men working for a month to produce only 115,000 square feet of glass.

The man whose name became most closely associated with assembly-line production was Henry Ford. He was convinced that every American should be able to own an automobile. The trick was in quantity production of a basic, unchanging model. In his Detroit plant Ford created an assembly line that could roll out 1,000 chassis a day (left) for "Model T" Fords. By 1926 he had made 15 million Model T's. The price was then under $300. More than any other auto manufacturer, he had put America on the road.

Mighty results followed the age of mass production. It increased concentration of ownership. Only a few companies in each industry could really compete, for only a few could afford multimillion-dollar plants. Mass production also spurred the search for customers in the millions to earn back the high costs of the machines. In that way it encouraged the growth of advertising and salesmanship. It reduced the workers to what one called "privates in the industrial army." Finally, it changed the look of the land itself and the life styles of people throughout the country.

Questions for Discussion

1. How did industrial leaders after the Civil War change American industry?
2. How did Rockefeller eliminate competition in the oil industry?
3. Where did industry secure the labor needed for large-scale and rapid industrialization?
4. Why was Henry Ford able to manufacture a car for less than $300?
5. How did the work of Edison and Bell affect industrialization?
6. Has luck helped our industrialization? How?

The Coming of the Indian Reservations 1850–1890

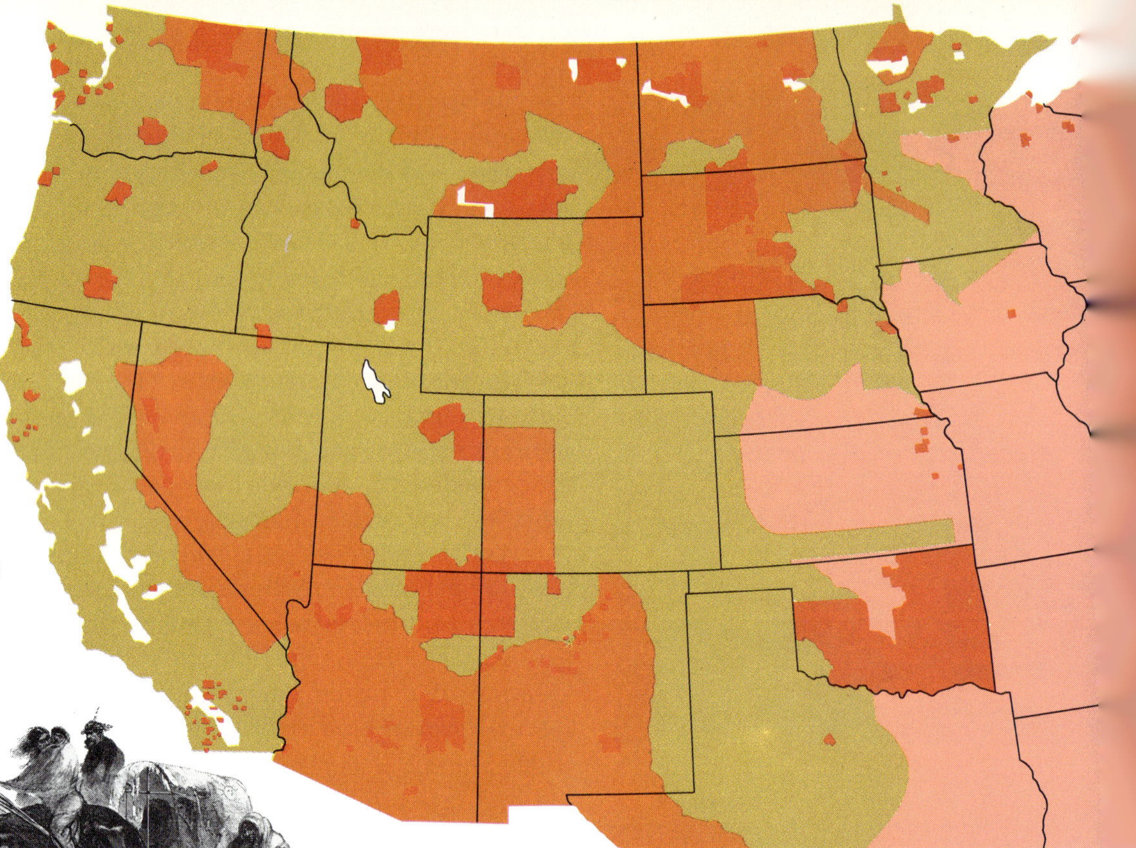

- Area ceded before 1850
- Area ceded 1850–1870
- Area ceded 1870–1890
- Reservations 1890

Harper's Weekly, DECEMBER 26, 1868

HAYNES STUDIO, INC.

Right: Train passengers fire at a herd of buffalo. Beginning in 1872 and continuing for a decade, amateur and professional buffalo hunters killed more than a million buffalo each year. Left: After the hideless buffalo carcasses had rotted away, the bones were collected and sold to fertilizer companies for $5 a ton. Bone collecting became a source of income for local farmers, like the Dakota Territory residents in this 1886 photograph.

Industry Transforms the West and the South

After 1865 industrial plants were to be found mainly in the area east of the Mississippi. But much of the food for their workers, as well as the natural resources, came from the Far West, beyond the Mississippi and Missouri rivers. Between 1865 and 1900 a West of farms, mining towns, and lumber camps replaced much of the open space that the mountain men had first mapped. Those who stood in the way were shoved aside. The Plains Indians were unfortunate enough to have been standing in the way.

The subduing of the Plains Indians began when the great buffalo herds were destroyed. We have already seen how the tribes depended on the large shaggy beasts for the needs of life, and how their culture rested on buffalo-hunting. But when railroads brought whites into the Plains in great numbers, the buffalo were doomed. White passengers shot them for sport from special trains (left). Hunters mowed them down for their bones and hides, to sell to dealers in fertilizers and robes. Before railroad days the herds sometimes looked like great, moving brown rivers. But by 1882 a hunter, after witnessing the slaughter of a herd, wrote, "A man could have walked twenty miles upon their carcasses." Soon all but a handful were gone.

For Plains Indians this meant that they must either live on rations provided by the United States government or steal beef from white settlers. But sometimes they did not have the first choice. The government Indian agent might cheat the tribesmen by holding back food that he was supposed to give them and selling it to others for his own profit. Or, for a bribe, he might permit other whites to sell the Indians unlawful guns and whiskey. So some hungry Indians did steal. Others became drunk and troublesome. Sooner or later there would be a clash between whites and Indians. Then troops would move in, and a tribe would go on the warpath. Despite the well-publicized victory over General Custer at the Battle of the Little Big Horn, the end of these struggles was always the same. In time the Indians would surrender to the better-armed white soldiers. They would walk the trail of captivity to the reservation (map, upper left).

In 1887, by a law known as the Dawes Act, the United States encouraged the division of tribal lands into individual farms. But most Indians did not want to give up their tribal way of life for the white man's pattern of individual property in land. The Dawes Act

LIBRARY OF CONGRESS

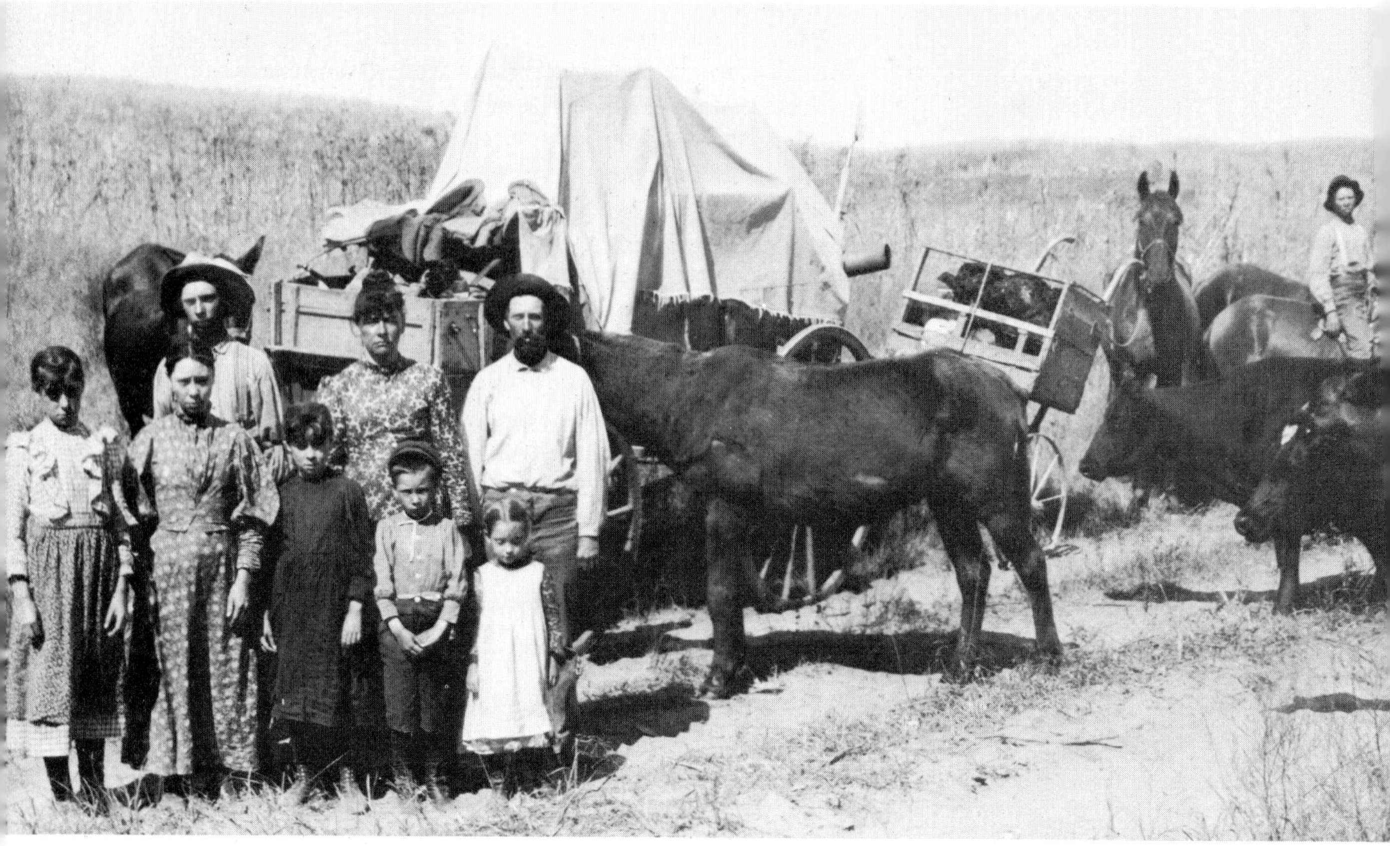

NEBRASKA STATE HISTORICAL SOCIETY

UNIVERSITY OF OKLAHOMA LIBRARY, WESTERN HISTORY COLLECTIONS

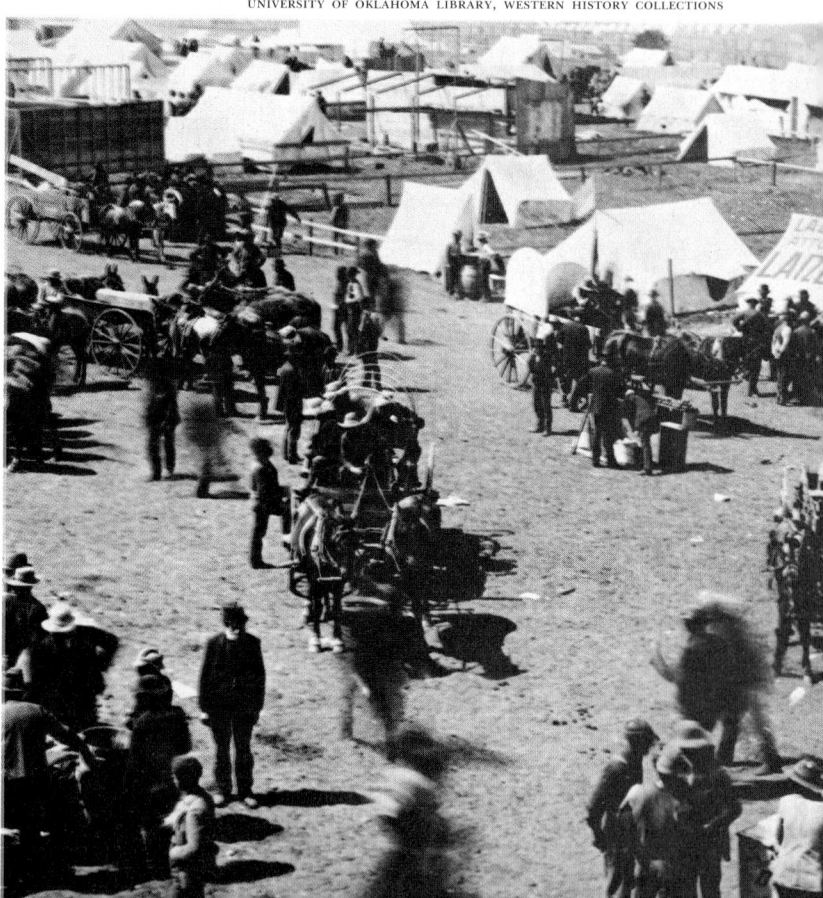

Above: Although Nebraska was admitted to the Union in 1867, nearly 20 years later open farmlands still lured pioneers. In 1886 this family arrived in central Nebraska's Custer County. Right: One of the last two sections of Indian Territory was thrown open officially to settlers at noon on April 22, 1889. By that evening Oklahoma City had a population of 10,000—nearly all living in tents. Guthrie, about 30 miles to the north and seen here 5 days after the opening, had a population of 15,000. In time Congress created the Oklahoma Territory and, in 1907, Oklahoma was admitted to the Union.

began a long and sad history of governmental attempts to solve the Indian "problem," a problem created by destroying the Indians' livelihood and culture.

The Opening of the Plains: The Final Frontier

Most Americans thought that if an Indian refused to become a farmer, it was because he was lazy. In their eyes farming was noble work that fed mankind and opened wild lands to progress. Despite such beliefs, individual farmers in the Far West, like the pioneers at the upper left, were soon facing great hardships because agriculture was becoming big business. The nation wanted to see the unused lands of the West put to productive use. People rushed to take up land and make it pay profits in the same way that they rushed to build railroads and steel mills.

In 1862 Congress passed the Homestead Act. It gave a free 160-acre farm to any adult male citizen who would claim one and actually live on it for five years. By 1900 about 80 million acres of public land had been given away. Yet that was only a start. Another 180 million acres went to the railroads, and 140 million acres were given to the states by the Federal government. Many of these went into the nearly 4.5 million farms added to the economy between 1860 and 1910. Nothing seemed to satisfy the land hunger of Americans. In 1889 Oklahoma—once supposed to be preserved as Indian Territory—was opened to homesteading. Thousands of men crowded to the starting line on opening day. At the crack of a signal gun, they whipped their horses into a frantic race to be first at the choicest locations. Overnight, Oklahoma got a population and tent-and-shack towns like Guthrie (left).

But not all of the public domain went to the settler who wanted only a homestead. Land speculators and ranchers bought huge tracts from the states. In a number of cases, false homestead claims were put together to make giant-sized domains for single owners. Mining and lumbering companies also got huge shares as the public domain was carved up like a roast. A single company in Florida, for example, bought 2 million acres of forest lands.

Before the Civil War the Republican Party had demanded "free soil." The idea was to save the land of the Far West for individual family farms and not permit it to be turned into plantations. Yet after the war the 160-acre farmer in the Far West found that he

Above: In 1902 this farmer in Walla Walla, Washington, used horses—33 of them—to pull his wheat-harvesting machine. Above right: At the same time some farmers had converted to steam power. These two steamers, pulling water wagons as well as plows, carved furrows in the North Dakota plains. Run day and night, they could plow 50 to 60 acres a day, but sparks from the fire boxes were serious fire hazards.

was a small man in a world of landowning giants who increasingly used machinery to replace the work formerly done by men and horses.

Farming Becomes a Big Industry

Just as invention increased the output of industrial workers, marvels of invention stood ready to help the farmer produce more. Machinery was creating an agricultural revolution. There were threshers, harvesters, combines, binders, cultivators, huskers, shellers, and other factory-built devices that made huge savings in human effort. A farmer of 1830 had to work 61 hours to harvest 20 bushels of grain by hand. In 1900 he could do the same work in 3 hours. In 1850 a man needed 21 hours to harvest a ton of hay. Half a century later the time was 4 hours. At first the power for these machines came from farm work animals (above, left). Steam-driven equipment (above, right) was some inprovement. In 1901 a gasoline engine powered the first tractor. Within 40 years mechanical inventions had driven the horse and the mule from all but the poorest farms.

Meanwhile, new and better seeds were being developed. Improvements in the breeding of cattle raised the quality of livestock. Research in agriculture was carried on in several places. The Department of Agriculture, which became a full-fledged Cabinet depart-

STATE HISTORICAL SOCIETY OF WISCONSIN

ment in 1889, did scientific studies in its laboratories. Through officials known as county agents, it spread word of the results to farmers. Agricultural colleges were beginning to open their doors. The Morrill Act of 1862 gave land grants to such colleges to further their work. Farming was no longer a calling that depended entirely upon the whims of nature for good harvests.

A steadily shrinking share of the whole United States population managed to keep feeding the country and other parts of the world as well. Wheat harvests rose to more than half a billion bushels each year. The huge loaf in the advertisement (right) symbolizes the power of agriculture.

Yet all these mechanical improvements cost the farmer a good deal. On the plains he needed barbed wire for fencing. He paid large sums of money for the great machines that helped him plant, tend, and harvest his crops and for the special feeds that produced healthy hogs and fat chickens. In those parts of the West which were too dry, he needed to irrigate his lands. He paid for the cost of building and running the railroads through the freight charges that came out of his pocket. The more he produced of his own crop, however, the lower the prices that he received tended to fall. He was operating in a big-business economy. Success went to those farmers who could make large investments in special equipment and who could combine with others

Below: In this ad the Duluth Imperial Flour Company used the ballooning craze to advantage.

453

to control the prices of their products. Some farmers were able to become successful large-scale operators. But those with small holdings struggled constantly to keep out of debt. They were like hand-loom weavers competing with textile factories.

The Cattle Kingdom Becomes an Industry

In the Southwest a thriving "cattle kingdom" arose. It, too, was part of an "industrial revolution" in food production. It began because great natural resources were available. On the grasslands still in the public domain, a skinny calf could grow into a fat beef animal. His owner would not have to pay anyone a cent for this: Public-land prairie grass was free, like air and water.

Modern technology joined natural resources after the Civil War. At that time railroads were built to points in Kansas and Missouri. Then it was possible for cowboys to drive their owner's herds northward (immediate right) over the cattle trails (map, center) to the railhead towns like Dodge City. The herd would be sold to meat packers at a good profit to their owner. After a rail trip to the Chicago stockyards and processing plants (far right), they would become steaks for meat-hungry Easterners. Americans now ate Texas red meat with their Minnesota white bread.

The workers in the cattle industry were quite special. Like the mountain man before him, the cowboy was a colorful individual. He did hard, dangerous, often lonely work. Night and day, rain and shine, he ran risks from stampedes or accidents. For this he received only $30 a month.

Yet his work was done outdoors. It tested him constantly as a man. And it allowed him individual freedom: There was no assembly-line method for roping a steer. Thousands of cowboys, black and white, preferred their tough and carefree life to any other. In modern times movies and television have made the cowboy in his picturesque "ten-gallon" hat, chaps, and boots a symbol of honor and freedom.

The heyday of the cattle kingdom was short. The free-grazing lands became overcrowded. Owners were forced to move northward—but there, winter blizzards could wipe out herds left in the open all year. Soon cattlemen realized that they would need to buy and fence land, build barns, buy feed, and take good care of their stock. This required capital. Millionaires and

UNIVERSITY OF OKLAHOMA LIBRARY, DIVISION OF MANUSCRIPTS

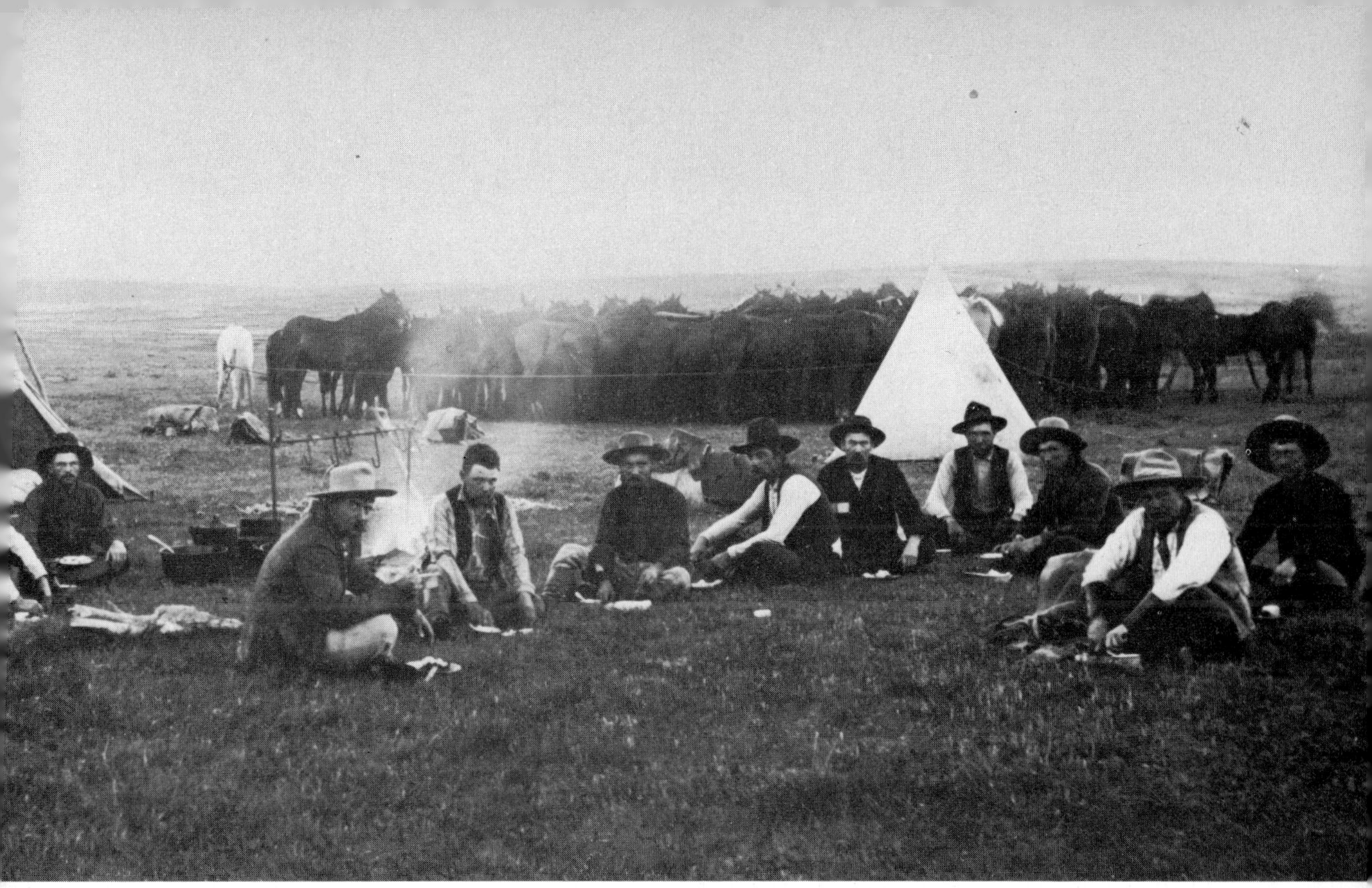

Above: Oklahoma cowboys pause during a roundup in the 1890's. Right: By 1900 the Union Stockyards in Chicago were the world's largest. Left: By 1910 the railroad had reached Lubbock, Texas, where this drive is headed.

BOTH: LIBRARY OF CONGRESS

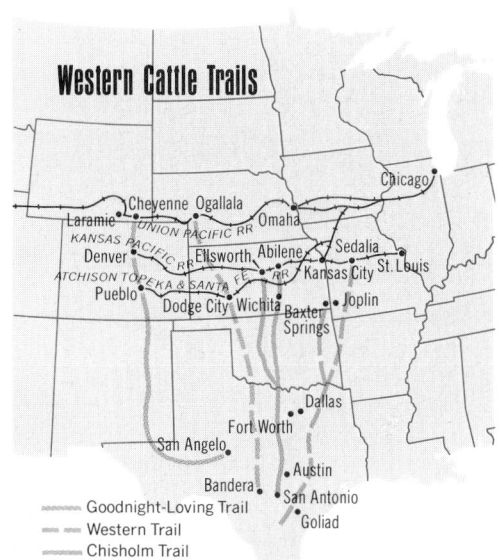

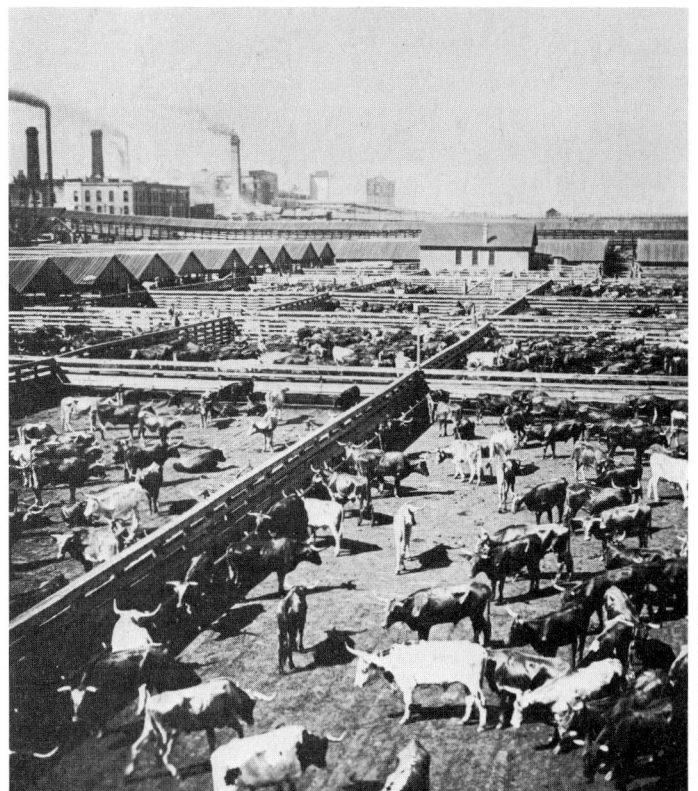

BOTH: LIBRARY OF CONGRESS

Above: After the discovery of gold in Alaska, thousands made their way to Dyea, a village that became a supply center and a starting-off point for the trek to the northern mining fields. Left: The Homestake Mine in Lead, South Dakota, photographed here in 1900, was one of the largest gold mines in the world. South Dakota led the nation in gold production after 1920.

corporations began to appear as important ranch owners in the cattle country. Even for those cattlemen whose holdings were not extensive, ranching was basically a business by 1910. It still had some of the color of cowboy days, but it was clearly part of an industrial process for mass producing meat.

The Growth of the Mining Industry

The mining frontier also gave way to a businesslike scene. The earliest miners in the days of 1849 in California could work with simple tools like picks, shovels, and washbasins. If a prospector made a lucky find, he could become rich overnight. For this reason new gold and silver discoveries always attracted a horde of footloose individuals with large hopes and small amounts of money for equipment. Each gold or silver "strike" pulled thousands to the new "diggings." Up to the century's end, news of a "strike" started a rush. Thousands would be off to the Black Hills of South Dakota, to Denver or Leadville in Colorado, to Virginia City, Nevada, and even, in 1897, to Alaska, like the hopeful fortune-seekers at left.

But soon it was necessary to go deeper into the earth for gold and silver. Nor was all the mining for these precious metals only. Lead, copper, and other basic industrial metals were also dug out of the western earth. To get at them thousands of feet of shafts and tunnels had to be dug like honeycombs in the hearts of mountains. They had to be braced with timber and ventilated by machine-driven fans. In addition, the metals deeper in the earth were more firmly embedded in rocks or ores. Smelters—places which refined ore—were great factories for crushing and chemically treating these ores in order to extract their valuable contents. The costly processes of modern mining and refining gradually brought large corporations into the field and began to crowd out the lone-wolf types.

So the mining town—such as Lead, South Dakota (lower left), or Denver, Colorado, or Butte, Montana, or Bisbee, Arizona, or Boise, Idaho—became a part of the new western scene. Around these towns the mountains still stood in purple majesty. But in the streets there was ugliness. Piles of slag, discarded rock, were visible. So were chimneys that belched unpleasant-smelling smoke into the air. So were streams, discolored by refinery waste materials poured carelessly into them. So

were ugly shacks in which the underpaid, hard-working miners lived. The miners soon formed unions and conducted strikes. Labor struggles became especially sharp in mining towns, where frontier violence was still a tradition. The result of producing copper, lead, iron, and precious metals for the new industrial and banking world was a West far different from the one which Lewis and Clark had gazed upon.

By the last years of the nineteenth century, men were beginning to realize how fast the West was changing. They worried about it for many reasons. If it vanished the American character, which was formed in a day of open land, might change.

The Beginnings of Conservation

Some far-sighted lawmakers began to worry that we might be using our natural resources so rapidly that they would disappear in a short time. They pressed for national action to reserve oil and timberlands, to dam streams so that floods did not wash away good soil, and to do other things to manage the country's natural wealth. Such men were the founders of the **conservation** movement. Hand in hand with them worked individuals and groups who simply wanted to save the great beauty of the American land for the future.

Even before the 1890's conservationists began to win some victories. Yellowstone National Park was created in March of 1872. In 1890 Yosemite National Park was authorized by Congress. Thereafter, Presidents such as Theodore Roosevelt fought for and obtained the right to set aside—that is, keep from settlement or unrestricted commercial use—nearly 150 million acres of forest land. During Roosevelt's two terms of office, the number of national parks was doubled, and in 1916 the National Park Service was created to operate them.

While conservationists worked at preserving the West, tourists, like the sightseer at left, came out in increasing numbers to look in awe at its marvels. Both the Grand Canyon and the auto were wonders—one natural, the other man-made. Could they live together?

As the frontier West disappeared, the imaginary West became more popular in books, on the stage, and, after about 1910, on movie screens. In the 1890's a popular entertainment was "Buffalo Bill's Wild West Show" (right). Buffalo Bill was the nickname of William F. Cody. He had been an army scout and had taken care

Above: William F. Cody first took his Wild West Show on tour in 1883. Until he retired in 1894, Buffalo Bill gave thousands of people around the world their first impression of America's West. Left: This tourist, in his 1902 open Toledo, was free to enjoy a timeless view of the Grand Canyon alone. Shortly, mass production of the automobile allowed thousands of tourists to visit this sight each year.

of horses for a freight-wagon company. He had served as a deadly buffalo hunter, providing meat for railway work gangs. A friend of his wrote a play called *Scouts of the Prairies*. Bill starred in it and liked it so much that he went into show business himself. He and his friends did riding, roping, and shooting tricks for cheering audiences. Urban Americans enjoyed sharing, in imagination, a past of brave crack shots gunning down "redskins."

Industry Begins to Build a New South

The hand of industry reached into the South to change its ways, too. After 1877 southern leaders began to blame their section's poverty on the fact that it depended too greatly on the cotton crop for its wealth and paid too much to northern manufacturers for goods made from southern raw materials. In the 1880's a southern editor, Henry W. Grady, used to make a speech about a southern funeral which was held in a forest of pine trees near iron deposits and good pasture land for sheep and cattle. The man, said Grady, was buried in a pine coffin from Cincinnati put together with nails made in Pittsburgh. He wore a coat from New York, shirt and pants from Chicago, and shoes from Boston. The South furnished nothing but the corpse and the hole in the ground.

Men like Grady argued that the South should encourage the growth of industries. Southern factories would give jobs to southern workers. Their labor forces would eat food grown on southern farms. The taxes their owners paid would build better schools and roads. The South would prosper like the thriving North.

This argument had been rejected by southern planters up to 1860. But the men in command of the "new South" led it in a new direction. They encouraged factory and railroad-building, mining, lumbering, and steelmaking. Cigarette manufacturing became a major southern industry. The number of cotton spinning and weaving mills (immediate right) in the Carolinas surged upward. By the turn of the century Birmingham, Alabama—founded only in 1871—had become the "Pittsburgh of the South." And in Florida, Louisiana, and the Gulf States, Southerners worked at producing coal, oil, lumber, and other industrial products. The South's main cities proudly held industrial fairs. They boasted of their electric lights, streetcars, and fine homes. Their newspapers no longer sneered at

Manufacturing, formerly scorned as unsuitable for a southern gentleman, was recognized as a profitable investment around the turn of the century. The Birmingham, Alabama, steel mill (above) and tin factory (right) employed thousands. The South became a major textile manufacturing center as raw cotton was sent to southern mills like this one in Greensboro, North Carolina (below).

ALL: BROWN BROTHERS

money-grubbing Yankees who lacked the leisurely grace of Dixieland. Instead, they crowed over the hustling spirit of southern businessmen.

The South of slavery, religious revivals, Confederate flags, and mountain feuds became a land where factories, like those at the top of page 461, were familiar. But the expected prosperity did not come. Most major industries still remained outside the South or were owned by northern businessmen. Moreover, in order to lure industrial capital southward, southern states kept taxes low. Nor did they discourage the use of poorly paid labor of all ages and both sexes. Their police officials often helped employers to chase away organizers of labor unions, a practice not restricted to the South. Negroes, a big share of the southern populace, got a tiny share of factory jobs.

The new South welcomed economic change. But it remained conservative about social change. So it remained a section of special problems, even as it blended into the industrial environment.

Questions for Discussion

1. What were the steps in the destruction of the Plains Indians?
2. In what way were the purposes of the Homestead and Dawes Acts similar? Why did both have only very limited success?
3. Why did both farming and ranching tend to become "big business?"
4. Why did wheat prices tend to drop as the Great Plains became more and more settled?
5. Why have stories of the West remained a familiar part of American folklore?
6. What advantages to Southerners did Henry Grady see in industrializing the South? Why did industrialization fail to bring prosperity to the South?

Chapter Review

Social Studies Term

conservation

Summary Questions for Discussion

1. Why did many people think an industrial fair was the proper way to celebrate the nation's centennial birthday in 1876?
2. Why did steel, oil, and coal become the building blocks of modern industry? Look at the graph on page 443. If growth remained constant what would

have been the figures for 1960?
3. Why did the self-made man become an American ideal?
4. Why were changes in transportation and communication part of rapid industrialization?
5. Why are interchangeable parts and assembly lines essential features of mass production?
6. How did Andrew Carnegie and John D. Rockefeller change the average American's way of life? Did they improve it? Why?
7. Why was the United States able to feed both itself and a large part of the world even while the sons and daughters of farmers moved to the cities in large numbers?
8. Why did the idea of conservation get such a late start in the United States? What did the conservationists want to do besides save natural resources?

Pictures as Historical Evidence

Compare the pictures in this chapter with those in Chapter 11. Then, using the pictures alone as evidence, comment on the following generalization. The industrial development that took place in the United States between 1865 and 1914 hardly differs from the industrial development that took place in the United States between 1800 and 1860.

Map Study

Study the maps on pages 445, 448, and 455. How does the map of transcontinental railroads help to explain why the era of the great drives on the western cattle trails was so short-lived? How does it help to explain why the Indians who lived in the part of the United States shown on page 448 ceded more and more of their land to the government and were forced onto reservations?

For Further Reading

Captains of Industry, by Bernard A. Weisberger. New York: American Heritage Publishing Co., Inc., 1966.

Indians of the Plains, by Eugene Rachlis. New York: American Heritage Publishing Co., Inc., 1960.

Leaders of Labor, by Roy Cook. Philadelphia: J. B. Lippincott Co., 1966.

Railroads in the Days of Steam, by Albert L. McCready. New York: American Heritage Publishing Co., Inc., 1960.

16
A Nation of Cities

The great civilizations of history have had their foundations in cities. Athens, Rome, Paris, Alexandria, Timbuktu, and Cuzco are examples of European, African, and South American urban centers of trade, learning, religion, and political life. They were built by kings, popes, and emperors. In the modern United States, mighty new cities were created by the forces of an industrial society.

Chicago was made "the gem of the prairie" by its many railroads. Minneapolis, Milwaukee, and St. Louis grew rich as their businessmen turned the cattle and wheat of the Great Plains into beef and flour. Pittsburgh became a capital for steelmakers who grew as powerful as monarchs. Other cities reflected the nation's industrial wealth in different ways.

All these centers attracted swarms of people. In 1860 only one American in four lived in a place with a population of more than 2,500. By 1910 four out of every nine lived in such a place. By 1970 this figure had grown to seven out of ten. Most of these urbanites were in great metropolitan centers or their suburbs—little communities on the big town's outskirts.

The growth of a village of a few hundred souls into a community of many thousands of families caused great changes in social behavior. In political life, for example, voters could no longer have personal acquaintance with every candidate. They therefore tended to vote more by party label than by "shopping" among office seekers. Economically, cities depended heavily on new inventions and gigantic construction projects to feed, house, and transport thousands of people each day. That meant a steady rise in the complexity and cost of local government. It spelled a need for more experts in office and higher taxes.

But a great bridge, power plant, or subway tunnel was more than a high-priced piece of engineering. It was a monument to man's skills, as much as a cathedral or a pyramid. And a crowded city, as seen in the painting at the right, was more than population figures. It was a mixing bowl of many peoples and many styles of living. Despite its problems, metropolitan America was—and is—a great achievement of many different humans working together.

As you read, think about these questions:
1. How did the cities change between 1865 and 1914?
2. How can cities be made healthy, safe, and pleasant places to live?

A 1913 street scene—noisy crowds, rickety tenements, and a traffic jam.

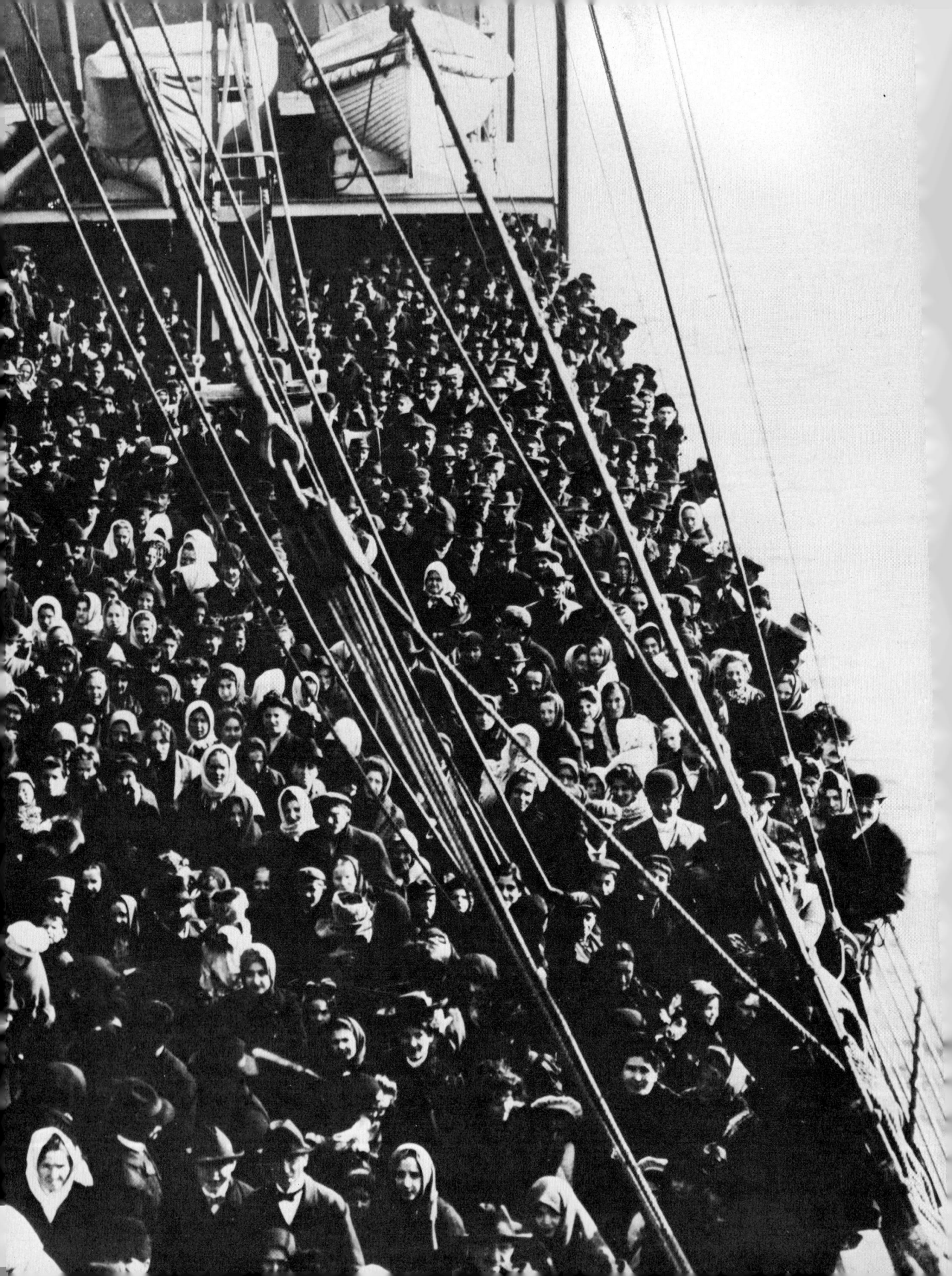

New Citizens for New Cities

Thousands of the newcomers to the cities were American country boys and girls. They were drawn by the bright lights, the hopes of quick fortunes, and the simple wish to change their lives. But thousands of others were European immigrants (opposite page). From 1870 onward the tide of migration rose. The graph at the left shows the changes in the number of immigrants every five years between 1860 and 1935. It depicts the long-run climb toward a high point just before World War I.

The newcomers were attracted here by many forces. Transportation in the Steam Age was quick and cheap. A ticket to the New World promised a new farm, a new job, and a new chance. But the pull of American opportunity was matched by the push of political and religious persecution at home. Russian Jews, German socialists, and Polish and Italian peasants were among those driven across the oceans by harsh laws and hard times. By 1914 over 70 per cent of the new arrivals came from southern and eastern Europe.

In the 1880's Americans welcomed new arrivals. The inscription on the Statue of Liberty, put up in New York harbor in 1886, said that the great copper figure lifted her lamp "beside the golden door" for "huddled masses yearning to breathe free." But the golden door was closed to some. A law of 1882 barred Chinese laborers from entering the country. Later, in 1907, Japanese immigrants also were largely shut out.

In the 1890's demands began to be heard for limiting the number of immigrants admitted from all countries. Between 1921 and 1924 a new system was established which severely limited immigration from Asia and eastern and southern Europe. But until then places like New York's Ellis Island, where new arrivals were given medical and other tests for admission, were crowded with men and women from dozens of countries, seeking their future in America.

Not all immigrants crossed the seas. Many came from Canada and other Western Hemisphere nations. And as the twentieth century began, there was a kind of "immigration" within the United States. Thousands of Negroes moved to the cities of the South and the North in search of industrial jobs. They, too, fled from harsh laws and rural poverty, as some European migrants did. When World War I cut off European immigration, blacks came North in ever greater numbers to meet the demand for labor.

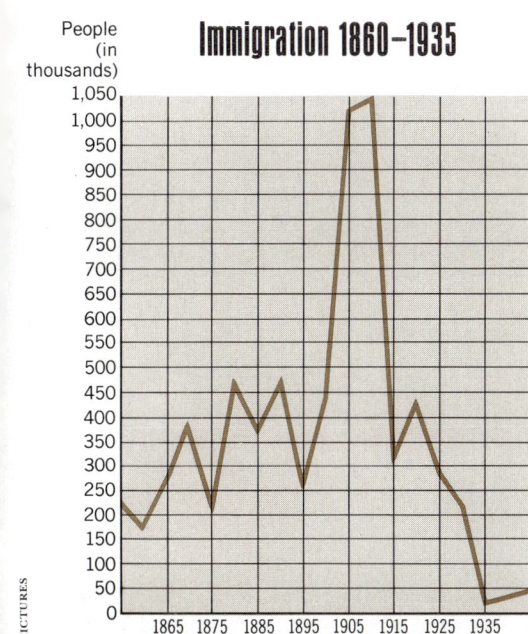

In 1906 immigrants crowd the deck of a ship arriving at Ellis Island.

NEW YORK PUBLIC LIBRARY, GENEALOGY DIVISION

GEORGE EASTMAN HOUSE

Getting a Start in the City

Boom times always spurred immigration, and depression always reduced it. The graph on page 467 shows the deep cuts made after the panics of 1873, 1893, and 1929. This was a natural reaction. When business was poor and jobs were scarce, a newly arrived urban immigrant was in trouble. His first business always was to get work. "America does not begin," said one foreigner, "until a man is a workingman."

The immigrant who had just arrived was, in some ways, like a pioneer of frontier days. He did not have to build a cabin and clear land in a dangerous wilderness. But he had to find work and a place to live in new surroundings, where every face was strange, where he did not know the language, and where he was often without a penny. He or she needed plenty of courage and energy.

There were different ways of solving these problems. Some nationalities formed immigrant aid societies to meet the "greenhorns" and help them find shelter and ways of earning bread. There were also employment agencies (below, left) which advertised jobs that were open. If the immigrant obtained a job, he paid the agency part of his first wages. Sometimes a fellow countryman—speaking their own language—would round up a group of immigrants on the dock. Then he would lead them to a boarding house and later to a construction gang or factory that was hiring. In turn, he collected a fee from the employer. Or a businessman—who might be from the "old country" himself—would find lodgings for the newcomers and then give them work to do at home, like artificial flower-making (above left).

At first both jobs and living quarters were likely to be low-grade. Samuel Gompers, an American labor leader, came from England at the age of thirteen in 1863. His family's first new-world apartment was full of the stench of a nearby slaughterhouse.

New Americans and a New America

In 1890 a New York newspaper reporter said that a map of the city colored to show nationalities would have "more stripes than on the skin of a zebra, and more colors than any rainbow." New York was only one of many American communities where immigrants gave different "colors" to national life by their customs. A dragon dance in San Francisco's Chinatown was

Below: In 1910 new arrivals in New York City—immigrants from overseas, Negroes from the South, farmers lured by the big city—wait outside an employment agency. Left: It was not unusual for immigrant families to work long into the night for a little extra money. This family, living in a New York tenement in 1912, earned income by making wreaths of artificial flowers.

something new for visiting rural Americans to see (lower right). So were streets decked with flowers in an Italian neighborhood on a saint's day or a parade of Irishmen stepping along to "The Wearing of the Green" on St. Patrick's Day. So were signs in Greek, Yiddish, and Spanish or the smells of Hungarian or southern country Negro dishes cooking in apartment kitchens.

Even though people clung to their old habits, **Americanization** went on, especially for immigrant children. They were learning to behave like Americans in the way they talked, dressed, and played. These things were learned from playmates, newspapers, and other unofficial means of education. In school they were taught American history and government and told that their share in democracy was equal to that of native-born citizens. For youngsters like those at the right, the public schools and the streets were gateways to becoming immigrants no more.

Some old-stock Americans were frightened. They did not have faith that the United States could quickly absorb millions of strangers. They especially objected to people from the eastern and southern European countries. **Nativists** (those favoring limits on the rights of the foreign-born) claimed that these Latin and Slavic peoples could never really learn the "American" ways established by English colonists two centuries earlier. They accused the recent immigrants of furnishing most of the country's poor, criminals, and dishonest voters.

But other native-born citizens refused to share this attitude. They argued that the United States was not just an Anglo-Saxon nation. It was, and should be, a great melting pot, where people from every nation could live together in peace and freedom. True Americanism meant accepting peoples' right to be different. Although laws limiting the number of immigrants allowed into the country were passed in the 1920's, American nativism grew weaker in the long run.

Questions for Discussion

1. What groups added to the population growth of the larger cities of the United States?
2. Why was immigration to the United States slower in times of depression than in times of prosperity?
3. How did immigrants join together to help each other after they arrived in the United States?
4. How were European immigrants Americanized?

The largest number of immigrants from Asia—primarily from Japan and China—settled in California. Many chose to live in San Francisco's Chinatown and to continue cultural traditions like the dragon dance in the festival below. Oriental children were introduced to American traditions in public school. Pupils from the three major races make up the elementary school class in the picture at the right, taken in San Francisco in 1919.

M. BARTON COLLECTION

CULVER PICTURES

Building the Modern Metropolis

While the Flatiron Building was under construction (right), New Yorkers stood a safe distance away waiting for the wind to crumble it. In 1904 immigrants bought groceries from street venders along New York's Mulberry Street (below).

BOTH: LIBRARY OF CONGRESS

The rise of the modern city was proof that men can sometimes use applied scientific knowledge to solve special social problems. A growing urban population had to be fitted into a fairly small area. A city of over a million people, like Chicago in 1890, had a population equal to one-fourth of the whole United States in 1790! One way of housing a growing population was to expand upward: to stack people on top of each other in their homes and at their jobs.

The **tenement** house was a dwelling containing apartments for many families. Such a building need not be unpleasant. But in fast-growing cities in the late nineteenth century, profit-hungry builders were allowed to put up buildings several stories high on very small lots. This left no space between tenements for light and air. In addition, nothing stopped greedy landlords from putting many large families on each floor and providing only one water tap or bathroom for all of them. The reporter and photographer Jacob Riis found 192 adults and children in a single New York tenement house. Dirt collected and disease bred in the narrow, dark, stuffy hallways. The danger of fire was great. Many cruel disasters led some cities to pass laws trying to improve tenement-house conditions. But good or bad, the many-storied dwelling was part of the urban scene.

In the 1880's another important development took place. Architects learned how to construct a building around a steel framework that could rise to dizzying heights. Such "skyscrapers" appeared in Chicago as early as 1885. The one at right is New York's Flatiron Building, twenty stories high, completed in 1902. At that time it was the wonder of the city.

Skyscrapers were too costly to be used profitably for housing. They rose in the business districts and were used for offices. They depended on other inventions, too, like electric elevators and powerful water pumps. Yet, thanks to such developments, thousands of office workers did something miraculous as an everyday, unnoticed occurrence. They performed their jobs a tenth of a mile or more straight up in the air!

Urban Transportation and Essential Services

Nineteenth-century engineers used steel, electricity, and steam to conquer great distances, as with the Atlantic cable or the transcontinental railroad. But they also employed the same resources to permit

the quick, safe movement of many thousands of people on short but frequent journeys to and from work.

In 1883, for example, the Brooklyn Bridge (upper right) was opened. It was an iron bridge, hung from great towers by cables of twisted wire. This was the best and most secure kind of bridge yet made for handling floods of heavy traffic while leaving room underneath for passing ships. The bridge was built by two great engineers, German-born John A. Roebling and his son Washington Roebling. The father was killed and the son crippled in accidents which occurred during its construction. Today their bridge still stands and carries cars and trucks instead of horse-drawn wagons. It is their memorial.

An elevated railroad, like the one at lower right, was first built in New York City in 1867. It was considered a fine invention, except by those underneath who were showered with cinders from its smokestacks. But a solution to that problem came after 1888. In that year, in Richmond, an inventor showed a practical way of running electrically powered cars over tracks in the street. By 1903 New York had converted its "el" to electric power. Like hundreds of other cities, it also had fleets of electric street cars.

Besides reaching for the heavens, urban man also dug down into the earth to make his new kind of life possible. Big cities first had to dig beneath the surface level to find space for the huge tunnels necessary to bring water for thousands of people and carry away waste products. The scene at top far right shows a trench for a sewer being dug in Savannah, Georgia. Soon it became clear that underground electric cables were necessary to avoid having forests of poles and wires to carry the current for telephones and electric lighting systems. Poles with live wires were found to be very dangerous when storms knocked them over.

Soon pipes for carrying steam and gas for cooking also became part of the world beneath the streets. New York went so far as to put a whole transportation network below ground when a private company completed the city's first subway system in 1904.

The Need for Urban Planning

In the early history of the United States, there had been towns whose growth was planned. Puritan villages had grown in a pattern controlled by the leaders of the close-knit community. Congress had hired Pierre

MUSEUM OF THE CITY OF NEW YORK, J. CLARENCE DAVIES COLLECTION

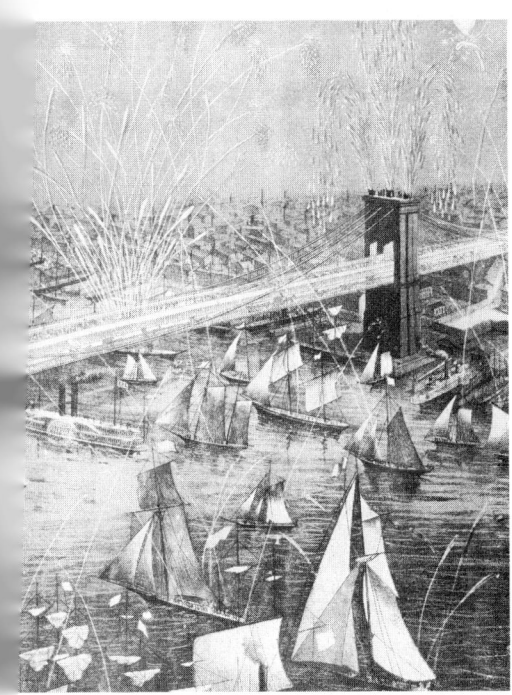

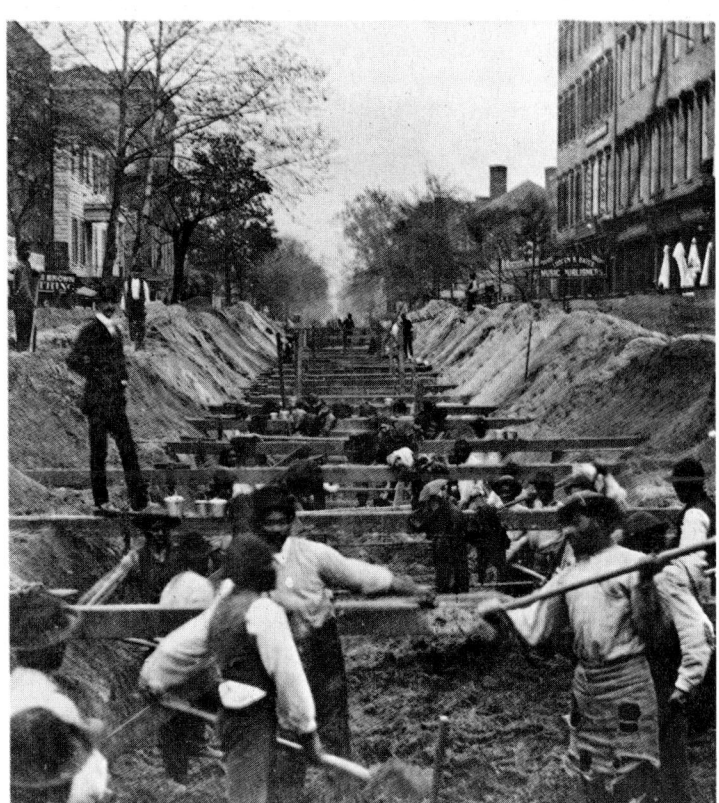

Right: Sewer construction in Savannah, Georgia. Above: Fireworks mark the opening of the Brooklyn Bridge. Below: New York's Third Avenue "el" around 1880.

MRS. BRYON DEXTER COLLECTION

CULVER PICTURES

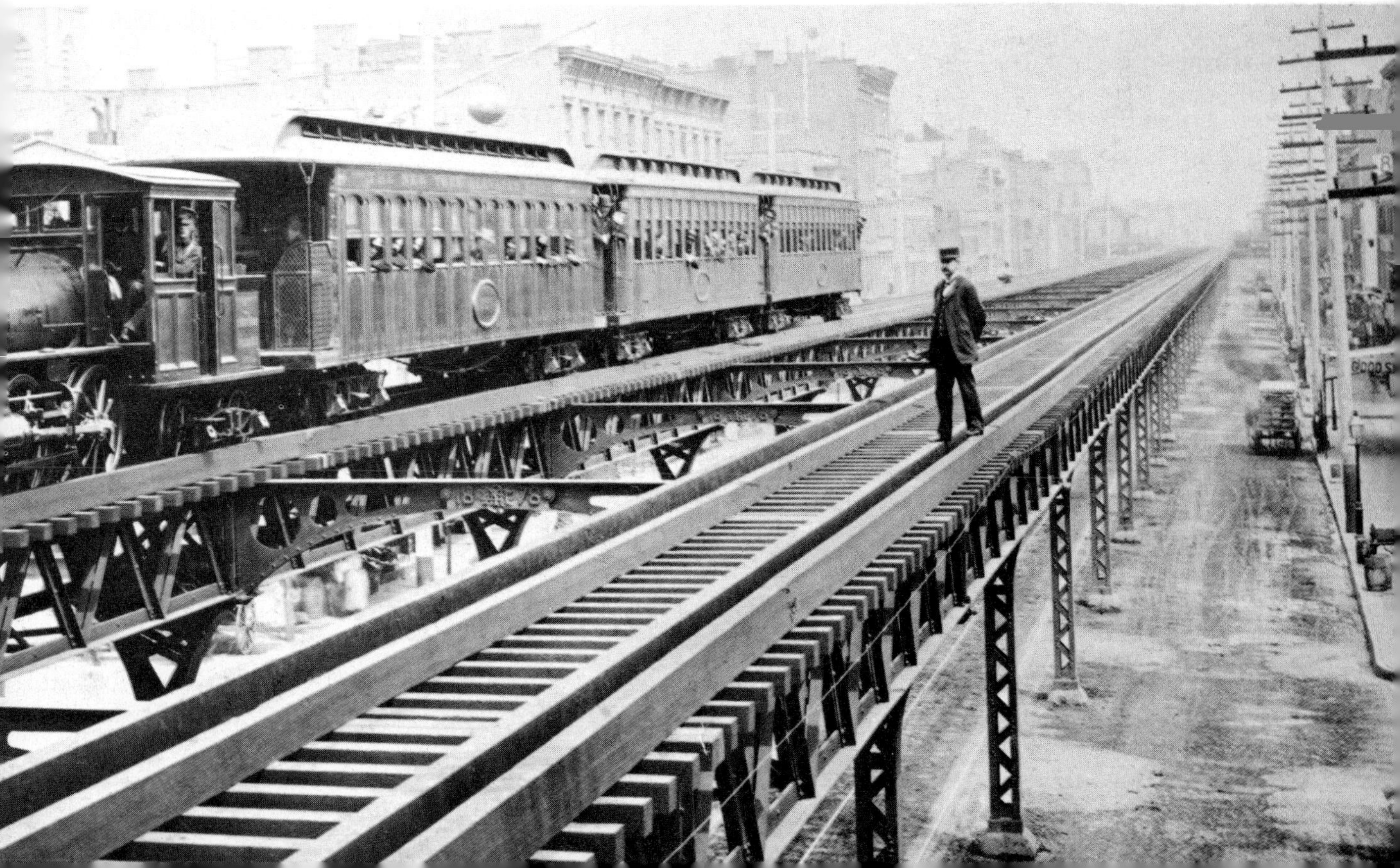

New York's Pennsylvania Railroad Station, seen here under construction in the early 1900's, became a famed architectural landmark as well as an important transportation center.

SMITHSONIAN INSTITUTION

L'Enfant to prepare a design for Washington, D.C. But the fast-growing industrial cities of the late nineteenth century were different. They had no single group of men with the power or the wish to lay out a model city. The result was often disorderly, ugly urban areas where factories, cheap housing, stores, telephone poles, and car tracks jammed every inch of space.

But there were some attempts to change this picture. Several kinds of urban planning emerged. Some cities enacted laws which **zoned** their land, by requiring factories and homes to be built in separate areas. Cities also provided **building codes** (laws which set minimum standards for space and conveniences, such as plumbing and lighting, in new buildings). Such laws were not always well enforced, but they were a beginning.

In addition, cities and corporations put up buildings for public use which were designed to lift spirits and express the outlook of their era. One example was the lofty Pennsylvania Railroad terminal in New York (left). Its great interior spaces and steel columns honored the power of the railroads and industry in much the same way that a royal palace glorified a prince.

Finally, some cities even tackled the job of saving open space for recreation in natural surroundings. In the 1850's New York planned a "central park" in the middle of Manhattan. It gave the task of design to a talented landscape architect, Frederick L. Olmsted, who, one observer said, "paints with lakes and wooded slopes." Olmsted tried to lay out a park (right) which would give city dwellers "pleasurable and soothing relief" from buildings. Its many acres of ponds, hills, trees, and rocks still do exactly that.

There were two parts to the new science of city planning. It aimed to make cities beautiful. And it also tried to foresee and provide for a city's future needs in housing and **public utilities**, such as mass transportation, power, and light.

Questions for Discussion

1. What technological developments made skyscrapers possible?
2. What were the early attempts to solve the problems of transportation into the cities and within the cities themselves?
3. Why did some cities feel that zoning was necessary?

In addition to Central Park, Frederick Olmsted designed the grounds of the Capitol in Washington, D.C., and many college campuses, including Princeton, Yale, and Stanford.

MUSEUM OF THE CITY OF NEW YORK

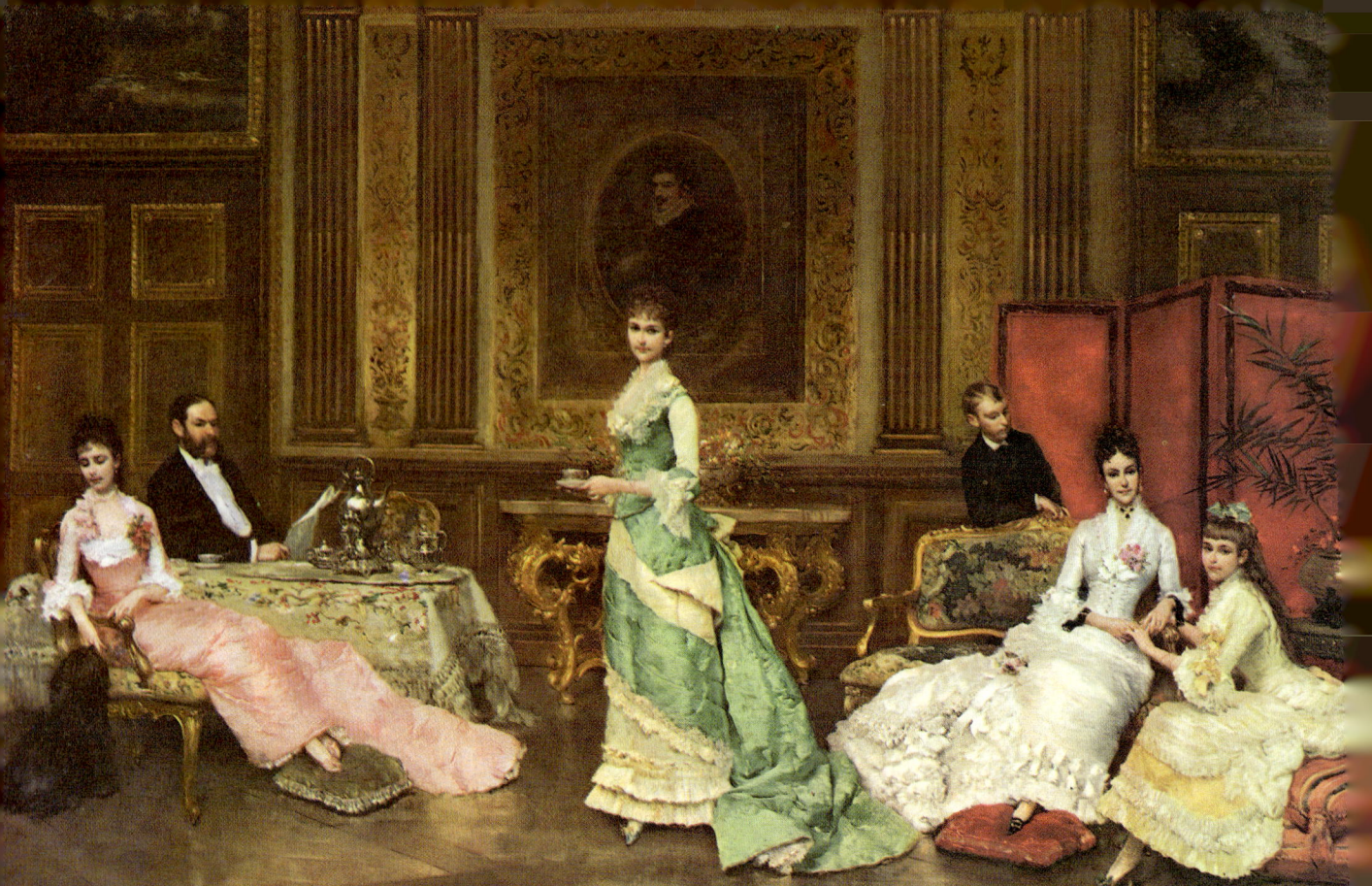

MRS. VINCENT ASTOR COLLECTION

The Gulf Between the Rich and the Poor

The city showed its inhabitants many varieties of life. Some of its scenes were educational and amusing. But others were deeply shocking. For the city made the gap between rich and poor more visible than it had ever been in America. In Chicago, for example, there was a slum neighborhood, known as the "Sands," in existence before the Great Fire of 1871. It was full of garbage heaps, saloons, dark alleys where robbers lurked, neglected and dirty children begged or wandered, and old buildings where people occupied "damp, dark, ill-ventilated, vermin-infested underground rooms." Yet not far from the Sands was a stretch of Lake Michigan shorefront later known as the Gold Coast. Along its clean, well-lighted streets stood mansions like that of Cyrus McCormick, the great reaper manufacturer. In the many rooms of these homes, servants glided over imported carpets, carrying out the wishes of people who surrounded themselves with fine furniture and lovely works of art. The two pictures at the top suggest the width of the gulf between rich and poor. Every big city had—and often still has—such contrasting districts.

MUSEUM OF THE CITY OF NEW YORK, JACOB A. RIIS COLLECTION

In 1888 a book entitled *Looking Backward* by Edward Bellamy appeared. Its hero falls into a deep sleep and awakens in the year 2000 to find a perfect world of equality and justice. In trying to describe the society of his own time, he compares it to a coach. The masses of mankind dragged this coach, he says, up a hilly, sandy road. Their backs ached, their feet bled, they choked with dust. But hunger drove them on. A few fortunate beings sat on top of the coach. In the city those who pulled the coach and those who rode it were within easy view of each other.

The Urban Poor

The life of the urban poor was described by an immigrant using another grim image: "My people do not live in America. They live underneath America. America goes on over their heads." The sweatshop worker, the peddler, and the unemployed clerk or factory hand all lived at a standard far below that of luckier Americans. A poor family in a rural area at least had some home-grown food and the air and sunlight of an outdoor life. The slum dweller and his

In the nineteenth century wealthy families often commissioned grand family portraits. Top left, striking a "casual" pose in formal dress, is the William Astor family in 1875—at home in the huge family mansion on Fifth Avenue. Not very many families could afford to keep up with the Astors: In 1890 fewer than 10 per cent of America's families earned more than $380 a year. Jacob Riis, a Danish immigrant, was among the first to document life among the poor with photographs. He hoped that when Americans actually saw the miserable living conditions in a city slum, they would demand that something be done about it. His photographs, like the one above of an immigrant family in 1910, did much to stir the conscience of the nation.

479

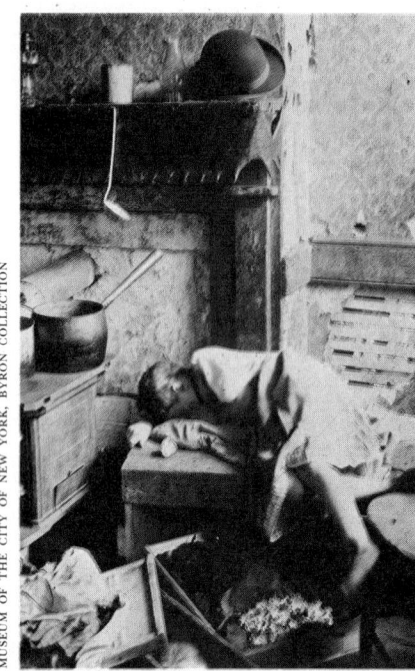

The exhausted child above rests after making artificial flowers. Photographer Lewis Hine urged child labor laws by concentrating on the plight of tenement children. Below, a boy picks through a garbage can in search of valuables. At the right, children somehow ignore their surroundings and enjoy a baseball game.

children had neither, as the pictures at left clearly show. The child sleeping in the crowded tenement probably was one of those of whom Jacob Riis wrote. Their "lullaby" was the squeak of the pump in the hall which was the only source of water for a number of families. Deprived of proper air and nourishment, thousands fell victim to diseases like tuberculosis, which affects the lungs. Entire neighborhoods were known as "lung blocks." Rats and roaches carried other germs which killed many young children before they reached school age.

The little boys and girls who did survive often had duties that cut their childhood brutally short. They took care of infant brothers and sisters while both parents went in search of work. Or they themselves found jobs or sold flowers or matches or other small items from sidewalk stands, or became newsboys or shoeshine boys, in order to add to the slim family income. Whatever playtime they had, they spent in the streets (right).

Many brave men and women in slums, both in the early 1900's and nowadays, held families together and survived. Many tough-spirited youngsters rose from such an environment to success. But the discouragements were huge. Thousands were tempted to turn to drink or to crime in search of some escape from the brutal facts of existence. A life of poverty was a grim training school. It strengthened some people and broke others. But its overall cost to society, because of the sickness and waste of life it created, was far too high.

The basic ideal of America was that hard work, learning, responsibility to the community, and faith in free government would be rewarded with success. Family love and religion were supposed to be great builders of character. It was hard for the urban poor to hold to these beliefs while they endured their grim daily experiences.

The Pleasures of the Rich

Those to whom success was given—the rich—lived with a special glitter. Their money bought a great deal in the early twentieth century when prices were low and taxes were light. So even a millionaire who gave freely to charity had plenty left to spend. He might live in a mansion like that of banker Jay Cooke, which had 72 rooms. He might travel by private railroad car

or even have a yacht, like J. P. Morgan's *Corsair*. The amusements of the very rich were the theater and the opera, driving, hunting occasionally, and, for those not forbidden by a pious objection to gambling, going to the race track. Their meals were eight or ten-course affairs of soup, fish, poultry, roasts, vegetables, fruits, cheeses, puddings, cakes, and ices. Their children were educated at private schools or by tutors.

The scale of living of the super-rich is shown by a party given in the 1890's. The 72 guests sat around an oval table covered with flowers. In its center was an artificial lake. On the lake's surface swam four live swans. They were kept from flying away by a network of golden wires surrounding the lake.

The novelist Mark Twain, with Charles Dudley Warner, wrote a book about such extravagance, and called it *The Gilded Age*. A famous social scientist, Thorstein Veblen, referred to such spending as "conspicuous consumption." The meaning of both these

Beginning in 1884 the upper crust of Chicago society flocked to the annual running of the Derby. Held at an exclusive racing club, Washington Park, the event became far more social than sporting. The year of the painting below — 1893 — was also the year of the Columbian Exposition in Chicago, celebrating the 400th anniversary of Columbus' discovery of America. The elegant couple at the far right are spending an evening at an expensive New York café in 1905.

terms is explained by the custom, called a potlatch, of some Pacific Coast Indians. A potlatch is a feast given by a tribesman. At its end he gives away or else destroys as many valuable things as he can simply to show that he is rich enough to afford it. For America's wealthy classes the period from 1870 to 1914 might be described as the Age of the Big Potlatch.

ART INSTITUTE OF CHICAGO, FRIENDS OF AMERICAN ART COLLECTION

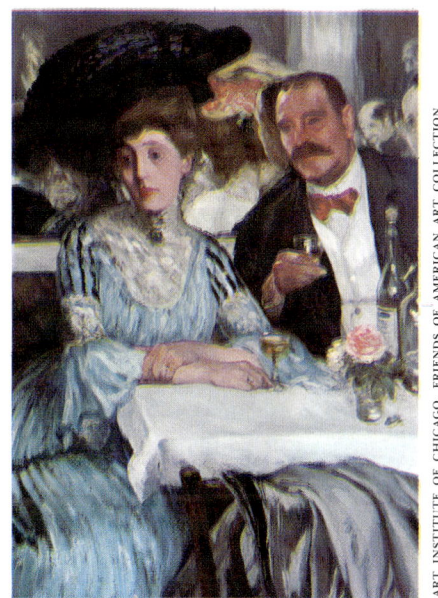

The Growing Middle Class

The greatest number of urban Americans, however, did not live in slums or in mansions. They were members of the middle class. It is hard to be exact about who belonged to this class. It refers to those who are neither rich nor poor—which is the way most people think of themselves. It also has something to do with ways of making a living. People were apt to think of **white-collar workers** (those whose jobs do not involve working with their hands) as middle class no matter what their income was. But well-paid **blue-**

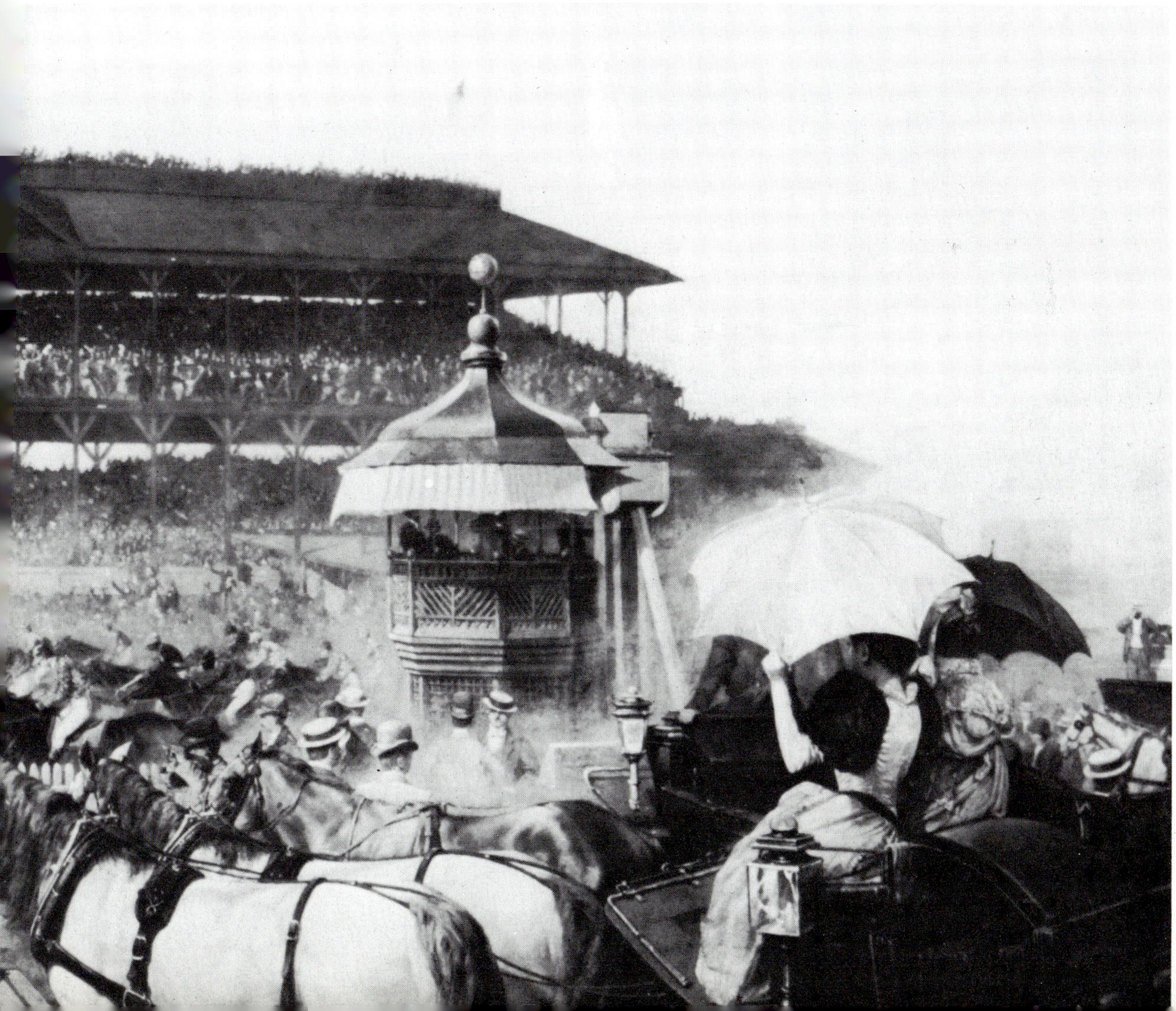

CHICAGO HISTORICAL SOCIETY

Owning a home like the one at the right was the goal of many Americans. The proud owners of this home—with the shutters arranged "just so"—are posing at the side. Americans also longed for time and money to spend for leisure. Below, an editor of a New York newspaper takes his family bicycling through their neighborhood in 1891 and a family picnics on a crowded New York beach around 1920.

LIBRARY OF CONGRESS, CURRIER COLLECTION

MUSEUM OF THE CITY OF NEW YORK, BYRON COLLECTION

CULVER PICTURES

collar workers (those whose jobs involve working with their hands) living in a spacious city apartment or a small house in a factory town were members of the middle class also.

Professional men and businessmen, such as doctors, lawyers, store owners, and managers, set the basic tone of urban middle-class America in this period. Some historians refer to them as the upper middle class and to low-paid white-collar workers and skilled industrial blue-collar workers as the lower middle class. Sizable numbers of families in the upper middle class, seeking space and cleanliness, began to move from the cities into the suburbs around 1900 and thereafter.

Their homes, like the one at the left, were neat and roomy but not as grand as those of the rich. The grounds outside were kept neatly trimmed. Inside there might be water colors done by ladies of the family, vases of flowers on tables, a piano, and many lamps, rugs, small statues, and souvenirs of travel.

The center of life was the family. Father was expected to be a good provider, and mother and the children, in turn, were expected to listen respectfully to him. He was a severe figure, but he might relax on weekends, like the man taking his household out for a spin on bicycles (far left) or to the beach (lower left).

Members of the middle class were extremely serious about doing socially approved things in order to set a proper example for others. Lower middle-class members worked especially hard at this because they did not have much money and therefore had to show by their behavior that they were not like the poor. In most middle-class homes children were scrubbed nearly skinless on Saturday night and marched off in starched clothes to church on Sunday morning. Liquor and gambling were frowned upon. If the family income permitted servants, there were a few — a cook, a laundress, a handyman for the yard. But idleness was discouraged, and everyone had chores. Engagements were long, and marriages were expected to be permanent.

The middle-class citizen amused himself in various ways. He might patronize the minstrel show or the music hall but rarely the "highbrow" opera. Upper and lower middle-class members both enjoyed professional baseball and outdoor excursions in the park or at the county fair but avoided horse races. The well-off mid-

dle-class household had Shakespeare and the Bible on its bookshelves, but its members did most of their reading in the daily newspapers.

The middle-class American was proud of modern progress, especially as shown in his electric lights and his telephone. He took pride in his country and his religion. He was kindly, but had little room for understanding other lands, other cultures, and other classes. He belonged to an age when improvements in life seemed natural and expected, and problems were thought of as small and few. It was an innocent and self-confident era, now gone.

Questions for Discussion

1. Why was the gulf between the rich and poor more apparent in urban than in rural areas?
2. What did Veblen mean by "conspicuous consumption?"
3. Who set the style of middle-class urban American life in the late nineteenth and early twentieth centuries?
4. Why, around 1900, did the movement of people to the suburbs begin?
5. What were some of the values treasured by the average urban middle-class family?

Chapter Review

Social Studies Terms

Americanization, nativists, tenement, zoned, building codes, public utilities, white-collar workers, blue-collar workers

Summary Questions for Discussion

1. What factors explain the change-over from a mainly rural to a mainly urban United States?
2. Why did European immigrants to United States cities have to face some of the same problems American pioneers had faced in the wilderness?
3. Why did nativists strongly object to large-scale immigration from eastern and southern Europe?
4. Why did New York become the nation's largest city? What factors were responsible for the rapid growth of Chicago?
5. How did the desire for high profits lead to substandard housing in many northern cities? What actions were taken by city governments to correct housing abuses?
6. Why was it important to so many people that they

not only *be* wealthy but also that they *show* they were wealthy?
7. Why did people in the middle class seek out some forms of entertainment but avoid others?
8. How has family life changed since 1910? Which values have changed? Which have not?
9. How did the growth of large cities tend to change government and other forms of social behavior?
10. What problems faced by city governments from 1850 to 1900 have not been solved?

Pictures as Historical Evidence

Look at the pictures of colonial cities such as Boston, Philadelphia, and Charleston in Chapter 4. Next study the pictures of American cities in this chapter. Then answer the following question, using only pictures as evidence. Were the cities of the late nineteenth and early twentieth centuries more like colonial cities or more like American cities in the 1970's?

Graph Study

Study carefully the graph on page 467. About how many immigrants came to the United States each year between 1860 and 1865? between 1915 and 1920?

Why did the number of immigrants drop sharply just before 1915 and again after 1920? Why did immigration drop dramatically during World War I but not during the Civil War? What factors other than war tended to affect the number of people coming to this country?

Where could you find information about the number of people who immigrated to the United States after 1935?

For Further Reading

America's Immigrants, by Rhoda Hoff. New York: Henry Z. Walck, Inc., 1967.

McTeague, by Frank Norris. New York: Fawcett World Library, 1968.

Our Oriental Americans, by Ed and Helen Ritter and Stanley Spector. St. Louis: Webster Division, McGraw-Hill Book Company, 1965.

Passage to the Golden Gate, by Daniel and Samuel Chu. New York: Doubleday & Company, Inc., 1967.

To America, by Eleanor B. Tripp. New York: Harcourt, Brace & World, Inc., 1969.

17
An Age of Reform

On July 4, 1892, an exciting political convention met in Omaha, Nebraska. Its aim was to found a new national party. The delegates chosen to attend knew well that they had gathered on the anniversary of the birth of the United States as a free country. They deliberately adopted a **platform** (a statement of a party's goals and ideas) which they believed to be as revolutionary and as necessary as the Declaration of Independence. "We meet," it said, "in the midst of a nation brought to the verge [edge] of moral, political and material ruin." It went on to charge, "The fruits of the toil of millions are boldly stolen to build up colossal fortunes for a few."

It was 116 years since 1776 and only 27 since the end of the Civil War, which had saved the Union and overthrown slavery. What had happened to produce a platform so full of angry accusations?

The men at Omaha who were starting the People's Party, the Populists, had an answer. The nation had grown in wealth and productive power faster than it could handle the social problems that swift change created. As one Populist writer expressed it, our science had gotten beyond our conscience.

The beginnings of industrialism before the Civil War had prodded the American conscience and resulted in reform movements to make society more just. Then the slavery question seemed to swallow all others. But after 1865 a mighty spurt of industrialization and urbanization raised new and difficult questions. Did a gigantic corporation, with a whole community's economic health depending on it, have the right to manage its "private" property without public regulation? How could there be equality among Americans when some were paupers and some multimillionaires? What was needed to provide government of the people, by the people, for the people in gigantic cities?

If such challenges could not be answered, reformers believed, the people's representatives in government would be dwarfed by powerful industries, as the cartoon at right suggests. New ways had to be found to save the old ideals of 1776.

As you read, think about these questions:
1. What problems did urbanization bring to America?
2. What did both business and labor gain by combining into larger organizations?
3. Why do third parties arise in American politics? Do they serve a useful purpose?

Joseph Keppler attacked the power of big business in this 1889 cartoon.

Reform Comes to the City

Thomas Nast, the staff artist of Harper's Weekly *from 1862 to 1886, launched his attack on the Tweed Ring in 1869. Powerful Nast cartoons, like the four on this page, helped lead to the downfall of Tweed and his henchmen in 1871.*

ALL: NEW YORK PUBLIC LIBRARY, PICTURE COLLECTION

In the nation's growing cities, honest governments bent like overloaded bridges under new strains. One strain was caused by the huge profits made by those who got contracts, licenses, and **franchises** (rights or privileges granted by a government) to build public works. City governments were supposed to award these "plums" to the best and cheapest producers. But the great sums involved tempted some businessmen to bribe officials. In return for illegal payments, franchises were awarded to a favored, dishonest few.

A second strain on honesty came when populations were so big that voters rarely knew their officials in person and were, therefore, unable to check up on them. And a third arose because the poverty and unfamiliarity with city life of both native and immigrant urban newcomers made them welcome any kind of help. Political machines took advantage of these developments to build power for themselves.

A machine was usually organized as a political "club." It had workers in the neighborhoods who gave poor voters free coal and food, helped them to find jobs and housing, and amused them with picnics and entertainments. In return, votes were given without question to machine candidates. Therefore, the machine could control elections and put its men in important offices. Then it could make its deals with those willing to pay.

Political machines were controlled by a strong leader, or **boss**. Mayors, city lawmakers, and judges were his puppets. An outstanding example of a boss was New York City's William Marcy Tweed (right). Tweed's base was a Democratic club known as Tammany Hall. Its mascot was a tiger. Between 1862 and 1871 Tammany's tiger ripped millions of dollars from New Yorkers. Tweed's men sold contracts for city work to companies which then overcharged the city treasury. Public taxes paid both bribe-givers and bribe-takers. Eventually, however, Tweed was exposed by newspapers and magazine cartoons (left), and sent to jail.

Yet machines and bosses appeared again, in New York and other cities. They helped handle problems of urban poverty and growth which old-fashioned city governments often failed to do. The bosses knew how to speak and act plainly. But the bosses were not Robin Hoods, taking from the rich to give to the poor. Corruption raised the cost of government to everyone. It bred contempt for law and encouraged crime. Angry

Born in New York in 1823, the son of a chairmaker, William Marcy Tweed entered politics as an officer of a volunteer fire company. The Tweed Ring is estimated to have stolen between $20 and $200 million from New York City. For example, the city paid one of Tweed's friends $179,729.60 for 3 tables and 40 chairs! In 1871 the New York Times *began to publish such shocking figures. Boss Tweed, however, was more concerned about Thomas Nast: "My constituents don't know how to read, but they can't help seeing them damned pictures." Tweed was stunned when Nast refused his $500,000 "scholarship" to study art abroad. When the Ring collapsed Tweed's top associates escaped punishment. Tweed himself spent a year in jail. Arrested on another charge in 1875, Tweed escaped to Spain where he was recognized from a Nast cartoon and returned to New York to await trial. He died there in a city jail in 1878.*

WALLACE KIRKLAND

The daughter of a well-to-do businessman, Jane Addams had planned to become a doctor but failing health forced her to drop out of medical school. This photograph was taken around the time she founded Hull-House at the age of 29. Concerned young people from all over the country came to be residents at Hull-House. In addition to giving immediate help to the neighborhood, they led broader reform movements that got results: child labor laws, a juvenile court, a factory inspection law. Jane Addams supported reform political candidates in Chicago and throughout the nation. She also worked for a lasting peace and remained against war even after the United States entered World War I. At the age of 71 she became the second American to be awarded the Nobel Peace Prize.

reformers began to insist that city dwellers deserved better urban rule.

There were several ways to reform cities. One was to spend money and energy to elect honest men. Victorious reform candidates could then arrest some of the more obvious machine lawbreakers. But sooner or later the public would lose interest and the bosses would return. The basic causes of corruption had to be attacked.

Therefore, reform mayors, such as Cleveland's Tom Johnson (1901–1909) or Detroit's Hazen Pingree (1889–1896), modernized city government in ways that cut the roots of machine power. They fought to have utility companies publicly owned or regulated, so that profiteers could not overcharge the cities. They tried to have city services run by experts who were selected by competitive examination. This principle of a professional **civil service** helped prevent the machine from filling public offices with its henchmen.

Along with this "scientific" or "progressive" urban reform, such mayors as Johnson and Pingree moved to improve the conditions of the poor so that the boss could no longer win elections by offering bread and coal to workers in exchange for votes.

Jane Addams and the Settlement House

One device for helping slum dwellers better their lives was the **settlement house.** This was a new kind of community center right in the slum which offered services to the poor, especially immigrants. One of the first of such centers was Hull-House, founded in Chicago in 1889 by Jane Addams (left). At Hull-House she started classes in sewing, child care, and English. There was help for working mothers with babies. There were free medical clinics (upper right) and gymnasiums and singing clubs (lower right) to keep youngsters off the streets. The goal was not to give just charity but a helping hand in adjusting to American urban life.

Jane Addams' work was a threat to a local boss like Johnny Powers (upper right), leader of Chicago's tough 19th Ward. Powers tried hard to get rid of Hull-House, and Jane Addams tried to beat him at the polls. Both failed. But their struggle was part of a widespread battle for urban betterment.

Questions for Discussion

1. How did a political machine get and hold power?
2. How did reformers change urban America?

NEW YORK PUBLIC LIBRARY, GENEALOGY DIVISION

CHICAGO HISTORICAL SOCIETY

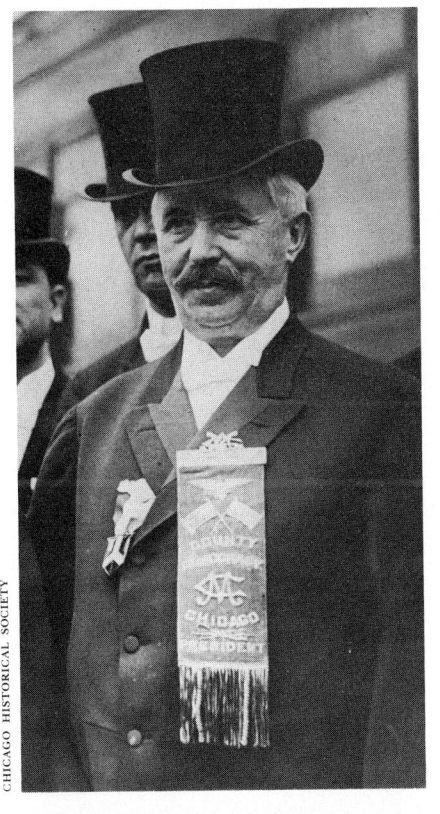

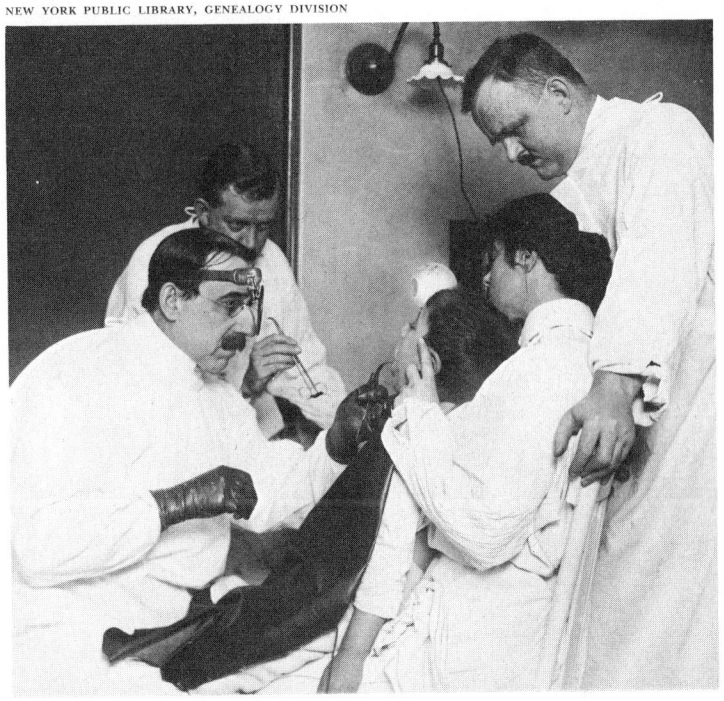

In 1910 Johnny Powers (left) was still a Ward boss, but his power over the poor had been weakened by Hull-House activities like this clinic (above) and singing class (below).

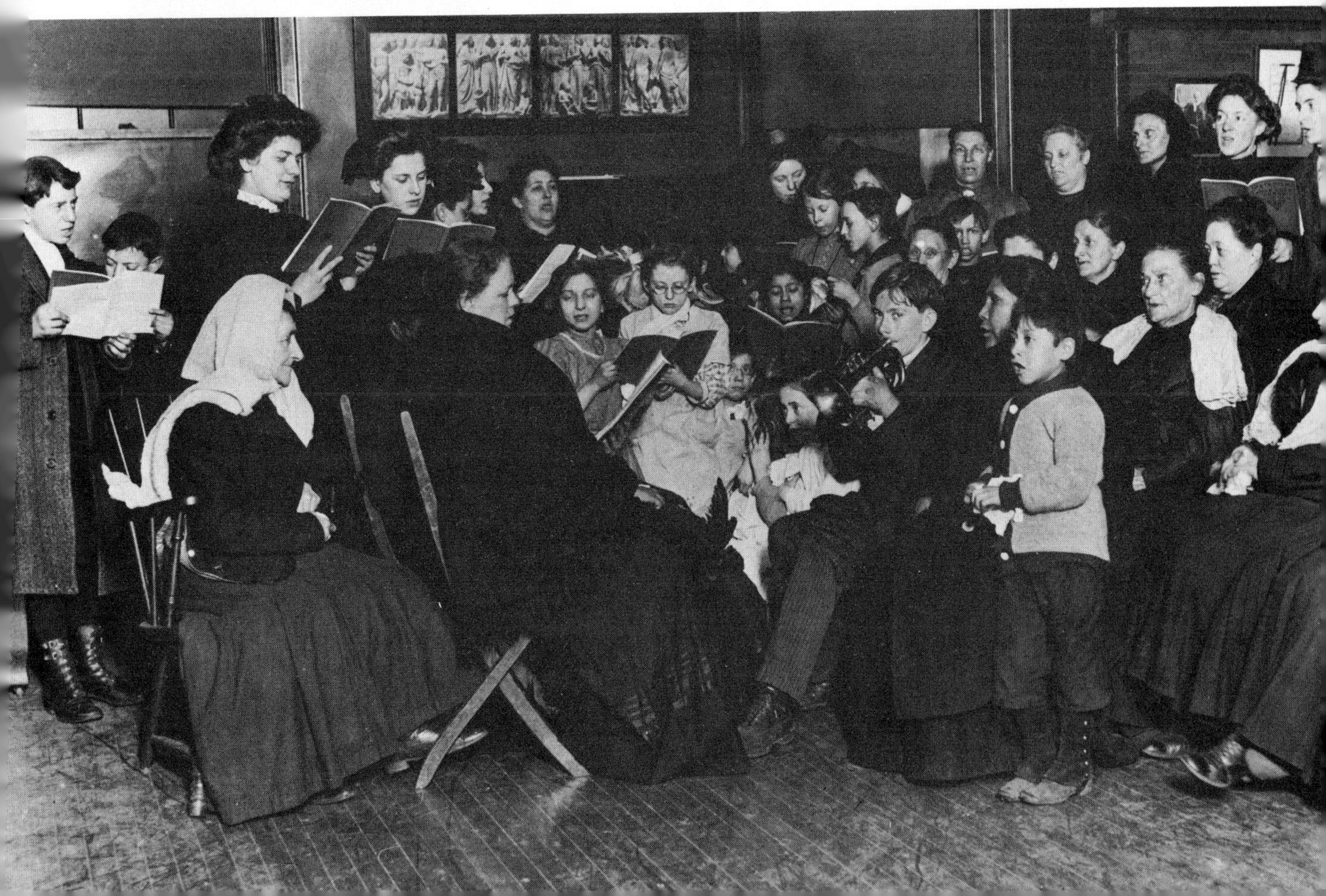

Factories where workers toiled long hours for low wages under bad conditions were called sweatshops. The one at right employed men and women to make clothes. Children were sought after by employers because they could be paid even less. Lewis Hine photographed the boys below breaking coal in a Pennsylvania mine.

BROWN BROTHERS

BOTH: GEORGE EASTMAN HOUSE

Labor Organizes

The march of industrial progress often left people behind. Among these people were laboring men and women. In some ways they were better off than their forefathers had been. Thanks to mass production, they ate better, dressed better, and had more physical comforts than pioneers. But the same mass production system also created brutalizing working conditions.

Certain hard-driving manufacturers saw wages not as a payment for the wealth created by the workingman's efforts, but simply as a production cost. Like all other such manufacturing costs, big businessmen thought wages must be cut to the bone in order to raise profits. So workers, except in a few states which forbade such a practice, worked twelve or fourteen hours a day. Though the pace of work speeded up, pay was kept at rock-bottom levels.

Women were paid less than men for the same work. Children were paid even less. As late as 1906, when some states already had passed laws prohibiting the employment of children under 14 (lower left), nearly 2 million youngsters were still working for as little as 25 cents a day. A poet wrote, "We grind in our mills the bones of the little ones."

Finally, workers ran grave risks of industrial accidents and diseases. They got tuberculosis in the foul air of sweatshops (upper left), were slowly poisoned by chemical fumes, lost fingers and hands in unguarded machines, or were buried in collapsing mineshafts. A worker was an unprotected soldier in a continual battle.

These dangers were horribly illustrated by an episode in New York City in 1911. The Triangle Waist Company, occupying the top three floors of a ten-story building, caught fire. Its 500 screaming employees, mostly immigrant girls, tried to fight the blaze or flee. But the single fire escape collapsed. Rotten water hoses burst. No money had been spent on safety equipment. So the girls, some burning like torches, flung themselves from the windows to the sidewalk far below. The disaster spurred the passage of laws requiring safer factories and providing for inspection and punishment of violators. But it came too late for 147 dead Triangle victims.

Labor Leaders Seek Reform Through Unionization

Working men and women did not just wait for legislators to make things better. They organized to fight for their rights. Some joined unions, like the parading

In another Lewis Hine photograph, this slum dweller is taking rags she has collected to a dealer who will pay her a few pennies.

Above: Terence Powderly, head of the Knights of Labor, in 1886. Below: New York garment workers parade to recruit new members for their union.

BROWN BROTHERS

New York lady garment workers (lower left), and demanded better treatment and higher wages. Early unions were composed of workers in the same trade in the same city. Before the Civil War some national unions were formed by uniting many such local groups into a single, nationwide body. Soon after 1865 labor leaders attempted a further step—to link national unions together into a really large organization, "a union of unions," which would have as much power as huge corporations.

In 1869 a garment worker, Uriah Stephens, founded a secret society—The Noble and Holy Order of the Knights of Labor. The union's secret rituals gave the members a sense of importance and shared responsibility. But spreading the word about a society whose members were sworn to secrecy presented quite a problem. Terence V. Powderly (upper left) succeeded Uriah Stephens as Grand Master Workman of the Knights in 1879. Within two years the secrecy was abandoned and membership began to grow.

The Knights hoped to organize all working people in the United States. Thus united, the Knights could demand political action to bring about fair play in industry by general reforms to improve society. It favored such reforms as more free land for farmers and an increase in the supply of currency to make borrowing easier. Through such steps, it thought, more Americans could go into business for themselves. The Knights even hoped to start its own factories. The workers in these factories would not be hired laborers slaving for capitalists, but craftsmen, cooperating in ownership and sharing the profits among themselves. These dreams of ending the wage system altogether ignored economic realities. The nation would not return to production in small shops and give up the efficiency of large-scale industry with a mass labor force of wage-earners. Naturally, these ideas led to conflicts with management—and to strikes. The Knights staged a number of successful strikes in the 1880's. However, organizational weaknesses and the rise of stronger unions led to the decline of the Knights.

Sharply opposed to the Knights' philosophy was Samuel Gompers (right). By 1877 he was president of Local 144 of the Cigarmakers Union, where he fought for "trade unionism, pure and simple." Gompers wanted all unions to be composed of men sharing a special skill, even if that meant creating several such **craft**

unions within one industry. In contrast, **industrial unions** bring together all workers in one industry—as, for instance, today's United Auto Workers includes clerks in auto factories as well as men on the assembly line. Gompers believed that unions should use strikes and boycotts to make employers grant increased wages, shorter hours, and safer working conditions. Gompers called these reforms a fair share for labor, a "better tomorrow." But Gompers did not want unions to have political goals, nor try to change the economic system. He only wished to soften employers' harshness.

In 1886 Gompers and others persuaded a number of craft unions to enter a new organization, the American Federation of Labor. He became its first president. Until his death in 1924, he worked tirelessly, writing thousands of speeches and letters, helping to form new craft unions for the AF of L and to win public support for labor's demands.

The Strike as a Weapon

Gompers' "bread and butter" unionism included using the workingmen's very real power of refusing to work until their demands were met. This was not always easy. In the early days of unions, strikes were often poorly planned. They were broken easily when workers grew hungry and returned to their jobs on the employer's terms. It was necessary to plan carefully, collect dues, and build up treasuries from which to feed striking laborers before this weapon could be effective.

Nor were employers always willing to wait for strikers to get tired and discouraged. Sometimes they barred them from returning—a practice called a **lockout**—and gave their jobs to new men, who were known as strikebreakers. The strikers, in turn, marched before the factories as pickets to bar the strikebreakers (whom they called "scabs") and to call public attention to their cause. Sometimes pickets and scabs would clash, and violence would result. One such incident led to a tragedy and a violent national debate.

During a strike at the McCormick Harvester plant in Chicago in 1886, police were on hand to protect strikebreakers. When a fight erupted between pickets and the strikebreakers, the police opened fire and killed several workers. A mass protest meeting, announced in bilingual posters (next page), was called in Haymarket Square. In Chicago at this time, there was a small group of anarchists. This particular group of anarch-

AFL-CIO

Samuel Gompers traveled around the country helping to organize the AF of L. He posed for this photograph in the midst of a visit to strike-torn West Virginia coal mines.

ists believed that justice would be won only by the destruction of government, beginning with the assassination of top officials. While the Haymarket meeting was in progress, someone—never found—threw a bomb which exploded in the midst of a squad of policemen, killing a number of them. The police immediately arrested eight known anarchists and anarchist sympathizers. They were accused of responsibility for the murders because of the ideas they taught. They were hurriedly tried and convicted. Four were hanged. Many leading Americans, however, objected strongly to the idea that men should be executed simply for advocating certain violent deeds, without any proof whatever that they actually committed them. So the Haymarket riot and trial left the whole country angry, divided, and shaken.

Worse violence was to come in the 1890's. In 1892 at Andrew Carnegie's Homestead steel plant, near Pittsburgh, gun-play between strikers and scabs brought new deaths. Two years later there was a railroad strike in Chicago. The rail owners got an **injunction** (a court order commanding a person to do or stop doing something) forbidding the strike. But the workers defied it. Some of them, or possibly some hoodlums, set fire to millions of dollars' worth of railroad property. President Cleveland sent Federal troops to Chicago to "keep order," which broke the strike.

In the fire and gun-play in Chicago, Homestead, and elsewhere, many worried Americans saw strikes as a dangerous form of industrial warfare. They feared that capital and labor might eventually be locked in a new civil war. Workers would be on one side and police or troops on the other, as in the bayonet-to-belly confrontation (right) during a textile strike in Lawrence, Massachusetts, in 1912.

Despite these worries, only a handful out of many hundreds of strikes each year ended in bloodshed. Unions, especially those in the AF of L, continued to grow, reaching a membership of over 2.5 million by 1914. Though some employers continued to battle labor with lockouts and injunctions, a growing number found it sensible to accept the right of workingmen to bargain for better conditions through their unions. Samuel Gompers himself was invited to join the National Civic Federation, an organization of businessmen devoted to promoting industrial peace through discussion and fair play. Soon he was an associate of top-hatted re-

Below: Twenty thousand hastily printed handbills announced the Haymarket protest rally. The main speaker was the editor of a radical German-language newspaper. Right: In January 1912 factory workers in Lawrence, Massachusetts, carry American flags as a symbol of their constitutional right to protest peacefully. As the strikers ran out of money, they began sending their children to friends and relatives in other cities. Police realized this would prolong the strike and seized 40 children on a train bound for Philadelphia. Parents who tried to intervene were clubbed. This act of police brutality won sympathy for the workers. Shortly, the strike was settled in their favor.

Century Magazine, APRIL 1893

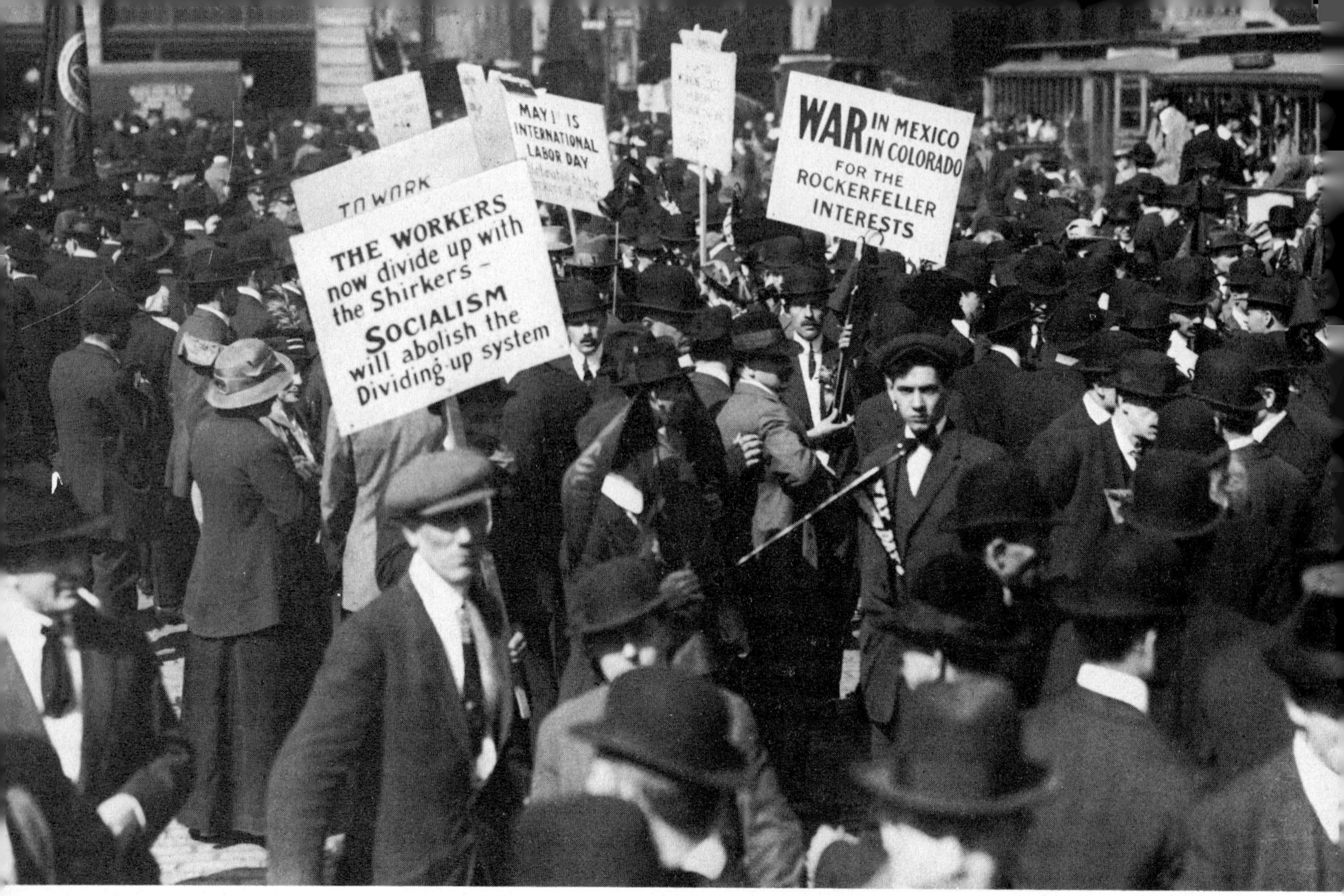

UPI

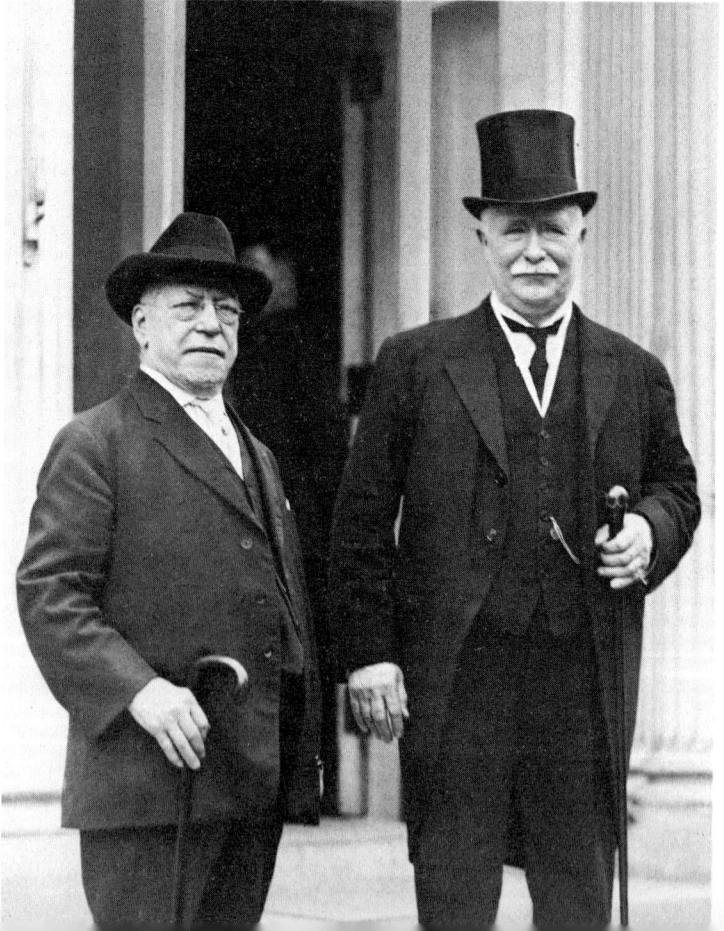

Right: Under the leadership of Samuel Gompers, the AF of L won wide acceptance among management as well as craftsmen. During World War I Gompers served on the Council of National Defense and was a frequent White House visitor. Here, a year before his death in 1924, Gompers posed outside the White House with the prime minister of New Zealand. Above: The organizers of the IWW were far more radical. They were convinced, and said so in the preamble to their constitution, that, "The working class and the employing class have nothing in common." The IWW sponsored a number of successful strikes and won considerable support among unskilled workers. Here, IWW members and supporters rally in New York City on May 1, 1914.

LIBRARY OF CONGRESS

spectable citizens and even visited the White House (lower left).

The Labor Movement Splits

This change did not please everyone concerned with labor's welfare. There were **socialists** who were convinced that a capitalist system would never divide the fruits of industry fairly among all members of society. Socialists argued that the basic means of production, such as factories, mines, and railroads, should be owned by the government. Government should also take responsibility for the distribution of wealth and for all large-scale economic decisions, instead of allowing the lure of profit to determine what was produced where, when, and by whom. Socialists hoped to persuade voters to elect them to office to carry out these reforms.

Other socialists fought the system by helping to form the "union of unions" in 1905, the Industrial Workers of the World. The IWW believed that workers should bring about socialism but not through political action. All workingmen should belong to "One Big Union" (right). When the time was ripe, all could stop work together in a general strike that would completely tie up the nation. Then the working class could take the machines from the capitalist owners who, they said, "stole" most of the wealth or profit created by factory workers. Until that day there could only be war between the laboring and the owning classes. This radical view of how to make a good society became dominant in the IWW after 1908. It had little support among most Americans, but the IWW's spirited posters, songs, and slogans made converts among unskilled laborers. In addition, the IWW was successful in organizing certain workers, such as farmhands and lumberjacks, whom the AF of L had ignored. Despite a few strikes won by the IWW, however, American workingmen believed, like Gompers, that the wage and profit system was here to stay. So both sides moved slowly toward industrial peace.

The goal in this IWW poster never became a reality. The union leaders hoped to create a single industrial union so that a complaint by one set of workers in a single shop could bring on a strike that would paralyze an entire industry. Ultimately, a signal from the "One Big Union" could halt industrial production across the country.

Questions for Discussion

1. Why was mass production both an advantage and a disadvantage to American workers?
2. What methods were used by employers against labor unions? How did the unions fight back?
3. Why did socialists, unlike other labor reform groups, reject capitalism?

Puck MAGAZINE, SEPTEMBER 7, 1904

Although the subject of many attacks like this 1904 cartoon, the Standard Oil trust was one of many. Excluding railroads, in 1896 less than a dozen companies had over $10 million in assets; by 1903 there were over 300 such giants.

The Beginning of a New Politics

As we saw in Chapter 11, economic changes raise new political issues. In the 1890's national parties had to deal with problems created by the industrial boom of the 1870's and 1880's.

At the roots of many of these problems was the difference between a corporation's legal form and its tremendous power. For example, the directors of a railroad company were only a few men with a few votes. But by raising freight rates, they could wipe out the profits of thousands of farmers who used the road to ship grain to market. By giving one industrial shipper a special low price, they could help him to undersell competitors and drive them out of business. By contributing to political campaigns, they could get favorable laws passed by grateful legislators. By employing the most able as well as the best paid lawyers, they stood a good chance to win cases in court. And what was true for railroads was true for other corporations doing essential jobs for whole communities.

Competition among producers was supposed to keep prices down and quality up. Yet around 1880 individual companies in the same industries began to combine, creating near-monopoly conditions. Customers then had no choice of companies from which to buy and no power to influence company policy. The greatest such combination was John D. Rockefeller's strong, efficient Standard Oil Company. By 1882 it had bought almost all of its competitors. Through a legal device known as a **trust** (a combination of companies for the purpose of reducing competition and controlling prices throughout an industry), Standard Oil ran many companies as a single organization. Like an octopus (left), it strangled opportunities for the few independent refiners left in business. Soon trusts were formed in coal, steel, copper, sugar refining, meatpacking, and many other vital industries. Many people asked how could society have any control over such "monsters." They squeezed small producers out of business, set prices of needed goods, and made decisions deeply affecting the public. Yet they were controlled by only a handful of wealthy directors who owned most of their stock. Slowly, Congress moved into action. In 1887 it created the Interstate Commerce Commission to regulate interstate railroad rates. In 1890 it passed the Sherman Antitrust Act, which made it illegal for individuals to combine "in restraint of trade," that is, to interfere with others' rights to do business freely. Yet,

at first, the ICC had very little power to enforce its rules. Because business continued to have immense political as well as economic power, the Sherman Act was almost never used—except against labor unions—throughout the 1890's.

The Populist Crusade

The first sweeping political program for national reform came from the People's Party. Its founders were cotton and wheat farmers, hard-hit by falling prices. After first forming political clubs to express their complaints, they became convinced that neither major party was really listening. So in 1892 they merged these clubs into a new party.

The problems of Populists were high prices for the things they bought—combined with low prices for the crops they sold. They blamed this squeeze on the power of organized wealth and drafted a platform that included broad reforms. First, they wanted the government to increase the available money and credit by coining—that is, making into currency—more of the plentiful silver from western mines. That would lower interest rates and raise the price of farm products. Next, the Populists wanted the government to limit the power of trusts to make excessive charges. As a first step they called for government ownership of the railroads and the telephone and telegraph systems. They also wanted a **graduated income tax** (a tax on people's income that rises as income increases) to distribute the nation's wealth more evenly and to make the rich pay a larger share of government costs.

Finally, Populists wanted to make certain that politicians listened to the people and not just to corporation lobbyists. So they urged election of Senators directly by the people instead of by state legislatures, the secret ballot, and other measures to give voters more of a direct voice in government.

In 1892 the Populists won a million popular votes. In 1896 they nominated the man already chosen by the Democrats, William Jennings Bryan of Nebraska. A spellbinding speaker (right), he won the Democrats' nomination with an emotion-charged speech in favor of coining more silver and denouncing the government's policy of using only gold as money. He concluded with a thundering cry, "You shall not crucify mankind upon a cross of gold!" In his campaign against the Republican candidate, William McKinley (left), Bryan chose to

In 1896 William McKinley ran a safe, dignified campaign from his front porch while a superb Republican organization gave out buttons (left) and bombarded the public with cartoons (bottom). This Puck cartoon represents William Jennings Bryan and his supporters as fools and makes special fun of their demand for free coinage of silver at a ratio of 16-to-1 with gold. Bryan traveled 18,000 miles and gave more than 600 speeches (below) in a losing cause.

ALL: CULVER PICTURES

emphasize only this silver question. Since currency control was a complex economic question, Bryan's opponents were able to dismiss his simple ideas about economics as those of a windbag.

In a close popular vote, Bryan was defeated. He was to run twice more as a Democrat. The People's Party gradually faded away, but its reforming ideas and spirit lived on.

New Political Parties Are Formed

In many states after 1900, a movement generally known as "progressivism" was born. Like the Populists, Progressives hoped to fit American democracy to a modern age. But unlike Populists, Progressives believed that complicated national economic questions could not be settled directly by the people. Instead, they proposed that experts, responsible to publicly chosen officials, should manage society's business. Progressives would not have liked Bryan's statement, "The people of Nebraska are for free silver and I am for free silver. I will look up the arguments later."

A typical Progressive governor was Wisconsin's Robert La Follette, shown campaigning at right. During his term in office from 1901 to 1905, La Follette tried to make Wisconsin a "laboratory of democracy." He created special commissions to regulate railroads and utilities. Their members were often scholars from the faculty of the state university; thus La Follette brought the best brains of the academic community into public service. He fought for fairer taxes and election laws. He led the legislature to the passage of laws providing safer factories, shorter working hours for women and children, and improved conservation of resources. La Follette believed that the American political and economic machinery was still basically sound. It needed only some fixing and an informed public to make it work well.

Another reformer, Eugene V. Debs (left), did not share La Follette's faith in the capitalist system. Debs was an Indiana-born railroad worker and union leader who became a socialist after much reading in jail, where he was put in 1894 for defying an antistrike injunction. As a socialist he believed that real economic equality was not possible under a system of private ownership of productive property. The urge for profit would always rise above the spirit of community. The fruits of growth would not be shared. Only government

Above: Robert La Follette broke with state party bosses and campaigned for progressivism. Left: Socialist Eugene V. Debs, campaigning for President in 1912, received over 900,000 votes.

Puck MAGAZINE, JANUARY 13, 1904

The 1904 cartoon above by Joseph Keppler is titled "Jack and the Wall Street Giants" and shows a contemporary view of Teddy Roosevelt battling all the monster-trusts. Actually, Roosevelt did not favor dissolving all trusts, only those he considered "bad." But his actions as President made him a symbol of the progressive movement. Seen at right delivering one of his rousing speeches, Roosevelt sought the Republican nomination again in 1912. Defeated, he bolted his party and headed the new Progressive Party which lost to the Democrats.

ownership of factories, railroads, mines, and all industries would guarantee fair play. Debs' good humor and sense of brotherhood won him many supporters, even among people who voted against him during his five unsuccessful tries for the Presidency.

Reform from the White House

The dawn of the twentieth century turned the average American's thoughts to the future. The national mood of desire for social improvement grew. Reform-minded Americans had blind spots. They overlooked the plight of blacks in the United States. As we shall see in the next unit, they welcomed the growth of an American empire as well as nativist attacks on immigrants of non-Anglo-Saxon stock.

But they also listened when crusading newspaper and magazine reporters, known as **muckrakers**, exposed corruption in government and business. They often voted for progressive mayors and governors. And in Theodore Roosevelt they found a President who expressed their feelings in the same way that Andrew Jackson had for individualistic, westward-moving Americans 70 years before.

Roosevelt was no ordinary reformer or ordinary man. Born into a wealthy New York family, he had a keen mind, sharpened by a Harvard education. He read widely and wrote easily. He was also a naturalist, conservationist, outdoorsman, athlete, and even had been a cowpuncher on his own western ranch. Before he was forty he was a combat hero of the Spanish-American War. He had done all this and still served in government jobs, from New York City Police Commissioner to Assistant Secretary of the Navy.

In 1900 Roosevelt was elected Vice-President with McKinley. Some big businessmen and party bosses were worried about what the energetic young reformer might be planning. To their horror an assassin's bullet cut down McKinley in 1901 and Roosevelt did become the Chief Executive. However, the American public liked "Teddy," or "T.R." He was rich and educated, but could box, ride, and shoot like a man. He was not a socialist, but he said that trusts must be controlled by the national government to help people obtain a good life. In the early years of his administration, people were ready to support him when he took on the giants of Wall Street (left).

Roosevelt used his superb enthusiasm (right) and

the prestige of the Presidency to put pressure on Congress for progressive Federal legislation. Laws passed during his terms of office strengthened railroad regulation, provided for national inspection of meats and medicines to protect consumers, and set aside new conservation areas. The Justice Department was also given power to move against the trusts under the Sherman Act, and Roosevelt did not hesitate to threaten to use his authority to "bust the trusts." Actually, he did not "bust" many. Roosevelt wanted just enough reform to head off more drastic changes by "radicals."

The high tide of national progressivism came under Woodrow Wilson, a progressive Democrat elected in 1912. Under Wilson a new antitrust act was passed, and an enforcement body, the Federal Trade Commission, was created to protect the public from unfair business practices. A Federal Reserve System was established to provide some control over the nation's banks. Other laws between 1913 and 1916 restricted child labor, extended loans to farmers, improved the working conditions of merchant sailors, and provided an eight-hour day for railroad workers. Meanwhile, the states completed ratification of the Sixteenth and Seventeenth Amendments, providing for an income tax and direct election of senators.

By 1916 progressivism rode high. But the way had been prepared by the long years of patient work of early urban, state, and national crusaders. Then war clouds filled the sky, and the progressive movement took a back seat to preparation for conflict.

Questions for Discussion

1. How did the growth of large corporations give great economic and political power to a few men?
2. Why were most supporters of the Populist Party farmers and miners?
3. Which reforms favored by the Populists were favored by more radical political parties? Which reforms were eventually supported by one of the two major parties?
4. What reforms did Robert La Follette introduce into the government of Wisconsin?
5. How did the political ideas of Eugene Debs differ from those of Robert La Follette?
6. What reforms made during the Presidencies of Theodore Roosevelt and Woodrow Wilson entitled them to be called progressives?

Chapter Review

Social Studies Terms

platform, franchises, boss, civil service, settlement house, craft unions, industrial unions, lockout, injunction, socialists, trust, graduated income tax, muckrakers

Summary Questions for Discussion

1. How did big-city political machines and newly arrived immigrants help each other?
2. How did reform mayors try to undercut the power of political machines?
3. Why did Samuel Gompers have greater success at forming a lasting national labor union than Terence V. Powderly?
4. Why was violence sometimes a part of labor disputes?
5. Consider Article I, Section 8 of the Constitution, enumerating [listing] the powers of Congress. Tell in your own words what powers Congress has to regulate business.
6. Why are the nation's railroads under such tight government regulation?
7. What was significant about the time and place of the meeting of the Populist Party convention in 1892?
8. In what ways were the ideas of the Populists similar to those of some third parties or other political groups today?

Pictures as Historical Evidence

Look at the cartoon on page 489. How does this cartoon get its message across? Now look at the pictures on page 494–495. Which of these pictures would most likely convince viewers that reform of labor practices was necessary? Why?

For Further Reading

Jane Addams of Hull-House, by Winifred E. Wise. New York: Harcourt, Brace & World, Inc., 1963.

Labor on the March, by Joseph L. Gardner. New York: American Heritage Publishing Co., Inc., 1969.

Samuel Gompers, by Bernard A. Weisberger. Morristown, N.J.: Silver Burdett Company, 1967.

The Haymarket Affair, by Corinne J. Naden. New York: Franklin Watts, Inc., 1968.

Theodore Roosevelt, by John A. Garraty. New York: American Heritage Publishing Co., Inc., 1967.

ISSUES PAST AND PRESENT

What Is the Responsibility of the Government for the Welfare of Its Citizens?

Many of the services which our city, state, and national governments provide for us, like delivering the mail, building streets and roads, and educating the young, we take for granted. It is hard to believe that there was once a time when people either had to do these things for themselves or make arrangements to have them done. Can you imagine each family in America having to make private, individual arrangements for the education of its children?

The impact of rapid industrialization and urbanization in the 50 years after the Civil War led many people to demand that governments accept responsibility for doing even more jobs than the ones just mentioned. These reformers wanted the government to use tax monies to help individuals get jobs and medical care and to provide money for food and shelter when times were hard or when people became too old to work. In time governments, at many different levels, did indeed accept such responsibility. Now, care for people in their old age, medical help for the elderly and the poor, and payments of money to people who do not have jobs are all part of huge government programs. But this role for the government is as unacceptable to millions of Americans as it is acceptable to millions of others. Whenever such help was first seriously proposed and considered, a debate was set off which raised questions that people still argue about fiercely. Here are some of those questions:

1. How much responsibility does government have for the welfare of all its citizens?
2. Who should get welfare? Who should pay for it?
3. Do people lose some of their freedom if they look to the government for help? Why?

Accidents That Just Happen

In the years when corporations, factories, and the machines in those factories were all growing to giant size, industrial workers were often the victims of terrible fires and other accidents. William Hard was one of many writers troubled by the hardships such disasters caused workers and their families. He tried to arouse the government to take action to lessen the effects of these hardships.

WILLIAM HARD:
INJURED IN THE COURSE OF DUTY, 1907

Let us take a typical accident. On the 18th of February, 1901, John Zolnowski, with a fellow worker named Behrens, was working in a big open-hearth furnace in the plant of the

Illinois Steel Company in South Chicago. The vast interior of the furnace was dark, and the men were guided to their gloomy task by the dim flare of a torch. Suddenly, without warning, without any fault on the part of the men, without any fault on the part of the company, a column of inflammable gas was shot into the steep-sided furnace in which the men were working. No one ever discovered who released the gas or for what purpose. Escape for the two men was impossible. The column of gas rushed at the torch and exploded into flame. In an instant a long, thick finger of fire was playing on the bodies of the men. Behrens was at once burned to death. Zolnowski was hideously disfigured and permanently disabled.

What does the law say to Zolnowski? It says to him that, though he was not in any way to blame for the accident, neither was his employer in any way to blame for it. And it says to him that therefore he alone must bear the whole burden of it. He took the risk of such accidents when, because he needed food and clothing, he took a job in the steel industry. He had nothing coming to him.

Most accidents are like Zolnowski's. They just happen. And if an accident just happens, the whole financial burden of it is placed on the shoulders of the employee. The law does not place that burden, the burden of agony, of sorrow, of financial loss, on the steel industry, which cannot be operated without such happenings. The steel industry pays for its iron ore. It pays for its coke. It pays for its limestone. But it does not pay for its accidents. The burden of accidents is thrown upon the employee.

1. Why did Zolnowski have to bear all the burden of the accident?
2. What does the author think ought to be done?

The Need for New Rules

The following words are from a speech that Woodrow Wilson gave in 1912 when he was running as the Democratic Party's candidate for the Presidency. His opponent in that election was Theodore Roosevelt.

WOODROW WILSON: *THE NEW FREEDOM*, 1912

We have come to a very different age from any that came before us. In this new age we find, for instance, that our laws with regard to the relations of employer and employee are often wholly out of date and impossible. They were passed for another age, which nobody now living remembers. The employer is now generally a corporation or a huge company

of some kind. The employee is one of hundreds or of thousands brought together, not by individual masters whom they know and with whom they have personal relations, but by hiring agents of one sort or another. Workingmen are gathered together in great numbers to work in giant factories. They generally use dangerous and powerful machinery, over whose repair and renewal they have no control.

New rules must be written with regard to their duties and their rights, their duties to their employers, and their duties to one another. Rules must be written for their protection, for their compensation when injured, for their support when disabled.

We must not match power against weakness. The employer is generally, in our day, as I have said, a powerful group. Yet the workingman, when dealing with his employer, is still, under our present law, an individual.

We used to think, in the old-fashioned days when life was very simple, that all that government had to do was to put on a policeman's uniform and say, "Now don't anybody hurt anybody else." We used to say that the ideal of government was for every man to be left alone and not interfered with, except when he interfered with somebody else. But we are coming to realize that life is much more complicated now and new approaches are necessary. The law has to step in and create conditions under which we can live decently.

> "Compensation" is something given or received to pay or make up for what someone else has lost or had taken.

1. Why did Wilson believe that the United States was in a new age?
2. What did Wilson think ought to be done?

Helping Ourselves

In 1923 when the United States was very prosperous, businessmen were widely admired and envied. The words of Henry Ford were listened to with respect by many Americans. These words on "the American system" are adapted from his autobiography.

HENRY FORD: *MY LIFE AND WORK*, 1923

Law can never be more than a policeman. You cannot have a whole country thinking that Washington is a sort of heaven where men know everything and have power over everything. If a nation thinks that way, you are educating that country into a dependent state of mind which promises bad things for the future. Our help does not come from Washington.

The welfare of the country is squarely up to us as individuals. That is where it should be and that is where it is

safest. Governments can promise something for nothing but they cannot deliver. It is work and work alone that can continue to deliver the goods—and that, down in his heart, is what every man knows.

Our present system, always clumsy, often stupid, and in many ways not perfect, has this advantage over any other—it works. Our system stands. Is it wrong? Of course it is wrong, at a thousand points! Is it clumsy? Of course it is clumsy. By all right and reason it ought to break down. But it does not.

Through work and work alone may health, wealth, and happiness inevitably be secured. There is no reason why a man who is willing to work should not be able to work and be paid for the full value of his work. But if he contributes nothing, he should take away nothing. He should have the freedom of starvation. We are not getting anywhere when we insist that every man ought to have more than he deserves.

1. Compare Henry Ford's ideas about welfare with Woodrow Wilson's. With whom do you agree? Why?

In the early years of the 1930's, less than ten years after Henry Ford wrote the previous selection, a terrible economic depression swept across the United States. Many factory workers lost their jobs. Many of those who lived on farms could not produce enough food or earn enough money to feed themselves and their families. A Federal Emergency Relief Administration was set up to help them. The woman who wrote the next selection was one of the relief administrators.

A Man Who Saw Ghosts

"Relief" means either money or goods given to those who need help.

LOUISE V. ARMSTRONG:
WE TOO ARE THE PEOPLE, 1938

The old people, and the sick or crippled or otherwise helpless cases, were the first to come to us when the Relief Office opened. They made up the major part of our direct relief load. A family of two received $8.40 a month, and so on up to families of ten or more. I have heard many complaints about people "living in luxury" on relief. I have never seen any of these people.

In October 1933 the government announced that various surplus goods would be made available for distribution to relief cases. We decided to send men on relief with the truck drivers to make the deliveries. I selected, for the first man to go on this duty, one of the auto mechanics whom I had known a long time and knew to be honest. The morning after the first day he had spent delivering out in the country, he

came into my office looking like a man who had seen ghosts.

This man was in desperate need himself. He had a wife and five children and no job. He was in danger of losing his house in town. In an effort to save it, he had rented it and had moved with his family to a run-down farm on the outskirts of the city. Later, however, his place was saved with a government home loan.

"I thought we were poor enough," he told me, "but I wouldn't of believed what I seen yesterday if I hadn't of saw it. I've lived here in the county all my life, but always in town. I didn't know what it was like out there in them hills and woods—folks with a bunch of kids and old folks—living in shanties that ain't fit for pigs—sometimes without even no floor, only dirt. I had a hard time making some of 'em understand about the pork. Some thought I was trying to sell it to 'em, and when I said not, they wanted to know if it was really for them, and finally I sez it was a present from the government. A lot of 'em—especially the old folks—broke down and cried. I guess all some of 'em has to eat is potatoes and beans and bread, and not any too much of that. Some said they hadn't tasted meat for months."

1. What different kinds of government help are mentioned in this selection?
2. In what ways does the author indicate that she favored government help for the poor?

A "government home loan" was a kind of loan to homeowners begun in 1933. The government was authorized to loan $3 billion in the form of mortgages to homeowners who were in debt and therefore in danger of losing their homes.

Building a New Foundation

With these words President Franklin D. Roosevelt tried to answer those who said that the poor were "living in luxury" and that the government was spending too much money to help people who should have been helping themselves. Franklin D. Roosevelt was President from 1933 until his death in 1945. These words were spoken when he was running for a second four-year term in the White House.

On March 4, 1933, Roosevelt became President of a nation in the grip of a disastrous depression.

FRANKLIN D. ROOSEVELT: *CAMPAIGN SPEECH FOR RE-ELECTION*, 1936

The first thing before us on that famous March 4, 1933, was to give aid to those overtaken by disaster. We did that, and we are not ashamed of giving help to those who needed help. We furnished food relief, drought relief, flood relief, and work relief. Some people call these things waste. Some people ridicule the government agencies we set up. But you and I know that they are the agencies that have substituted

food for starvation, work for idleness, hope instead of dull despair.

Some people call these things meddling and interference. You and I know them to be new stones in a foundation on which we can build a safer, happier, more American America.

We will not be content until all our people fairly share in the ever-increasing ability of America to provide a high standard of living for all its citizens.

1. What did Roosevelt state as the goal of his programs?
2. What role did he think government should play?

The Effects of Welfare

The author of the following selection was the unsuccessful Republican candidate for the Presidency in 1964. In a book that he had written four years earlier, when he was United States Senator from Arizona, he set forth his reasons for opposing large-scale government welfare programs.

BARRY GOLDWATER:
CONSCIENCE OF A CONSERVATIVE, 1960

Think of what happens to the person who receives government welfare payments. For one thing he puts himself in debt to the Federal government. In return for benefits he grants to the government the ultimate in political power, that is, the power to grant or withhold from him the necessities of life as the government sees fit. Even more important, however, is the effect on him—the elimination [loss] of any feeling of responsibility for his own welfare and that of his family and neighbors. A man may not at that time, or ever, realize the harm he has done to his character. Indeed, this is one of the great evils of Welfarism—that it changes the individual from a dignified, hard-working, self-reliant person into a dependent animal creature without his knowing it. There is no way to avoid this damage to character under the Welfare State.

Let us not reduce charity to a mechanical operation of the Federal government. Let us, by all means, encourage those who are fortunate and able to care for the needs of those who are unfortunate and disabled. But let us do it in a way that promotes the spiritual as well as the material well-being of our citizens. Let us do it in a way that will preserve their freedom. Let welfare be a private concern. Let it be promoted by individuals and families, by churches, private hospitals, religious service organizations, community charities, and other institutions that have been set up for this purpose.

"Welfarism" refers to a social system in which the government takes on the primary responsibility for the well-being of its citizens.

1. According to Goldwater what happens to the person who accepts government welfare payments? Why?
2. Who does he believe should be responsible for caring for those in need? Why?

Poverty Amidst Wealth

The book from which the following words were taken is credited with inspiring President John F. Kennedy to declare a war on poverty.

MICHAEL HARRINGTON: *THE OTHER AMERICA*, 1963

There is an America we all know celebrated in speeches and advertised on television and in the magazines. It has the highest standard of living the world has ever known. There exists another America. In it live somewhere between 40 million and 50 million citizens of this land. They are poor. Here are the unskilled workers, the migrant farm workers, the aged, the minorities, and all the others who live in the other America. They are hungry. They are without adequate housing and education and medical care. Even more basic, this poverty twists and deforms the spirit. The American poor are pessimistic and defeated. They are the victims of mental suffering.

Here is a familiar story that comes from those blind to poverty and its causes: "The poor are that way because they are afraid of work. And anyway they all have big cars. If they were like me (or my father or my grandfather), they could care for themselves. But they prefer to live on government handouts and cheat the taxpayers." But the real explanation of why the poor are poor is that they made the mistake of being born to the wrong parents, in the wrong section of the country, or in the wrong racial group. They have never had a chance to get out of the other America.

Here is one form of the vicious circle of poverty. The poor get sick more than anyone else in the society. That is because they live in slums, jammed together under unhealthy conditions. They have inadequate diets, and cannot get decent medical care. When they become sick, they are sick longer than any other group in the society. Because they are sick more often and longer than anyone else, they lose wages and work, and find it difficult to hold a steady job. And because of this, they cannot pay for good housing, for a nutritious [healthy] diet, for doctors. At any given point in the circle, particularly when there is a major illness, they are likely to move to an even lower level and to begin the cycle, round and round, toward even more suffering.

In a nation that could provide every citizen with a decent life, it is an outrage and a scandal that there should be such misery.

There is only one institution in the society capable of acting to abolish poverty. That is the Federal government. The state governments in this country cannot deal with the problem of poverty. The cities are not now able to deal with poverty. Each day they become even less able. Private agencies of the society simply do not have the funds to deal with the other America. So, there is no place to look except toward the Federal government. Only the Federal government has the power to abolish poverty.

We can now fulfill the age-old dream: Poverty can now be abolished. How long shall we ignore this other America in our midst? How long shall we look the other way while our fellow human beings suffer? How long?

1. How does Harrington define "the other America?"
2. According to Harrington what causes a person to become poor or stay poor?
3. Who does Harrington believe should be responsible for eliminating poverty? Why?

Making a Policy Decision

You have now read a number of selections, each of which proposed an answer to the question of what is the responsibility of the government for the welfare of its citizens. As you can see, the question has been hotly debated for nearly a hundred years.

Imagine that you are on a television panel debate along with Woodrow Wilson, Henry Ford, Louise Armstrong, Franklin D. Roosevelt, Barry Goldwater, and Michael Harrington. They have all had a chance to speak. Their speeches were what you have just read. It is your turn now. While you have been listening, you realize that your answer must cover four questions:

1. Will there always be a need for some form of social assistance for some people? Who? Why?
2. What is the best way to give whatever amount of help you think necessary?
3. Who should pay the costs?
4. Who on the panel do you most closely support and with whom do you most strongly disagree? Why?

1784 First American Ship Reaches China

1853 Perry Arrives in Japan

1867 Alaska Purchased from Russia

1882 Chinese Exclusion Act Passed

1823 Monroe Doctrine Announced

1856 Walker President of Nicaragua

1868 Burlingame Treaty with China

UNIT VI
The United States Becomes a World Power

1900 Boxer Rebellion in China

1904 Roosevelt Corollary to Monroe Doctrine

1917 United States Enters World War I

1898 Spanish-American War Begins

1903 Construction of Panama Canal Begins

1914 World War I Begins

1919 Treaty of Versailles

Growing rapidly in size and wealth after independence from Britain, the United States soon became one of the world's most powerful nations. By the end of the nineteenth century, most of the other great nations were the hubs of immense empires that spread around the globe. Now Americans began to ask if the United States should have an empire too. Part of the debate that took place about this question opens Unit VI in *Interpreting the Past*.

The stage for the American drama of expansion in the 1800's extended to the borders of Canada and Mexico, from the Atlantic to the Pacific. Chapter 18 tells of how the limits of that stage were stretched to islands in the Pacific, to Alaska, and to countries in the Far East. Chapter 19 describes the nation's growing involvement in the affairs of Caribbean islands and Latin American lands south of the Rio Grande. Chapter 20 discloses that even when Americans tried hard, they could not remain aloof from the affairs of the European countries from which most of their ancestors had come. Their involvement in a war that spread from Europe to the entire world renewed interest in a question that had concerned even Washington, Adams, and Jefferson: What should be America's role in the world? This question, which has troubled Americans particularly since the beginning of the Vietnam War, is examined at the end of this unit in *Issues Past and Present*.

TOP, LEFT TO RIGHT:
U. S. NAVY LIBRARY
DEWOLF PERRY COLLECTION
BROWN BROTHERS
LIBRARY OF CONGRESS
Collier's, SEPTEMBER 22, 1900
NEW YORK *World*
NEW JERSEY HISTORICAL SOCIETY
BOTTOM, LEFT TO RIGHT:
LIBRARY OF CONGRESS
LIBRARY OF CONGRESS
HAYES MEMORIAL LIBRARY
LIBRARY OF CONGRESS
SMITHSONIAN INSTITUTION
IMPERIAL WAR MUSEUM
LIBRARY OF CONGRESS

INTERPRETING THE PAST

The Argument over Empire

"Expansionists" were those who favored the continued territorial growth of the United States.

Even before they began to call themselves Americans, the people who came to the land that became our country thought of themselves as people of destiny. That destiny, some said, was to establish the Kingdom of God in the New World. Others spoke of making Christians of the "savage" Indians. After independence destiny to some meant setting an example of liberty and democracy for all the world to see, admire, and follow. Later, ambitious expansionists spoke and wrote of overspreading the continent until the settlements of "civilized" men had reached the Pacific Ocean. When the United States actually did reach the Pacific, many people were willing to give up the idea of a destiny that went any further. Their main concern was to perfect the society that existed within our borders. Others had visions which were not so geographically limited.

Between April and August of 1898, the United States won decisive military victories over Spain which left it in control of the Philippines, Puerto Rico, Cuba, Guam, and Wake Island. Even before the Spanish-American War, Americans had long debated the desirability of building an overseas empire. Sudden ownership of so many islands simply brought the debate to a head. As you read the two selections below about that debate, keep these questions in mind:

1. How does a man's view of the meaning of history influence his thinking?
2. At the end of the Spanish-American War, what were the central issues in the debate about America's role in the world?

The Flag Marches On

The speech from which this selection is taken was delivered in September of 1898 by Albert Beveridge, a leader of the Republican Party who soon became a powerful United States Senator from Indiana.

ALBERT J. BEVERIDGE: *THE MARCH OF THE FLAG*, 1898

Our God has planted on this soil a mighty people. He has given a glorious history to His chosen people. This history has been made heroic by our faith in our mission and our future. It is the history of soldiers who carried the flag across blazing deserts and through hostile mountains, a history of a people who overran a continent.

Those who do not want the United States to annex foreign lands tell us that we ought not to govern a people without

their consent. I answer, "That rule of government applies only to those people who are capable of self-government." We govern the Indians without their consent. We govern our territories without their consent. We govern our children without their consent.

We are just doing what our fathers did. We are just pitching the tents of liberty farther westward, farther southward. We are just continuing the march of the flag!

The march of the flag! In 1789 the flag of the Republic waved over 4 million souls in 13 states, plus territory which stretched to the Mississippi. The timid people of that day said that no new territory was needed, and, at that time, they were right. But Jefferson bought Louisiana, which swept from the Mississippi to the mountains. The march of the flag began!

Then Texas answered the bugle calls of liberty, and the march of the flag went on! And at last, we went to war with Mexico and the flag swept over the southwest, over California, past the Golden Gate to Oregon on the north.

And now, our President today plants the flag over the islands of the seas, which will be our outposts of commerce, our fortresses of national security. The march of the flag goes on!

Today, we are raising more crops than we can eat and making more than we can use. Therefore, we must find new markets for our products. And so, while we did not need the territory taken during the past century at the time we got it, we do need what we have taken in [the Spanish-American War of] 1898, and we need it now.

Puerto Rico and the Philippines produce what we consume, and consume what we produce. They sell sugar, coconuts, fruit, and timber of great worth. They buy flour, clothing, tools, machinery, and all that we can raise and make. Their trade will one day be ours.

There are so many important things to be done—canals to be dug, railways to be laid, forests to be cut, cities to be built, fields to be farmed, markets to be won, ships to be launched, peoples to be saved, civilizations to be proclaimed.

Wonderfully, God has guided us. We cannot retreat from any soil where He has unfurled our flag. It is our duty to save that soil for liberty and civilization.

1. What does Beveridge want the United States to do? Why?
2. How does he answer those who criticized a policy of annexation?
3. Would you agree with Beveridge? Why?

The Duties of a Democracy

When Carl Schurz made the speech from which the following words are taken, the Treaty of Paris ending the war between Spain and the United States had already been signed. By the treaty Spain had ceded Puerto Rico, the Philippine Islands, and Guam to the United States and given complete control of Cuba to the United States. But the treaty had not been approved by the United States Senate, as required by the Constitution. A former Senator and journalist, Schurz was a powerful figure in the Republican Party who sought to influence the coming vote in the Senate.

CARL SCHURZ: *AMERICAN IMPERIALISM*, 1899

It is said that we should annex certain islands taken from Spain in the recent war. It is nearly time to make a decision on the matter.

Our government was, in the words of Abraham Lincoln, "the government of the people, by the people, and for the people." To make this republic the example and guiding star of mankind was the noblest of ambitions. Such was our ambition just a short year ago.

Then came the Spanish War. When our forces occupied foreign territory, a loud demand arose that the conquests, even the Philippines, should be kept. "Why not?" was the cry. Has not the job of the republic almost from its beginning been one of territorial expansion?

The question is not whether we *can* do such things, but whether we *should* do them. If we do we shall, for the first time since the abolition of slavery, again have two kinds of Americans: first-class Americans, who have the privilege of taking part in government, and second-class Americans, who are to be ruled by the first-class Americans.

If we do we shall change the government of the people, by the people, and for the people, for which Abraham Lincoln lived, into a government of the strong over the weak.

Inevitably, we shall want new conquests to protect those conquests we already have. We shall have new conflicts on our hands, almost without knowing how we got into them. It has always been that way, and it always will be. This means more and more soldiers, ships, and guns.

We are told by some that our industries must have new markets, and that we need colonies all over the world to give us those markets. More markets? Certainly. But do we, civilized people, believe that we must own the countries with which we wish to trade? It is an absurd and barbarous idea.

We are told that great power is necessary for us to get our share of the trade with China. Therefore, we must have

"Barbarous" means uncivilized or savage.

the Philippines. But does trading with China really require us to have the Philippines? Do we have to make a great show of power to get our share? Trade is developed not by the best guns, but by the best merchants.

We are told that it is time for us to become a "world power." Well, we *are* a world power now, and have been for many years. Is it necessary for a world power, in order to be such, to have its finger in every pie? Must we have the Philippines in order to become a world power?

It is said that the Filipinos and the Puerto Ricans are not able to govern themselves as independent countries. They may answer that this is their own business and that they are at least entitled to give it a try. I frankly admit that if they are given the chance to govern themselves, their conduct will be far from perfect. Well, the conduct of no people is perfect, not even of our own. They may have bloody civil battles. But we, too, have had our Civil War. They may have troubles with their wild tribes. So did we, and we treated our wild tribes [the Indians] in a manner not to be proud of.

We should keep our troops on those islands only until their people have set up governments and organized forces of their own to keep order.

If this democracy remembers its pledges and thinks clearly about its duties to itself and to others, and then resists the temptation of conquest, it will achieve the grandest triumph of the democratic idea that history knows of.

1. What does Schurz want the United States to do? Why?
2. What dangers did Schurz see in having an empire? Have any of his fears been realized?

Evaluating Opinions

Each of the selections which you have just read is an attempt at persuasion. The public has to evaluate or judge such attempts in order to decide what policies it will support and what candidates for office it will vote for. This is not an easy task, for it demands, first, that we clearly understand the issue and, then, that we learn the appropriate facts upon which to base a decision. People of opposing viewpoints often see the issue in very different ways. For instance, how does Beveridge define the issue? How does Schurz? Did their view of American history influence their thinking? Do these men have similar or different ideas about what the United States' role in the world ought to be? Explain.

18 The United States in the Pacific

On an August day in 1784, a small merchant ship entered the harbor in Canton, China, flying an unfamiliar banner at her masthead. Few Cantonese could know that it was the flag of the new United States of America. Three years before the Constitution was written, the red, white, and blue had been carried into the far Pacific. By 1917, as the map at right shows, the United States was a major power in that ocean.

Today the United States is a global giant. The Stars and Stripes fly over American military posts in more than 25 countries. Twice in 20 years American armed forces have fought in land wars in Asia. In addition, there is hardly a country in the world that has not seen American businessmen, teachers, engineers, doctors, and technicians at their work.

In part this is because of swift, deep changes in the world since 1945. But it is also the continuation of a story that began with the little *Empress of China* bobbing into Canton in 1784, halfway around the world from her home port of New York.

Certain forces kept pushing Americans outward. Even as British colonial subjects, they had been adventurous sailors and traders in distant waters. When the United States, as a free nation, began to add new territory, its merchants grew ambitious for new markets. In addition, there was a strong American sense of religious mission, or special duty for the benefit of others. Many nineteenth-century Americans believed that God had chosen them to bring Christianity to the "heathen." Finally, as the United States industrialized, many of its citizens came to believe in a new version of this idea. For the good of humanity, "backward" peoples, who lacked railroads, telegraphs, factories, and other signs of "progress," should be improved by "advanced" nations.

Such beliefs led the United States and other strong, modernized countries to move toward **imperialism** (a policy of extending a nation's control over other peoples, either by actually taking over and ruling their territories or by making them dependent economically). The belief in Manifest Destiny which led America across the continent did not permit stopping at the water's edge.

As you read, think about these questions:
1. How did the opening of new markets in the Pacific lead the United States to acquire land overseas?
2. What problems arose from acquiring such land?

The Beginnings of Imperialism

The voyage of the *Empress of China* was a huge success. She returned home with a cargo which earned a profit of $38,000. Soon other ships were leaving northeastern United States ports for China. Often they went around Cape Horn and stopped on the Pacific Coast for furs. Then, partway across the Pacific, they would stop again at the Hawaiian Islands for fresh food and water. So Oregon, California, Hawaii, and China were linked together by American traders even before the first three belonged to the United States.

At first American ships brought the Chinese furs and special plants used in making medicines and perfumes. After industry came to New England, the cargoes were likely to be cotton cloth, hardware, and other manufactured goods. Tea, china, and silk were brought back to Boston and New York wharves in exchange. The actual buying and selling was done by American businessmen who lived for a time in China and often learned Chinese manners, language, and business customs. They returned with jade earrings, silk robes, and ivory fans for their Yankee brides.

But there were some drawbacks. The Chinese were unwilling to have foreigners in their country. Until 1840 they forced foreign businessmen to trade only in one port, live in special neighborhoods, and deal with only a few specially chosen Chinese merchants. West-

ern nations would not allow the Chinese government to make such rules, even on Chinese soil, when they had modern arms and the Chinese did not. In 1840 Great Britain fought the first of a series of small wars with China. After each war the defeated Chinese emperor would have to sign a treaty allowing trading rights in ports such as Shanghai, Canton, and Hong Kong (upper right) to foreign powers. The Chinese government would also have to accept the presence of missionaries trying to win its subjects away from Chinese religion. Foreign governments demanded, too, that their citizens accused of committing crimes in China be tried in special non-Chinese courts.

The United States did not join in these wars, but it did share in the advantages gained by them. In 1844 the United States and China signed a commercial treaty which gave the United States certain trading privileges in that vast land. Ten years later the American navy took a hand in the process of "opening up the Orient."

Commodore Perry Opens Japan

Japan was even more isolated than China. Only one European ship a year could visit one port. With western merchants eager for enlarged Far Eastern trade—as they had been since Columbus' day—some western

From the time that trade with the West had begun in the sixteenth century, China tried to limit western influence by confining merchants to certain areas. Contacts between Chinese and European public officials, like the meeting seen at left, were polite, formal, and not very frequent. The big break for English merchants came in 1842 when the Chinese were forced to sign a treaty opening two more ports. Similar treaties with other western nations, including the United States, soon followed. By 1854 the port of Hong Kong, seen above, was jammed with clipper ships and side-wheel steamers.

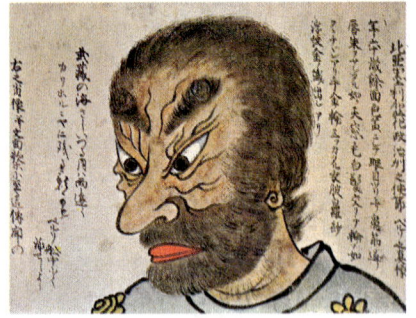

HONOLULU ACADEMY OF ARTS

CARL BOEHRINGER COLLECTION

The ship at right is a woodblock print by a Japanese artist who also included the ship's dimensions and the number of arms on board in the box at top right. The water color below shows Perry's fleet off present-day Yokohama. The note at left begins, "This morning I have seen for the first time the black ships of the barbarians."

MR. AND MRS. HAROLD GREHAN, JR., COLLECTION

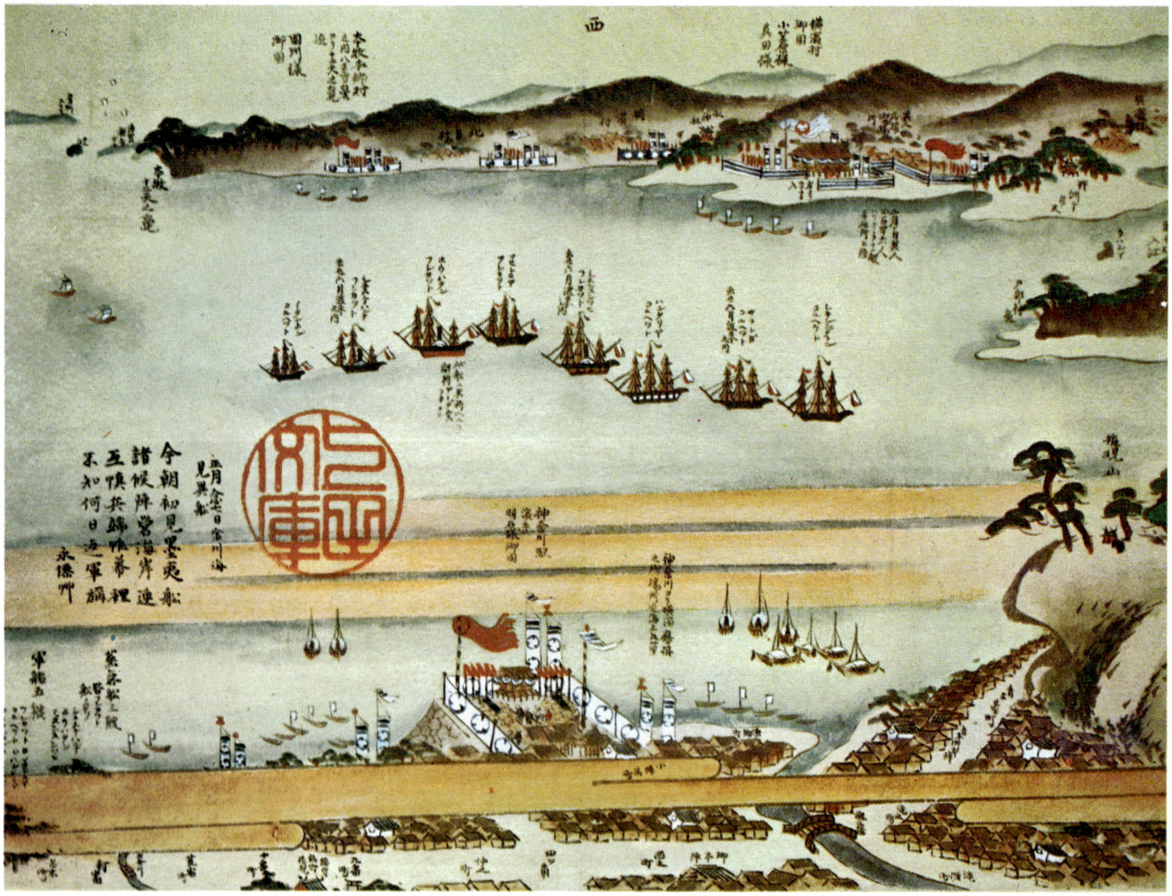

530

country was bound to try to force open Japan's door.

The United States became involved through its busy whaling industry. Its whaling vessels roamed the Pacific in pursuit of the great sea creatures, which provided valuable oil. Some of these ships were wrecked on Japan's coasts. The survivors were imprisoned by the Japanese as foreign "invaders." In 1852, therefore, President Millard Fillmore sent a naval expedition under Commodore Matthew C. Perry (right) to "request" a treaty that would protect shipwrecked American sailors from seizure. But Fillmore also believed, like his fellow members of the Whig Party, that a navy should not just fight battles, but help the nation's commerce to grow. So Perry was also to try to get one or more Japanese ports opened to American trade.

Perry conducted his errand with great skill. He was told to be tough if needed, but not to involve the United States in war. In July of 1853 he sailed his ships boldly into forbidden Tokyo Bay and ignored Japanese orders to leave. He refused to see minor Japanese officials, but remained hidden in his cabin and sent word that he had a letter from the President to the emperor and would deliver it in person only to someone of the highest rank. Six tense days passed before this game of bluff worked.

A meeting was held between the Japanese and Americans. The Americans displayed many gifts, including industrial products, tools, guns, a camera, and even a model steam train which chugged around a circular track, carrying solemn Japanese noblemen. Japanese artists sketched Perry, the American sailors, and the American ships (left) in the style of their country.

Perry left Japan to give the Japanese time to think over his offer. When he returned the following February, Japanese leaders were convinced of the advantages of commerce, industry—and arms! They signed a treaty opening two ports to Americans and admitting United States diplomatic officials into their country. This opened a long period of American-Japanese trade and also began a steady march by Japan toward modernization. Young America had helped to stimulate the growth of a new power in Asia.

Prophets of Imperialism

By the eve of the Civil War, the United States itself was becoming a Pacific power. It had treaties with

LIBRARY OF CONGRESS

Before his successful mission to Japan, Commodore Matthew C. Perry was better known as the younger brother of Oliver Hazzard Perry, the naval hero of the War of 1812. Compare the 1848 daguerreotype above with the portrait of Perry on the opposite page drawn by an unknown Japanese artist.

China and Japan. In Hawaii, an ideal stopping-off point for ships bound across the Pacific, American influence was growing swiftly. American missionaries had set up schools and were becoming educational advisers to Hawaii's kings. American businessmen had made Hawaii another frontier. They owned sugar plantations and trading firms and were playing a large role in directing the islands' economic life. They were Hawaiian citizens, but only in the way that early Texas settlers had been "Mexican" citizens.

Some Americans believed that Manifest Destiny called for American leadership in Asia as well as North America. A few actually wanted to take over some Asian territory to provide bases for American naval and merchant vessels—places to make repairs and to get fuel, supplies, and protection. On returning home Commodore Perry urged that the United States take Okinawa, annex Hawaii, and establish a **protectorate** (a relationship of protection and partial control by a superior power over a dependent country or region) over Formosa. His feelings were not shared by Congress, for while many people favored some form of expansion, few would go so far as to advocate annexation of overseas territories.

Some expansionists urged that the United States treat Asian nations with the respect given to other governments. Townsend Harris, American consul general to Japan in 1858, worked hard for a trade agreement more favorable to the Japanese, and got it. Anson Burlingame, who became American minister to China in 1861, was anxious to prevent the great powers from carving up China's lands among themselves. He was so good at presenting Chinese views to foreign diplomats that when the emperor wished to send a mission to western nations in 1867, he asked Burlingame to head it. In 1868 Burlingame, accompanied by his staff (right), arranged a treaty with the United States by which each country allowed free entry to citizens of the other country.

HAYES MEMORIAL LIBRARY

Men like Harris and Burlingame did not object to the growth of American influence in Asia. But they believed that trans-Pacific trade would achieve this result in such a way as to help both countries.

Seward Snags Alaska

The chief advocate of United States imperialism in the 1860's was hawk-beaked Secretary of State William

In 1867 the retiring American minister to China, Anson Burlingame, was appointed to head China's first diplomatic mission to western nations. The United States signed a treaty with his mission in part to provide cheap labor for the building of the transcontinental railroad.

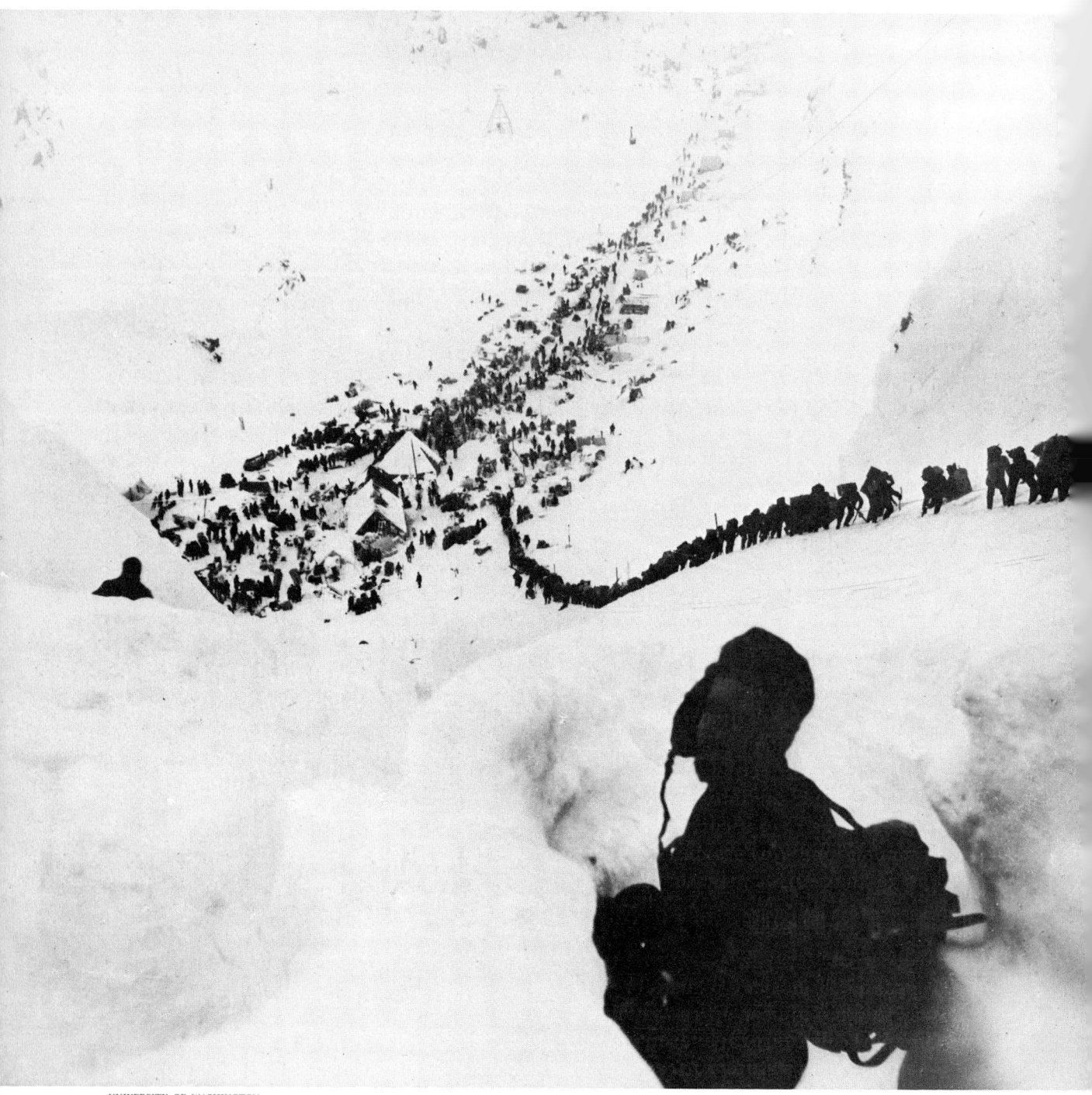

William H. Seward (top, right), who arranged to buy Alaska, did not guess its real value. In 1897 gold prospectors rushed to the coastal town of Dyea. From there they had to cross Dyea Canyon (right) and the Chilkoot Pass (above) to reach the mining fields. In the winter some miners hired Chilkat Indians to carry packs as they struggled single file up the 1,200 steps cut out of the hard snow.

H. Seward (upper right). He was a lawyer from upstate New York who served as governor for one term before entering the Senate in 1849.

As Secretary of State from 1861 to 1869, Seward saw his biggest task (after the Civil War ended) as one of helping American traders, bankers, and manufacturers to bring progress, through their goods and skills, to the non-industrialized world. He thought it would require the peaceful American take-over of lands with good raw materials, customers for American products, and ports located along trade routes for American ships. At different times he tried to get the Congress to buy Cuba, Puerto Rico, the Virgin Islands, Santo Domingo, and Hawaii. But he only won permission to annex the Midway Islands, two tiny dots of land west of Hawaii (see map, page 527).

He did, however, score one huge success. In 1867 he learned that the Russians wanted to sell Alaska, their only North American colony. Its fur trade was no longer profitable, and besides, the czar feared that the weak Russian navy could not protect it in case of a war with Russia's biggest rival at that time, Great Britain. Swiftly, Seward opened talks with the Russian ambassador. A price of $7.2 million was finally arranged.

Seward's real problem was to persuade Congress to vote the money to carry out the treaty. Most Congressmen thought of Alaska as a "dreary waste of glaciers, icebergs, . . .and walruses." But Seward persisted and won. In 1896, long after his death, his faith was rewarded. Gold was struck in the "dreary waste," and thousands of prospectors (left and lower right) rushed there in search of fortune. Sixty-three years later, in 1959, Alaska became a state, with still untapped wealth in fish, lumber, coal, natural gas, oil, and other natural resources. In time almost all the islands that Seward wanted became American-owned or American-dominated.

Island-Grabbing Across the Pacific

In the 25 years after Seward left office, the United States reached out for stepping stones across the Pacific. As early as 1873 a cartoonist showed America and Russia reaching for new territory and keeping a sharp eye on each other (page 537, top). In 1878 the United States had signed a treaty with the native king of the Samoan Islands, giving Americans a naval base

CULVER PICTURES

LIBRARY OF CONGRESS

at Pago Pago. (In 1899 the United States annexed some of the islands, and Germany took the rest.) In 1887 Hawaii gave the United States exclusive trading privileges and the right to refuel and repair warships at Pearl Harbor. By 1890 more than 90 per cent of Hawaii's exports came to the United States.

As the 1890's began the prosperous American sugar growers of Hawaii faced some hardships. Since 1875 their sugar had been admitted duty-free to the United States, where it faced little competition. But in 1890 Congress lowered duties on Cuban sugar and also gave subsidies to American producers, in order to cut sugar prices. Such favoritism was a harsh blow to the Hawaiian planters. The price which they received for a ton of sugar dropped from $100 to $60. In addition, a new monarch, Queen Liliuokalani (right), took the throne and tried to reduce the influence of Americans in the government. This drew all of the islands' American businessmen together in resistance.

BROWN BROTHERS

Early in 1893 they proceeded to stage a bloodless revolution. Help arrived when landing parties from a United States cruiser went ashore to "preserve order" and keep Hawaiians loyal to the queen from interfering. Americans in Hawaii occupied government buildings, declared Liliuokalani deposed, and set up a temporary government. Then the Austins and Houstons of the Hawaiian Republic followed the Texas example and asked the United States to annex them.

Their wishes were delayed because a treaty was still under consideration in the Senate where a fierce argument raged over annexation. When Democrat Grover Cleveland, who opposed new territorial additions, took office in 1893, he withdrew the treaty from the Senate and even tried, without success, to get the temporary government to step down. But in 1898 the McKinley administration easily completed the work of annexation. By then the United States, through war, had taken up the **white man's burden** (the idea that white men had a duty to civilize "backward" peoples of other races).

Questions for Discussion

1. What products did the Americans sell to the Chinese and the Chinese sell to the Americans?
2. What were the purposes of Perry's visits to Japan?
3. Why did Seward purchase Alaska?
4. How did the United States acquire Hawaii?

Louis Choris, a young Russian on a round-the-world voyage in 1816, painted the water color of Honolulu below. Four years later the first Christian missionaries from America were shocked to find that Honolulu had "not one white cottage, no church spire, not a garden." But their families stayed on and came to dominate the island's economy. The 1873 cartoon at right shows Uncle Sam's growing interest in the Sandwich Islands, as the Hawaiian Islands were then known. At left is Queen Liliuokalani who tried to assert native control and was deposed after just two years as queen.

By 1904, when the photograph at right was taken, Alfred T. Mahan had seen his philosophy on the importance of sea power win worldwide acceptance. In December 1907 President Theodore Roosevelt sent a naval fleet of 16 battleships and 12,000 men on a round-the-world cruise. Seen below, the fleet visited 20 nations before returning in February 1909. Roosevelt hailed the cruise as "The most important service that I rendered to peace."

LIBRARY OF CONGRESS

U. S. NAVY

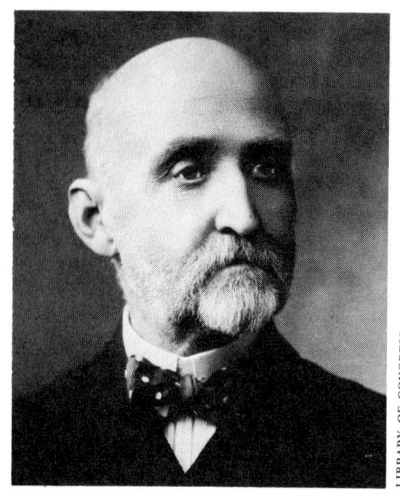

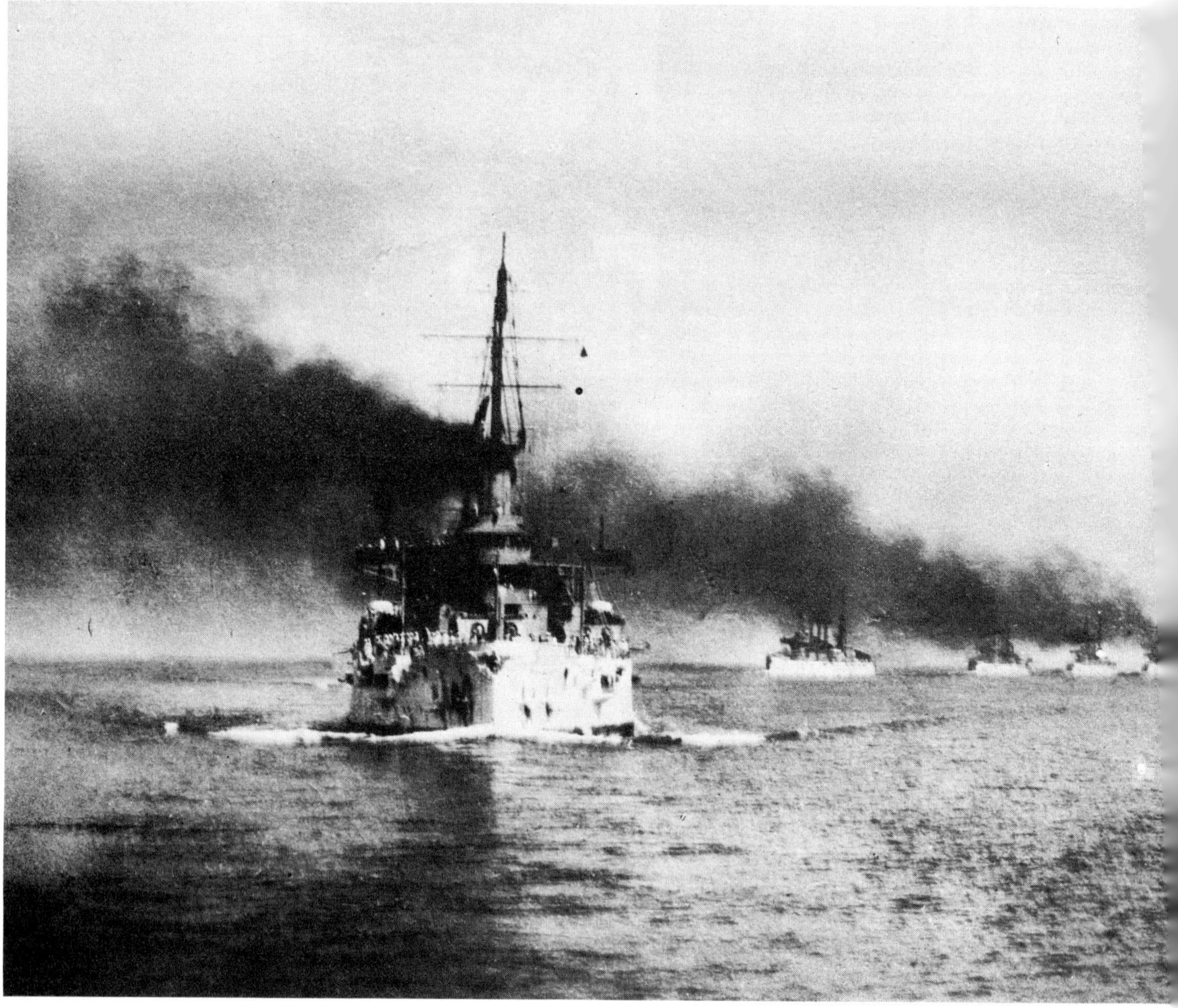

A New Global Power

By 1890 American businessmen and officials already had a great deal of influence in Asian countries. This was a kind of imperialism, limited to using economic and diplomatic pressure. Before the United States could become a full-fledged imperialist power—with colonies of its own or areas which it "protected" by actually ruling their peoples—Americans had to change some of their customary beliefs. One such deep-rooted attitude was a dislike of permanent large armies and navies.

But this feeling began to change, so far as the navy was concerned, around 1890. Pressure mounted to build an up-to-date fleet. Some of that pressure came from **jingoism** (an exaggerated national pride that approves of tests of military strength). Some came from manufacturers who hoped to profit by building new warships. And some was created by businessmen who were beginning to worry about a hidden danger of industrial growth. What if America's farms and factories produced too much for its own people to consume? Unsold goods would pile up; factories would close down; depression would grip the land. The United States must be sure of having other markets. The answer, to some, was in more foreign sales.

Building a Modern Navy

But trade on the high seas needed protection. This was the argument of Captain Alfred T. Mahan (top, left) in an 1890 book, *The Influence of Seapower on History*. Captain Mahan claimed that history's leading powers at different times—Spain, Holland, England—had owned great merchant fleets and unbeatable navies. Benjamin Tracy, Secretary of the Navy, echoed Mahan's influential work when he said, "The sea will be the future seat of empire. And we shall rule it."

Tracy spurred a program of construction that converted the navy from a group of aging wooden ships to a fast, powerfully armed force of armor-plated vessels. Only an industrial nation such as the United States or Great Britain or Germany could afford to build and keep a modern fleet, with its huge demands for steel, complex machinery, coal, and oil. So when President Theodore Roosevelt sent the new United States fleet (left), painted white for peace, on a good-will cruise around the world in 1907, he was announcing that America had become a mighty power both militarily *and* industrially.

Dewey, Manila, and the Philippines

Like a racing car gathering speed, the United States rushed toward actual possession or control of overseas territories. Two years before the twentieth century began, the arguments for a big navy, overseas bases, and world leadership were put to an actual test.

In April of 1898 a crisis between the United States and Spain over the future of Cuba burst into war (see the following chapter). Halfway around the world from Cuba, a small squadron of American warships in Asian waters was already under secret orders from Assistant Secretary of the Navy Theodore Roosevelt. In the event of war with Spain, it was to rush to Manila and attack Spain's fleet in the Spanish-owned Philippine Islands. On May 1, only a week after Congress declared war, Admiral George Dewey (top, left) carried out his mission with astounding success. In a short battle (upper right) the Spanish fleet was wiped out without any American losses.

Then a problem arose. In August Spain surrendered. What should the United States do with the Philippines? After much soul-searching President McKinley found an answer. He told of how he prayed in the White House at midnight for God's help. We could not, he said, give them back to Spain without dishonor. We could not let commercial rivals like France or Germany seize them. Nor could we leave them alone, for they were "unfit for self-government.... There was nothing left...but to take them all, and to educate the Filipinos, and uplift and Christianize them."

But some Filipinos, led by General Emilio Aguinaldo (below, left) who had been fighting against the Spaniards, did not think themselves "unfit for self-government." They had welcomed liberation from Spain and had expected to become a free nation. When they learned of American plans for annexation, they revolted. This gave a new, unexpected look to the glories of empire. Suddenly, American soldiers were fighting in jungles and villages against Asians like the prisoners shown below, right. They were battling guerrilla warriors who met superior weapons with cunning and courage and melted back among their own people when pursued. It was three years before the rebellion was broken. The horror stories that reached the United States about the conduct of American troops shocked the nation into a hot debate on what imperialism would actually do to American ideals.

Below: Emilio Aguinaldo led the Filipinos against Spanish rule and then against American rule.

CULVER PICTURES

At top left is Admiral George Dewey, hero of the Battle of Manila Bay, seen in the painting above. The photograph below shows Filipinos held prisoners by the American army.

The Anti-Imperialists Take a Stand

The election of 1900 was considered a test of public feeling on imperialism. A vote for McKinley, running for re-election, was supposedly a vote for empire. The arguments for empire in the Pacific were summed up vigorously by a young Senator from Indiana, Albert J. Beveridge, in the words, "The Pacific is our ocean."

But voices of opposition were raised by a group of Americans which included businessmen like Andrew Carnegie, authors like Mark Twain, and political leaders like former President Cleveland. These anti-imperialists argued that Americans were facing an impossible choice. They could not annex islands like the Philippines and admit them to the Union, for even the anti-imperialists believed that "tropical people" were not ready for self-rule. Yet to take in peoples without the promise of eventual statehood would deny the basic American promise of liberty and equality for all men. Moreover, empire would force on the United States a huge army and navy. There would also be an "army" of colonial officials, tempted to corruption—super-bosses in the making. And empire's profits would go to a few great organizers of trusts in hemp, sugar, tobacco, lumber, and other tropical products.

Anti-imperialists felt strongly that the war in the Philippines would betray everything the United States stood for. They published bitter cartoons (left) and pamphlets. "We have desolated homes and burned villages," said one, "and...we have created hatred of ourselves in the breasts of millions of people." The platform of an anti-imperialist league, organized in 1899, rang out, "We deny that the obligation of all citizens to support their Government in times of grave National peril applies to the present situation."

But the anti-imperialists lost, as McKinley won the election. In the long run neither the evils foreseen by the anti-imperialists nor the benefits promised by the imperialists came entirely to pass. After 1916 the United States allowed the Philippines greater self-government. Finally, in response to Filipino demands, Congress agreed to free the islands in 1946.

The Open Door Policy

In the early twentieth century, the policies of major industrial nations toward China showed how it was possible to extend economic control over an area without actually occupying it. In 1899 England, Germany,

This 1899 cartoon makes a strong case against imperialism by emphasizing the horrors of American policy in the Philippines.

Russia, and Japan, by then a powerful modern state, were making demands that went well beyond the trading of former years. Each wanted special trading and military privileges at certain ports. Each wanted a particular Chinese region reserved for its own businessmen to carry on profitable activities. Such a region was called a **sphere of influence.**

John Hay, America's Secretary of State from 1898 to 1905, feared that the United States might be shut out of China's markets and investment opportunities. So he proposed that all major powers agree to an "Open Door" policy in their spheres. They should give businessmen of all countries equal rights. Hay also urged other nations not to cut up China by annexing their spheres. Since no nation was willing to disagree publicly, Hay announced they all had agreed. The United States thus appeared as the defender of China's **territorial integrity** (the right of a nation to have its boundaries respected by all other nations).

But the United States would use troops in China when necessary. In 1900 a Chinese patriotic society known as the Boxers began a rebellion. Its members were young Chinese nationalists, tired of seeing the imperial rulers give in to foreigners. They began to attack and kill western businessmen and their western employees as well as missionaries and their Chinese converts. The Europeans fled to their embassies in Peking, where the Boxers surrounded them (right). An international force, including 2,500 United States soldiers and marines, finally fought its way into Peking. The uprising collapsed and China's territorial integrity seemed insured when the international force withdrew.

Nevertheless, China continued to suffer the fate of a weak power among strong ones. Japan in particular became more and more influential in North China. The United States and Japan agreed, by the Root-Takahira Agreement of 1908, to respect China's territorial integrity and recognize each other's rights to do business in China. The engineers, bankers, and manufacturers of both nations continued to play a dominating role in China's life.

Questions for Discussion

1. Why was there an outcry around 1890 to create a large navy?
2. What was the purpose of Hay's Open Door policy?
3. Why did the United States intervene in China?

In this Chinese print done for propaganda purposes, fierce Boxer troops use bayonets, sabers, cannon, and dynamite to drive the hated foreigners from Tientsin. After the rebellion collapsed the city was governed for seven years by an international commission.

BOTH: NEW-YORK HISTORICAL SOCIETY

This grocery store owner in San Francisco's Chinatown posed for a photograph next to his display of fresh vegetables.

When East Meets West

While adventurous nineteenth-century Americans sought their fortunes in China, thousands of Chinese crossed the Pacific in the opposite direction for the same reason. At first they came to look for gold in California in 1849. Then many settled in the West's growing towns. Few had the money to buy a farm, and so many Chinese became cooks and laundrymen. American pioneers often thought such jobs unmanly, but Chinese men did not think it was only women's work to feed people or do laundry. Beginning in 1868 Chinese laborers, willing to work for low wages, came in large numbers to help build the West's railroads. In 1870 about 90 per cent of California's agricultural labor was Chinese. Some moved eastward to settle in other American states. But the bulk of Chinese immigrants to the United States remained in the Pacific and Rocky Mountain states.

The Chinese gave American life a special flavor. Their homes and shops (far left) brought exotic foods, incense, pictures, carvings, and other arts of a civilization thousands of years old to raw pioneer settlements. Yet the Chinese people were not welcomed by Americans.

In part the Chinese tendency to live in neighborhoods of their own came from their strong sense of family and community. But the hostility of Americans also drove them together. Too often white Americans scorned Oriental peoples and cultures. The Chinese who worked for "coolie" wages, though they had no control over what they were paid, were accused of deliberately choosing a standard of living lower than that of Americans. Other racial accusations were made. Their "odd" clothes, food, and religion were unjustly mocked. Soon anti-Chinese riots broke out. Workingmen, who were led to believe that their low wages were the direct result of Chinese competition, burned Chinese shops and beat and killed their owners (left). Finally, western states demanded that further Chinese immigrants be barred.

In 1882 Congress willingly passed a Chinese Exclusion Act forbidding the immigration of Chinese laborers. Yet the Burlingame Treaty had given each nation's citizens the right to travel and live freely in either country. President Arthur argued that the United States could not break its word and vetoed the measure. It was repassed over his veto. Only Chinese businessmen, diplomats, and scholars could enter the

This 1880 newspaper sketch shows the anti-Chinese riot in Denver.

United States now. Court decisions denied all Chinese the right of naturalization. No western nation's peoples were so humiliated.

Around 1900 Japanese immigrants began to arrive in the West. They became farm workers and gardeners; many soon owned their own farms and businesses. The same anti-Oriental feelings that barred Chinese were again aroused. Californians now demanded that the Japanese, like the Chinese, be excluded as "undesirable." The government of Japan prevented this embarrassment by signing a "Gentlemen's Agreement" with the United States in 1907. Under it Japan itself would not allow its laborers to emigrate to America, so no insulting anti-Japanese law was needed.

By 1910 it was clear that many Americans were willing to sell to Oriental customers and generously provide schools, hospitals, missions, and charity to poverty-stricken Oriental peoples—provided that they stayed on their own side of the Pacific!

Questions for Discussion

1. What economic opportunities attracted Chinese immigrants to the United States?
2. Why was the Chinese Exclusion Act passed? Do you think cultural conflict was involved? Why?
3. What was the purpose of the "Gentlemen's Agreement" worked out between the United States and Japanese governments in 1907?

Chapter Review

Social Studies Terms

imperialism, protectorate, white man's burden, jingoism, sphere of influence, territorial integrity

Summary Questions for Discussion

1. What were the forces that led the United States to become a major power in the Pacific?
2. Why did Westerners accused of crimes in China object to being tried in Chinese courts?
3. Why were the Chinese at a disadvantage in trying to keep foreigners out of their country?
4. How did the United States share in the gains made by foreigners in their wars with China without itself taking part in those wars?
5. Can a nation cut itself off from all other nations, having little or no trade or other contact with them? Is such a policy desirable? Why?
6. Why did some Americans want the United States to

acquire territories overseas even before all of the land in their own country was settled?
7. Did Seward purchase Alaska for the same reasons that Jefferson purchased Louisiana? Defend your answer.
8. How did Americans gain control of Hawaii's commerce, land, and government?
9. Why was the settlement of Americans in lands outside the borders of the United States nearly always followed by annexation? Why was violence nearly always a part of this process?
10. Why did a revolution break out in the Philippines after the United States won them from Spain?
11. Were American laborers fair in blaming Chinese immigrants for low wages in certain industries? Why?
12. Why do the customs of the peoples of other nations often seem "odd" to Americans?
13. Who was more far-sighted and wise: the prophets of imperialism or the anti-imperialists? Why?

Map Study

Study the possessions acquired by the United States on the map on page 527. Which major nations shown on the map might be concerned about the growth of American power in the Pacific? Why?

For Further Reading

Commodore Perry in Japan, by Robert L. Reynolds. New York: American Heritage Publishing Co., Inc., 1963.

George Dewey, by Frederika Shumway Smith. Chicago: Rand McNally & Co., 1963.

Hawaii, by Oscar Lewis. New York: Random House, Inc., 1954.

Hawaii, Fiftieth Star, by A. Grove Day. New York: Duell, Sloan and Pearce, 1966.

Here Is Alaska, by Evelyn Stefansson. New York: Charles Scribner's Sons, 1959.

The Alaska Gold Rush, by May McNeer. New York: Random House, Inc., 1960.

The Boxer Rebellion, by Christopher Martin. London: Abelard-Schuman Limited, 1968.

William McKinley, by Edwin P. Hoyt. Chicago: Reilly & Lee Books, 1967.

19

The United States and Latin America

When the United States began life as a nation, Europeans had been colonizing the Western Hemisphere for almost three hundred years. Spain, France, Portugal, Holland, and England had helped themselves freely to gold, silver, fish, furs, timber, and the fertile lands of both American continents. They had fought frequently over these riches. It seemed likely that they would go on doing so. In that case it was probable that the new little republic would soon be crushed by the continuing rivalry of European giants in the New World.

Yet from the beginning some American statesmen worked to avoid this fate. They dreamed of a day when the United States itself would be too strong to be threatened. History worked on their side. From 1792 to 1815 Europe's major powers were busy with problems of war and revolution at home. During that time revolutionary ideas reached the peoples of the Spanish colonies in Latin America. They too took up arms—as the thirteen English colonies had done—and declared themselves independent nations. In 1823 the President of the United States, James Monroe, seized this favorable opportunity to declare that Europeans must not return as conquerors.

This was a boastful statement from a small nation. Between that year and 1898 the United States added the strength that allowed it to back up the Monroe Doctrine. Year by year, its stunning economic growth gave weight to the arguments of its diplomats. The building of a modern navy gave the United States supremacy on the waters once sailed by the New World's explorers and sea fighters.

A new era began in 1900. Now, other nations realized that the United States was an international giant. The United States and its citizens used this might to get deeply involved in the affairs of other American states (map, right). United States diplomats soon claimed to speak for the entire hemisphere. United States dollars, troops, and cannon were major forces in the lives of its southern neighbors. Not until after World War I did the United States move toward more cooperative Latin American policies.

As you read, think about these questions:
1. Why did the United States become involved in Latin America?
2. What caused the United States policy in Latin America to change between 1812 and 1917?

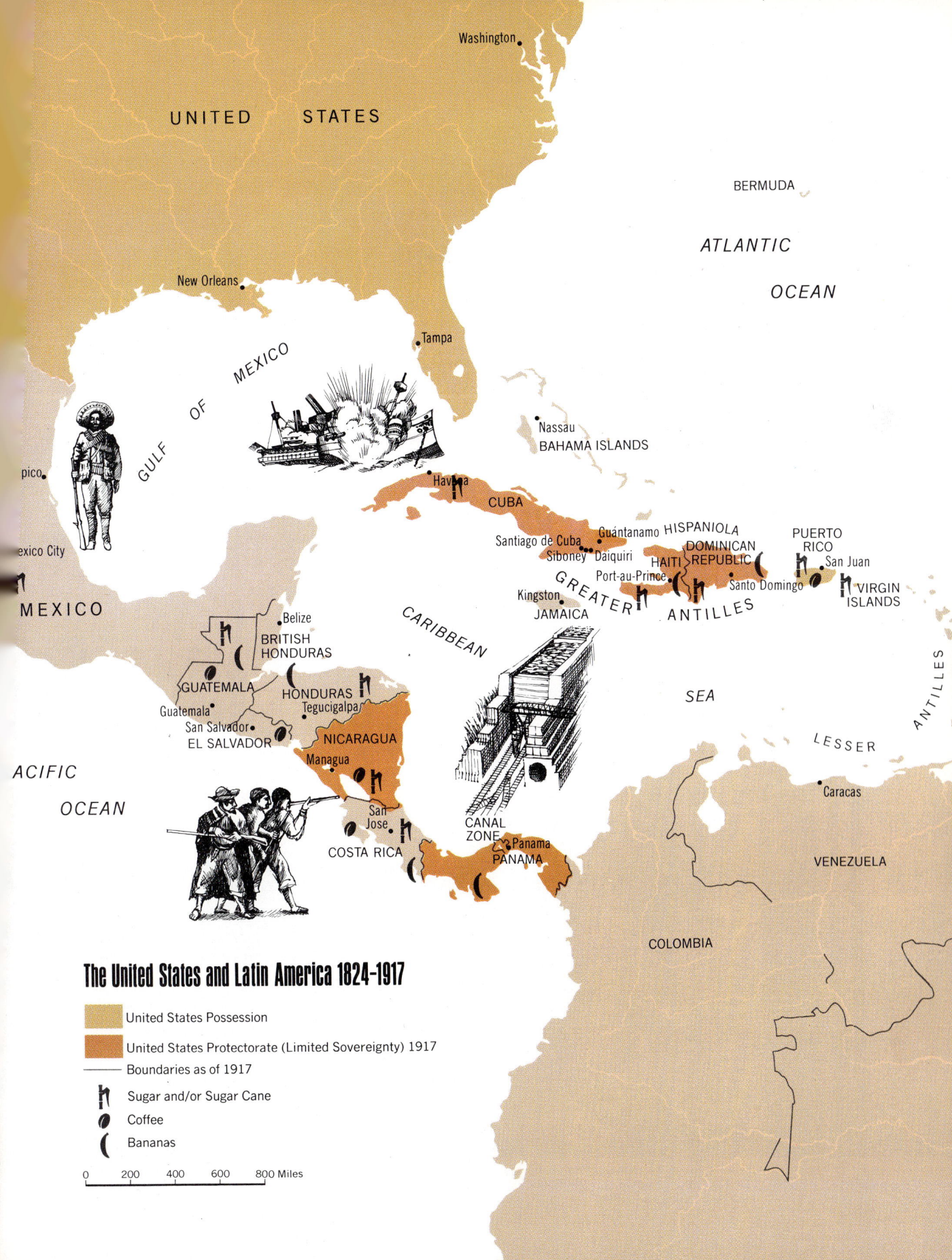

This cartoon appeared in *Puck* less than a month after Theodore Roosevelt was inaugurated. It foretold the tough-minded interpretation he was to give to the Monroe Doctrine. In the cartoon's caption Europe is saying, "You're not the only rooster in South America." Uncle Sam replies, "I was aware of that when I cooped you up."

An Awakening Interest

In 1821 Secretary of State John Quincy Adams felt pleased. The breakaway of Spain's New World colonies had reduced the threat that he feared most—European armies poised to attack the United States from European possessions close to its borders. Moreover, with Spanish trade restrictions lifted, United States merchants were finding good customers in Latin America.

But by 1823 clouds had gathered on Mr. Adams' horizon. In 1815 the monarchs of Prussia, Russia, and Austria formed a "Holy Alliance" for putting down revolutions—especially democratic revolutions—everywhere. In 1821 the Russian czar suddenly claimed that Alaska extended southward into the Oregon territory. Moreover, there was talk of Spain, with French help, attempting to win back its South American colonies. Was a new round of European expansion in the Americas about to begin?

Adams had one piece of comforting information. In order for Spain to reconquer its colonies, Great Britain, mistress of the seas, would have to remain neutral. But Great Britain had no wish to see its old enemy, Spain, regain power or to allow any other European nation to grow dangerously strong by taking American lands.

Knowing this, Adams and President James Monroe drew up a statement that became known as the Monroe Doctrine. In a message to Congress in December 1823, Monroe declared that the United States did not wish to see Europeans spread their political system to the Western Hemisphere by interfering with governments that had already declared their independence. While the United States recognized the right of European countries to keep their remaining American colonies, the Americas were no longer "subjects for future colonization by any European power."

Monroe did not make threats. Nor did he claim that the United States should be supreme in the Americas. Later Presidents were to give the Monroe Doctrine a jingoistic interpretation, like that expressed in the 1901 cartoon at left. But in 1823 Adams and Monroe were more concerned with the security of the United States than with strutting. The Monroe Doctrine was probably not responsible for the fact that Russia did not press its Alaskan claims or that Spain did not attempt to regain its lost colonies. Yet such a declaration was bold and revolutionary. It proposed a new policy,

barring the mighty countries of Europe from any new imperial adventures in Latin America.

American Adventurers in Latin America

In the early 1850's Central America began to tempt certain United States citizens. Some were wealthy businessmen, like Cornelius Vanderbilt who hoped to build rail, steamboat, and canal lines across Central America to the gold fields of California. They needed land and special legal rights, much like those later granted by urban bosses to transportation promoters in American cities. Most Central American rulers were willing to sell such rights and pocket the money themselves. They were often dictators with little popular support and in danger of being overthrown by some other "strong man."

A second group of "Yankees" wanted to do more than just make deals with Central American rulers. They wanted to replace the rulers. Many were Southerners who believed that Manifest Destiny made it easy, natural, and right for them to enter a Latin American nation with a few followers and seize control of it by their skill and daring. A few were secretly encouraged by southern politicians who saw an opportunity to add slave territory. Little bands of such adventurers, called "filibusters," slipped out of the United States for raids on Cuba, Mexico, or points south.

The only successful filibuster, for a short time, was William Walker (top, right). Tennessee-born, he was trained in law and medicine but later became a New Orleans journalist. The doctor longed for greatness. In 1855, with the approval of Vanderbilt, Walker and some fifty "emigrants" sailed for Nicaragua. There, he joined and became the leader of a small guerrilla force in revolt against the government. In four months his troops captured the capital. Walker, who later made himself president, had great visions of uniting the Central American states, introducing slavery, and digging a canal from the Atlantic to the Pacific.

Then his dream collapsed. Walker quarreled with Vanderbilt and seized the property of Vanderbilt's company in Nicaragua. But Vanderbilt struck back by financing an invasion of Nicaragua by its neighbors. By April 1857 Walker was defeated and forced to return to New Orleans. In 1860, on another invasion, he was captured and died—aged 36—before a firing squad.

LIBRARY OF CONGRESS

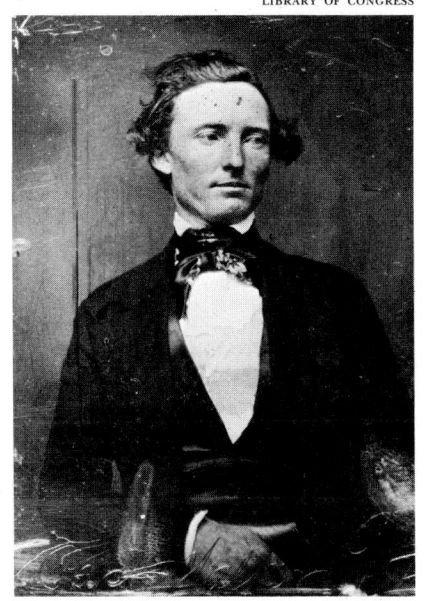

Left: William Walker's filibustering campaign in Nicaragua was not his first. In 1853 he led a force into Lower California, declared it independent from Mexico, and named himself president. Mexican troops forced him out, but his actions were so popular in the United States that a jury acquitted him of violating the neutrality laws. His invasion of Nicaragua was supported by American interests there, and, in May 1856, the United States recognized Walker's group as the official government of Nicaragua. Below: Troops loyal to Walker land at Virgin Bay, Nicaragua. They were on their way to fight a coalition of Central American forces financed by another American—Cornelius Vanderbilt. Walker was forced to flee, but he was welcomed as a hero in many parts of the United States. His attempts to regain control of Nicaragua ended when he was sentenced to death—before a firing squad—by a Central American military court.

CULVER PICTURES

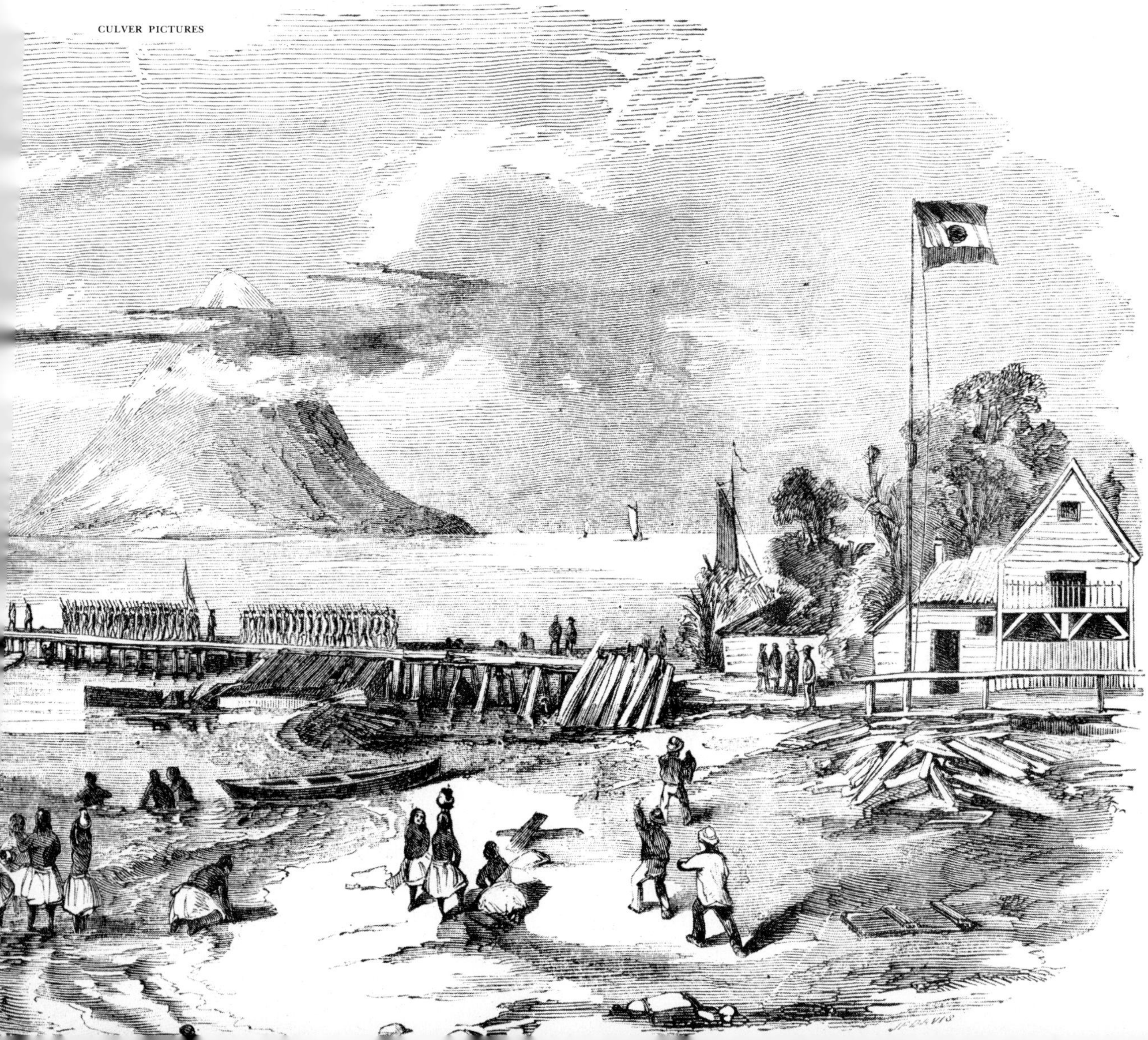

This 1897 Puck *cartoon was titled "Patient Waiters Are No Losers." A confident Uncle Sam expects Cuba, Canada, and Hawaii to fall into America's basket.*

A Growing Interest in Cuba

Other nations saw nothing romantic in Walker. They feared that such filibusters were the drum majors of a steady American march southward. Their fears seemed justified in 1854, when three American ambassadors in Europe met in the Belgian town of Ostend and drew up a secret report on Cuba for the Secretary of State. They suggested that if Spain refused to sell Cuba the United States then would have the right, "by every law, human and divine," to seize it. The report was leaked to the press and became known as the Ostend Manifesto. It created such a furor that the Secretary of State was forced to announce that the United States had no intention of seizing Cuba.

Yet actually long before 1854 Cuba had tempted Americans. Even John Quincy Adams had declared that a law of "political gravitation" would make it drop like an apple into the American basket (cartoon, top left) as soon as its "unnatural" connection to the Spanish tree was broken.

After the Civil War Americans revived their interest in Cuba's harbors, mines, forests, ranches, and plantations. Secretary of State Seward tried to buy

Several times in the 1890's the United States found itself on the brink of war over disputes involving Latin America. In addition, Latin Americans resented the high American tariffs on their goods. This 1897 Puck *cartoon suggests why the "romance" between the United States and Latin America was in trouble.*

Cuba as well as other Caribbean islands, but failed. Busy with Reconstruction and encouraging economic growth, the lawmakers had no interest in island-grabbing. At that time and in the 1880's, Americans were more concerned with adding markets than adding territory to the United States. James G. Blaine, Secretary of State from 1889 to 1892, urged a reduction of tariffs on animal hides, sugar, and other products of Latin American countries if those countries would agree to buy more American-made goods.

Then, in 1895, a rebellion broke out in Cuba against Spain. In waging their guerrilla war, the rebels burned plantations, ambushed Spanish troops, and assassinated officials. In turn, the Spaniards arrested and tortured suspected rebels. In order to keep an eye on Cuban villagers, the Spanish army put civilians in prison camps where thousands died of hunger and disease.

Questions for Discussion
1. Why was the Monroe Doctrine announced?
2. What role did filibusters play in the affairs of Central American countries?

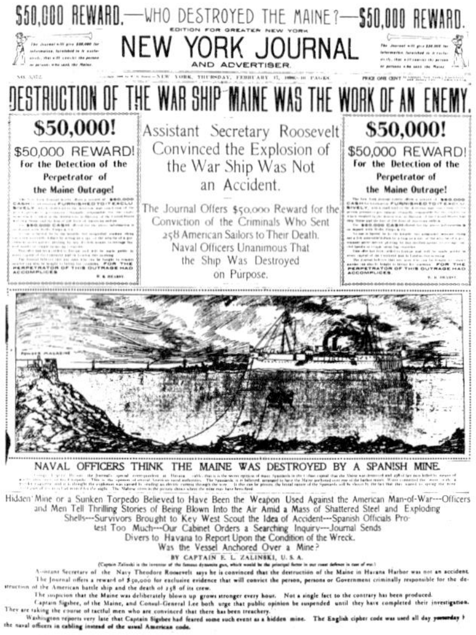

$50,000 REWARD.—WHO DESTROYED THE MAINE?—$50,000 REWARD.

EDITION FOR GREATER NEW YORK

NEW YORK JOURNAL

AND ADVERTISER.

NEW YORK, THURSDAY, FEBRUARY 17, 1898.

PRICE ONE CENT

DESTRUCTION OF THE WAR SHIP MAINE WAS THE WORK OF AN ENEMY.

$50,000!

$50,000 REWARD!

For the Detection of the Perpetrator of the Maine Outrage!

Assistant Secretary Roosevelt Convinced the Explosion of the War Ship Was Not an Accident.

The Journal Offers $50,000 Reward for the Conviction of the Criminals Who Sent 258 American Sailors to Their Death. Naval Officers Unanimous That the Ship Was Destroyed on Purpose.

$50,000!

$50,000 REWARD!

For the Detection of the Perpetrator of the Maine Outrage!

NAVAL OFFICERS THINK THE MAINE WAS DESTROYED BY A SPANISH MINE.

Hidden Mine or a Sunken Torpedo Believed to Have Been the Weapon Used Against the American Man-of-War---Officers and Men Tell Thrilling Stories of Being Blown Into the Air Amid a Mass of Shattered Steel and Exploding Shells---Survivors Brought to Key West Scout the Idea of Accident---Spanish Officials Protest Too Much---Our Cabinet Orders a Searching Inquiry---Journal Sends Divers to Havana to Report Upon the Condition of the Wreck. Was the Vessel Anchored Over a Mine?

BY CAPTAIN E. L. ZALINSKI, U. S. A.

(Captain Zalinski is the inventor of the famous dynamite gun, which would be the principal factor in our coast defence in case of war.)

Assistant Secretary of the Navy Theodore Roosevelt says he is convinced that the destruction of the Maine in Havana Harbor was not an accident.

The Journal offers a reward of $50,000 for exclusive evidence that will convict the person, persons or Government criminally responsible for the destruction of the American battle ship and the death of 258 of its crew.

The suspicion that the Maine was deliberately blown up grows stronger every hour. Not a single fact to the contrary has been produced.

Captain Sigsbee, of the Maine, and Consul-General Lee both urge that public opinion be suspended until they have completed their investigation. They are taking the course of tactful men who are convinced that there has been treachery.

Washington reports very late that Captain Sigsbee had feared some such event as a hidden mine. The English cipher code was used all day yesterday by the naval officers in cabling instead of the usual American code.

CULVER PICTURES

HENRY E. HUNTINGTON LIBRARY

CHICAGO HISTORICAL SOCIETY

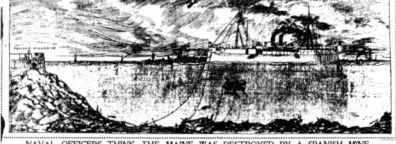

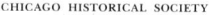

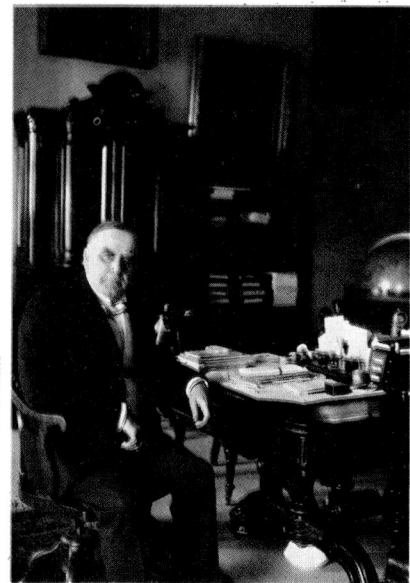

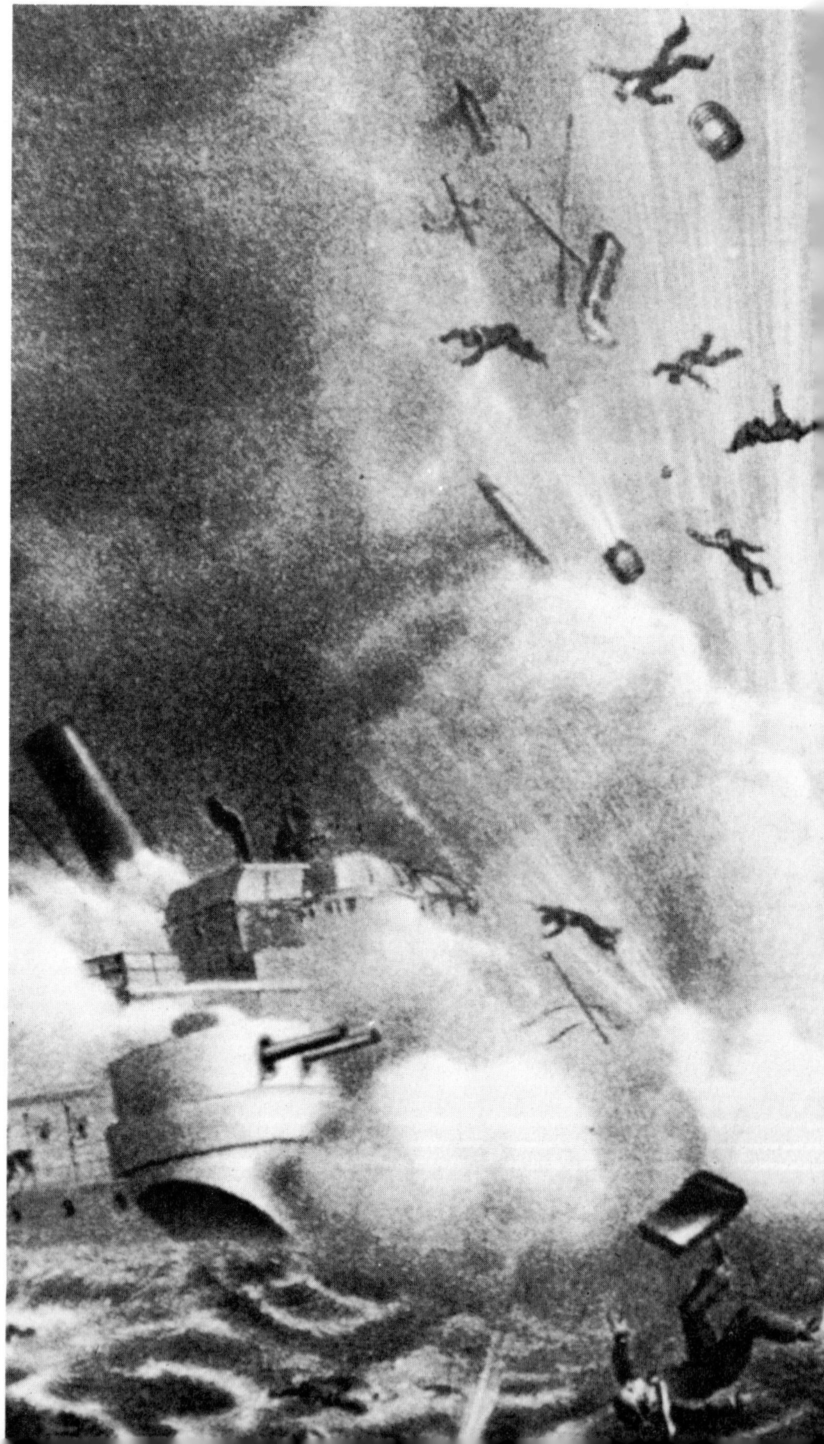

The New York Journal *(top) announces Spain is responsible for the sinking of the* Maine. *Gaudy paintings (right) fed the nation's growing demand for revenge. Within two months President William McKinley (above) asked for a declaration of war.*

The Spanish-American War

The horrors of the Cuban revolution were reported to Americans in the newspapers which were becoming an important part of city life. For two cents the average man got local and world news, news of sports and theater, advertisements, cartoons, stories, and advice-columns. Before movies, radio, or televison, millions of people looked to the newspaper to entertain them and to show them how the rest of the world lived. The press, therefore, had great power to shape public opinion and habits. Some of its power, as we saw, was used to expose political and urban evils. But a number of editors—sometimes the same ones who were political crusaders at home—also ran exaggerated news stories of bloody crimes and the private sins of people in public life. This kind of sensational journalism (sometimes known as yellow journalism, after a popular cartoon character known as "Yellow Kid") played a major role in determining foreign policy.

The New York *World*, owned by Joseph Pulitzer, and the New York *Journal*, of William Randolph Hearst, had as many as 300,000 daily readers and sold their news services to papers across the country. They competed for sensational news by publishing stories of Cuban atrocities in blood-spattered detail. They ran cartoons showing Spain's General Valeriano Weyler as a butcher or a gorilla. They staged "stunts" like that of the *Journal*, which sent a man to Havana to rescue an imprisoned eighteen-year-old Cuban rebel girl. He did so by sawing through the bars of her cell and getting her out disguised as a boy. Then he crowed to a record-breaking number of readers, "I have set free the beautiful captive of Monster Weyler."

Because of such stories, a wave of enthusiasm for Cuban independence swept the country. Joined with it was a wish to test America's "fitness" by battle. But not all Americans were in favor of war. President McKinley (lower left) kept urging the Spanish government to grant Cuba self-rule, but made no threats. But on the night of February 15, 1898, while on a peaceful visit to Havana's harbor, the United States battleship *Maine* exploded and sank (left), killing 260 of her men. To this day no one is sure what happened. But the *Journal* (upper left) and other jingoistic papers were quick to decide that the Spanish had planted an underwater mine to sink the ship. The war fever now became incurable. "Remember the Maine!" became a battle cry that drowned out voices of caution and compromise.

War and Invasion

McKinley sent an **ultimatum** (a statement threatening serious penalties if its terms are not accepted) to Spain. It demanded an end to the reconcentration camps and an immediate truce. On April 9, 1898, the Spanish government agreed to all of McKinley's demands. But it was too late. The hard-pressed McKinley had given in to the prowar hysteria and two days later asked Congress for a declaration of war. It was easily passed. An amendment by Colorado's Senator Henry Teller was added, promising that the United States would not annex Cuba.

The United States thus began the war with high spirits and idealism, but little preparation. Volunteers rushed to enlist and were hastily sent to training camps in Florida. There, because no summer uniforms were ready, they sweltered in tropical heat in woolen shirts. Some of their food was spoiled canned meat, which dishonest packers had sold to the government. The scandal of the "embalmed beef" helped to get Federal meat inspection provided for by law—but not until eight years later! There were barely enough ships to carry the attacking force to Siboney and Daiquiri, in Cuba, at the end of June. Almost no ships were available to follow with food and medical supplies. Siboney and Daiquiri had no wharves and warehouses, and the Americans were not equipped to build them. The photograph (right) shows Americans moving inland from Daiquiri toward their objective, the capital city of Santiago. Fortunately for the United States, the Spaniards did not counterattack.

At sea the picture was brighter. The naval building program of the 1890's proved valuable, as powerful American ships bottled up Spain's Atlantic fleet in Santiago harbor. On July 3 Admiral Pascual de Cervera led his few cruisers and destroyers in an effort to break out. In a few hours American guns turned every one of them into a flaming wreck. Four centuries of Spanish history in New World waters had come to an end.

The Battle for Santiago

Two days before this naval battle, American units on land had battled their way to the outskirts of Santiago, suffering heavy losses. Among the hard-hit outfits was a part of the First United States Volunteer Cavalry, nicknamed the Rough Riders, proudly commanded by Lieutenant Colonel Theodore Roosevelt

Rainy nights, land crabs, and mosquitoes greeted American forces in Cuba.

(left) and the Negro Tenth Cavalry (right) commanded by Lieutenant John J. Pershing. On July 1, 1898, the Americans charged a hotly defended Spanish position called Kettle Hill. Roosevelt spurred his horse up and down the battlefield, urging his men on. When Kettle Hill had been secured, the infantry began the charge up nearby San Juan Hill. Roosevelt called on his men, who were cheering the San Juan Hill charge, to hit the next line of Spanish trenches.

On July 17 Santiago surrendered. But the American army was in as much danger from victory as it would have been from defeat. Malaria, yellow fever, and other diseases swept the ranks, killing far more men than Spanish bullets had done. Only the surrender of Spain on August 2, and the troops' return to the United States, prevented disaster.

In the peace treaty Spain gave the United States the Philippines for $20 million. The United States also got Puerto Rico and the Pacific island of Guam. The question of the fate of Cuba and Puerto Rico was troublesome. Under the Teller Amendment the United States had agreed not to annex Cuba, but after the war enthusiasm for Cuban freedom cooled. A majority in Congress wanted some control over Cuban affairs. An amendment, offered by Connecticut's Senator Orville Platt, was added to a 1901 bill providing money for the army. Under the amendment Cuba had to sign a treaty with the United States, promising to make no agreements which would give any other nation control of its affairs. Cuba was not to borrow more money than it could quickly repay. If the United States thought it necessary, Cuba had to let United States forces land in order to protect life and property. And Cuba had to agree to lease land for naval bases to the United States. Cuba remained a protectorate until the Platt Amendment was repealed in 1934.

As for Puerto Rico, Americans were unwilling either to set the island free or to absorb its people into the United States as equal partners. In 1901 Puerto Rico was made a colony. In 1917 its people were granted United States citizenship. In 1952 it became a self-governing commonwealth within the United States.

Questions for Discussion

1. What part did "yellow journalism" play in bringing the United States into war with Spain?
2. How did the war with Spain affect Puerto Rico?

To John J. Pershing the Battle of San Juan Hill had great meaning. "White regiments, black regiments [right], regulars, and Rough Riders [above], representing the young manhood of the North and the South, fought shoulder to shoulder, unmindful of race or color, unmindful of whether commanded by an ex-Confederate or not, and mindful only of their common duty as Americans."

WIDE WORLD PHOTOS

PANAMA CANAL COMPANY

NATIONAL ARCHIVES

The Course of Empire

Building the Panama Canal was a fantastic problem in engineering. Teddy Roosevelt, however, was determined to "make the dirt fly on the Isthmus." Colonel George Goethels engineered the project while Dr. William Gorgas brought malaria and yellow fever under control. At the height of activity, 56,000 men worked on the canal. At the Culebra Cut (top), 6,000 workers, 60 million tons of dynamite, and 140 locomotives pulling 3,700 flat cars removed 100 million cubic yards of material—30 million as the result of landslides. The locks (far left) were arranged side-by-side in pairs for two-way traffic. Today an average size ship pays about $6,000 to pass through the canal, but the shorter route saves it as much as $50,000.

After 1900 the United States had a giant's strength in the Caribbean and began to use it. Its first step was to bring part of the Isthmus of Panama—the narrow neck of land joining North and South America—under the Stars and Stripes in order to dig a canal through it. The United States had long been interested in such a canal. When, in 1898, it gained possessions to protect in both the Atlantic and the Pacific, it became absolutely urgent that its navy could move quickly from one ocean to the other.

Panama was then part of the Republic of Colombia. In January 1903 the United States signed a treaty with Colombia which would put a six-mile-wide strip of the isthmus under American control. The United States agreed to pay $10 million immediately and make annual payments thereafter. For months, however, the Colombian government in Bogotá hesitated to sell this part of its territory. President Theodore Roosevelt fumed in a private letter: "I do not think that the Bogotá lot of jack rabbits should be allowed permanently to bar one of the future highways of civilization."

Then mysterious things happened. A small group of Panamanian nationalists, opposed to Colombian rule, made contact with individuals who had friends in the United States government. In November the rebels seized Panama City and proclaimed an independent republic. An American cruiser, sent to the area by Roosevelt before the revolt, appeared at the nearby port of Colón, where Colombian soldiers were preparing to land to crush the uprising. The cruiser had orders to protect American travelers in Panama by preventing fighting. Instead, it used the threat of its mighty guns to prevent the Colombians from retaking their own soil. Helplessly, Colombia watched the United States recognize the Republic of Panama. Two weeks later Panama signed a treaty giving the Americans control over a ten-mile-wide zone across the isthmus.

While the Panamanian national revolt was not started by Roosevelt, he clearly insured its success by his intervention. And later Roosevelt would claim proudly, "I took the Canal Zone."

Building the canal was not easy. For ten years American army engineers assaulted the difficult jungle landscape with giant machines (left), while American health officers battled epidemics. The canal was opened in August 1914, an American triumph in a world that had just plunged into war.

ALL: BROWN BROTHERS

American companies built homes (above and left) in Latin America for the white Americans who worked as company managers and their families. To attract investment Latin American governments often gave American companies tax-free land. In return, a company like United Fruit built schools, hospitals, and homes for its native workers—who were paid far more than they could earn in locally owned businesses.

A New Kind of Investment

Even before the United States became *the* naval power in the Caribbean, it cast a long economic shadow across Central America. American citizens moved there to build and operate railroads, lumber camps, plantations, mines, and oil wells, much as other Americans had settled undeveloped areas of the United States. A good example of a young man who went south of the border instead of west to the frontier was Brooklyn-born Minor Keith.

In 1871 at the age of 23, Keith went to Costa Rica to help his older brother build a railroad. The brother died, but by 1890 Keith managed to finish the line. Partly in order to have freight for it to carry, he tried planting bananas on some land he owned. His banana plantations were as big a success in Costa Rica as tobacco plantations had been in colonial Virginia. Before long Keith was importing goods to trade for bananas, providing ships to carry bananas to the United States and other countries, and buying new banana lands in Guatemala and El Salvador.

In 1899 Keith helped to found the giant United Fruit Company. Some of its activities are shown at left. Like other American-owned companies in the Americas, it played an important role in the lives of the small Western Hemisphere nations. American corporations provided jobs, introduced modern services and ideas such as refrigeration and electricity, and in a few cases provided medical care and education for their Latin American employees.

But even at its best such **paternalism** (acting as a father might toward his children) was widely resented. It was a constant reminder of outside control. Managers and engineers from the United States enjoyed luxuries made possible by the work of people whose basic poverty remained unchanged. Many American corporations interfered in local politics by putting their wealth and influence behind rulers who would cooperate with them. And behind that influence was the likelihood that if American economic interests were threatened the American companies could ask for—and usually get—United States sailors and marines sent to their aid.

Keith made Central America his home and married the daughter of a former president of Costa Rica. From 1900 to his death in 1925, Keith developed a sizable railway system linking Central America with Mexico.

Parading United States marines became a familiar sight in Latin America.

His scheme encouraged economic growth by providing transportation for the cocoa, coffee, and fruits raised in the countries through which the railroad passed. Keith was an American adventurer, like William Walker, but he fulfilled his dreams with rails and dollars, not guns.

The Roosevelt Corollary

A challenge to the Monroe Doctrine arose when Latin American nations borrowed money from European bankers and governments. If Latin American countries failed to repay these loans, their creditors had a ready-made excuse for tough action. In 1902, for example, Venezuela failed to pay sums which it owed to several European nations. As punishment British, German, and Italian naval forces blockaded Venezuelan ports.

At first Theodore Roosevelt saw no threat. "If any South American state misbehaves toward any European country," he wrote, "let the European country spank it." But in 1904, when the Dominican Republic seemed about to go bankrupt, he changed his mind. "I have about the same desire to annex it as a gorged boa constrictor might have to swallow a porcupine wrong-end-to." He had no desire to see the little Caribbean country occupied by the nations to whom it owed money, but he did not want to take it over for the United States either. So he announced to Congress a **corollary,** or addition, to the Monroe Doctrine. Any Western Hemisphere nation that could keep order and pay its debts would not be interfered with. But if it failed in these civilized responsibilities, the United States would act as an "international police force." It would be peacekeeper and bill collector for the Europeans. Roosevelt forced a special treaty on the Dominican Republic. Under it a United States official collected Dominican import duties, paid the republic's overdue bills with some of the revenue, and "gave" the rest back to the Dominican government.

Under the Roosevelt Corollary the United States soon began to occupy other small neighbors. It assumed the right to supervise their tangled finances or protect lives and property during revolutions and civil wars. But the protection tended to last a long time, during which the countries involved were, for all practical purposes, United States protectorates. In 1912 marines (like those at left) landed in Nicaragua and remained,

569

In March 1916 Brigadier General John J. Pershing led a large United States force into Mexico to find and punish Pancho Villa. Pershing did not receive the cooperation he expected from Mexican government troops. In fact, clashes with them were nearly as frequent as those with the elusive Villistas. Eleven months and $130 million later, Pershing was ordered home.

except for a brief trial withdrawal in 1925, until 1933. They went ashore in the Dominican Republic in 1916 and stayed until 1924. They took over Haiti during a 1915 revolt and did not leave until 1930.

The United States defended such blunt use of its power as necessary to prevent Latin America from being divided, like Africa or parts of Asia, among European powers. Often leaders of the Latin American countries asked for United States troops to protect their own power. But because of these occupations, hatred for the "colossus [giant] of the North" remained a strong force in Latin American life even after the United States moved toward a more cooperative policy.

Mexican-American Relations

United States relations with its closest southern neighbor, Mexico, took a turn for the worse in 1911. For some decades Mexico had been ruled by a dictator named Porfirio Díaz. Díaz encouraged foreign investors to develop Mexico's resources. By 1910 a billion United States dollars were invested in Mexican railroads, ranches, mines, and oil wells. Over 40,000 Americans—businessmen, workers, and their families—lived in Mexico. But the average Mexican saw little of the profit made by this use of his country's natural wealth.

In 1911 a revolution broke out that overthrew Díaz. Several Mexican leaders, including Venustiano Carranza and Francisco "Pancho" Villa (right, top and bottom), fought among themselves to see who would replace Díaz. In February 1913 another dictator, Victoriano Huerta, got control of the government. While these leaders and their armies fought for power, thousands of Mexicans and some foreign residents, including Americans, were killed and injured.

President Woodrow Wilson hoped to influence Mexican politics without large-scale American intervention. What he wanted was a government which would be constitutional and democratic, but strong enough to protect life and property. He tried various methods to weaken Huerta, whose one-man government he did not approve of. In April 1914 a minor incident involving the arrest of some American sailors at Tampico led Wilson to order the bombardment and occupation of that city by United States forces. War was barely averted through **arbitration** (the process by which those involved in a dispute voluntarily submit their differ-

Right: Francisco "Pancho" Villa, standing third from the right, was considered something of a Robin Hood by his followers. He adopted the name Francisco Villa, after a famous outlaw, early in his career. Below: Villa controlled the national government for brief periods during the Mexican Revolution. This photograph, with Villa in the center and his sometime ally Emiliano Zapata on his left, was taken at the National Palace.

BOTH: CULVER PICTURES

ences to the judgment of others and agree to accept their verdict).

Wilson appeared to have scored a gain when Huerta was forced out and replaced by Carranza late in 1915. But Carranza could not control the turbulent Mexican revolution either. Wilson's hand was now forced by Pancho Villa. On March 9, 1916, Villa's men—who had already murdered a number of Americans in Mexico—crossed into Columbus, New Mexico. There, they killed seventeen United States citizens.

An outraged United States mobilized a small army for an expedition to punish Villa. Under General John J. Pershing (page 570) they pursued Villa, intending to break up his force. Carranza was furious. He did not like Villa, but neither did he like an American invasion. Pershing's men toiled through a hot, difficult campaign in rugged country, but failed to capture Villa in any of his mountain hideouts.

The Mexican government continued to insist that the Americans leave. But before a second war with Mexico could take place, other events changed the picture. By January 1917 the United States was dangerously close to war with Germany. The troops were brought home to prepare for that conflict, and the policing of Mexico was left to Mexicans.

In 1917 the United States became involved in a war among the world's great powers. Almost a century had gone by since the end of the War of 1812, the last such war to involve Americans. But the America of 1917 was no longer a little republic caught up in the clashes of giant European powers. It was no longer the country of 1823 that declared its separation from Europe's affairs in the Monroe Doctrine. Instead, the United States now had far-flung strategic interests to guard. Therefore, after a hundred years when most American problems were domestic, a new period began, in which foreign developments became increasingly important. As the twentieth century went forward, treaties, wars, and big military expenditures tended to take more of the spotlight in United States history.

Questions for Discussion

1. How did Theodore Roosevelt insure the success of the Panamanian revolt from Colombia?
2. What natural resources in Latin America attracted the interest of American businessmen?
3. Why did Roosevelt announce his corollary?

Chapter Review

Social Studies Terms
ultimatum, paternalism, corollary, arbitration

Summary Questions for Discussion
1. Why did Monroe and Adams want to end European commercial and military rivalry in Latin America?
2. Why did some Latin American dictators or "strong men" cooperate with American businessmen in the development of Latin American resources?
3. How did an early Spanish surrender prevent disaster for the American army in Cuba?
4. How did the United States gain control over a zone of land for the construction of a canal across Panama?
5. How did the Panama Canal add to the commercial and military strength of the United States?
6. Why were many American corporations resented by Latin Americans?
7. How did the Roosevelt Corollary lead the United States to play the role of "policeman" in Latin America?
8. What was the purpose of Pershing's expedition into Mexico? Why was Carranza angered by this expedition? What put an end to the expedition?

Pictures as Historical Evidence
Which pictures in this chapter would provide evidence for, and which would tend to disprove, the hypothesis that the United States has always followed a "hands-off" policy in Latin America?

Map Study
Look at the map on page 551. What reasons for building the Panama Canal did the United States have after 1900 that it did not have in 1890?

For Further Reading
Island in the Crossroads: The History of Puerto Rico, by M. M. Brau. Garden City, New York: Doubleday & Company, Inc., 1968.

Teddy Roosevelt and the Rough Riders, by Henry Castor. New York: Random House, Inc., 1954.

The Land Divided, The World United: The Story of the Panama Canal, by Paul Rink. New York: Julian Messner, 1963.

The Spanish-American War, by Allan Keller. New York: Hawthorn Books, Inc., 1969.

20

World War I

On June 28, 1914, two pistol shots cracked loudly in a street in Sarajevo, a city in the province of Bosnia. The shots were fired into the chest of an Austrian archduke by a young Serbian to protest the condition of Serbians like himself living under Austro-Hungarian rule in Bosnia (see map, page 583). Few people in the United States had heard of Sarajevo, Bosnia, or Serbia, and few were interested when the newspapers the next day reported the archduke's death. Yet those shots changed the lives of Americans for all time to come, just as they changed the destiny of the whole world. The assassination triggered a world war, which became history's biggest conflict up to then.

At its end, in November 1918, more than 8.5 million soldiers had died. Millions of civilians had also perished from disease, cold, and hunger. Billions of dollars' worth of farms, factories, homes, mines, and ships had been blown up or sunk. Three empires were overthrown by revolution. Riots and civil war threatened orderly government in the lands of the exhausted winners as well as in the defeated nations.

Americans in 1914 believed that Europe's wars were not their affair. But the United States, with its industrial strength and worldwide trade, could not escape becoming involved. In 1917 it entered the war and shared in the bloodshed. In 1919 its President took part in the peacemaking. After that, although the nation tried to withdraw from world affairs, it was never again possible for thinking Americans to be entirely uninterested in the fate of peoples on the rest of the globe.

Changes swept the United States in wartime. Figures of industrial and farm production zoomed, and so did the size of the Federal government. Debates over progressive reforms gave way to calls for unity and victory. People and ideas were on the move—blacks to industrial jobs in the North, women from homes into war work, and nearly 2 million young men in uniform to France. Many returned with changed views of themselves, their goals, their country, and their world. The shots at Sarajevo set off an explosion symbolized by the shellburst in the battlefront photograph at left. World War I was the smashup of an entire way of life.

As you read, think about these questions:
1. Why did the United States become involved in World War I?
2. How did the war change the United States?

During World War I a bursting shell lightens the sky on the Western Front.

The Great War Begins

Why did one political murder start so much destruction? The answer is that Europe's major powers—Austria-Hungary, Russia, Germany, France, and Great Britain—had strengthened themselves in two ways. First, they had tried to outdo each other in building deadly military forces. France, Russia, Germany, and Austria-Hungary had huge land armies. Germany was also in an armaments race with England in which each nation tried to build the biggest warships in the world. Besides raising such walls of steel, the great powers formed alliances. Under these, if one member became involved in war, the others would have to go to its aid. But that meant that one nation's quarrel was sure to drag others in.

The alliance system was the result of the way in which European foreign affairs had been carried on since early modern times. Kings and princes were accustomed both to fighting and to making bargains with each other. As they were often related by marriage, these were, in a way, family feuds and partnerships. The gorgeously uniformed diplomats and generals (like the whirling dancers at left) who did the bargaining and fighting for royalty were a link to the feudal past. But the alliance system was dangerously rigid.

How the system worked is shown by what happened between June 28 and August 4, 1914. Immediately after the assassination Austria-Hungary sent a diplomatic note to Serbia with stiff demands. Serbia agreed to all of the demands, except those that threatened its sovereignty. Austria was not satisfied with the Serbian reply and declared war. But Russia believed itself to be the protector of "brother" Slavs in Serbia, and so declared war on Austria. Germany, allied to Austria, had to prove to its partner that it would keep its word. Germany therefore declared war on Russia. Since Russia was allied with France and Great Britain, these two nations joined the combat. So it went, until most nations of Europe and the world had lined up with either the Central Powers, chiefly Germany and Austria-Hungary, or the Allied Powers, chiefly Russia, France, and Great Britain.

Trench Warfare Leads to a Stalemate

The war astonished everyone by rapidly becoming a quagmire. Before 1914 the generals had planned and trained for fast, decisive drives that would destroy the enemy armies. But their plans failed to work. A

Above: Czar Nicholas II of Russia and his only son Alexis in 1913, four years before they were both executed during the Russian Revolution. Left: The Hofbal—the dance given annually by Austrian Emperor Franz Joseph—in 1900.

On July 1, 1916, Allied infantrymen—like the Scottish troops above—climbed out of their trenches to begin an offensive against German positions along the Somme River. The British alone suffered 60,000 casualties the first day. A poet watching the first day's battle from an observation post wrote, "I am staring at a sunlit picture of Hell." Neither side had gained any significant territory when the battle finally ground to a halt on November 18.

huge Russian thrust into East Prussia ended in the last week of August, when the Germans almost wiped out the invaders at Tannenberg (see map, page 583). A surprise German invasion into northern France was turned back at the Battle of the Marne in early September. Eight weeks after the war's opening, each side had failed to make a knockout blow.

Now the war, especially on the Western Front, became a stalemate with neither the Germans nor the French and English able to make a winning move. Powerful artillery and machine guns made it impossible for even the bravest infantry charges (left) to break through the lines. Great offensives by both sides bogged down in a few weeks. Casualties were in the hundreds of thousands. The "victors" of such battles captured only a few miles of scarred ground.

Things went better for the Central Powers in the East. Turkey had entered the war on their side, cutting off Russia from Allied help by way of the Black Sea. Russia was not a major industrial power and could not stand the steady drain of continuous warfare. By 1916 its great manpower was useless. Its armies lacked ammunition, trucks, medicines, clothing, and food. War-weary, a growing number of Russians blamed the czar for their predicament.

In March of 1917 a revolution overthrew the czar. In October of that year the Bolsheviks, the founders of Russian **communism** (a theory of government which generally supports communal ownership of all the means of production and specifically advocates the overthrow of the capitalist class by the working class), seized control of the revolution. Eager to get an exhausted nation out of the war, the new communist government signed the Treaty of Brest-Litovsk (see map, page 583) in March 1918.

By early 1917 the war had become a monster, devouring millions of dollars and thousands of lives a day, with no end in sight. No victory could repay any nation for what it was losing. Yet governments on both sides had whipped up people's feelings with propaganda that identified the enemy with all the evil in the world. They had promised their suffering people victory. They could not consider a compromise peace. And so the slaughter (upper right) went on and on.

Question for Discussion

1. What caused war to break out in 1914?

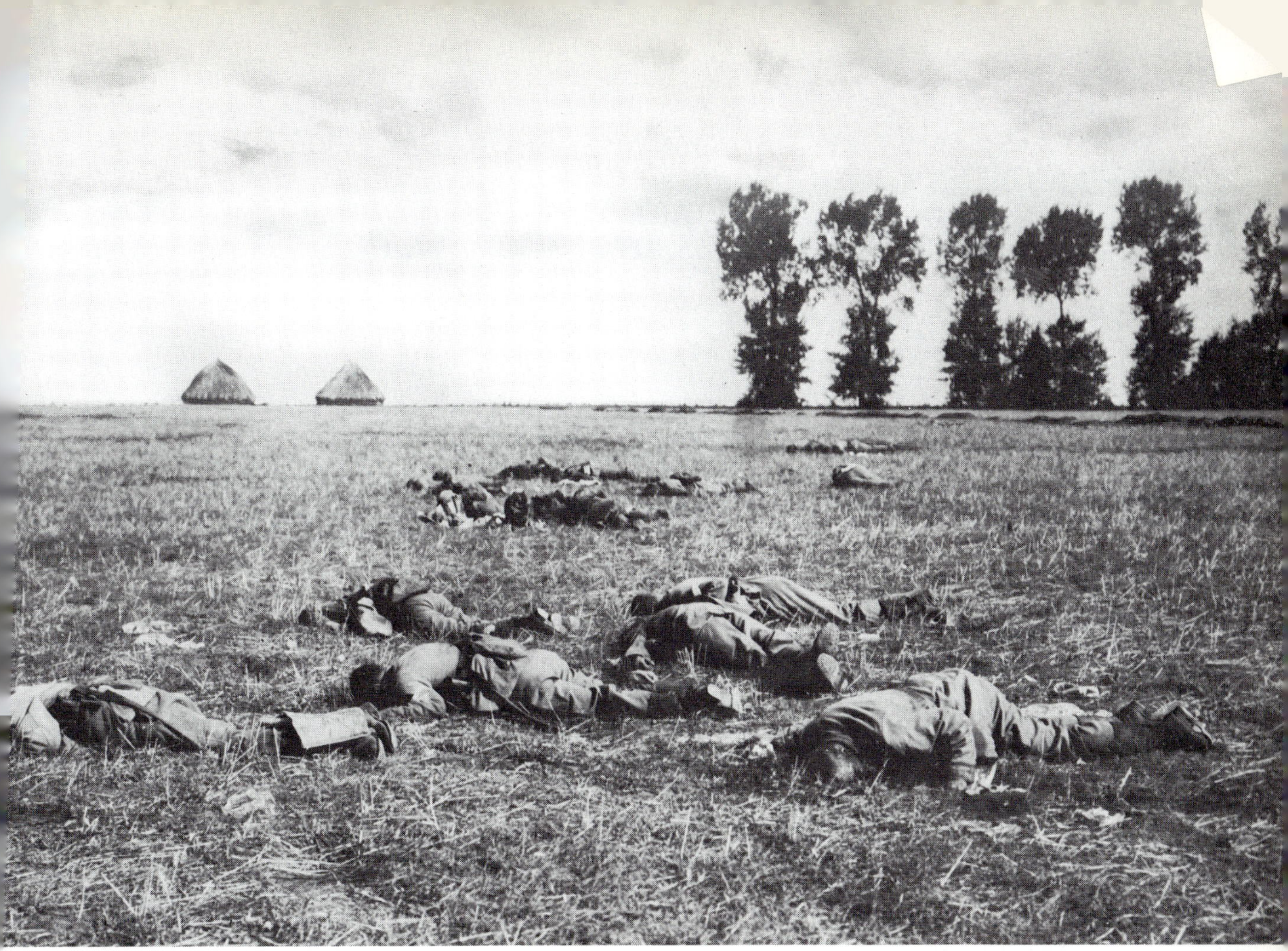

L'Illustration, NOVEMBER 21, 1914

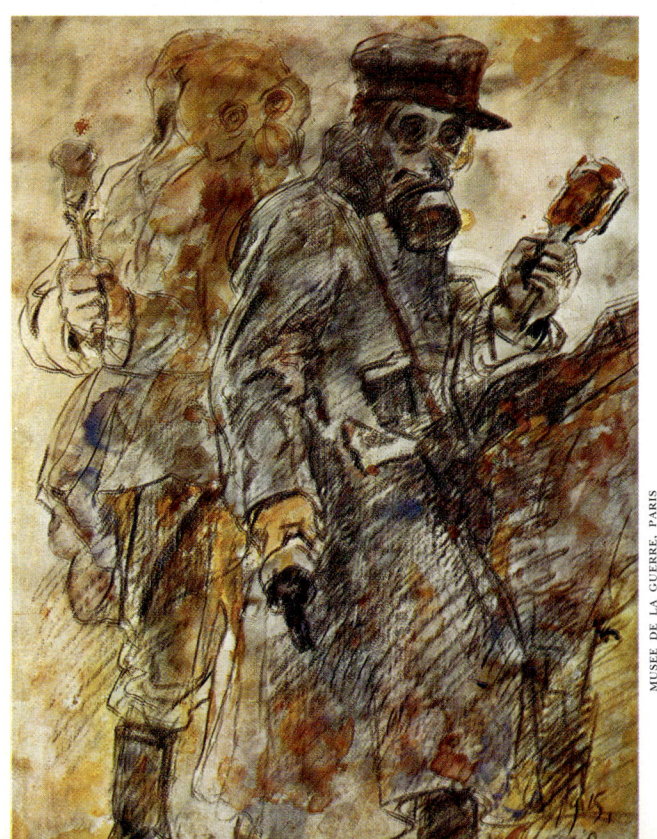

Above: After the first few months of war, fields of dead lay on the European countryside. These are German soldiers killed at the First Battle of the Marne. In the first month alone, approximately 200,000 Frenchmen died. Right: Poison gas was introduced as a weapon by the Germans early in 1915 and soon adopted by the Allies. This 1915 painting shows soldiers wearing masks to prevent exposure to the deadly poison.

MUSEE DE LA GUERRE, PARIS

LUSITANIA SUNK BY A SUBMARINE, PROBABLY 1,000 DEAD;
TWICE TORPEDOED OFF IRISH COAST; SINKS IN 15 MINUTES;
AMERICANS ABOARD INCLUDED VANDERBILT AND FROHMAN;
WASHINGTON BELIEVES THAT A GRAVE CRISIS IS AT HAND

NEW YORK PUBLIC LIBRARY

NEW YORK PUBLIC LIBRARY

New York American

WAR WITH GERMANY

EUROPEAN PICTURE SERVICE

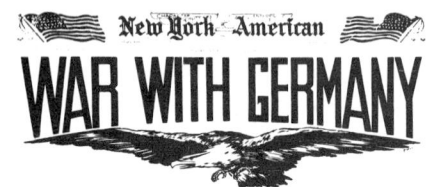

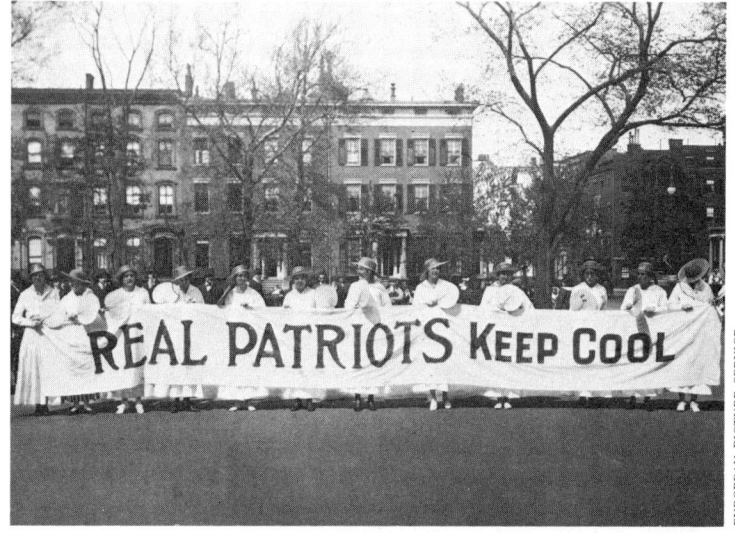

L'Illustration, MAY 1917

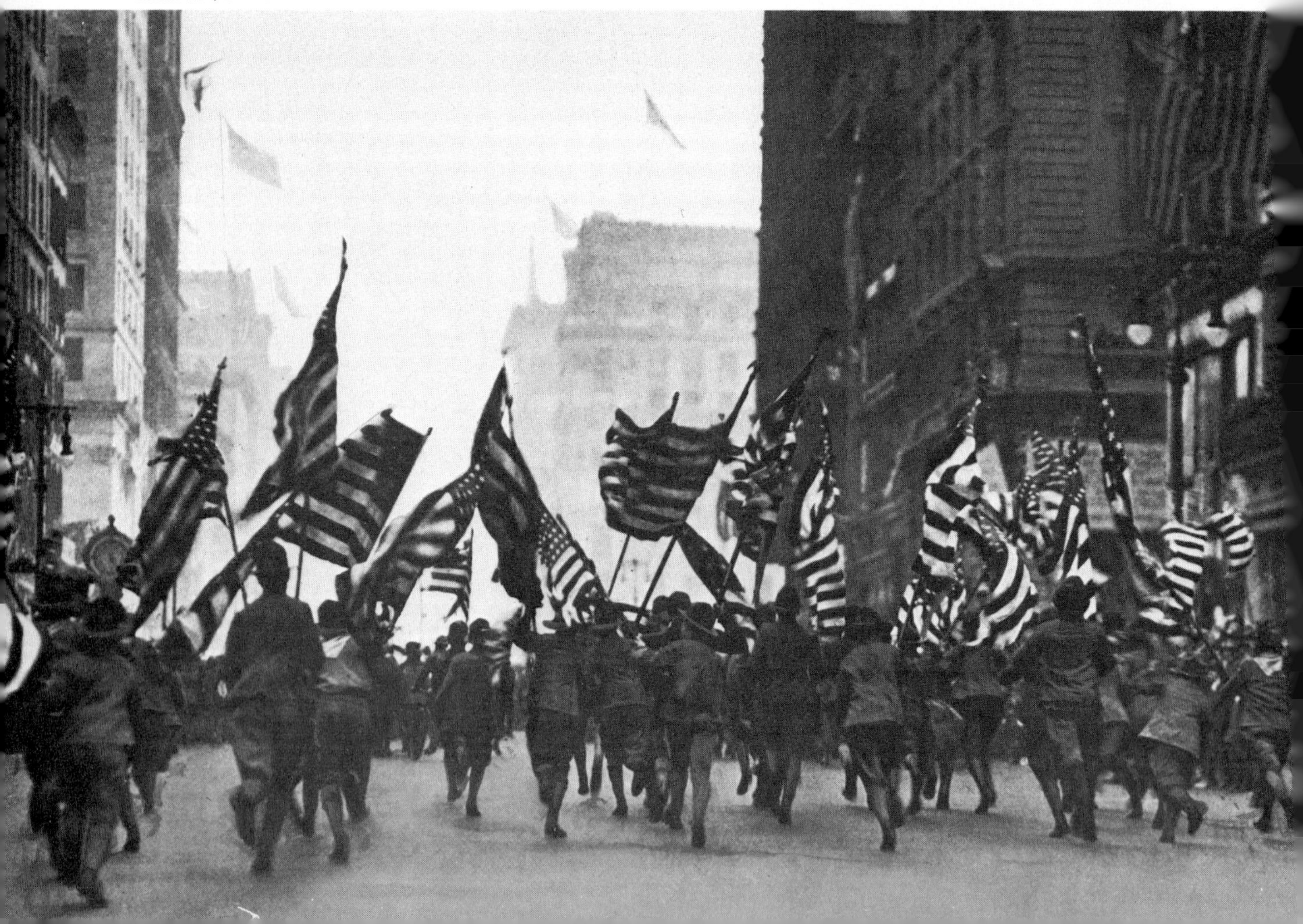

The United States Enters the War

Most Americans at first hoped to stay neutral, despite generally pro-British sympathies among editors and other public opinion makers. But neutrality was quickly endangered because of the new technology of war. Since the British surface fleet controlled the sea lanes, it could stop neutral merchant ships. The German counterweapon was the recently invented submarine, or U-boat, which attacked without warning from under the sea, leaving the crew and passengers of a torpedoed ship to their fate.

In May of 1915, as the headline (upper left) proclaimed, a U-boat torpedoed the unarmed British ocean liner *Lusitania*, killing 1,198 people, 128 of whom were Americans. Horror swept the country. Some Americans called for immediate war, while **pacifists** (opponents of war and violence as a means of settling disputes) urged that the country keep cool (center left).

President Wilson did not give in to the cry for war in 1915. But neither would he agree to prohibit trade or travel. The historic right of neutrals was to enjoy free commerce, except for guns, explosives, and other weapons, with all **belligerents** (warring parties). But since the British blockade of Germany was completely effective, only the Allies could get supplies from the United States. Moreover, when the Allies began to run short of money, American bankers made loans to them so that they might continue to keep American factories busy with war orders. Thus, playing by the traditional rules of neutrality had made America moneylender and arms-maker for one side only.

Still Wilson continued to protest the illegal blockade tactics of both Great Britain and Germany. But after the sinking of the *Lusitania*, he demanded that Germany end unrestricted submarine attacks. Fearing American intervention, the Germans agreed. In May of 1916 Wilson was hailed as the man who defended America's rights, yet kept it out of war.

But in February of 1917 the Germans gambled that all-out submarine warfare would finally give them such a quick victory that it would not matter if the Americans entered the war. They announced the resumption of unrestricted submarine attacks. In the next two months eight American ships were sunk. On April 2 Wilson sadly took the final step and asked Congress for a declaration of war. He did not stress threatened American interests. Instead, he made the issue moral and worldwide. "The world," he said, "must be made

On May 1, 1915, the day the Lusitania *sailed from New York, the German embassy in Washington put out a warning that anyone traveling on a ship flying the British flag did so at his own risk. Yet the sinking of the* Lusitania *off the Irish coast stunned the American public (top). The Woman's Peace Party marched to cool the growing war fever in the country (top, right). Nearly two years later President Woodrow Wilson asked Congress for a declaration of war. The war resolution passed the Senate April 4, 1917, and the House gave approval two days later. The nation, including these flag-waving Boy Scouts marching down New York's Fifth Avenue (left), voiced its agreement.*

safe for democracy." Inspired by Wilson's statement of idealism, Congress declared war by an overwhelming vote. Under forests of waving flags, America said goodby to neutrality.

Over There

It was nearly fifteen months before Americans reached France in any important numbers. The original plan of the Allied High Command was to use American units as replacements for battered portions of British and French armies. But the United States commander, tough General John J. Pershing, who had fought in Cuba and chased Villa in Mexico, insisted that a separate United States army be organized. Parts of this American Expeditionary Force (AEF) got their first taste of battle in 1918. In March of 1918 the Germans launched a final all-out drive. By late May they crunched to within 75 miles of Paris. As summer drew near fresh infantrymen in United States uniforms poured into the trenches to relieve weary French warriors. In hard-fought battles at Cantigny, Chateau-Thierry, and Belleau Wood, they helped to check the last German offensive (map, right).

In September the AEF launched its first independent effort, a four-day assault that wiped out a German strong point around St. Mihiel. On September 26 it began a massive offensive in the Argonne forest. Forty-seven days later the Germans, in retreat everywhere, surrendered. In those six and a half weeks the million-man United States force had lost almost 50,000 killed in action and over 200,000 wounded.

But even in the short time that Americans were in action, they learned that twentieth-century warfare was not a matter of gallant charges up San Juan Hill. In 1918 it was crouching in trenches (left) full of muddy water and swollen corpses. It was steady bombardment that broke men's nerves. It was a choking death by poison gas or entrapment in the barbed wire strung between opposing trench lines. It was long lines of ambulances delivering wounded men to makeshift hospitals (right). Sherman's description of war as hell was fulfilled to the letter.

The Home Front

As our own Civil War shows, prolonged wars change societies in unexpected ways. Before April 1917 American foreign policy had been directed at such

NATIONAL ARCHIVES

Above: Of the 100,000 black soldiers sent overseas, about 80,000 were assigned to segregated units that did the hard, dirty work behind the lines. The Secretary of War said the Army did not intend to settle the "so-called race question." A mayor warned black troops leaving for France not to "get any new fangled ideas about democracy." Those who did reach the front—in segregated units—fought bravely. These men of the 369th Infantry were at the front for 191 days straight—longer than any other American regiment. Many returned to fight racism in America. Right: American wounded during the first day's fighting in the Argonne forest rest in a bombed-out French church.

NEW YORK PUBLIC LIBRARY

World War I

- Central Powers
- Allied Powers
- Furthest Military Penetration by Central Powers
- Neutral Countries
- German Submarine War Zone 1915
- × Battle Sites

When the United States entered World War I, journalist George Creel was appointed to head the Committee on Public Information. He recruited speakers, writers, artists, and film-makers to mobilize public opinion against the enemy. The cartoon below appeared in a Brooklyn magazine in 1917. Some individuals overreacted to the committee's message. Many loyal American citizens lost their jobs just because their names were German. School boards banned the teaching of German in public schools. Laws were passed officially changing the name of sauerkraut to "liberty cabbage."

LIBRARY OF CONGRESS

limited objectives as forcing the enemy to give up submarine blockades. But once Congress had declared war, official propaganda began to encourage the idea that the enemy was scarcely human. A typical war editorial said that we were "dealing with madmen, whose sole purpose is to kill."

Such attitudes stirred passions that made dissent almost impossible. A strong Espionage Act of 1917 and a Sedition Act of 1918 lashed out at opponents of the war. The IWW and the Socialists both had resisted the call to arms. They believed that the struggle was between the capitalists who controlled all the great powers and the workers who did the fighting, suffering, and dying, no matter which side won. Because of this opposition, IWW leaders were arrested and jailed, crippling the organization. Eugene V. Debs, the Socialist leader, was sentenced to Federal prison for speeches against the draft.

Many Americans of German origin lived in the shadow of distrust. It was believed, quite falsely, that they would prove loyal to Germany rather than to the United States, as the cartoon at left suggests. Germans were not imprisoned, but a tremendous wave of anti-German feeling surged through the country.

The actual work of preparing for battle soon showed the importance of massive organization. In 1861 the North waited two years to draft men. In 1917 the nation turned almost at once to this means of filling the ranks. Volunteering was encouraged by patriotic songs and posters (right). But the draft remained the basic manpower policy. In the year and a half that the United States spent at war, about 4 million men were taken from every section, class, and trade, and put in uniform. About 2 million of them were sent overseas.

Raising a labor force was another big task. Some of the "slack" was taken up by urging women to work in factories and offices. The Wilson administration also took additional steps to attract workers. One such move was to create a War Labor Board, with representatives from industry, unions, and government. It proposed standards for working conditions at camps and bases and on other projects being built for the government. It mediated, or settled, disputes over wages and hours in critical industries. It also recognized the workmen's right to organize. In return, Samuel Gompers, one of the Board members, gave the AF of L's pledge not to strike during the war. Gompers was jubilant over what

NEW-YORK HISTORICAL SOCIETY

Below: This poster encouraged young men to join the struggling Army Air Service. Not until 1918 did any Army Air Service units see action. But during the last seven months of the war, American fliers made an important contribution to the Allied offensive. With 26 enemy planes to his credit, Eddie Rickenbacker was the leading American ace. Left: Five massive Liberty and Victory Loan drives financed about two-thirds of the cost of the war. This poster was aimed at recent American immigrants. Directed by the advertising and entertainment industries, all the drives were huge successes. Persons who refused to buy often were publicly ridiculed and even assaulted.

LIBRARY OF CONGRESS

he believed to be a great gain. Capital and labor were wartime partners, pulling in harness. But Gompers' critics reminded him that government, though its authority in this field was limited, held the reins.

New Engines of War

In all wars each victim must suffer pain, fear, and grief as an individual alone. Yet the war of 1914 to 1918 tended to make the process of fighting and dying more mechanical, as inventors who hoped to end the stand-off between attack and defense came up with new, scientific ways of destruction.

Aerial bombardment was one new horror. Early in the war the Germans sent dirigibles to bomb London. These were cigar-shaped airships, kept aloft by lighter-than-air hydrogen gas. Unlike the stationary observation balloon being walked into position (right), the "Zeppelins" (so named for their inventor, Count Ferdinand von Zeppelin) had motors which made them self-propelled. They did not do much damage, but frightened the noncombatant population which suddenly found itself in danger. Far more destructive was the development of long-range artillery with gigantic guns like the one at far upper right.

Airplanes became steadily more deadly. In 1903 the Wright brothers' first plane just skimmed the ground for 120 feet, carrying one man at about 35 miles per hour. By 1918 planes with 2-man crews, machine guns, and bombs were flying 2 miles high at 95 miles per hour. Crude as these first fighters and bombers were, they were a step ahead in man's conquest of time and space. Wartime aeronautical research and development led to the building of the first planes to fly the Atlantic, in May of 1919. Other modern weapons included poison gas and tanks (lower right). In order to get better death-dealing machines, governments willingly paid the huge costs of such engineering marvels, from thousands of manhours preparing designs to numerous experiments and tests.

At sea destroyers and submarines hunted each other with torpedoes and depth-bombs. Their crews, like those of other new war-machines, became dehumanized themselves. No longer did men battle face to face, like heroes of legend. They risked their lives bravely, true. But they fought from great distances and killed enemies—often women and children—whom they never saw.

Above: German soldiers walk a small observation balloon to its launch site in a hayfield. The balloon carried 2 observers aloft to a height of about 2,000 feet. Right: In January 1916 the British try out a secret weapon—first used in the Somme offensive 9 months later. When the new weapon was being shipped around England undercover, it was explained away as a water tank, and the name "tank" stuck. Far right: Early in the war a French pilot and his spotter await combat over the Champagne front. Above right: By 1918 the Germans had developed a gun that shelled Paris from a distance of 75 miles.

LIBRARY OF CONGRESS

HAUPTSTAATSARCHIV, MUNICH

ETABLISSEMENT CINEMATOGRAPHIQUE DES ARMEES

ALL OTHERS: BROWN BROTHERS

SMITHSONIAN INSTITUTION

CULVER PICTURES

Perfecting the Technology of Manufacturing Arms

Perhaps the most impressive technological feat of the war was the power of industry to mass produce weapons. The task of supplying gigantic armies and navies was so enormous that American machine-power was as welcome to the Allies in April of 1917 as the promise of American manpower to come.

Building war plants and shipyards was itself a long process. United States factories did not hit full productive stride until 1918. Then they poured out floods of war material. As a single example, the nation produced 43 airplanes in 1914 — and 14,000 in 1918, although only 1,800 of these were ready in time to be shipped to France before the fighting was over.

Assembly-line procedures (left) and round-the-clock work hours were the keys to these marvels. But in addition, the economy was thoroughly organized from the top. The government ran the railroads. It set limits on civilian use of food and fuel. It established priorities in the purchase of scarce raw materials — that is, it made lists of who should be allowed to buy available supplies first, second, third, and so on. Through a War Industries Board, it assigned responsibility for producing different items to various manufacturers. More than 500 war agencies ran the industrial "front." Washington became the headquarters of a "super-trust," so full of businessmen that the Secretary of the Interior wrote to a friend, "It is easier to find a great cattle king or automobile manufacturer or a railroad president or a banker at the Shoreham [a Washington hotel] than it is to find him in his own town."

A great change was taking place. Americans had rejected the arguments of Socialists who called for national ownership and economic planning. In 1914, by the Clayton Antitrust Act, Congress had approved a Federal effort to keep competition alive in industry. Yet just four years later, under the spur of war, the country accepted massive government regulation and combined efforts by companies that were peacetime rivals. Some men wondered if the same sacrifices might not someday be made for non-warlike purposes.

Questions for Discussion

1. What was the AEF? Who was its commander?
2. How did World War I change the nature of warfare?
3. Did life in America change during the war? How?

In March 1918 Bernard Baruch was put in charge of the War Industries Board. For two years he was a virtual economic dictator. He had the power to regulate all industries that were in any way connected with the war. For example, new regulations on corsets saved 8,000 tons of steel a year for the war effort. The Board also fixed prices — at levels that allowed businesses to make huge profits. Crash programs to manufacture heavy arms were begun (left). Thousands of blacks left the South to take factory jobs. About a million women (far left) joined the labor force. However, the American artillery, tank, and airplane construction programs were so slow that they had no effect on the war.

An Uncertain Peace

On January 8, 1918, while American armies were still in training, Woodrow Wilson outlined fourteen points that he believed would end the system of armaments, alliances, national jealousies, and colonial economic rivalries that had brought on the disastrous war. These points included an end to secret treaties, freedom of the seas, the lowering of international tariff barriers, **disarmament** (the reduction or abolition of weapons and armed forces), a fair adjustment of colonial claims with the interests of colonial peoples in mind, and **self-determination** (the right of people to decide their own political future) for the national groups within the Turkish and Austro-Hungarian empires. Finally, there was to be a League of Nations to guarantee the freedom and boundaries of all nations. Wilson believed that acceptance of his program might actually make World War I the war that ended all wars.

As reported in the international press, the Fourteen Points had a powerful impact, especially among the Germans. Many of them realized that they were losing the war. They found Wilson's terms irresistible. The surrender terms were not so harsh as those that England or France had been demanding. Everyone knew that the old national order of 1914 was crushed. What should replace it? The Bolsheviks in Russia offered one choice: working-class revolution everywhere and international communism. Wilson promised something less drastic. He proposed an international society of nations under constitutional governments elected by all classes. Such nations, he believed, would solve their disputes peacefully.

Assuming that Wilson spoke for the Allies, some German officials opened secret negotiations with him for an armistice. Wilson insisted that the German people first be freed of autocratic rule. In the first week of November revolts broke out in Germany. On November 9 the kaiser resigned and a German Republic was proclaimed. Its leaders asked for, and were granted, an armistice, which took effect at 11 A.M. on November 11, 1918. The next day a war correspondent wrote, "Last night, for the first time since August in the first year of the war, there was no light of gunfire in the sky.... The Fires of Hell had been put out." At the front (far left) and in cities (left), cheering thousands celebrated the end of the long plunge into the hell of total war.

Left: At the front members of the American 64th Infantry react to news of the armistice. Above: In July 1919 American veterans march through the Arc de Triomphe in Paris to celebrate peace.

A week after the armistice President Woodrow Wilson announced that he would lead the United States delegation to the peace conference in Europe. This photograph was taken before he sailed from New York on December 4, 1918. Wilson was the first American President to travel to Europe during his term in office.

Woodrow Wilson and the Treaty of Versailles

Early in December a confident, smiling Wilson (left) sailed for Paris to take personal charge of the United States delegation at the peace conference. In the streets of every European city he visited, he was welcomed with signs (right) and cheering crowds. The people of Europe believed that "Veelson," chief of the still fresh and powerful United States, could really bring about the kind of world described in the Fourteen Points.

But when the President met with the prime ministers of France, Great Britain, and Italy at the Palace of Versailles (bottom, right), just outside Paris, he received some rude shocks. For one thing, self-determination ran head-on into secret wartime treaties that promised certain territories to the winners, regardless of the nationality of their peoples. Moreover, many nationalities in Central Europe were still hopelessly intermingled. So nations, such as Czechoslovakia and Poland, created or restored at the peace conference out of parts of Germany and Austria-Hungary had their own discontented minorities.

No agreement could be reached on tariff reduction. There was no fair adjustment of the claims to Germany's colonies. Instead, these were simply divided among the winners. The British would not promise freedom of the seas, and the French would not disarm. Both countries still feared Germany too much to risk the hard-won advantages of victory. Finally, France and England demanded harsh punishment for the beaten enemy. By the Treaty of Versailles which was finally drawn up, Germany was branded as the only nation responsible for the war and was forced to disarm almost completely. Though stripped of its merchant marine and coal and iron lands, it was still ordered to pay heavy **reparations** (payments for damages) to its enemies. Impoverished, the German people felt betrayed and bitter and soon became ripe for troublemakers.

Wilson was not at fault because the final treaty was so far from his hopes. He fought as best he could for his Fourteen Points. Nor was it a case of the statesmen of Europe being basically wicked. The fact was that age-old social and national conflicts could not be solved by kind words and good will.

Wilson bargained away some of his Fourteen Points to keep one hope. The treaty created a League of

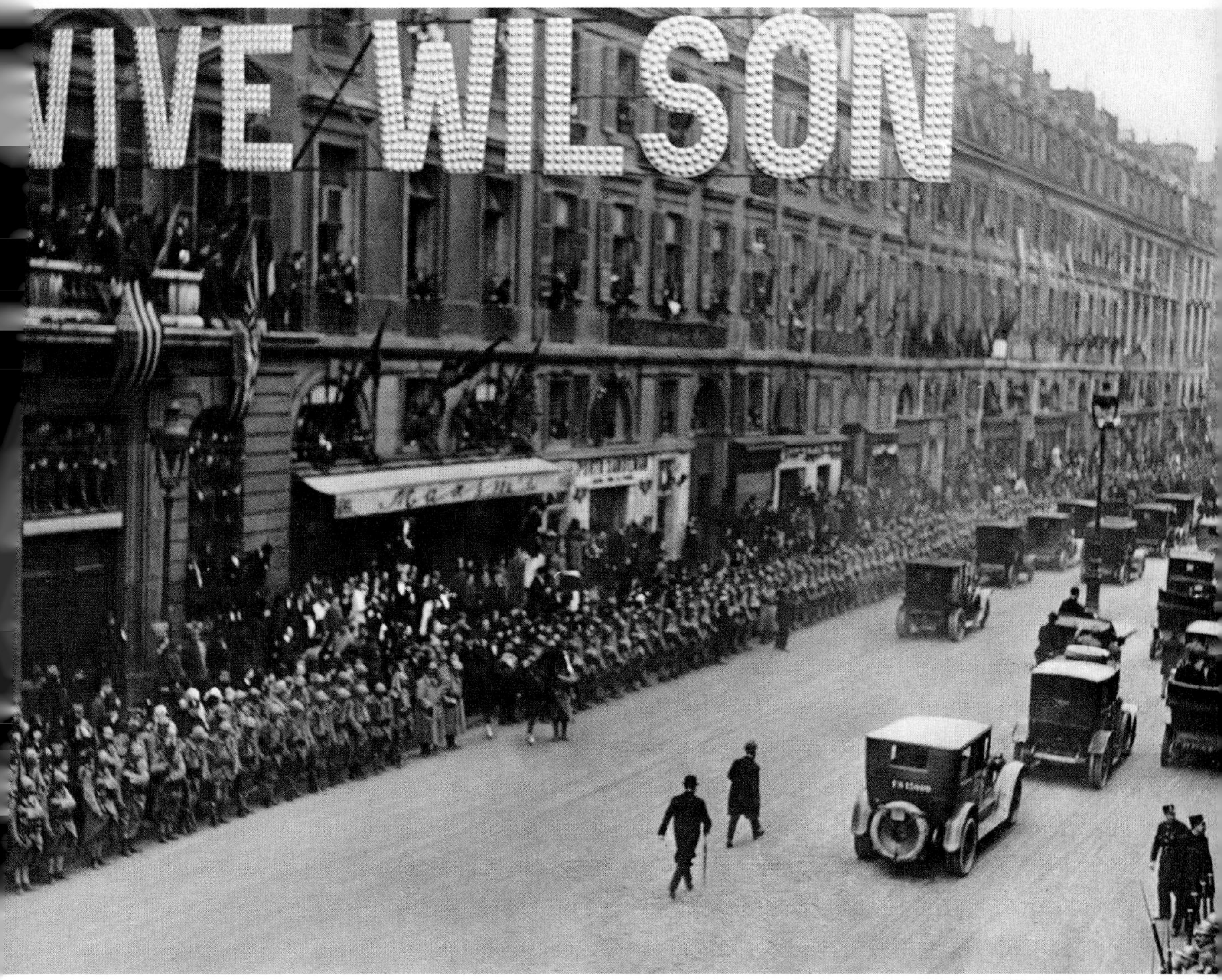

NATIONAL ARCHIVES

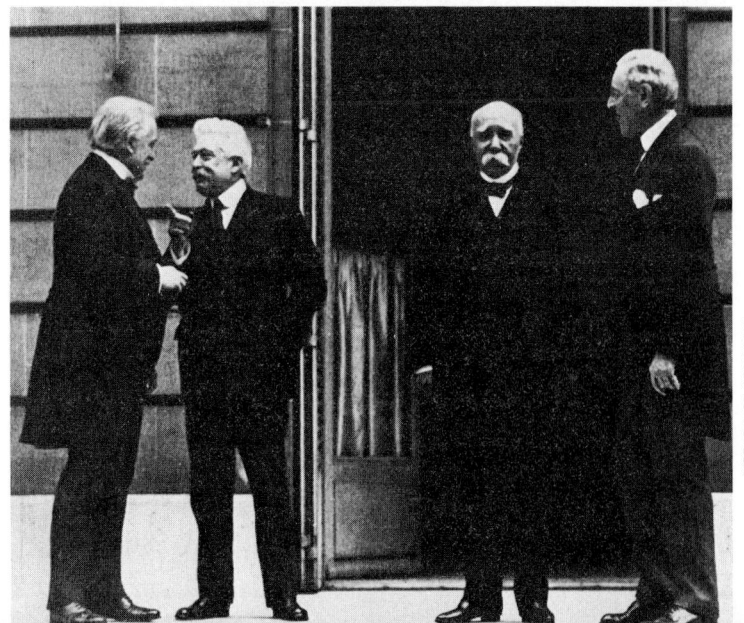

Above: Parisians erected this electric sign along the route of Wilson's motorcade. Right: The Big Four at the Versailles Peace Conference—David Lloyd George, Vittorio Orlando, Georges Clemenceau, and Woodrow Wilson. The European leaders scorned Wilson's peace plan. Said France's Clemenceau, "Mr. Wilson bores me with his Fourteen Points; why, God Almighty has only ten."

LIBRARY OF CONGRESS

Nations with headquarters in Switzerland. With this parliament of mankind in existence, Wilson believed that problems left by the treaty might be talked out instead of hammered out by gunfire.

Woodrow Wilson—Statesman Defeated

The Treaty of Versailles was signed June 28, 1919. Wilson immediately returned to get the United States to ratify it and so accept membership in the League. But he came back to an America in which opposition to the treaty had been hardening. Some Senators objected to Wilson's failure to consult them during the Versailles negotiations. Various nationality groups resented parts of the treaty that they thought unfair to their countrymen. Progressives, who had hoped that Wilson was leading them to a more just world, were outraged at his seeming willingness to accept a brutal victor's peace. Finally, some voters believed that involvement in the League would drag the United States into future European power struggles, disguised as peace-keeping efforts. They did not want, as one said, to "send our armed forces wherever and whenever a super government of foreigners sitting in Switzerland orders."

Some, though not all, of the Treaty's opponents wanted the United States to follow a policy of **isolationism** (a national policy of not getting involved in the political or economic affairs of other countries). They believed that the United States could exert its greatest influence in the world by setting a good example of democracy at home. They would do this best by avoiding Europe's wars and arms burdens. Wilson's defenders argued that no nation was safe any longer without some international peace-keeping organization such as the League of Nations, any more than individuals were really safe without police and courts. Nonetheless, anti-League Senators, led by Henry Cabot Lodge, Chairman of the Senate Foreign Relations Committee, added reservations or limit-setting changes to the treaty. The most serious denied any American "obligation" to protect member nations in the League unless Congress agreed.

Wilson could have accepted this language and gotten the treaty ratified. But Lodge was a political enemy, and Wilson also felt that such limits were dishonorable. The United States must be forced, if need be, to enter the League as a full partner, with nothing

In September 1919 the English magazine Punch *ran this cartoon showing President Wilson trying to drag a reluctant United States into the League of Nations.*

BRONSTRUP IN *The San Francisco Chronicle*, 1919

"I know I'm at the end of my tether," said President Woodrow Wilson, but "the trip is necessary to save the treaty." He was certain that his personal appeal to the people would result in a public demand for Senate ratification. Below, the President and his party arrive in San Diego. Shortly afterward Wilson's ill health forced an abrupt end to the tour. The cartoon at right is one of many inspired by the Senate's defeat of the treaty.

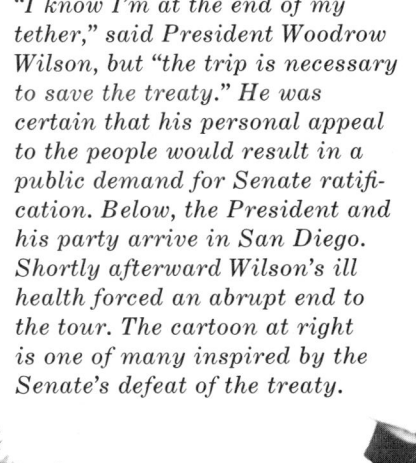

TITLE INSURANCE AND TRUST COMPANY, SAN DIEGO

held back (cartoon, page 594). He decided to go over the Senate's head and appeal directly to the people to "see the thing through."

In September 1919 he began an extensive trip by train around the country. In 3 weeks he traveled 9,500 miles and made 37 speeches in 29 cities. But the strain of overwork took its toll on a man of 62 and led to tragedy. On September 25, at Pueblo, Colorado, Wilson became so ill that he had to be rushed back to Washington. A few days afterward, he suffered a paralytic stroke. For months he was too sick to conduct business or receive reports. Yet he sent word to Democratic Senators not to give in and accept the treaty with reservations. When it came to a vote, they loyally joined with those Senators who opposed the treaty in any form and defeated ratification. So ended Wilson's dream. Was he a blind, stubborn man? Or was he ahead of his time? Men would ponder that question when war broke out again, twenty years later.

Questions for Discussion

1. What were the main ideas in Wilson's Fourteen Points? Why were many Germans eager to accept a peace based on Wilson's Points?
2. Where was the conference to write a peace treaty held? Who were the Big Four powers at that conference? What part did Wilson play in the conference?
3. For what reasons was it difficult to realize the goals of all of the Fourteen Points? Why did Wilson agree to sacrifice some of them?
4. Why did some groups in the United States oppose ratification of the Treaty of Versailles? Why did Wilson oppose "reservations" and other changes in the treaty?
5. What was the purpose of Wilson's 1919 trip throughout the United States?

Chapter Review

Social Studies Terms

communism, pacifists, belligerents, disarmament, self-determination, reparations, isolationism

Summary Questions for Discussion

1. What did the events following the assassination of the Austrian archduke in June 1914 show about the alliance system's ability to maintain peace?

2. Why did Russia withdraw from the war in March 1918?
3. Why did the war continue even after both sides knew they would gain little by a victory?
4. Did the official policy of neutrality followed by the United States until 1917 actually benefit the Allied powers? Why?
5. Was the German strategy of resuming unrestricted submarine warfare in 1917 wise? Why?
6. Why did the Socialists and the IWW oppose the entry of the United States into the war?
7. Does war tend to result in the limiting of freedom? Why? How?
8. Why did the Allied powers win World War I?
9. How did discontent with the peace settlement which followed World War I contribute to the coming of World War II?
10. Was Wilson right in fighting so hard for a League of Nations and for United States membership in that League? Why?

Pictures as Historical Evidence

Which pictures in this chapter would support the following generalization? Explain why. World War I was a total war in which the efforts of citizens as well as soldiers were an essential part of the war effort.

Map Study

Look at the map on page 583. Find the boundary line set by the Treaty of Brest-Litovsk. Who did the treaty favor? Why?

For Further Reading

Bitter Victory: A History of Black Soldiers in World War I, by Florette Henri. Garden City, New York: Doubleday & Company, Inc., 1970.

John J. Pershing, by Arch Whitehouse. New York: G. P. Putnam's Sons, 1964.

The Military History of the Lusitania, by Louis L. Snyder. New York: Franklin Watts, Inc., 1965.

The Story of World War I, by Robert Leckie. New York: Random House, Inc., 1965.

They Flew to Glory, by Robert Sidney Bowen. New York: Lothrop, Lee & Shepard Co., Inc., 1965.

World Citizen: Woodrow Wilson, by Jules Archer. New York: Julian Messner, 1967.

ISSUES PAST AND PRESENT

What Should Be America's Role in the World?

Patriotism

Ready or not, by the end of the Spanish American War the United States found itself one of the world's great economic, military, and political powers. Before 1898 many Americans had tried to keep the United States apart from the rest of the world. After 1898 they found it increasingly hard to do so. The wars, revolutions, and economic troubles of other nations that once had seemed to affect Americans no more seriously than mild illnesses had a way of becoming raging international epidemics that did not stop at American coastlines. As a result, for more than 70 years Presidents, other politicians, journalists, and citizens have been trying to find an answer to the perplexing question: What should be America's role in the world? In seeking answers Americans have found it necessary to ask themselves other difficult questions such as:

1. What values should the United States stand for?
2. Should the United States try to prevent crises in other parts of the world that may lead to violence?
3. Do Americans have an obligation to help other peoples in time of peace? If so, how?

Like Frederick Jackson Turner, whose views you read on pages 254 to 255, the novelist Frank Norris was one of the first Americans to write of the significance of the passing of the frontier. The selection below was published in the same year the author died.

FRANK NORRIS: *THE FRONTIER IS GONE*, 1902

Is it not possible that we can find in this great destiny of ours something a little better than just battle and conquest, something a little better than just trading our products for theirs? Is it not possible to hope that a new patriotism, one that shall include all peoples, may win out in the end? The past seems to show that this is a goal toward which we are moving.

Consider how patriotism began. At the very first the ties of birth held men together and the first feeling of patriotism was the love of family. But the family grows, expands, and becomes the clan. Patriotism is then devotion to the clan, and the clansmen will fight and die for the supremacy of the clan.

Then comes the time when the clans, tired of the roving life of herders, halt a moment and settle down in a chosen spot. The tents are exchanged for permanent dwelling houses, and the camp of the clan becomes at last a city. Patriotism is then pride in one's city.

The city extends its adjoining fields. They take in outlying

towns and other cities. Finally, the state comes into being. Patriotism no longer is confined within the walls of the city, but is enlarged to take in a larger area. But boundaries fade and states join other states, and at last the nation is born. Patriotism becomes a national thing, a far larger, broader, truer feeling than family patriotism. The word "brother" may be applied to men we cannot see and do not know, and a countryman is one of many millions of fellow countrymen.

We have reached this stage at the present, but the progress will not stop here. Will it not go on, this story of civilization, this destiny of races? Will it not go on until at last we who now proudly call ourselves Americans, supreme in conquest, whether of battleship or of bridge-building, may realize that the true patriotism is the brotherhood of man, and know that the whole world is our nation and all people our countrymen?

1. How does Norris explain the development of patriotism?
2. For what new meaning of patriotism does he want Americans to strive?
3. Do you agree with Norris? Why?

Democracy and the World

The aim which Frank Norris set forth in the previous selection seemed to be rudely pushed aside by the great world war which broke out in 1914. In 1917, when the United States became involved in that war, President Wilson tried to explain to Americans—and to the world—what he thought Americans were fighting for.

WOODROW WILSON: *WAR MESSAGE TO CONGRESS*, 1917

We are glad, now, to fight for the final peace of the world and for the liberation [freedom] of its peoples, including the German people. We are glad to fight for the rights of nations large and small and for the privilege of men everywhere to choose their way of life. The world must be made safe for democracy. Its peace must be planted upon the foundations of political liberty. We have no selfish purposes to serve. We desire no conquest. We are but one of those nations fighting for mankind.

There are many months of fiery trial and sacrifice ahead of us. It is a fearful thing to lead this great peaceful people into war. It is especially fearful to lead it into the most terrible and disastrous of all wars, in which civilization itself seems to be at stake. But what is right is more precious than peace. We

shall fight for the things which we have always carried nearest our hearts. Those things are democracy, the right of people to have a voice in their own governments, and the rights and liberties of small nations. To such a task we can give our lives and our fortunes. We can give everything that we are and everything that we have. We have the pride of those who know that the day has come when America is privileged to spend its blood and its might for the principles that gave it birth and happiness and the peace which it has treasured. God helping it, it can do no other.

1. What main goal were Americans fighting for in 1917?
2. What did Wilson expect Americans to get from such an effort? What did he expect them to give?
3. Are Wilson's goals ones you would support? Why?

America and Freedom

Wilson's aims for the United States in 1917 were not achieved. In the 1930's war broke out again in many places on the globe. In the speech from which these words were taken, President Franklin D. Roosevelt set forth some of the reasons why, in 1941, we were becoming deeply involved in World War II. That war had begun in Europe two years before when Germany had invaded Poland. At the time this speech was made, the United States had not declared war against Germany or Japan. But Americans were already giving large amounts of aid to future allies such as France, England, and China.

FRANKLIN D. ROOSEVELT: *THE FOUR FREEDOMS*, 1941

At no time before now has American security been as seriously threatened from outside our borders as it is today.

Since the permanent formation of our government under the Constitution, most of the periods of crisis in our history have had to do with affairs here at home. Fortunately, only one of these—the four-year war between the states—ever threatened our national unity.

It is true that before 1914 the United States often had been disturbed by events in other continents. But in no case had a serious threat been raised against our national safety or our independence.

Even when world war broke out in 1914, it seemed to contain only small threats of danger to our own American future. But, as time went on, the American people began to realize what the downfall of democratic nations might mean to our democracy.

Our national policy in affairs here at home has been based

upon a decent respect for the rights and the dignity of all our fellow men within our borders. Likewise, our national policy in foreign affairs has been based on a decent respect for the rights and dignity of all nations, large and small.

We are pledged to full support of all those brave peoples, everywhere, who are resisting aggression [invasion] and are thereby keeping war away from the Western Hemisphere.

In the future days, which we seek to make secure, we look forward to a world founded upon four essential human freedoms. The first is freedom of speech and expression—everywhere in the world. The second is freedom of every person to worship God in his own way—everywhere in the world. The third is freedom from want, which means securing for every nation a healthy peacetime life for its people—everywhere in the world. The fourth is freedom from fear, which means a worldwide reduction of armaments to such a point that no nation will be in a position to begin a war against any neighbor—anywhere in the world.

This nation has placed its destiny in the hands and heads and hearts of its millions of free men and women, and its faith in freedom under the guidance of God. Freedom means the supremacy of human rights everywhere. Our support goes to those who struggle to gain those rights or keep them.

1. According to Roosevelt how did twentieth-century national crises differ from the crises of earlier centuries?
2. Are Roosevelt's "four freedoms" goals you think Americans ought to seek for people everywhere? Why? How?

The Point IV Program

The United States was the only major world power not to be ravaged by the widespread destruction of World War II. After the war ended many Americans felt that even in peacetime we should take an active role in using our resources to prevent the takeover of weaker nations by more powerful nations. In 1949 President Harry Truman announced a program that he hoped would help achieve that goal.

HARRY TRUMAN: *POINT IV PROGRAM*, 1949

More than half the people of the world are living in conditions approaching misery. Their food is inadequate. They are victims of disease. Their economic life is primitive and stagnant. Their poverty is a handicap and a threat to them and to more prosperous areas.

For the first time in history, men possess the knowledge and the skill to relieve the suffering of these people. I believe that we should make available to peace-loving peoples the benefits of our technical knowledge in order to help them realize their dreams for a better life. Our aim should be to help the free peoples of the world, through their own efforts, to produce more food, more clothing, more houses, and more machines to lighten their burdens.

This should be a cooperative task in which all nations work together through the United Nations wherever possible. It must be a worldwide effort for the achievement of peace, plenty, and freedom. The old imperialism—exploitation for foreign profit—has no place in our plans.

"Exploitation" here means the taking advantage of colonial peoples.

Experts in different fields can bring about tremendous improvements. For example, the health of the people of many foreign nations has been greatly improved by the work of United States engineers in setting up modern water-supply systems. The food supply of many areas has been increased as the result of the advice of United States agricultural experts.

We hold out before the peoples of these areas the promise of a better future through the democratic way of life. It is vital that we move quickly to make that promise come true.

1. What role did President Truman want the United States to play in the postwar world?
2. What resources did he want the United States to use to achieve that goal?
3. Would you support Truman's policy today? Why?

Dealing with Communism

The following selection is taken from a speech made by the Republican Senator from Arizona, Barry Goldwater, on July 14, 1961, in the United States Senate.

BARRY GOLDWATER: *VICTORY IN THE COLD WAR*, 1961

The President of the Senate is the Vice President of the United States.

"Mr. President, I should like to see us get on the right track, once and for all, in our approach to foreign policy matters. And I believe the first step is for the President of the United States to declare officially that it is our purpose to win the Cold War, not merely wage it in the hope of attaining a standoff....

"Mr. President, it is really astounding that our government has never stated its purpose to be that of complete victory over the tyrannical forces of international communism. I am sure that the American people cannot understand

why we spend billions upon billions of dollars to engage in a struggle of worldwide proportions unless we have a clearly defined purpose to achieve victory. Anything less than victory, over the long run, can only be defeat, degradation, and slavery. Are these stakes not high enough for us? Is not this reason enough for us to fight to win?

"I suggest that our failure to declare total victory as our fundamental purpose is a measure of official timidity that refuses to recognize the all-embracing determination of communism to capture the world and destroy the United States. This timidity has sold us short, time and time again."

1. What does the author think should be the main goal of American foreign policy?
2. Is this goal similar to, or different from, the goals announced by Wilson, Roosevelt, and Truman in the previous selections? Why?

Haves and Have-Nots

Many countries that were colonies of European powers won or were given their independence from those powers in the years after World War II. Most of them were like the countries described in a brief sermon by Dr. Ralph W. Sockman, a leading radio preacher of that time. He did not state directly how the United States should help those countries, but instead relied upon his statistics to carry the message.

RALPH W. SOCKMAN:
HAVE AND HAVE-NOT NATIONS, 1960

Picture the world's population, now over 2.5 billion, compressed to the scale of a single town of 1,000 inhabitants. In such a town 60 persons would represent the population of the United States; 940 persons would represent the rest of the world. In the town as a whole about 300 would be Christians; 700 would not be. At least 80 persons out of the town's 1,000 people would be Communists and 370 would be under Communist domination. 303 persons in the town would be white; 697 would be nonwhite. The 60 Americans would expect to live 70 years; the non-Americans less than 40 years. The 60 Americans would have one-half of the town's entire financial income and the 940 others would share the other one-half. And almost one-half of the non-American population would not be able to read and write.

There is our world situation reduced to a scale which our imaginations can grasp. And color the picture with the consideration that now this world-town of 1,000 persons is being

stirred by a revolution of rising expectations. The poor, the hungry, the sick now know about the better life being enjoyed by the favored few in America.

Explosive forces and exploding populations are on the move. The direction these take will determine the life or death of the human race. Can we be unconcerned about the big issues confronting our world?

1. About what per cent of the people of the world are citizens of the United States? What fraction of the world's income do they receive?
2. What does the author mean by a "revolution of rising expectations?"
3. What does he seem to want Americans to do?

In Search of Leadership

In the 1960's the United States became involved in a war in Vietnam, a country that in 1954 had been divided into Communist and non-Communist areas. Many Americans interpreted our participation as one more example of our selfless use of force to prevent a Communist takeover of a weak country. Others saw it as a modern example of selfish imperialism. More than any other event of the 1960's, the war caused Americans to debate the role of their country in the world. The author of the following selection was a United States Senator and a leading participant in that debate.

J. W. FULBRIGHT: *THE PRICE OF EMPIRE*, 1967

When he visited America a hundred years ago, Thomas Huxley wrote, "I cannot say that I am in the slightest degree impressed by your bigness, or your material resources, as such. Size is not greatness, and territory does not make a nation. The great issue is what you are going to do with all these things." The question is still with us and we seem to have come to a time of historical crisis when its answer can no longer be put off.

We have not become a traditional empire yet. The old values remain—the optimism, the individualism, the rough-hewn equality, the friendliness, and the good humor. There also is still the inventiveness and the zest for life, the caring about people and the sympathy for the underdog. In addition, there is the idea, which goes back to the American Revolution, that maybe—just maybe—we can set an example of democracy and human dignity for the world.

That is something which none of the great empires of the past has ever done—or tried to do—but we were bold

A "traditional empire" was one in which territories were ruled by force for the benefit of the mother country.

enough to think that we might be able to do it. And there are a great many Americans who still think that we can do it — or at least they want to try.

They do not accept the view that because other great nations have pursued power for its own sake — a pursuit which has ended in decline or disaster — America must do the same. They think we have some choice about our own future and that the best basis for exercising that choice is the values on which this republic was founded.

This does not mean that other countries must adopt our values or that we should force our values on anybody. But it does require us to conduct ourselves so that our society does not seem hateful and evil to others.

The world has no need, in this age of nationalism and nuclear weapons, for a new imperial power. But there is a great need for moral leadership — by which I mean the leadership of decent example. That role could be ours.

1. What values does the author believe caused the United States to become a great nation?
2. What does the author believe to be the proper role for the United States in the world? Would you agree? Why?

Values as a Guide to Making Decisions

In trying to answer difficult questions about what peoples or nations should do, it is almost always necessary to try and determine what values are worth supporting. As you may have noticed, each of the authors of the previous selections based his opinion on those values which he held to be the most important. Go through these selections, and the two selections from *Interpreting the Past* at the beginning of this unit, and after each author's name list the values upon which he based his decision. Then answer these questions:

1. Which of the authors was most concerned about survival?
2. Which of the authors thought the most important value was the perfecting of democracy at home?
3. Which of the authors thought democracy ought to be brought to other peoples?
4. Which of the authors thought we had a responsibility to prevent international crises from erupting?
5. Which of the authors thought we should aid other countries in peacetime?
6. What do you think ought to be America's role in the world? Why?

1920 Women's Suffrage Granted

1921 Washington Armament Conference

1925 Scopes "Monkey" Trial

1928 Kellogg-Briand Pact Outlaws War

1920 Era of "Normalcy" Begins

1922 Mussolini Seizes Power in Italy

1927 Lindbergh Flies the Atlantic

UNIT VII
The
Twenties and Thirties

1931 Japan Invades China

1933 Hitler Gains Power in Germany

1936 Spanish Civil War Begins

1929 Great Depression Begins

1932 Roosevelt Elected President

1935 Congress Passes Social Security Act

1939 World War II Begins

Like a thunderbolt, the stock market crash of October 1929 ended a decade of sunny prosperity and began a decade of gloomy depression at home and growing turmoil in Europe and Asia. Prosperity was turned into poverty, gaiety into grimness. Unit VII gives us a picture of the contrasting halves of that period.

It begins, in *Interpreting the Past*, with impressions of the 1920's by historians who lived through those years. Chapter 21 presents a more detailed look at the way Americans worked and played in that decade. It also tells how Americans wrestled with questions of right and wrong in an era of rapid technological change. Chapter 22 describes the 1930's, the decade of the "Great Depression." What was happening in the rest of the world from 1920 to 1940, and how the country reacted to it, is the subject of Chapter 23. Though economic troubles at home continued to claim the attention of most people in the 1930's, fires of war began to sweep through Africa, Europe, and Asia. By the end of the decade, much of the world was at war.

In a time, like today, when the past seemed to offer little guidance for a fast-changing present and an uncertain future, it was natural to ask: Should Americans follow the ways of the past? This is the question examined at the end of the unit in *Issues Past and Present*.

TOP, LEFT TO RIGHT:
WIDE WORLD PHOTOS
LIBRARY OF CONGRESS
NEW YORK PUBLIC LIBRARY
WIDE WORLD PHOTOS
BIRNBACK PUBLISHING COMPANY
LIBRARY OF CONGRESS
WILLIAM GROPPER IN *New Masses*
BOTTOM, LEFT TO RIGHT:
OHIO HISTORICAL SOCIETY
WIDE WORLD PHOTOS
NATIONAL ARCHIVES
UPI
WIDE WORLD PHOTOS
HARVARD COLLEGE LIBRARY
NATIONAL ARCHIVES

INTERPRETING THE PAST

The Twenties

The Joys of Speculation

Some decades of American history are remembered for an event so far-reaching in its importance that the course of the nation was to be changed forever by it. In the 1770's that event was the Revolutionary War. In the 1840's Texas was annexed and the Mexican War added vast amounts of territory in the West.

The 1920's was a decade marked neither by war nor by territorial expansion. But many historians agree that what happened to the nation in the twenties had as much meaning to the future of the country as the wars and territorial expansions of earlier decades. As you read the following sources, consider these questions:

1. What were the lives of Americans like in the 1920's?
2. How did the 1920's change the nation?

Frederick Lewis Allen, magazine editor and author of one of the best books about the twenties, wrote the following selection at the end of the decade.

FREDERICK LEWIS ALLEN: *ONLY YESTERDAY*, 1931

In tropical Miami in the summer and autumn of 1925, the whole city became one insane real estate market. Something happened to the minds of supposedly sensible men and women when they caught the most raging fever of real estate speculation which had attacked the United States in many years. There were said to be 2,000 real estate offices in Miami and 25,000 salesmen selling house lots or acreage. The highway to Miami was clogged with automobiles from every part of the country. A traveler caught in a traffic jam counted the license plates of eighteen states among the sedans and flivvers waiting in line. Hotels were overcrowded. People were sleeping wherever they could lay their heads. Everybody was making money on land, prices were climbing to incredible heights, and those who came to scoff remained to speculate.

Nor was Miami alone booming. The whole strip of coastline from Palm Beach southward was being developed into an American Riviera. The fever spread to Tampa, Sarasota, St. Petersburg, and other cities and towns. People were scrambling for lots all through the state.

Yes, the public bought. By 1925 they were buying anything, anywhere, so long as it was in Florida. Natives of Florida, visitors to Florida, and good citizens of Ohio and Massachusetts and Wisconsin who had never been near Florida made out their checks for lots. People from Florida were doing

"Flivver" is a slang term meaning an old or cheap car.

The "Riviera" is the famous resort area in the south of Italy and France.

most of the shouting. But the hysteria [frenzied excitement] which centered in their state was a national hysteria, enormously increased by the crowds of people from outside the state who wanted to make easy money.

Another fever of the 1920's was stock market speculation. In March 1928 it was infecting the whole country. Stories of fortunes made overnight were on everybody's lips. One doctor said that his patients were talking about the market and nothing else. Wives were asking their husbands why they were so slow and why they were not getting in on all this, only to hear that their husbands had bought 100 shares of American Linseed stock that very morning.

By the summer of 1929 the prices of shares of stock had soared far above the stormy levels of the winter before. Factories were running at full blast. This was a new era.

The American could spin wonderful dreams. His dreams were of a romantic day when he would sell his stock at a fabulous price and live in a great house and have a fleet of shining cars and take it easy on the sands of Palm Beach. And when he looked toward the future of his country, he could see an America set free from poverty and toil. He saw roads swarming with millions upon millions of automobiles. He saw airplanes darkening the skies. He saw lines of high-tension wires carrying from hilltop to hilltop the electric power to give life to a thousand labor-saving machines. He saw skyscrapers thrusting above one-time villages. He saw vast cities rising in great masses of stone and concrete and roaring with traffic—and smartly dressed men and women spending, spending, spending with the money they had won by being far-sighted enough to foresee, way back in 1929, what was going to happen.

1. Did most of the people who bought real estate or stock intend to keep it for a long time? Why?
2. Why did so many people believe that the value of the real estate and stock they bought would never stop rising?

Prohibition

The manufacture, transportation, sale, and drinking of alcoholic beverages was prohibited by the Eighteenth Amendment to the Constitution, which went into effect in 1920. Though most Americans probably approved of Prohibition at that time, many did not. Violation of the law which put the amendment into effect was common. In fact, it was so widespread that many of those who approved of Prohibition in 1920 began by 1930 to favor the repeal of the Eighteenth Amendment. The following poem has many versions. Who the original author was is not

certain, but one writer assigns it to Franklin P. Adams, a noted humorist, who published it in his column in the New York World *in 1931.*

FRANKLIN P. ADAMS: *PROHIBITION*, 1931

Prohibition is an awful flop.
  We like it.
It can't stop what it's meant to stop.
  We like it.

It's left a trail of graft and slime,
It's filled our land with vice and crime,
It don't prohibit worth a dime,
  Nevertheless, we're for it.

1. From the poem what hypothesis might you make about enforcing the law on Prohibition? Why?

"Graft" is the using of one's official position to gain special advantages or money. During Prohibition many officials allowed the illegal sale of alcoholic beverages for which they received payment and special favors.

Flashy, Sad, and Misinterpreted

The article from which the following words were taken was written for a special issue of American Heritage, *a leading magazine of American history, by one of its editors.*

BRUCE CATTON: *THE RESTLESS DECADE*, 1965

The decade of the 1920's was at one and the same time the flashiest, the saddest, and the most misinterpreted era in modern American history.

It was flashy because it was full of restless life in a time when all of the old rules seemed to be gone. It was sad because many things that Americans were certain about in 1920 were either gone forever or going fast. It was misunderstood because so many of its interpreters became so fascinated by the things that floated around on the surface that they could not see anything else.

Many of the words that have been written about it are wrong. It was, we are told, the period when *everybody* did fantastic things. Everybody hated Prohibition, bought liquor from bootleggers, made terrible gin in the bathtub and worse beer in the basement. Everybody danced the Charleston. Everybody bought stocks or real estate in Florida on credit and expected to become rich before they grew old. Everybody, to sum it all up, was off on a very long spree. The typical figure of the era was the Flapper, the girl who bobbed her hair and wore short skirts and climbed in and out of open cars driven by college boys in coonskin coats. It makes an entertaining

"Bootleggers" are dealers in illegal liquor.

"Bobbed" means cut short.

picture, but it is only a partial picture.

The first thing to remember is that the word "everybody" describes too many people. There were a lot of people in the United States in the 1920's, and most of them were serious, hard-working people who did their best to earn a living, bring up their children, live decently in the best way they knew, and put away a few dollars for their old age. Most of them never saw the inside of the places where liquor was sold unlawfully. Most never really tried to make gin or beer at home. Anyone over the age of 26 who danced the Charleston regretted it immediately—only the young could really do it. Most people accepted Prohibition, and its repeal was never seriously considered until after the twenties had ended. Certainly the vast majority of people bought neither stocks, bonds, nor Florida real estate.

Nevertheless, the twenties did have their own peculiar character—because they were years of unending change. The world was shifting gears, starting to move with bewildering speed. The destination was not clear, but the speed itself was breathtaking.

The age of the automobile was arriving. The change it was going to make on America—change for city, town, and countryside, for ways of living—could already be seen. The airplanes and electronics that would change the world forever were appearing. The age of mass communications was here.

The twenties were not like anything ever seen before—or since. They were years that no one who lived through them can ever forget. They were also a time nobody in his senses would care to repeat. You do have to say one thing for them: When the great catastrophe of World War II came, ten years after the twenties had ended, the people the twenties had raised proved to be strong enough to stand the shock.

1. For what reasons does the author feel that the twenties have been a "misinterpreted era?"
2. Describe in your own words what the author felt most Americans of the twenties were like.
3. What are some of the factors that caused the twenties to be "years of unending change?"

Summary Question

1. How does Frederick Lewis Allen's evaluation of the 1920's differ from Bruce Catton's evaluation?

21

The Golden and Not-So-Golden Twenties

The saxophones moan, the clarinets giggle, the drums go bangety-boomp! And the flapper (left)—a young girl who has dropped old-fashioned ways and does not care who knows it—kicks up her heels. The nineteenth-century pioneers of women's rights would not recognize this short-skirted, short-haired "new woman" of 1926. It is equally hard to imagine her willing, older partner as a descendant of Puritans or frontiersmen. Thus the two free-swinging figures represent one of the themes of the 1920's—a sharp, radical break with the past.

America took on its modern look almost overnight. It became a land crowded with highways, billboards, radios, movies. Automobiles were not new in 1920, but after that year they poured out of factories in such numbers that they changed the look of the American countryside. Suburbs and advertising were known in 1910. But by 1925 all big cities seemed to be in a race to spread outward, and advertisements appeared to leap from every magazine page.

Quick change was the rule in everything from business and entertainment to family life. Yet a curious thing took place. The more things changed, the more some people lived in "old-fashioned" ways and defended time-honored beliefs. Any group of people faced with upheaval feels some fright. So it was natural that some Americans of the 1920's tried to keep things as they had been by shutting the gates on immigration, or banning new ideas from the schools, or withdrawing from the world's affairs.

Yet often these same people enjoyed other parts of modern progress. They were cautious about new social customs but loved new gadgets and wanted bigger incomes. They cheered the growth of their communities. Not *all* change was a threat.

Meanwhile, other men and women of the twenties accepted certain changing ideas but feared that America was sacrificing its former ideals in the rush to get rich. Reactions to life in the 1920's were varied. But almost everyone shared one special feeling. It was a sense that they had crossed a dividing line that made their times unlike any ever before experienced by Americans.

As you read, think about these questions:
1. In the 1920's why did some people welcome change while others opposed it?
2. What changes brought by the twenties proved to be most permanent?

In the 1920's cartoons by John Held, Jr., popularized the flapper image.

WIDE WORLD PHOTOS

Presidential candidate Warren Harding poses with the Chicago Cubs (below). President Harding greets a young admirer (above). President Calvin Coolidge (far left) chats with Herbert Hoover.

BOTH: OHIO HISTORICAL SOCIETY

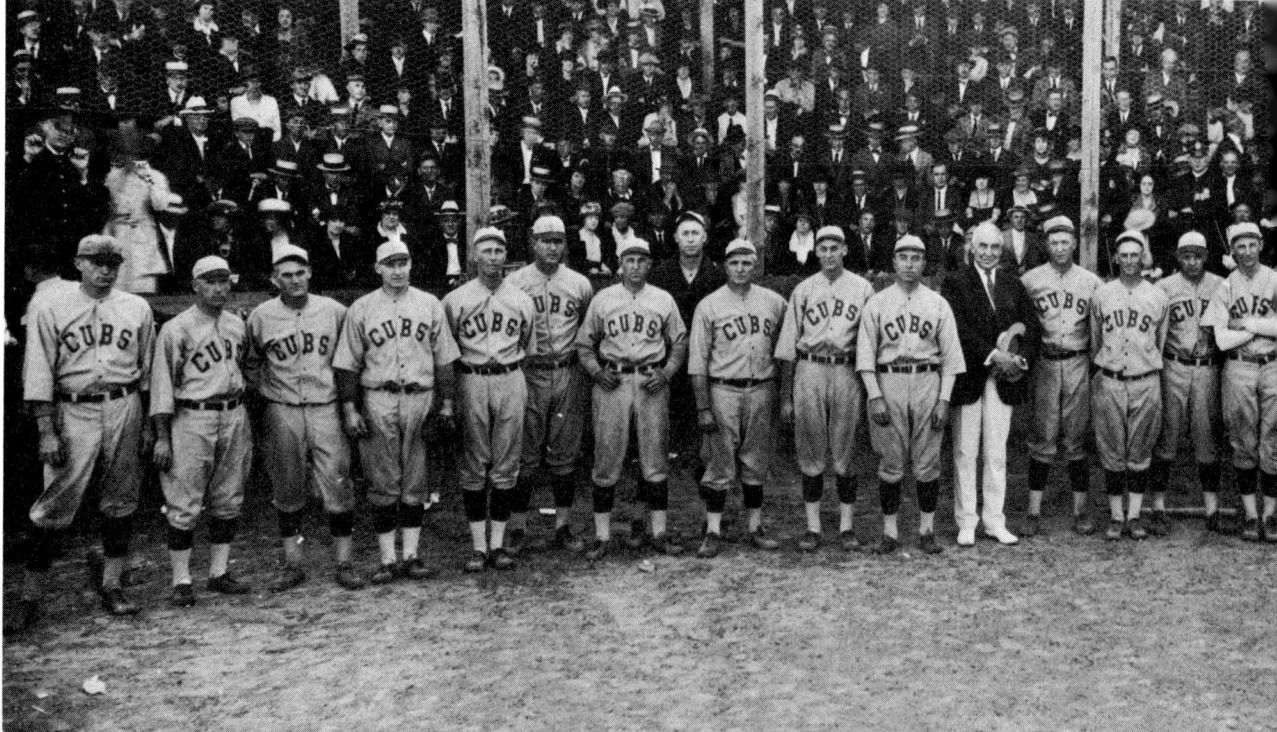

"The Business of America Is Business"

It would be difficult to find two more different men than Woodrow Wilson and Warren G. Harding, who succeeded Wilson as President in 1921. Wilson was an ex-professor, accustomed to lecturing others, especially on their duties. Harding was a likable, easygoing, small-town newspaper owner, at ease bouncing a child or greeting a visiting baseball team (left). He had few strong ideas of his own on any issue and called only for a return to "normalcy"—a quiet pace after the Progressive and wartime crusades.

Although Harding himself was not politically corrupt, he appointed some of his friends to high posts. They betrayed him by taking bribes in return for doing illegal government favors. The President and the country were just beginning to learn of these scandals when Harding suddenly died in August of 1923.

Calvin Coolidge (far left), Harding's Vice President and successor, was not involved in the scandals. His fellow Americans viewed him as a healthy example of the simple life. Actually, Coolidge was a college graduate and a Massachusetts corporation lawyer before entering politics. But in an age when the Presidential "image" was becoming more important, it helped him to look and sound like a Vermont farmer who never wasted a word or a nickel. In 1924 he ran for re-election on the slogan "Keep Cool With Coolidge." His opposition was divided between a conservative candidate nominated by a badly split Democratic Party and Robert La Follette, the candidate of a new third party that followed Progressive traditions. Coolidge won a decisive victory.

"Normalcy" and "keeping cool" meant a sharp departure from the Progressive policies of reforming and regulating the economy. Taxes on corporations were cut to the bone, leaving business with more money to invest, while Congress voted almost no funds to allow the Federal government to enforce antitrust and other Progressive laws. Both Harding and Coolidge had as their Secretary of Commerce Herbert Hoover (far left), a brilliant engineer and organizer. Under him the Department of Commerce encouraged companies in the same industry to form "trade associations." It then provided them with information on markets, prices, new inventions, and sources of raw materials. This increased the efficiency in each industry—but also discouraged competition by independent outsiders.

The thinking behind such policies was that indus-

EWING GALLOWAY

Above: Cars crowd New York's Fifth Avenue in 1921. Below: In 1928 hundreds of racing enthusiasts on their way to the Maryland Hunt Club steeplechase created this traffic jam.

CULVER PICTURES

trial prosperity would create wealth not just for businessmen but for all consumers: laborers, farmers, and even the poor. No further national action to deal with social problems was needed. As Coolidge himself said, "The business of America is business."

America Becomes a Machine Civilization

And business roared on! The industrial machinery tuned to wartime pitch in 1918 soon began to produce civilian goods again. But the boom of the 1920's differed from those of earlier times. In addition to **capital goods** (basic economic building blocks, such as steel girders and farm machines), more and more **consumer goods** (things used directly by individuals) were being produced. These included not just everyday items like canned vegetables and workshirts, but also a long list of new devices to save labor and increase personal pleasure: toasters, radios, vacuum cleaners, refrigerators, and cosmetics. Certain older industries like coal-mining suffered because of overproduction and aging machinery as well as because of competition from the oil industry. But newer ones like moviemaking, electric utilities, and aviation were making eye-catching upward leaps.

In order to sell new goods, especially luxuries, advertising itself became a big business. Its leaders claimed that their work was necessary to create the demand that kept factory wheels turning. Without "ads," said one man, the nation would have to "turn back the page to medieval times." For many yesterday's luxury became today's necessity. Along with advertising as an encouragement to buying came the **installment plan.** This allowed customers to buy an item with a small down payment and a written promise to pay the rest later in weekly or monthly sums. Credit buying had been common in business and farming. Used for more personal spending, it soon changed the basic American ideas about the value of thrift toward a new belief which stressed consumption.

The new industry that had the biggest effect on the economy was the manufacture of automobiles. When cars first appeared in the 1890's, they were sold as luxuries (right). But assembly-line procedures, easy credit, and advertising had made them commonplace by 1929, when more than 23 million private cars were in use in the United States. The manufacture of automobiles used up 20 per cent of the steel, 80 per cent of

In this 1904 ad appealing to the upper classes, Ford promises an "8 actual horsepower" motor.

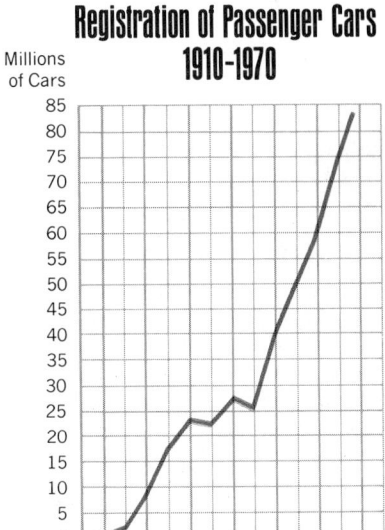

617

the rubber, and 90 per cent of the oil produced in the United States each year. It also created millions of other jobs in the oil and highway industries.

The Growth of Suburbia

Along with its huge economic impact, the automobile had revolutionary effects on society. A car gave any man, regardless of section, class, or background, a 40-mile-an-hour magic carpet to go wherever he wished. It gave young people who were "keeping company" a chance to escape the supervision of older eyes. It thus changed manners and morals by loosening family control of behavior. It also speeded up the pace of American life by encouraging family travel. The America of settled towns and time-honored habits became a land of wheeled wanderers.

The automobile also put suburban living within the reach of the middle class. In the nineteenth century only the well-off businessman could buy a "country retreat." But inexpensive automobiles allowed the ordinary worker to seek fresh air and greenery for himself and his children. He no longer had to live near his job. The automobile sparked a suburban real estate boom which has yet to slow down. Builders bought vacant lands near highways (top right) and put up new homes, spurring economic growth still further.

Because the homes of the new suburbia had to be low priced for mass sale, they were built on small lots which threw them close together. It was also cheapest to build many houses, with identical features, from a common plan. Thus many—though not all—suburbs had a monotonous, crowded look (lower right).

Suburban growth deeply affected the future of urban centers. Cheap open land, needed for future growth, began to vanish under rows of houses. Big cities began to lose income for needed services as their former taxpayers left at sundown after using city facilities while at work. The villages to which suburbanites rushed were not much better off. They could not build new schools, roads, and power and water systems fast enough to satisfy explosively growing needs.

Henry Ford and men like him produced a cultural revolution. They were responsible for giving new forms to the American city, landscape, and family. As one Midwesterner said, the changes in America could be explained "in just four letters—A-U-T-O!"

Top right: In 1922 real estate developers discuss plans for a new project—Westwood Village—near Santa Monica Boulevard in California. Right: This photograph, taken in the 1920's, shows suburban Queens, New York.

SECURITY FIRST NATIONAL BANK

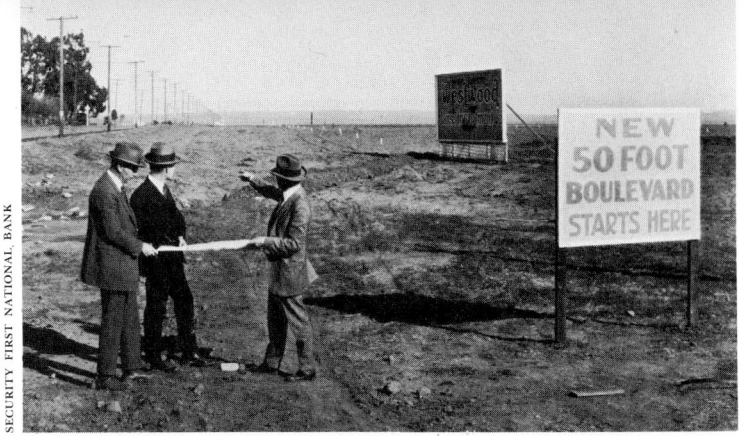

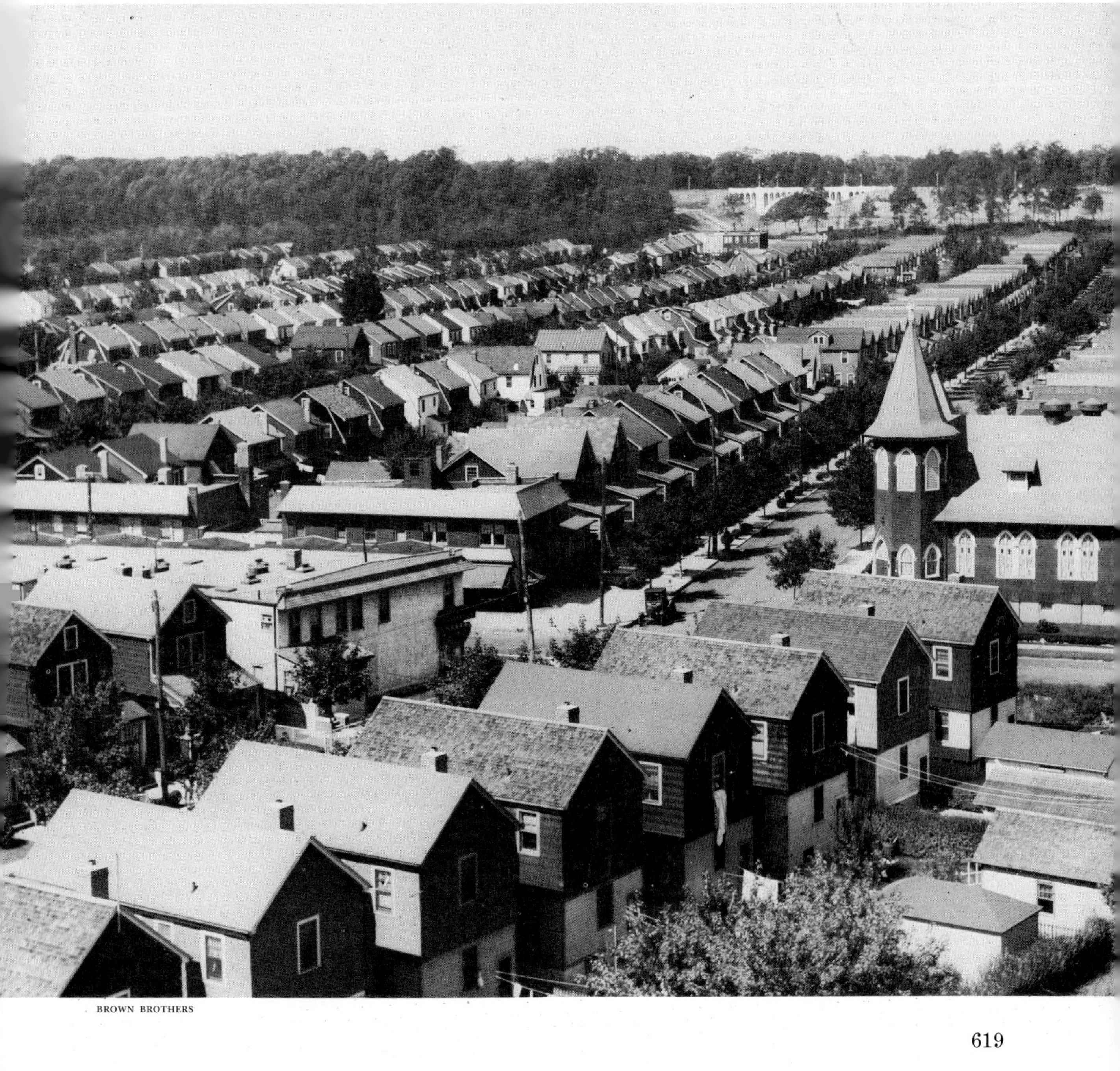
BROWN BROTHERS

NEGROES HAVE COME NORTH TO STAY; FIND CHANCE FOR INDEPENDENCE HERE

The Negro Comes to the City

The city, however, had not lost its attraction for ambitious and talented young men and women in the twenties. This was especially true for blacks, who were now moving cityward in great numbers.

In New York City a community called Harlem showed both the possibilities and the frustrations that urban blacks would experience in the years to come. Most Negroes who sought city opportunities found only low-paid and unskilled jobs, often as servants. But there was a middle class of black businessmen and a black artistic community, too. These groups were drawn to Harlem, an upper Manhattan neighborhood which had once been a white suburb. As Negroes moved into Harlem's streets, frightened and prejudiced whites left in droves. Soon Harlem was mostly black.

To live there brought pride to Negroes. Many businessmen, poets, novelists, painters, musicians, and scholars achieved both prosperity and fame. They also enjoyed closeness to each other in Harlem and felt like the poet Langston Hughes. He wrote that when he returned to Harlem after a long trip away, he "took a deep breath and felt happy again." Best known of all to whites were great jazz musicians, like Duke Ellington (upper left). Jazz, originally created by New Orleans blacks, became a popular part of American culture and was eventually admired all over the world.

Harlem's day of glory was short. The community began to develop severe problems. Whites elsewhere in the city would rarely sell or rent living space to Negroes. New York's growing Negro population, therefore, crowded into Harlem. Slum conditions (lower left) developed as landlords proved unwilling or unable to prevent decay. Most blacks, in addition, still faced huge handicaps in finding rewarding work. So unemployment, poverty, disease, and crime grew. By 1935 Harlem was the nation's largest **ghetto** (a slum section of a city inhabited almost entirely by a minority group who cannot move out because of poverty and discrimination).

Questions for Discussion

1. How did the Harding and Coolidge administrations help some businesses but hinder others?
2. How did the automobile change America?
3. Why did black urban communities tend to become ghettoes?

During the 1920's Harlem became almost exclusively a black community. A number of Negro intellectuals and artists became Harlem residents. Black writers, like poet Langston Hughes, won praise from white and black critics alike. Whites visited Harlem to hear musicians like Duke Ellington (top left) perform. The most famous night spot was the Cotton Club, which catered exclusively to whites. Harlem became a symbol of the Jazz Age and the "New Negro." Yet most blacks who came to Harlem found poor housing (bottom left) and few jobs. To pay the high rents many families were forced to crowd into small apartments, which led to still worse conditions. From 1923 to 1927 Harlem's death rate was 42 per cent higher than the city's. However, Harlem's glamorous image during the twenties overshadowed its social problems.

BROWN BROTHERS

UNDERWOOD & UNDERWOOD

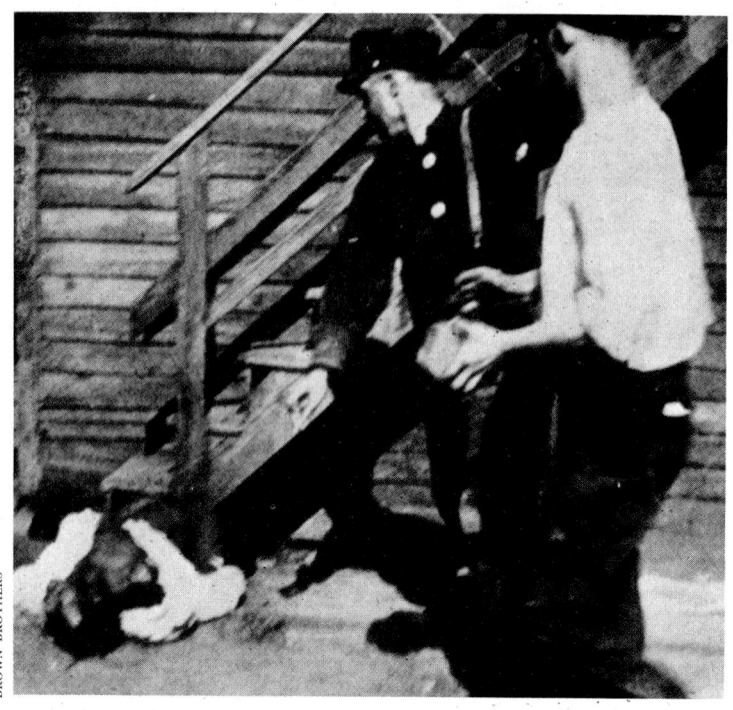

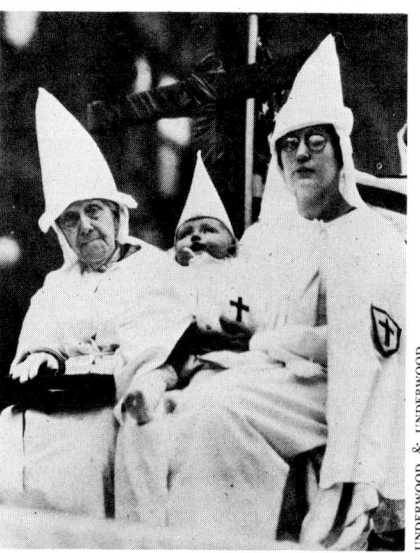

Above: Whites murder a Negro during the 1919 Chicago race riots. Right: Three generations of Klansmen pose in 1925.

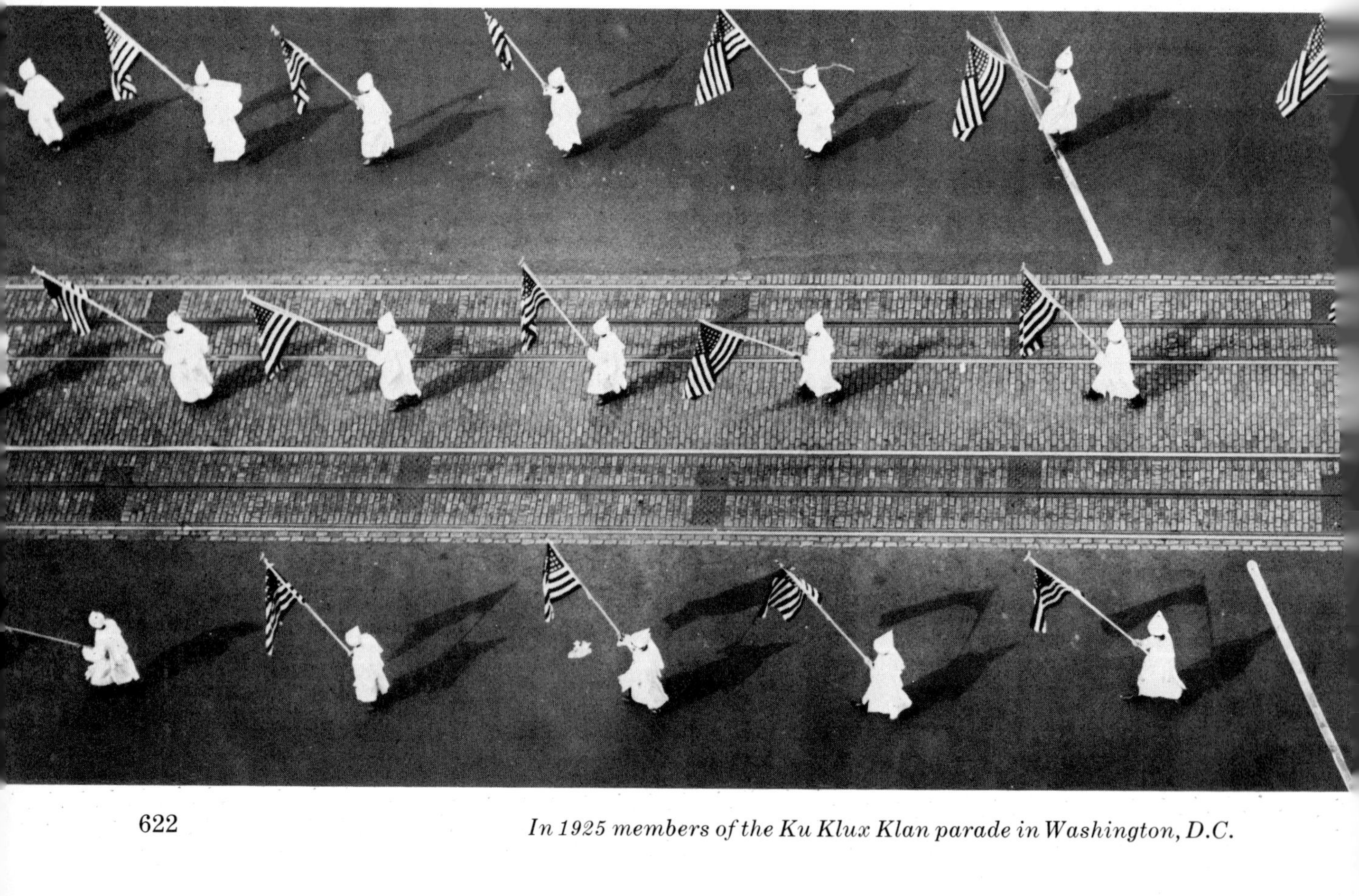

In 1925 members of the Ku Klux Klan parade in Washington, D.C.

An Era of Reaction

The steady march to urban areas kept up. By 1920 less than half of the American population lived in rural communities. As small-town America's ways vanished, some Americans fought back against modernizing influences.

Not all anger at change came from villages. White big-city dwellers, for example, objected to the growing numbers of blacks in their midst. In 1919 there was a "red summer" of race riots. Between June and December, 76 Negroes were lynched in some 25 riots. The worst was in Chicago. It began with an unimportant fight between white and black youths on a bathing beach. But wild rumors soon led to nearly a week of street battles between gangs of both races. Before the National Guard restored peace, 15 whites and 23 blacks died and over 500 people were injured.

The most outspoken foes of Negroes, however, were members of the Ku Klux Klan, which was revived in 1915. The new Klan, however, was not limited to the South. Nor were its targets only Negroes. Its slogan was "native, white, Protestant," and by 1920 it opposed Catholics, Jews, foreigners, and radicals, who, it said, were trying to "take over" America. The reborn organization quickly grew to a membership estimated in 1923 to be 5 million. It was a powerful political force in Texas, Louisiana, Oklahoma, Maine, Kansas, and Indiana. Klan political machines helped to elect or defeat governors and Congressmen from 1920 to 1925. In 1928 the Democrats nominated Alfred E. Smith, a New York Catholic, for President. Klan opposition was one of the reasons why seven southern states broke their tradition of voting Democratic and voted instead for the Republican candidate, Herbert Hoover, guaranteeing his election.

Though the Klan was strongest in rural areas, it did win big-city recruits. The hooded, parading figures (bottom left) in Washington, D.C., were part of an assembling of 40,000 Klansmen from all parts of the nation. The Klan was probably guilty of terroristic acts against its "enemies," though its leaders always denied it. Yet the Klan appealed not only to violence. It gave some poorly educated men and women who were fearful of change a sense of sharing the burden of defending their way of life. But by 1930 most Americans were not convinced that Americanism belonged to any one race, nationality, religion, or set of ideas. In addition, important Klan leaders were found guilty

Ellis Island (below), in New York's harbor, became an immigrant processing station in 1891. From then on the vast majority of immigrants to America were processed there. Following World War I immigration to the United States increased dramatically. In 1920, 430,000 people emigrated to America. The next year the number rose to 805,000. This 1923 cartoon (left) by Pulitzer-Prize-winning cartoonist Rollin Kirby anticipated the harsh Immigration Act of 1924. Secretary of State Charles Evans Hughes is saying to potential European immigrants, "I sympathize with you, Madame, but I cannot associate with you."

of political corruption and murder. Between 1923 and 1930 the Klan shrank to a tiny handful.

The Golden Door is Closed

There was still another reaction to the waves of change washing over America. The nation ended its historic practice of admitting almost unlimited numbers of European immigrants. As we saw in previous chapters, there had long been complaints against wide-open immigration. But during World War I suspicions of foreigners grew stronger than ever. Propaganda suggested that even innocent-looking neighbors might be German spies in disguise. After the Russian Revolution it was easy to transfer such fears to possible Communist sympathizers. A New York newspaper said, in 1919, "All over the country, alien or foreign-born agitators are carrying on in many languages...the Bolshevist and IWW propaganda for the overthrow of the government."

A great "Red Scare" (Communists were known as "reds") gripped the land. While it lasted thousands of **aliens** (people who are not citizens of the country in which they are living) were rounded up and hundreds were deported, even in cases where there was no proof of wrongdoing. Meantime, Congress hammered out an immigration restriction policy. It took final form in a law of 1924.

Under this law the number of Europeans admitted as immigrants in any one year after 1928 was to be only 150,000. Each nation would have a quota based on the number of its people or their descendants in the American population in 1920. The less time a nation's emigrants had been in the United States, of course, the fewer descendants they had. So the law successfully cut down the quotas of those southern and eastern European countries which had only recently contributed large numbers of new Americans. As an example, five times as many places were saved for British newcomers as for Italians. Unused spaces on a generous quota could not be transferred to another nation. Congress had designed the law to keep America's "flavor" Anglo-Saxon.

No longer did long lines of future United States citizens throng New York harbor's Ellis Island (lower left). The poem on the Statue of Liberty's base reads, "I lift my lamp beside the golden door." In the 1920's the golden door was closed most of the way.

The Scopes Trial

Sometimes a small incident in history is important because it stands for something much bigger. In 1925 a trial in little Dayton, Tennessee, became a famous event because it summed up the decade's clash between old and new points of view. The accused was a young biology teacher named John Scopes. He had broken a new state law that forbade the teaching of Charles Darwin's 65-year-old theory of evolution.

One part of the theory held that man was an animal who had evolved into his present form over millions of years and was related to the apes, whom he resembled. To Fundamentalists—Christians who read the Bible as a factual record of events, like a newspaper—this idea was wicked. It made a lie out of the Biblical story of how God created Adam and mankind.

The issue was not simply what Scopes did. Supporters of the law believed that if the Bible could be questioned then all religion, patriotism, family love—things that held society together—might be fatally challenged. Surely, a free community had the right to protect itself against poisonous ideas.

But opponents of the law claimed that, if a majority anywhere could ban ideas which they disliked from schools, they would end progress. Humanity, they said, had climbed upward from savagery only by questioning accepted wisdom. Free men needed free minds and the free speech protected by the Constitution.

The American Civil Liberties Union helped Scopes by hiring one of the country's foremost criminal lawyers, Clarence Darrow (bottom right), to defend him. William Jennings Bryan (top right), Democratic candidate for President in 1896, 1900, and 1908, volunteered to prosecute for the state. Not only was Bryan himself a Fundamentalist, but he felt that he was defending the right of people to keep their world as it was and as they wished it.

The trial became a circus. The national press called it "monkey business" and made it a battle between "city slickers" and "hayseeds." Fundamentalism won an empty victory. Scopes was found guilty. But as years passed the law was widely ignored.

Questions for Discussion

1. Why did the Klan lose power by 1930?
2. How did the quota system change immigration?
3. What were the main issues in the *Scopes* trial?

APE

NEANDERTHALER

SOCRATES

DEFENDER OF THE FAITH
(*U. S. A., 20th Century*)

Responding to pressure from Fundamentalist groups, the Tennessee legislature passed an anti-evolution law, certain that the governor would veto it. He signed it, certain that school districts would ignore it. They did. But the American Civil Liberties Union wanted to test the law in court. John Scopes, a 24-year-old unmarried teacher, reluctantly agreed to deliberately break the law. The trial's most dramatic moment came when Clarence Darrow (below) called the prosecutor, William Jennings Bryan (right), to the stand. Darrow's attack on Fundamentalist beliefs and the 100° heat combined to break Bryan; five days after the trial ended, he died. Scopes was found guilty, but a higher court set aside his penalty—a $100 fine.

BOTH: UPI

The Roaring Twenties

High on the list of forces shaping life in the twenties was Prohibition. In 1919 the Eighteenth Amendment was ratified. It prohibited the manufacture, sale, and transportation of intoxicating liquor one year after ratification. After a century of crusading against "demon rum," America had gone dry.

Many spokesmen for the amendment had been Progressives. They thought that outlawing liquor would improve the quality of national life. Drunkenness cost society millions of dollars each year in accidents, crime, lost jobs, and broken homes, they said.

But times were changing in 1920. Numerous Americans, especially urbanites, saw no harm in moderate drinking. Above all, they believed that to drink or not to drink was a personal choice. The government had no right to determine personal **morality** (judgments about right and wrong). So they ignored the law and bought illegal "booze" or made their own "home brew."

This created problems. In rural areas illegal liquor could be made in small, hidden distilleries. But city dwellers usually had to buy it. Their suppliers, known as "bootleggers," most often smuggled in liquor from abroad. Even frequent raids by police and Treasury agents (center right and bottom right) failed to keep bootlegging from thriving as a business.

But an illegal business lacks protection for both buyers and sellers. Those who are strong and without conscience can quickly take over. A bootlegger did not compete with rivals by price cuts or advertising. He did not sue nonpaying customers in court. Instead, in extreme cases, he hired gunmen to "rub them out." Soon gangs of killers were fighting each other in the streets for control of a city's liquor business, as the photo (top, far right) taken after a Chicago gangland massacre shows.

The best known gangster in the nation was Chicago's Al Capone (top right). Using his many millions of dollars of illegal profit each year, he bribed officials to look the other way. His gunmen were the army of an "empire" of boats, trucks, warehouses, and "speakeasies," that is, nightclubs that illegally sold drinks. Capone himself avoided arrest and had a fine home in Florida. Crime, like everything else in the 1920's, had become a big, well-organized business.

"Wets" and "drys"—Prohibition's enemies and supporters—blamed each other for its failures. Whoever was at fault, it was impossible to enforce and the

CHICAGO HISTORICAL SOCIETY

Right: State troopers nab a bootlegger and his illegal booze. Above: Federal Prohibition agents pose with some captured distilling equipment. Above right: Al Capone, who assumed control of Chicago's underworld in 1925, was finally jailed in 1931 on charges of income tax evasion.

WIDE WORLD PHOTOS

UNDERWOOD & UNDERWOOD

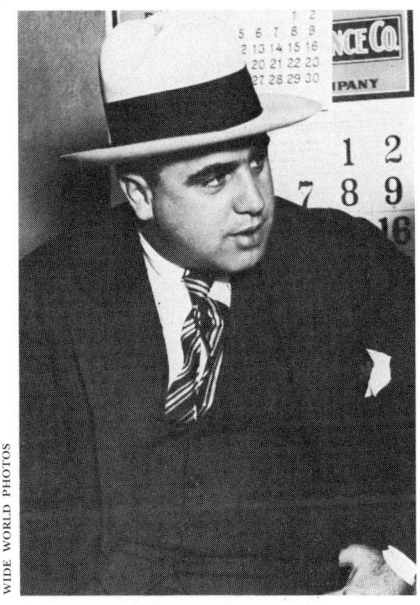

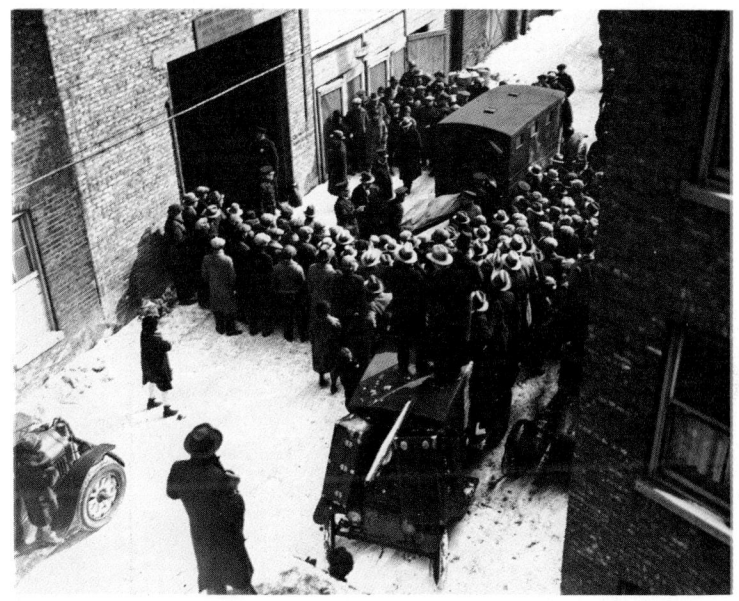

Above: On St. Valentine's Day 1929 crowds gather after seven Chicago mobsters were gunned down by a rival gang.

UPI

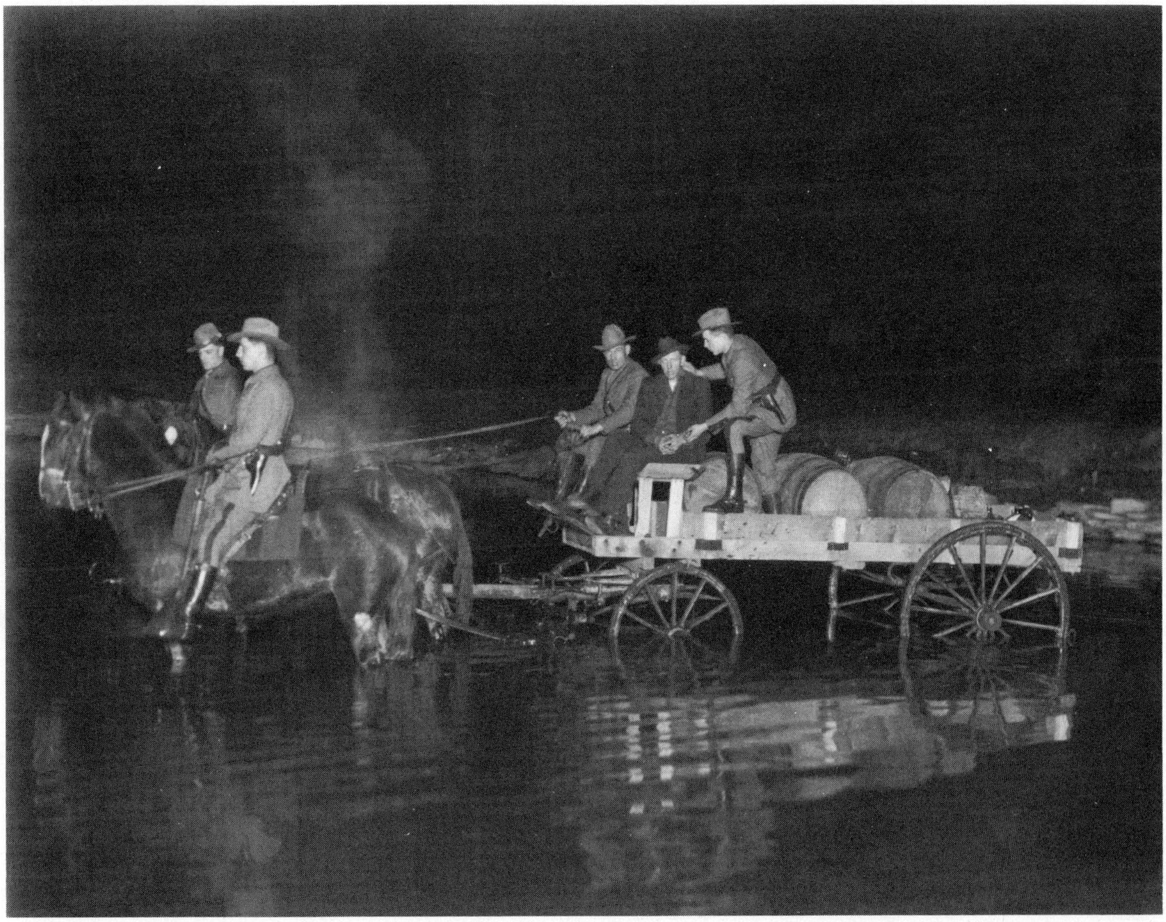

In 1922 a Chicago policewoman (in the white skirt) arrests four young ladies at the beach. They were charged with offending public decency by wearing daring new one-piece bathing suits. Just a year later one-piece suits were very fashionable. Notice the interested male bystanders, properly attired in two-piece swim suits, in the background.

country tired of it. Its repeal was voted in 1933. Organized crime went on, but Capone's career ended about the same time as Prohibition.

The New Woman

In August 1920 the Nineteenth Amendment, giving women the vote, took effect. Like the Eighteenth which brought Prohibition, it came after a long battle that went back to the first reform era of the 1830's and 1840's. Like that amendment, it also was intended to purify national life.

This was because women, as mothers, were supposed to be the special caretakers of the finer things in life. While men did the practical work of the world in shops and offices, women taught the children religion and morals and decorated their homes with things of beauty. In the Progressive era, when many women became pioneers in education, social work, and reform activities, it was believed that such work was natural to them because of their "finer instincts." With their ballots many now thought they would clean up politics, too.

But the "new woman" of the twenties surprised everyone. She saw that being worshiped for having a special kind of womanly goodness could be a trap, forcing her into certain kinds of "pure" behavior. What she wanted was the same freedom as a man to choose her way of life and her personal habits. She might try to improve society. Or she might choose a profession, along with—or instead of—a husband and children. But she insisted on changing old patterns of behavior to suit her individual tastes. She smoked, danced, wore make-up, drank, and did things that only "wicked" women did in her mother's youth. She even wore daring bathing suits (left) without shame!

The heroines admired by young women in the 1920's were a new American type. There was Gertrude Ederle, who swam the English Channel through cold, tricky, dangerous tidal currents. There was the slim pilot Amelia Earhart, the first woman to fly the Atlantic. In the world of entertainment, there were movie stars with rosebud lips and come-hither eyes, like Clara Bow or Theda Bara.

Not every girl was a flapper or a new woman. But the new feminine styles of behavior, widely shown in newspapers and movies, were copied by country as well as city girls. When small-town misses appeared at

dances with bare knees and painted lips, they were saying that in changing times they would no longer automatically accept their parents' answers to such questions as: "How should I behave? What is my position in life? Where do I fit in?"

An Age of Hero Worship

One reason for the breakdown in older community standards was the rise of rapid mass communication. Local preachers, politicians, and editors had to compete for respectful attention with nationally known experts interviewed on radio or in the big-city papers. Often they lost.

One definition of a community is a group of people who share something. Using that definition, the **mass media** (any means of public communication, such as newspapers, radio, and movies, reaching a large audience) were actually building a nationwide community. All Americans were coming to share in the news instantly reported over the airwaves, in print, or in newsreels. Journalism made millions of people "eyewitnesses" to events and "acquaintances" of newsmaking figures.

Since sensational news did not happen every day, the media created celebrities—people made famous through appearance in news columns—in sports and entertainment. Great events did not occur each morning. But George Herman (Babe) Ruth played baseball (middle right) from April to October. He was a superathlete, exciting to watch as his mighty swing drove the ball out of sight for one of his yet-unmatched 714 home runs. But the millions of words written about the Babe's actions on and off the field were as sensational as his playing. He was the "Sultan of Swat," the "Bambino," the hero of youth. When he ate too many hot dogs one day, he had "the bellyache heard 'round the world." He was better known to millions of newspaper readers, who never saw him in person, than their own neighbors.

Sports heroes grew so important that when a member of a minority group entered their ranks it could affect the status of the whole group. Jesse Owens, a brilliant black track star, won many medals for the United States team in the 1936 Olympics in Berlin. His tremendous official welcome home (lower far right) did not solve the problems of America's Negroes. But his triumphs, like the victories of heavyweight cham-

Above: After Charles Lindbergh's solo flight across the Atlantic in 1927, New York welcomed him with a spectacular ticker-tape parade. Right: In 1920 Babe Ruth swats one during his first season with the New York Yankees. He became the greatest drawing card ever in American sports. Below: Excluded from many sports teams, Negroes formed their own—the National Negro Baseball League in 1920, the Harlem Globetrotters in 1927. However, Jesse Owens' 1936 Olympic victories forced the nation to recognize the abilities of a great black athlete.

pion Joe Louis, gave millions of ordinary blacks and whites a moment of common pride in a Negro's deeds. That was something new in American life.

The greatest hero of the twenties was a young flier named Charles A. Lindbergh. On May 20, 1927, he took off from New York, alone in a radioless, single-engined airplane for a nonstop flight across the Atlantic. No one had yet achieved this. From the moment Lindbergh was airborne, newspapers followed his progress. For 33 hours the little *Spirit of St. Louis* droned across the vast Atlantic. Reports by people who had spotted the plane made bigger headlines every hour. By the time the weary pilot touched down to a smooth landing in Paris, almost everyone in the United States—flappers and Fundamentalists, bankers and coal miners, the foreign-born and *Mayflower* descendants—joined in the rejoicing.

The real person behind the headlines often differs from the image. Lindbergh himself was actually a talented expert in aeronautics. His flight was brave, but planned to the last drop of gasoline and ounce of weight—a precise scientific experiment. Yet the press called him "Lucky Lindy." Or they said he was the "Lone Eagle," the daredevil against the sea. For one moment they made him the American of the individualistic past, like the cowboy or the mountain man. The true Lindbergh was a pioneer of modern flight.

Questions for Discussion

1. Why was Prohibition hard to enforce? How was it connected with organized crime? When did it end?
2. Why did the supporters of the Eighteenth and Nineteenth Amendments believe that these amendments would improve the quality of national life? Would you agree? Why?
3. What new freedoms did some women demand—and get—in the 1920's?
4. How did the mass media help to build a sense of community in the entire nation? How did they create news as well as report it?
5. For what was each of the following famous: Babe Ruth, Jesse Owens, Joe Louis, Gertrude Ederle, Amelia Earhart, Charles Lindbergh?

Chapter Review

Social Studies Terms

capital goods, consumer goods, installment plan, ghetto, aliens, morality, mass media

Summary Questions for Discussion

1. What factors combined to make the twenties a decade of rapid change in the United States?
2. What did Coolidge mean by his slogan, "The Business of America Is Business?"
3. In the twenties how did businessmen justify the large amount of money spent on advertising? Do you believe such expenditures are justifiable today? Why?
4. Why did the automobile have such a revolutionary effect on the lives of Americans in the 1920's?
5. In what ways did the cities provide opportunities for some Negroes and hardships for others?
6. Was change or fear of change responsible for racial violence? Explain.
7. Do you think there should be quotas on immigration? Explain.
8. Think about the *Scopes* trial. Who should decide what is to be taught in schools? Why?
9. Why did both the Eighteenth and Nineteenth Amendments to the Constitution fail to accomplish some of the hopes of their supporters?

Pictures as Historical Evidence

Which pictures would support the following generalization? The American way of life in the 1920's and today are alike. Explain your choices.

For Further Reading

America and the Jazz Age, by Fon W. Boardman, Jr. New York: Henry Z. Walck, Inc., 1968.

Langston Hughes, by Milton Meltzer. New York: Thomas Y. Crowell Company, 1968.

The American Heritage History of the 20's and 30's, by Edmund Stillman. New York: American Heritage Publishing Co., Inc., 1970.

The Great Gatsby, by F. Scott Fitzgerald. New York: Charles Scribner's Sons, 1925.

The Many Worlds of Herbert Hoover, by James P. Terzian. New York: Julian Messner, 1966.

The Search for Amelia Earhart, by Fred Goerner. Garden City, New York: Doubleday & Company, Inc., 1966.

Time of Trial, Time of Hope: The Negro in America, 1919 to 1941, by Milton Meltzer and August Meier. Garden City, New York: Doubleday & Company, Inc., 1966.

22
The Great Depression Tests American Democracy

The twenties were a time of optimism, of a nation joyriding in new automobiles. The thirties, however, opened with a crash and then despair. In 1930 the United States plunged into the deepest depression in its history. Month after bitter month, the figures grew more frightening. By the end of 1932 half the nation's productive machinery was idle. Twelve million workers had no jobs. Hundreds of banks had closed, losing their depositors' lifetime savings forever. Farmers could find no buyers for their crops and saw their homes and lands taken for unpaid debts. City families huddled in shanties in vacant lots. Men trudged the roads in a desperate search for a job, like the wanderer at left. Thousands of Americans paid attention to radical critics who said that only the abandonment of capitalism and democracy would revive the stricken land.

Though shocked and shaken by the economic collapse, the American people did not give up. They had believed that the business leaders of the twenties were magicians, who brought progress with a wave of the wand. Now, they seemed to realize that these "heroes" were human, like themselves.

Americans chose new political leadership. They tackled hard social questions, instead of waiting for prosperity to provide automatic answers. The questions were those asked by reformers and progressives since industrialism began: What is society's responsibility to the helpless? How should wealth be distributed? What sacrifices are necessary to renew cities and save natural resources? How should the Constitution's balancing of the rights of individuals, local communities, and the Federal government be changed to keep up with changing times? Many voices gave conflicting, angry answers. There was tension as the country struggled back to its feet. At the end of the decade, a new world war broke out. Wartime prosperity returned to "cure" the depression—but left the big questions unanswered.

Those who lived through those years—your parents and grandparents—remember them as full of argument and experiment. They were painful times— but exciting and challenging, too.

As you read, think about these questions:
1. In what ways did the depression test American democracy?
2. Did the American political system change during the 1930's? If so, how?

Alone, weary, and broke, a depression victim moves on in search of work.

WIDE WORLD PHOTOS

UNDERWOOD & UNDERWOOD

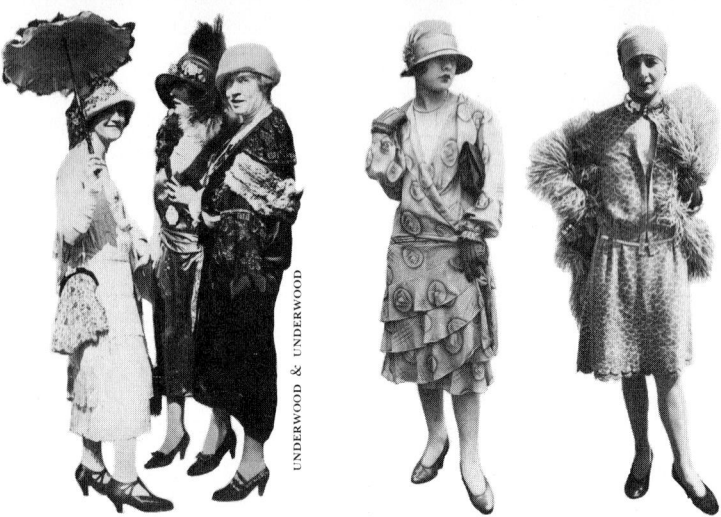

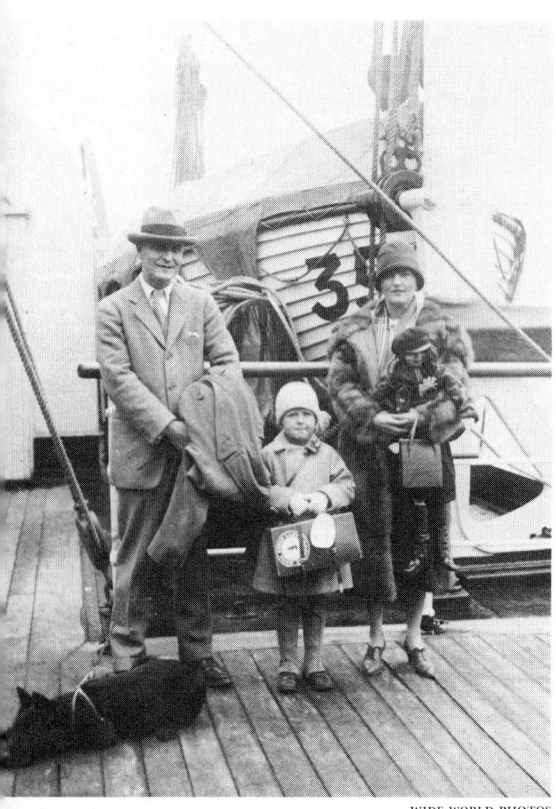

To many Americans the 1920's meant a frantic social whirl. Fashions (above and below left) reflected the frivolous, spendthrift tone of the era. Socialites and celebrities enjoyed outdoor parties at large country estates (below).

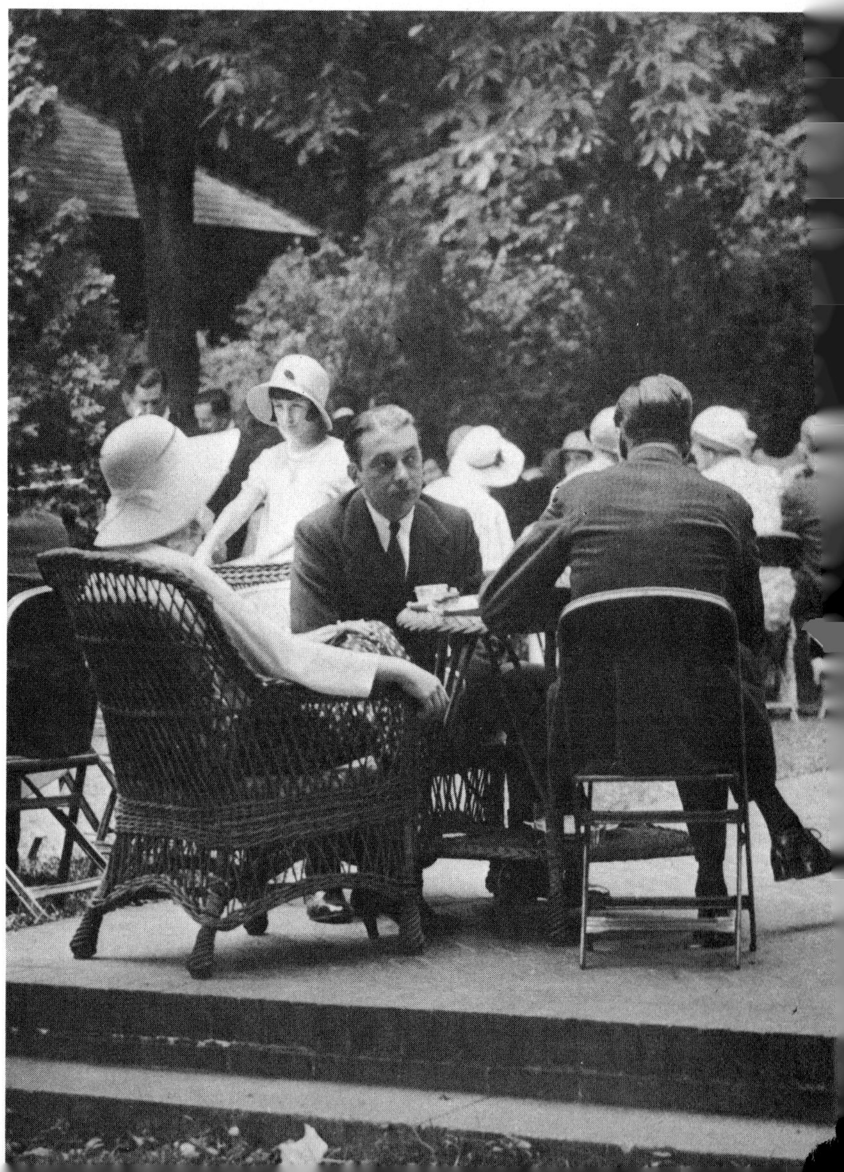

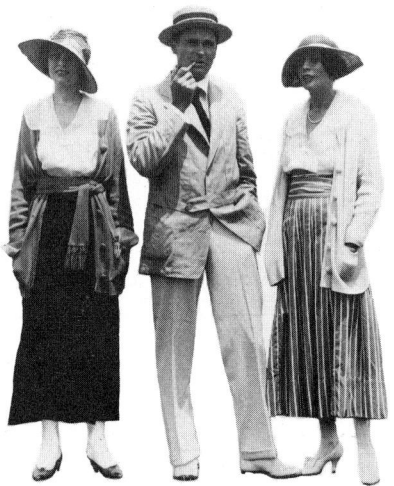

Top: In 1926 F. Scott Fitzgerald, his daughter Scottie, and wife Zelda return to America after two years in Europe. Through his novels and widely publicized social life, Fitzgerald emerged as a spokesman for, and typical product of, the Jazz Age—a term he coined to describe the twenties.

Boom and Bust

Part of the boom of the twenties was caused by real economic growth. But much of it was due to speculation. Speculation differs from ordinary business operations by offering quicker and higher profits, but bigger losses if the buyer guesses wrong.

As we saw in Chapters 9 and 11, speculation in land and in the **stocks** (shares of ownership in a company) of banks, railroads, and canals had long been part of the nation's history. In the twenties speculation in industrial stocks became popular. It was not undertaken by businessmen only, but involved hundreds of thousands of new customers from all walks of life. It even became part of the nation's way of life.

Shares of stock can be a reasonable, safe investment. They entitle their owners to **dividends,** or a part of the profits. When buying stock people are expecting that the value of each share will rise and that they will receive increased dividends.

Around 1925 a wave of optimism swept the **stock market,** where shares are traded. Speculators began to pay higher and higher prices for certain stocks—so high that future earnings could probably not repay the cost for many years. Yet the owners of these stocks were not worried. They believed that so long as stock prices were rising, they could always sell their stocks, if necessary, and make immediate profits without waiting for a single dividend. Like holders of banknotes in Jackson's time, they had fortunes—in "paper profits." Rising stock prices and dividends allowed thousands to live like the glittering, playful rich (left).

Everyone admired wealth. Even Calvin Coolidge, admired for his thrifty personal habits, did not discourage the big "bull market"—one in which everyone is buying and prices are rising. Democrats and Republicans alike approved of it. In 1929 John J. Raskob, Chairman of the Democratic National Committee, wrote an article claiming that anyone, by putting a few dollars a month into stocks, could have a handsome income in a few years. Its title was, "Everybody Ought To Be Rich." Such statements encouraged men with modest incomes to borrow money to invest. This demand for stocks drove prices still higher. More people crowded onto the get-rich-quick merry-go-round.

The Stock Market Crashes

In the election campaign of 1928, Herbert Hoover confidently told the country that, under Republican

leadership, it would soon see the day "when poverty will be banished." Hoover won, but one year later the boom collapsed and poverty flooded the land.

On October 24, 1929, a wave of selling swept the stock market, forcing prices down. When everyone is eager to sell, buyers need pay little for what they want. This fall in prices cut the value of stocks held by speculators. In order to make sure of having enough to meet their debts, they frantically sold more stock. This sent prices tumbling still further. By October 29 entire fortunes had been wiped out. A lawyer drew a symbolic sketch (right) of the buildings on Wall Street in New York, home of the country's biggest stock exchange, crashing in ruins.

Suddenly, there was no money to spend, and the country began to suffer. Some experts had warned that, even without the crash, a crisis had been in the making because Coolidge prosperity had not reached everyone. A day was bound to come when the business companies, whose stocks brought such high prices, would run out of customers who could afford to buy their products.

While the bull market had been surging higher and higher, the prices received by United States farmers for their crops had sunk steadily. More and more farm owners were unable to pay their bills. Nor were all industries thriving. Some were producing more than they could sell. Some were hurt by changes in technology, like coal mining which lost customers as gasoline and electric engines steadily replaced steam power. Although most workers' wages had risen, many workers—especially in the "sick" industries—were suffering cuts in their pay envelopes, long layoffs, or periods when there was no work at all. In "booming" 1929, 67 per cent of all American families made $3,000 a year or less (graph, right). That sum left little extra to buy new goods, which would keep industry humming and, in turn, provide jobs for a growing population.

Questions for Discussion

1. What are the "paper profits" on a share of stock? Can there also be "paper losses?" Why?
2. How did speculation help to bring on the stock market crash?
3. Why did some people believe, even before 1929, that the nation was headed for an economic crisis?
4. Does the graph at right help to explain the depression? How?

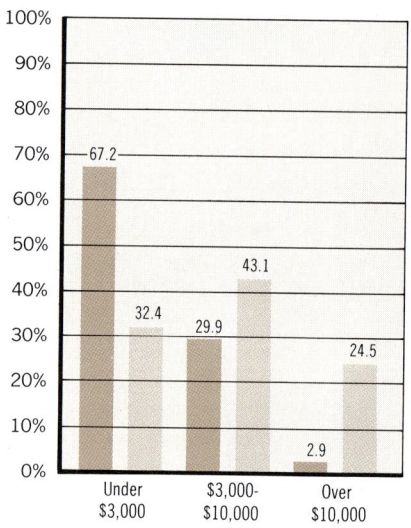

Income Distribution 1929

	Under $3,000	$3,000–$10,000	Over $10,000
Families and Unattached Individuals	67.2	29.9	2.9
Percentage of National Income	32.4	43.1	24.5

James Rosenberg, a lawyer and amateur artist, titled this grim sketch of Wall Street's collapse, "October 29, Dies Irae." Dies Irae is a medieval Latin hymn describing the Day of Judgment.

A Nation Crippled and Desperate

In a modern economy all groups are closely interdependent. What happens to one is felt by all soon. In good times this is a source of strength. A rise in wheat prices means that Kansas farmers buy more automobiles. This, in turn, opens up more jobs on the assembly line for Detroit workers. But in the depression the same process worked in reverse. As companies laid off men, families cut down their grocery buying. This cutback in spending caused farm prices to sink further. As jobless families drew savings out of banks, many of the banks had to close their doors. Those who had not yet withdrawn their money lost it forever. Each closed factory was a blow to all the businessmen who sold it raw materials and parts. Each family without a breadwinner bought less of everything, from toys to telephone service. They gradually became unable to pay their property taxes, so that local governments had less to spend on **relief** (money or goods given to those who need financial help). Eventually, all Americans, except a lucky few, suffered from the crash.

Statistics recorded the decline. Motor vehicle output, the key element in Coolidge prosperity, sank from 4.5 million in 1929 to 1.1 million in 1932. In the same three-year period, new investments declined from $10 billion to $1 billion, and **national income** (the total of what everyone in a nation earns in a year) from $87 billion in 1929 to under $40 billion in 1933.

But statistics do not show the human pain of the depression. There are no units to measure the bitterness of men standing in bread lines (upper right). No adding machine can total the shame of people living in shanties in vacant lots (lower right)—people who believed that poverty was not a misfortune, but a disgrace. Now it was *their* disgrace.

A magazine article of 1932 told how there was "slow starvation" in Philadelphia. In St. Louis people dug for food in garbage piles in the city dump. Families lived for days on stale bread or spoiled vegetables picked up around markets. State and city welfare agencies were overpowered. Their small sums of money could do very little for whole armies of needy citizens.

Depression in Rural Areas

Conditions were little better outside the cities. Americans had once believed that the farmer would never suffer from poverty because he could grow his own food, on his own land, with his own labor. But the

Below: Many families, unable to find work during the depression, lived in this shantytown—called Camp Thomas Paine—in Manhattan. Similar shantytowns, often bitterly nicknamed Hoovervilles, became common in many cities.

CULVER PICTURES

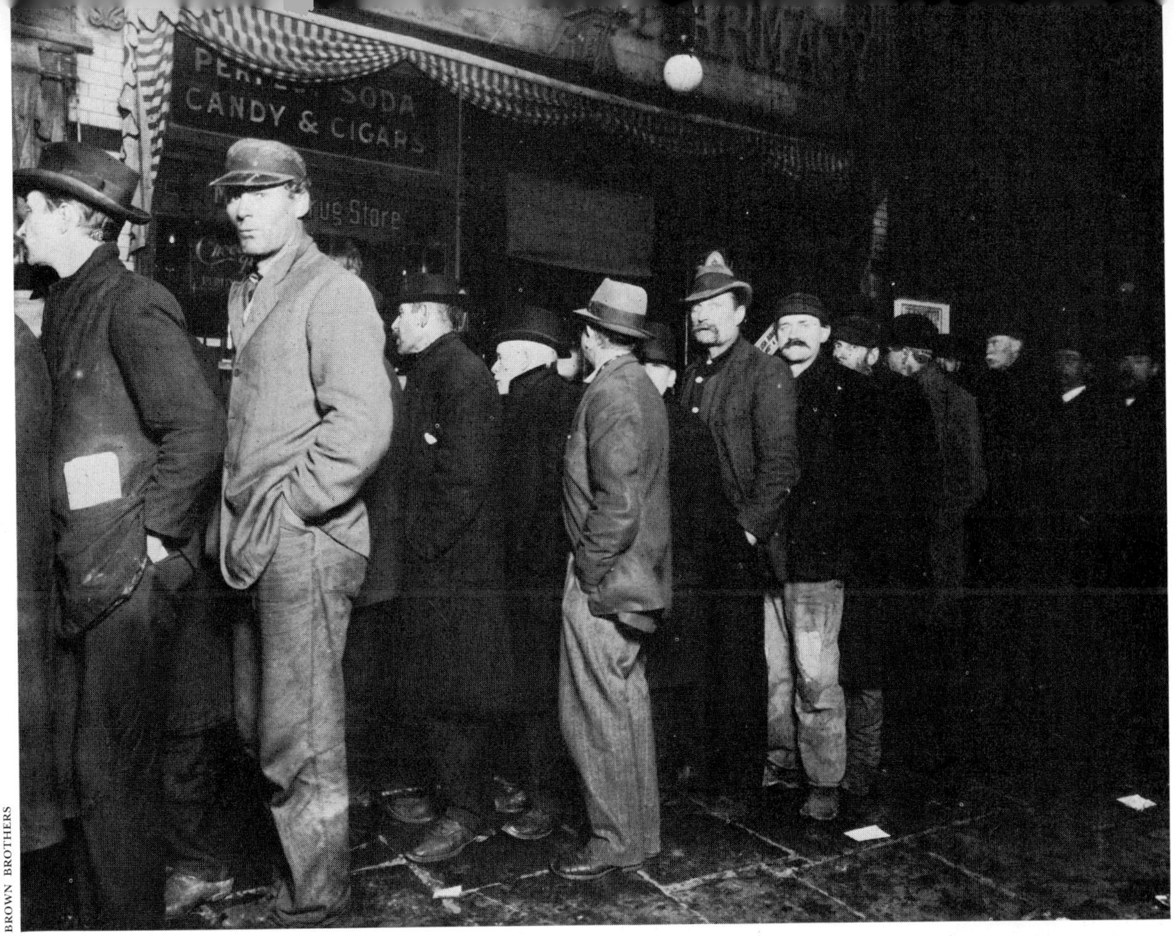

BROWN BROTHERS

WIDE WORLD PHOTOS

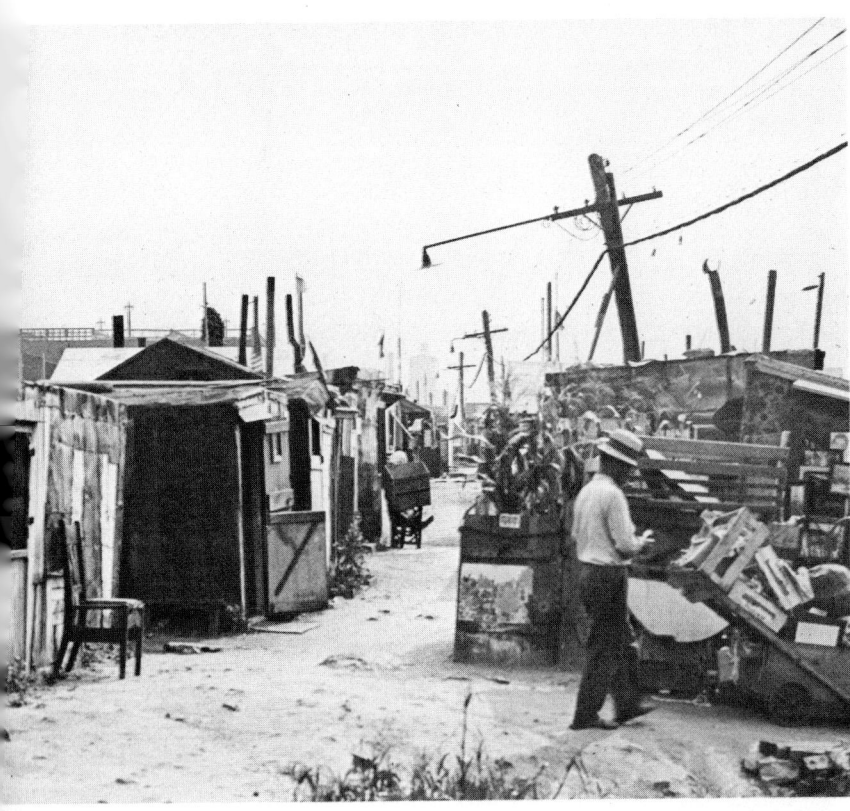

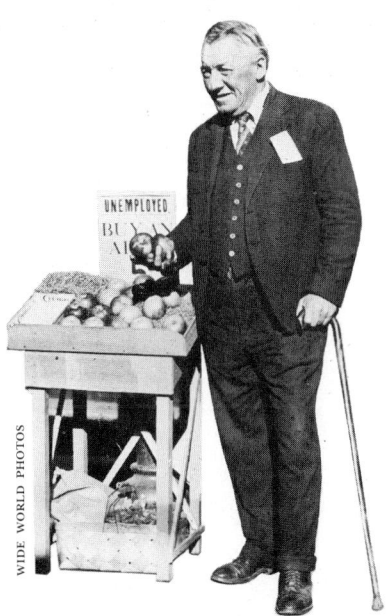

Top: Bread lines, often sponsored by local charity organizations, kept many from starvation. Above: In 1931 a man who was once a near-millionaire tries to earn a few pennies by selling apples.

BOTH: FARM SECURITY ADMINISTRATION

industrial-age farmer of 1929 could not survive without equipment. He was in debt for his various machines, as well as for his land. And when he lost income steadily and could make no payments, he could be forced off his farm. As agricultural prices fell lower and lower, that was the fate of thousands of independent farmers, men whom Jefferson had once called "the chosen people of God."

A specially tragic fact was that in some places crops brought in so little that growers could not afford to harvest or ship them. So, while city people starved, apples rotted on the ground in Oregon and mutton was fed to the buzzards in Montana. The nation became aware of the fact that poverty existed in the midst of plenty.

To make matters still worse, tremendous droughts hit the Great Plains in the early 1930's. Farmers watched helplessly as the dried-up soil was blown away by high winds. Huge "dust storms" blackened the skies. Week after week, "the sun blazed down on thousands of square miles once green but now dun-colored and grassless," as one man recalled. Many families, "discouraged and beaten, began to load their few possessions into trucks or trailers and go east or west, anywhere to escape disaster" (left). They were refugees as much as those in the Civil War who fled from invading armies had been.

Many farmers from Texas, Oklahoma, and Arkansas headed toward California to find work as harvest hands, picking other men's crops. For these "Okies" and "Arkies," the end of the line was often a barren migrant labor camp. Here, they ended the westward migration begun in hope by their pioneer grandfathers.

Drift Toward Chaos

As distress clamped the land in its grip, some Americans seemed ready for strong action. Protest marches of the unemployed shuffled through city streets. Farmers threatened to use force to prevent courts from seizing debtors' property. Visions of re-enactments of Civil War draft riots and Shays' Rebellion disturbed many civic leaders, especially since Communists exploited the outraged feelings of depression victims. It seemed possible that Communists and Socialists together would poll a huge vote in 1932.

Such talk alarmed the Hoover administration into reacting violently against a group known as "bonus

During the autumn and winter of 1933 dust storms in the Great Plains blackened midday skies, buried farm machinery, and killed livestock. By 1939 more than 200,000 people had abandoned their farms to search for food and work. Many were lured to California by exaggerated tales of large farms that needed workers. Some were lucky and found jobs harvesting crops. They were paid next to nothing and housed—while they were working—in leaky shacks or tents. Those without jobs tried to keep their jalopies (left) in running condition and camped each night along the roadside (below), struggling to survive. The tension between the local population and the "inferior" migrants often resulted in violence.

marchers." After World War I Congress promised veterans a bonus, a special reward, payable in 1945. In 1932 unemployed ex-servicemen asked for immediate payment of this money. They said that it would help them through the crisis and that their spending would give business a lift. About 20,000 veterans, calling themselves the Bonus Expeditionary Force (BEF), came to Washington to petition Congress. On June 17 the Senate killed a bill which would have met the BEF's demands. Most returned home when Congress rejected this appeal. But some 2,000 camped out in unsightly tents and shacks near the Capitol. Hoover refused to recommend early payment of the bonus and would not even meet delegates from the BEF. On July 28, 1932, frightened by rumors of a planned **insurrection** (open revolt), Hoover ordered the army to remove the threadbare lobbyists. With tear gas and bayonets, troops in full combat gear dispersed the unarmed men and set their camp ablaze (above, left and right).

Hoover was condemned for a lack of pity for the distressed. This was not entirely fair. He was eager to relieve misery and spur recovery. But Hoover favored neither a vigorous use of the Federal government's power nor **deficit financing** (the spending of more money than is provided by taxation). Hoover felt that Amer-

ica's special strength was in the time-tested ability of its individual citizens and local communities to solve their problems wisely and independently. He wanted businessmen to agree voluntarily not to cut prices, lay off workers, or in other ways make hard times worse. He would lend Federal money to companies for investments or to states and cities for relief, but held back on more direct action by Washington.

The country demanded bolder steps. In the Presidential election in November, Hoover was defeated, carrying only six states against his Democratic rival, Franklin D. Roosevelt. But the Socialist and Communist parties combined won even fewer votes than the Socialists alone had in 1920. Americans were ready for a change. But they only wanted what Roosevelt called a New Deal—not a brand-new political game.

When the United States Army was ordered to force the Bonus Army from Washington, D.C., much of the action was within view of the nation's Capitol. The troops (above left) were under the personal command of Army Chief of Staff Douglas MacArthur. They put the torch to the packing boxes, egg crates, automobile bodies, and pup tents in which thousands of the bonus marchers had lived for months (above).

Questions for Discussion

1. Why do hard times in industry cause hard times in rural areas?
2. Why did some crops rot or go unharvested even though there were hungry people in many places?
3. Who were the "Okies" and "Arkies" of the 1930's?
4. Why did Hoover not want the Federal government to actively intervene to end the depression?

BOTH: FRANKLIN D. ROOSEVELT LIBRARY, HYDE PARK

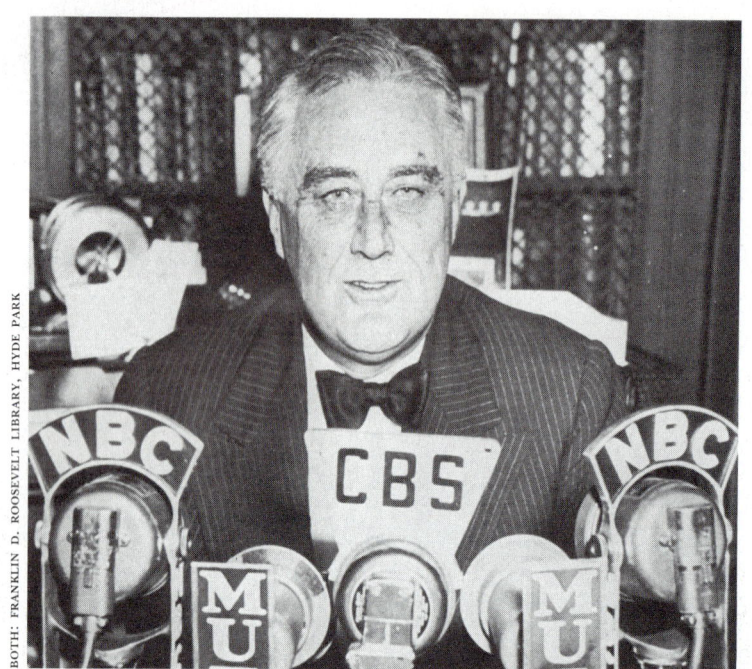

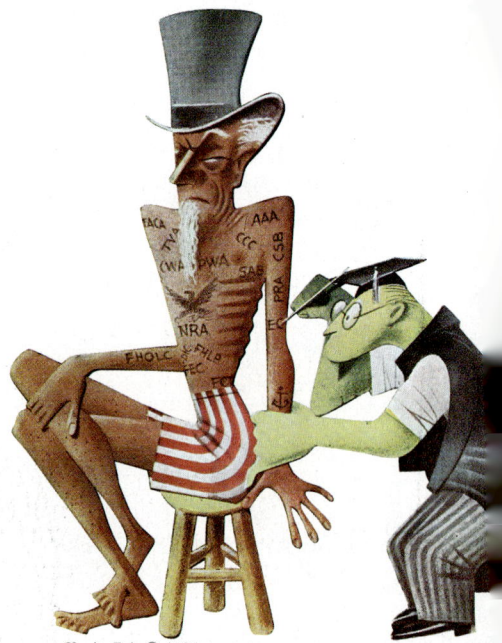

Below: In October 1932 Franklin D. Roosevelt (back seat, right) campaigns in Indiana. Right: This 1934 cartoon shows Dr. Braintrust tatooing Uncle Sam with the initials of New Deal programs. Above: From the library of his home FDR seeks votes for New Deal Congressional candidates in 1938.

Vanity Fair © 1934 CONDE NAST PUBLICATIONS

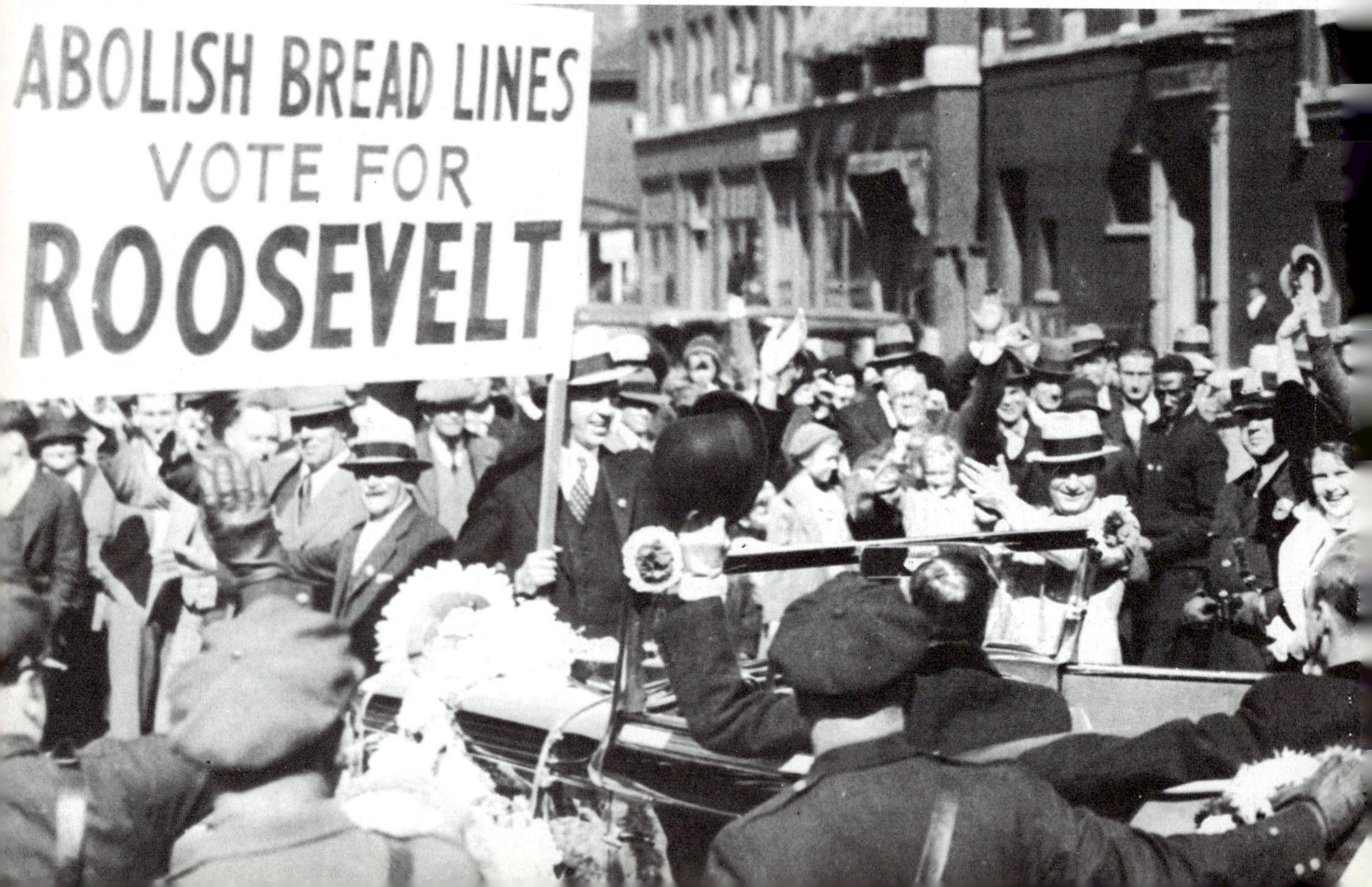

The New Deal

Franklin D. Roosevelt was a good symbolic choice to lead a nation that needed courage to fight its way out of despair. He himself had battled back from a crippling attack of polio in 1921. Though bound to a wheel chair and leg braces for the rest of his life, he gamely refused to quit politics. Instead, he won election as New York's governor in 1928 and 1930 and in 1932 went from there to the White House.

In 1933 Roosevelt judged that the country wanted a strong President to get things moving and to break the grip of terror. "The only thing we have to fear," he said in his inaugural address, "is fear itself.... This Nation asks for action, and action now."

"Action now" was what the nation got. Roosevelt was given sweeping emergency powers. He almost immediately declared a "bank holiday" to give government examiners a chance to eliminate unsound banks and to restore faith in the value of the dollar. Then he brought a stream of special advisors to Washington. Most were young university professors. Hence they were nicknamed the "Brain Trust," and provided good targets for cartoonists (left). In the New Deal's first hundred days, lights burned late as the Brain Trust boldly planned war on the depression. At first Congress enacted everything the reformers proposed.

The immediate goal of 1933 planning was to get people back to work. Early programs bore down on this task and spent freely to achieve it. One measure set up a Public Works Administration (PWA) and gave it $3.3 billion for immediate work on projects such as constructing roads, bridges, tunnels, post offices, and government office buildings. A Federal Emergency Relief Administration (FERA) got $5 billion to help feed and house the jobless. In his first morning of work, its director, Harry L. Hopkins, authorized the spending of several million dollars. A Civilian Conservation Corps (CCC) swiftly put thousands of young men between the ages of 18 and 25 to work in national and state forests planting trees, fighting fires, and building dams.

When the PWA, FERA, CCC, and other New Deal "alphabetical agencies" were under attack, they were brilliantly defended by a man with another well-known set of initials—FDR. When he grinned at crowds or addressed them on the air (far left) as "my friends" and spoke of "your government," they believed he meant it. As his wife said, "There was a real dialogue [conversation] between Franklin and the people."

The New Deal in the Cities

Between 1934 and 1938 the New Deal settled down to making long-range changes in American life. New and lasting relationships were created between the Federal government and local governments and directly between the Federal government and the people. A complete new view of public responsibility for social needs was forged. Its results could actually be seen in the changing American landscape.

A new look came to the nation's cities as the PWA built libraries, hospitals, schools, and government office buildings. Yet by 1935 unemployment was still a huge problem. Some New Dealers found the PWA pattern of help too slow. Under it cities and states proposed improvements. Then, if Washington approved, private companies were awarded contracts and hired workers. A new approach was tried by the creation of the Works Progress Administration (WPA). Despite the similar initials, WPA worked differently from PWA. It put men on relief directly to work as employees of the Federal government.

Between 1935 and its ending in 1943, the WPA spent $11 billion on over a million projects. It employed a total of 8.5 million men, including some who were clearly not used to heavy construction work, like the bespectacled worker (left).

In the frontier nation artistic activities had been considered leisure-time frills, less important than the work of helping the country grow by farming or business enterprise. Thus there was resistance to the idea of supporting the arts with government funds. Nevertheless, from 1935 to 1938 the WPA was permitted to sponsor music, art, drama, and writing "projects." The artists employed decorated public buildings with paintings, such as that at upper right done for the Department of the Interior. But by 1938 Congress had cut off further funds for the arts projects.

Another New Deal experiment was the entry of the Federal government into the housing business. An act of 1937 created a United States Housing Authority (USHA), which lent money to low-income communities for the construction of housing projects. These were supposed to be temporary dwellings for slum families who could not yet afford to move to privately owned apartment houses, where rents had to be high enough to return profits to the owners. The projects begun by USHA did not meet growing low-cost housing needs.

WPA employees, like those above seen at work in 1940, were paid more than they could get on relief, but far less than workers with jobs in private industry.

DEPARTMENT OF INTERIOR

Most WPA projects, like the one at left, were geared to manual labor. During its 8-year history the WPA built over 600,000 miles of highway and constructed, repaired, or improved some 124,000 bridges, 125,000 public buildings, 8,000 parks, and 800 airport landing fields. In addition, the WPA sponsored projects in the arts. The painting above, "Building of a Dam" by William Gropper, is part of a mural contracted by the WPA. Critics charged the WPA with inefficiency, extravagance, and political corruption. Supporters claimed that the WPA eased the unemployment crisis and produced results that benefited the entire nation.

BOTH: CULVER PICTURES

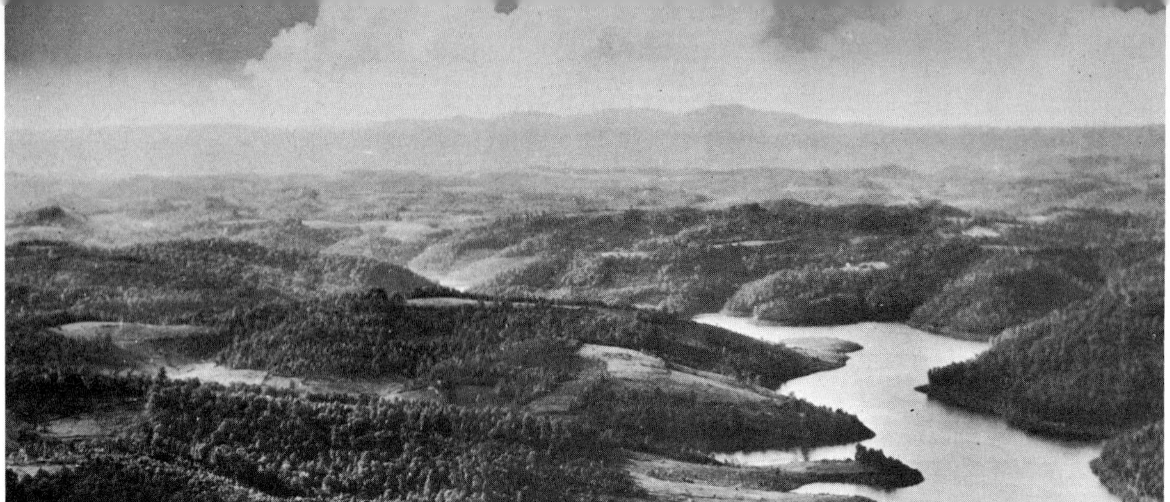

TVA

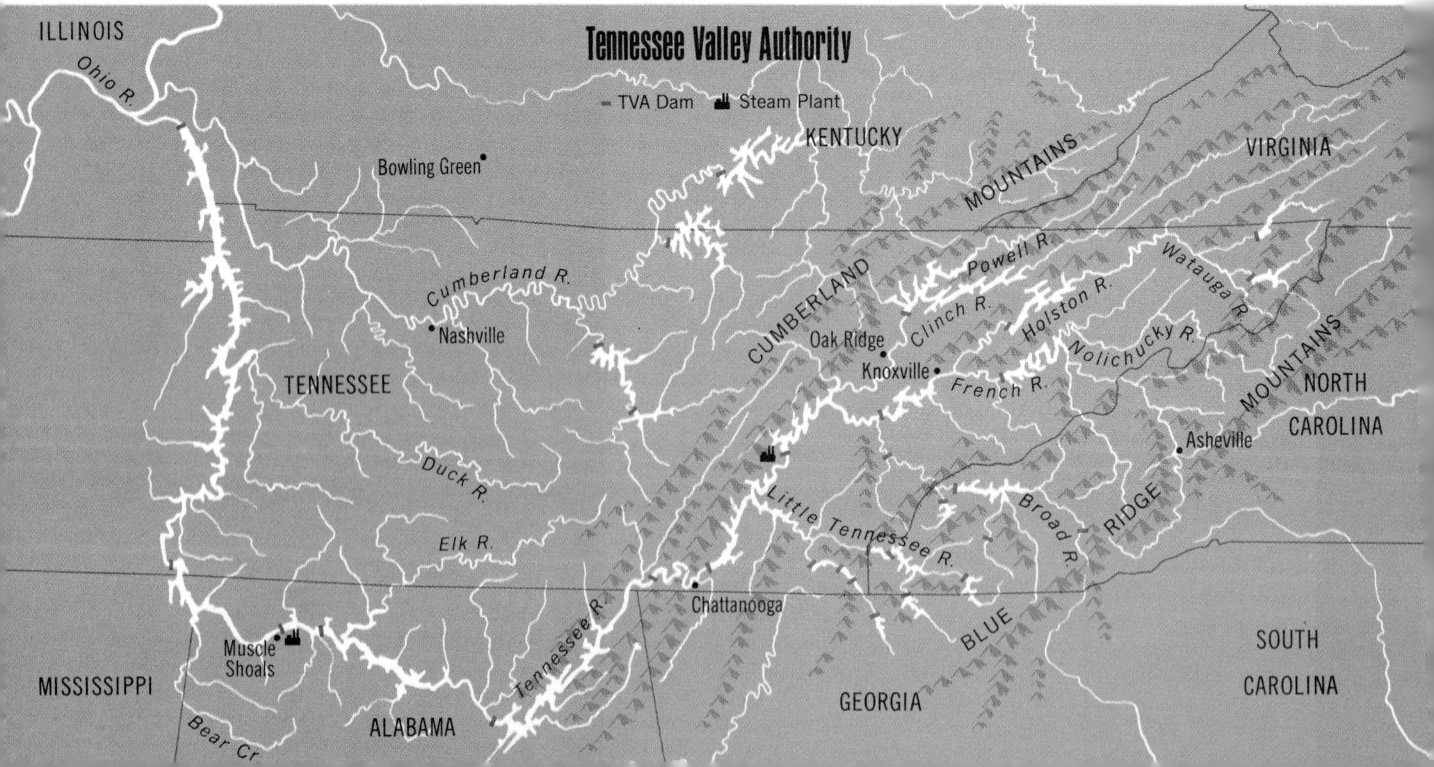

Tennessee Valley Authority
TVA Dam
Steam Plant
ILLINOIS
Ohio R.
KENTUCKY
Bowling Green
MOUNTAINS
VIRGINIA
Powell R.
Watauga R.
Cumberland R.
CUMBERLAND
Clinch R.
Holston R.
Nashville
Oak Ridge
Nolichucky R.
Knoxville
TENNESSEE
French R.
MOUNTAINS
NORTH
CAROLINA
Asheville
Duck R.
Broad R.
RIDGE
Little Tennessee R.
Elk R.
Chattanooga
Tennessee R.
Muscle Shoals
BLUE
SOUTH
CAROLINA
MISSISSIPPI
GEORGIA
ALABAMA
Bear Cr

The TVA Act established a government-owned corporation to develop an area almost as large as England. Twice before, similar acts had passed Congress, only to be vetoed by Presidents Coolidge and Hoover, who thought that government should never compete with private industry. But no private company, especially in 1933, had the money for such a huge project. The 1942 photograph below shows men at work on a dam site. At left is a major TVA dam.

But they were further signs of a growing partnership between Washington and metropolitan regions. Federal money devoted to social planning and improvement became a large part of every big city's income.

The New Deal and the Country

The farmer, too, received the New Deal's attention. Various laws gave farm owners **subsidies** in the form of different kinds of payments. These were sometimes given for conservation activities, such as letting some acres remain unplanted to restore the fertility of the soil. Sometimes the government bought and stored surplus crops. What mattered most was that the Federal government took responsibility for helping agriculture.

In 1937 Congress also began to help migrant farm workers, sharecroppers, and other tenant farmers. A law created the Farm Security Administration (FSA). The FSA supervised conditions in migrant camps and retrained some families for industrial work and a new start in the cities. It lent tenant farmers money to buy their own land and helped them to organize cooperative groups to buy low-cost electric power, machinery, supplies, and the services of doctors and dentists.

The most spectacular New Deal achievement was the creation, in 1933, of the Tennessee Valley Authority (TVA). TVA's mission was to remake an entire mountain region, covering parts of several states, over many years. First, it built a string of dams (left) on the rampaging Tennessee River. These harnessed the rapids and controlled floods by storing excess water in rainy seasons and releasing it in dry periods. The tamed river and its tributaries formed an inland waterway connecting the valley with the Great Lakes and the Ohio and Mississippi river systems (map, lower left). With such good water transportation available, industry was encouraged to move into the fast-changing area.

Water, roaring through gates in the dams, turned turbine wheels to generate hydroelectric power. This was sold at low cost. Soon lights twinkled and news broadcasts crackled in once-lonesome mountain towns and farmhouses which had never before enjoyed the benefits of electricity. TVA also manufactured chemical fertilizers, sold them cheaply, and offered instruction on how to use them.

Over a twenty-year period the region's income increased nearly 200 per cent. But the change in outlook meant more than dollars and cents. An Alabama editor rejoiced that his people had "caught the vision of their own powers." And one of TVA's first directors, David Lilienthal, said simply, "Democracy is on the march in this valley."

The New Deal and Organized Labor

Under the New Deal the American labor movement also scored important gains. In the 1920's it had slowed down. Many employers had fought back hard and fiercely with "union-busting" tactics. They fired union organizers, forced workers to join company unions controlled by management, and hired toughs to beat and threaten would-be strikers into surrender.

Labor unions had not considered Roosevelt an especially friendly figure in 1932. But they soon drew comfort from the open good wishes of members of his administration. New Deal warmth toward labor was shown by many incidents, such as that depicted at the upper right in which Frances Perkins, Secretary of Labor (and first woman Cabinet member), shook hands with an enthusiastic steelworker.

In 1935 Congress passed the National Labor Relations Act (NLRA). The act forbade certain unfair labor practices. These included most company activities designed to interfere with union organization. Workers could ask for an election to choose a union and unions could negotiate for many benefits, including the **closed shop,** or the right to insist that only union men be hired. Or the workers might try for a **union shop,** under which anyone could be hired by the employer but would then have to join the union representing that shop. A National Labor Relations Board (NLRB) was set up to supervise elections and hear complaints. It could demand an injunction to force an end to unfair dealings by employers. For years workers had bitterly felt that judges were allies of "the bosses." Now the shoe was on the other foot.

Though the NLRB was supposed to be a neutral umpire, many of its early decisions tended to favor the union at the employer's expense. Complaints were widespread that the Wagner Act, as the NLRA was known, tipped the balance of power too far in labor's direction.

Whether or not such charges were justified, it was

Above: Frances Perkins, Secretary of Labor during Roosevelt's entire Presidency, won the respect of union men across the country. Here, she is greeted by Pittsburgh steelworkers. Right: During the 1930's auto workers organized an industrial union and tried to win recognition from management. In early 1937 they tried something new—a sit-in, which kept management from using strikebreakers. This photograph shows workers at a General Motors body plant in Flint, Michigan. The 40,000 strikers were supported by the CIO and its head, John L. Lewis, who bargained with the companies on behalf of the United Auto Workers. After 44 days General Motors and Chrysler both agreed to recognize the UAW.

BROWN BROTHERS

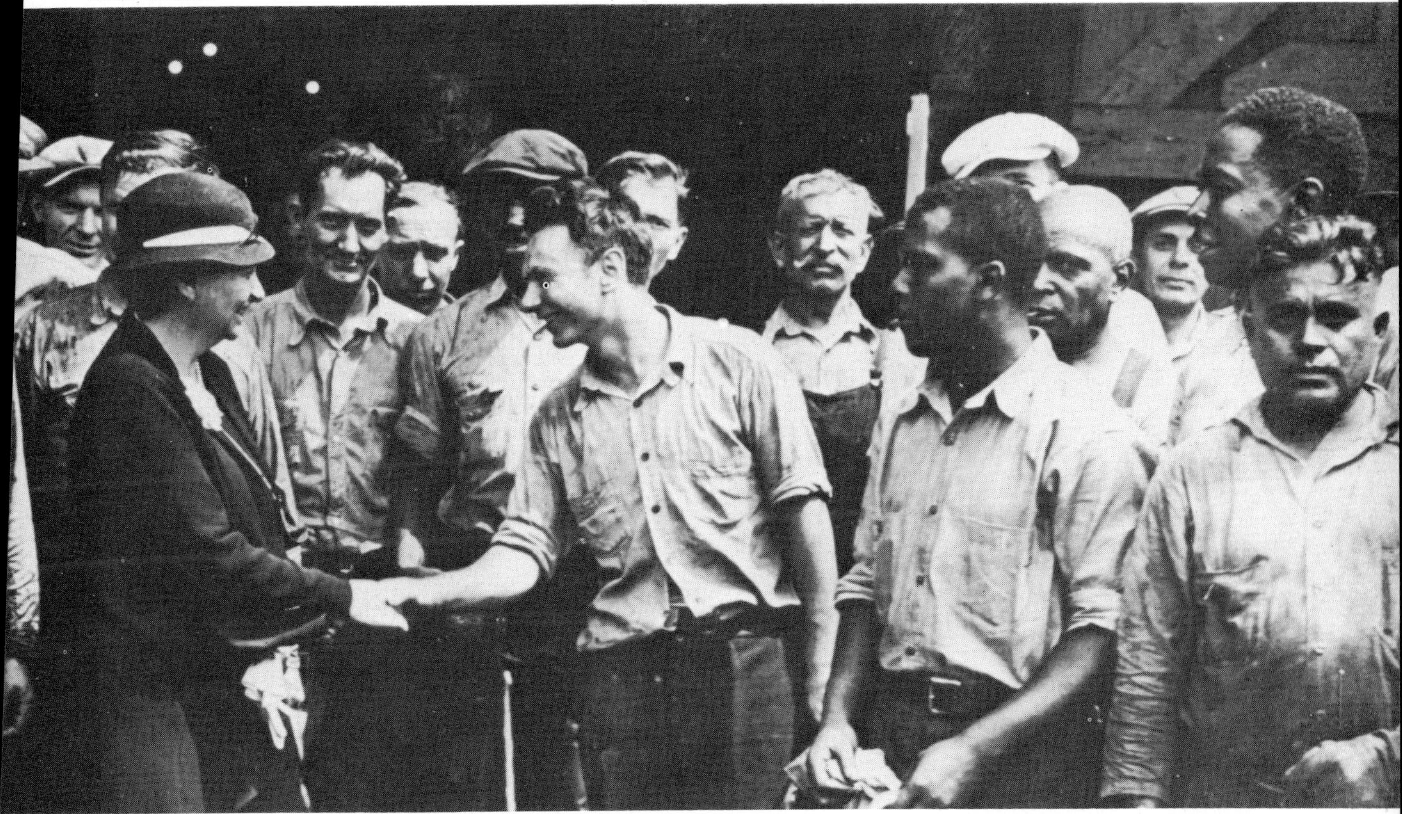

LIBRARY OF CONGRESS

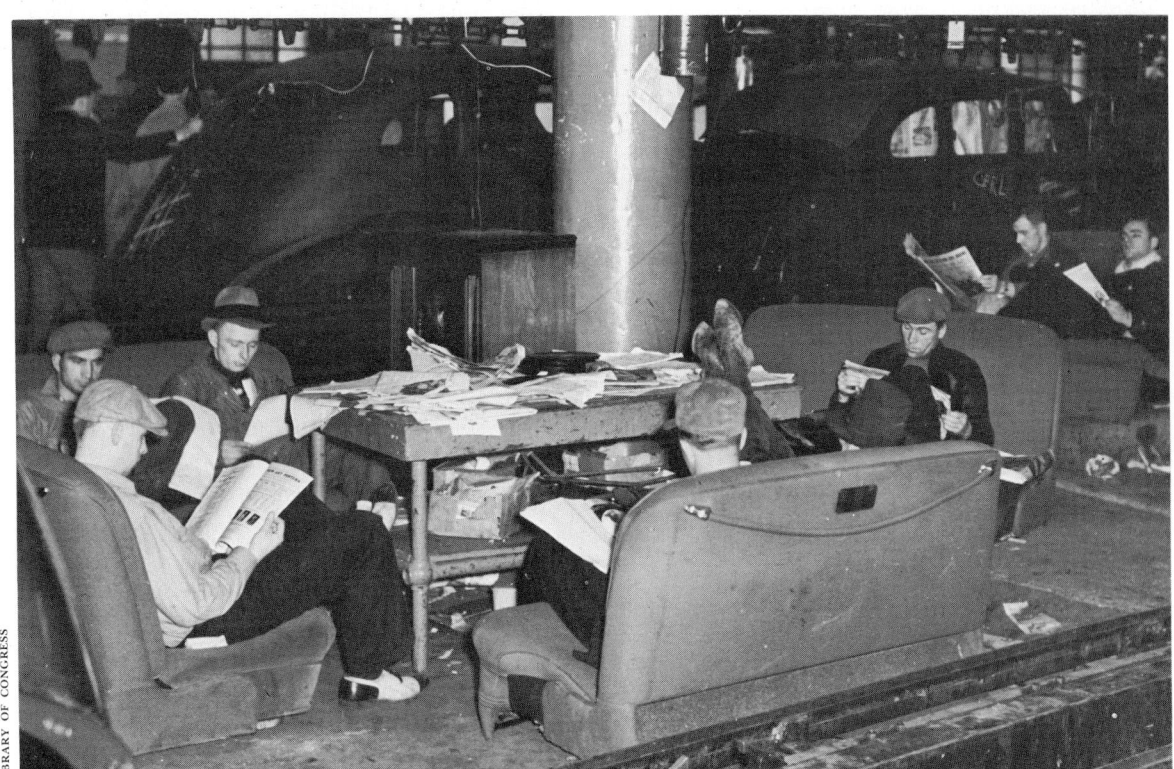

EDWIN MARCUS IN *The New York Times*

Frustrated by the Supreme Court declaring major New Deal legislation unconstitutional, FDR announced—on February 5, 1937—his plan to reorganize the Federal judiciary. During the five months of bitter debate that followed, FDR was accused of corrupting the Constitution and trying to destroy judicial independence.

BROWN BROTHERS

a fact that labor was getting support from the Federal government. This encouraged unions to undertake vigorous organizing campaigns. A split over tactics in 1935 led to the birth of a new national body, the Congress of Industrial Organizations (CIO). The AF of L was built around craft unions of workers sharing a particular skill while the CIO's basic unit was the industrial union of all workers in a given industry. After twenty years of rivalry about which form of organization would triumph, the AF of L and CIO merged in 1955. By then some 16 million workers were enrolled in the unions controlled by the AFL-CIO.

The New Deal—A Watershed in History

Sometimes the New Deal simply brought progressivism up to date. Many of the laws it proposed added to the list of measures taken early in the century to limit the power of great corporations and to make sure that they kept the public's health and safety in mind. Banking and the stock market were placed under strict supervision. New Federal agencies were created and old ones strengthened to regulate the aviation, radio, electric power, natural gas, shipping, and trucking industries.

Unlike these laws, another type of New Deal legislation tried wholly new social experiments. Some won acceptance, while others were later dropped. An example of a New Deal experiment which became permanent is the Social Security Act of 1935. Under it a **payroll tax** is collected from employers and employees. The money is used to provide pensions for workers who reach retirement age, as well as financial help for widows, orphans, the blind, and other people who need a hand. Parts of the law also encouraged the states to create similar funds to pay benefits to workers during jobless periods. Some European nations already had similar plans, but for Americans the Social Security Act was a break with the past. The tradition of an era of plenty was to leave such planning entirely to individuals. Yet the majority accepted the argument that in a modern, interdependent society, where misfortune could strike anyone through no fault of his own, some provision on a larger scale had to be made. The Social Security program is now in its fourth decade of successful operation.

Reform movements in American politics very often have a short life. In 1936 Roosevelt won an overpower-

ing victory at the polls. He got the electoral vote of all but two states—Maine and Vermont. Yet in the next two years he could not prevent rising resistance in Congress to further New Deal measures. Early in 1937 he submitted a measure calling for an enlargement of the Supreme Court. He hoped to appoint new justices, who would be more sympathetic to New Deal measures than the "nine old men" who had declared the National Industrial Recovery Act (NIRA) and the Agricultural Adjustment Administration (AAA) unconstitutional. But a large section of public opinion was angered by what seemed to be an attempt to "pack" the Court with judges friendly to the President, and thus destroy the balance between the branches of the Federal government (cartoon, lower left). FDR's plan was beaten soundly in Congress.

In the following year, while other Roosevelt-inspired bills failed to be passed by a Congress with a mind of its own (cartoon, upper left), the President decided to challenge some of his conservative Congressional opponents. During the spring of 1938, he called for Democratic voters in **primary elections** (elections held to choose party nominees) to defeat certain incumbent, office-holding, Congressmen who stood in the way of further New Deal developments. Despite his plea, the same citizens who had elected FDR in 1936 returned his opponents to office in 1938. To make matters worse, the economy slumped and unemployment shot up again in that year.

By 1939 things began to change. Europe went to war that September. Even earlier, however, military orders from European governments began to set factory wheels in motion. Congress also voted a large expansion of United States naval and air forces in preparation for the coming crisis. The beginning of an era of war and global responsibility restored prosperity and changed the issues of the day.

Because of this no one to this day knows for sure whether the New Deal by itself would have succeeded in curing the depression or what would have happened after 1938 if the war had not come along. As events developed, however, the need for a huge government and long-range economic and social planning remained, and later Presidents continued to meet the need. Even though the New Deal of 1933 to 1937 may have ended, the nation never returned to a "normalcy" like that of the 1920's. Like the 1890's which saw the closing of the

FRANKLIN D. ROOSEVELT LIBRARY, HYDE PARK

Most members of the upper class thought that FDR—who was himself upper class—had betrayed them. This 1938 cartoon expressing that view was captioned, "Mother, Wilfred wrote a dirty word!"

frontier, the many changes of the 1930's marked a great dividing line in the nation's history.

Questions for Discussion

1. What was Roosevelt's Brain Trust?
2. What was the purpose of the "bank holiday" declared by Roosevelt soon after his inauguration?
3. How did Roosevelt's and Hoover's views on the role of the Federal government during the depression differ?
4. What agencies were set up by the New Deal to handle unemployment problems? What kind of work did they do?
5. How did the New Deal extend help to farmers?
6. How did the TVA illustrate the power of the Federal government to change the lives of people in an entire region of the United States?
7. In what ways did New Deal measures give direct help to industrial workers and unions?
8. Whom is the Social Security Program designed to help? Who provides the money for it?
9. Why did many people oppose Roosevelt's plan to increase the membership of the Supreme Court?
10. How did the coming of war in Europe help to bring the Great Depression to an end?

Chapter Review

Social Studies Terms

stocks, dividends, stock market, relief, national income, insurrection, deficit financing, subsidies, closed shop, union shop, payroll tax, primary elections

Summary Questions for Discussion

1. What were some of the causes of the depression?
2. Why did the depression affect nearly all of the people in the United States?
3. In the 1930's why was money for relief not available to local governments just when they needed it most?
4. How should the BEF have been treated?
5. What problems must be solved to turn a depressed economy into a prosperous one?
6. Why did most Americans reject radical solutions to the problems brought by the depression?
7. How do some government leaders use deficit financing in an attempt to solve economic problems?
8. Was Roosevelt an able leader in a time of national crisis? Explain.

9. In what ways was the New Deal a continuation of the progressive tradition in American politics? In what ways did it depart from that tradition?
10. What problems of American life in the 1930's were left unsolved by the New Deal?
11. How did the depression change the relationship between the government and the individual? What other changes brought about in the 1930's have become permanent features of American life?
12. Do you favor or disapprove of massive government involvement in the American economic system? Explain.

Pictures as Historical Evidence

Is there any pictorial evidence in this chapter to support the generalization that the New Deal greatly extended the Federal government's activities? Explain.

Graph Study

1. Look at the graph on page 640. Does such a pattern of income distribution by itself pose any problems for a highly industrialized society? Explain your answer.
2. Compare the graph showing income distribution in 1929 on page 640 with the graph showing income distribution in 1968 on page 744. On the basis of the two graphs alone, make a hypothesis about why there might or might not have been a depression in 1968.

For Further Reading

Franklin Delano Roosevelt, by Wilson Sullivan. New York: American Heritage Publishing Co., Inc., 1970.
The Grapes of Wrath, by John Steinbeck. New York: The Viking Press, Inc., 1939.
The Herbert Hoover Story, by Catherine Owens Peare. New York: Thomas Y. Crowell Company, 1965.
The Story of Eleanor Roosevelt, by Margaret Davidson. New York: Four Winds Press, 1968.
Thirties: America and the Great Depression, by Fon W. Boardman. New York: Henry Z. Walck, Inc., 1967.

23

Between Two World Wars

When the Treaty of Versailles went down to defeat in the Senate in 1919, it seemed that the United States had said a loud "No!" to any role in the postwar world's affairs. But that was only part of the truth. The United States might disband its 4-million-man army and reduce its great navy in 1919. But the economic power that had already drawn the United States into the network of international relations continued to limit any American desire to withdraw from world affairs, as did the conscience of those who thought American power must help a battered Europe (cartoon, left).

Postwar America was rich, and Europe was poor. The world needed—and got—American loans and American goods, at a profit to American bankers and businessmen. The Republican leadership of the twenties encouraged such loans and exports. They knew that foreign investments and profits from trade were hurt by wars or arms races, which destroyed wealth and crippled commerce. So the Harding and Coolidge administrations willingly arranged disarmament and antiwar treaties among the great powers. Yet they gave no pledge of using American might to guarantee the agreements reached.

This attitude matched their policies at home. Government should help business—but limit the active use of its own power as much as possible. According to historians, the twenties were an era of isolationism. But this kind of "isolation" did not prevent American diplomatic activities designed to protect United States investments and markets abroad.

This diplomacy worked well until 1930 when world prosperity collapsed. International stability, or steadiness, crashed down with it. Strong new leaders, especially in Italy and Germany, challenged the Treaty of Versailles which had left France and Great Britain as Europe's dominant powers. Japan drove toward a commanding position in the Pacific that would bar western powers from a share in Asia's wealth.

The United States was forced to make a choice. It could wait out events and make new "deals" to preserve stability or it could defend the existing order, but at the risk of war. These were the hard, hotly debated choices of the stormy thirties.

As you read, think about these questions:
1. What role did the United States play in keeping the world peaceful from 1919 to 1941?
2. How can nations best cooperate to maintain peace?

This World War I anniversary poster argues against American isolationism.

The Legend of Isolation

The failure of the United States to join the League of Nations meant that American voices did not ring out in the debates at Geneva nor did its flag appear along with those of other nations as part of the League's standard (upper right). But Americans did take part in conferences called by certain nonpolitical bodies under the League. In addition, there were permanent American observers in Geneva to serve as eyes and ears for the United States government.

Moreover, in July of 1921, President Harding called for a conference of nine nations—all with colonial holdings—to meet the next year in Washington. The first subject for discussion was naval disarmament. Fleets of mighty battleships then were like today's bombers and ballistic missiles. Only great nations could afford them and even they groaned under the heavy cost. The United States itself could not slim its Federal budget without reducing its navy. So when the sessions opened, the United States Secretary of State, Charles Evans Hughes, surprised everyone. Not only did he propose limits on future naval shipbuilding, but he urged that the United States, Great Britain, and Japan actually scrap a total of over a million tons of warships. Two historians noted that Hughes, in a few words, "proceeded to sink more ships than all the admirals in the history of the world." Eventually, a Five-Power Treaty was signed, setting quotas of naval strength for the naval "Big Three" (the United States, Britain, and Japan) and for France and Italy as well.

The Washington Conference also tried to "freeze" the balance of power in Asia. The United States, Britain, Japan, and France (which governed Indochina as a colony) agreed to recognize the boundaries of each others' possessions in the Pacific. All nine nations present pledged to continue the Open Door in China and to continue to guarantee China's territorial integrity.

The United States had made no commitment to enforce these Washington agreements for dividing seapower and sharing Asian raw materials and markets. Yet its sponsorship of the conference, like its taking part in some of the League's work for international welfare, was a long way from "isolation."

American Business Goes Overseas

Meanwhile, American dollars marched abroad. World War I created a basic change in the position of

WOODROW WILSON HOUSE, WASHINGTON, D.C.

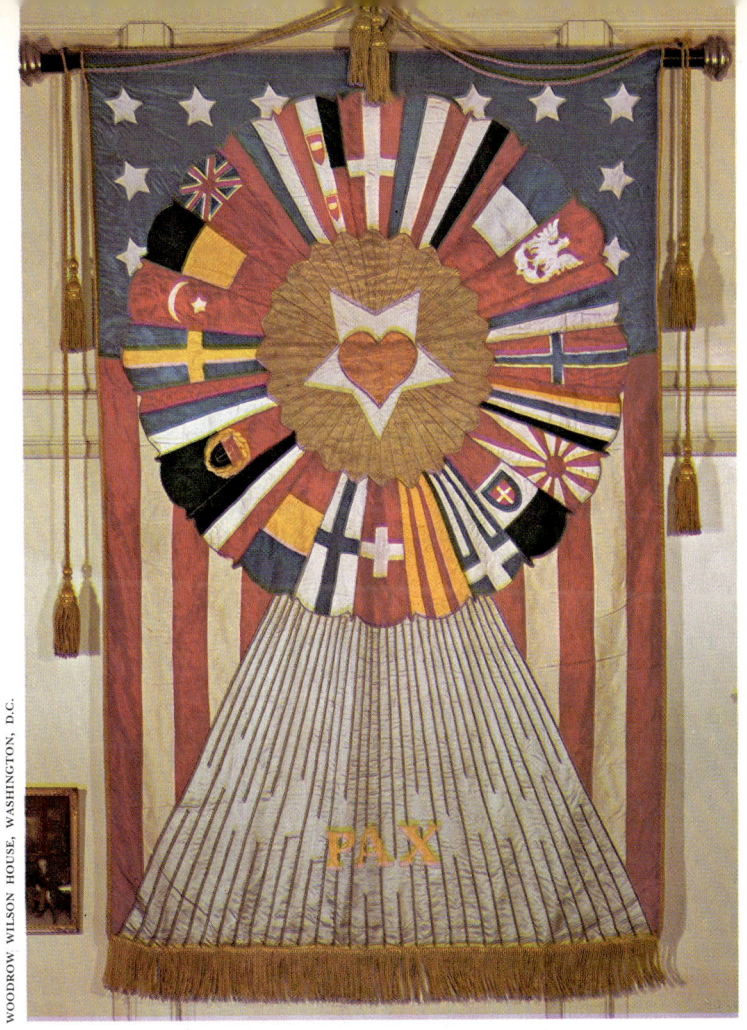

Whether America should join the League of Nations, represented by its flag at left, became an issue in the 1920 Presidential election. Democratic candidate James Cox favored American membership. Republican candidate Warren Harding's campaign slogan was "America first!" However, since Harding also spoke vaguely of favoring an "association of nations," the candidates' positions were not as clearly defined as the cartoon below indicates.

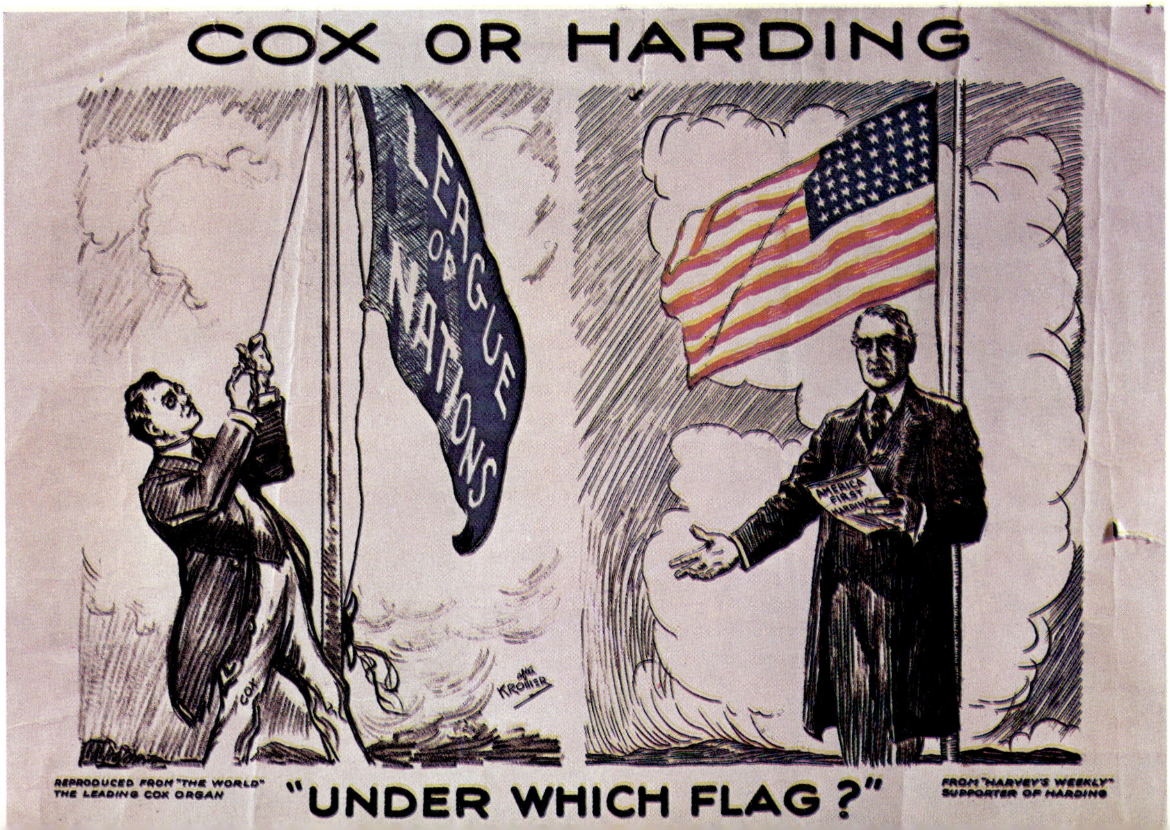

NEW-YORK HISTORICAL SOCIETY

MUSEUM OF MODERN ART

Above: In the late 1920's a group of artists who found a special beauty in buildings and machinery emerged. Charles Sheeler's American Landscape *conveys a feeling of awe and excitement about industrial America. Right: American companies trying to attract foreign markets used tested advertising techniques. This ad appeared in a 1928 French magazine. The reader is told that AC spark plugs allowed Charles Lindbergh — a hero in France as well as America — to cross the Atlantic.*

PAS un ennui avec la bougie A. C. C'est elle qui a permis à Lindbergh de franchir l'Atlantique, c'est elle qui a permis à Bugatti de gagner la Targa Florio. C'est elle qui vous permettra de rayer les ennuis d'allumage de vos préoccupations. Celle qu'il faut à votre voiture existe chez votre garagiste, demandez-la lui.

BIBLIOTHEQUE NATIONALE

the United States. It became a **creditor nation.** Once, young America had borrowed money from Europe's bankers to build its railroads and canals. Now, American **financiers** (large investors or financial experts) were moneylenders to the world. They made their loans by buying the **bonds** of foreign companies and local governments. A bond is a written promise to pay back the money loaned at the end of a set time, usually twenty or more years. Meanwhile, the bondholder receives interest each year. By the mid-1920's American bond purchases provided funds to build railroads in Poland, housing developments in Austria, and public utilities in Tokyo. American dollars were also helping to drill oil wells in Arabia and open rubber plantations in Malaya. Soon world prosperity rested in good part on billions of dollars in American loans. That same prosperity helped American industry too, for it made it possible for the people of other countries to purchase an increasing amount of goods — such as spark plugs — made in American factories.

Busily, the Department of Commerce encouraged overseas investments. Secretary Hoover proudly described the Department's agents in 57 foreign offices as "hounds for foreign sales." European farmers plowed their acres with American tractors. Asian workers rode to their jobs on American-made bicycles or streetcars. Latin American secretaries pounded out their letters on American typewriters. Children everywhere cheered the heroes of American movies.

Sometimes American companies built plants abroad to take advantage of low foreign taxes and cheap foreign labor. These investments also put money, in the form of wages and payments to suppliers, into the world economy. Despite such help, foreigners did not earn enough through sales of their own goods to other countries to pay for what they bought from the United States. In addition, high American protective tariffs tended to keep foreign products off American shelves. But Congress did not see that these tariffs were becoming a serious international problem.

The Search for Peace

The United States had a stake in keeping the world prosperous. This meant keeping the world peaceful. Only nations that were productive and safe could offer good markets in the long run.

The realization that profits and peace might be

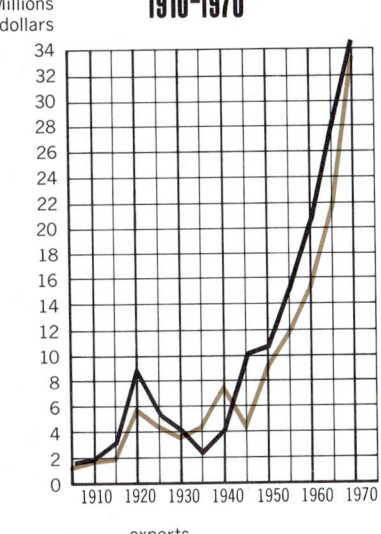

United States Foreign Trade 1910-1970

— exports
— imports

(includes merchandise, gold, and silver)

WIDE WORLD PHOTOS

A number of events in the 1920's seemed to indicate that nations really wanted to insure world peace. Below: President Warren G. Harding (standing at center) delivers an address welcoming delegates from eight nations—Great Britain, Japan, France, Italy, Holland, Portugal, Belgium, and China—to the Washington Disarmament Conference. Right: On January 17, 1929, President Calvin Coolidge signs the Kellogg-Briand Pact, committing the United States to the peaceful settlement of disputes. By 1934 some 64 nations had agreed to the provisions of the pact. Opposite page: The Women's International League for Peace and Freedom produced this broadside during the 1920's as part of their campaign against an international arms race.

CULVER PICTURES

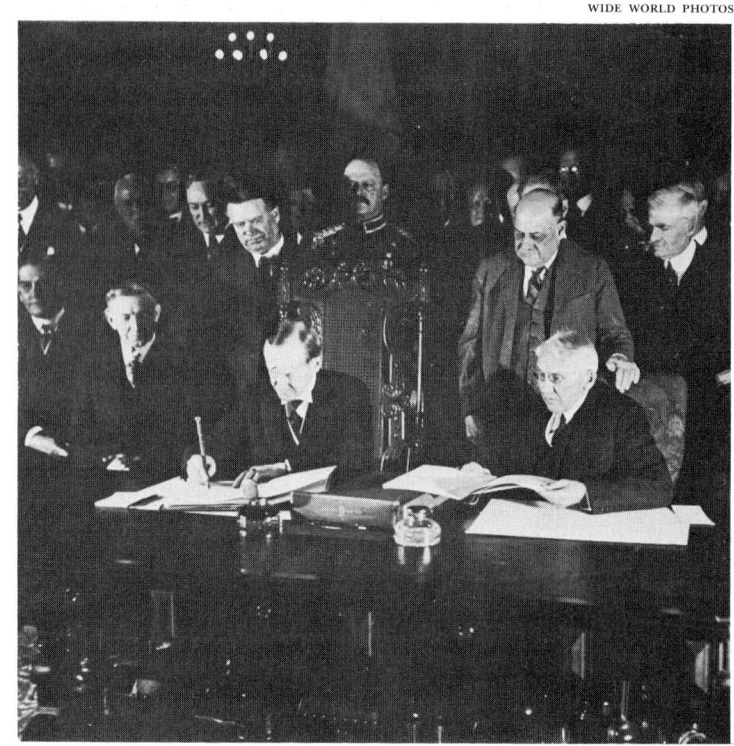

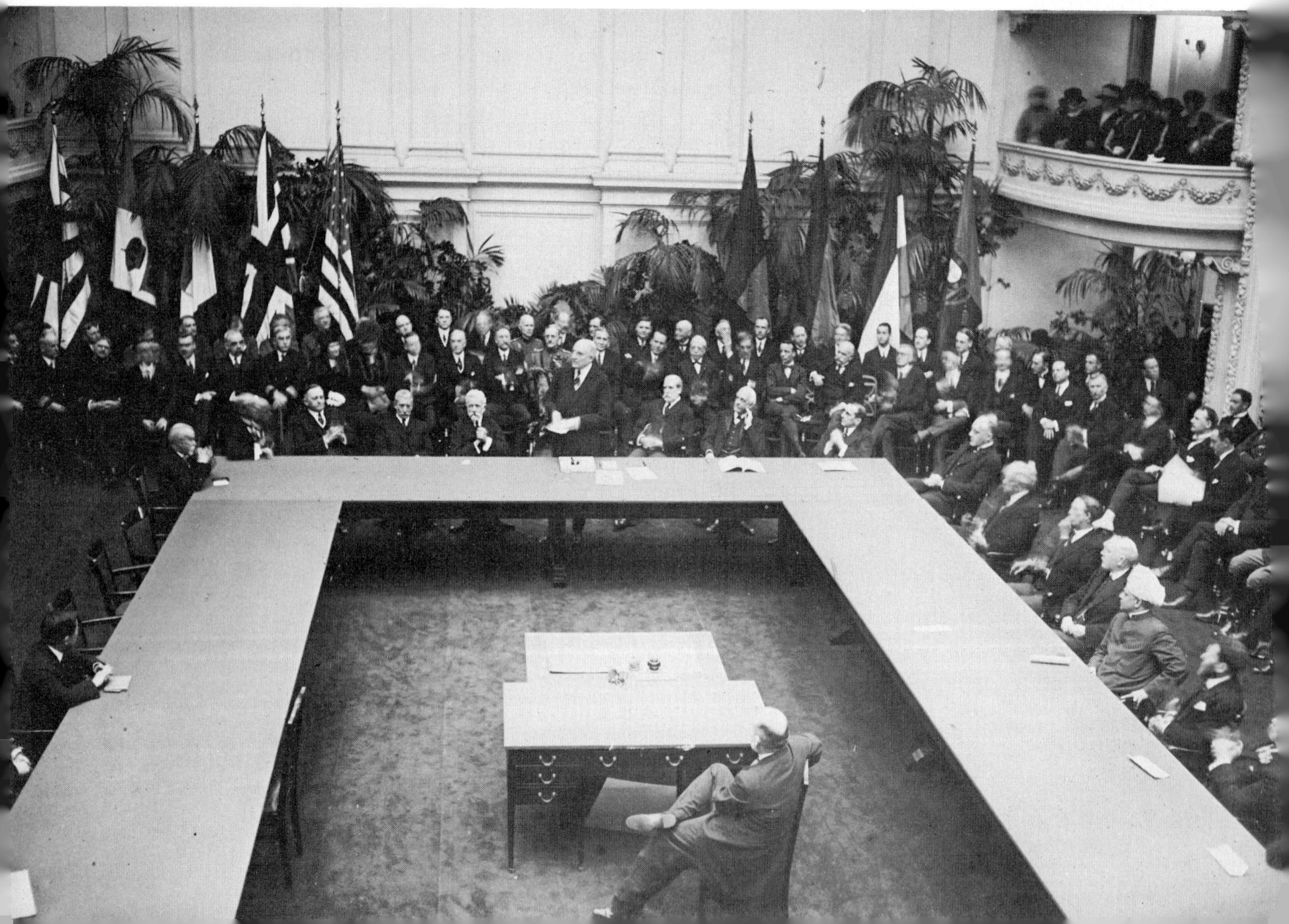

linked helped to strengthen the pacifist movement in the United States. Pacifist organizations had existed since the early days of American reform movements. Their members held many different views. Some were Christians whose reading of the Bible told them that killing another person was never justified. Some were nonreligious believers in human reason; they simply saw war as an insane way to "solve" problems. Socialists held that wars only enriched capitalists who produced the weapons at the expense of the workers who did the fighting. After World War I pacifism became popular. Many distinguished business and educational leaders joined such groups as the American Committee for the Outlawry of War and urged the United States to lead in banishing armed conflict from the world. In 1928 they won a victory.

Secretary of State Frank Kellogg had gotten a proposal from the French for an agreement that the United States and France would never go to war against each other. Kellogg did not wish to commit the United States to a treaty with France, but neither did he wish to offend Paris with a refusal. He saw a way to solve his problem and please the pacifists at one and the same time. He suggested to France's foreign minister, Aristide Briand, that they sign a treaty which would condemn and renounce war—give it up—as a way of settling disputes and invite all the great powers to join them.

Neither France nor any other nation could well refuse. It would be like refusing to condemn sin! So on August 27, 1928, 15 nations signed the Kellogg-Briand Pact (upper left). The next year Kellogg, who privately thought many pacifists were unrealistic "fools," received the Nobel Peace Prize. Eventually, more than 60 nations signed the pact.

Nothing, of course, could force nations to obey the treaty. Yet it was historically important that anti-war feeling all over the world was strong enough to compel governments to bow in its direction.

Questions for Discussion

1. In what ways did Americans profit by purchasing the bonds of foreign countries? How did those countries profit from the sale of these bonds?
2. What was the connection between economic prosperity and world peace?
3. What victories did the pacifists win in the 1920's?

The United States and Latin America

When the twenties began United States marines still occupied Nicaragua, the Dominican Republic, and Haiti. But the Republicans soon began to move away from the pattern of using United States armed forces in Latin American nations. In 1923 Secretary Hughes said that he hoped to keep the peace of the hemisphere "not by arms but by mutual respect and good will."

The change came partly because of the growing dislike of war. But it also was due to the changing beliefs of progressive businessmen. They now felt that it was better to have solidly established governments in the Americas—even if they were sometimes unfriendly—than constant "brushfires" of revolution to be stamped out by United States troops.

The new policy was first applied in 1924 by withdrawing the marines from the Dominican Republic. The next year saw them pull out of Nicaragua as well. However, in 1927, a revolt against dictator Adolfo Díaz brought the "leathernecks" pouring down the gangplanks once more. But this time Henry L. Stimson, a distinguished corporation attorney and public servant, was sent down as a "trouble-shooter." He talked things over with both sides and got consent to free elections supervised by the United States in return for the "rebels" laying down their arms and Díaz completing his term of office. The marines (right) stayed on duty until 1933, however, to handle the guerrilla fighters of one leader, Augusto Sandino, who refused to enter the arrangement.

In Mexico, in 1927, President Plutarco Calles demanded that American companies owning oil wells and mines in his country return these valuable subsoil properties to the Mexican people. Many of the owners, who had paid heavily for developing their holdings, were outraged and joined Secretary Kellogg in denouncing Calles as a "Bolshevik." But Coolidge once again kept cool. He sent Dwight W. Morrow, a partner in the mighty J. P. Morgan banking house, to Mexico City as United States ambassador. Morrow took great pains to be friendly and made no threats. He even got Charles A. Lindbergh to fly down for a good-will visit to show how much Americans thought of Mexico. Morrow, meanwhile, worked out a compromise with Calles.

The Good Neighbor Policy

Herbert Hoover continued the new look in hemisphere diplomacy. Immediately after his election he

BOTH: U.S. MARINE CORPS

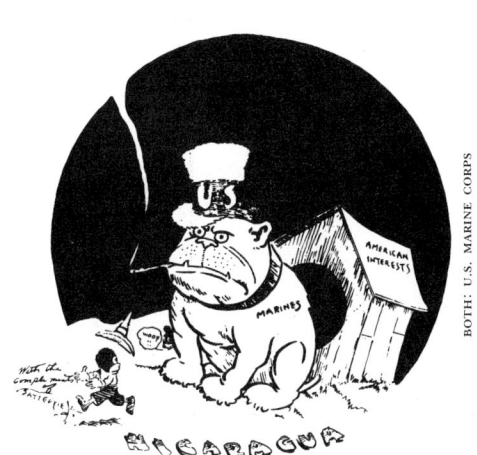

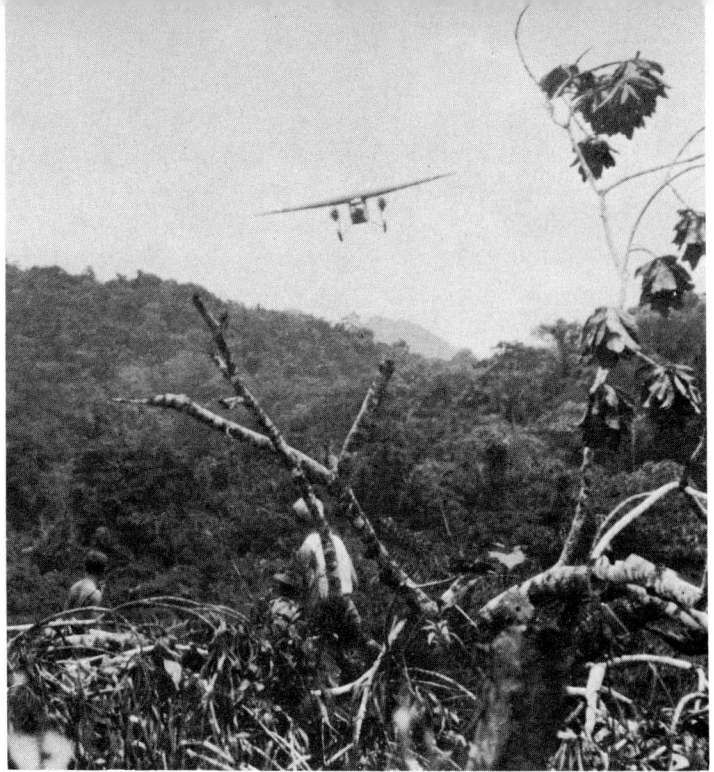

The cartoon above boasts that United States marines will protect American interests in Nicaragua. At right, marines wait for a plane to drop supplies. Below, they pose in a native village.

NATIONAL ARCHIVES

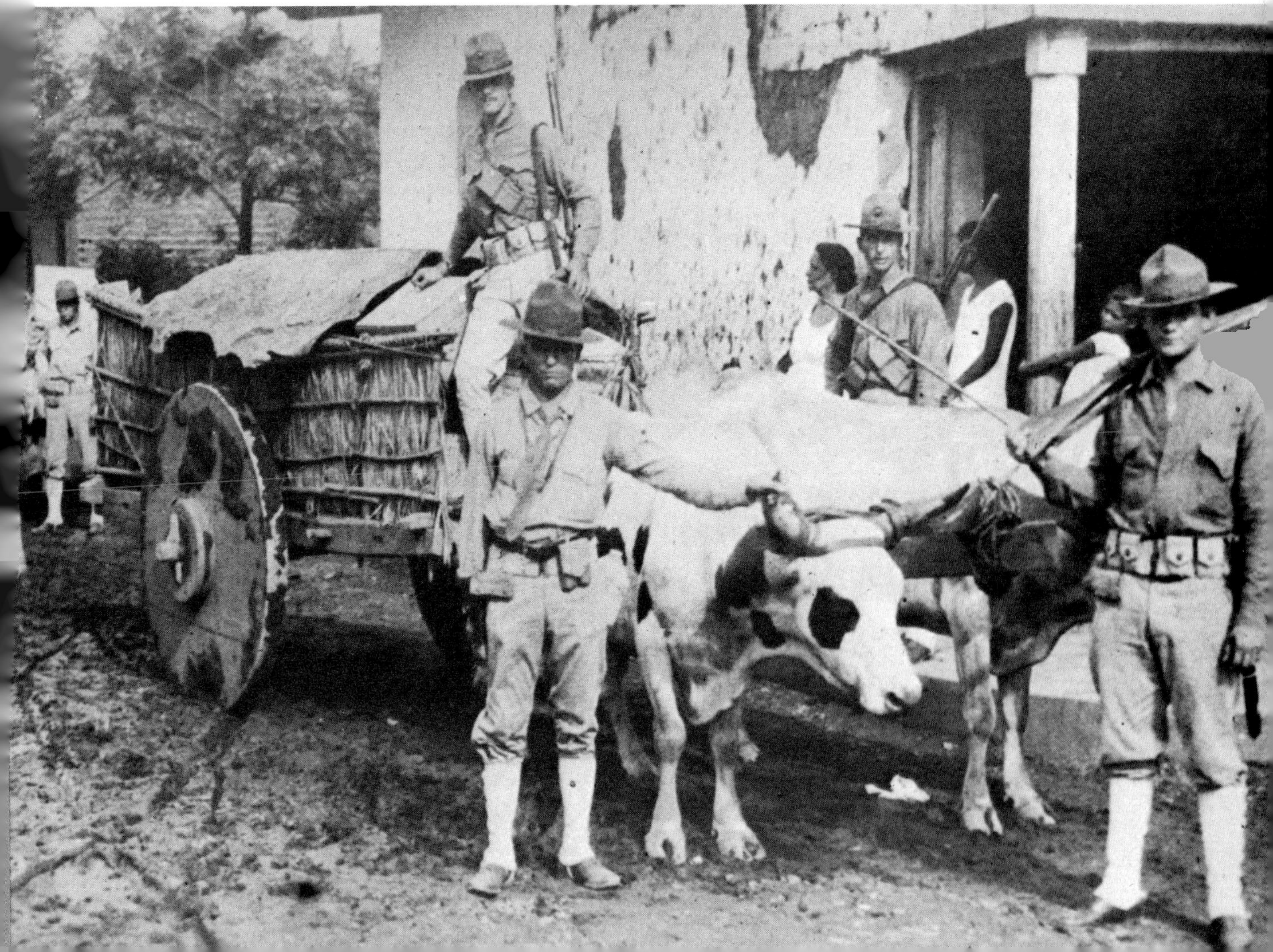

took a good-will tour of Latin American nations (far right). His Secretary of State, Henry L. Stimson, made it clear that the Monroe Doctrine would no longer be used to justify the invasion of other American republics. The Roosevelt administration took up in 1933 where Hoover and Stimson left off.

In his inaugural address FDR spoke of his wish to "dedicate this Nation to the policy of the good neighbor." He was speaking of American relations with all countries. But his words were taken to refer especially to southern neighbors. He and his Secretary of State, Cordell Hull, soon backed friendly words with deeds. Between 1933 and 1936 the United States withdrew all forces from Haiti and Nicaragua and renounced its treaty rights to intervene in Cuba and Panama except to protect United States citizens.

The nation also began a program of economic development in Puerto Rico, whose people had been made United States citizens by the Jones Act of 1917. Finally, in 1938, the United States signed a treaty with Mexico accepting the **expropriation** (seizure of property) of American companies in return for agreed sums of money, known as **compensation.**

Meanwhile, in 1934, Congress passed the Trade Agreements Act, which amended the Tariff Act of 1930. It allowed the President to negotiate individual trade agreements with other countries and to lower tariffs on a reciprocal basis—favor for favor. For example, if Argentina would agree to lower its duties on American flour, the United States would reduce the tariff against Argentine beef. Though this program was worldwide, it was especially helpful to Latin American countries, which depended heavily on a brisk trade with their mighty northern neighbor.

The change in United States hemispheric policies did not end all of Latin America's problems. Not every one sang *Viva Roosevelt* (right). Poverty, illiteracy, and tyranny remained problems threatening Latin American well-being—problems still too much ignored by the rich United States. Yet the picture was changing.

Presidents Hoover and Roosevelt each tried to change the image of the United States in Latin America. Hoover took a pre-inaugural tour of Central and South America (right). Although he coined the term "Good Neighbor Policy," it was Roosevelt who captured the imagination of Latin Americans. When he visited Argentina in December 1936, Roosevelt was hailed as el grand democrata. A song in praise of Roosevelt was set to a Latin American beat (above). Roosevelt did remove United States troops from Central American countries and established a non-intervention policy. But the United States did little to improve the social and economic condition of the people, and much of their resentment remained.

Questions for Discussion

1. What changes were made in the United States foreign policy in Latin America in the 1920's? Why?
2. If there is financial compensation, is the expropriation of foreign companies a fair practice? Why?
3. What did the Trade Agreements Act do?

L'Illustration, 1917

The Gathering Storm

When Woodrow Wilson dreamed of the League of Nations, he hoped that its member states would all be like the most progressive Allied countries. They would have elected governments and guarantees of individual freedom. More important, they would recognize the time-honored rules of international trade and borrowing, would keep treaty promises, and would respect the rights of other governments, like law-abiding citizens in a community of nations.

But in the fourteen years after 1919, new political systems arose which violated all these principles. The first was Russian Communism. The Bolshevik faction of Russia's Social Democratic Party seized power in November 1917. Under Leon Trotsky and Nikolai Lenin (above right), who soon took dictatorial control, they executed the czar and began to make overwhelming changes in Russian life. In addition, they took steps which badly shook the entire European diplomatic pattern, under which governments recognized rights of other nations to rule within their own boundaries

and newly chosen leaders lived up to agreements made by those who ruled before them. First, Bolsheviks proclaimed that Russia was now the "homeland" of worldwide Communist revolution. Communist Russia would encourage and help workers in all capitalist countries to overthrow their rulers. Thus the Bolsheviks automatically made Russia the enemy of non-Communist governments everywhere. Next, they declared that they would keep no treaties and repay no loans made by the czarist government. The "capitalist" governments believed that the Bolsheviks were declaring themselves to be outlaws. They responded by trying to help anti-Bolshevik "White" Russians to overthrow the "Reds." But by 1921 the Bolsheviks had won their bloody civil war at a tremendous cost in suffering in their torn land. Americans contributed to famine relief for the Russians, but the United States did not officially recognize the new government until 1933.

Gradually and suspiciously, Russia—renamed in 1922 the Union of Soviet Socialist Republics—and the

In March 1917 mobs overran the streets of Petrograd (left), forced the czar to abdicate, and launched the first democratic government in Russian history. In a nearly bloodless takeover the Bolsheviks ended Russia's experiment in democracy in November and named Vladimir Ilyich Lenin (above) to head the government. He was convinced that his program of "bread, peace, land" would solve the country's problems. His first economic plans included a huge government-financed industrialization program, as the poster above indicates. The words on the poster reflect Lenin's dedication to worldwide Communist revolution: "There is a spectre haunting Europe, the spectre of Communism."

Hitler used mass rallies to inspire loyalty and create an appetite for war. Below, he arrives at Nuremberg in September 1934.

other powers re-established contact. Lenin was succeeded in 1924 by Joseph Stalin, a brutal tyrant, who nonetheless was willing to put off international revolution and make deals with other nations in order to strengthen Russia. Even then the Soviet Union remained a disturbing force in Europe.

The Rise of the Dictators

Democratic government also collapsed in Italy. That country suffered deeply from postwar unemployment and unsolved social problems. Numerous leaders, including the Communists, arose with "miracle cures." One leader, Benito Mussolini (lower right), had his followers organized into a party that he named Fascist. In 1922 Mussolini led thousands of Fascists in a march on Rome and frightened Italy's king into naming him prime minister. Soon he seized dictatorial powers. He became an international figure when he began to argue that Italy was "cheated" out of its share of the world's colonial wealth by France and Great Britain. Someday, he said, Italy must conquer what rightly belonged to it.

Then it was Germany's turn. The Republic established after the kaiser fled in 1918 was in constant trouble. Communists tried to overthrow it in 1919. At the other extreme certain parties of Germans, bitter

in defeat, charged that the Republic was too soft on Bolsheviks and other radicals and must return to reverence for German military tradition and honor. One such group was the National Socialist German Workers' Party (abbreviated to Nazi) led by Adolf Hitler. Hitler shrieked his message to thousands of hysterical, uniformed followers at huge rallies (below left). Germany, he charged, had been "stabbed in the back" in 1918 by Bolsheviks and Jews. Both must be driven out of German life and replaced by clean-cut members of the "pure" German race, like the Nazi youth in the poster (upper left).

At the start of the 1930's the depression spread to Europe. It drove many people, including Germans, to seek extreme remedies for extreme distress. In 1932 thousands of them voted for the Nazis. In January 1933 Hitler became chancellor. At once he began to jail and kill his rivals. He also announced plans to tear up the Treaty of Versailles, rebuild the army, and unite all Germans in Europe under one flag. Now there were two dictator-controlled nations ready to use armies to change the map of Europe and Africa. But before Mussolini marched or Hitler came to power, the first shots against world order were fired halfway around the globe, in Asia.

Hitler assumed the title Führer *and made effective use of mass media to spread his message. The poster at the far left reads, "The German student fights for Führer and Nation." Notice the swastika, adopted as the official emblem of the Nazi Party in 1935. In Italy Benito Mussolini also assumed a title meaning leader—*Il Duce. Below, *in January 1936 he reviews some of the 250,000 men he sent to conquer Ethiopia.*

Five months after Japanese troops invaded the northern Chinese province of Manchuria in September 1931, they had established control. Conquering the rest of China proved more difficult, even though China was in the midst of a civil war between the Nationalists led by Chiang Kai-shek and the Communists led by Mao Tse-tung. But each side fought the Japanese, most often using guerrilla tactics. The Japanese attacked Shanghai in January 1932. Six months later their officers, seen at right, were wearing bullet-proof vests to protect them from sniper fire. The Japanese soldiers seen below at right are prodding captured Chinese guerrillas with bayonets.

Japan Invades China

In the 1920's Japan faced a growing economic crisis. Its population of 80 million was increasing. Yet its home islands were no bigger than California. Japan had taken giant steps in industrialization, but needed huge stocks of raw material and millions of overseas customers in order to keep its machines working and its people employed. Since the raw materials were not present in Japan, its businessmen were tempted by nearby China which had great untapped resources plus throngs of possible consumers for Japanese-made goods. In their eyes China was economically part of their "front yard" as surely as Latin America was economically tied to the United States.

Yet Japan's ambitions to make China an economic colony ran head-on into obstacles. There was a rising wave of Chinese nationalism that led to boycotts and demands for the withdrawal of all foreigners. Besides, European and American businessmen in China would not give up their treaty privileges. Japan could meet this problem in two ways. It could try to negotiate new treaties concerning China with other powers. Or it could follow the advice of its **militarists** (those who glorify war). They argued that Japanese troops should simply smash into China and take it over!

By 1931 the militarists had won a commanding influence in Japanese affairs. That September they struck. A train carrying Japanese soldiers was blown up by a bomb in Mukden in the rich Chinese province of Manchuria. Using this "incident" as an excuse to "restore order," the Imperial Japanese Army quickly and efficiently overran Manchuria (lower left). They set up their own ruler, renamed the region Manchukuo, and annexed it to Japan.

The United States Secretary of State, Henry L. Stimson, saw that the whole Asian balance of power was in danger if Japan got away with its **aggression** (attack). He tried to get the United States and the League of Nations to join in some kind of punishment, such as an embargo. But neither the League nor President Hoover would risk war with Japan. The best Stimson could do was to refuse diplomatic recognition, official acceptance, of Manchukuo.

The End of Peace in Europe

Now Europe's peace collapsed in six whirlwind years. In 1933 Germany quit the League. In 1935 it

began to re-arm, in violation of the Treaty of Versailles, and in 1936 marched into the Rhineland, an area that was supposed to remain "neutralized" under the treaty. In 1938 the Nazis invaded and annexed Austria and then seized parts of Czechoslovakia. In 1939 Hitler swallowed the rest of Czechoslovakia and made it plain that Poland was the next country due to have its German minority "liberated" by conquest. All these victories came without a shot, as unprepared Britain and France kept backing down rather than face Hitler's huge forces of infantry, tanks, and bombers.

Meanwhile, in 1935 Italy overran the brave, barefoot warriors of Ethiopia, in East Africa. In 1937 and 1938 Japan seized all of helpless China's coastal provinces. China's Open Door was closed.

A few people outside of Germany, Italy, and Japan admired these acts of aggression. Some thought well of Fascism's energy and power, compared to the slow-moving democracies. A number of vigorous anti-Communists believed that Hitler would save Europe from Communist Russia. And others felt that Germany and Italy had been harshly treated by the Treaty of Versailles and had fair claims in Europe.

But most free men were disgusted by Nazism. Under Hitler's flag ugly things bloomed—**anti-Semitism** (prejudice against, and persecution of, Jews), the crushing of truth, free thought, and justice. And yet Hitler and his "bullies" were winning. Was a world ruled by aggressors a nightmare about to become true?

American feelings came to a boil during the Spanish Civil War. In 1936 General Francisco Franco led the Spanish army in a revolt against the "Loyalists" who had established a Republic of Spain in 1931. Germany and Italy at once supported him with "volunteers"—actually well-armed air and ground forces of their own. The Loyalists—whose government included Communists—got some outmoded equipment from the Soviet Union, which had little to spare.

Many strongly anti-Communist Americans sympathized with Franco's rebels. Yet thousands of non-Communists truly believed that aggression must be checked in Spain to preserve freedom everywhere. Inspired by cartoons like that at left, some of them—and many Communists as well—joined the International Brigades. Like the Americans arriving in Paris (upper right), the International Brigades were made up of volunteers for the Loyalists from all over the world.

Loyalist sympathizers pictured the Spanish Civil War as part of a romantic worldwide struggle against Fascism. This drawing by William Gropper appeared in a magazine called New Masses.

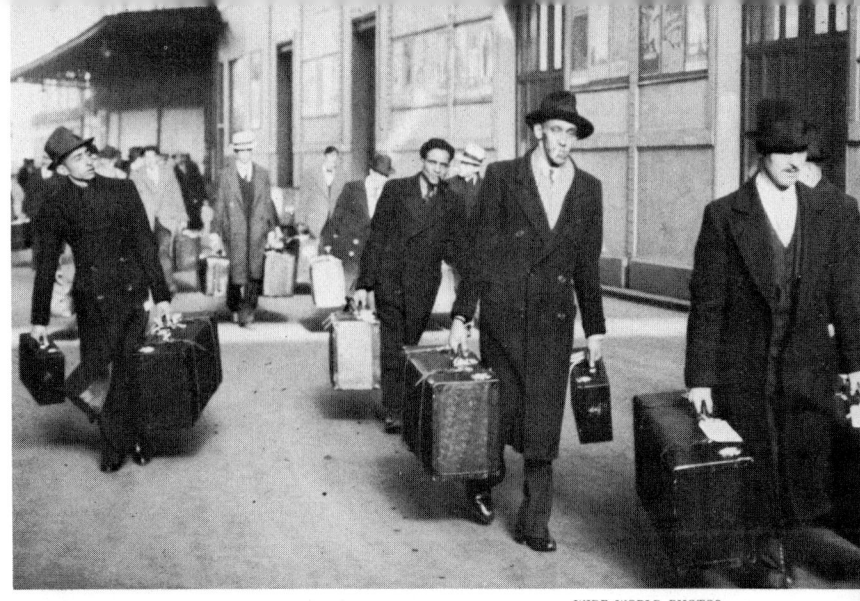

Right: In February 1937 Americans arrive in Paris on their way to join the Abraham Lincoln Battalion in Spain. About 4,000 American volunteers fought for the Loyalists during the war. Below: Robert Capa's photograph of a Loyalist soldier at the instant of death captures the grim reality of the Spanish Civil War.

WIDE WORLD PHOTOS

ROBERT CAPA, MAGNUM

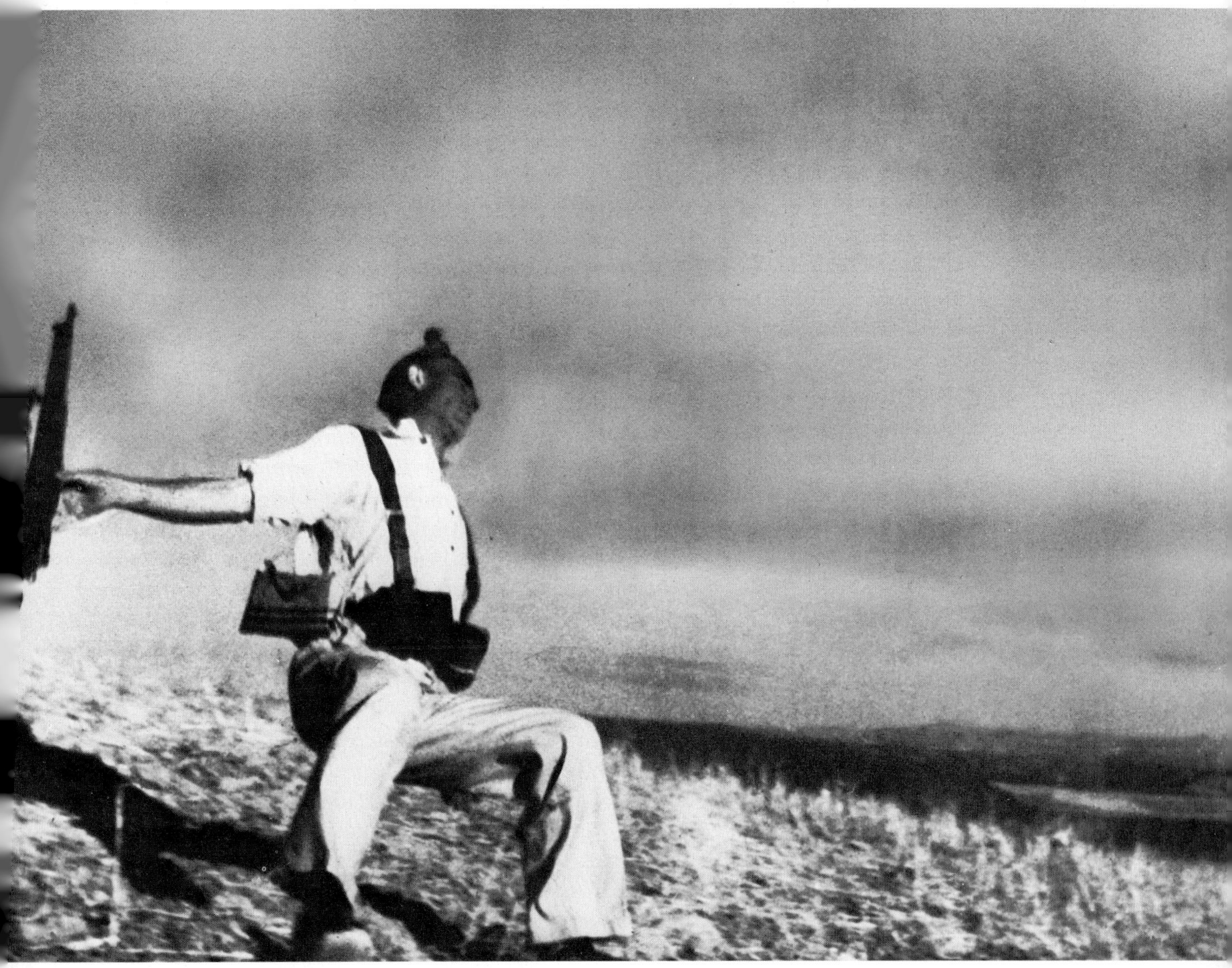

On August 14, 1936, President Roosevelt made a campaign speech at Chatauqua, New York. He spoke of the danger of being drawn into war and declared, "I hate war." The Chicago Tribune cartoon seen above questioned the sincerity of Roosevelt's speech. Notice the comparison to Woodrow Wilson's 1916 campaign slogan—"He kept us out of war."

Before Franco finally won in 1939, hundreds of these young men found graves in Spanish earth.

Isolationism Abandoned

It was a strange fact that just when aggressors were tearing up treaties, Americans finally reached a mood of genuine isolationism. The depression cut foreign trade and investments and forced the United States to be concerned above all with its own severe problems. In the 1930's Americans came to realize the important part which arms sales and loans to the Allies played in ending American neutrality between 1914 and 1917. A congressional investigating committee under Senator Gerald P. Nye concluded that "the lure of the profits" in munitions shipments was a root cause of American involvement in war.

Wilsonian idealism was forgotten. The depression generation did not want a re-run of "America's Road to War." Congress therefore passed three Neutrality Acts between 1935 and 1937. Under them, if war, or civil war, broke out anywhere, Americans were barred from selling or delivering munitions or lending money to the belligerents.

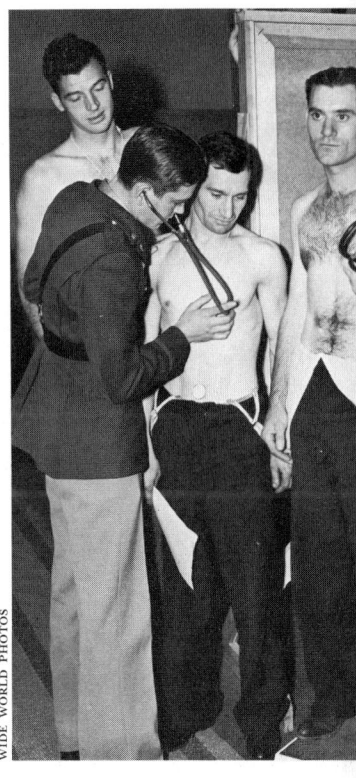

In September 1940, as the Senate debated the nation's first peacetime draft law, mothers of draft-age men lobbied against the bill by staging a "Death Watch" in the Senate reception room (above). Congress passed the law and, on October 29, 1940, a blindfolded Secretary of War, Henry L. Stimson (above left), drew the first of the numbers that determined the order in which men would be drafted. Two of Chicago's first draftees received their physicals on November 18, 1940 (above).

By 1938, with the stamping of German boots shaking Europe, these laws were under attack. One argument against them was that in a world being shrunk by rapid transportation, no nation could afford to ignore the breakdown of peace anywhere. To ex-Secretary of State Stimson, isolation was "a fantastic impossibility." And Secretary Hull voiced a second argument against the laws. Since aggressors had a head start in the arms race, Great Britain and France—in case of war—could only catch up by imports from the United States. An embargo on both sides would therefore play, Hull said, "into the hands of those nations which have taken the lead in building up their fighting powers."

Despite such pleas, isolationist feelings remained strong. But in one swift year, starting in the summer of 1939, the picture changed dramatically. That spring Great Britain and France decided that they had to make a stand. They promised Poland aid if it were attacked. In August Hitler and Stalin, supposedly the deadliest of enemies, astonished the world by signing a non-aggression pact under which Germany and Russia agreed not to go to war against each other. Now Ger-

many was temporarily safe against a war on two fronts. On September 1 it threw a bruising attack at Poland. Two days later the French and British declared war on Germany, but had to stand by powerlessly as the German blitzkrieg, or lightning war, overpowered the Poles in 21 days. Three weeks after the German attack, Russia drove into Poland from the east. In a ten-week period from April to mid-June 1940, waves of Nazi armor rolled over Denmark, Norway, Holland, Belgium, and France. The British army in France barely escaped capture at Dunkirk, on the coast of France, and fled to England, leaving most of its equipment behind.

Now the United States faced a critical choice. Most Americans wanted a British victory—but still hoped to stay neutral. Yet without a great deal of American help, Britain was certain to lose. Most Americans also did not want the burden of building up costly armed forces. Yet an unprepared America would be in serious trouble in a world threatened by aggression. These opposed feelings caused political leaders to act in ways that sometimes seemed to border on dishonesty.

Some cartoonists pictured President Roosevelt as talking peace but planning war. In 1939 FDR asked Congress to change the neutrality laws to allow American help to flow to France and England. In the autumn of 1940 he ran successfully for re-election for a third term. During the election campaign he stood firmly behind legislation which provided for the first peacetime conscription law in the nation's history. The draft was strongly objected to by many, including American mothers of draft-age men. But Roosevelt was able to use his popularity to carry the nation toward a wartime footing. Originally meant to run for only one year, the draft law was renewed late in 1941 by only one vote in Congress. No one knew that the nation had less than three months of peace left.

Questions for Discussion

1. Why did the Russian Communists automatically become the enemy of non-Communist nations?
2. What conditions in Germany contributed to Adolf Hitler's rise to power?
3. Why was Japan interested in expansion into China? What were the obstacles to this expansion?
4. What were the arguments for and against the Neutrality Acts?

Chapter Review

Social Studies Terms

creditor nation, financiers, bonds, expropriation, compensation, militarists, aggression, anti-Semitism

Summary Questions for Discussion

1. What factors or events made isolation unworkable in the 1920's? in the 1930's? Would isolation be a good policy now? Why?
2. Is military power an essential part of world leadership? Why?
3. Which nations were the major threats to world peace in the 1930's? Which will be the major threats to peace in the 1970's? Defend your answer.
4. Is disarmament a good way to insure peace? Why?
5. What are the reasons for the United States' special interest in the political affairs and well-being of Latin Americans?
6. Was the Good Neighbor Policy a change from the principles of the Monroe Doctrine? Explain.
7. What was the reaction in the United States and Europe to the Bolshevik takeover of Russia?
8. Why was so little action taken to stop aggression in the 1930's?

Graph Study

Look at the graph on page 665. What hypothesis can you give to explain why from 1940 to 1945 exports rose sharply while imports fell?

For Further Reading

Franco and the Spanish Civil War, by Laurence E. Snellgrove. New York: McGraw-Hill Book Company, 1968.

From Tsar to Commissars, by Kaye M. Teall. New York: Julian Messner, 1966.

Hitler and Nazism, by Louis L. Snyder. New York: Franklin Watts, Inc., 1961.

Russia in Revolution, by E. M. Halliday. New York: American Heritage Publishing Co., Inc., 1967.

The Desperate Years. by James D. Horan. New York: Crown Publishers, Inc., 1962.

The Rise and Fall of Adolf Hitler, by William L. Shirer. New York: Random House, Inc., 1961.

The Three Worlds of Latin America, by Donald E. Worcester. New York: E. P. Dutton & Co., Inc., 1963.

ISSUES PAST AND PRESENT

Should Americans Follow the Past?

More than any other decade since the 1920's, the 1960's were for young Americans a decade of questioning the values and ways inherited from their parents. The readings below will give you an opportunity to examine the values of different decades since 1900 and to reflect on your own values. Sometimes even worthwhile values like freedom and order may conflict with each other. Individuals must then decide which values are the most important and which are less important. As you read each selection, consider the following questions:

1. How have American values changed during the last 70 years?
2. What values inherited from earlier times should be preserved? Which should be cast aside?
3. Which values are most important? least important?

Fundamental Rules

To understand some of the values that have helped to determine American ways, we will begin with a reading by a financier written at the turn of the century. Henry Clews, the author of the following selection, was actually born in England, but he came to the United States at the beginning of the Civil War and decided to stay. He became a very successful financier and in 1877 established his own business.

HENRY CLEWS:
THE WALL STREET POINT OF VIEW, 1900

It does not require a great genius to make money. The accumulation [gathering] of wealth is an easy matter. It does not require education, the right ancestors, or dignified manners. Luck has little to do with it. Any man or woman may become wealthy, if he or she begins in the right way. The opportunities for making a fortune are very numerous in this country, if certain basic rules are followed.

The first step to getting a fortune lies in hard work. I could give you no better advice than that given by Benjamin Franklin: "Save something each day, no matter how little you earn." Make your work count for all that you can. Always save some part of your wages, and then be on the lookout for good investment opportunities. If you do this wisely, your money will begin to accumulate, double, triple, and in a few years, perhaps, you may be a millionaire.

The beginning is the most difficult. Lay a good foundation for your fortune. Be brave, be generous, be helpful, be honest, do not overwork, keep in good health, cultivate [develop] your

mind, be pure. To these good habits add thrift, and you need not fear. You cannot fail.

I would say to all fathers and mothers, teach your children the value of money. When they are old enough, make them understand the worth of a penny. From the child's savings bank in the playroom to the millionaire's bank account is not a long step. It is a short and easy span.

1. What was Clews' idea of a successful life?
2. What values did Clews favor?
3. Do you like Clews' values? Why?

During the 1920's The American Magazine, *with more than 2 million readers, had a monthly column called "The Family's Money." The articles were written by their readers. The following is typical of many that were submitted.*

The Simple Life

MR. C. M.:
WE SAVE MORE THAN HALF OF OUR INCOME, 1926

I am a teacher and receive a salary of $2,500 for nine months of teaching. Starting with $1,500 savings at the time of our marriage three years ago, my wife and I have increased our savings to almost $6,000. Our monthly budget is approximately as follows:

Income

Salary	$250.00	
Interest from investments	30.00	
Total		$280.00

Expenditures

Rent	$ 35.00	
Food	25.00	
Clothing	20.00	
Entertainment and Education	10.00	
Insurance	8.00	
Fuel	5.00	
Light, Water, and Telephone	4.50	
Medical	3.00	
Charity	2.50	
Laundry	2.00	
Total		$115.00
Savings		$165.00

We are fortunate in renting a neatly furnished, comfortable, modern four-room house for $35 per month. Although not located in the most exclusive section of the city, it is in a good neighborhood and has a yard with trees and a garden. We are just turning 25 and have plans for more schooling and hopes for a better position before we shall own our own home.

My wife is an excellent cook and our simple foods are well-cooked and attractively served. We buy potatoes and apples by the bushel and canned foods by the case, thereby making a good saving. For vitamins during the winter, we use lettuce now and then and drink milk at least once a day.

My wife is an expert seamstress. She has her own electric sewing machine and makes all her own dresses. Since taking a few lessons in hat designing, she makes pretty hats at a cost less than half that of the ready-made kind.

Our town does not offer the great variety of entertainment to be found in a large city. Occasionally, we go to a good play or a recital, and perhaps twice a month go out to a movie, a dance, or a card party. Our best entertainment, however, comes from reading, hiking, and listening to the radio. We use both the school and the city libraries, and a constant stream of books and magazines passes through our hands.

We keep a few hundred dollars in a savings bank in case of need, but as soon as $750 is accumulated we invest $500 in bonds bearing a higher rate of interest than the bank pays.

Frequently, our friends ask us how we manage to save so large a slice of our small income. The answer is simple: Our wants are few. We find that most of our real pleasures cannot be measured in terms of money. Therefore, with us, saving requires little sacrifice and becomes almost automatic. We try to practice the virtue of being content and happy in the present, but we are always looking forward toward the future and trying to plan for it too.

1. What values seemed to be important to this couple?
2. Are they the same values that seemed important to Henry Clews? Explain your answer.

The Big Trouble

When the 1930's brought times of trouble, even couples like those in the previous selection had a hard time paying their bills. But life became even harder for families like those in the next reading. The selection was recorded by a college professor who for a time traveled with boys and girls wandering around the country in search of some kind of a living. The exact number of boys and girls who were forced to find a living this way is not known, but the number was estimated at the time to be in the hundreds of thousands.

THOMAS MINEHAN:
BOY AND GIRL TRAMPS OF AMERICA, 1934

"It wasn't so bad at home," says the boy from Texas to me, "before the big trouble came. We got along pretty good. Dad, of course, never was very well. He was in World War I and he got some kind of sickness, but he couldn't get a pension. He was always sick for about a month every year, and so he had to look for a new job each time he got well.

"But we got along swell before the big trouble came even if there were seven of us kids. I shined shoes in a barber shop. Jim carried papers. And Marie took care of Mrs. Rolph's kids. Mother always did some sewing for the neighbors. We had a Chevie and a radio and a piano. I even started to high school mornings, the year the big trouble came.

"Dad got sick as usual but we never thought anything of it. When he comes to go back to work he can't get a job, and everybody all of a sudden seems to be hard up. I cut the price of shines to a nickel, but it didn't help much. I even used to go around and collect shoes and shine them at the houses or take them away, shine and return them, but even then some weeks I couldn't make a dime. Mrs. Rolph's husband got a cut in pay and she fires Marie. Jim had to quit the paper route because he lost all his cash customers and the others never paid. Nobody wanted Mother to sew anything. And there we were, seven kids and Dad and Mother, and we couldn't make a cent like we could before the big trouble came.

"But the big trouble came, and there we were. Oh, we tried hard enough, and everybody did their best. Marie made the swellest wax flowers. The kids peddled ironing cloths. Mother tried to sell some homemade baked goods. And Dad did everything. We did our best, I guess, but it wasn't good enough, for the big trouble had come and nobody had any money.

"Dad gave up pipe smoking in the fall. All last winter we never had a fire except once a day when Mother used to cook some mush or something. When the kids were cold, they went to bed. I quit high school but the kids kept going to school because it didn't cost anything and it was warm there.

"In February I went to Fort Worth. Mother used to know a man there, and she thought maybe he could help me get a job. But he was as hard up as anybody else. I didn't want to return home and pick bread off the kids' plates so I tried to get work for a farmer for my board. Instead, I got a ride to California. Near Salinas, California, I worked in the lettuce fields, cutting and washing lettuce. I made $32 and I sent $10 home. But that was my first and last pay check. I got chased

In the 1930's many American homes still did not have central heating.

out of California in June. Since then, I just been traveling."

1. What values did the boy and his family want to preserve both before and after the depression came?
2. What hypothesis can you make about how the depression might have changed the values of young people?

Living It Up

The author of the following reading was a newspaperman who lived in a foreign country for nine years. When he came back to the United States in the middle of the 1950's, Look magazine assigned him to take a trip across the country with his wife, Sim, and write about what he saw.

WILLIAM ATTWOOD:
STILL THE MOST EXCITING COUNTRY, 1955

When we started this trip we had some doubts about riding around the country in our swanky-looking British sports car. We feared that it might set us apart from the people we wanted to talk to. They might think we were wealthy and treat us with shyness.

Our doubts quickly evaporated when we stopped for the night in a second-rate motel south of Washington, D.C. The lady who ran the place appraised our car with a fleeting glance. "Cute," she said. "We bought our daughter one like it for Christmas—a Corvette—so she'd have something to run around in. It's bigger than yours. Here's your room key. That'll be five dollars."

More people are making more money than ever before in America. But that is not the main reason you see so much plush living in unexpected places. Wages and salaries have risen—but not that much faster than the cost of living. The secret of America's prosperous look is not so much that people are making big money, but that they are spending it lavishly. Everybody seems to be living it up—and paying for it later. Thanks to installment buying, things that foreigners cannot begin to dream about are within everyone's reach. I remember when mink coats and Cadillacs were signs of wealth. Today they just mean you are deeper in debt.

No one can deny that too many Americans are still ill-housed, ill-clothed, and ill-fed. But there are no longer as many of them as there were in the depression. The big story today is not that they exist, but that their numbers are dwindling so rapidly. Will prosperity last? Does anybody know where we are headed? How will it end?

To "appraise" means to determine the value of something.

We heard these questions, but only from businessmen over 40 years old. Americans who were grown-up during the depression, and who remember what it felt and looked like, are concerned about the future. The others are confident that prosperity is here to stay. The younger generation that never saw or only dimly remembers a bread line will tell you that we are safe from another depression.

Their attitude disturbed a middle-aged chain-store manager in Arizona. "Young people don't give a second thought to going into debt these days," he told us. "They figure the government will take care of them somehow if they go broke or lose their jobs. They just don't know what a depression means."

Are Americans happier? Maybe, maybe not. "The more money I make," said a truck driver near San Diego, "the more payments I seem to take on. There's no let-up."

Of course, we Americans like our new comforts and our new toys. But time and again on this trip, Sim and I met people who could not find words to explain that purpose and direction were missing from their lives. I suspect that, like the suffragette who wanted something and thought it was the ballot, a lot of Americans want something and think it is color television.

Today I think we Americans are chasing a lot of things, and not all of them have price tags. In an increasingly mechanized society, more people are discovering that they need some kind of creative outlet—and they are doing something about it. In town after town, we found thriving amateur dramatic societies, symphony orchestras, art groups, and sculpture classes; and nearly all had sprung up since World War II.

Everything sold in grocery stores is designed to save the housewife time and trouble. They are even selling bottled iced tea and complete pre-cooked dinners. Many women find time to take jobs that sometimes double the family income. Childless couples—and others, too—have found that with both adults in the family earning money, they can afford luxuries that would otherwise be out of reach. And among the luxuries are appliances that cut housekeeping chores down to the point where an eight-hour-day outside job is no hardship. I remember one week in which we met three different women who were keeping house and pursuing successful careers.

1. Why did Attwood feel that American ways were different from what they had been in earlier times?
2. How was the outlook of young people on economic matters different from their parents' outlook?

The Wrong Kind of Everything

There are now some 38 million Americans who are between 14 and 25. Never before in American history have the young been so numerous—or so loud in their challenge of the ways of the past. The author of the following selection was one adult who attempted to evaluate the meaning of the rebellion of youth.

EDA J. LESHAN: *WHAT? AMERICANS HATE KIDS?* 1968

American youths are highly visible in their flashy clothes. They are often barefoot and unshaven. They frequently wear beads. They appear to have little regard for property. Most of all, they anger us by asking just the questions we want least to hear. They also anger us because they can see clearly just where we have failed.

I am speaking of the young people who want to know how we can travel to the moon but so pollute our water and our atmosphere that life becomes endangered. I am speaking of those who wonder aloud at our turning this nation into one huge highway. These young people ask why we insisted on teaching them about the Constitution when, as a nation, we have absolutely refused to follow its requirements in regard to men of different color.

And then, too, they have proved to be so unthankful. We gave them everything money could buy. The first generation raised in wealth, they have all the things their parents and grandparents worked so hard to get for them. And here they are, telling us it is the wrong kind of everything. They turn their backs on the three-bathroom house and the secure future in the family business. Some of them even reject the graduation-present sports car. They care nothing at all about material possessions. They tell us such possessions do not bring happiness.

They tell us that it is what is inside a man that counts, not the color of his skin. We know that when they say "brother," they really mean it. They explain that warfare is an outdated way of settling disputes if we want to preserve human life. Most of all, they question the meaning of our lives. They are more deeply committed to our own ideals than we ever were. They have dared to tune us out.

1. Why does the author feel that young people of the sixties acted differently than their parents?
2. What ways of living of the older generation were being questioned by the younger? Why?
3. According to the author what values do today's youth hold in high regard?

Who Could Ask For More?

A viewpoint about American ways and personal values can also be expressed in music. Pete Seeger is among the songwriters best known for songs that express personal values.

PETE SEEGER: *MY RAINBOW RACE,* 1970

One blue sky above us, one ocean lapping all our shores,
One earth so green and round, who could ask for more?
And because I love you I'll give it one more try
To show my rainbow race it's too soon to die.

Some folks want to be like an ostrich: bury their heads in the sand,
Some want to take the easy way: Poisons, bombs! They think we need 'em.
Don't they know you can't kill all the unbelievers. There's no shortcut to freedom.

One blue sky above us, one ocean lapping all our shores,
One earth so green and round, who could ask for more?
And because I love you I'll give it one more try
To show my rainbow race it's too soon to die.

Go tell—go tell all the little children!
Go tell mothers and fathers, too:
Now's our last chance to learn to share what's been given to me and you.

One blue sky above us, one ocean lapping all our shores,
One earth so green and round, who could ask for more?
And because I love you I'll give it one more try
To show my rainbow race it's too soon to die.

1. To what does the term "rainbow race" refer?
2. What ways of acting or values does Seeger reject?
3. What is Seeger's message? Do you agree or disagree? Explain your answer.

Summary Questions

1. Which of the values mentioned in the previous selections are worth maintaining today? Why?
2. Which of the values mentioned in the previous selections would you like to scrap? Why?
3. What values not mentioned in any of the selections do you feel should be followed by Americans? Why?

1941 Japan Attacks at Pearl Harbor

1945 Germany and Japan Surrender

1950 Korean War Begins

1955 King Assumes Lead of Civil Rights Movement

1944 D-Day, Allies Land in France

1947 Marshall Plan Announced

1954 School Segregation Declared Unconstitutional

UNIT VIII
A Changing Society in a Changing World

1962 Cuban Missile Crisis

1965 Johnson Intervenes in Vietnam

1969 Man Walks on the Moon

1961 Peace Corps Begins

1963 President Kennedy Assassinated

1967 Black Riots Erupt in Many Cities

1970 Congress Lowers Voting Age

In previous units you have learned how rapid change has made a deep impact on American life. Though this change often led to unsettled lives and even occasional conflict, the ability of the American people to survive change was rarely doubted. But the period of history beginning with World War II brought change so far-reaching that many Americans began to wonder if the nation was going to be overwhelmed by it. Much of this change was caused by an explosion of technology that threatened, for the first time, to become man's master and destroyer instead of his servant.

In *Interpreting the Past*, which begins Unit VIII, the significance of technology in American life is debated. Chapter 24 tells the story of World War II, the most technological — and most terrifying — of modern wars. World War II ended with the dropping of a weapon of unheard of destructive power, the atomic bomb. Even after the war ended, the bomb's mushroom-shaped cloud seemed not to disappear but to hover over events inside as well as outside the borders of the United States.

Progress in solving the nation's problems since 1945 is the subject of Chapter 25, while Chapter 26 tells of the ways the United States has exercised its power in a rapidly changing world. At the end of the unit, in *Issues Past and Present*, the problem of handling our machine-age environment is explored.

TOP, LEFT TO RIGHT:
NATIONAL ARCHIVES
WIDE WORLD PHOTOS
U. S. MARINE CORPS
WIDE WORLD PHOTOS
UPI
WIDE WORLD PHOTOS
NASA
BOTTOM, LEFT TO RIGHT:
U. S. COAST GUARD
CULVER PICTURES
UPI
PEACE CORPS
WHITE HOUSE
UPI
NAACP

INTERPRETING THE PAST

The Significance of Technology

Technology has been such an important part of American life that many people have thought of technology's progress as an important measure of our progress as a nation. Even people in foreign countries have thought of the United States as a Promised Land or a world power because of its staggering ability to produce and consume an unending stream of goods—from airplanes to automobiles, from telephones to televisions, from tractors to toys.

Today machines are all around us. They have become as much a part of our environment as trees and buildings. They perform in a jiffy a million jobs that once took hours of hard manual labor. Whisk—the lawn is mowed. Whisk—an elevator flies up 90 stories. Whisk—a jet screams across the sky. They are used even for purely social purposes. Want to find a date who is like you? Ask your friendly computer. But if machines seem to be the solution to some problems, they seem to be the cause of others. Americans are seeking answers to questions like these:

1. What impact has scientific industrial technology had in shaping our lives?
2. Do we need to curb or expand the use of technology? Why? How?

American Technology

By 1880, when the following speech was made, technology was widespread enough to touch almost every aspect of American life. The following selection was taken from the speech made by Robert Thurston when he became president of the American Society of Mechanical Engineers.

ROBERT THURSTON:
ADDRESS TO AMERICAN SOCIETY OF MECHANICAL ENGINEERS, 1880

We Americans receive from all lands their most ambitious and hard-working people. We send to all lands the best devices for creating the most essential comforts and the greatest luxuries. The United States is looked upon as the home of all clever and effective "labor-saving" devices. It is the home of the finest wood-working machinery. Foreign nations imitate our designs. The American steam engine has revolutionized the manufacturing of steam engines all over the world. The introduction of navigation by steam here led to the construction of steam vessels everywhere. Our mowers and reapers gather the harvests of every field from Oregon to

Maine and from Great Britain to the most distant countries of Europe. They are even seen among the half-barbarians of farthest Asia. And thus in thousands of ways modern civilization, which is reaching its highest development in this new world, is reaching out to touch and to renew life in every other nation.

1. In what ways did the author think technology had influenced the past?
2. What did he expect technology to accomplish in the future?
3. Has Thurston been proven correct? How?

Man and Machine

When an engine was added to the buggy, the "horseless carriage" was born. The assembly line helped to make the car available to the common man. But what was it like to work on the assembly line? In the following reading Roderick Nash gives his answer.

RODERICK NASH: THE NEW INDUSTRIAL ORDER, 1970

October 7, 1913, Highland Park, Michigan: As Henry Ford and his executives watched tensely, a rope attached to a Model T's chassis tightened and inched it across a 250-foot track on the factory floor. Workmen kept pace, adding part after part. Five hours and fifty minutes later, a finished car rolled off the line under its own power. The Ford men were pleased. Their previous production record had been cut in half.

A few months later, the Highland Park plant produced 600 cars in a single working day. Soon the average time per car fell to 93 minutes. The unbelievable day of a car-a-minute was just ahead.

While there was much to celebrate in the success of Ford and those who worked with him in the automobile industry, some problems of the new industrial order could not be denied. On the assembly line work became mindless drudgery [boring and unpleasant work]. The old-time craftsman had been entirely responsible for a finished product. He could take pride in his work. But the man whose labor consisted of tightening several nuts on a moving chassis in no sense "made" a car. He was a machine, and if possible he was replaced by one. Even the $5-a-day minimum wage Ford promised for a day's work could not change that. The individual was lost in an economic system no longer dependent upon his special skill.

1. What did increasing the speed of production mean to the average factory worker?
2. Compare the viewpoints of Thurston and Nash.
3. In what direction is technology moving today?

Science and the Future

During World War II the government spent huge sums of money for technological development, especially of weapons. At the end of the war Vannevar Bush, a leading scientist in the wartime Office of Scientific Research and Development, gave his views of what technology or applied science could mean for mankind.

VANNEVAR BUSH: *ENDLESS HORIZONS*, 1946

Advances in science when put to practical use mean more jobs, higher wages, shorter hours, and more abundant crops. They also mean more free time for recreation, for study, for learning how to live without the deadening drudgery which has been the burden of the common man for ages past. Advances in science also will bring higher standards of living. They will lead to the prevention or cure of disease. They will promote conservation of our limited national resources, and will assure means of defense against aggression.

Our population increased from 75 million to 130 million between 1900 and 1940. In some countries the same increase has brought famine. In this country the increase has been accompanied by a more abundant food supply, better living, more free time, longer life, and better health. This is mainly the result of three factors—a vigorous people who, in this democratic society, are not afraid to try out new ideas, our great natural resources, and the advance of science and its application.

1. Reread Bush's last paragraph. Would you agree with the three reasons he gives for why Americans have been able to increase the quality of their life while their numbers were growing? Why?
2. In what ways does Bush think technology will influence the future?
3. How does Bush's point of view differ from Nash's?

Was He Free? Was He Happy?

The author of the following poem was born in England in 1907 and came to the United States in 1939. He became an American citizen in 1946 and won the Pulitzer Prize for poetry in 1948.

W. H. AUDEN: *THE UNKNOWN CITIZEN*, 1940

(To JS/07/M/378 This Marble Monument Is Erected by the State)

*He was found by the Bureau of Statistics to be
One against whom there was no official complaint,
And all the reports on his conduct agree
That, in the modern sense of an old-fashioned word, he was a saint,
For in everything he did he served the Greater Community.
Except for the War till the day he retired
He worked in a factory and never got fired,
But satisfied his employers, Fudge Motors Inc.
Yet he wasn't a scab or odd in his views,
For his Union reports that he paid his dues,
(Our report on his Union shows it was sound)
And our Social Psychology workers found
That he was popular with his mates and liked a drink.
The Press are convinced that he bought a paper every day
And that his reactions to advertisements were normal in every way.
Policies taken out in his name prove that he was fully insured,
And his Health-card shows he was once in hospital but left it cured.
Both Producers Research and High-Grade Living declare
He was fully sensible to the advantage of the Installment Plan
And had everything necessary to the Modern Man,
A phonograph, a radio, a car and a frigidaire.
Our researchers into Public Opinion are content
That he held the proper opinions for the time of year;
When there was peace, he was for peace; when there was war, he went.
He was married and added five children to the population,
Which our Eugenist says was the right number for a parent of his generation,
And our teachers report that he never interfered with their education.
Was he free? Was he happy? The question is absurd:
Had anything been wrong, we should certainly have heard.*

A "Eugenist" is a scientist who studies hereditary factors and population control.

Summary Questions

1. How would you answer the questions in the next-to-last line of the poem? Do you believe these questions are truly absurd? Why?
2. Did technology help to make *JS/07/M/378* the kind of person he was? Why?
3. What is your view of modern technology? Explain.

24
World War II

The Bible says that in the sixth hundredth year of Noah's life, "all the fountains of the great deep [were] broken up," and a flood swept the earth and destroyed every living thing that was not in the ark. When the waters went down and dried up, a whole new life began for mankind.

World War II deserves that kind of poetic language to describe its impact. It was more than a large-scale replay of World War I. While World War I had changed the past, World War II seemed almost to wipe it out. The use of far-ranging aerial bombardment not only killed millions of noncombatants, but for six years smashed cities, which were the proud achievements of many centuries of European civilization, into junk-piles.

The war also set free revolutionary forces of nationalism in Asia and Africa. After 1945 a weakened Europe could no longer check a rush toward independence by its former possessions. Thus 500 years of world mastery by European colonial empires came to an end, completing a process begun by Americans in 1776.

Finally, the war closed with the blazing explosion of the atomic bomb in the skies over Japan. As an official United States document said, it was "the most terrible weapon ever known in human history, one bomb of which could destroy a whole city." This unbelievably destructive power opened an era of international relations unlike any ever known before.

For the United States all of this had enormous importance. In one sense, World War II was a triumph for America. A nation divided and crippled by the depression in 1933 was able, only ten years later, to perform miracles of production for one, unifying purpose—to give the best to "our fighters" (left). Yet the victory of 1945 over the Axis powers—Germany, Italy, and Japan—left the United States the only powerful and still unscarred nation on the entire globe. There was no escape, as in 1919, from the heart-aching burden of preventing chaos in the world, at least in the immediate future. There was no chance even to pretend that the United States could return to a simple, isolated past.

As you read, think about the following questions:
1. Why did the United States enter World War II on the side of the Allies?
2. How did World War II differ from previous wars?

This World War II poster urges civilians to support their fighting men.

U. S. AIR FORCE

The Storm Breaks

After the shattering Nazi victories of 1940, the United States moved swiftly toward arming itself. Congress passed both a multibillion dollar program for building up American armed forces and a peacetime draft act. Meanwhile, the situation was critical for Britain. Its cities staggered under daily pounding by waves of Nazi bombers (left), while submarines feasted like sharks on the merchant ships whose cargoes kept the island kingdom from starvation.

Roosevelt was convinced that a British collapse would be a disaster. But while American public opinion had moved away from the isolationism of the Neutrality Acts, it was not yet ready for combat. Roosevelt, therefore, had to devise steps short of war to help the hard-pressed British fighting under Prime Minister Winston Churchill's leadership. In January 1941 the President proposed a dramatic new idea called lend-lease. He explained it with a little story. If a man's house were afire and he needed a hose, said FDR, any good neighbor would lend him one. All the neighbor would expect was the return of the hose or a replacement when the fire was out. Roosevelt wanted congressional authority to produce $7 billion worth of military hardware to lend the British as their "hose." It could be repaid in arms or other goods at the war's end. After sharp debate Congress enacted lend-lease in March. The United States was now a non-belligerent partner of Great Britain. In time, lend-lease aid went to Russia, China, and other Allies.

The headlines of 1941 blared forth shock after shock. In April and May Hitler conquered Yugoslavia and Greece. In June he tore up his pact with Stalin and attacked Russia. As Hitler's power grew United States neutrality wore thinner. In August Roosevelt and Churchill signed the Atlantic Charter, agreeing on the kind of world they hoped for after "the final destruction of Nazi tyranny." Then, since it was pointless to manufacture lend-lease goods only to have them sunk at sea, the United States moved to help the thinly stretched British navy guard the Atlantic supply line. American warships began to conduct submarine-spotting patrols in the North Atlantic. After some were fired on, they received orders to "shoot on sight" any German or Italian undersea craft. November 1941 found the United States in an undeclared naval war with Germany. Then, suddenly, lightning struck halfway around the world, in the Pacific.

From July 1940 to June 1941 Germany tried to bomb Britain into surrender.

Japanese militarists assumed undisputed control of the government when General Hideki Tojo became Prime Minister in October 1941. They continued, however, to try to hide their preparations for war. When Tojo delivered a warlike speech to the legislature on November 17 (above), Japanese censors translated the speech into a plea for "Pacific peace." Japan's attack on Pearl Harbor ended any hopes for peace in the Pacific. The United States Pacific fleet was severely crippled. An enormous explosion broke the Arizona *(right, center) in half, killing 1,100 men.*

Pearl Harbor and War with Japan

Defeat in 1940 stripped Hitler's enemies of the power to protect their overseas possessions. Japan's expansionists, like General Hideki Tojo (left), looked hungrily at French Indochina, British-ruled Malaya and Burma, and the Dutch East Indies (map, page 716). All were rich in rubber, tin, oil, and other materials sorely needed by Japan's industrial economy.

Only the United States stood in the way. The United States was strongly pressing Tokyo to get out of China and threatening an embargo on its own exports of vital industrial materials to Japan. Even the few remaining pro-peace moderates in Japan's government, however, could not support a pullout from China. It would be denounced as a disgraceful surrender.

The impatient generals were ready to move. In July 1941 Japan occupied French Indochina. The United States struck back with an embargo on gasoline, copper, and scrap iron. The Japanese moderates begged their government for a final chance to negotiate a Pacific settlement. The moderates got their chance—with conditions. A surprise attack against the Americans would be readied—and put into execution if talks produced no results by December 1.

But on November 26 Washington informed the Japanese ambassadors that it had not changed its stand. There would be no Pacific pact or lifting of the boycott until Japan left both Indochina *and* China. To the United States this was part of its historic support of a free China. To the Japanese it was a demand: "Surrender, or be destroyed economically." Secret orders sent Japanese carriers steaming to a point north of Hawaii.

At 7:55 A.M. on Sunday, December 7, their planes caught the American base at Pearl Harbor unprepared. Within 2 hours columns of oily smoke marked the graves of 3 battleships (right), many smaller ships, 188 aircraft, and nearly 2,400 soldiers and sailors. The next day an angry President Roosevelt, denouncing Japan's sneak blow, got a declaration of war from Congress. Japan's allies, Germany and Italy, then declared war on the United States. Once more the end of the road to battle had been reached.

Questions for Discussion

1. Why did the United States give aid to Britain?
2. Why did the Japanese attack Pearl Harbor?

Mobilization for Victory

In one way there was more home-front unity in World War II than in 1918. There were almost no antiwar radicals. It was also taken for granted that all but a tiny minority of German-Americans were loyal. Thus American **pluralism** (a pattern of many faiths and different nationalities living peacefully together) seemed stronger in the 1940's than ever.

But there was a glaring exception. On the West Coast lived 110,000 Americans of Japanese birth or descent. During the early months of 1942, Japan was winning the war's opening battles. Fears were expressed that a Japanese force might land on the United States Pacific Coast and that Japanese descendants living there would support it. Nothing whatever in the past behavior of Japanese-Americans supported such a belief. But behind it was a long history of prejudice against Orientals. With strong support from local authorities, the army, in April 1942, ordered all West Coast Japanese to prepare in 48 hours for removal to "relocation centers," which were not unlike prison camps. Forced to sell their homes and property at once, for whatever price was offered, the Japanese-Americans obeyed orders (right). Some later were allowed to leave the camps for jobs in other parts of the country. Despite this bitter experience, almost all the Japanese in America expressed only a desire to prove their loyalty. Moreover, 8,000 Nisei (children born in the United States of Japanese parentage) enlisted in the armed forces, like the infantrymen of the much-decorated 442nd Regimental Combat Team (top right).

Other home-front nonwhite minorities had both good and bad experiences. Blacks found some industrial jobs open to them which had been closed before. Yet as they moved into wartime boom towns, crowding resulted in tension and violence. In Detroit an interracial fight in a crowded park on a hot June Sunday in 1943 led to a riot which left 38 dead and 500 wounded. In Los Angeles Mexican-American civilian youths were beaten by mobs (including off-duty servicemen) in a 1943 outbreak. Thus racial conflicts continued beneath the surface of wartime unity. Yet the minority races were strengthening their position for the future by the economic gains of war prosperity.

The Arsenal of Democracy

War is a mighty machine that speeds up social changes. As we have seen, since the end of the nine-

NATIONAL ARCHIVES

LIBRARY OF CONGRESS

By nightfall on December 7, 1941, the FBI had arrested some 1,300 "potentially dangerous" Japanese aliens in California. By spring, the civil liberties of all Japanese-Americans living on the West Coast had been suspended.

U. S. ARMY

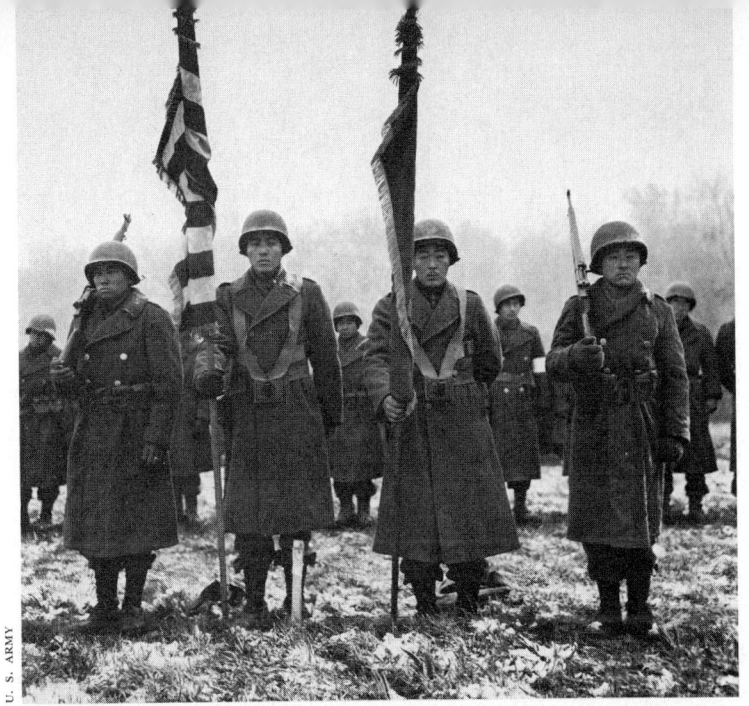

In February 1942 California's Attorney General, Earl Warren, called for military action to "protect this state from the Japanese situation." Beginning in April some 110,000 Japanese-Americans—half of them under 20—were ordered to relocation centers (below). From there they were transferred (left, below) to barracks surrounded by barbed wire. Exceptions were made for Japanese-American citizens willing to join the army. The 442nd Combat Team (left) posed for this photograph in 1944 while receiving citations for bravery.

LIBRARY OF CONGRESS

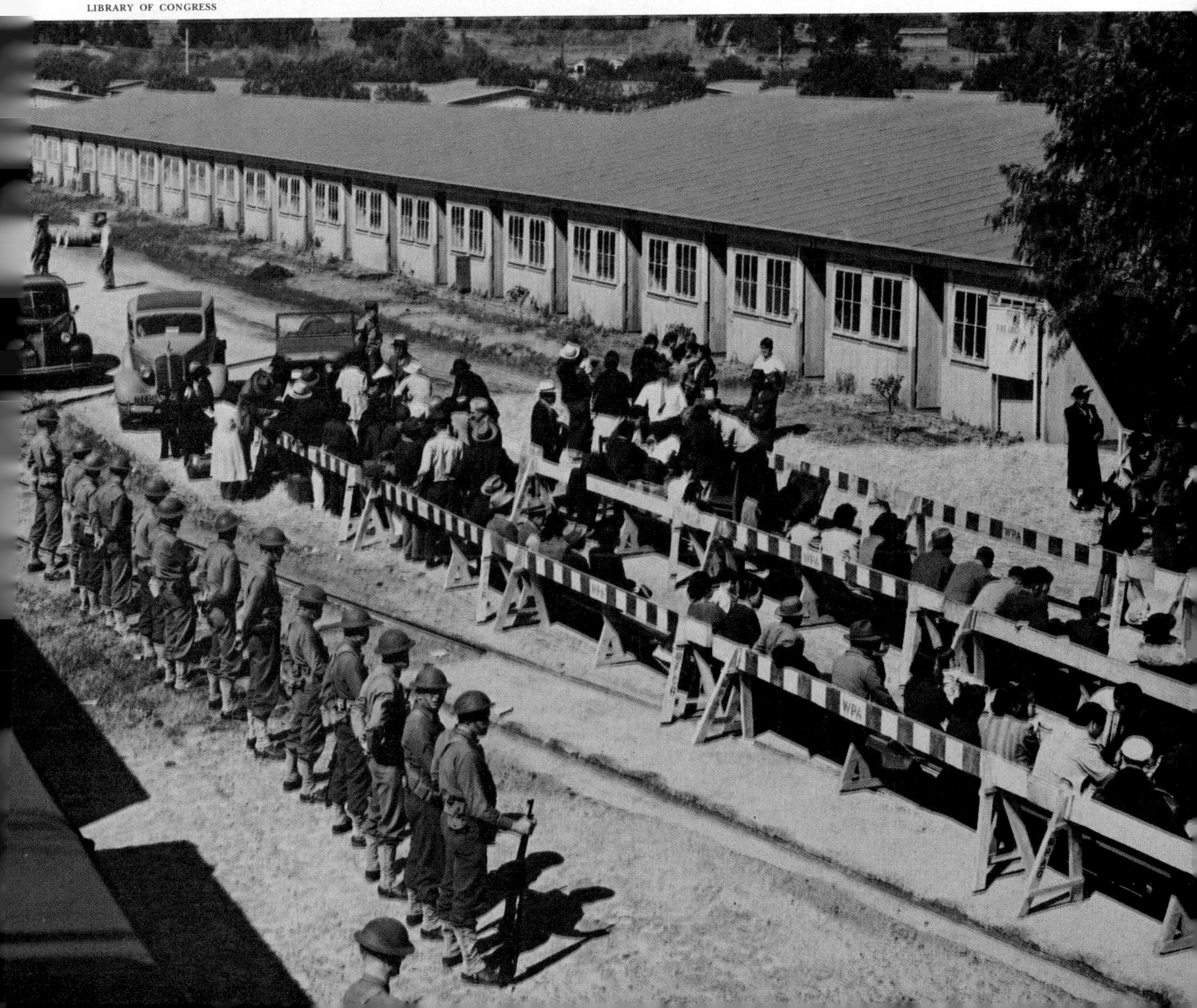

teenth century, the United States was moving rapidly in new directions. People were leaving farms for cities. The economy of many small, competing companies was shifting to one of large, powerful corporations regulated by a large, powerful government. A society based on thrift, hard work, family closeness, and community loyalty was adjusting to an age of mass salesmanship, movement, and high spending.

From 1942 through 1945 these movements increased in force. As in World War I, wartime government agencies, staffed by businessmen and their lawyers, managed the economy. They assigned raw materials and production tasks to factories. They rationed civilian goods such as tires, gasoline, and meat, and, for the first time in history, set ceilings on how high wages and prices could go.

The movement to the city became a stampede. In West Coast shipyards (right), midwestern tank and airplane factories, southwestern refineries and munitions plants—everywhere—an industrial army fought the battle of production in round-the-clock shifts. Housing problems became critical. Ugly rows of boxlike "homes," boarding houses, and trailer camps sprang up. Like the swollen towns around army camps, they were full of a quickly moving population, cheap stores, and places of entertainment.

All of this change shook up families and communities. Children changed schools many times. Religious ties were weakened as people moved in and out overnight. A wartime factory town had no local customs.

Instead, it was something like frontier life. But the old frontier drew families together for protection. Wartime living tended to scatter them. Father might be in uniform overseas and mother in a factory. The children stayed with relatives too old to work or with sitters. The millions of women who answered the nation's call in industrial jobs (upper right) were an advance guard of liberated women. Yet the change pulled up an important social anchor. The question of how family duties were shared between working husbands and wives remained unanswered. It was one of many such problems that would linger on to become important in postwar American life.

America Prospers While Europe Burns

In one way America did *not* change during the war, as compared to the nations of Europe. While the

Right: The United States Army recruited women workers with posters like this one. WOW stood for Woman Ordnance (military weapons and ammunition) Worker. The millions of women who flocked to defense plants inspired the popular song, "Rosie the Riveter." Below: Workers place the deck on a freighter hull. When that task was finished the freighter was launched and completed in the water so that a new hull could be started. During the war American shipyards set amazing production records—6,500 naval vessels, 64,500 landing craft, and 5,400 cargo ships.

FRANKLIN D. ROOSEVELT LIBRARY, HYDE PARK

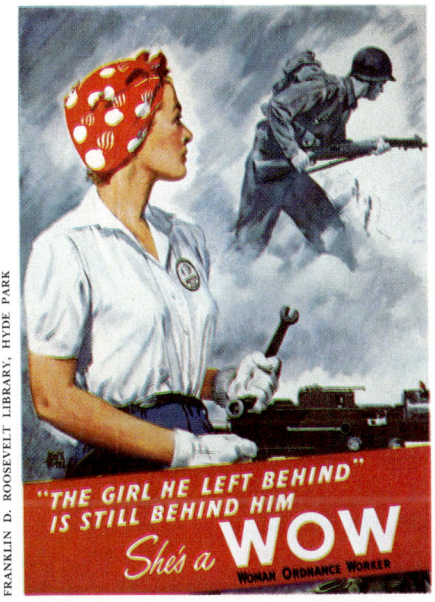

HANS MIETH, *Fortune*

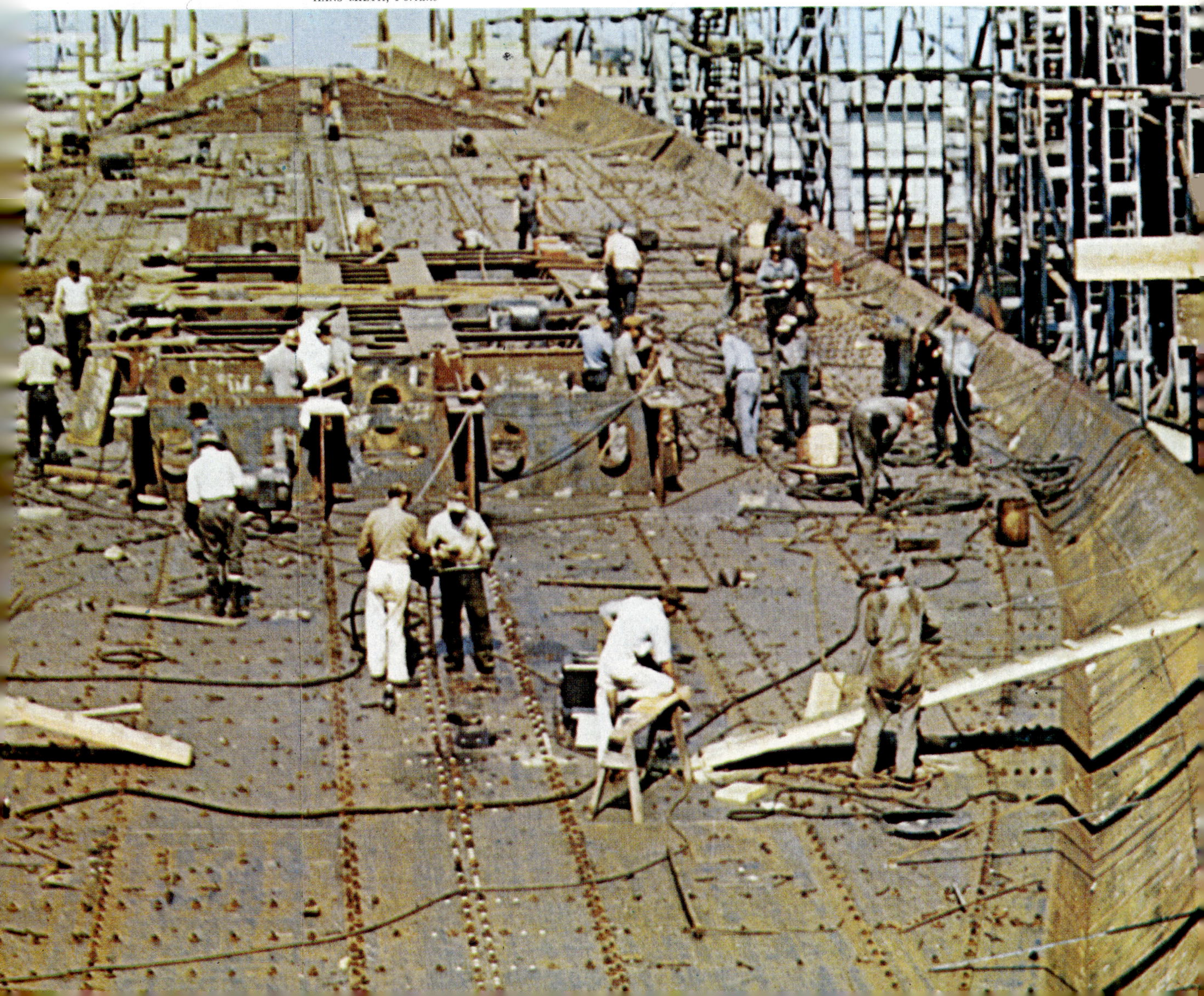

Germany's invasion of Russia in June 1941 completely surprised the Red Army. By the end of September it had suffered 2.5 million casualties. The German policy toward the civilian population was to offer a choice—enslavement or annihilation. A German photographer took the picture at right of a cottage—probably the home of a peasant who resisted the Nazis—burning in a Russian village. By contrast, American cities came through the war unscarred. Civilians were certainly affected by the war. Food, shoes, and gasoline were rationed; some luxuries like cameras disappeared from stores. But most civilians were earning more money than they had ever thought possible. Between 1941 and 1945 the United States government spent twice as much as it had spent in its entire previous history.

DR. ALFRED OTT

FAIRCHILD AERIAL SURVEYS

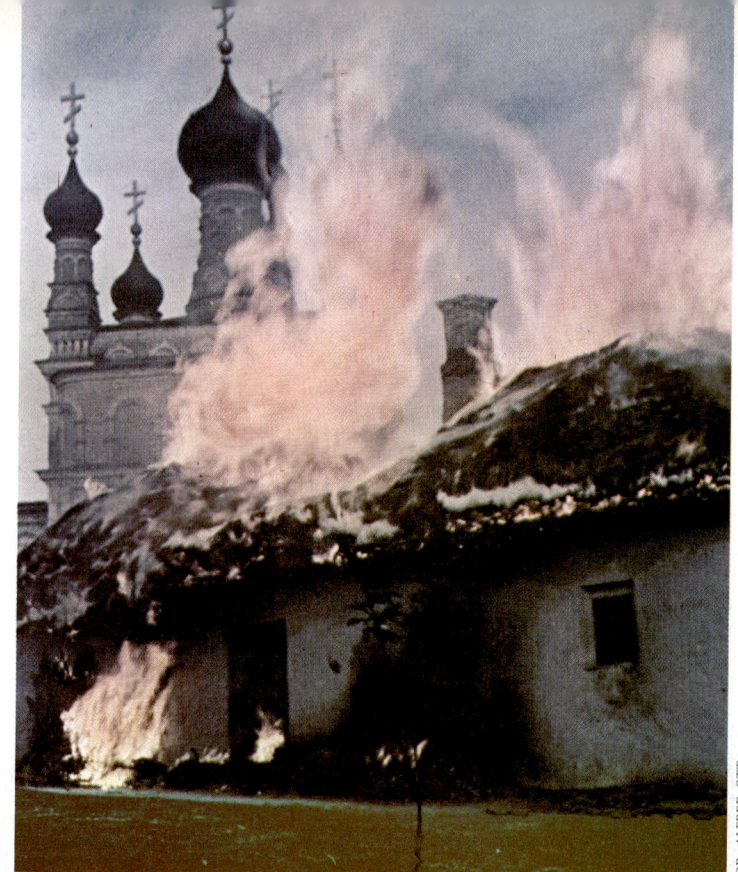

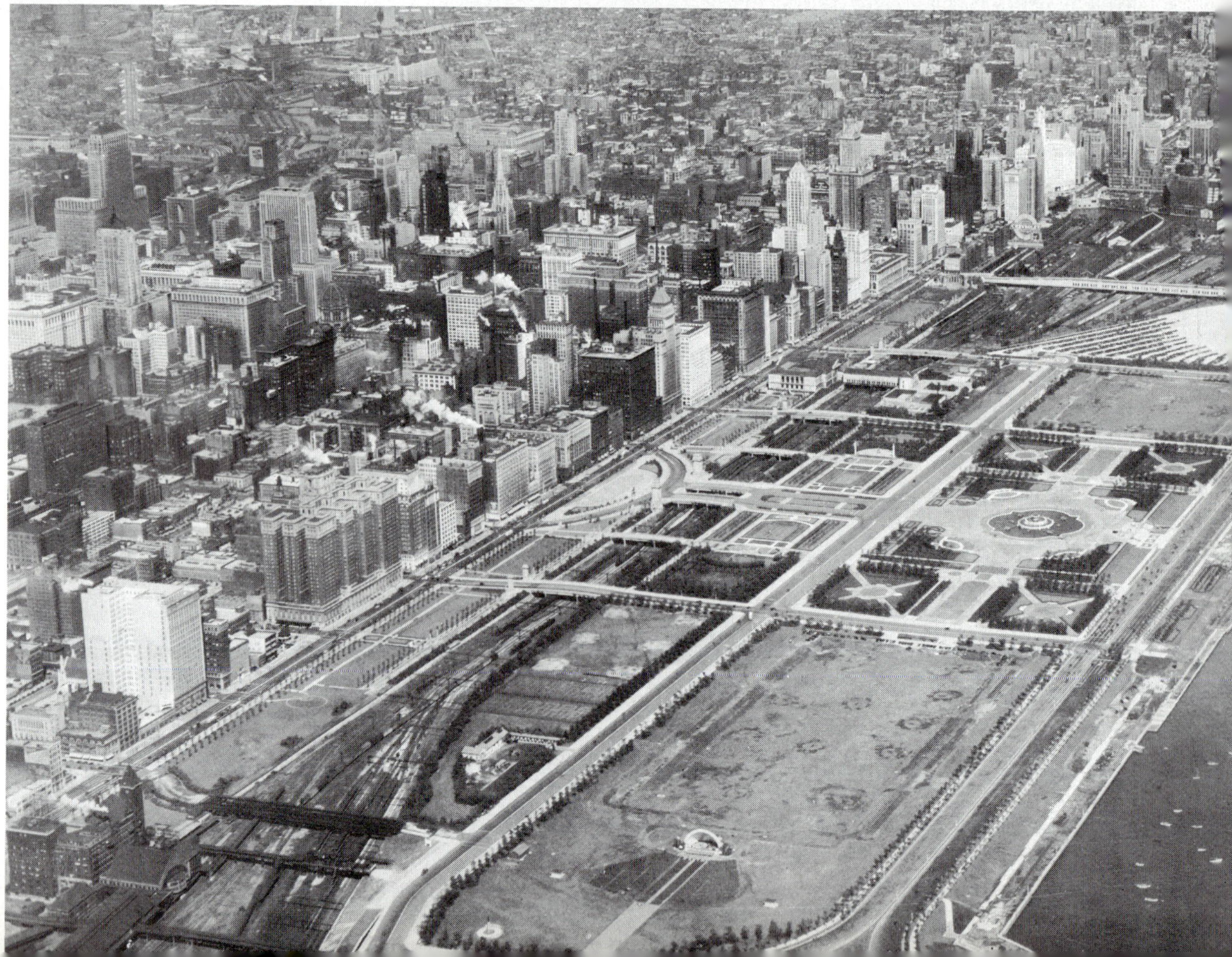

fighting battered them like some gigantic wrecking machine, the United States remained untouched, a healthy giant among wounded victims.

From the summer of 1940, Nazi bombers pounded England's cities and factories. The English struck back with air raids on Nazi-occupied Europe. Later their planes were joined by those of the Americans. By 1944 as many as a thousand bombers a night rained explosives on all the elements of industrial civilization—on dams, electric plants, highways, rail lines, power lines, mines, shipyards, and oil refineries. In eastern Europe land and air battles between Russians and Germans scorched the good earth and destroyed thousands of villages (upper left).

Throughout Europe war production was kept up only by starving the civilian economy. Fuel, food, power—all were severely rationed, that is, the government decided how much of certain goods a citizen was to have. Everyone had books of stamps which entitled them to buy only a certain ration or portion. Threadbare families shivered in unheated, unlit, half-ruined apartment buildings. They ate dried vegetables and coarse bread and drank substitute coffee. They got only a few ounces of meat, butter, or sugar each week. Few saw eggs, milk, or fresh fruits. Many survived only by stealing, using the illegal "black market," or selling themselves for any purpose to occupying armies. This was the world that European teenagers knew from 1939 to 1945.

In contrast, America flourished. Between 1940 and 1945 it turned out nearly 300,000 planes, over 64,000 landing craft, 5,000 cargo ships, 102,000 tanks and self-propelled guns. Yet in no war year was even half the total national production devoted to war goods. American cities, like dynamic Chicago (left), were whole and thriving.

Despite light rationing and some discomfort, civilian Americans found the war a time of jobs, savings (in the form of war bonds), and future hopes. By 1945 Americans were the world's rich relatives. This fact shaped American feelings toward other peoples in a special way.

Questions for Discussion
1. Why were Japanese-Americans relocated in 1942?
2. What changes in the United States were speeded up by World War II?

Victory in Europe

The actual fighting raged in two theaters of operations, Europe and the Pacific. In both of them the military story for the United States, Britain, Russia, China, and the other nations allied with them was one of struggling along a comeback road from defeat.

In September 1942 Germany had reached its greatest expansion (map, right). Hitler's divisions were besieging Stalingrad (now Volgograd), deep in Russia, and moving southward around the eastern end of the Black Sea, toward the rich oil fields of the Middle East. Other German troops had gone to Libya, in North Africa, to take over the fighting from the Italians there. Under the brilliant General Erwin Rommel, their Afrika Korps launched an early 1942 offensive that carried its tanks streaking across desert sands into Egypt. Only one more push seemed necessary to send the Germans beyond the ancient pyramids which had looked down on so many other conquerors. Then Rommel could cut the Suez Canal and pinch off a vital supply route of Britain's empire.

But in October the tide began to turn. The Russians held on at Stalingrad. They even counterattacked and surrounded the enemy. In January 1943 the entire Nazi siege force surrendered. Meanwhile, the British in Egypt launched a huge offensive at El Alamein (upper right) on October 23. Two weeks later a great fleet landed British and American forces in French Morocco and Algeria. The pro-German French government in these provinces quickly surrendered. Rommel was squeezed between forces advancing into Tunisia from two directions. His supplies were cut off by Allied control of the air over the Mediterranean. In June 1943 his battered force—its tanks and planes useless from lack of gas—gave up. For the second time in four months, a whole German army was bagged.

In July 1943 Allied armies landed in Sicily. In September they attacked the Italian mainland. Mussolini already had been forced out of office. The Italians shortly surrendered. The first enemy was out of the war. But the Germans dug in and stubbornly defended mountain strongholds such as Monte Cassino. The Allies inched forward but by June 1944 the Americans had taken Rome (left).

The Great Invasion Begins

The Nazi empire began to crumble. Helped by a stream of American lend-lease supplies, the Russians

Above: In October 1942 the British launch an offensive against Rommel. *Left:* On June 5, 1944, Americans occupy Rome.

World War II in Europe

IMPERIAL WAR MUSEUM

UPI

U. S. ARMY

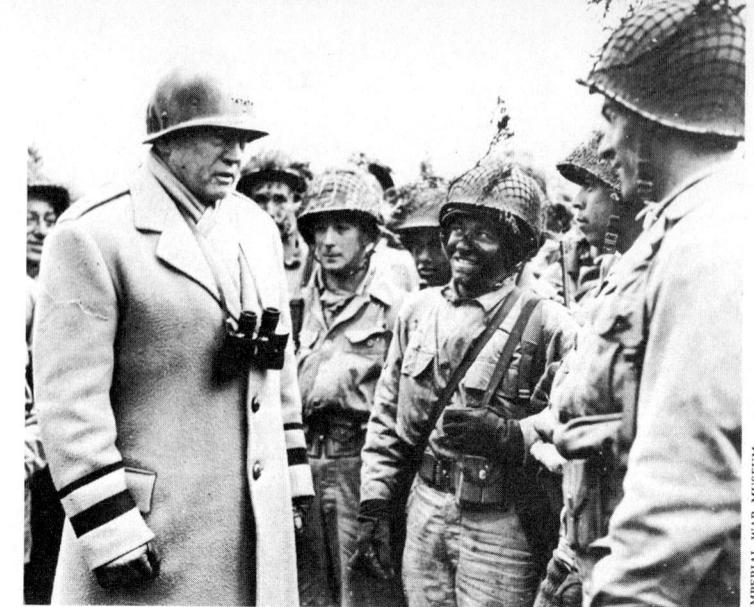

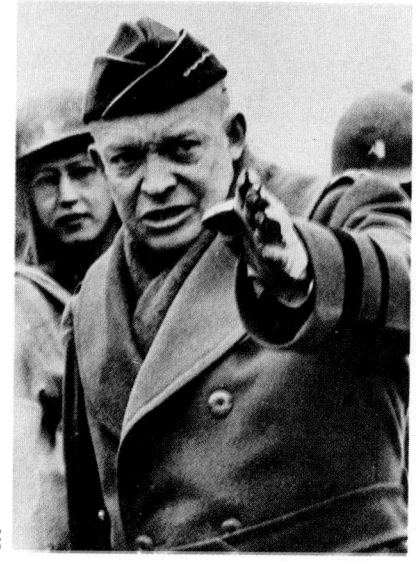

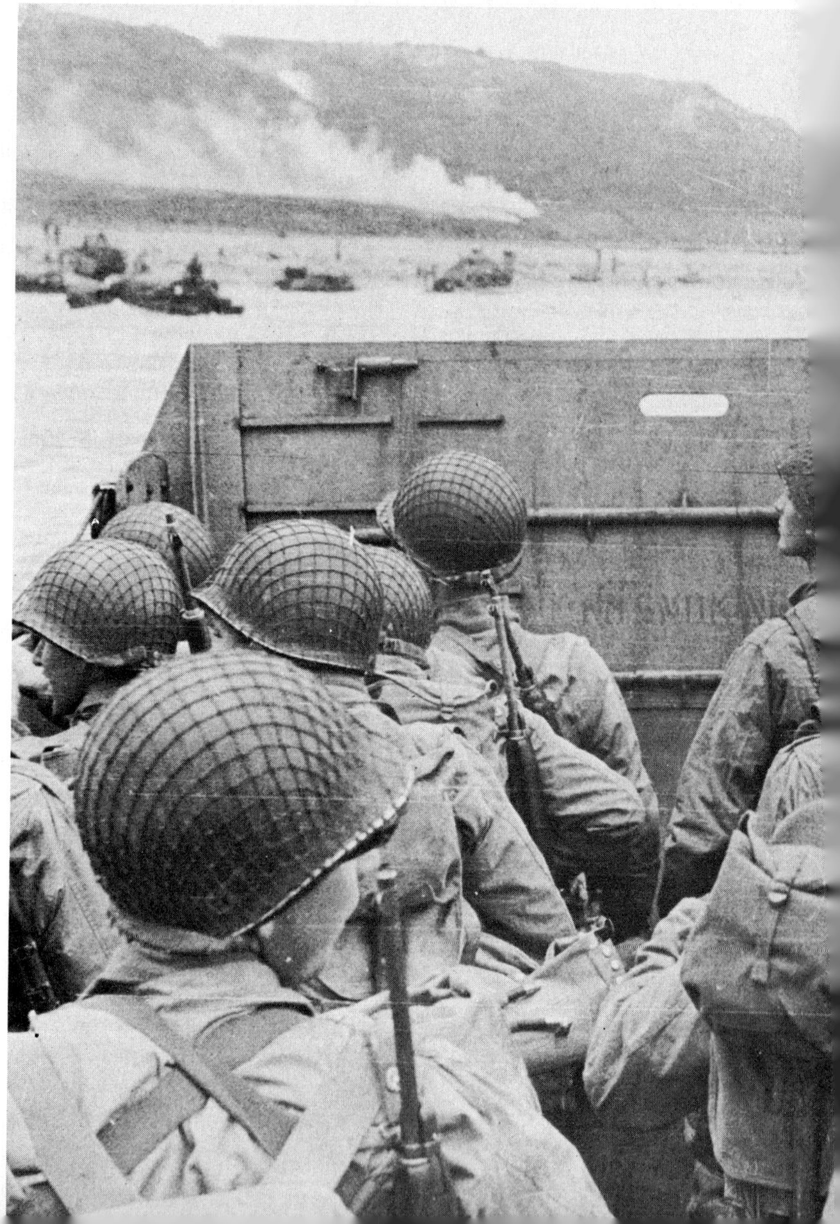

General Dwight D. Eisenhower (above) became Supreme Commander of Allied Forces in January 1944. He supervised the planning of Operation Overlord, the largest amphibious operation in history. On D-Day 176,000 troops and 4,000 landing craft (right), aided by 600 warships and 11,000 planes, headed for 5 separate points along the Normandy coastline. The Allies suffered heavy casualties, but D-Day was a success. A little more than a month later, General George S. Patton (above right), a tank commander with a reputation for ruthless efficiency, was pushing his Third Army across western Europe at a record-setting 40 miles a day.

pushed the Germans back along a thousand-mile long front in the war's biggest battles involving millions of men. By the end of 1944 they had liberated most of their country and were in Poland, Rumania, Czechoslovakia, Hungary, and even the eastern part of Germany itself.

Germany bled from many wounds. It had to pour reinforcements into Italy. In the occupied countries, fierce attacks by underground resistance fighters blew up trains and supply dumps and pinned down thousands of troops on guard duty. Allied air raids grew greater daily. The Germans, unable to replace vital losses, concentrated their airplanes over Germany for a fierce defense of their home skies. But the price was loss of air control everywhere else. And this became a key element in the plans of the Allied high command to end the war by invading western Europe and striking at the Nazi heartland directly.

All through the spring of 1944, an army of more than 2.5 million men, with a crushing weight of supplies, was concentrated in England. Day after day, it trained for an attack on the heavy fortifications along the French coastline across the English Channel. The commander of this force of Americans, British, Poles, Free French, and men from every country conquered by Nazis and from British Commonwealth nations, was General Dwight D. Eisenhower (far left).

D-Day, the secret day chosen for the assault, was set for June 6, 1944. In the early morning hours, commanders gave their tense troops final instructions. Then thousands of planes roared out to smash German positions and every possible route of reinforcements. Paratroopers dropped in to seize key bridges and crossroads behind the Germans. As dawn lightened the sky, an armada of fighting ships and landing craft (lower left), under an umbrella of fighters, crossed the channel. Men poured ashore and in the teeth of savage machine gun and artillery fire fought their way inland past barbed wire obstacles and land mines. By nightfall 2,000 had paid with their lives for a beach-head. But the walls of Hitler's fortress were breached.

The Road to Victory

The British and Americans poured supplies into the area they controlled, then broke out explosively in a massive assault. While Allied truck convoys steadily fed gasoline and ammunition to advancing armored

columns, German supplies and reinforcements were blasted off the roads by unceasing aerial assault. By August 25 Paris had been freed. Ten days earlier another Allied landing had been made, this time on France's Mediterranean coastline. By November German columns were reeling backward toward their own frontiers and all of France was liberated.

In December the Germans struck back with a vicious counteroffensive in Belgium. The "bulge" they drove into American lines gave the battle its name. But this last desperate thrust ran out of steam. The Germans were tough, veteran fighters and well-led. But they were up against equally good soldiers who now had overwhelming superiority in weapons. In March 1945 the Rhine was crossed and the invasion of Germany from the West was on. On April 25 the Americans met the Russians advancing from the East. American tanks (right) were rolling into Austria and Czechoslovakia as well as into Germany and the Red Army was fighting its way into Berlin, block by block, leveling the city to rubble.

In his underground headquarters in Berlin, Hitler finally realized that the end had come. On April 30 he committed suicide, and loyal followers burned his body. One after another, Nazi generals surrendered their surrounded, exhausted forces. The final, unconditional surrender of all remaining German forces took place on May 8, which thus became V-E Day (Victory in Europe).

All over Europe millions, like the cheering Frenchmen (far right), celebrated the end of Hitler's rule. The Nazis had imprisoned, starved, and tortured millions of their enemies both inside and outside of Germany. Moreover, Hitler had planned the systematic extermination, primarily by gassing, of all European Jews. The task was almost complete when advancing Allied armies liberated his "death camps." The twentieth century thus saw the unbelievably brutal revival of **genocide**, the deliberately planned destruction of an entire people. It was for this especially that some of the leading Nazis were tried as "war criminals" at Nuremberg in 1946, found guilty, and executed.

Questions for Discussion

1. What battles were turning points in the war in Europe?
2. What was D-Day? When was it?

U. S. ARMY

In April 1945 American tanks enter gutted Magdeburg, Germany.

On V-E Day—May 8, 1945—Parisians march through the Arc de Triomphe jubilantly waving flags of the Allied nations.

NATIONAL ARCHIVES

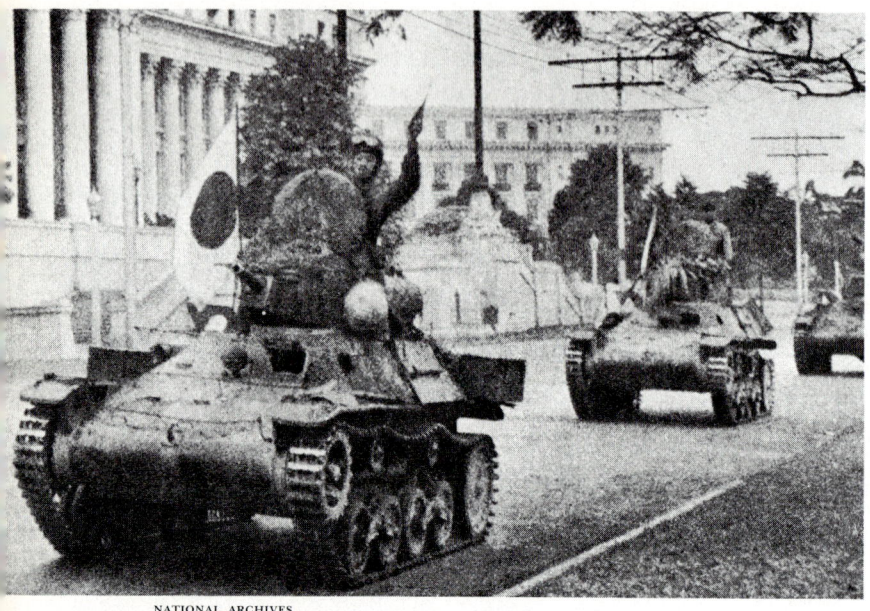

Left: Japanese tanks parade past the Filipino legislature in Manila. This photograph was used in a Japanese propaganda pamphlet called, "Victory on the March." Right: On February 29, 1944, in the midst of his struggle to return to the Philippines, General Douglas MacArthur views the results of heavy naval bombardment.

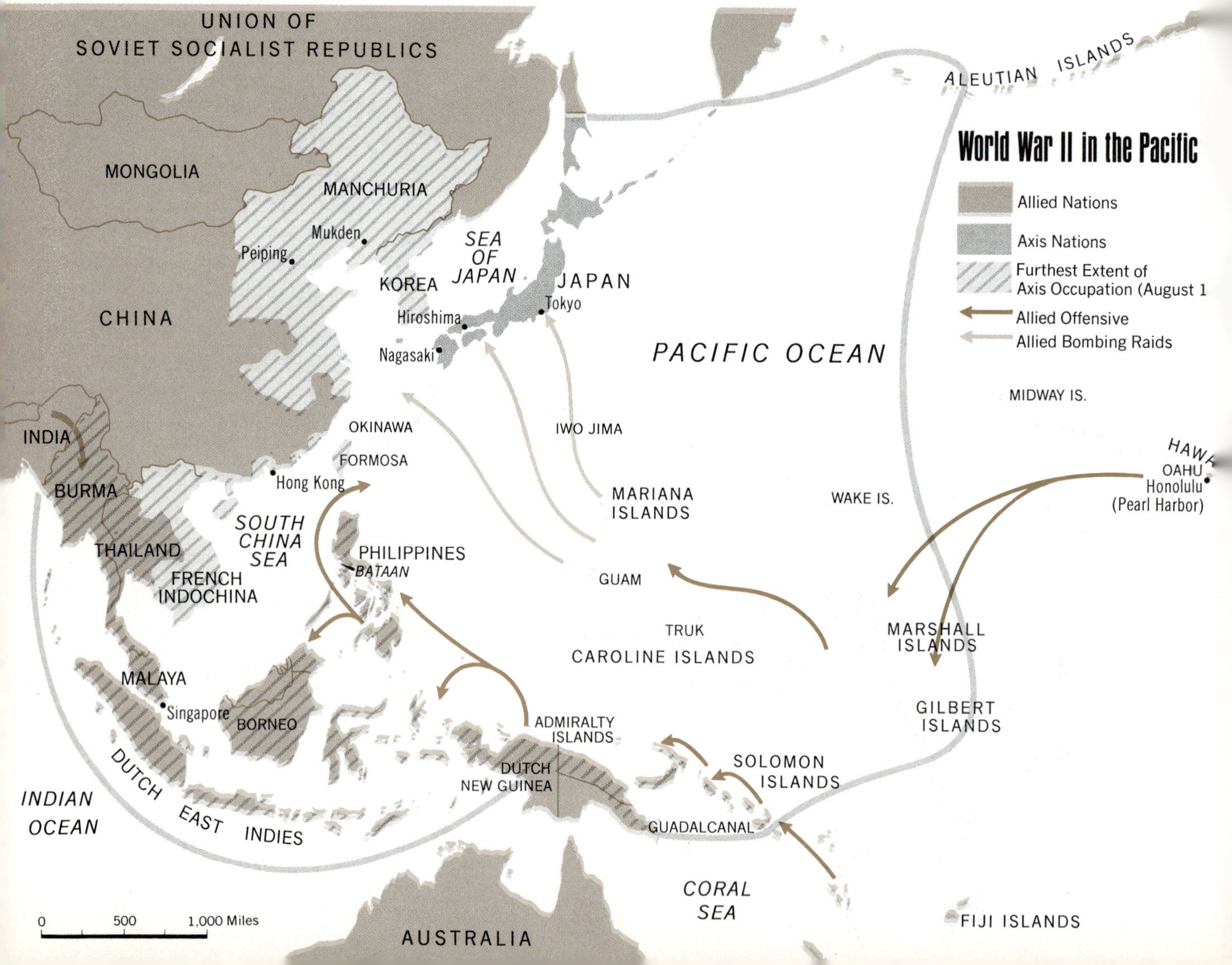

Victory in the Pacific

The war in the Pacific, like the war in Europe and Africa, began with enemy triumphs (map, left). The battle plan of the Japanese had been to strike quickly and paralyze the American fleet. With that done they could overrun the weak defenses of the Philippines, the Dutch East Indies, Malaya, and Burma. In the first six months of Japan's war, this timetable worked brilliantly.

Japanese amphibious (land and sea) forces, supported by waves of fighters and bombers, overran Guam and the Wake Islands and landed in the Philippines—all in the first week of their attack. Soon Japanese tanks rolled through Manila (upper left). Four months later hollow-eyed, starving American and Filipino defense forces surrendered first at Bataan and later at Corregidor. Their commander, General Douglas MacArthur (left), was not captured with them. He was ordered to escape to Australia and to take charge of all Allied forces in the Southwest Pacific. He did so, darting through enemy-infested waters in a small torpedo-boat and vowing, "I shall return."

It did not look as if he would. The Japanese astonished the world with their speed and skill. They captured all Malaya, including the great British fortress of Singapore, by mid-February 1942. They occupied Burma and cut off China from the world except by a perilous air route over the towering Himalaya Mountains. They took the Dutch East Indies by the end of April with only light casualties to themselves.

Japan was in a commanding position now. It could, if it chose, appeal for the friendship of the Asian peoples in what it called its "co-prosperity sphere." If Japan could hold out, negotiate peace terms with weary Allies, and then share the fruits of its industry with those who supplied its raw materials, it might become the champion of a powerful "Asia for Asians" movement.

But Japan's militarists fumbled this chance. They treated their possessions harshly and exploited the local peoples like any other imperialists. Movements for national independence in each Japanese-occupied land became anti-Japanese as well as anti-European. Moreover, the Japanese army and navy reached too far. They landed on islands off the northwest coast of Australia to cut off that island continent from help and possibly soften it for invasion. But this stretched their seaborne supply lines dangerously thin.

Carrier War in the Pacific

Japan's downfall, in fact, came through a new kind of warfare that attacked its lines of communication, thousands of miles long, instead of capturing territory or destroying its mainland armies. The key was control of the air. Surface ships could not survive aerial attack without protecting planes of their own. Aircraft carriers, not battleships, were now queens of the sea. Naval battles would now be fought by forces hundreds of miles apart, sending out planes (upper and lower right) to destroy each other's floating airbases. The first such sea fight, near Midway Island, in June 1942, turned the tide in the Pacific. A huge Japanese fleet moved out to capture Midway. But American planes found and sank the four Japanese carriers in the striking force. The invasion armada thereupon turned back without having fired a shot at a United States surface vessel.

In carrier warfare the United States was bound to win. Its shipyards poured out more than 2 dozen full-sized carriers and over 70 smaller "escort" carriers. A two-part strategy took shape. First, the American navy should win mastery of the air. In great battles near the Mariana Islands and the Philippines between June and November of 1944, Japan lost 7 carriers and thousands of planes and experienced pilots. With these gone American air power easily found Japanese battleships and cruisers and sank or crippled them. By spring of 1945 the Japanese navy was finished as a combat force.

The second part of America's Pacific strategy was a campaign of "island-hopping." An island would be seized and developed as a base from which bombers and submarines could swarm out to assault Japanese merchant vessels and strong points. Meanwhile, strength would be built up to take another island closer to Japan. Eventually, Japan itself would be brought under air attack. Many of its island outposts, as well as its armies on the Asian mainland, could be ignored or "by-passed." They would be starved out as Japan's ships were sent to the bottom.

It was not an easy technique. Except for the Philippines, occupied in October 1944, all the islands assailed were small. And all were bitterly and bravely defended. Thousands of soldiers and marines died in assaults (lower right) on dots of coral. But by spring of 1945 Americans had taken Iwo Jima and Okinawa.

Below: Marines move out against the Japanese on Tarawa, the largest of the Gilbert Islands. The fighting there in November 1943 was so bloody that the island became known as "Terrible Tarawa." Of the 5,600 marines who landed there, 991 were killed and 2,311 were wounded. Of the 4,500 Japanese defenders, only 17 came out alive. Right: Lieutenant Commander William Draper, a navy combat artist, painted these planes pounding Japanese-held islands in the Pacific in March 1944. The planes were flying in support of General MacArthur's invasion force. Below right: Another Draper painting, "Planes Return," portrays the recovery of a strike force in May 1944.

U. S. MARINE CORPS

BOTH: COMBAT ART SECTION, U. S. NAVY

719

U. S. ARMY

Left: Fifteen seconds after the first successful detonation of an atom bomb, this awesome sight filled the predawn sky in New Mexico. The bomb had been dropped from a tower. After the blast all that was left of the tower site was a crater, 1,200 feet wide and 25 feet deep at the center. There was nothing in it except little green glass beads which had been formed out of the sand by the fantastic heat from the explosion. Below: The photograph of Hiroshima gives some idea of the terrible physical destruction of the city. Nearly 60 per cent of the city's total area all but disappeared. Some 40,000 buildings vanished.

They were now within fighter-plane range of Japan and were able to protect fleets of B-29 Super-Fortresses which flew from the Marianas to drop millions of tons of explosives on the Japanese main islands.

The Atomic Age Begins

July 1945 saw the end at hand. Japan's factories were crippled, its cities gutted, and hundreds of thousands of its civilians dead as a result of great bombing raids. But the final blow to Japan did more than end the long struggle. It opened a new era of fear for mankind.

Only a handful of Americans knew in 1945 that the United States had worked for more than three years on a terrifying new weapon. This was a bomb which used the enormous force created by the splitting of atoms of the element uranium to produce an explosion powerful enough to wipe out a city in one blast.

The possibility of creating such a bomb had first been brought to American attention in 1939 by several distinguished European scientists who were refugees from Fascism and Nazism. The Italian Enrico Fermi, the Hungarians Leo Szilard, Eugene Wigner, and Edward Teller, and the German Albert Einstein had all learned of experiments in atom-splitting. They realized that the process had military possibilities, and dreaded the thought of Hitler's scientists giving him this weapon. During the war some of them, along with American scientists, worked at super-secret factories which spent $2 billion doing the necessary research experiments and assembling a bomb that would work by nuclear fission, or atom-splitting. On July 16, 1945, they had one ready to test in New Mexico. It exploded with a searing blast of fire "brighter than a thousand suns," as one observer remembered. The United States had two more such A-bombs (for atom) ready. Each had the power of 20,000 tons of TNT. The most powerful ordinary bombs then in use contained one or at most two tons of this explosive.

On April 13, 1945, President Roosevelt (re-elected a fourth time in 1944) suddenly died. His successor, Harry S. Truman, was now told of the A-bomb and advised by his military leaders to use it to frighten Japan into immediate surrender. They argued that otherwise it would be necessary to invade Japan, causing countless casualties on both sides. But some scientists who had developed the bomb thought that such an

U. S. AIR FORCE

appalling weapon should not be used if the Japanese could be brought to their knees by continuing the air and sea blockade. After a top-secret debate, Truman made his decision: The bomb would be used.

On August 6, 1945, a B-29 dropped an A-bomb over Hiroshima, an industrial town with a population of about 350,000. A mushroom-shaped pillar of cloud shot 40,000 feet into the air. Beneath it a fireball killed 70,000 people in a few seconds and turned what was once a thriving city into a charred wasteland. Later as many as 100,000 more Japanese—the exact number is uncertain—died of illness from the deadly radiation that followed the explosion. On August 8 Russia hurried to join the kill by declaring war on Japan. On August 9 a second A-bomb hit Nagasaki, killing an estimated 50,000 more Japanese. The Imperial Government asked for peace terms. On September 2 Japanese officials signed a document of surrender aboard an American battleship in Tokyo Bay.

The cruelest and costliest war in history was over. But amid the triumph there was concern. The A-bomb had opened a frightening possibility—that man might go on to develop weapons powerful enough to destroy his own species. The fireball in the skies over Hiroshima and Nagasaki might stand for the dawn of a new day when men would be forced to build a peaceful world. Or it might symbolize the final blaze that would wipe out mankind.

Questions for Discussion

1. What mistakes did the Japanese make in their plans for the conquest of Asia?
2. Why was the Battle of Midway such an important battle in the war in the Pacific? What was unusual about this battle?
3. Why was the capture of Iwo Jima and Okinawa so important to the United States?
4. What arguments convinced President Truman that he should use the atomic bomb against Japan?

Chapter Review

Social Studies Terms

pluralism, genocide

Summary Questions for Discussion

1. In what ways did the United States join the war against the Axis powers even before it declared war on them?

2. Was it reasonable for Japan to feel that it needed to conquer other lands in Asia? Why?
3. Why did the United States declaration of war against Japan lead to the declaration of war against Germany and Italy?
4. Contrast the lives of civilians on the home front in the United States and in Europe.
5. In your opinion what factor was most responsible for the Allied victory in World War II?
6. What was the worst example of genocide in the war?
7. Describe the purpose of the strategy of "island-hopping."
8. Why were the Japanese able to conquer so much territory so quickly?
9. Was President Truman's decision to use the A-bomb a wise one? Defend your answer.

Pictures as Historical Evidence

Look through the pictures in Chapter 13, *The Civil War*, and in Chapter 20, *World War I*, as well as in this chapter on World War II. In what ways was each of these wars alike? In what ways were they different?

Map Study

Look at the map on page 711. Why was the Battle of El Alamein of great importance? What prevented Hitler from defeating England as easily as he had Belgium, Holland, and France? Why was Hitler's attack on Russia very foolhardy?

Look at the map on page 716. Why was it difficult and costly to defeat Japan?

For Further Reading

Air War Against Hitler's Germany, by Stephen W. Sears. New York: American Heritage Publishing Co., Inc., 1964.
Carrier War in the Pacific, by Stephen W. Sears. New York: American Heritage Publishing Co., Inc., 1966.
Men of Valor: The Story of World War II, by Earl Schenck Miers. Chicago: Rand McNally & Co., 1965.
The History of the Atomic Bomb, by Michael Blow. New York: American Heritage Publishing Co., Inc., 1968.

CONSTANTINE MANOS, MAGNUM

NASA

25
An Age of Challenge and Change

In 1945 the United States plunged into the troubled stream of world history. There are two reasons for this. One is that the end of World War II left the nation an unharmed giant in a wrecked world—a giant with a responsibility for using its strength wisely.

But there is another reason as well. It was made clear when astronauts aboard an Apollo spacecraft took the first pictures of earth from many thousands of miles out in space. At last men could actually see that their planet was a small, cloud-wrapped ball, mostly covered with water. National boundaries were invisible. Mankind was clearly one family.

Americans have led in changing the course of modern history by building a technology which has transformed not only their own country, but vastly accelerated the growth—and problems—of the rest of the world. American engineers have led in building communications equipment that can flash pictures from one part of the globe to any other in an instant. American scientists have developed wizard-like chemical compounds to reduce hunger and disease and electronic brains that solve problems in split seconds.

But Americans—like other peoples—have not solved social problems as easily as technical challenges. Like the anti-Vietnam War demonstrators in Washington, D.C. (far left) Americans have disagreed among themselves as to how to find peace abroad. Peace at home has not been easily achieved either. The drive of nonwhite minorities for equality in the United States has produced protests and demonstrations and also has influenced elections. Those demanding changes in the distribution of wealth and power—both at home and in other parts of the globe—were saying that society would have to change in the age of the rocket. The unanswered question was "how." While most of the pressure for—and against—change was peaceful, there were tragic exceptions. In the "long, hot summers" of 1964 through 1968, riots raged in the black ghettoes of American cities. Moreover, three leaders in the struggle for peaceful change were cut down by assassins' bullets—President John F. Kennedy in 1963 and Martin Luther King, Jr. and Robert F. Kennedy in 1968.

Left: July 1969—At Cape Kennedy Apollo 11 lifts off for the moon. Far left: November 1969—In Washington, D.C., some 400,000 demonstrators ask for "Peace Now."

As you read, think about these questions:
1. What problems did American cities face after 1945?
2. How has technology caused both progress and problems?

The Exploding Metropolis

Each challenge of the new era grows out of an enormous speeding up of some earlier trend in our history. The mushrooming growth of the suburbs is an example. Americans began to flow toward the cities in record numbers in the 1870's. Half a century later, in the 1920's, the automobile began to accelerate suburban growth. After World War II the movement to suburbia became a stampede.

Census takers no longer speak only of "cities." There is now a unit of measurement known as a **metropolitan area**. Each includes a central city, surrounded by many smaller suburbs. Out of an American population of about 200 million in 1970, an estimated 135 million—nearly 70 per cent—live in 225 such metropolitan areas. Within them the suburbs have been growing in population 5 times as fast as the central cities. There are even great **megalopolises** or "strip cities" in which the suburbs around one center melt into those around another, in a continuous belt of homes, shops, offices, and factories.

Suburbs are of many kinds. Some have expensive homes, surrounded by spacious lawns and screened by trees. Others are carefully planned "total" communities, like Reston, Virginia (far right). Yet most of the millions of suburbanites have exchanged crowded, beehive-like city apartment buildings for equally uniform rows of "country" homes (right). In an age of population growth so great that it is called an "explosion," it is almost impossible to find the open spaces in urban areas that once were common to Americans and formed the basis for individuality. This fact has created a gap in thought between urbanites and those Americans still living in more rural regions.

Most suburbs have been predominantly or entirely white. This was partly because suburban homes were too costly for most nonwhite Americans. It was also due to deliberate refusals by many homebuilders in suburban towns to sell to nonwhites. But the census of 1970 showed a significant change. Between 1965 and 1970 nearly 800,000 blacks had moved to the suburbs.

The Growing Threat of Urban Decay

While suburbs were growing after 1945, inner cities were undergoing a mixture of decay and growth. The decay came in old neighborhoods abandoned by people who were bound for suburbia. Newcomers to the city took their places. Like the immigrants who had

Poor long-range planning—or none at all—has marred many suburbs (above). In 1961 Robert E. Simon began construction of a planned town—Reston, Virginia— to include clusters of homes, apartments, recreational facilities, stores, and industries. By 1971 some 10,000 people lived in Reston (right), and construction was continuing under the supervision of Gulf Oil Corporation. Simon had gone $45 million in debt and was forced to sell to Gulf in 1967.

BURK UZZLE, MAGNUM

WILLIAM A. GRAHAM

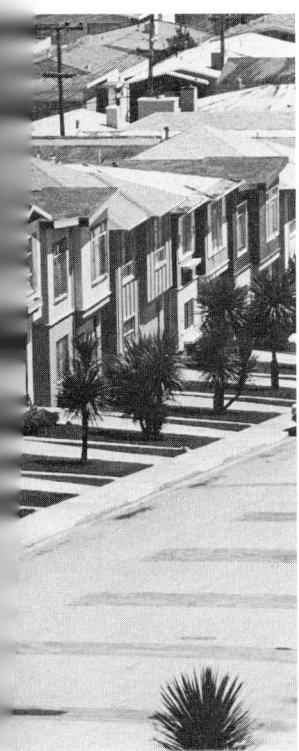

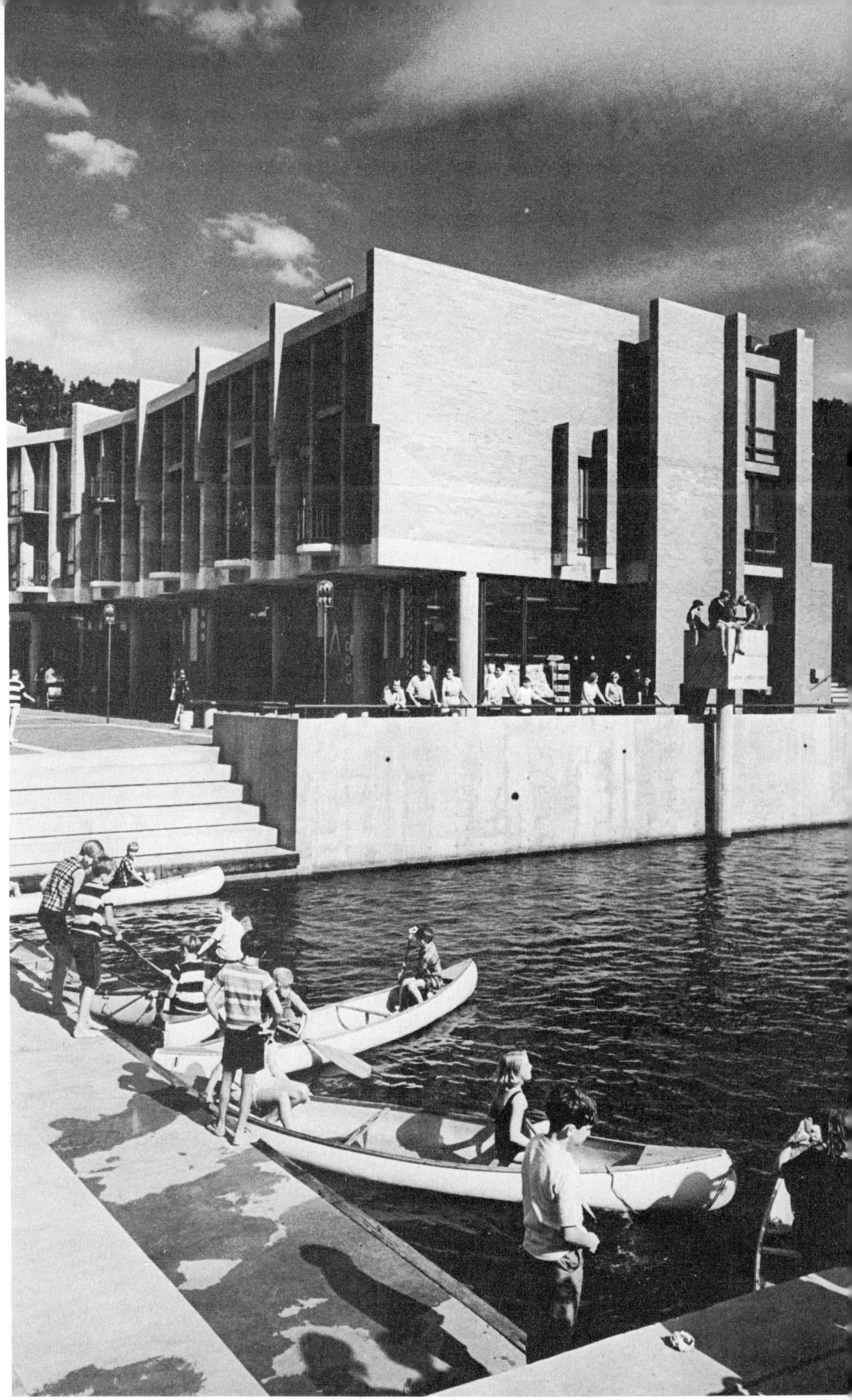

flocked to the cities early in the twentieth century, these fresh arrivals were often poor. Many were nonwhite. But after 1945 rising costs made it unprofitable to repair or replace city dwelling places, except for those who could afford high rents. This at least was the claim of many building owners—who did not live in the city themselves and who permitted their apartment houses, like those at bottom right, to become unfit to live in. Tenant complaints of broken windows, peeling paint, and electric, plumbing, and heating systems that did not work went unanswered. Buildings completely uninhabitable were not replaced. A black child in New York's Harlem pointed to a burned-out building and told a reporter, "When a building burns down, it's just left there. . . .Kids like to play around these lots. It's dangerous but it's fun."

But meanwhile, other parts of the inner city were doing well. Business corporations with headquarters in downtown areas spent freely, and with good taste, to put up beautifully modern steel, chrome, and glass skyscrapers (top right). In 1947 the Federal government began a new program of urban renewal. It gave financial help to city governments and private builders to replace decayed neighborhoods with shopping plazas, cultural centers housing theaters and museums, some elegant private homes, and public housing projects for people of middle income and for the poor.

Such renewals did not solve a basic urban housing problem. They often destroyed low-income housing, which was not replaced. They encouraged the building of expressways to carry automobiles into the business and shopping districts. These superhighways also swept away old dwellings in their path. The cities were becoming divided between handsome areas where affluent people did business and were entertained and the blighted slums of the poor. One of the city's great attractions—a variety of neighborhoods containing different income levels and styles of life—was disappearing. Yet city governments could not halt the process without new powers and more money. They lacked both.

Governing Urban America

Urban America's financial problems and political problems were tangled together. Within the boundaries of a sprawling metropolitan area such as Los Angeles

ELLIOTT ERWITT, MAGNUM

American cities face a serious crisis. Urban planners have designed low-cost housing (above right) to ease slum conditions. Often the result has been the destruction of neighborhoods and the creation of a vertical slum. Middle-income residents have fled to homes outside the center city (left). Most businesses continue to build new city offices (above), but some are beginning to head for suburbia.

Urban sprawl goes unchecked in Los Angeles (above) and many other cities.

WILLIAM GARNETT

(left) would be a number of suburban communities and parts of several counties. Each had its own government and its own services, such as school districts and police, sanitation, and welfare departments. The people in these towns might get more for their local real estate taxes by combining such services and sharing equipment and experts. But there was little governmental or legal machinery allowing for such deals between local governments.

The central cities faced especially serious problems. The residents whom they lost to the suburbs were usually well-educated young people with rising incomes. These "emigrants" now paid taxes to the suburban towns that they called home. Yet when they came into the city by day to work or to attend sports events or theaters in the evening, they still required costly services: street lighting, sewers, police and fire protection. The people who found it hard to move—the aged, the poor, the handicapped—could pay little in taxes, yet needed public hospitals, welfare agencies, and special schools more than suburbanites did. Where would cities find money? There were limits on how heavily they could tax those who already paid heavy state and Federal taxes. Moreover, the taxing power of cities was often limited by state charters written by rural legislators in an earlier day.

Increasingly, cities turned to the Federal government, which collected the largest share of the nation's taxes. Congress responded with many acts. Besides the urban renewal program, it passed laws in 1961, 1965, and 1966 which helped cities to plan for and build highways, schools, and mass transit systems. Congress also created a new Cabinet department in 1966, the Department of Housing and Urban Development, to supervise such efforts. Its first Secretary was Robert Weaver, the first Negro to hold Cabinet rank. But the creation of a new partnership among the cities, the states, and Washington, is still unfinished business.

Questions for Discussion

1. What percentage of Americans live in metropolitan areas?
2. How did the growth of suburbs cause problems for inner cities?
3. Why were city governments unable to solve the problems they faced after 1945? In what ways did the Federal government try to help them?

Below: In 1957 Governor Orval Faubus posted National Guardsmen outside Central High School in Little Rock, Arkansas, to prevent integration. On September 23, after a Federal court had ordered the guardsmen removed, a jeering mob of whites greeted the black students. Two days later the school was integrated as some 12,000 Federal troops stood by to prevent violence. Right: In August 1963 James Meredith became the first Negro to graduate from the University of Mississippi.

Minorities: The Struggle for an Equal Share

Governing the American city is one challenge which the past has handed on to the present. Another was stated by John Brown in 1859. "This Negro question," he said, "the end of that is not yet." A century later it was still not ended.

A milestone was reached, however, on May 17, 1954. On that day the Supreme Court ruled on a suit brought by some Topeka, Kansas, Negro citizens, aided by the National Association for the Advancement of Colored People, against segregated schools. Unanimously, the nine judges overturned the 1896 decision in *Plessy v. Ferguson* that "separate but equal" public facilities were constitutional. A segregated education, said the 1954 court, was by its very nature a badge of inequality—and a violation of the Fourteenth Amendment.

To get the decision enforced was not as easy as winning the case. Many Southerners cried "Never!" In 1957, when Little Rock, Arkansas, was ordered to admit nine black students to a formerly all-white high school, jeering mobs threatened the Negro youngsters (left). President Eisenhower reluctantly had to call out the National Guard to bar violence. In 1962 a Federal court ordered the all-white University of Mississippi to admit James Meredith (left, above). But once again it took troops to get him safely onto the campus, after a riot which killed two. But it was done. And in 1967 Thurgood Marshall, chief lawyer for the NAACP, was himself named by southern-born President Lyndon Johnson as the first Negro Justice of the Supreme Court.

The battle was slow. Many southern school districts "integrated" by admitting tiny handfuls of black students to a single school. Some had not done so at all sixteen years after the *Brown v. Board of Education of Topeka* case. Nor was the South alone resisting. In northern cities schools in black neighborhoods had almost completely black student bodies. They were subject to **de facto segregation** (segregation in fact, but not by law), though not **de jure segregation** (segregation by law). Efforts to change this pattern by moving children, in buses, to schools outside their neighborhoods met bitter white resistance almost everywhere and some black resistance too.

Yet black Americans had won important victories under law. The legal road to betterment was slow but it led somewhere. Other roads were tried as well.

Protest—Peaceful and Violent

Besides legal attacks on segregation, Negro Americans sought other weapons of protest. A landmark year for black resistance was 1955. The Negro community of Montgomery, Alabama, decided to boycott the city's segregated buses. The leader of the movement was an eloquent young minister, the Reverend Martin Luther King, Jr. (upper right). A year later the bus company gave in and desegregated their vehicles. King, meanwhile, had become a national figure. His plan of action called for nonviolent resistance. Blacks should refuse to obey unjust laws. But they should accept the penalties and neither strike back at their enemies nor hate them. Eventually, this essentially Christian behavior would force white America to listen to its conscience and change its ways.

In the first half of the 1960's these tactics worked. Black college students protested discrimination with "sit-ins." They would enter a segregated restaurant or other public place and refuse to leave until served or arrested. They were supported by Negro boycotts of businesses which practiced discrimination and by massive "demonstrations"—peaceful parades and meetings—of black and some white citizens.

In some southern communities resistance was furious. Demonstrators in Birmingham, including women and children, were blasted by high-pressure firehoses and attacked by police dogs. But such brutality backfired on those who used it. A horrified American public watched these events on national television newscasts. They reacted, as King predicted, with support for the demonstrators. Many cities abandoned their Jim Crow laws. In 1964 Congress passed a strong new Civil Rights Act prohibiting segregation in many public places and racial discrimination in employment.

Yet progress remained slow, especially against racial discrimination in employment and housing. Some blacks, particularly youthful ones, called for policies other than integration and nonviolence. One strong black separatist group, known as the Black Muslims, rejected Christianity, saying that it was a white man's religion and urged blacks to run their own farms and businesses and have as little as possible to do with white "devils." A leading Black Muslim spokesman, until he broke with the group in 1964 and was later murdered, was a man known as Malcolm X (upper left). In 1966 a young black **militant** (a person

BERT SHAVITZ, PIX

CHARLES HARBUTT, MAGNUM

Top: Malcolm X, born Malcolm Little in 1925, was a brilliant organizer and speaker for black rights. His eloquent Autobiography *was published after his murder in 1965. Above: Before his death Martin Luther King, Jr., had planned to lead poor people of all races in a march on Washington. In June 1968 some 50,000 people participated in the Poor Peoples' Solidarity Day March.*

In March 1965 King led thousands from Selma to Montgomery, Alabama (above), dramatizing a voter registration drive and objecting to harassment of blacks (below).

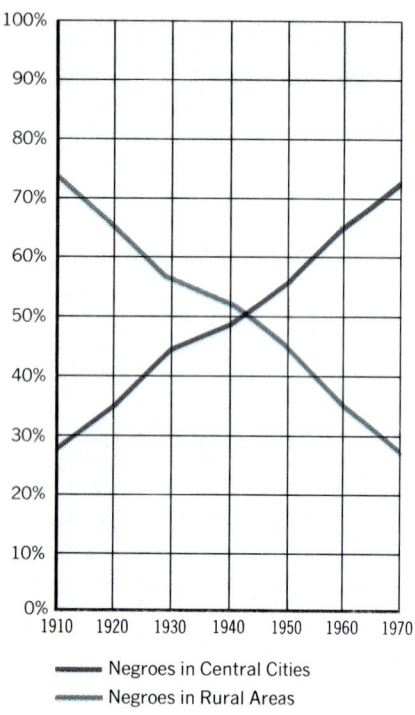

Distribution of Negro Population

- Negroes in Central Cities
- Negroes in Rural Areas

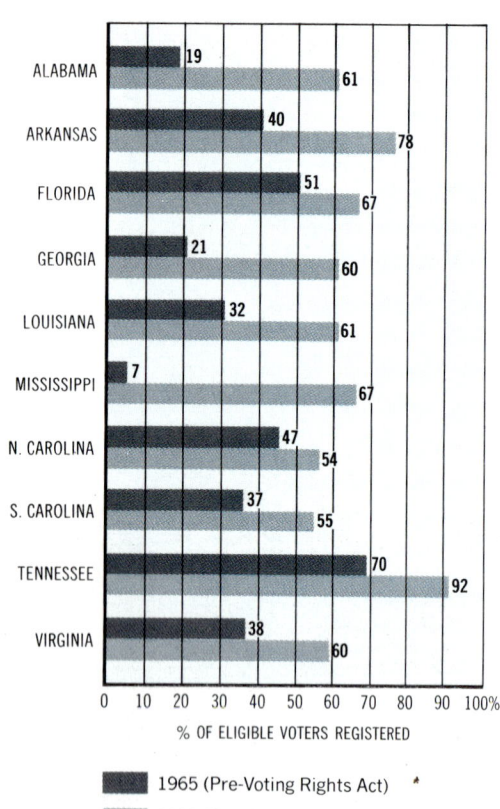

Negro Voter Registration in the South

State	1965	1969
ALABAMA	19	61
ARKANSAS	40	78
FLORIDA	51	67
GEORGIA	21	60
LOUISIANA	32	61
MISSISSIPPI	7	67
N. CAROLINA	47	54
S. CAROLINA	37	55
TENNESSEE	70	92
VIRGINIA	38	60

% OF ELIGIBLE VOTERS REGISTERED

- 1965 (Pre-Voting Rights Act)
- 1969 (Post-Voting Rights Act)

who calls for strong, sometimes violent, political action) named Stokely Carmichael told Negroes to follow only black leadership and seek "black power." He did not say whether this power was to be gained through votes, boycotts, or other means. But members of another group, calling themselves the Black Panthers, were quite clear. They denounced nonviolence, carried guns, and threatened their "oppressors" with guerrilla warfare.

New Political and Economic Power

Moderate black leaders, like Roy Wilkins, Whitney Young, James Farmer, and Bayard Rustin, warned that this attitude was dangerous. Violence could defeat itself by producing a "backlash" of white resistance to further Negro advancement. These advocates of "cooling it" urged blacks to use another route to their goals — political power. That was the traditional way of immigrant groups. In 1965 it was made easier in the South by the passage of a Voting Rights Act. This act permitted the Federal government to supervise the enrollment of black voters who were denied their rights by local officials. Black registration in the South soon rose (graph, left) and had results, such as the election of Charles Evers (top right) as mayor of Fayette, Mississippi.

In the North some blacks began to organize to make more effective use of their vote in cities where they often were close to a majority. Between 1967 and 1970 their political efforts elected black mayors in Cleveland, Ohio (lower right), Gary, Indiana, and Newark, New Jersey. Though these mayors had some white support, their election showed that Negroes, like Italians, Jews, and Irishmen before them, could put members of their own ethnic group in local offices.

The use of economic pressure — or "green power" — also remained an important tactic, not only for blacks but for all minorities. In California a new union of almost entirely Mexican-American grape-pickers struck against working conditions in 1965. Their dynamic leader, Cesar Chavez (far right), urged a nationwide sympathy boycott of California grapes. Many important public figures supported him. By 1970 the grape-growers gave in and recognized the union. For Chavez, a devoted believer in nonviolence, this was important proof that the way of peaceful protest did not lead to a dead end.

ALL: UPI

Above: In July 1969 Charles Evers becomes the first black mayor of a Mississippi town since Reconstruction. Below: Cleveland's Mayor Carl Stokes celebrates his re-election in November 1969. Right: In July 1970 John Giumara, a leading California grape-grower, recognizes Cesar Chavez' union.

Right: Puerto Ricans living in New York celebrate Puerto Rican Day in 1965. Below: American Indians may be the most deprived minority in the country. Their unemployment rate is 10 times the national average; 3 out of 4 Indian families earn less than $3,000 a year. In 1969, 89 Indians occupied Alcatraz Island, proclaimed it Indian Territory, and announced plans to build a center for American studies. The Federal government cut off their water and electricity supplies but did not try to remove the Indians forcibly. By 1971 Indian plans for the island seemed doomed, and only a handful lived on Alcatraz.

CHARLES HARBUTT, MAGNUM

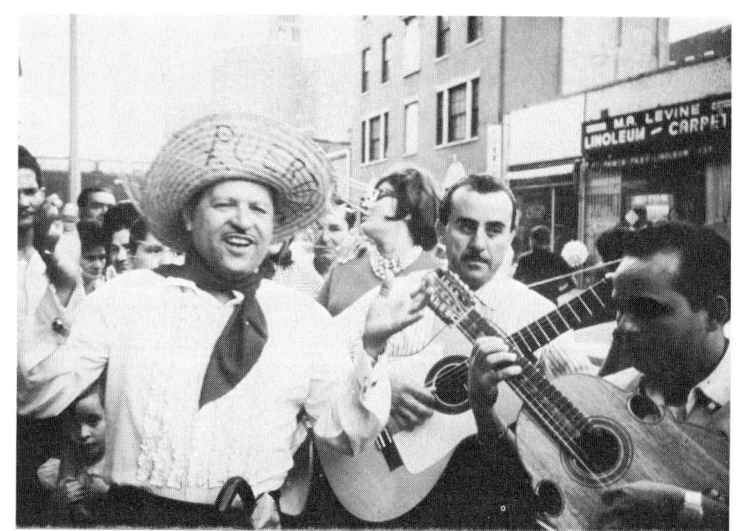

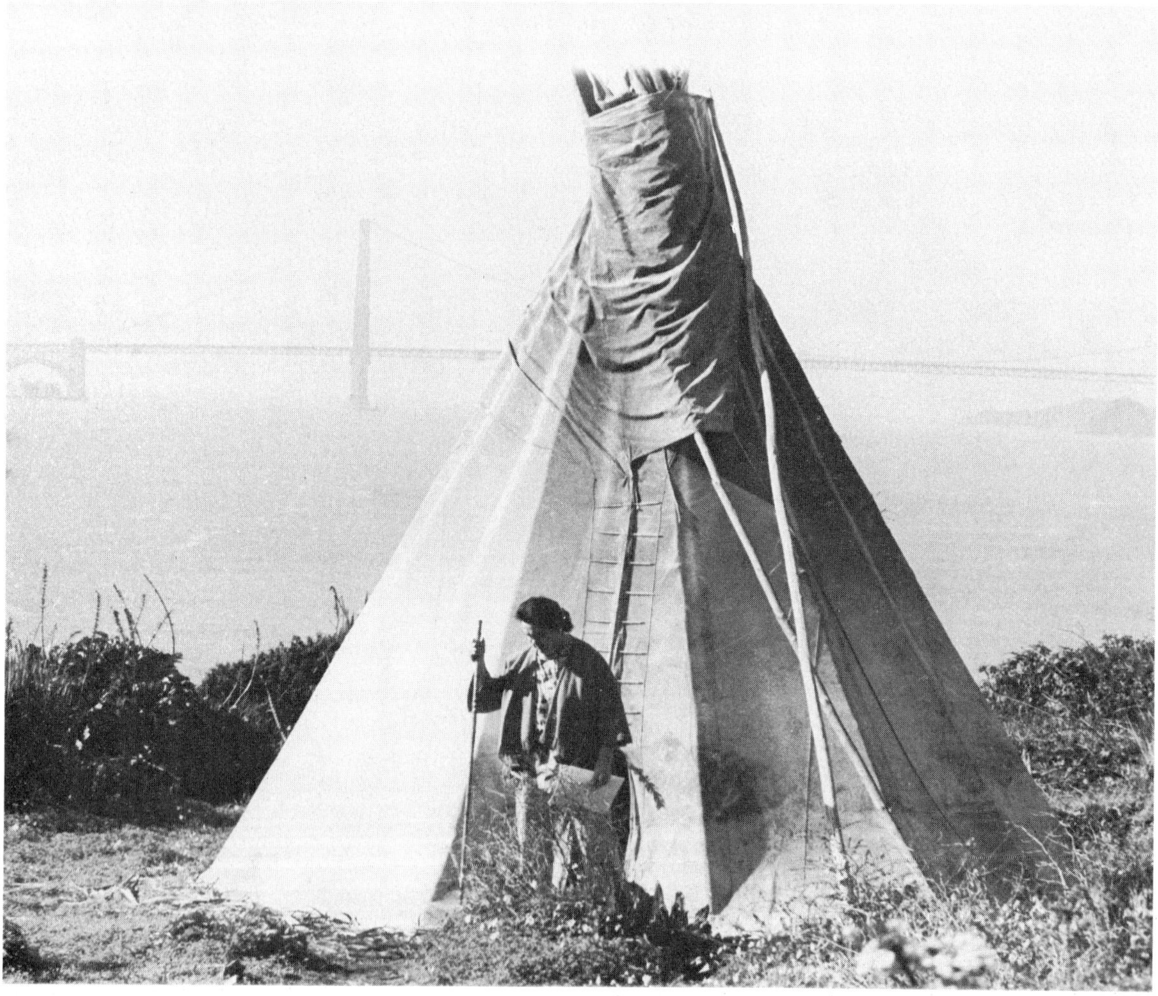

UPI

A New Pride in an Old Heritage

In appealing for national sympathy for the fruit and vegetable-pickers, Chavez did not play down their Mexican background. The strikers' slogan, *Viva La Huelga* (Hurrah for the Strike), was printed everywhere in Spanish. This illustrated a new attitude on the part of American minorities. For many years the model held up to them was that of the melting pot. Their members might rise in life as they gained in education and income. But as they did so, they were expected to give up their "foreign" eating habits, dress styles, and customs. Successful Americans were alike!

In the 1960's, however, racial and national minority groups objected to such a notion of Americanization. Some Negroes—whether or not involved in protests—wore "Afro" hairstyles and African robes and jewelry to school (right) or work. Other "outsiders," too, looked for ways to resist what they believed was a forced conformity. Indian civil-rights organizations demanded that the Federal government stop spending money on Indian welfare and training programs planned by whites. The dollars should go instead to tribal councils to spend on Indian-run self-help programs. A number of Indians even occupied Alcatraz Island in San Francisco Bay (lower left). It contained only an abandoned Federal prison. The Indians claimed the island and set up an independent commune which attracted attention across the country.

Many of New York's million Puerto Ricans were becoming proud of their culture and taking part in festivals and celebrations that stressed their Spanish past (top left). This search for **cultural identity** (knowledge of who you are and pride in your ethnic background) was coupled with political demands for a voice in running educational and medical programs in Puerto Rican neighborhoods. These activities were denounced by many Americans—including some members of such minority groups—who believed that the special strength of the United States lay in keeping different peoples peaceably together. A degree of conformity, they argued, was a price worth paying for so rare an achievement.

During the 1960's black history was introduced in many schools. Here, elementary students illustrate aspects of African culture for their classmates.

Questions for Discussion

1. Why was the decision in *Brown v. Board of Education of Topeka* so important to blacks?
2. What is a sit-in? a boycott? a demonstration?

Technology: Promise and Threat

BOTH: UPI

In the years since 1945, mankind's scientific knowledge has increased tremendously. The United States, as a wealthy nation possessing the universities and laboratories to train thousands of scientists, has contributed much to this "information explosion." The technological breakthroughs of the past 25 years, if wisely used, promise all mankind a happier life.

Some advances have freed men from the age-old grip of pain and early death by disease. There are new vaccines and antibiotics—drugs which destroy germs but do not harm other microscopic organisms essential to life. Such "miracle medicines" have made death by infection from wounds and injuries rare. They have almost wiped out former killers like diphtheria and polio. Blood banks as well as new surgical techniques have made possible operations which save the lives of sick people once hopelessly doomed. Transplants of healthy organs to replace diseased ones are in the experimental stage.

The lowering of the death rate has contributed to the continued expansion of the population. Science has helped to increase food production with powerful chemical fertilizers which enable farmers to grow bigger crops, using less land and labor. New drugs and sprays also protect crops and livestock from insects and diseases that once wiped out the food supplies of whole communities.

Scientists even look beyond the day when the earth's small land area will no longer be able to feed a swollen world populace. In deep-sea exploration vehicles (left) they are experimenting with growing food on the ocean floor and increasing the harvest of fish. The seabed may also yield new sources of oil and coal to replace shrinking stocks of these energy-producing minerals.

Atomic reactors, burning nuclear material, may be the power plants of the future. They may operate factories which produce synthetics to replace resources now becoming more scarce.

The most spectacular of man's recent scientific accomplishments have been the United States manned landings on the moon (right). Although these and other space explorations undertaken by the United States and the Soviet Union promise no large-scale immediate benefits to mankind, they excite people everywhere. They seem to prove that humanity has limitless power to solve "insoluble" technical problems.

Far left: The Deepstar-4000, a new kind of vehicle for underwater research (top), can carry 3 men to a depth of 4,000 feet. The Navy Electronics Laboratory in San Diego is using it for research in marine biology and geology. In 1970 a team of 5 women scientists tested human ability to live underwater for an extended time. Deep beneath the Caribbean Sea, Dr. Sylvia Barle (bottom), the head of the team, gathers samples of plant life. Below: In May 1969 Tom Stafford and Eugene Cernan descended to within 9 miles of the moon's surface in this lunar module before rejoining John Young in the command module of Apollo 10. Below left: During the first 2 minutes of its historic flight, Apollo 11 booster rockets propelled the craft to an altitude of 38 miles. Left: On July 20, 1969, Neil Armstrong became the first man to walk on the moon. He was joined by Edwin Aldrin, while Michael Collins circled the moon in the command ship.

ALL: NASA

RENE BURRI, MAGNUM

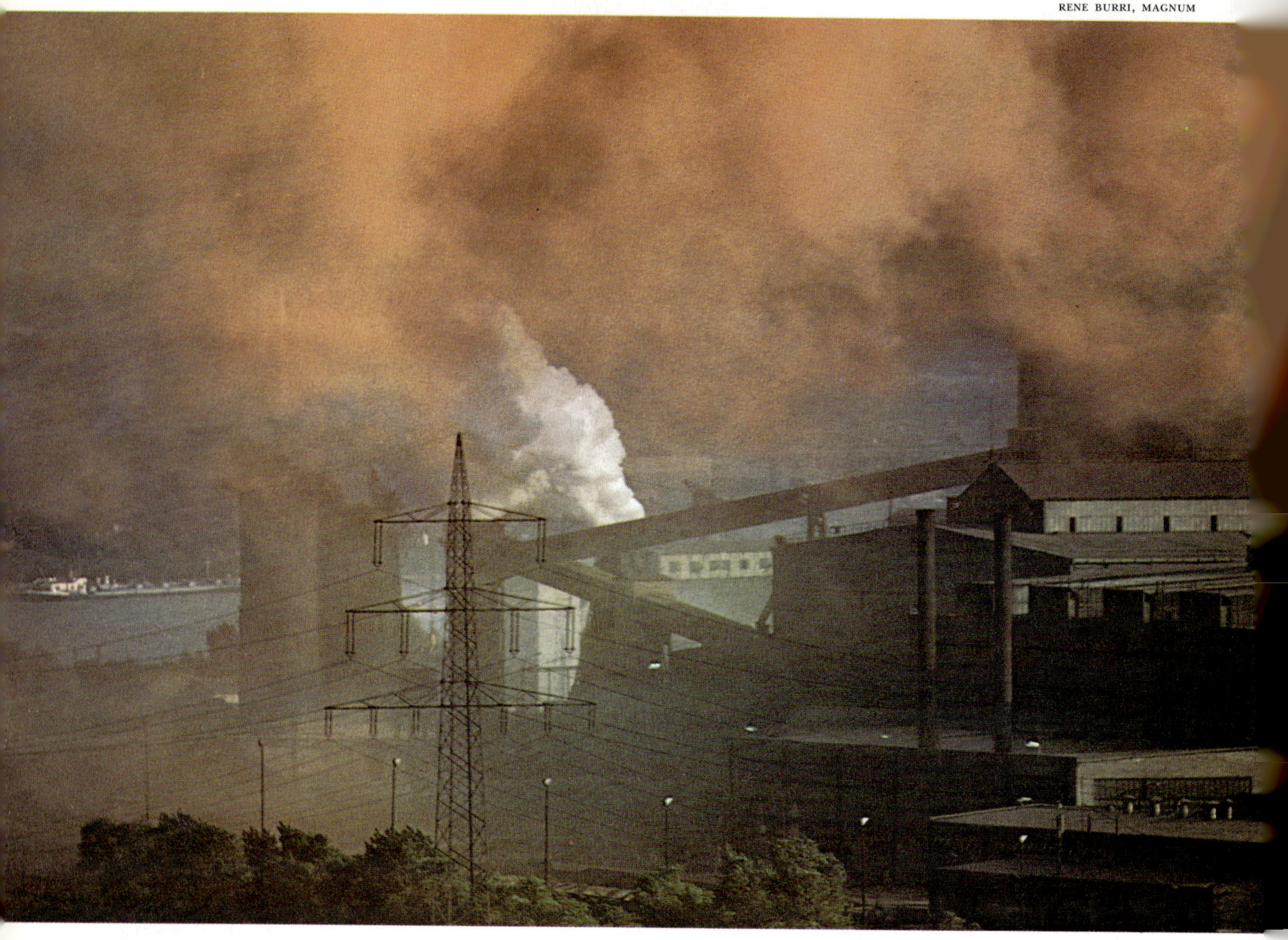

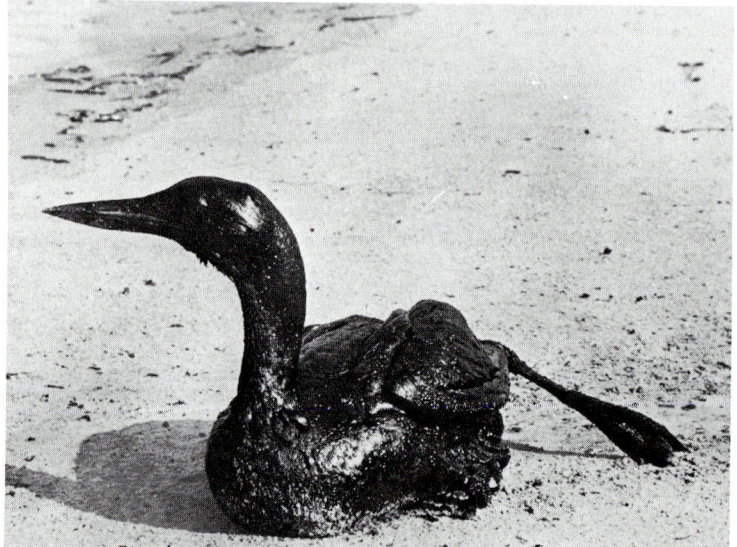

For years scientists have been warning that man must take steps to curb pollution or face the possibility of having no air to breathe nor water to drink. As the 1970's began their message finally seemed to be reaching large numbers of people. Laws were passed requiring companies to curb their pollution of the air and water. On April 22, 1970, Earth Day programs were held to enlist the aid of individual citizens. As scientists urged further action it remained to be seen whether companies and consumers would sacrifice profits and conveniences to insure the future of life on earth.

Los Angeles Times PHOTO

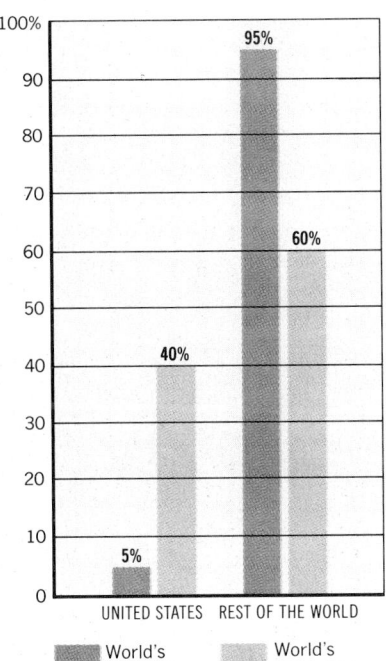

Use of Natural Resources 1970

- World's Population
- World's Resources

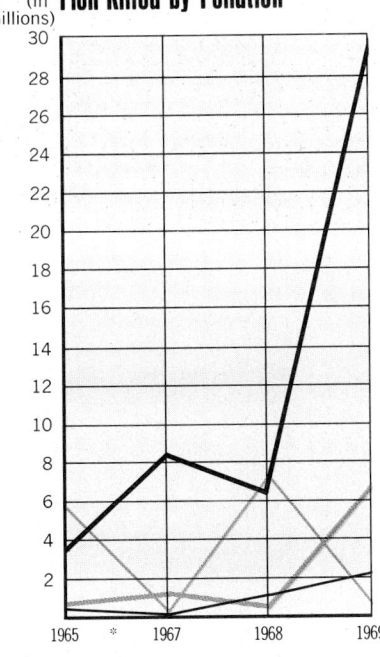

Fish Killed by Pollution

Sources of Pollution:
- Agricultural Operations
- Industrial Operations
- Municipal Operations
- Transportation Operations

*figures not available for 1966

The Problems of Progress

Postwar Americans, however, made an astonishing discovery about technology. Early in the century they firmly believed that any invention which saved time or effort was good for humanity. But around 1965 scientists began to sound a warning. Too much so-called progress was becoming dangerous. As conservationists had long warned, large-scale industry consumed natural resources at a furious rate (graph, upper left). But worse yet, it even endangered such basic necessities as pure air and water.

Millions of automobile engines and factory chimneys belching waste gases into the air over crowded cities (far left) helped to create a serious problem of lung and heart disease. Industrial and human waste products discharged into once-clean rivers and lakes wiped out fish (graph, lower left) and made the water unfit to swim in or to drink without heavy chemical treatments. Sometimes dramatic accidents made the problem highly noticeable—as, for example, when an oil tanker spilled its cargo of thick, greasy petroleum which coated the feathers of sea birds who died by the thousands (far left). But such **pollution** of the environment in heavily built-up areas was a constant process even when it did not make headlines. Each step of technological advance changed the **ecology** of a region—the natural balance among living things. As an example, phosphates dumped into streams as industrial waste products overstimulate the growth of algae. As the algae multiply they consume so much oxygen that the fish are denied their normal supply and die off. Thus industrial processes often have unforeseen side-effects which upset the ecological balance.

Much technology is new, but the basic human problem of how to use it is old. An ancient Greek myth tells of a brilliant inventor named Daedalus. He built two pairs of feathered wings, held together by wax. With them he and his son Icarus escaped from a tyrant who held them prisoner. But Icarus flew too close to the sun. The wax melted, and he fell to his doom. Man might soar into the heavens—or destroy himself by not respecting the godlike powers of nature. The choice was his—to be Daedalus or Icarus.

Poverty and Plenty

Quite clearly, the problem of sharing the fruits of progress still called for human judgment. Ameri-

cans of the 1960's learned that poverty continued to exist in their land of plenty. Curiously, this poverty was partially due to progress itself.

Post-1945 economic growth created high-paying jobs in new industries. Factory workers drove costly automobiles and bought home freezers and camping trailers. Members of a new white-collar class of experts—engineers, technical editors, salesmen of complex equipment, and professors—lived well. They spent freely on "highbrow" entertainments like the opera (far right) and on cameras, record players, books, travel, and other luxuries for leisure-time use.

But the parade was passing some people by. Those who could quickly learn new technical skills could share in prosperity, especially if they were young and willing to move quickly from place to place. But millions did not fit this description. Youths with poor schooling could not easily qualify for highly skilled jobs. Neither could workers who were displaced by increasing **automation.** In a highly sophisticated automated system of production, machines are no longer tended by humans but guided by electronic "brains," supervised by one or two experts at a control panel. Whole areas were sometimes hard-hit when their basic industries were automated. In the Appalachian Mountains thousands of veteran coal miners were made idle both by automation and by a declining need for coal. They remained in the countryside where they had grown up—unable or unready to move or to find new work. Farmers who could not afford expensive machinery and fertilizers were forced off the farms and into low-paying jobs. They did not fit into modern agriculture.

Such people were the poor of the technological age. Pensions and welfare payments kept most, but not all of them, from actual starvation. But they and their children lacked balanced diets, good medical care, and the skills necessary to climb out of poverty. In spite of its ability to better the human condition, technology, without proper guidance, could create a social environment of inequality (graph, right), just as it could cause a polluted physical environment.

Culture and Conflict

The pace of change in the short span of history between 1945 and 1970 was unbelievably swift. This fact lay behind the so-called "generation gap." A whole

New York City—Celebrities at the Metropolitan Opera and unemployed men outside their temporary home.

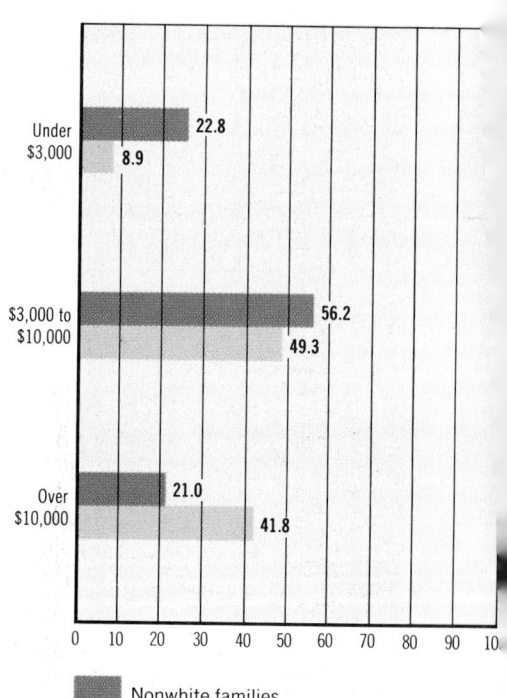

Income Distribution of Families 1968

Under $3,000: 22.8 (Nonwhite), 8.9 (White)
$3,000 to $10,000: 56.2 (Nonwhite), 49.3 (White)
Over $10,000: 21.0 (Nonwhite), 41.8 (White)

■ Nonwhite families
□ White families

ELLIOTT LANDY, MAGNUM

History's largest "happening" took place on a 600-acre farm in Bethel, New York, during three days in August 1969. At least 400,000 young people, attracted by a cast of top rock artists, managed to get to the Woodstock Music and Art Fair (above). The huge turnout and the warm gentle atmosphere—in spite of rain and lack of food and sanitation facilities—surprised even the sponsors of the festival. Critics condemned the widespread use of drugs and casual nudity, but even they were amazed that not one robbery nor violent fight occurred. Perhaps most important, Woodstock made the nation aware that a large community of youth rejected traditional values. Subsequent rock festivals were marred by violence and, in 1970, two well-known stars died from overdoses of drugs. But thousands of young people—some disillusioned by a society that permits poverty, racism, and war to exist—continued to search for new ways of living (right).

CHARLES HARBUTT, MAGNUM

population grew up with experiences unknown to previous generations. The pioneer parents who faced the hardships of the frontier could show their sons and daughters how to build a cabin, trap a squirrel, or plant a garden. But the father and mother who lived through World War II could not tell their children how to face the knowledge that the world might be blown up in hours or poisoned in a few years.

Children had once learned about life by listening to aunts, uncles, grandparents, and the wise men of their town or neighborhood. Books and movies might stretch their imaginations. But the "real" world they would someday enter was a territory known and mapped by principals, teachers, ministers, doctors, lawyers, and other elders. Even when children made fun of adults, they knew that.

Television helped to change that pattern. Once television became common children lived in a different world. From infancy they spent many more hours watching it than they spent with older people. Television gave them a different feeling about space and time than any earlier generation. It brought them, in split seconds, words and events from Europe, Asia, Africa—or the moon! Such places were as much a part of the "real" world as the house next door. As one critic said, television made the world a "global village" where everything happened at once.

This led to a constant questioning of the wisdom and authority of the past by young people. Because they felt that older people could not possibly understand their emotions, they looked for experiences that were their very own. Young people have always felt this way—but never with so much reason. In the 1960's rock music, psychedelic lights and posters, "freaky" clothes and long hair that were the same for boys and girls, and experimentation (often dangerous) with drugs were part of a new culture. So were campus rebellions and protests. This culture of mass rock festivals (upper left) and hippie communes (lower left) was concerned with "now" and with complete personal freedom. It clashed with the "old" culture that put a value on things that had been useful to parents in their time, such as planning for the future, saving, and using reason and good judgment, and following those ways that had worked in the past.

Despite many conflicts, the generations still communicated. They had no choice. Young people would

some day grow old and have their own children. In March 1971 Congress proposed the Twenty-sixth Amendment, which lowered the voting age to eighteen in Federal, state, and local elections. In little more than two months the amendment was ratified by the required number of states.

Questions for Discussion

1. Discuss some ways that science and technology have improved the lives of people in the United States. In what ways are scientists and technologists working to improve life in the future?
2. Why did some people believe progress to be a cause of poverty and environmental problems?
3. What was the so-called generation gap of the 1960's? What were thought to be its causes?

Chapter Review

Social Studies Terms

metropolitan area, megalopolises, *de facto* segregation, *de jure* segregation, militant, cultural identity, pollution, ecology, automation

Summary Questions for Discussion

1. What problems have been solved by technology and science? Why have they been unable to solve all our problems?
2. What ties exist between suburbs and inner cities? What will be the effect on inner cities if Americans continue to move to the suburbs?
3. Do you live in a city? What needs to be done to make it a better place in which to live?
4. What Supreme Court decision was overturned by the decision in *Brown v. Board of Education of Topeka?* Why was it difficult to enforce the decision in the *Brown* case?
5. Why is the problem of integrating schools a northern problem as well as a southern problem?
6. Why was resistance to the desegregation of southern schools ineffective in some places?
7. Which of the methods used by members of minority groups to gain equality and justice were most effective? Defend your answer.
8. Who were some of the leaders in the movement to obtain justice and equality for minorities in the United States? Why did some of them call for separation from whites rather than integration with whites?

9. What political gains were made by Negroes between 1945 and 1970? What methods were used to make these gains?
10. Why did some people believe that America's cultural pluralism should be preserved? In what way did members of some minority groups try to preserve their cultural identity?
11. Is the generation gap real or imaginary? Give reasons for your answer.

Pictures as Historical Evidence

Which pictures in this chapter would provide evidence for, and which would provide evidence against, the following generalization? The American way of life from 1945 to 1970 was marked by an acceleration of earlier trends in our history.

Graph Study

Study the graph on page 736. Which state's political life would you expect to be most changed as a result of the 1965 Voting Rights Act? Why? Which of the states do you think would be least affected? Why?

Study the graph on resource consumption on page 743. What hypothesis do you think best explains why the 5 per cent of the world's population who live in the United States consume 40 per cent of the world's resources?

For Further Reading

Americans in Space, by the Editors of American Heritage. New York: American Heritage Publishing Co., Inc., 1965.

Black Americans, by Earl Schenck Miers. New York: Grosset & Dunlap, Inc., 1969.

Conquest of the Moon, by Felix Sutton and Alvin Maurer. New York: Grosset & Dunlap, Inc., 1969.

Fighters for a New World, by Thilo Koch. New York: G. P. Putnam's Sons, 1969.

Growing Up Black, by Jay David. New York: William Morrow & Co., Inc., 1968.

Martin Luther King, Jr., by Edward Preston. Garden City, New York: Doubleday & Company, Inc., 1968.

President from Missouri, by Ralph G. Martin. New York: Julian Messner, 1964.

Triumph and Tragedy: The Story of the Kennedys, by the Editors of Associated Press. New York: Associated Press, 1968.

26
An Uncertain World

In the last week of April 1945, deep in wartime Germany, two tanks approached each other, then halted. Their crews climbed out, grinned, and shook hands all around. One tank was Russian, the other American. That night their meeting made happy news for millions of newspaper readers all over the world. Armies of these two great allies had united to cut the fading Nazi empire in half. Soon the victorious nations would build a new, free, and better world.

Sixteen years later, on an August night in Berlin, other American troops on guard in their "sector" or part of Berlin strained their ears anxiously as they heard odd sounds in the darkness. Berlin was deep in East Germany which was now a **satellite** state controlled by an anti-American Soviet Union. When dawn came the sounds were explained. East German soldiers had built a crude wall, which can be seen beyond the barbed wire in the photograph at left, sealing off their part of the city. The wall was to keep thousands of East German, anti-communist refugees from fleeing each year to West Berlin. The wall actually divided Berlin. But it was symbolic of a dividing line through Germany, through Europe, and through the world.

The wartime alliance between Russia and the West was long over in 1961. It broke up less than two years after the war's end. Joseph Stalin had shown no intention of letting democracy exist anywhere within the shadow of Russian power. He began a program of expanding that power, arguing that he only wished to protect the Soviet Union from the foreign enemies who had attacked it twice since the revolution of 1917.

In response, the United States, claiming to act as the defender of world freedom, re-armed and took an active part in supporting anti-communist governments throughout the globe. Soon both superpowers were deep in an arms race. Both built alliances which extended far beyond their borders. Russian-American rivalry throughout the 1950's and 1960's influenced the fate of peoples and governments everywhere. It led fighting men of the United States into battle and death once more. It kept the entire world living in fear of nuclear war. The future was as uncertain as it was challenging in a divided world.

As you read, think about these questions:
1. What have been the chief obstacles to global peace since the end of World War II?
2. How can such obstacles be overcome in the future?

West Germany installed barbed wire to avoid trouble near the Berlin Wall.

Europe 1970

- Warsaw Pact Nations
- North Atlantic Treaty Organization (Also included: United States and Canada)
- Not members of either alliance

The Clash of Superpowers

The end of the war left the Russians in control of much of eastern Europe. In 1944 they had seized the little Baltic nations of Estonia, Latvia, and Lithuania. By 1946 they had taken parts of Poland and East Prussia. By 1948 they controlled most of the Balkan countries (map, left). In the countries their troops had "liberated," they set up puppet communist regimes controlled from Moscow. In these satellite nations all those who did not put Russian interests first were suppressed.

Gradually, the British and American governments became convinced that the Soviet Union was doing more than simply acting like a great power in its own sphere of influence. They decided that the Russians wanted what Winston Churchill had called "the indefinite expansion of their power." A growing number of Americans who had been sympathetic to Russia during the war were coming to share this view.

It was suspected that Russia was sending "volunteers" from Yugoslavia and Albania to support a guerrilla uprising against the Greek government. In March 1947 President Harry S. Truman (left) decided that the moment had come for action. The Greek government was getting weaker. While it was scarcely a perfect democracy, Truman believed that if Greece fell the communists would soon threaten neighboring Turkey. So Truman asked Congress for $400 million in military aid for Greece and Turkey. Truman claimed that "totalitarian [dictatorial] regimes imposed upon free peoples by direct or indirect aggression" weakened peace everywhere, and thus American security. After some debate Congress granted his request. The United States now became committed to defending anti-communist nations against attack or communist-led revolutions. In addition, the nation gave billions of dollars in aid through the Marshall Plan to bolster the battered economies of non-communist, western European countries.

The new position of the United States was soon tested by the Russians. In June 1948 they barred Allied road and rail traffic through their zone of occupied Germany, thus cutting off all supplies. They hoped to starve the western powers' garrisons in West Berlin (and the West Berliners in the process) and force them into the humiliation of leaving. But the American response was to send great fleets of transport planes to supply the city by air (upper left). For a

In 1945, Germany was divided into 4 sectors—American, British, French, and Russian. Berlin, inside the Russian sector, was divided similarly. When Russia closed Allied access routes to Berlin in June 1948, President Truman (above) decided to try airlifting supplies. By December, 200 C-54 transport planes were flying in and out of Berlin each day (above left). The Russians did not lift the blockade until May 1949—when they were certain the Allies could supply Berlin by air indefinitely. More than 2 million Berliners owed their lives to the pilots who had made 276,926 flights to bring them 2.3 million tons of supplies.

Under the leadership of Mao Tse-tung (above), state-controlled communes nearly tripled food production by 1958. Russian technology spurred industry (below).

time the world held its breath, fearing that if the Russians shot at the American planes a new war would start. But after 321 nerve-racking days the Russians backed down and lifted the blockade.

Civil War in China

Halfway around the world in Asia, things did not go nearly as well for the Truman Doctrine of defending nations against communist-led revolutions. In China a civil war, which ended with a communist victory in 1949, overturned nearly half a century of American policy. The United States had always tried to keep a friendly Chinese government in power. This was the idea behind the Open Door policy. Moreover, the United States had fought Japan, in large part, to prevent Japanese control of China's land, people, and economy.

During the 1930's China had actually become divided between two governments. Chiang Kai-shek, the dictatorial leader of the Kuomintang or Nationalist Party, united many quarreling provincial warlords behind him to fight the Japanese after 1937. But he could not always count on popular support. Many of his lieutenants were loyal to him only because he did not investigate their corrupt deeds. Meantime, the Chinese Communists had entrenched themselves in the northeastern provinces of the country. They were dictatorial, disciplined, and dedicated. Until 1945 the Kuomintang and the Communists were allies against the invading Japanese.

But after 1945 both Nationalist and Communist groups claimed the right to govern all of China. The United States sent one of its ablest soldiers, General George C. Marshall, to try to work out an agreement between them. But he failed. War broke out early in 1947, and it soon became clear that Chiang was losing. The United States believed that nothing could save him except full-scale intervention. Unwilling to make such a commitment, the United States watched as Chiang was driven back and fled to Taiwan (Formosa) in 1949. All it could do was to continue to recognize his government as the only official government of China. There were now two Chinese governments—the Communist Peoples' Republic of China on the mainland and the Republic of China in Taiwan.

The Chinese Communists promptly embarked on a program of industrial development (lower left) and mass propaganda (right). Though China's "loss" was at

Before Russia and China quarreled, Peking celebrated a visit by Khrushchev.

first thought to be a victory for Russia, the Chinese Communists soon showed that they were more interested in their own fate than in Soviet needs. Though they accepted much-needed Russian help at first, by the late 1960's they had broken with Russia and were competing with Moscow for control of Communist parties everywhere.

The Korean War

Then, in 1950, another part of Asia exploded. Since the end of World War II the former Japanese possession of Korea (map, right) had been jointly occupied by Russian and American troops. In each occupation zone a different Korean government was chosen. When both Russia and the United States pulled out, the dividing line between their armies became the boundary between two hostile Korean nations. Suddenly, on June 25, 1950, forces of the Communist Republic of North Korea smashed across the border, the 38th parallel, and invaded South Korea.

Harry S. Truman was no man to back away from a fight. He asked for an emergency session of the United Nations Security Council. Russia boycotted the session. The Security Council then voted to send a UN peacekeeping force to Korea under the command of General Douglas MacArthur. Over 90 per cent of the troops were American and South Korean.

At first the North Koreans, with their Russian equipment, nearly pushed the Americans and South Koreans into the sea. Then General MacArthur (seen with Truman at upper left) turned the tide and sent the Communist forces reeling back across the 38th parallel. Instead of stopping there, he pressed on into North Korea to "punish the aggressors." The Chinese Communists began to warn that they would not stand for UN forces approaching their border with North Korea. In late November 1950 the Chinese Communist troops broke through the American lines and drove United States soldiers and marines back below the 38th parallel once more.

For the American people this was a shocking experience. A second shock came when the United States did not at once launch air attacks on enemy bases and supply routes inside China. This was the desire of General MacArthur, who believed that in war there was "no substitute for victory." But the President and the highest military command, the Joint Chiefs of

Top: At Wake Island in October 1950, General MacArthur assures President Truman that the Chinese will not enter the Korean War.

Lower left: President-elect Eisenhower, who had promised during the campaign to visit Korea and end the war, tours battlefield sites with General James Fry in December 1952. Right: Refugees fleeing from the enemy pass by American infantrymen on their way into battle.

Asia 1970

- Southeast Asia Treaty Organization (Also included: United States, United Kingdom, France, New Zealand)
- Communist Nations
- Officially Neutral Nations
- Contested Areas

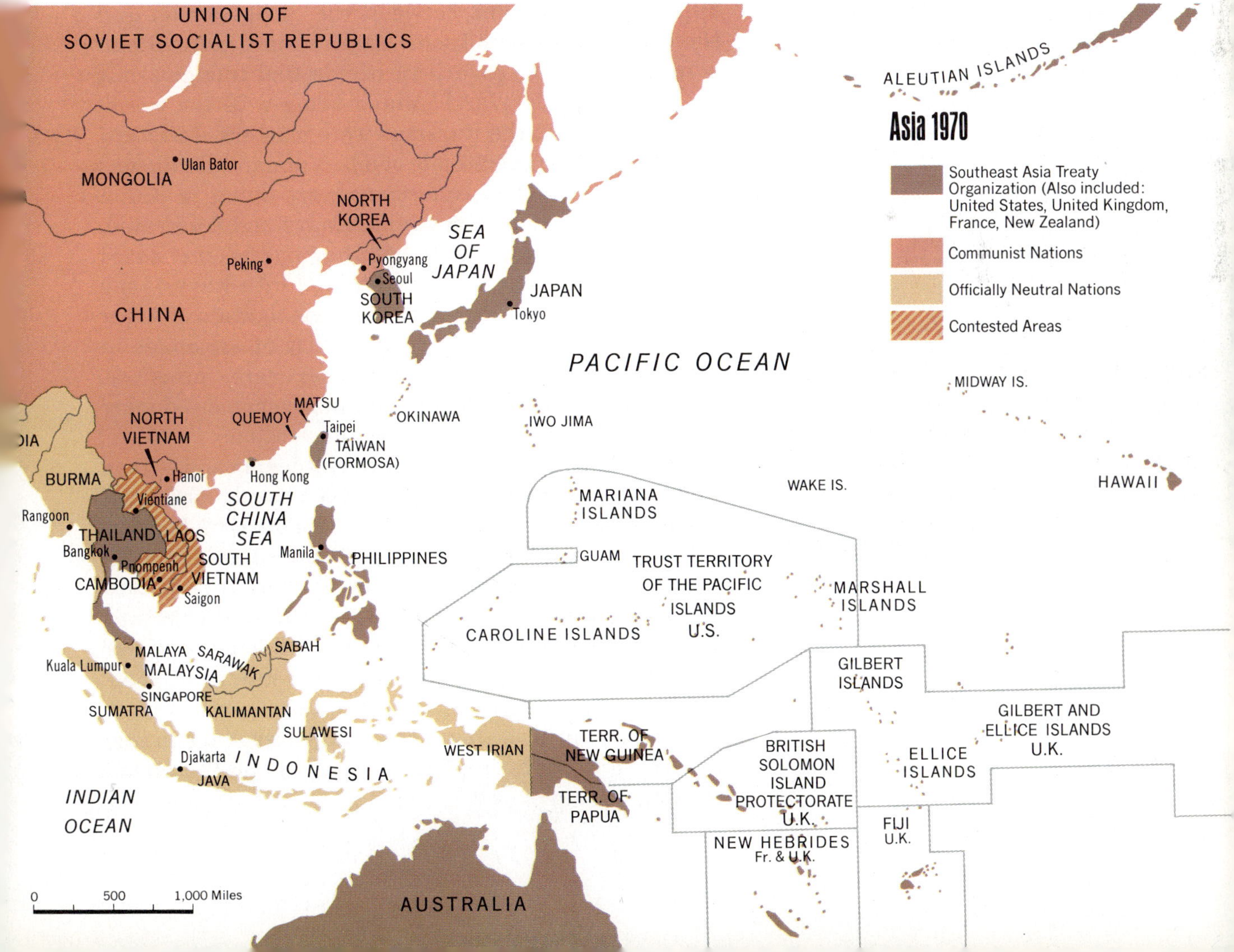

Staff, feared that such action might provoke Russia into starting a devastating atomic war in defense of its communist ally. When MacArthur publicly protested this decision, the peppery President fired him.

So the war surged back and forth. Neither side could "win" without the risk of starting a third world war. It was now clear to both sides that the best way out was to negotiate a settlement calling for a return to the pre-1950 state of affairs. In June 1951 the Communists agreed to negotiate an armistice. Only a very popular American could sponsor a "no-win" stand-off without facing charges of a "sell-out." Such a man was Dwight D. Eisenhower, elected President in November 1952. Eisenhower visited Korea, then authorized peace talks which lasted two years before an armistice was signed in 1953. In this new kind of war 33,000 Americans died.

The Politics of Containment

The **Cold War** (the long conflict without all-out military commitment between the Soviet Union and the United States) had some harsh results in American political life. The American people had thought that the end of World War II would bring a better world. Instead, by 1952 the Russians were masters of eastern Europe and had the atomic bomb. Mainland China was a communist nation. Americans were dying in Korea and paying huge military bills. Angry and frustrated, many Americans decided that they had been cheated and betrayed. Such feelings were fed by a wave of spy trials, beginning in 1948 with the investigation of Alger Hiss. A few people were found guilty of espionage in atomic plants. To some these cases were "proof" of widespread communist influence in government during the Roosevelt and Truman administrations.

Such feelings divided Americans deeply and set the stage for the rampage of Senator Joseph McCarthy (left) through national life from 1950 to 1954. McCarthy's specialty was wild accusations of communism against both obscure bureaucrats and highly respected government officials like General Marshall. For a time McCarthy's unfounded attacks met with much popular support. In 1954 he even went so far as to insult some of his fellow Senators and to question the army's patriotism. He was then **censured** (severely criticized in a public vote) by his fellow Senators and thereafter ignored.

During the 1950's many people lost their jobs and were subject to public ridicule because of a communist witch hunt led by Senator Joseph McCarthy. However, not one communist was found, not one spy was convicted, and not one person was indicted for a crime as a result of his charges.

The years from 1955 to 1960 were fairly peaceful. Eisenhower's popularity calmed the country. His Secretary of State, John Foster Dulles (right), first spoke of "rolling back" communism, but settled instead for "containing" it. To do so he traveled tirelessly around the world, logging nearly 500,000 air miles and building up an alliance system. In 1947–1948 the United States had helped to form the Organization of American States (OAS)—a defensive alliance system in the Americas. In 1949 the United States entered the North Atlantic Treaty Organization (NATO) with the major non-communist European powers (map, page 752). All members were pledged to mutual defense against an attack on any one member. To NATO Dulles added a Central Treaty Organization (CENTO) in the Middle East and a Southeast Asia Treaty Organization (SEATO). By the end of 1960 the once "isolationist" United States was committed to defend more than two dozen non-communist countries ringed around the borders of Russia and China. It had military bases in many of them.

Cuba—Cold War Hot Spot

In 1959 Nikita Khrushchev, new head of the Soviet government, visited the United States. Both he and Eisenhower talked of **peaceful coexistence** (the idea that despite the difference between communism and democracy Russia and the United States would not interfere in each other's domestic affairs and would respect each other's sphere of influence), thus letting each nation, and the world, live in peace. The Cold War seemed to have thawed. But between 1960 and 1962 it heated up again. In one sizzling week it threatened full war. This time the scene was in Cuba.

In January 1959 the young Cuban revolutionist Fidel Castro seized control of the island from the dictator Fulgencio Batista. Mock trials, execution of his political enemies, and quarrels with the United States followed. Castro moved toward closer relations with Russia and finally announced that he was a Communist. In April 1961 the newly elected President John F. Kennedy backed the United States Central Intelligence Agency's (CIA) attempt to overthrow Castro by training and landing in the Bay of Pigs a force of Cuban anti-Castro, anti-communist exiles. The CIA expected a general revolt to follow. Instead, the invaders were quickly captured and killed, and the

As Secretary of State, John Foster Dulles insisted that the United States build up its supply of nuclear, rather than conventional, weapons. Then the United States could threaten any communist aggressor with massive nuclear retaliation. This policy, known in full as "brinksmanship," was designed to avoid small wars around the world. Eventually, the scheme proved unrealistic and unworkable. Ironically, an alliance forged by Dulles led America into a war in Southeast Asia fought only with conventional weapons.

WIDE WORLD PHOTOS

JIMMY SCOTT FROM *Topaze*, SANTIAGO, CHILE

This cartoon, which appeared in a South American publication, implies that Castro was to blame for the head-on confrontation between Kennedy and Khrushchev during the Cuban Missile Crisis. One major result of the confrontation was that Castro learned that the United States would not tolerate offensive missiles in Cuba and the Russian government would not risk war to protect Cuba's right to have missiles.

American role in the affair was revealed. Many Americans objected (top, far right) to an act of rather clumsy aggression, no matter how noble its motives.

Khrushchev may have thought that Kennedy, having gambled and failed in Cuba, would be unwilling to face a new involvement there. During the summer of 1962 Russia began to ship Soviet medium and long-range missiles to the island. But when American aerial intelligence took photos of the missile sites, Kennedy met the situation head on. On October 22, 1962, he gravely announced to the world an American naval blockade of Cuba. Russian vessels carrying the missiles to Cuba would be turned back (bottom right). The OAS backed the American stance while the United States presented its case to world opinion in the UN. For a few tense days everyone waited to see how the Russians would respond. Would an angry shot in Cuban waters be the signal for a nuclear exchange that would kill millions? Finally, Khrushchev backed down and agreed to move the missiles.

Actually, both Russia and the United States could now launch terrible hydrogen explosives against each other from their homelands or from submarines. This itself made both sides ease up after 1962 and seek disarmament talks. Besides, both superpowers had problems of their own. Communist China had sharply broken with Russia which it charged was no longer a "true" communist country. Even former satellite nations like Yugoslavia and Albania refused to follow the Soviet lead in many matters. And the United States was learning, in a far-away place called Vietnam, that its ability to control events around the globe was limited.

The War in Vietnam

Like Korea, Vietnam was a divided land. It was part of the former French colony of Indochina, split "temporarily" when the French left in 1954. The northern half, governed from Hanoi, was a communist dictatorship. South Vietnam, whose capital was Saigon, was ruled by a series of inept and often corrupt governments dominated by generals. Opponents of the Saigon rulers organized a guerrilla army, called the Viet Cong. It began to attack villages and gain control of the countryside.

The United States believed that a Viet Cong victory would topple South Vietnam into the arms of commu-

Above right: In April 1961 pro-Castro sympathizers picket the White House to protest the Bay of Pigs Invasion. *Above:* In November 1962 President Kennedy announces to the nation that the Russians have agreed to withdraw their missiles from Cuba. *Right:* The United States Navy made certain that Russia kept its promise. Here, the United States destroyer *Dahlgren* (in the background) tails a Soviet freighter carrying missiles out of Cuba. In return for the Russian withdrawal, President Kennedy pledged that the United States would not attempt another invasion of Cuba.

Below: In 1966 United States troops take up defensive positions in a Mekong Delta rice paddy. By 1971, under Nixon's Vietnamization plan, most of the fighting in the Delta had been turned over to the South Vietnamese. Above: Opponents of the war protest that the United States does not have the right to intervene in a Vietnamese civil war. Defenders of the war pointed to the "domino theory:" If South Vietnam fell to the communists, other Asian nations would follow.

nism, and that other southeast Asian nations might follow. Beginning with the Eisenhower administration, Washington furnished military equipment and advisers to bolster the Saigon government. Hanoi, meanwhile, aided the Viet Cong. In 1963 President Kennedy sent the first combat troops. In 1964 President Lyndon Johnson, who had become President when President Kennedy was assassinated, became convinced that without stepped-up American intervention the Viet Cong would win. Johnson thereupon ordered United States bombers and infantrymen (left) into action.

The Vietnam War was unlike any ever fought by Americans before. There was no front line. The "enemy" wore no uniforms and looked like the friendly villagers. Even the regular North Vietnamese army units easily melted into the countryside. The military adopted the strategy of clearing whole areas of pro-Saigon people, then bombing and burning those regions in the belief that only Viet Cong remained in them. So the war went on cruelly and without a decision for years. By 1970 the war was still costing the United States $30 billion a year. By 1971 over 45,000 Americans and countless Vietnamese had lost their lives.

The war divided the United States bitterly. Demonstrations, particularly by the young (top left), were held, in which thousands denounced their government's policies. Counter-demonstrations by defenders of the war angrily criticized the lack of patriotism of their antiwar opponents.

Opposition ran so high that in 1968 Johnson ended bombing of North Vietnam and started peace talks in Paris. Total military victory might no longer be the goal, but he refused to withdraw support from the Saigon government. After the 1968 Presidential election, Nixon put in force a plan, known as Vietnamization, to slowly withdraw American combat troops and turn the fighting back to the South Vietnamese. In the spring of 1970 American and South Vietnamese troops attacked enemy sanctuaries in Cambodia. In February of 1971 the Americans gave air and logistical support to a South Vietnamese attack against enemy supply lines in southern Laos.

Questions for Discussion

1. Why did the United States oppose the spread of Russian power and influence in Europe?
2. Why has the United States fought in Asia?

The Search for Peace

Much of the history of the last 25 years has not involved only superpowers. One of the era's greatest developments was the end of colonialism. Because the ability of European nations to resist national revolutions in their colonies was fatally weakened by World War II, more than 50 new nations have emerged since 1945. Each major power wanted to win the friendship and support of the newcomers in this "third world." But this meant that quarrels among small nations or revolutions within their borders could threaten to involve the great powers in war.

The part of the third world of developing nations nearest to the United States was Latin America. None of these were "new" nations. But many of their peoples suffered from poverty and disease. During the 1950's there were charges that the United States had used its influence in Latin America to support anti-communist governments that it believed friendly even if they were not democratic. Such charges gained some strength when the CIA helped to overthrow a government in Guatemala in 1954 that was buying arms from communist sources.

President Kennedy sought to meet such suspicions

in 1961 by offering to "sister republics south of the border" what he called an "alliance for progress—to assist free men and free governments in casting off the chains of poverty." This meant that the United States would lend money to Latin American governments to help them with programs of land reform, economic development, and other steps to raise public health and living standards. Cheering crowds on a Kennedy 1962 tour of Mexico (upper left) showed that the "Alliance" had revived good will toward the United States. President Johnson sent marines briefly into the Dominican Republic to "protect lives" in 1965, during what he described as a communist uprising. Thereafter, the OAS took over peacekeeping responsibility and supervised elections for a new government.

From 1965 on, the growing American involvement in Vietnam proved such a financial drain that the United States had to cut back its aid to developing Latin American countries.

Helping Developing Nations

Developing lands needed both materials and skills to raise their living standards. They had to have such

Above left: Residents of Mexico City respond enthusiastically to President Kennedy and Mexican President Mateos in 1962. Above: In April 1965 President Johnson sent 20,000 troops to the Dominican Republic to restore order. Johnson later defended his action by saying, "We don't propose to sit here in our rocking chair with our hands folded and let the Communists set up any government in the Western Hemisphere." However, communist involvement in the revolt was questionable, and many Latin Americans resented the United States intervention.

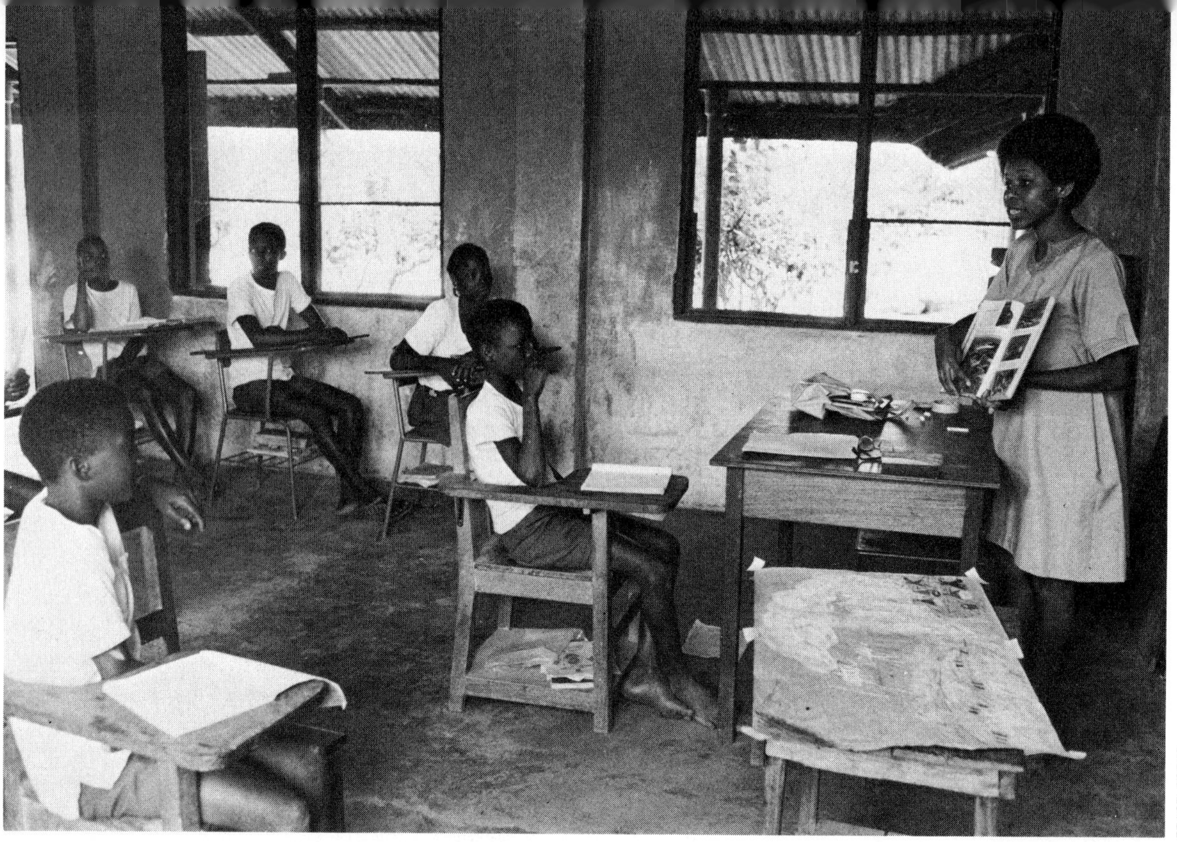

PEACE CORPS

Thousands of Peace Corps volunteers have worked in countries like Liberia (above), Togo (below), or Colombia (right). Recently, fewer have volunteered—perhaps because of a growing concern over America's domestic problems.

WIDE WORLD PHOTOS

RAY WITLIN, BLACK STAR

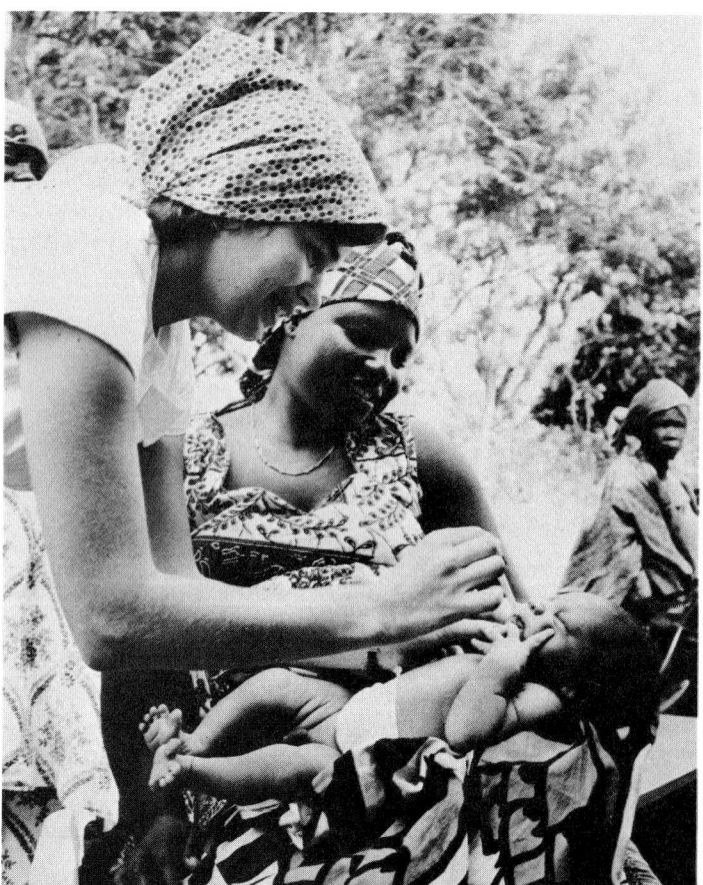

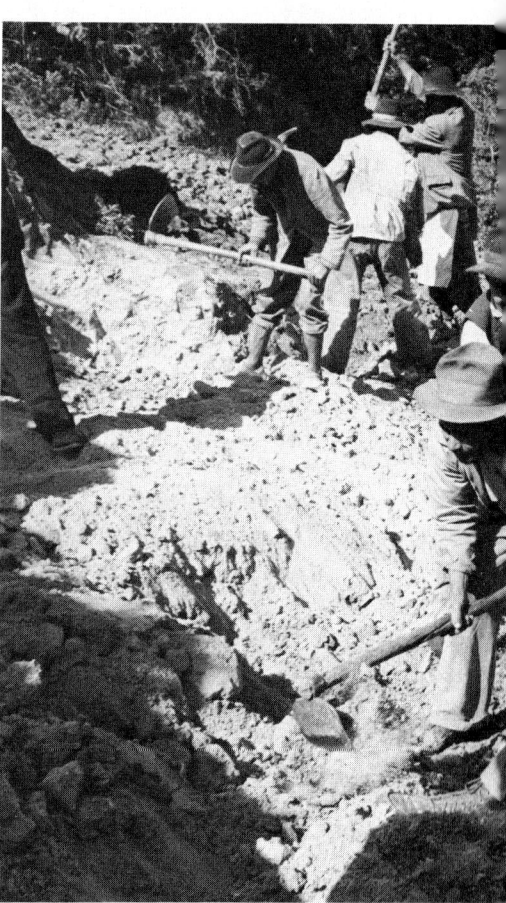

basic building blocks of a modern industrial economy as dams, power plants, roads, fertilizer factories, and schools. Helping them to get these things was smart Cold War politics. It made allies and, by raising living standards, it prevented revolutions which might unexpectedly replace friendly governments with hostile ones. It was also good business for industrially advanced nations to help poorer neighbors raise their incomes and thus become better customers. For such reasons the United States had been providing economic aid to underdeveloped nations since 1948. But President Kennedy suggested still another reason in his 1961 inaugural address. He pledged help to "those peoples in the huts and villages of half the globe struggling to break the bonds of mass misery... not because the Communists may be doing it, not because we seek their votes, but because it is right. If a free society cannot help the many who are poor, it cannot save the few who are rich."

One way of extending such help was through loans and gifts to governments. Another dramatic method proposed by Kennedy in 1961 was the Peace Corps. Under this program Americans do not simply provide dollars to nations needing help. They give of their own effort. Peace Corps volunteers enlist for two years to work in a country as teachers, surveyors, medical technicians, or farming experts (left). They receive only $75 per month and live as much as possible like the people with whom they work.

This new kind of foreign service stirred up a wave of youthful idealism. Inside the first year of the Peace Corps, nearly 13,000 people had volunteered for rugged physical and academic training to prepare for their assignments. As one of them said, the Corps gave a "chance for personal contact instead of dollar diplomacy."

Toward a New World Order

In April 1945, when the last shots of World War II were being fired in Europe, the United Nations was created by a conference of the anti-Axis powers at San Francisco. Like the League of Nations, it was man's hope for a peaceable world. In part it was supposed to be a debating body where arguments, not bombs, solved the family quarrels of the human race. Soon after its birth the United Nations moved into permanent headquarters in New York City.

The United Nations has achieved some success in its efforts to relieve hunger in underdeveloped areas. Here, UNICEF workers distribute powdered milk to the Masai in Kenya.

The UN, however, was not able to prevent the Cold War, the arms race, and many small wars, as well as larger ones such as Korea and Vietnam. Part of the reason lies in the way the UN is organized. It is not a world government. The five great powers permanently represented on the fifteen-member Security Council (the United States, Britain, the Soviet Union, France, and Nationalist China) have the power to veto either further debate or action in the Security Council. Even the General Assembly of all member nations has little power to enforce its decisions. It does, however, provide a place for nations to meet, debate, and negotiate settlements. There is an International Court of Justice but, as it only hears cases which the disputing nations want heard, its influence is small. The UN has no permanent army. In some cases UN peacekeeping forces have been created out of troops "loaned" by several member nations. These armies have enforced truces in the Middle East, the Congo, Indonesia, and other trouble spots. UN observers have also supervised international agreements between India and Pakistan. But basically the UN, like the United States under the Articles of Confederation, has only those powers which member states are willing to give it.

Yet the UN does much work for peace that is not concerned with settling disputes. Agencies under its authority work to build a climate of prosperity and health for all mankind, from which comes good will and tolerance. A body known as the Economic and Social Council (ECOSOC) supervises efforts to improve worldwide standards of living, health, and human rights. It also promotes international cooperation in science, education, and the arts.

Agencies working with or under ECOSOC include the Food and Agricultural Organization (FAO), which helps nations improve their crop production. The World Health Organization (WHO) sends doctors, nurses, and health workers to developing nations. The United Nations Childrens' Emergency Fund (UNICEF) provides medicines and vaccines for 750 million children. It distributes milk and food (left) and runs educational campaigns to teach people how to prevent disease.

The United Nations Educational, Scientific, and Cultural Organization (UNESCO) helps nearly half the world's children who have little or no schooling. It provides money to train teachers and build libraries, thus attacking illiteracy and ignorance. UNESCO also

This photo of United Nations headquarters shows the Secretariat (rising 39 stories), the General Assembly building (with the domed top), and the UN library (in the foreground). The Secretariat, headed by a Secretary-General and staffed by an international body of civil servants, is responsible for administering UN programs all over the world. The Secretary-General also has the power to submit any matter that he considers a threat to world peace to the Security Council. If the Council decides to take military action, all UN members are obligated to supply the Council with whatever it considers necessary to restore peace.

arranges cooperation among scientists of many nations doing research in deep-sea exploration or other matters where national boundaries must be crossed for effective study. Just as the confederation of the thirteen states laid the foundation for the American nation before there was a Constitution, perhaps the UN's work will create the framework of a peaceful world before there is a world government.

Americans should be especially good at making the transition to a new world order. Dwight D. Eisenhower, speaking to the UN in September 1960, reminded the delegates of something special about the impact of our past. "Here in this land," he said, "in what was once a wilderness, we have generated a society and a civilization drawn from many sources. Yet out of the mixture of many peoples and faiths we have developed unity in freedom.... This concept of unity in freedom, drawn from the diversity of many racial strains and cultures, we would like to see made a reality for all mankind." Thus, he said, the world might build a "true peace—a peace in which all peoples may progress constantly to higher levels of human achievement. The means are at hand. We have but to use them with a wisdom and energy worthy of our cause."

Questions for Discussion

1. What is meant by the expression "third world?" How did the United States try to win friends for itself in the third world?
2. What methods were used by Presidents Kennedy and Johnson to keep Latin American countries in the non-communist camp?
3. What are some of the successes and failures of the United Nations? How is it organized to help maintain a peaceful world? What other types of work does it attempt to do?
4. What are some United Nations organizations that are not directly concerned with the settlement of disputes? What humanitarian work do these organizations do?

Chapter Review

Social Studies Terms

satellite, Cold War, censured, **peaceful coexistence**

Summary Questions for Discussion

1. Why were many Americans disappointed in their hopes for a peaceful world after 1945?

2. Why was the Berlin Wall both a reality and a symbol?
3. In what confrontations with Soviet power has the United States achieved a clear-cut victory? Defend your answer.
4. Should the United States give assistance to the undemocratic governments of non-communist countries? Why?
5. Was the victory of the communists in China a long-range gain for the Soviet Union? Why?
6. In what ways have our problems in foreign policy caused problems here at home?
7. What was meant when our foreign policy was described as one of "containment?"
8. What confrontation did the Americans and Russians have over Cuba in 1962? How can such confrontations best be prevented?
9. How did the United States become increasingly involved in Vietnam after 1954? Why was the war there unlike any ever fought by Americans before? Why did the war divide Americans at home?
10. How could the United Nations be made a more effective organization for insuring world peace?
11. What can Americans do to achieve the objectives announced by Eisenhower on page 770?

Map Study

1. Study the map on page 752. What geographical reason would help to explain why Berlin has been a Cold War hot spot?
2. What strategic purposes might President Truman have been trying to attain when he gave military aid to Greece and Turkey?
3. Study the map on page 757. What geographical problems did the United States face in trying to contain communism in China? in Korea? in South Vietnam?

For Further Reading

Dwight D. Eisenhower, by Malcolm Moos. New York: Random House, Inc., 1964.

Kennedy & Johnson, by Evelyn Lincoln. New York: Holt, Rinehart & Winston, Inc., 1968.

The Story of the United Nations, by Katharine Savage. New York: Henry Z. Walck, Inc., 1962.

The World of Tomorrow, by Kenneth K. Goldstein, New York: McGraw-Hill Book Company, 1969.

ISSUES PAST AND PRESENT

How Should We Handle Our Environment?

Very soon after the first settlers came to the land that was one day to become the United States, they began to change the environment. With tools which they brought ashore from their ships, they cleared the land of trees and plowed the soil. Though the environment could be a rich provider of life's essentials, it was treated by many as if it were an enemy. They thought the forests, for example, harbored wild beasts and even wilder men. Unless the forests were destroyed, men could not survive. When the bounty of nature was nearly exhausted, there was always a new frontier to take advantage of.

Then America became a vast urban, industrial civilization of more than 200 million people. Though there are still vast stretches of wilderness, the mass movement of peoples to escape our endangered environment is no longer possible. Questions, like the following, that once went unasked must now be squarely faced.

1. Is there a difference between human problems and environmental problems? Which is more important? Why?
2. Should we try to shape our environment to fit human needs, or should we try to leave it in a "natural" state? Why? How?

Wrong Side Up

The author of the following selection was a western newspaperman and writer of stories.

JOSEPH K. HOWARD:
MONTANA, HIGH, WIDE, AND HANDSOME, 1943

One day in the spring of 1883, a farmer, John Christiansen, was plowing his fields in North Dakota. He looked up to find that he was being watched by an old and solemn Sioux Indian.

Silently, the old Indian watched as the dark soil curled up and the prairie grass was turned under. Christiansen stopped, leaned against the plow handle, pushed his black Stetson hat back on his head, and rolled a cigarette. He watched, amused, as the old Indian knelt, thrust his fingers into the plow furrow, measured its depth, and fingered the sod and the buried grass.

Then the old Indian straightened up and looked at the farmer. "Wrong side up," he said, and went away.

For a number of years, that was said to be a very funny story indeed, showing the ignorance of the poor Indian. Now, there is a marker on Highway 10 in North Dakota on the spot

where the words were spoken—a little reminder to the white man that his red brother was not so dumb.

1. What did the Indian mean by his brief comment?
2. Why is the Indian now thought to be smarter than people believed him to be in 1883?
3. Do you agree with the Indian? Why?

Peace and Strength in the Wilderness

The frontier in the United States had scarcely officially disappeared in 1890 before men began to search for new frontiers. The rapid and often ruthless development of the nation's natural resources after the Civil War was such a new "frontier" for millions of Americans. Some, like the author of the next selection, tried to find the good things that go with an unspoiled environment by retreating now and then into the wilderness.

GEORGE S. EVANS: *THE WILDERNESS*, 1904

When you go into the wilderness, a feeling of quietness and peace begins to take hold of you, almost without knowing it. You explore deep canyons, climb vast mountains, push into shaggy forests, follow the meanderings of wild streams. Your step becomes lighter, your eyesight better, your hearing sharper. Your brain becomes more active. You get a new view of life. You acquire the ability to decide which things are worthwhile. Your judgment becomes keener. You now understand that man is the product of his environment. You think of the civilization you have left behind. Seen through the eyes of the wilderness, how stupid and silly it all seems.

Whenever work and pleasure become boring, go to the wilderness. It will turn you from a weakling into a man. When you leave the dusty road and "hit the trail," you will have new courage to live your life. You will get new strength. You will soon behold all with a peaceful soul.

1. According to Evans why did man get a new view of life when in the wilderness?
2. What else did the author believe the wilderness added to human life? Do you agree? Why?

Dependence upon Nature

The word conservation is associated more closely with Theodore Roosevelt than with any other President. Soon after his inauguration in 1901, Roosevelt announced that the conservation of natural resources would be one of the main concerns of his Presidency. By speaking about conservation to a conference of state governors, Roosevelt helped to put the topic squarely into the national spotlight.

THEODORE ROOSEVELT:
ADDRESS TO THE GOVERNORS, 1908

The natural resources of our country are in danger of exhaustion if we permit the old wasteful methods of exploiting them to go on.

When people rise from savagery to civilization, and as the needs of the average man become greater, this average man demands more from the natural resources of the country. As the average man demands more, he is apt to lose the sense of his dependence upon nature. He lives in big cities. He works in industries that do not bring him into close touch with nature. He does not realize the demands he is making upon nature. For instance, he finds that it is cheaper to build his house of concrete than of wood, learning only in this way that he has allowed the woods to become exhausted.

We cannot, when the nation becomes fully civilized and very rich, continue to be civilized and rich unless the nation shows more foresight than we are showing at this time.

In the past we have allowed the individual to injure the future of the nation for his own profit. The time has come for a change. As a people we have the right and the duty to protect ourselves and our children against the wasteful development of our natural resources.

Any father who thinks ahead earnestly desires and strives to leave his son prepared for the struggle of life. So this nation should earnestly desire and strive to leave to the next generation the national resources unexhausted.

1. According to Roosevelt why were many Americans unaware that their welfare depended upon nature?
2. How did Americans respond to Roosevelt's warning?
3. Would you agree today with Roosevelt that the United States cannot "continue to be civilized and rich unless the nation shows more foresight than we are showing at this time?" Why?

A Talk with an Ant

The author of the following reading, Don Marquis, was a poet and journalist who worked for the New York Sun *between 1912 and 1922. To his delighted readers he introduced the characters of Archy, a cockroach, and Archy's friend Mehitabel, a cat. At night, when Marquis was not at his typewriter, Archy typed letters to Marquis, his "boss," by hurling himself headfirst onto the typewriter keys. With great effort Archy could operate the lever to shift to a new line of type, but of course he could not shift for capital letters. This letter from Archy to his boss was published in 1935 in the book,* the lives and times of archy and mehitabel.

DON MARQUIS: *WHAT THE ANTS ARE SAYING*, 1935

dear boss i was talking with an ant
the other day
and he handed me a lot of
gossip which ants the world around
are chewing over among themselves
here is what the ants are saying

america was once a paradise
of timberland and stream
but it is dying because of the greed
and money lust of a thousand little kings
who slashed the timber all to hell
and would not be controlled
and changed the climate
and stole the rainfall from posterity   "Posterity" means future generations.
and it wont be long now
it wont be long
till everything is desert
from the alleghenies to the rockies
the deserts are coming
the deserts are spreading
the springs and streams are drying up
one day the mississippi itself
will be a bed of sand
ants and scorpions and centipedes
shall inherit the earth

men talk of money and industry
of hard times and recoveries
of finance and economics
but the ants wait and the scorpions wait
for while men talk they are making deserts all the time
getting the world ready for the conquering ant
it wont be long now it wont be long
till earth is as barren as the moon
and sapless as a mumbled bone

dear boss i relay this information
without any fear that humanity
will take warning and reform
          archy

1. What did Archy believe Americans were doing to the environment?
2. Do you think Archy's fears are correct? Why?

The Science of Ecology

At the end of the 1960's the word ecology *took its place alongside* conservation *as a word familiar to most Americans. The selection is from* Newsweek, *a leading national news magazine.*

NEWSWEEK: *OUR RAVAGED ENVIRONMENT*, 1970

With the coming of the Industrial Revolution, man developed powerful new skills in the exploitation of nature—and also new excuses for using them. For as technology grew so did the need for sources of energy to run it. As wealth expanded so did population. Man began to overpower his environment.

Modern man seems all the time to be cursed with new ways of self-destruction. He came out of World War II armed with nuclear weapons that soon gave him the power to wipe out all human life. His population has since grown at a rate that could threaten disaster all over the world. And now he has come face to face with a new man-made peril, the poisoning of his natural environment with harmful doses of chemicals, garbage, fumes, noise, sewage, heat, ugliness, and urban overcrowding. Nearly unnoticed, pollution has already spread so far that a few scientists say only a drastic cure can prevent devastation as complete as that of nuclear war. There is enough danger to cause a sudden boom in the science of ecology, which examines the precarious relationships between living things and their surroundings. Most important of all, the general public has become so angry and alarmed that it has prodded political leaders into proclaiming conservation of the environment as the chief task of this decade—and perhaps of the rest of the century.

For every American the decay of the environment has become a personal experience—a glass of water bitter with impure substances, a mountain view obscured by haze, the foul smell of industrial smoke or automobile exhaust, the boom of jets or the rumble of trucks so loud that the noise can damage the ear.

The villians are consumers who demand new, more, faster, bigger, cheaper playthings without counting the cost in a dirtier, smellier, sicklier world.

"Precarious" means delicate or fragile.

1. According to the article what was the relationship between increased technology and the use of natural resources? Why?
2. According to the author who is responsible for pollution? Do you agree? Why?
3. What should be the responsibility of the consumer?

As the United States entered the 1970's, debate increasingly centered on some of the practical problems of improving the environment. The following selection is from the magazine National Review.

They Is We

NATIONAL REVIEW: *WHO PAYS FOR ANTI-POLLUTION?* 1970

Who is going to pay for all the environmental cure we are now promising ourselves? The general feeling seems to be that "They" are going to foot the bill—that is, "government" and "Big Business." But the money spent by government to end pollution will come from taxes that *we* pay. Since there is a limit to tax money, the portion of tax money spent on anti-pollution must cut down somewhat the portion spent for other things that we may need or want. The anti-pollution money spent by business will be part of the cost of doing business and thus will be added onto the cost of the product or service that we, the consumers, will pay. In paying for anti-pollution, then, "They" turns out to be "We."

We will face the fact that we can't have everything. We want clean air, land, and water, but *we—we—* are going to have to pay for it. So we shall then begin asking ourselves: How much anti-pollution do we want, compared to other things we also want? Obviously, we want things clean enough so that they won't kill us all off or shorten our lives by half or spread horrible plagues or surround us with ugliness. To prevent even these possible disasters is clearly going to cost a lot. But are we really ready to pay the multiplied taxes and zooming bills in order to get that last 5 per cent of gloop out of the air of our cities so that it will come to our lungs like the breezes on a mountain top?

We men are also part of nature, changing and shaping nature as nature in turn shapes us. There is no Time Machine that can return us to a clean, pure past—which, as it happens, never existed in the first place.

1. What is the author's main message to the reader?
2. Do you agree that controlling the environment will require hard choices? Why?

Summary Questions

1. How serious do you think our environmental problems are?
2. What do you think ought to be done about these problems—by you? by your family? by industry? by government?

The Declaration of Independence

When in the Course of human events, it becomes necessary for one people to dissolve the political bands which have connected them with another, and to assume among the Powers of the earth, the separate and equal station to which the Laws of Nature and of Nature's God entitle them, a decent respect to the opinions of mankind requires that they should declare the causes which impel them to the separation.

We hold these truths to be self-evident, that all men are created equal, that they are endowed by their Creator with certain unalienable Rights, that among these are Life, Liberty and the pursuit of Happiness. That to secure these rights, Governments are instituted among Men, deriving their just powers from the consent of the governed, That whenever any Form of Government becomes destructive of these ends, it is the Right of the People to alter or to abolish it, and to institute new Government, laying its foundation on such principles and organizing its powers in such form, as to them shall seem most likely to effect their Safety and Happiness. Prudence, indeed, will dictate that Governments long established should not be changed for light and transient causes; and accordingly all experience hath shown, that mankind are more disposed to suffer, while evils are sufferable, than to right themselves by abolishing the forms to which they are accustomed. But when a long train of abuses and usurpations, pursuing invariably the same Object evinces a design to reduce them under absolute Despotism, it is their right, it is their duty, to throw off such Government, and to provide new Guards for their future security. — Such has been the patient sufferance of these Colonies; and such is now the necessity which constrains them to alter their former Systems of Government. The history of the present King of Great Britain is a history of repeated injuries and usurpations, all having in direct object the establishment of an absolute Tyranny over these States. To prove this, let Facts be submitted to a candid world.

He has refused his Assent to Laws, the most wholesome and necessary for the public good.

He has forbidden his Governors to pass Laws of immediate and pressing importance, unless suspended in their operation till his Assent should be obtained; and when so suspended, he has utterly neglected to attend to them.

He has refused to pass other Laws for the accommodation of large districts of people, unless those people would relinquish the right of Representation in the Legislature, a right inestimable to them and formidable to tyrants only.

He has called together legislative bodies at places unusual, uncomfortable, and distant from the depository of their Public Records, for the sole purpose of fatiguing them into compliance with his measures.

He has dissolved Representative Houses repeatedly, for opposing with manly firmness his invasions on the rights of the people.

He has refused for a long time, after such dissolutions, to cause others to be elected; whereby the Legislative Powers, incapable of Annihilation, have returned to the People at large for their exercise; the State remaining in the mean time exposed to all the dangers of invasion from without, and convulsions within.

He has endeavoured to prevent the population of these States; for that purpose obstructing the Laws of Naturalization of Foreigners; refusing to pass others to encourage their migration hither, and raising the conditions of new Appropriations of Lands.

He has obstructed the Administration of Justice, by refusing his Assent to Laws for establishing Judiciary Powers.

He has made Judges dependent on his Will alone, for the tenure of their offices, and the amount and payment of their salaries.

He has erected a multitude of New Offices, and sent hither swarms of Officers to harass our People, and eat out their substance.

He has kept among us, in times of peace, Standing Armies without the Consent of our legislature.

He has affected to render the Military independent of and superior to the Civil Power.

He has combined with others to subject us to a jurisdiction foreign to our constitution, and unacknowledged by our laws; giving his Assent to their acts of pretended legislation:

For quartering large bodies of armed troops among us:

For protecting them, by a mock Trial, from Punishment for any Murders which they should commit on the Inhabitants of these States:

For cutting off our Trade with all parts of the world:

For imposing taxes on us without our Consent:

For depriving us in many cases, of the benefits of Trial by Jury:

For transporting us beyond Seas to be tried for pretended offences:

For abolishing the free System of English Laws in a neighbouring Province, establishing therein an Arbitrary government, and enlarging its Boundaries so as to render it at once an example and fit instrument for introducing the same absolute rule into these Colonies:

For taking away our Charters, abolishing our most valuable Laws, and altering fundamentally the Forms of our Governments:

For suspending our own Legislature, and declaring themselves invested with Power to legislate for us in all cases whatsoever.

He has abdicated Government here, by declaring us out of his Protection and waging War against us.

He has plundered our seas, ravaged our Coasts, burnt our towns, and destroyed the lives of our people.

He is at this time transporting large armies of foreign mercenaries to compleat the works of death, desolation and tyranny, already begun with circumstances of Cruelty & perfidy scarcely paralleled in the most barbarous ages, and totally unworthy the Head of a civilized nation.

He has constrained our fellow Citizens taken Captive on the high Seas to bear Arms against their Country, to become the executioners of their friends and Brethren, or to fall themselves by their Hands.

He has excited domestic insurrections amongst us, and has endeavoured to bring on the inhabitants of our frontiers, the merciless Indian Savages, whose known rule of warfare, is an undistinguished destruction of all ages, sexes and conditions.

In every stage of these Oppressions We have Petitioned for Redress in the most humble terms: Our repeated Petitions have been answered only by repeated injury. A Prince, whose character is thus marked by every act which may define a Tyrant, is unfit to be the ruler of a free People.

Nor have We been wanting in attention to our British brethren. We have warned them from time to time of attempts by their legislature to extend an unwarrantable jurisdiction over us. We have reminded them of the circumstances of our emigration and settlement here. We have appealed to their native justice and magnanimity, and we have conjured them by the ties of our common kindred to disavow these usurpations, which, would inevitably interrupt our connections and correspondence. They too have been deaf to the voice of justice and of consanguinity. We

must, therefore, acquiesce in the necessity, which denounces our Separation, and hold them, as we hold the rest of mankind, Enemies in War, in Peace Friends.

We, therefore, the Representatives of the united States of America, in General Congress, Assembled, appealing to the Supreme Judge of the world for the rectitude of our intentions, do, in the Name, and by Authority of the good People of these Colonies, solemnly publish and declare, That these United Colonies are, and of Right ought to be Free and Independent States; that they are Absolved from all Allegiance to the British Crown, and that all political connection between them and the State of Great Britain, is and ought to be totally dissolved; and that as Free and Independent States, they have full Power to levy War, conclude Peace, contract Alliances, establish Commerce, and to do all other Acts and Things which Independent States may of right do. And for the support of this Declaration, with a firm reliance on the Protection of Divine Providence, we mutually pledge to each other our Lives, our Fortunes and our sacred Honor.

The Constitution of the United States

We the people of the United States, in Order to form a more perfect Union, establish Justice, insure domestic Tranquility, provide for the common defence, promote the general Welfare, and secure the Blessings of Liberty to ourselves and our Posterity, do ordain and establish this CONSTITUTION for the United States of America.

Article I

LEGISLATURE

Section 1. All legislative Powers herein granted shall be vested in a Congress of the United States, which shall consist of a Senate and House of Representatives.

House of Representatives

Section 2. The House of Representatives shall be composed of Members chosen every second Year by the People of the several States, and the Electors in each State shall have the Qualifications requisite for Electors of the most numerous Branch of the State Legislature.

Qualifications for Representatives

No Person shall be a Representative who shall not have attained to the Age of twenty-five Years, and been seven Years a Citizen of the United States, and who shall not, when elected, be an Inhabitant of that State in which he shall be chosen.

Method of Apportionment

Representatives and direct Taxes shall be apportioned among the several States which may be included within this Union, according to their respective Numbers, which shall be determined by adding to the whole Number of free Persons, including those bound to Service for a Term of Years, and excluding Indians not taxed, three fifths of all other Persons. The actual Enumeration shall be made within three Years after the first Meeting of the Congress of the United States, and within every subsequent Term of ten Years, in such Manner as they shall by Law direct. The Number of Representatives shall not exceed one for every thirty Thousand, but each state shall have at Least one Representative; and until such enumeration shall be made, the State of New Hampshire shall be entitled to chuse three, Massachusetts eight, Rhode-Island and Providence Plantations one, Connecticut five, New-York six, New Jersey four, Pennsylvania

eight, Delaware one, Maryland six, Virginia ten, North Carolina five, South Carolina five, and Georgia three.

When vacancies happen in the Representation from any State, the Executive Authority thereof shall issue Writs of Election to fill such Vacancies.

The House of Representatives shall chuse their Speaker and other Officers; and shall have the sole Power of Impeachment.

Section 3. The Senate of the United States shall be composed of two Senators from each State, chosen by the Legislature thereof, for six Years; and each Senator shall have one Vote.

Immediately after they shall be assembled in Consequence of the first Election, they shall be divided as equally as may be into three Classes. The Seats of the Senators of the first Class shall be vacated at the Expiration of the second Year, of the second Class at the Expiration of the fourth Year, and of the third Class at the Expiration of the sixth Year, so that one-third may be chosen every second Year; and if Vacancies happen by Resignation, or otherwise, during the Recess of the Legislature of any State, the Executive thereof may make temporary Appointments until the next Meeting of the Legislature, which shall then fill such Vacancies.

No person shall be a Senator who shall not have attained to the Age of thirty Years, and been nine Years a Citizen of the United States, and who shall not, when elected, be an Inhabitant of that State in which he shall be chosen.

The Vice President of the United States shall be President of the Senate, but shall have no vote, unless they be equally divided.

The Senate shall chuse their other Officers, and also a President pro tempore, in the absence of the Vice President, or when he shall exercise the Office of the President of the United States.

The Senate shall have the sole Power to try all Impeachments. When sitting for that purpose, they shall be on Oath or Affirmation. When the President of the United States is tried, the Chief Justice shall preside: And no person shall be convicted without the Concurrence of two thirds of the Members present.

Judgment in Cases of Impeachment shall not extend further than to removal from Office, and disqualification to hold and enjoy any Office of honor, Trust, or Profit under the United States: but the Party convicted shall nevertheless be liable and subject to Indictment, Trial, Judgment, and Punishment, according to Law.

Section 4. The Times, Places and Manner of holding Elections for Senators and Representatives, shall be prescribed in each state by the Legislature thereof: but the Congress may at any time by Law make or alter such Regulations, except as to the Places of Chusing Senators.

The Congress shall assemble at least once in every Year, and such Meeting shall be on the first Monday in December, unless they shall by Law appoint a different Day.

Section 5. Each House shall be the Judge of the Elections, Returns and Qualifications of its own Members, and a Majority of each shall constitute a Quorum to do Business; but a smaller number may adjourn from day to day, and may be authorized to compel the Attendance of absent Members, in such Manner, and under such Penalties, as each House may provide.

Each house may determine the Rules of its Proceedings, punish its Members for disorderly Behavior, and, with the Concurrence of two thirds, expel a Member.

Each House shall keep a Journal of its Proceedings, and from time to

time publish the same, excepting such Parts as may in their Judgment require Secrecy; and the Yeas and Nays of the Members of either House on any question shall, at the Desire of one fifth of those Present, be entered on the Journal.

Neither House, during the Session of Congress, shall, without the Consent of the other, adjourn for more than three days, nor to any other Place than that in which the two Houses shall be sitting.

Members' Compensation and Privileges

Section 6.   The Senators and Representatives shall receive a Compensation for their Services, to be ascertained by Law, and paid out of the Treasury of the United States. They shall in all Cases, except Treason, Felony, and Breach of the Peace, be privileged from Arrest during their Attendance at the Session of their respective Houses, and in going to and returning from the same; and for any Speech or Debate in either House, they shall not be questioned in any other Place.

No Senator or Representative shall, during the Time for which he was elected, be appointed to any civil Office under the Authority of the United States, which shall have been created, or the Emoluments whereof shall have been increased, during such time; and no Person holding any Office under the United States shall be a Member of either House during his continuance in Office.

Money Bills

Section 7.   All Bills for raising Revenue shall originate in the House of Representatives; but the Senate may propose or concur with Amendments as on other bills.

Presidential Veto and Congressional Power to Override

Every Bill which shall have passed the House of Representatives and the Senate, shall, before it become a Law, be presented to the President of the United States; If he approve he shall sign it, but if not he shall return it, with his Objections, to that House in which it shall have originated, who shall enter the Objections at large on their Journal, and proceed to reconsider it. If after such Reconsideration two thirds of that House shall agree to pass the bill, it shall be sent, together with the objections, to the other House, by which it shall likewise be reconsidered, and if approved by two thirds of that House, it shall become a Law. But in all such Cases the Votes of both Houses shall be determined by Yeas and Nays, and the Names of the Persons voting for and against the Bill shall be entered on the Journal of each House respectively. If any Bill shall not be returned by the President within ten Days (Sundays excepted) after it shall have been presented to him, the Same shall be a Law, in like Manner as if he had signed it, unless the Congress by their Adjournment prevent its Return, in which Case it shall not be a Law.

Every Order, Resolution, or Vote to which the Concurrence of the Senate and House of Representatives may be necessary (except on a question of Adjournment) shall be presented to the President of the United States; and before the Same shall take Effect, shall be approved by him, or being disapproved by him, shall be repassed by two thirds of the Senate and House of Representatives, according to the Rules and Limitations prescribed in the Case of a Bill.

Congressional Powers

Section 8.   The Congress shall have Power To lay and collect Taxes, Duties, Imposts and Excises, to pay the Debts and provide for the common Defence and general Welfare of the United States; but all Duties, Imposts and Excises shall be uniform throughout the United States;

To borrow money on the credit of the United States;

To regulate Commerce with foreign Nations, and among the several States, and with the Indian Tribes;

To establish an uniform Rule of Naturalization, and uniform Laws on the subject of Bankruptcies throughout the United States.

To coin Money, regulate the Value thereof, and of foreign Coin, and fix the Standard of Weights and Measures;

To provide for the Punishment of counterfeiting the Securities and current Coin of the United States;

To establish Post Offices and post Roads;

To promote the Progress of Science and useful Arts, by securing for limited Times to Authors and Inventors the exclusive Right to their respective Writings and Discoveries;

To constitute Tribunals inferior to the Supreme Court;

To define and punish Piracies and Felonies committed on the high Seas, and Offenses against the Law of Nations;

To declare War, grant Letters of Marque and Reprisal, and make Rules concerning Captures on Land and Water;

To raise and support Armies, but no Appropriation of Money to that Use shall be for a longer Term than two Years;

To provide and maintain a Navy;

To make Rules for the Government and Regulation of the land and naval forces;

To provide for calling forth the Militia to execute the Laws of the Union, suppress Insurrections and repel Invasions;

To provide for organizing, arming, and disciplining the Militia, and for governing such Part of them as may be employed in the Service of the United States, reserving to the States respectively, the Appointment of the Officers, and the Authority of training the Militia according to the discipline prescribed by Congress;

To exercise exclusive Legislation in all Cases whatsoever, over such District (not exceeding ten Miles square) as may, by Cession of particular States, and the acceptance of Congress, become the Seat of Government of the United States, and to exercise like Authority over all Places purchased by the Consent of the Legislature of the State in which the Same shall be, for the Erection of Forts, Magazines, Arsenals, dock-Yards, and other needful Buildings;—And

To make all Laws which shall be necessary and proper for carrying into Execution the foregoing Powers, and all other Powers vested by this Constitution in the Government of the United States, or in any Department or Officer thereof.

Section 9. The Migration or Importation of such Persons as any of the States now existing shall think proper to admit, shall not be prohibited by the Congress prior to the Year one thousand eight hundred and eight, but a tax or duty may be imposed on such Importation, not exceeding ten dollars for each Person.

Limits on Congressional Power

The privilege of the Writ of Habeas Corpus shall not be suspended, unless when in Cases of Rebellion or Invasion the public Safety may require it.

No Bill of Attainder or ex post facto Law shall be passed.

No capitation, or other direct, Tax shall be laid unless in Proportion to the Census or Enumeration herein before directed to be taken.

No Tax or Duty shall be laid on Articles exported from any State.

No Preference shall be given by any Regulation of Revenue to the Ports of one State over those of another: nor shall Vessels bound to, or from, one State, be obliged to enter, clear, or pay Duties in another.

No Money shall be drawn from the Treasury, but in Consequence of Appropriations made by Law; and a regular Statement and Account of the Receipts and Expenditures of all public Money shall be published from time to time.

No Title of Nobility shall be granted by the United States: And no Person holding any Office of Profit or Trust under them, shall, without the Consent of the Congress, accept of any present, Emolument, Office, or Title, of any kind whatever, from any King, Prince, or foreign State.

Limits on Powers of the States

Section 10. No State shall enter into any Treaty, Alliance, or Confederation; grant Letters of Marque and Reprisal; coin Money; emit Bills of Credit; make any Thing but gold and silver Coin a Tender in Payment of Debts; pass any Bill of Attainder, ex post facto Law, or Law impairing the Obligation of Contracts, or grant any Title of Nobility.

No State shall, without the Consent of the Congress, lay any Imposts or Duties on Imports or Exports, except what may be absolutely necessary for executing its inspection Laws: and the net Produce of all Duties and Imposts, laid by any State on Imports or Exports, shall be for the Use of the Treasury of the United States; and all such Laws shall be subject to the Revision and Control of the Congress.

No State shall, without the Consent of Congress, lay any duty of Tonnage, keep Troops, or Ships of War in time of Peace, enter into any Agreement or Compact with another State, or with a foreign Power, or engage in War, unless actually invaded, or in such imminent Danger as will not admit of delay.

Article II

EXECUTIVE

President

Section 1. The executive Power shall be vested in a President of the United States of America. He shall hold his Office during the Term of four years, and, together with the Vice-President, chosen for the same Term, be elected, as follows:

Election of President

Each State shall appoint, in such Manner as the Legislature thereof may direct, a Number of Electors, equal to the whole Number of Senators and Representatives to which the State may be entitled in the Congress: but no Senator or Representative, or Person holding an Office of Trust or Profit under the United States, shall be appointed an Elector.

Electors

The Electors shall meet in their respective States, and vote by Ballot for two persons, of whom one at least shall not be an Inhabitant of the same State with themselves. And they shall make a List of all the Persons voted for, and of the Number of Votes for each; which List they shall sign and certify, and transmit sealed to the Seat of the Government of the United States, directed to the President of the Senate. The President of the Senate shall, in the Presence of the Senate and House of Representatives, open all the Certificates, and the Votes shall then be counted. The Person having the greatest Number of Votes shall be the President, if such Number be a Majority of the whole Number of Electors appointed; and if there be more than one who have such Majority, and have an equal Number of Votes, then the House of Representatives shall immediately chuse by Ballot one of them for President; and if no Person have a Majority, then from the five highest on the List the said House shall in like Manner chuse the President. But in chusing the President, the Votes shall be taken by States, the Representation from each State having one Vote; a quorum for this Purpose shall consist of a Member or Members from two-thirds of the States, and a Majority of all the States shall be necessary to a Choice. In every Case, after the Choice of the President, the Person having the greatest Number of Votes of the Electors shall be the Vice-President. But if there should remain two or more who have equal votes, the Senate shall chuse from them by Ballot the Vice-President.

The Congress may determine the Time of chusing the Electors, and the

Day on which they shall give their Votes; which Day shall be the same throughout the United States.

No person except a natural-born Citizen, or a Citizen of the United States, at the time of the Adoption of this Constitution, shall be eligible to the Office of President; neither shall any Person be eligible to that Office who shall not have attained to the Age of thirty-five years, and been fourteen Years a Resident within the United States. *Qualifications of President*

In Case of the Removal of the President from Office, or of his Death, Resignation, or Inability to discharge the Powers and Duties of the said Office, the same shall devolve on the Vice President, and the Congress may by Law provide for the Case of Removal, Death, Resignation, or Inability, both of the President and Vice President, declaring what Officer shall then act as President, and such Officer shall act accordingly, until the disability be removed, or a President shall be elected. *Succession to the Presidency*

The President shall, at stated Times, receive for his Services a Compensation, which shall neither be increased nor diminished during the Period for which he shall have been elected, and he shall not receive within that Period any other Emolument from the United States, or any of them. *Compensation*

Before he enter on the execution of his Office, he shall take the following Oath or Affirmation:— "I do solemnly swear (or affirm) that I will faithfully execute the Office of President of the United States, and will, to the best of my Ability, preserve, protect, and defend the Constitution of the United States." *Oath of Office*

Section 2. The President shall be Commander in Chief of the Army and Navy of the United States, and of the Militia of the several States, when called into the actual Service of the United States; he may require the Opinion, in writing, of the principal Officer in each of the executive Departments, upon any subject relating to the Duties of their respective Offices, and he shall have Power to Grant Reprieves and Pardons for Offenses against the United States, except in Cases of Impeachment. *Powers of the President*

He shall have Power, by and with the Advice and Consent of the Senate, to make Treaties, provided two thirds of the Senators present concur; and he shall nominate, and by and with the Advice and Consent of the Senate, shall appoint Ambassadors, other public Ministers and Consuls, Judges of the supreme Court, and all other Officers of the United States, whose Appointments are not herein otherwise provided for, and which shall be established by Law: but the Congress may by Law vest the Appointment of such inferior Officers, as they think proper, in the President alone, in the Courts of Law, or in the Heads of Departments. *Making of Treaties*

The President shall have Power to fill up all Vacancies that may happen during the Recess of the Senate, by granting Commissions which shall expire at the End of their next Session. *Vacancies*

Section 3. He shall from time to time give to the Congress Information of the State of the Union, and recommend to their Consideration such Measures as he shall judge necessary and expedient; he may, on extraordinary occasions, convene both Houses, or either of them, and in Case of Disagreement between them, with respect to the Time of Adjournment, he may adjourn them to such Time as he shall think proper; he shall receive Ambassadors and other public Ministers; he shall take Care that the Laws be faithfully executed, and shall Commission all the Officers of the United States. *Additional Duties and Powers*

Section 4. The President, Vice President and all civil Officers of the United States, shall be removed from Office on Impeachment for, and Conviction of, Treason, Bribery, or other high Crimes and Misdemeanors. *Impeachment*

JUDICIARY

Courts, Judges, Compensation

Jurisdiction

Trial by Jury

Treason

FEDERAL SYSTEM

Privileges and Immunities of Citizens

Article III

Section 1. The judicial Power of the United States, shall be vested in one supreme Court, and in such inferior Courts as the Congress may from time to time ordain and establish. The Judges, both of the supreme and inferior Courts, shall hold their Offices during good Behaviour, and shall, at stated Times, receive for their Services, a Compensation, which shall not be diminished during their Continuance in Office.

Section 2. The judicial Power shall extend to all Cases, in Law and Equity, arising under this Constitution, the Laws of the United States, and treaties made, or which shall be made, under their Authority;—to all Cases affecting ambassadors, other public ministers and consuls;—to all cases of admiralty and maritime Jurisdiction;—to Controversies to which the United States shall be a Party;—to Controversies between two or more States;—between a State and Citizens of another State;—between Citizens of different States,—between Citizens of the same State claiming Lands under Grants of different States, and between a State, or the Citizens thereof, and foreign States, Citizens or Subjects.

In all Cases affecting Ambassadors, other public Ministers and Consuls, and those in which a State shall be Party, the supreme Court shall have original Jurisdiction. In all the other Cases before mentioned, the supreme Court shall have appellate Jurisdiction, both as to Law and Fact, with such Exceptions, and under such Regulations as the Congress shall make.

The trial of all Crimes, except in Cases of Impeachment, shall be by Jury; and such Trial shall be held in the State where the said Crimes shall have been committed; but when not committed within any State, the Trial shall be at such Place or Places as the Congress may by Law have directed.

Section 3. Treason against the United States, shall consist only in levying War against them, or in adhering to their Enemies, giving them Aid and Comfort. No Person shall be convicted of Treason unless on the Testimony of two Witnesses to the same overt Act, or on Confession in open Court.

The Congress shall have power to declare the Punishment of Treason, but no Attainder of Treason shall work Corruption of Blood, or Forfeiture except during the Life of the Person attainted.

Article IV

Section 1. Full Faith and Credit shall be given in each State to the public Acts, Records, and judicial Proceedings of every other State. And the Congress may by general Laws prescribe the Manner in which such Acts, Records and Proceedings shall be proved, and the Effect thereof.

Section 2. The Citizens of each State shall be entitled to all Privileges and Immunities of Citizens in the several states.

A Person charged in any State with Treason, Felony, or other Crime, who shall flee from Justice, and be found in another State, shall on demand of the executive Authority of the State from which he fled, be delivered up, to be removed to the State having Jurisdiction of the crime.

No Person held to Service or Labour in one State, under the Laws thereof, escaping into another, shall, in Consequence of any Law or Regulation therein, be discharged from such Service or Labour, but shall be delivered up on Claim of the Party to whom such Service or Labour may be due.

Section 3. New States may be admitted by the Congress into this Union; but no new State shall be formed or erected within the Jurisdiction

of any other State; nor any State be formed by the Junction of two or more States, or parts of States, without the Consent of the Legislatures of the States concerned as well as of the Congress.

Admission and Formation of New States Governing of Territories

The Congress shall have Power to dispose of and make all needful Rules and Regulations respecting the Territory or other Property belonging to the United States; and nothing in this Constitution shall be so construed as to Prejudice any Claims of the United States, or of any particular State.

Section 4. The United States shall guarantee to every State in this Union a Republican Form of Government, and shall protect each of them against Invasion; and on Application of the Legislature, or of the Executive (when the Legislature cannot be convened) against domestic Violence.

Federal Protection of the States

Article V

AMENDMENTS

The Congress, whenever two-thirds of both Houses shall deem it necessary, shall propose Amendments to this Constitution, or, on the Application of the Legislatures of two-thirds of the several States, shall call a Convention for proposing Amendments, which, in either Case, shall be valid to all Intents and Purposes, as part of this Constitution, when ratified by the Legislatures of three-fourths of the several States, or by Conventions in three-fourths thereof, as the one or the other Mode of Ratification may be proposed by the Congress; Provided that no Amendment which may be made prior to the Year One thousand eight hundred and eight shall in any Manner affect the first and fourth Clauses in the Ninth Section of the first Article; and that no State, without its Consent, shall be deprived of its equal Suffrage in the Senate.

Article VI

CONSTITUTION AS SUPREME LAW

All Debts contracted and Engagements entered into, before the Adoption of this Constitution, shall be as valid against the United States under this Constitution, as under the Confederation.

This Constitution, and the Laws of the United States which shall be made in Pursuance thereof; and all Treaties made, or which shall be made, under the Authority of the United States, shall be the supreme Law of the Land; and the Judges in every State shall be bound thereby, any Thing in the Constitution or Laws of any State to the Contrary notwithstanding.

The Senators and Representatives before mentioned, and the Members of the several State Legislatures, and all executive and judicial Officers, both of the United States and of the several States, shall be bound by Oath or Affirmation to support this Constitution; but no religious Test shall ever be required as a qualification to any Office or public Trust under the United States.

Article VII

RATIFICATION

The Ratification of the Conventions of nine States shall be sufficient for the Establishment of this Constitution between the States so ratifying the same.

Done in Convention by the Unanimous Consent of the States present the Seventeenth Day of September in the Year of our Lord one thousand seven hundred and Eighty seven, and of the Independence of the United States of America the Twelfth. In Witness whereof We have hereunto subscribed our Names.

Articles in Addition to, and Amendment of, the Constitution of the United States of America, Proposed by Congress, and Ratified by the Legislatures of the Several States, Pursuant to the Fifth Article of the Original Constitution.

FREEDOMS

Speech, Press, Assembly, and Petition

Amendment I [1791]

Congress shall make no law respecting an establishment of religion, or prohibiting the free exercise thereof; or abridging the freedom of speech, or of the press; or the right of the people peaceably to assemble, and to petition the Government for a redress of grievances.

RIGHT TO BEAR ARMS

Amendment II [1791]

A well regulated Militia, being necessary to the security of a free State, the right of the people to keep and bear Arms shall not be infringed.

QUARTERING OF SOLDIERS

Amendment III [1791]

No soldier shall, in time of peace, be quartered in any house, without the consent of the Owner, nor in time of war, but in a manner to be prescribed by law.

FREEDOM OF PERSONS

Warrants, Searches, and Seizure

Amendment IV [1791]

The right of the people to be secure in their persons, houses, papers, and effects, against unreasonable searches and seizures, shall not be violated, and no Warrants shall issue, but upon probable cause, supported by Oath or affirmation, and particularly describing the place to be searched, and the persons or things to be seized.

CAPITAL CRIMES

Protection of the Accused

Amendment V [1791]

No person shall be held to answer for a capital or otherwise infamous crime, unless on a presentment or indictment of a Grand Jury, except in cases arising in the land or naval forces, or in the Militia, when in actual service in time of War or public danger; nor shall any person be subject for the same offence to be twice put in jeopardy of life or limb; nor shall be compelled in any criminal case to be a witness against himself, nor be deprived of life, liberty, or property, without due process of law; nor shall

Compensation

private property be taken for public use, without just compensation.

TRIAL BY JURY

Accusation, Witnesses, Counsel

Amendment VI [1791]

In all criminal prosecutions, the accused shall enjoy the right to a speedy and public trial, by an impartial jury of the State and district wherein the crime shall have been committed, which district shall have been previously ascertained by law, and to be informed of the nature and cause of the accusation; to be confronted with the witnesses against him; to have compulsory process for obtaining witnesses in his favor, and to have the Assistance of Counsel for his defence.

CIVIL LAW

Amendment VII [1791]

In suits at common law, where the value in controversy shall exceed twenty dollars, the right of trial by jury shall be preserved, and no fact tried by a jury, shall be otherwise reexamined in any Court of the United States, than according to the rules of the common law.

Amendment VIII [1791]

BAILS, FINES, AND PUNISHMENTS

Excessive bail shall not be required, nor excessive fines imposed, nor cruel and unusual punishments inflicted.

Amendment IX [1791]

RIGHTS RETAINED BY THE PEOPLE

The enumeration in the Constitution, of certain rights, shall not be construed to deny or disparage others retained by the people.

Amendment X [1791]

RIGHTS RESERVED TO THE STATES

The powers not delegated to the United States by the Constitution, nor prohibited by it to the States, are reserved to the States respectively, or to the people.

Amendment XI [1798]

JURISDICTIONAL LIMITS

The Judicial power of the United States shall not be construed to extend to any suit in law or equity, commenced or prosecuted against one of the United States by Citizens of another State, or by Citizens or Subjects of any Foreign State.

Amendment XII [1804]

ELECTORAL COLLEGE

The Electors shall meet in their respective States and vote by ballot for President and Vice-President, one of whom, at least, shall not be an inhabitant of the same State with themselves; they shall name in their ballots the person voted for as President, and in distinct ballots the person voted for as Vice-President, and they shall make distinct lists of all persons voted for as President, and of all persons voted for as Vice-President, and of the number of votes for each, which lists they shall sign and certify, and transmit sealed to the seat of the government of the United States, directed to the President of the Senate;—The President of the Senate shall, in the presence of the Senate and House of Representatives, open all the certificates and the votes shall then be counted;—The person having the greatest number of votes for President, shall be the President, if such number be a majority of the whole number of Electors appointed; and if no person have such majority, then from the persons having the highest numbers not exceeding three on the list of those voted for as President, the House of Representatives shall choose immediately, by ballot, the President. But in choosing the President, the votes shall be taken by states, the representation from each state having one vote; a quorum for this purpose shall consist of a member or members from two-thirds of the states, and a majority of all the states shall be necessary to a choice. And if the House of Representatives shall not choose a President whenever the right of choice shall devolve upon them, before the fourth day of March next following, then the Vice-President shall act as President, as in the case of the death or other constitutional disability of the President.—The person having the the greatest number of votes as Vice-President, shall be the Vice-President, if such number be a majority of the whole number of Electors appointed, and if no person have a majority, then from the two highest numbers on the list, the Senate shall choose the Vice-President; a quorum for the purpose shall consist of two-thirds of the whole number of Senators, and a majority of the whole number shall be necessary to a choice. But no person constitutionally ineligible to the office of President shall be eligible to that of Vice-President of the United States.

ABOLITION OF SLAVERY

Amendment XIII [1865]

Section 1. Neither slavery nor involuntary servitude, except as a punishment for crime whereof the party shall have been duly convicted, shall exist within the United States, or any place subject to their jurisdiction.

Section 2. Congress shall have power to enforce this article by appropriate legislation.

CITIZENSHIP

Due Process of Law

Amendment XIV [1868]

Section 1. All persons born or naturalized in the United States, and subject to the jurisdiction thereof, are citizens of the United States and of the State wherein they reside. No State shall make or enforce any law which shall abridge the privileges or immunities of citizens of the United States; nor shall any State deprive any person of life, liberty, or property, without due process of law; nor deny to any person within its jurisdiction the equal protection of the laws.

Apportionment

Right to Vote

Section 2. Representatives shall be apportioned among the several States according to their respective numbers, counting the whole number of persons in each State, excluding Indians not taxed. But when the right to vote at any election for the choice of electors for President and Vice-President of the United States, Representatives in Congress, the Executive and Judicial officers of a State, or the members of the Legislature thereof, is denied to any of the male inhabitants of such State, being twenty-one years of age, and citizens of the United States, or in any way abridged, except for participation in rebellion, or other crime, the basis of representation therein shall be reduced in the proportion which the number of such male citizens shall bear to the whole number of male citizens twenty-one years of age in such State.

Disqualification for Office

Section 3. No person shall be a Senator or Representative in Congress, or elector of President and Vice-President, or hold any office, civil or military, under the United States, or under any State, who, having previously taken an oath, as a member of Congress, or as an officer of the United States, or as a member of any State legislature, or as an executive or judicial officer of any State, to support the Constitution of the United States, shall have engaged in insurrection or rebellion against the same, or given aid or comfort to the enemies thereof. But Congress may by a vote of two-thirds of each House, remove such disability.

Public Debt

Section 4. The validity of the public debt of the United States, authorized by law, including debts incurred for payment of pensions and bounties for services in suppressing insurrection or rebellion, shall not be questioned. But neither the United States nor any State shall assume or pay any debt or obligation incurred in aid of insurrection or rebellion against the United States, or any claim for the loss or emancipation of any slave; but all such debts, obligations, and claims shall be held illegal and void.

Section 5. The Congress shall have the power to enforce, by appropriate legislation, the provisions of this article.

RIGHT TO VOTE

Amendment XV [1870]

Section 1. The right of citizens of the United States to vote shall not be denied or abridged by the United States or by any State on account of race, color, or previous condition of servitude.

Section 2. The Congress shall have power to enforce this article by appropriate legislation.

Amendment XVI [1913]

INCOME TAX

The Congress shall have power to lay and collect taxes on incomes, from whatever source derived, without apportionment among the several States, and without regard to any census or enumeration.

Amendment XVII [1913]

SENATORS
Election

The Senate of the United States shall be composed of two Senators from each State, elected by the people thereof, for six years; and each Senator shall have one vote. The electors in each State shall have the qualifications requisite for electors of the most numerous branch of the State legislatures.

Vacancies

When vacancies happen in the representation of any State in the Senate, the executive authority of such State shall issue writs of election to fill such vacancies: *Provided*, That the legislature of any State may empower the executive thereof to make temporary appointments until the people fill the vacancies by election as the legislature may direct.

This amendment shall not be so construed as to affect the election or term of any Senator chosen before it becomes valid as part of the Constitution.

Amendment XVIII [1919]

PROHIBITION

Section 1. After one year from the ratification of this article the manufacture, sale, or transportation of intoxicating liquors within, the importation thereof into, or the exportation thereof from the United States and all territory subject to the jurisdiction thereof for beverage purposes is hereby prohibited.

Section 2. The Congress and the several States shall have concurrent power to enforce this article by appropriate legislation.

Section 3. This article shall be inoperative unless it shall have been ratified as an amendment to the Constitution by the legislatures of the several States, as provided in the Constitution, within seven years from the date of the submission hereof to the States by the Congress.

Amendment XIX [1920]

FEMALE SUFFRAGE

The right of citizens of the United States to vote shall not be denied or abridged by the United States or by any State on account of sex.

Congress shall have power to enforce this article by appropriate legislation.

Amendment XX [1933]

TERMS OF OFFICE

Section 1. The terms of the President and Vice-President shall end at noon on the 20th day of January, and the terms of Senators and Representatives at noon on the 3d day of January, of the years in which such terms would have ended if this article had not been ratified; and the terms of their successors shall then begin.

Section 2. The Congress shall assemble at least once in every year, and such meeting shall begin at noon on the 3d day of January, unless they shall by law appoint a different day.

Succession

Section 3. If, at the time fixed for the beginning of the term of the President, the President elect shall have died, the Vice-President elect shall become President. If a President shall not have been chosen before the time fixed for the beginning of his term, or if the President elect shall

have failed to qualify, then the Vice-President elect shall act as President until a President shall have qualified; and the Congress may by law provide for the case wherein neither a President elect nor a Vice-President elect shall have qualified, declaring who shall then act as President, or the manner in which one who is to act shall be selected, and such person shall act accordingly until a President or Vice-President shall have qualified.

Section 4. The Congress may by law provide for the case of the death of any of the persons from whom the House of Representatives may choose a President whenever the right of choice shall have devolved upon them, and for the case of the death of any of the persons from whom the Senate may choose a Vice-President whenever the right of choice shall have devolved upon them.

Section 5. Sections 1 and 2 shall take effect on the 15th day of October following the ratification of this article.

Section 6. This article shall be inoperative unless it shall have been ratified as an amendment to the Constitution by the legislatures of three-fourths of the several States within seven years from the date of its submission.

REPEAL OF PROHIBITION

Amendment XXI [1933]

Section 1. The eighteenth article of amendment to the Constitution of the United States is hereby repealed.

Section 2. The transportation or importation into any State, Territory, or possession of the United States for delivery or use therein of intoxicating liquors, in violation of the laws thereof, is hereby prohibited.

Section 3. This article shall be inoperative unless it shall have been ratified as an amendment to the Constitution by conventions in the several States, as provided in the Constitution, within seven years from the date of the submission hereof to the States by the Congress.

TERM OF PRESIDENT

Amendment XXII [1951]

No person shall be elected to the office of the President more than twice, and no person who has held the office of President, or acted as President, for more than two years of a term to which some other person was elected President shall be elected to the office of the President more than once.

But this Article shall not apply to any person holding the office of President when this Article was proposed by the Congress, and shall not prevent any person who may be holding the office of President, or acting as President, during the term within which this Article becomes operative from holding the office of President or acting as President during the remainder of such term.

WASHINGTON, D.C.

Enfranchisement of Voters in Federal Elections

Amendment XXIII [1961]

Section 1. The District constituting the seat of Government of the United States shall appoint in such manner as the Congress may direct:

A number of electors of President and Vice President equal to the whole number of Senators and Representatives in Congress to which the District would be entitled if it were a State, but in no event more than the least populous State; they shall be in addition to those appointed by the States, but they shall be considered, for the purposes of the election of President and Vice President, to be electors appointed by a State; and they shall meet in the District and perform such duties as provided by the twelfth article of amendment.

Section 2. The Congress shall have power to enforce this article by appropriate legislation.

Amendment XXIV [1964]

POLL TAX

Section 1. The right of citizens of the United States to vote in any primary or other election for President or Vice President, for electors for President or Vice President, or for Senator or Representative in Congress, shall not be denied or abridged by the United States or any State by reason of failure to pay any poll tax or other tax.

Section 2. The Congress shall have the power to enforce this article by appropriate legislation.

Amendment XXV [1967]

SUCCESSION

Section 1. In case of the removal of the President from office or his death or resignation, the Vice President shall become President.

Section 2. Whenever there is a vacancy in the office of the Vice President, the President shall nominate a Vice President who shall take the office upon confirmation by a majority vote of both houses of Congress.

Section 3. Whenever the President transmits to the President pro tempore of the Senate and the Speaker of the House of Representatives his written declaration that he is unable to discharge the powers and duties of his office, and until he transmits to them a written declaration to the contrary, such powers and duties shall be discharged by the Vice President as Acting President.

Section 4. Whenever the Vice President and a majority of either the principal officers of the executive departments, or of such other body as Congress may by law provide, transmit to the President pro tempore of the Senate and the Speaker of the House of Representatives their written declaration that the President is unable to discharge the powers and duties of his office, the Vice President shall immediately assume the powers and duties of the office as Acting President.

Thereafter, when the President transmits to the President pro tempore of the Senate and the Speaker of the House of Representatives his written declaration that no inability exists, he shall resume the powers and duties of his office unless the Vice President and a majority of either the principal officers of the executive departments, or of such other body as Congress may by law provide, transmit within four days to the President pro tempore of the Senate and the Speaker of the House of Representatives their written declaration that the President is unable to discharge the powers and duties of his office. Thereupon Congress shall decide the issue, assembling within 48 hours for that purpose if not in session. If the Congress, within 21 days after receipt of the latter written declaration, or, if Congress is not in session, within 21 days after Congress is required to assemble, determines by two-thirds vote of both houses that the President is unable to discharge the powers and duties of his office, the Vice President shall continue to discharge the same as Acting President; otherwise, the President shall resume the power and duties of his office.

Amendment XXVI [1971]

VOTING AT AGE 18

Section 1. The right of citizens of the United States, who are eighteen years of age or older, to vote shall not be denied or abridged by the United States or any State on account of age.

Section 2. The Congress shall have power to enforce this article by appropriate legislation.

The United States Today

State	Admission Date	Total Area (Sq. Miles)	1970 Population
Alabama	1819	51,609	3,373,006
Alaska	1959	586,412	294,607
Arizona	1912	113,909	1,752,122
Arkansas	1836	53,104	1,886,210
California	1850	158,693	19,715,490
Colorado	1876	104,247	2,178,176
Connecticut	1788	5,009	2,987,950
Delaware	1787	2,057	542,979
Florida	1845	58,560	6,671,162
Georgia	1788	58,876	4,492,038
Hawaii	1959	6,450	748,575
Idaho	1890	83,557	698,275
Illinois	1818	56,400	10,977,908
Indiana	1816	36,291	5,143,422
Iowa	1846	56,290	2,789,893
Kansas	1861	82,264	2,222,173
Kentucky	1792	40,395	3,160,555
Louisiana	1812	48,523	3,564,310
Maine	1820	33,215	977,260
Maryland	1788	10,577	3,874,642
Massachusetts	1788	8,257	5,630,224
Michigan	1837	58,216	8,778,187
Minnesota	1858	84,068	3,767,975
Mississippi	1817	47,716	2,158,872
Missouri	1821	69,686	4,636,247
Montana	1889	147,138	682,133
Nebraska	1867	77,227	1,468,101
Nevada	1864	110,540	481,893
New Hampshire	1788	9,304	722,753
New Jersey	1787	7,836	7,084,992
New Mexico	1912	121,666	998,257
New York	1788	49,576	17,979,712
North Carolina	1789	52,586	4,961,832
North Dakota	1889	70,665	610,648
Ohio	1803	41,222	10,542,030
Oklahoma	1907	69,919	2,498,378
Oregon	1859	96,981	2,056,171
Pennsylvania	1787	45,333	11,669,565
Rhode Island	1790	1,214	922,461
South Carolina	1788	31,055	2,522,881
South Dakota	1889	77,047	661,406
Tennessee	1796	42,244	3,838,777
Texas	1845	267,339	10,989,123
Utah	1896	84,916	1,060,631
Vermont	1791	9,609	437,744
Virginia	1788	40,817	4,543,249
Washington	1889	68,192	3,352,892
West Virginia	1863	24,181	1,701,913
Wisconsin	1848	56,154	4,366,766
Wyoming	1890	97,914	328,591

★ State Capitals
● Major Metropolitan Centers
▨ Extended Urban Areas

Presidents of the United States

1789	GEORGE WASHINGTON,	*Virginia*
1797	JOHN ADAMS,	*Massachusetts, Federalist*
1801	THOMAS JEFFERSON,	*Virginia, Democratic-Republican*
1809	JAMES MADISON,	*Virginia, Democratic-Republican*
1817	JAMES MONROE,	*Virginia, Democratic-Republican*
1825	JOHN QUINCY ADAMS,	*Mass., Democratic-Republican*
1829	ANDREW JACKSON,	*Tennessee, Democratic*
1837	MARTIN VAN BUREN,	*New York, Democratic*
1841	WILLIAM H. HARRISON,	*Ohio, Whig*
1841	JOHN TYLER,	*Virginia, Whig*
1845	JAMES K. POLK,	*Tennessee, Democratic*
1849	ZACHARY TAYLOR,	*Louisiana, Whig*
1850	MILLARD FILLMORE,	*New York, Whig*
1853	FRANKLIN PIERCE,	*New Hampshire, Democratic*
1857	JAMES BUCHANAN,	*Pennsylvania, Democratic*
1861	ABRAHAM LINCOLN,	*Illinois, Republican*
1865	ANDREW JOHNSON,	*Tennessee, Republican*
1869	ULYSSES S. GRANT,	*Illinois, Republican*
1877	RUTHERFORD B. HAYES,	*Ohio, Republican*
1881	JAMES A. GARFIELD,	*Ohio, Republican*
1881	CHESTER A. ARTHUR,	*New York, Republican*
1885	GROVER CLEVELAND,	*New York, Democratic*
1889	BENJAMIN HARRISON,	*Indiana, Republican*
1893	GROVER CLEVELAND,	*New York, Democratic*
1897	WILLIAM McKINLEY,	*Ohio, Republican*
1901	THEODORE ROOSEVELT,	*New York, Republican*
1909	WILLIAM HOWARD TAFT,	*Ohio, Republican*
1913	WOODROW WILSON,	*New Jersey, Democratic*
1921	WARREN G. HARDING,	*Ohio, Republican*
1923	CALVIN COOLIDGE,	*Massachusetts, Republican*
1929	HERBERT HOOVER,	*California, Republican*
1933	FRANKLIN D. ROOSEVELT,	*New York, Democratic*
1945	HARRY S. TRUMAN,	*Missouri, Democratic*
1953	DWIGHT D. EISENHOWER,	*New York, Republican*
1961	JOHN F. KENNEDY,	*Massachusetts, Democratic*
1963	LYNDON B. JOHNSON,	*Texas, Democratic*
1969	RICHARD M. NIXON,	*New York, Republican*

Presidential Administrations

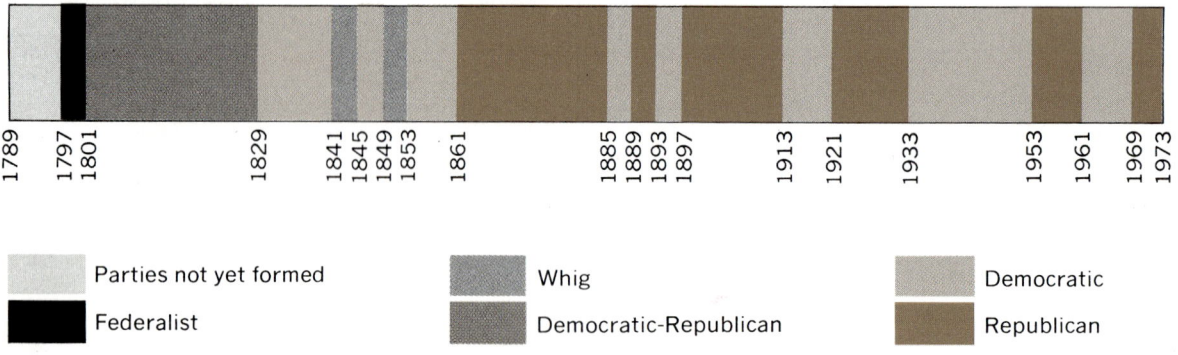

Acknowledgments

From CRISIS IN BLACK AND WHITE, by Charles E. Silberman. Copyright © 1964 by Random House, Inc. Reprinted by permission of the publisher. • Copyright 1951 by Langston Hughes. Reprinted from THE PANTHER AND THE LASH, by Langston Hughes, by permission of Alfred A. Knopf, Inc. • "A Case of Hypochondria," by Daniel J. Boorstin, from *Newsweek*, July 6, 1970. Copyright Newsweek, Inc. • GOD'S OWN JUNKYARD, by Peter Blake. Holt, Rinehart and Winston, Inc., 1964. • "Civilized World Plunging into Computerized Madness," by Stewart Udall, from *Newsday*, 1970. Reprinted with permission from Newsday, Inc. • From CONTEMPORARY CIVILIZATION, by Henry S. Commager. Copyright © 1964 by Scott, Foresman and Company. Reprinted by permission of the publisher. • "What We Must Do," by John Platt, from *Science*, Vol. 166, November 28, 1969. Copyright 1969 by the American Association for the Advancement of Science. • THE HUMAN ENVIRONMENT AND BUSINESS, by Henry Ford II. Weybright & Talley, Inc., a division of David McKay Company, Inc. • "If I Had A Hammer" (The Hammer Song), Words and Music by Lee Hays & Pete Seeger. TRO-© Copyright 1958 and 1962 Ludlow Music, Inc. New York, New York. Used by permission. • AN ANGRY MAN TALKS UP TO YOUTH, by K. Ross Toole. Universal Publishing and Distributing Corporation, 1970. • Copyright 1969 by Eric Sevareid, reprinted by permission of the Harold Matson Company, Inc. • Excerpt from LAND OF THE SPOTTED EAGLE, by Chief Standing Bear. Houghton Mifflin Company, 1933. • Adapted from BLACK POLITICAL POWER IN AMERICA, by Chuck Stone. Copyright © 1968, by C. Sumner Stone, used by permission of the publisher, The Bobbs-Merrill Company, Inc. • THE AFRICAN PAST, by Basil Davidson. Little, Brown and Company, 1966. • Adapted from pp. 160–164 in WAS AMERICA A MISTAKE? by Henry Steele Commager and Elmo Giordanetti. Copyright © 1967 by Henry Steele Commager and Elmo Giordanetti. Reprinted by permission of Harper & Row, Publishers, Inc. • "Explanation of the Black Psyche," by James O. Killen, from *The New York Times Magazine*, 1964. © 1964 by The New York Times Company. Reprinted by permission. • "Our Beginnings: A Lesson for Today," by Henry S. Commager, from *The New York Times Magazine*, January 26, 1941. © 1941 by The New York Times Company. Reprinted by permission. • "Our Declaration Is Still a Rallying Cry," by Henry S. Commager, from *The New York Times Magazine*, July 2, 1961. © 1961 by The New York Times Company. Reprinted by permission. • "Responsible for the Abuse of That Liberty," by Richard L. Tobin, from *Saturday Review*, January 13, 1968. Copyright 1968 Saturday Review, Inc. • "The Last of the Rugged Individualists," by Wayne Kernodle. Copyright © 1959, by Minneapolis Star and Tribune Co., Inc. Reprinted from the January 1960 issue of *Harper's Magazine* by permission. • "The Natural Limits of Slavery's Expansion," by Charles S. Ramsdell, from *Mississippi Valley Historical Review*, XVI (September 1929). • Excerpt from THE COMING FURY, by Bruce Catton. Copyright © 1961 by Bruce Catton. Reprinted by permission of Doubleday and Company, Inc. • From THE AUTOBIOGRAPHY OF MALCOLM X, reprinted by permission of Grove Press, Inc. Copyright © 1964 by Alex Haley and Malcolm X; copyright © 1965 by Alex Haley and Betty Shabazz. • "Separatism? We Are Separated—And That's the Cause of All Our Woes," by Whitney Young, Jr. Reprinted by permission of *Ebony Magazine*, copyright 1970 by Johnson Publishing Company, Inc. • From PORTRAITS AND PROTESTS, by Sarah N. Cleghorn. All rights reserved. Reprinted by permission of Holt, Rinehart and Winston, Inc. • From AMERICAN CAPITALISM, by Louis Hacker. Copyright © 1957 by Litton Educational Publishing Inc. Published by Van Nostrand Reinhold Company. • LIVING DOCUMENTS IN AMERICAN HISTORY, edited by John Anthony Scott. Copyright © 1963 by John Anthony Scott. Reprinted by permission of Washington Square Press, a division of Simon & Schuster, Inc. • MY LIFE AND WORK, by Henry Ford and Samuel Crowther. Doubleday and Company, Inc., 1923. • WE TOO ARE THE PEOPLE, by Louise V. Armstrong. Little, Brown and Company, 1938. • Reprinted by permission of G. P. Putnam's Sons from THE PRESIDENT SPEAKS, edited by Louis Filler. Copyright © 1964 by Louis Filler. • CONSCIENCE OF A CONSERVATIVE, by Barry Goldwater. Victor Publishing Co., Inc., 1960. • Reprinted with permission of The Macmillan Company from THE OTHER AMERICA, by Michael Harrington. © by Michael Harrington, 1962. • Reprinted by permission of G. P. Putnam's Sons from THE PRESIDENT SPEAKS, edited by Louis Filler. Copyright © 1964 by Louis Filler. • "National Radio Pulpit" by Ralph W. Sockman, February 1960. • Adapted from ONLY YESTERDAY, by Frederick Lewis Allen. Copyright 1931 by Frederick Lewis Allen; renewed 1959 by Agnes Rogers Allen. Reprinted by permission of Harper & Row, Publishers, Inc. • "The Restless Decade," by Bruce Catton, from *American Heritage*, August 1965. • Adapted and condensed from BOY AND GIRL TRAMPS OF AMERICA, by Thomas Minehan. Copyright 1934; © 1962 by Thomas Minehan. Reprinted by permission of Holt, Rinehart and Winston, Inc. • Excerpts from STILL THE MOST EXCITING COUNTRY, by William Attwood. Copyright © 1955 by William Attwood. Reprinted by permission of Alfred A. Knopf, Inc. • "My Rainbow Race," by Pete Seeger. © Copyright 1970 by SANGA MUSIC INC. All rights reserved. Used by permission. • "What? Americans Hate Kids?" by Eda Leshan, from *The New York Times Magazine*, December 1, 1968. © 1968 by The New York Times Company. Reprinted by permission. • Quoted with permission of the publisher from CALL OF THE WILD, by Roderick Nash. New York: George Braziller, Inc., 1970. • ENDLESS HORIZONS, by Vannevar Bush. Public Affairs Press, 1946. • Copyright 1940 and renewed 1968 by W. H. Auden. Reprinted from COLLECTED SHORTER POEMS 1927–1957, by W. H. Auden, by permission Random House, Inc. • MONTANA: HIGH, WIDE, AND HANDSOME, by Joseph Kinsey Howard, Yale University Press, 1943. • "What the Ants Were Saying" by Don Marquis. Copyright 1935 by Doubleday and Company, Inc. From the book THE LIVES AND TIMES OF ARCHY AND MEHITABEL, by Don Marquis. Reprinted by permission of Doubleday and Company, Inc. • "Our Ravaged Environment," from *Newsweek*, January 26, 1970. Copyright Newsweek, Inc. • "Who Pays for Anti-Pollution?" from *National Review*, February 10, 1970.

Glossary

Abolition The ending of slavery and slave trade; the act of doing away with any practice or **institution.**

Administration The persons who make up the executive branch of government during a President's term in office.

Aggression The action of a nation forcefully violating the rights of another nation, especially by invasion.

Alien A person who is not a citizen of the country in which he lives.

Alliance A formal agreement, usually between nations, to unite in a common cause.

Amendment A change.

Americanization The process by which a foreign-born person becomes a part of American culture.

Anarchy The absence of any government; political disorder and confusion.

Annex To add territory to an already existing state or country.

Anti-Semitism Prejudice against, and persecution of, Jews.

Arbitration The process by which the parties to a dispute submit their differences to an impartial party and agree to accept its verdict.

Aristocracy A hereditary privileged class; a state ruled by such a class.

Automation The operation or control of a process, equipment, or a system by mechanical and electronic techniques.

Autonomy Self-government or the right of self-government.

Bankrupt A condition in which a person is unable to pay his debts; financially ruined.

Barter economy An economic system based upon the "swapping" of goods. Compare with **market economy.**

Belligerents Warring parties.

Black codes Special laws for Negroes devised and enforced by whites.

Blockade The closing by force of a city, coast, harbor, or other area to traffic and/or communication.

Blue-collar worker A worker whose job involves manual labor.

Bond A certificate of debt issued by a government or corporation guaranteeing payment of the original investment by a specific date plus **interest.**

Boss A professional politician who controls a party or political machine.

Bounty A reward or payment, especially one given by a government.

Boycott To not use, buy, or deal with someone or something as a means of protest.

Building code The laws that establish minimum standards for new construction.

Bureaucracy The body of nonelected officials and administrators who work in the various bureaus or departments of government.

Capital The wealth, in the form of money or property, owned, used, or accumulated in business by an individual or a corporation.

Capital goods Machines and tools used in the production of other goods. Compare with **consumer goods.**

Capitalism An economic system based upon private ownership and control of the means of production, distribution, and exchange of wealth. Compare with **communism** and **socialism.**

Capitalist A person who has money or property invested in business enterprises.

Caste system A social system under which a person's **class** or **status** in society is unchangeable.

Censorship The practice of withholding certain information or ideas from the general public for moral, political, military, or other purposes.

Censure To express severe criticism or disapproval.

Civilization A level of human development marked by complex social, political, and economic systems and advances in the arts and sciences.

Civil rights The rights belonging to every person who is a citizen of the United States.

Civil service A system of appointing government employees on the basis of competitive examination rather than party loyalty. Compare with **spoils system.**

Clans Groups of related families.

Class A group of people who share a common role or position in society.

Closed shop A shop in which union membership is a requirement for hiring as well as for continued employment.

Coalition An **alliance**, especially a temporary one, of groups, parties, or nations.

Cold War A state of political tension and military rivalry between nations, stopping short of full-scale war; the state of such rivalry between the United States and the Soviet Union after World War II.

Colonist A person living in a permanent settlement ruled by a "mother" country, often his own.

Colony A permanent settlement ruled by a geographically separate country, often called a "mother" country.

Communism An economic system based upon total government control of the means of production, distribution, and exchange of wealth. Compare with **capitalism** and **socialism.**

Compensation Something given or received as payment for a loss, debt, or service.

Conciliation The process of creating good will.

Concurrent powers The powers shared by two or more governments. For example, Federal, state, and local governments all share the power of taxation.

Confederacy A loosely structured union of persons, parties, or states.

Confirm To give formal approval.

Confrontation A face-to-face meeting, usually hostile.

Conquistador A Spanish word meaning "one who conquers."

Conscription A military draft.

Consensus A general agreement.

Conservation The official preservation of natural resources.

Consumer goods Goods, such as food and clothing, that satisfy human wants and are not used in any further production process. Compare with **capital goods**.

Corollary An addition.

Craft union A union whose members share a common skill. Compare with **industrial union**.

Credit Confidence in a buyer's ability and intention to pay, which is shown by giving him goods or services without demanding immediate payment.

Creditor nation A nation that is owed money by other nations.

Cultural identity A person's knowledge and acceptance of his own cultural background.

Culture The sum total of the ways of living and the institutions of a society.

De facto **segregation** The practice of **segregation** within a society, but not as the result of laws requiring it. Compare with *de jure* **segregation**.

Deficit financing A government's spending of more money than is provided by taxation.

De jure **segregation** The **segregation** that exists within a society as the result of laws requiring it. Compare with *de facto* **segregation**.

Demilitarize To prohibit the establishment of military forces and installations.

Democracy A state ruled by the common consent of the people, obtained directly or through elected representatives.

Deport To send out of a country.

Depose To remove from office.

Deposits Money held in a bank account.

Depression A period of drastic economic decline during which business activity decreases, prices fall, and unemployment increases.

Dictator A ruler who has total authority without any limits or checks by others.

Diplomacy The art of conducting relations between nations.

Disarmament The reduction or **abolition** of military forces and weapons by a national government.

Disfranchisement The removal of the right to vote.

Dissent To think or feel differently; an opinion delivered by a Supreme Court Justice in opposition to the majority opinion of the Supreme Court.

Dissenter A person who opposes generally accepted practices; in colonial America the term usually referred to those who disagreed with church leaders.

Dividend A share of a company's profits received by a stockholder.

Duty A tax on imports and/or exports.

Ecology The scientific study of the natural balance among living things and their environment.

Economy The way in which members of a society manage production, distribution, and consumption of goods and services.

Electorate The body of qualified voters.

Emancipate To free from authority or influence; especially to free from slavery.

Empire A large area that includes a number of different territories ruled by a single authority.

Embargo A governmental suspension of all foreign trade; a suspension of foreign trade of a particular product.

Environment The physical and/or social surroundings of a particular locality or region.

Evidence The data on which a judgment or conclusion may be based.

Excise tax An indirect tax levied on the production, sale, or consumption of a product within a country.

Exclusive powers The powers held by only one level of government. For example, the power to conduct foreign affairs belongs exclusively to the Federal government.

Executive In government a person responsible for seeing that the laws are carried out; thus the President of the United States is the nation's Chief Executive.

Expansionism The policy of extending a nation's authority by acquiring new territories, without violating the sovereignty of any other nation.

Expropriation The seizure of property, especially by a government for public use.

Extended family A group consisting of parents, grandparents, children, adopted children, grandchildren, aunts, uncles, and cousins often living in the same area and sharing social rules.

Fact Something known with certainty. Compare with **opinion**.

Federalism A political system in which a union of states recognizes the authority of a central government in certain areas and retains its powers in other areas.

Feminist A person who demands that women be granted the same political, economic, and social status as men.

Financier A person who is skilled or engaged in dealing with money and **credit**.

Franchise A right or privilege granted a person by a government.

Frontier A region just beyond a settled area; any underdeveloped area or field, as in scientific research.

Generalization A principle or statement that applies to the whole or every member of a class or category.

Genocide The systematic, planned annihilation of a racial, political, or cultural group.

Ghetto A slum section of a city inhabited almost entirely by a minority group, often because of social or economic pressure.

Graduated income tax The taxation of greater incomes at a higher rate than smaller incomes.

Guerrilla warfare Waging a war by harassing a superior enemy force with hit-and-run tactics and avoiding large battles.

Hoard To hide or store supplies for future use.

Home rule The principle of self-government in domestic matters, usually in reference to a dependent territory or **colony**.

Hypothesis A statement used as a basis for argument

or reasoning; a premise from which a conclusion is drawn.

Ideology The body of ideas reflecting the goals of an individual, group, or culture.

Impeach To charge a public official, in the proper court, with misconduct in office.

Imperialism The policy of extending a nation's authority by acquiring new territories or by establishing political or economic influence over other nations.

Impressment The policy of forcing a person to serve in the military.

Indentured servant A person bound by a legal contract to work a fixed number of years without pay from his master.

Industrial revolution The social and economic changes brought about when the introduction of machines in production systems results in a shift from home industry to large-scale factory production.

Industrial union A union to which all the workers in a particular industry can belong, regardless of their skills. Compare with **craft union**.

Injunction A court order prohibiting a specific course of action or demanding a certain action.

Installment plan A **credit** system by which a debt is paid in fixed amounts over a definite period of time.

Institution An established organization, often dedicated to public service; an important, well-established way of behaving in a society.

Insurrection An open revolt.

Integration The coming together of all racial, religious, and other groups within the general body of society. Compare with **segregation**.

Interest The sum paid for the use of money or charged for the borrowing of money.

Isolationism A national policy of not getting involved in the political or economic affairs of other nations.

Jingoism An exaggerated national pride that supports an aggressive foreign policy.

Judicial review The right of the Supreme Court to determine if a law is constitutional.

Land speculator A person who invests in land in hopes that its value will rise sharply, thus enabling him to sell it for a large profit.

Leadership The ability to formulate a plan of action and convince others that they want to follow it.

Legislature A lawmaking assembly.

Literacy test A test of a person's ability to read and write, used by some states to prevent certain people from voting.

Lobbying The process of trying to get lawmakers to pass legislation that favors a special interest.

Lockout The closing of a plant by an employer to force the workers to meet his terms.

Logistics The procurement, distribution, care, and replacement of military weapons and personnel.

Lynching An execution without a trial, especially by hanging.

Manifest Destiny The nineteenth-century belief that the United States had the right and duty to expand throughout the North American continent.

Market economy An economic system in which the value of goods, services, and work is determined by demand and is expressed in terms of money. Compare with **barter economy**.

Mass media All means of public communication reaching a large audience.

Mass production The manufacture of large quantities of goods, using standardized designs that allow assembly-line techniques.

Megalopolis A region made up of several large cities and their surrounding areas which adjoin each other.

Mercenary A professional soldier hired by a country other than his own.

Metropolitan area A city and the suburbs surrounding it.

Militancy The willingness to fight or go to war.

Militant An aggressive person who is eager to fight, especially a political activist.

Militarist A person who supports or favors a warlike national **policy**.

Militiamen The male citizens of a state who are not members of the regular armed forces but are called to military service in emergencies.

Missionary A person sent to do religious or charitable work in a foreign country or territory.

Moderate A person who believes in and works for slow, orderly change in the established social or **political system**.

Monarchy A state ruled by a single authority, most often a king. See **sovereign**.

Monopoly The exclusive right to control the means of producing or selling a particular product or service.

Morality The evaluation of, or standard for evaluating, human conduct.

Muckraker A person who searches for and exposes corruption in government or business.

National income The total net earnings from the production of goods and services within a nation over a definite period of time; essentially, the sum of wages, profits, rents, and interest.

Nationalism An intense loyalty to, and feeling for, one's own nation.

Nativism A nineteenth-century political movement that favored the interests of native-born Americans over those of immigrants.

Naturalize To grant full citizenship to a person of foreign birth.

Negotiate To arrange or settle by discussion.

Neutrality A **policy** of not taking sides in a matter under dispute.

Nullification The action of declaring a law invalid.

Opinion A belief or conclusion held with confidence, but not necessarily supported by **fact**.

Ordinance A law, command, or order.

Pacifist A person who believes that war and violence should never be used as means of settling disputes.

Paternalism A policy of treating or governing people in a fatherly manner, especially by determining and providing for their needs without giving them any responsibility.

Payroll tax The taxation of wages, usually at a rate that is the same for all employees regardless of their salaries. Compare with **graduated income tax.**

Peaceful coexistence A theory that two or more nations with conflicting ideologies can exist in peace.

Pioneer A person who settles unknown or unclaimed territory; one who begins something new in any field.

Platform The formal statement of a political party's goals and ideas.

Pluralism A condition of society in which many ethnic, religious, and cultural groups exist within one nation, and each group preserves its distinct nature.

Polarization The movement of groups, forces, or interests toward two conflicting extreme positions.

Policy A plan of action.

Political system The way a society governs itself.

Poll tax A tax on people as a requirement for voting, used to discourage voting by the poor.

Pollution The contamination of soil, water, or the atmosphere by the discharge of harmful substances.

Popular sovereignty The principle that the people should have the final power to decide local or national **policy.**

Populists Members of a **reform**-minded American political party formed in the 1890's.

Precedent An example from the past; in law a judicial decision that may be used as a standard in later similar cases.

Prejudice An **opinion** about an idea, a person, or a group of people formed without knowledge or examination of the facts.

Pressure group Any group that tries to influence legislation through the use of **lobbying** techniques and **propaganda.**

Primary election An election held to nominate a political party's candidates for public office.

Profiteering Charging extremely high prices for goods that are in short supply.

Propaganda The circulation of information designed to arouse strong emotions for one side of a cause.

Protectorate The relationship of a strong nation to a weaker state or territory which it protects and partly controls.

Public domain The land owned and controlled by a state or Federal government.

Public opinion The beliefs held by members of a society on public issues.

Public works Construction paid for by taxes and beneficial to an entire community.

Public utilities Private business organizations subject to government control because they provide essential goods or services, such as water, electricity, transportation, and communication.

Racism The belief that one's own race is naturally superior to all others.

Radical A person who believes in and works for revolutionary change in the established social or **political system.**

Ratify To give formal approval.

Reconstruction The period during which the states of the southern Confederacy were controlled by the Federal government and forced to change their political and social institutions in order to be readmitted to the **Union.**

Reform To improve; a movement seeking improved social or political conditions without revolutionary change.

Refugee A person who flees from invasion or persecution.

Relief Money, food, or other help given by a government agency to those in poverty or need.

Reparations Payment demanded from a defeated nation for damages and injuries during a war.

Repeal To withdraw or cancel in a formal, official manner.

Repression The denial of **civil rights** in order to keep things under control.

Revenue The income received by a government from all sources.

Revolution A sudden, major change; a political revolution is the overthrow of one government and its replacement by another.

Satellite A nation that is dominated politically by another.

Secession The act of withdrawing formally from a political union.

Segregation The separation of a specific racial, religious, or other group from the general body of society. Compare with **integration.**

Self-determination The right of people to decide their own political future.

Self-sufficient Able to provide for oneself without the help of others; independent.

Settlement house A welfare center providing community services in a poor area.

Sharecropper A farmer who pays a share of his crop as rent.

Socialism An economic system based upon government ownership and control of most means of production and distribution. Compare with **capitalism** and **communism.**

Socialist A person who believes in **socialism**; a member of the Socialist Party.

Society A distinct group of people living together and having their own institutions and way of life.

Sociology The scientific study of human social behavior.

Sovereign Fully independent and self-governing; the head of government in a **monarchy.**

Speculation The engagement in business transactions involving the risk of huge losses but offering the chance of large gains.

Sphere of influence A region of a nation or territory in which another, more powerful nation dominates political and/or economic activities.

Spoils system The practice after an election of rewarding loyal supporters of the winning candidate with positions in government. Compare with **civil service.**

Staple crop A farm food grown or produced in a particular region and necessary for its livelihood.

States' rights All powers not delegated to the Federal government nor denied to the states by the Constitution; a political philosophy favoring limiting the powers of the Federal government and increasing the powers of individual states.

Status Rank or social position in the eyes of others.

Stock Shares of ownership in a company.

Stock market A place where stocks and bonds are bought and sold.

Strategy An overall plan; the science of military command as applied to overall planning and conduct of large-scale military actions.

Strike A work stoppage.

Subsidize To give financial help.

Subsidy Money given by a government to help or encourage a private agricultural or industrial undertaking.

Suffrage The right to vote.

Tariff A tax on imports.

Technology The application of science, especially to industrial or commercial purposes; all the skills and materials used to achieve societal goals.

Temperance The total avoidance of all liquor.

Tenement A run-down, low-rental apartment building or rooming house.

Territorial integrity The right of a nation to have its boundaries respected by all other nations.

Terrorist A person or group using violence and fear to achieve an end.

Theocracy A state ruled by religious leaders.

Title Proof of legal ownership.

Tribute Money or valuables paid by one ruler or nation to another for protection.

Truce A temporary agreement by opposing forces to cease firing.

Trust A combination of formerly independent companies for the purpose of achieving a **monopoly** or near-monopoly in a particular industry.

Tyrant An absolute ruler who uses his power in a cruel manner.

Ultimatum A final demand or set of terms issued by one party to a dispute, threatening serious penalties if the terms are not accepted.

Union An organization of wage earners for the purpose of improving their wages and working conditions; the United States of America; the northern states during the Civil War.

Union shop A shop in which union membership is a requirement for continued employment, but not for hiring.

Urban Having to do with, located in, or actually being a city.

Utopia A condition, situation, or place of social or political perfection.

Veto To forbid or reject with final authority.

Vigilantes Self-appointed policemen who also often act as judge and jury.

Welfare agency A government organization that seeks to improve the living conditions of people, especially the poor and the handicapped.

Welfarism The system under which a government assumes the responsibility for the economic and social well-being of all its citizens.

White supremacy The belief that the white man has a natural superiority over other races, particularly the Negro, and must keep them under control; exclusive white control of political, economic, and social life.

White-collar worker A worker whose job does not involve manual labor and who typically works in an office.

White man's burden The belief that white men have a duty to govern and care for the inferior non-white world population.

Zone A section of a city set aside by law for a certain type building or activity, such as a residential zone.

Pronunciation Key

The pronunciation system and key in this book is from THE AMERICAN HERITAGE INTERMEDIATE DICTIONARY © 1972 by American Heritage Publishing Co., Inc.

Throughout the Index **boldfaced** portions of the pronunciations correspond to the **boldfaced** entries of the key at left. The pages following a **boldfaced I** refer to an inquiry section. **Boldfaced** page references indicate pictures or captions.

ă **pat**/ā **ate**/âr **care**/ä **bar**/b **bib**/ch **chew**/d **deed**/ ĕ **pet**/ē **be**/f **fit**/g **gag**/h **hat**/hw **what**/ĭ **pit**/ī **pie**/ îr **pier**/j **judge**/k **kick**/l **lid**, **fatal**/m **mum**/n **no**, **sudden**/ng **sing**/ŏ **pot**/ō **go**/ô **paw**, **for**/oi **boy**/ou **out**/ŏŏ **took**/ōō **coo**/p **pop**/r **run**/s **sauce**/sh **shy**/t **to**/th **thin**/<u>th</u> **the**/ŭ **cut**/ûr **fur**/v **van**/w **wag**/y **yes**/ z **size**/zh **vision**/ə **ago**, **item**, **edible**, **gallop**, **circus**/

Index

A

Abolitionists (ăb′ ə lĭsh′ ə nĭsts), 320, **354–356, 360**, 361
Abrams v U.S., I 246–247
Adams, Franklin P., I 610
Adams, John, 111, I 138, 169, 204, 213, 214, 229, 796
Adams, John Quincy, 93, 240, 553, 556, 796
Adams, Samuel, 154, 155, 158
Adams-Onís (ăd′əmz ō′nĭs) Treaty, 238 (map), 240
Addams, Jane, **492, 493**
Advertising, **453**, 613, 617, **664**
Affonso (ə fŏn′sō), Dom, I 130
Africa
    Crusaders' trade with, 56
    El Alamein, battle of, 710, **711** (map), **711**
    Life in, **80–87**, 81 (map)
    Movement to return slaves to, 354
    Mussolini's invasion of Ethiopia, **675**, 678
    Nationalist movements in, 699
    Peace Corps in, **766**
    Portuguese exploration of, **58**, 59, 59 (map)
    Slave trade in, **78, 79, 88–93**, I 130–134
    Triangular trade, 108 (map), 109
    Tripoli, war with, **232, 233**
Agricultural Adjustment Administration Act (AAA), 657
Agriculture
    African, 82, 83
    Indian, **34, 35, 36, 42–43**
    Medieval European, 55, 56, **57**
    United States
        Big business, **452–453**, 454
        Chinese labor in, 547
        Colonial, 69, 104 (map), **112, 113, 118, 119, 120, 121**
        Department of, 452, 453
        In Depression of 1929, 637, 640, 642, **644**, 645
        Ecology and, 743 (graph), I 772–773
        Free-Soil Party, 358, 360, 451
        Homestead Act, **450**, 451, 452
        Increased production in, 575, 740
        Migration to industrial jobs from, 319, 347, 437, **469**, 706
        Morrill Act, 453
        New Deal legislation for, 653
        Populist party, **410, 411**, 488, **504, 505**, 507
        Protective laws for, 510
        Small farmers, 744
        In South, 271 (map), 347, 348, **349**
        Unionization of, 736, **737**, 739
        In West, 348, 350, **351**
    See also Cattle, Land; South
Aguinaldo (ä′gē näl′dō), Emilio, **540**
Airplanes, **585, 586, 587, 589**, 617, 631, **633**, 644, 699, **700**, 701, 709, 713, 714, **719, 752**, 753, 760, 763
Alabama
    In Civil War, 367 (map), 387 (map), 391 (map)
    Cotton frontier and admission as state, 270, 271 (map)
    First capital of Confederacy, 366
    Industry in, **460**
    Negro voter registration in, 736 (graph)
    Reconstruction in, 404 (map)
    Transportation in, 314 (map) 315 (map), 445 (map)
    T.V.A. in, 652 (map), 654
    In U.S. (1970), 794 (map)
    See also Civil Rights, South
Alamo, the, battle of, 284, **286, 287**
Alaska
    Admission as state, 196, 535
    Boundary of Oregon Territory, 291
    Exploration of, 74 (map), 76
    Gold, **457**, 534, **535**
    Indians: Chilkat (chĭl′kăt′), **534**; Eskimo, 29; Kwakiutl (kwä′kē ōōt′l), 46, **47**
    Russia, dispute with, 553
    Seward's purchase of, 535
    In U.S. (1970), 794 (map)
Albania (ăl bā′nē ə), 752 (map), 760
Albany, New York, 67, 72, 179, 309, 310, 794 (map)
    See also New York
Aldrin, Edwin, **741**
Algeria, in World War II, 711 (map)
Algonquin (ăl gŏng′kwĭn *or* ăl gŏng′kĭn) Indians, 32
Alien and Sedition Acts, 208, 229, 230, I 242–244
Aliens, deportation of in 1920's, 625
Allegheny Mountains, 104 (map), 189, I 252–253, I 257, 262 (map)
Allen, Frederick Lewis, I 608–609
Alliance for Progress, 764, 765
Allied Powers. *See* World War I, World War II
Amendments
    Development of, 201, 205, **208**
    1st, I 242–249, 788
    13th, 381, 790
    14th, 397, 399, 400, 411, 790
    15th, **396**, 397, 399, 400, 410, 411, 790
    16th, 510, 791
    17th, 510, 791
    18th, I 609–611, 628, 631, 791
    19th, 631, 791
    26th, 748, 793
    See also Bill of Rights, Constitution
American Civil Liberties Union, 626, **627**
American Committee for the Outlawry of War, 667
American Expeditionary Force (AEF), 582
American Federation of Labor (AF of L), 497–**501**, 584, 656
Anglo-Saxons, I 22–23, 333, 470, 568, **622**, 623, 625
Annexation. *See* Territorial Expansion
Anthony, Susan B., 321
Antietam (ăn tē′təm), battle of, 372 (map), 374, **375**
Anti-Federalists, 200, 201, 204, 222
Apache (ə păch′ē) Indians, 48, 275
Appalachian (ăp′ə lā′chē ən *or* ăp′ə lăch′ē ən) Mountains, 270, 744
Appomattox, **392**, 393
Arabs, 56, 80
Arapaho (ə răp′ə hō′) Indians, 275
Argonne (är′gŏn′) Forest, battle of, 582, 583 (map)
Arizona
    Exploration of, 277 (map), 278 (map)
    Gadsden Purchase, 296 (map), 297
    Indian reservations, 448 (map)
    Mining in, 457
    Transportation in, 445 (map)
    In U.S. (1970), 794 (map)
    See also Mexican War, New Mexico Territory, Southwest
Arkansas
    In Civil War, 367 (map)
    Compromises of 1820 and 1850, 358 (map)
    In Depression of 1929, **644**, 645
    Exploration of, 70
    Integration in, **732**, 733
    Negro voter registration, 736 (graph)
    Purchase of, 235 (map)
    Reconstruction in, 404 (map)
    Transportation in, **448**
    In U.S.: in 1853, 296 (map); in 1970, 794 (map)
    See also South
Armed Forces
    See individual wars
Arms race, 751, 767
    U.S. isolationists and, 680, 681
    See also Nuclear Power
Armstrong, Louise V., I 515, 516
Armstrong, Neil, **741**
Arnold, Benedict, 178, **179**
Arthur, Chester A., **210**, 547, 796
Articles of Confederation, 192, 195, 196, 197, **200**
Arts, public aid to, 650, **651**
Ashanti (ə shăn′tē), 80
Astor, William, **479**
Astronauts, 725, 726, 740, **741**
Atahualpa (ät′ ə wäl′ pə), 62, 63
Atlanta, Georgia, 314–315 (maps), 387 (map), 388, 413, 418, 445 (map), 794 (map)
Atlanta Compromise, 417
Atlantic Charter, 701
Atomic bomb
    Development of, **720**, 721
    Dropping of, 699, **720**, 721, 722
    See also Nuclear Power
Attucks, Crispus, **152**
Attwood, William, I 688–689
Auden, W. H., I 697
Austin, Stephen F. and Moses, 284
Austin, Texas, 288, **289**, 292 (map), 455 (map), 794 (map)
    See also Texas
Australia, in World War II, 716 (map), 717
Austria, 222, 553, 575, 583 (map), 665, 678, 711 (map), 714, 752 (map)
Automobile
    Effects of, **458**, 459, I 608–609, 613, 618, **619**, I 688, 691, I 695, 726, 728, **742, 743**
    Growth of industry, **616, 617**, 618, 642
    Henry Ford and, I 13, 447
    Unions, 497, 654, **655**
Axis (ăk′sĭs) Powers, 699
    See also World War II
Aztec (ăz′tĕk′) Indians, 29, 38, **39**, 53, 62, 65

B

Baird, Robert, I 252-253
Balboa (băl bō'ə), Vasco de, 62
Balloons, in World War I, 586, **587**
Baltimore, Lord, 114, **124**
Baltimore, Maryland, **104**, 214, **239**, 314 (map), 315 (map), 413, 794 (map)
Bancroft, George, I 138, 139
Banks
    Creation of state banks, 324
    In Depression of 1929, 637, 642, 649, 656
    Federal Reserve System, 510
    Hamilton's banking system, **220-222**
    Jackson's war with Second Bank, **323-325**
    Panic of 1837, **326-328**
    In World War I, 583
Banneker (băn'ĭ kər), Benjamin, **227**
Bara, Theda, 631
Barbados (bär bā'dōs), slavery in, **94, 95**
Baruch (bə rook'), Bernard, 589
Bataan (bə tän' or bə tän'), 717
Batista (bä tēs'tä), Fulgencio, 759
Battle Hymn of the Republic, 344, 368
Bay of Pigs, 759, **761**
Beaumont (bō' mŏnt), Gustave de, I 422
Beckwourth, James, 276
Belgium, 583 (map), 666, 682, 711 (map), 752 (map)
Bell, Alexander Graham, **444**
Bellamy, Edward, 479
Belleau (běl'ō) Wood, battle of, 582, 583 (map)
Benin (bě něn'), 80, 81
Benton, Thomas Hart, 283
Bering, Vitus, 74, 76
Berlin Airlift, 753
Berlin Wall, **750, 751**
Beveridge, Albert J., I 522, 523, 543
Biddle, Nicholas, 324
Bill of Rights, 201, 202, 204, 208, I **242-249**
    See also Civil Rights, Constitution
Birmingham, Alabama, **460**, 734, 794 (map)
Bisbee, Arizona, 457
Black, Hugo, I 247
Black Codes, 96, 101, **398, 399**
Blackfeet Indians, 275
Black Muslims (mŭz'lĭmz or mooz'lĭmz or moos'lĭmz), I 424-425, 734, 736
Black Panthers, 736
Black Power, 736
Blacks. *See* Negroes
Blaine, James G., 557
Bloomer, Amelia, 321
Bodmer, Carl, **267**
Boise, Idaho, 457
Bolsheviks (bōl'shə vĭks' or bŏl' shə vĭks'), 578, 591, 672, **673**
Bonus Army, **646, 647**
Boone, Daniel, 257, 262 (map), **263**
Boorstin (boor'stĭn), Daniel, I 12
Boston, Massachusetts, 104 (map), **110**, 111, 155, **164, 165,** 166, 179 (map), 313, 314 (map), 315 (map), 354, **355,** 356, 445 (map), 794 (map)
Boston Massacre, **152, 153**
Boston Tea Party, **158, 159**
Bow, Clara, 631

Bowie (bō'ē or boo'ē), Jim, 287
Boxer Rebellion, 544, **545**
Braddock, Edward, 146, **147,** 149
Brain Trust, **648,** 649
Breckenridge, John C., 366
Brest-Litovsk, Treaty of, 578, 583 (map)
Briand (brē änd'), Aristide, 667
Bridger, James, 276, **277**
Brinksmanship, 759
Brook Farm, 321
Brooklyn Bridge, 474, **475**
Brown, John, 344, **345,** 361, 363, **364,** 365
Bruce, Blanche K., **400**
Bry (brē or brī), Théodore de, **60, 62**
Bryan, William Jennings, 504, **505,** 507, 626, 627
Bryce, Lord James, I 253-254
Buchanan, James, 360, **361,** 796
Buena Vista, battle of, 292 (map), 293
Buffalo, 42, **48, 274,** 275, 448, 449
Buffalo, New York, 309
Buffalo Bill, **459,** 460
Bulge, battle of the, 714
Bull Run, battles of
    First, **370,** 372, 372 (map), **373**
    Second, 374
Bunker Hill, battle of, **164, 165,** 166
Burgoyne, John, 176, 179
Burke, Edmund, 157
Burlingame, Anson, 532, **533**
Burlingame Treaty, 532, **533,** 547
Burma, 702, 716 (map), 717, 757
Bush (boosh), Vannevar, I 696
Business
    Boycotts against, **734-737**
    Colonial, **68-69,** 70, **71, 72,** 104 (map), 108 (map), 109, **110, 111**
    In depressions, **326,** 327, 328, 637, 642, **643,** 646, 647
    Failure of Revolution to solve problems of, 189, 196
    In foreign countries, I 522-525, 526, **528-533,** 535, 543, 544, 554, **555, 556, 557, 566,** 567, 569, 570, 662, **664,** 665 (graph)
    Land, **194, 258,** 259
    Mass production, effects of, 444, **446, 447**
    Monopolies, **438, 439**
    Negro, 413, 418, **620,** 621
    Regulation of, **324, 325,** 352, 353, 488, 489, **502,** 503, 504, 507, **508, 509,** 510, 589, 656
    Trusts, **502-510**
    Urban, 490, 491, 728, **729**
    In World War I, **588,** 589
    In World War II, 706, **707,** 709, 718
    See also Factories, Industry, Labor, Open Door Policy, Pollution, Tariffs, Trade
Butte, Montana, 457
Byrd, William, II, 124, **125,** I 252

C

Cabeza de Vaca (kä bā'thä thä vä'kä), Alvar Nuñez, 74 (map), 75
Cabot, John, 66 (map), 67
Calhoun, John C., **359**
California
    Adams-Onís Treaty, 238 (map), 239
    Admission as state, 257
    In Civil War, 367 (map)

    In Compromise of 1850, 358 (map), 359
    In Depression of 1929, **644,** 645
    Exploration of, 74 (map), 76, 276, 277 (map), 278 (map), 279, **741**
    Gold in, 297, **298-303,** 377
    Growth of, **302,** 303, **619, 730**
    Immigration to, 469, 470, **471, 546,** 547, 548
    Indians: on Alcatraz, **738, 739;** reservations, 448 (map)
    In Mexican War, 291, 292 (map), 293-295, 296 (map)
    Spanish missions in, 63, **65**
    Trade with Orient, 528
    Transportation to, 278 (map), 300 (map), 445 (map)
    Unionization in, 736, **737**
    In U.S.: (1850), 296 (map); (1970), 794 (map)
    In World War II, **704,** 705
Calles, Plutarco, 668
Cambodia, 757 (map), 763
Camden, South Carolina, 182, **185**
Canada
    Diplomatic relations with U.S., 237, 239, 240, **556**
    French: exploration of, 70, 74 (map); immigration to U.S., 441, 467; loss of, 149
    Indians, 28 (map), **32**
    Niagara Conference, 418, 419, 420
    Northwest Passage, 66 (map)
    In Revolution, 179 (map)
Canal Systems, 308, 309, 313, 315 (map), 330-331, 334, 350, 554, **564, 565**
Cantigny (kän tē nyē'), battle of, 582, 583 (map)
Cape Horn. *See* Horn, Cape
Cape Kennedy. *See* Kennedy, Cape
Cape of Good Hope. *See* Good Hope, Cape of
Capitalism. *See* Business
Capone, Al, 628, **629,** 631
Carib (kăr'ĭb) Indians, 29, **60, 61**
Caribbean Islands, 61 (map), 72, **94, 95, 96, 97,** 99, 108 (map), 109, **550-574,** 551 (map)
    See also Cuba, Haiti, Puerto Rico
Carmichael, Stokely, 734, 736
Carnegie, Andrew, I 433, 438, **438, 443,** 543
Carranza (kə răn'zə), Venustiano, 570, 572
Carson, Kit, 276, 277 (map)
Cartier (kär tyā'), Jacques, 66 (map), 67
Castro, Fidel, 759, **760, 761**
Catholic Church, 62, 63, 65, 70, 114, 287
Catlin, George, 274
Caton, John Dean, I 330-331
Cattle, 65, 284, **285,** 288, 454, **455** (map), 457
Catton, Bruce, I 343, I 610-611
Central America, 29, 63, 301, 554, **555, 564-569**
Central Intelligence Agency, 759, 764
Central Powers, 577, 583 (map)
Central Treaty Organization (CENTO), 759
Cervera (thěr vā'rä), Pascual de, 560
Champlain (shăm **plān'**), Samuel de, 66 (map), 70
Chancellorsville, battle of, 372 (map), **384, 385**
Charleston, South Carolina, 98, 104 (map), 122, 123, 182, 185

804

(map), 262 (map), 313, 314 (map), 315 (map), **366**, **367**, 368, **372** (map), 378, 379, 387 (map), 391 (map), 445 (map)
Château-Thierry (shä tō'tē'ə rē), battle of, 582, 583 (map)
Chavez (chä'věz), Cesar, 736, **737**, 739
Cherokee (chěr'ə kē' *or* chěr'ə kē') Indians, 272, 273, 288
Chesapeake Bay, **183**, 185 (map), 186, 187, 237
Cheyenne (shī ăn' *or* shī ĕn') Indians, 45, 275
Chiang Kai-shek (chäng' kī'shĕk'), 676, 754
Chicago, Illinois, 314 (map), 315 (map), I 330–331, 445 (map), 454, 455 (map), **456**, 473, 478, **482**, **492**, **493**, 497, **498**, **622**, 623, 628, **629**, 631, 708, 709, 794 (map)
Chickasaw (chĭk'ə sô') Indians, 272, 273
Child labor, I 434, **441**, 480, 492, **494**
China
  In Asia (1970), 757 (map)
  Boxer Rebellion, 543, 544, **545**
  Burlingame Treaty with, 532, **533**, 547
  In Cold War, 758
  Communist take-over of, **754**, **755**, 756, 760
  Defensive Alliance against, 759
  In Korean War, 756, 758
  Open Door Policy, 543, 544, 662, 754
  Portuguese explorers in, 59 (map), 60
  Root-Takahira Agreement, 544
  U.S. trade with, 526, 527 (map), **528**, **529**
  In World War II, **676**, 677, 678, 701, 702, 716 (map)
Chinese-Americans
  Chinese Exclusion Act, **210**, 467, 547, 548
  Life in U.S., 469, 470, **471**, **546**, 547, 548
  Railroad laborers, **441**, **533**, 547
Chinook (shə **nook'** *or* chə **nook'**) Indians, 235
Choctaw (chŏk'tô') Indians, 272, 273
Churchill, Winston, 701, 753
Cincinnati, Ohio, 310, **311**, 314 (map), 315 (map), 350
Cities
  African, 82, 83
  Colonial, **68**, **69**, 70, 72, **73**, 106, **107**, **110**, **111**, 114, 116, **117**, 122, 123
  In Depression of 1929, 637, **640**, 642, **643**, 647, 650, 653
  Frontier: Pacific Coast, **302**, 303; Southwest, 288, **289**
  Ghettos in, I 10, I 518–519, **620**, 621
  Government and, 464, 637, 728, **729**, **730**, 731
  Growth of industrial, 313, I 330–331, I 432–435; Midwest, **350**, 351; Northeast, **346**, 347; river cities, **306**, 310, **311**; South, **460**, **461**, 462; West, **456**, **457**, 459
  Immigration and, **466**, 467, **468**, 469, 470, **471**, 479, **480**, **481**
  Indian: Aztec, 36, 39, 62; Mayan, 40, 41; North American, 42, 43
  Metropolitan areas, 464–486, 472–477, 613, 618, **619**, 726–731
  Negroes move to, 412, 413, I 425–427, **620**, 621, 736 (graph)
  Pollution in, I 12–13, 18, I 774–777
  Prohibition and, 628, **629**, 631
  Racial tension in, I 10, **622**, 623
  Reform in, 488–493
  Urban planning, 474, 475, **476**, **477**, 618, **619**, 726–731
  World War II move to, 706, **707**
  See also Ghettos, Pollution, Suburbs, specific cities, Technology
Civilian Conservation Corps, 649
Civil Rights
  Acts of, 399, **400**, 410, 734
  Alien and Sedition Acts, 208, 229, 230, I 242–244
  Amendments: Bill of Rights, 201; 13th, 381; 14th and 15th, **396**, 397, 399; 19th, 631
  Indians and: loss of, 209, 211, 272, 273; struggle for, **738**, 739
  Negro: Jim Crow laws, **410**, 411, 418; Ku Klux Klan threatens, **402**, 403, **622**, 623, 624; lynching, **402**, 403; segregation, **406**, 407; struggle for, **418**, 419, 420, I 422–427, 725, **734**, **735**, 736, **737**, 739
  In Reconstruction, 398, 399, **400**, **401**, 404 (map), 405
  Scopes trial, 626, **627**
  Voting Rights Act of 1965, 736
  In World War I, 584, **585**; Espionage Act, I 244–245, 584
  In World War II, 704, **705**
Civil War, 367 (map), 372 (map), 387 (map), 391 (map)
  Antietam, battle of, 374, **375**
  Appomattox, **392**, 393, 394
  Background of, I 340–343, **344–368**
  Blockade of South, 377, 378, **379**
  Bull Run, battles of, 370, 372, **373**, 374
  Chancellorsville, battle of, **384**, 385
  Fort Sumter, **366**, **367**, 368
  Gettysburg, battle of, **384**, 385
  Peninsula Campaign, **375**, **376**
  Petersburg, siege of, 390, **391**, 393
  Richmond, burning of, **392**, 393
  Sherman's march to Atlanta, **388**, **389**, 390
  Vicksburg, battle of, 385, **386**, 387, 390
  Wilderness, battle of, 390
Clark, George Rogers, 180, **182**
Clark, William, 234, 235
Clay, Henry, 290, **291**, 358, 359
Clayton Antitrust Act, 589
Clayton-Bulwer Treaty, 301
Cleghorn, Sarah N., I 434
Clemenceau (klĕm'ən sō'), Georges, **593**
Clermont, steamboat, 310, **311**
Cleveland, Grover, 498, 536, 543, 796
Cleveland, Ohio, 314 (map), 315 (map), 438, 439, 445 (map), 736, 794 (map)
Clews, Henry, 684, 685
Clinton, De Witt, 309
Coal, 437, **440**, **442**, 443 (graph), **460**, **494**, 497, 617, 640
Cody, William F., **459**, 460
Coinage, 200, 202, **220**, **221**, 222, 314, 377–378, 505–507
Cold War, I 602–603, 755, 759, **760**, **761**, 765, **766**, 767, 769
Collins, Michael, **741**
Colombia, 565
Colonies, American
  Founding of, 67, **68**, **69**, 70, 72, **73**
  In French and Indian War, 144–147
  Government by England, 142, 143, **150–167**
  Slaves in, 98–102, 118–121
  Structure of, 104 (map), **104–107**, 144 (map), I 254–255
  See also Articles of Confederation, Revolution
Colorado
  Exploration of, 74 (map), 75, 277 (map), 278 (map)
  Gold in, 457
  Transportation in, 445 (map)
  In U.S. (1970), 794 (map)
  See also West
Colt, Samuel, **316**, 317
Columbia, South Carolina, 387 (map), 388, **389**, 390, 391 (map), 794 (map)
Columbia River, 234, 235 (map), 277 (map), 278 (map)
Columbus, Christopher, 27, 29, **60**, 61 (map), I 128–129
Comanche (kə măn'chē) Indians, 274, 275, 317
Commager, Henry Steele, I 14, I 139–141
Committee on Public Information, **584**
Communism
  In China, 676, **754**, **755**, 756
  In Cuba, 759
  In Depression of 1929, 645, 647
  In Europe, 674, 675, 678
  In Korea, 756, **757**, 758
  In Latin America, **764**, 765
  In North Vietnam, 760, **762**, 763
  In Russian Revolution, 578, **672**, **673**, 674, 675
  U.S. relations with, 591, I 602–604, 625, 751, **752**, 753, 758, 759
  See also Cold War
Compromise of 1850, 358 (map), 359
Compromise of 1877, 404, **405**
Confederacy, 366, 367, 368, **370**, 371
  See also Civil War
Congress
  Party origins, **228**, 229, **350–353**
  Powers of, 199, 202, 208, 209, 220–222
Congress of Industrial Organizations (CIO), 654, **655**, 656
Connecticut
  In Civil War, 367 (map)
  Colonial, 104 (map), **107**
  Election of Washington, 213
  Free speech in, I 248
  Transportation in, 104 (map), 315 (map)
  In U.S.: in 1783, 188 (map); in 1970, 794 (map)
  See also North
Conservation, **458**, **459**, 460, 649, 653, I 774
Constitution
  Drafting of, **198–200**
  Free speech and, I 242–249
  Principles of, 202–211, 220–222
  Ratification of, 200–201
  Slavery and, 93, 356, 357, 359, **360**, **362–363**
  States' rights and, 344, 347, **352–353**

805

See also Amendments
Constitutional Convention, 192, 199
Constitutional Union Party, 366
Continental Congress
   Declaration of Independence, 170
   First, 158, 192
   Second, 163, 164, 169, 175–176, 180, 185, 189
   See also Articles of Confederation
Convention of 1818, 240
Coolidge, Calvin, **614**, 615, 639, 640, 642, 653, **666**, 668, **796** (graph)
Copley, John Singleton, 110
Copperheads, 382
Corn, 34, 41, **43**, **48**
Cornwallis, Charles, **183**, 186–187
Coronado, Francisco, 74 (map), 75
Corregidor (kə rĕg′ĭ dôr), 717
Cortés (kôr tĕz′), Hernando, 62
Costa Rica, **566**, 567, 569
Cotton, 269, **270**, 271 (map), 284, 288, 347, 348, 357, 359, **460**
Council Bluffs, Iowa, maps, 278, 445
Courts. *See* Judicial Power
Cowboys, **285**, 454, **455**
Cox, James, **663**
Creek Indians, 272
Creel, George, **584**
Crockett, Davy, **286**, 287
Crow Indians, **276**
Cuba, 61 (map), 62, I 522–525, 535, 536, 551 (map), 554, **556**, 557, **558**, 559, 560, **561**, 562, 563, 670, 759, **760**, **761**
Cumberland Gap, 262 (map)
Custer, George, 449
Czechoslovakia, 592, 678, 713, 714, 752 (map)

D

Dahomey (də hō′ mē), 82
Darrow, Clarence, 626, **627**
Darwin, Charles, 626
Davis, Jefferson, **366**, 371
Dawes Act, 449, 451
D-Day, 711 (map), **712**, 713
Debs, Eugene V., **506**, 507, 508, 584
Declaration of Independence, I 138–141, **142**, 143, 170, **200**
   Centennial, 437
Deerfield, Massachusetts, 144, **145**
Delaware, 104 (map), 112–113, 188 (map), 296 (map), 367 (map), 445 (map)
Delaware River, 174, 310
Democrats
   Compromise of 1877, 404, **405**
   Fight for home rule in South, 403
   Jacksonian, 323
   Presidential administrations, 796 (graph)
   Rise of, 290
   In slavery issue, 365, 366
Denmark, 682, 711 (map), 752 (map)
Denver, Colorado, 445 (map), 455 (map), 457, **547**, 794 (map)
Department of Agriculture, 452
   See also Agriculture
Department of Commerce, 665
   See also Business
Department of Housing and Urban Development, 731
   See also Cities
Depression

Background of, **638**, 639
"Bonus Marchers" and Federal troops, 644, **646–647**
Effect of, I 515–517, **636**, 637, 642, **643**, 680, I 686–689
In Europe, 675
Farmers and, 642, **644**, 645
Franklin D. Roosevelt and New Deal, I 515–517, **648–657**
1929 crash, 639, 640, **641**, 699
De Soto (də sō′tō), Hernando, 74 (map), 75
Detroit, Michigan, 104 (map), 189, 262 (map), 314 (map), 315 (map), 392, 492, 642, 704
Dewey, George, 540, **541**
Dias (dē′əs), Bartholomeu, 59
Díaz (dē′ɔs), Adolfo, 668
Díaz (dē′əs), Porfirio, 570
Disarmament, 593, 594, 662, 760
District of Columbia. *See* Washington, D.C.
Dodge City, Kansas, 455 (map)
Dominican Republic, 61 (map), 569, 570, 668, **765**
Doolittle, Amos, **160**
Douglas, Stephen A., 359, 362–363, 365
Douglass, Frederick, **355**, 356, I 422–423
Draft, 382, **383**, 584, 681, 682, 701
Drake, Sir Francis, 74 (map), 76
Draper, William, 718, **719**
Dred Scott v. Sandford, **360**
Du Bois (dōō **bois**′), William Edward Burghardt, 418, **419**, 420
Dulles, John Foster, **759**
Dunn, Harvey, **256**
Dust Bowl, **644**, 645

E

Earhart, Amelia, 631
Earth Day, **742**
East Africa, 80, 81 (map), 82
Easterbrooks, Prince, **162**
East Indies, 702, **716**, 717
Ecology. *See* Natural Resources
Economic and Social Council (ECOSOC), 769
Ederle (ā′dər lē), Gertrude, 631
Edison, Thomas, **444**
Education, 195, 202, 320, 406, **414**, **415**, 416, I 422–427, 428 (table), 732, 733
Egypt, 710, 711 (map)
Einstein, Albert, 721
Eisenhower, Dwight D., **712**, 713, 733, **757**, 758, 759, 763, 770, 796
El Alamein (ĕl äl′ə mān′), battle of, 710, 711 (map)
Electricity, 442, 464, 473, 474, **475**, 653
Elijah Muhammad, I 424–425
Ellicott, Andrew, 227
Ellington, Duke, **620**, 621
Ellis Island, **466**, 467, **624**
El Salvador (ĕl säl′və dôr′), 567
Emancipation Proclamation, 378–381
Embargo Act, 233
England
   In American colonies: exploration and settlement, 53, 59, 66 (map), 72, 74 (map), 76, 104–127, I 130–132; French and Indian War, 144–149; slave trade, 91, **94**, 95, 96, **98–102**

In Asia, 528–529, 543, 544, **545**
In Industrial Revolution, 307, 310, 313
In Latin America, 553, 569
In 1970, 757
In Revolution, 142, 143, **168–189**; background of, 150–166
In War of 1812, **236–240**; background of, 196, 197, **207**, **209**, 218, **222**, **223**, **233**
In West, 266, 279, 283, 288, **290–291**
In World War I, 577, **578**, 581, 583 (map), 592, 593, 594
In World War II, 682, **700**, 701, 702, 706, **710**, 711 (map), **712**, 713; background of, 661, 662, **666**, 674, 678, 681
Equiano (ĕk′wē ä′nō), Olaudah, 87
Ericson, Leif, 55
Espionage Act of 1917, I 244–245, 584
Estevanico (ĕs′tə vä′nĭ kō), 75
Ethiopia, 80, **675**, 678
Evers, Charles, **736**, **737**
Ewe (ā′va *or* ā′wä), 80
Executive power, 204–205
   See also System of Checks and Balances

F

Factories
   Automation in, 744
   Growth of, **312**, 313, **316**, 317; North, 347; South, 460, **461**, 462; West, 350, **351**, 457, 459
   Mass production in, **316**, 317, **436**, **437**, **440**, **441**, 444, **446**, **447**, **494**, **495**, **588**, 589, I 695–697, 706, **707**, 709
   Protective tariffs, 352, 353
   Women in, **317–319**
   In World War I, **588**, 589
   In World War II, 706, **707**, 709, 718
   See also Business, Industry, Labor
Fallen Timbers, battle of, 266
Fanti (făn′tē), 80
Farmer, James, 736
Farm Security Administration, 653
Fascism, **674**, 675, 678
Faubus, Orval, **732**
Federal Emergency Relief Administration, I 515–516, 649
Federal government. *See* Government of U.S.
Federalists
   And Alien and Sedition Acts, I 242–244
   End of, 290
   Hamilton and, **228–231**
   Rise of, 200, 201, 218
   Whiskey Rebellion and, 224
Federal Reserve System, 510
Federal Trade Commission, 510
Ferdinand, King, 60
Fermi (fĕr′mē), Enrico, 721
Filibuster, 554, **555**
Fillmore, Millard, 531, 796
Fish, 31–32, 34, **35**, **42**, **43**, 46, **47**, 67, 70, 71, 104 (map), 105, **108**, 109, 188, 189, 743 (graph)
Fisk, Jim, 414, 418
Fitch, John, 310
Fitzgerald, F. Scott, **638**
Fitzhugh, George, I 340
Five Power Treaty, 662
Flint, Michigan, 654, **655**
Florida

In Civil War, 367 (map)
Economy of, 271 (map), 460, I 608-611
Exploration of, 74 (map), 75
Indians and, **43, 261**
Negro voting registration, 736 (graph)
Purchase of, 238 (map), 240, 296 (map)
In Reconstruction, 404 (map)
Spain and, **188,** 189
In Spanish-American War, 560
Speculation in, I 608-611
Transportation in, 314 (map), 315 (map)
Food and Agriculture Organization (FAO), 769
Ford, Henry, I 13, 447, I 514-515, 618. *See also* Automobile
Ford, Henry, II, I 16
Formosa, 532
See also Taiwan
Fort Leavenworth, Kansas, 292 (map), 293
Fort McHenry, 239
Fort Sumter, **366, 367,** 368
Fort Ticonderoga, 163
Fourth of July, **219**
See also Declaration of Independence
France
Diplomatic relations with, 180, **194,** 222, 223, 227, **233-235, 288,** 661, 662, **666**
Exploration of New World, 66 (map), 67, **70,** 71, 74 (map), 75, 76, 105, I 130-132
In French and Indian War, **144-149**
In Haiti, **96, 97,** 99
Leaves Indochina, 760
Louisiana Purchase, 233, 234, **235**
In 1970, 752 (map)
In Revolution (American), 180, **181,** 182, **183, 186, 187**
In World War I, 578, **579,** 582, 583 (map), **587, 592, 593,** 594
In World War II, 682, 702, 711 (map), 712, 714, 715
Franco, Francisco, 678, 680
Frankfurter, Felix, I 247
Franklin, Benjamin, 114, 116, **116,** 158, **158,** 169, 180, **181,** 192, 211, I 684
Freedmen's Bureau, **398, 399,** 414
Free-Soil Party, 358, 360, 451
Frémont, John C., 276, 277 (map), 291, 293
French and Indian War, **144-149,** 180
Frobisher (frō′bĭ shər *or* frŏb′ĭ shər), Martin, 66 (map)
Frontier, I 252-255, **256-280,** 262 (map), 277-278 (maps), **450,** 451, 452
See also West
Fugitive Slave Act, 359
Fulani (fōō′lä nē *or* fōō lä′nē), 82, **82, 83**
Fulbright, J. W., I 604-605
Fulton, Robert, **310, 311**
Fundamentalists, 626, **627**
Furs, settlers and, 67, **70, 71,** 72, 104 (map), 105, 109, 188 (map), 189, 196, **274, 276,** 277 (map), 278 (map)
See also Buffalo

G

Gadsden Purchase, 296 (map), 297
Gage, Thomas, 161

Gallatin, Albert, I 333-334
Gama (gäm′ə), Vasco da, 59
Garrison, William Lloyd, I 340, 354, **355**
General Assembly, U.N., 769
George III, King of England, **142,** 143, 155, 157, 196, **204**
Georgia
In Civil War, 367 (map), 375, 387 (map), 388, 389
As colony, 104 (map), 144 (map)
Cotton and, **270, 271** (map), **271**
Indians and, 209, 211, 273
Industrialization and, **474, 475**
Negroes and, 413, 418, 736 (graph)
In Reconstruction, 404 (map)
In Revolution, 182, 185 (map), 188 (map)
Transportation and, 314 (map), 315 (map), 445 (map)
T.V.A., 652 (map)
In U.S. (1970), 794 (map)
See also Colonies, South
German-Americans, 114, I 130-132, 333, 336, 441, 584, 704
Germany. *See* Berlin Airlift, Berlin Wall, Cold War, World War I, World War II
Gettysburg, Battle of, **384,** 385, 387 (map)
Gettysburg Address, 371
Ghana (gä′nə), 80, 81 (map)
Ghent, Treaty of, 239
Ghettoes
Harlem, **620,** 621
Riots in, 725
Urban renewal in, 728, **729**
See also Cities
Gold, 62, 63, 67, 68, 75, 80, **82,** 297-303, 377, **456, 457, 534, 535**
See also Natural Resources
Goldwater, Barry, I 517, I 602-603
Gompers, Samuel, 469, 496, **497,** 498, **500,** 501, 584, 586
Good Hope, Cape of, 58 (map), 59
Good Neighbor Policy, 670, **671**
Gorgas (gôr′gəs), William, 565
Government of U.S.
In Articles of Confederation, 192, 195, 196, 197, 200
Centralization, need for, 199
In Constitution, **202-211**
Continental Congress establishes, 158, 163, 170, 176
Progressive reforms, 503, 504, 510
Slavery and, 352-353, 357-363
South secedes from, 366-368
Views on, I 512-519
Grady, Henry W., 460
Grand Canyon, 75, **458, 459**
Grant, Ulysses S., 294, 385, **386,** 387, 388, 390, 393, 796 (graph)
Grasse (gräs), François de, 186
Graves, Thomas, 186
Great Lakes, 66, **70,** 74 (map), 75, 76, 238 (map)
Great Plains, 42, 74, 234, 235 (map), **272-275,** 413, **644,** 645
Great Salt Lake, 276, 277 (map)
Greece, 701, 711 (map), 752 (map), 753
Greene, Nathanael, 185
Greenland, 55, 66 (map), 74 (map)
Greensboro, North Carolina, **460**
Greenville, Treaty of, 266
Grenville, George, 150
Gropper, William, 651, **678**
Guadalupe Hidalgo (gwä′*th*ä lōō′pä ē *th*äl′gō), Treaty of, 294, 296 (map), 297
Guam, I 522, I 524, 562
In World War II, 716 (map), 717, 757 (map)

Guatemala, 41, 567, 764
Guinea, 80, 81 (map), 88, 98
Guthrie, Oklahoma, **450,** 451

H

Hacker, Louis M., I 434
Haiti, **95-99,** 570, 668, 670
Hale, Nathan, 172
Hamilton, Alexander, **221**
Banking system, 221-223
And Constitution, 201
As Federalist, 229-230
Hampton Institute, 414
Hanoi (hä noi′ *or* hă **noi**′), North Vietnam, 760, **762,** 763
Hard, William, I 512-513
Harding, Warren G., **614,** 615, 662, **663, 666,** 796
Harlan, John Marshall, 411
Harlem, **412, 620,** 621, 728
Harmar, Josiah, 266
Harpers Ferry, 365
Harrington, Michael, I 518-519
Harris, Townsend, 532
Hawaii
Admission as state, 196
Annexation of, 536, **537, 556**
Trade with, 528, 536
In U.S. (1970), 794 (map)
U.S. business in, 532, 536
In World War II, 702, **703**
Hay, John, 544
Hayes, Rutherford B., 404, **405**
Haymarket Riot, 497, **498**
Hayne, Robert, **352,** 353
Hays, Lee, I 16
Hearst, William Randolph, **558,** 559
Held, John, Jr., **612**
Henry, Prince, 58, 59 (map)
Henry, Patrick, 125, 126, 155, **155,** 158, 201
Hine, H. G., **274**
Hine, Lewis, 480, **494, 495**
Hiroshima (hir′ō shē′mə *or* hĭ rō′shĭ mə), 720
Hispaniola (hĭs′pən yō′lə). *See* Haiti, Santo Domingo
Hiss, Alger, 758
Hitler, Adolf, **674-675,** 677-678, 681, 714
Hoban (hō′bən), James, 227
Hoboken, New Jersey, **346**
Holland
Exploration and settlement of New World, 66 (map), 67, 70, **72, 73,** I 130-132
In Europe (1970), 752 (map)
In Revolution, 180
Slave trade, 79, 91, **94,** 95
In World War I, 583 (map)
In World War II, **666,** 682, 702, 711 (map)
Holmes, Oliver Wendell
Abrams v. U.S., I 246-247
Schenck v. U.S., I 244-245
Holy Alliance, 553
Homer, Winslow, **319**
Homestead Act, **450,** 451-452
Homestead Steel Strike, 498
Honolulu, Hawaii, **537**
Hoover, Herbert, **614,** 615, 623, 639, 640, 645, 646, 647, **653,** 665, 668, **669,** 677, 796
Hopi (hō′pē) Indians, 49
Hopkins, Harry L., 649
Horn, Cape, 279, 300 (map)
Horses, Indians' use of, 275
House of Representatives, founding of, 199, 205, 209, 213
See also Government of U.S.

807

Housing
  In Depression of 1929, 642, **643**
  In industrial cities, **468, 472, 473, 479, 480, 481, 490-493**
  Racial discrimination in, effect of, **620,** 621, 734
  In suburbs, 618, **619,** 726, **727**
  U.S. Department of Housing and Urban Development, 731
  U.S. Housing Authority, 650, 653
  Urban renewal, 728, **729**
  In World War II, 706
Houston (hyōō′stən), Sam, 287-289, 290
Howard, Joseph K., I 772-773
Howe, William, 172-173, 176
Hudson, Henry, 66 (map), 67, 72
Hudson River, 179, 310, **311**
Hudson's Bay, 66 (map), 71, 74 (map)
Huerta (wĕr′tə), Victoriano, 570, 572
Hughes, Charles Evans, 624, 662, 668
Hughes, Langston, 11, 621
Hull, Cordell, 670, 681
Hull House, **492-493**
Humboldt River, 276, 277 (map)
Hungary, 713, 752 (map)
Hydrogen bomb, 760

I

Ibo (ē′bō), 80
Iceland, 55, 74 (map)
Idaho
  Exploration of, 277 (map), 278 (map)
  Indian reservations in, 448 (map)
  Industrial mining in, 457
  Transportation, 445 (map)
  In U.S. (1970), 794 (map)
  See also Oregon Territory, West
Illinois
  Admission as state, 195 (map), 196, 269
  In Civil War, 367 (map), 382
  Exploration of, 74 (map)
  German immigration to, 350
  Lincoln-Douglas debates, 362-363
  Mormons and, 279
  In Revolution, 182, 182 (map)
  Settlement of, **258, 267,** 275, I 330-331
  Springfield race riot, 418
  Transportation in, 314 (map), 315 (map), I 330-331
  See also Chicago, West
Immigrants
  Industrial Revolution and, **346,** 347, 350, I 432-435, **440, 441, 466,** 467 (graph)
  Life in U.S., I 18, 469, 470, **479, 480, 481, 490-493,** 495
  Reaction against, 467, 470, 547, 548, 613, 623, **624,** 625, **704,** 705
  See also Colonies, specific nationalities
Immigration Act of 1924, **624,** 625
Impeachment, power of, 209
Imperialism, debate on, I 332-335, 540, **542,** 543.
  See also Territorial Expansion
Import duties. *See* Tariffs
Impressment, 233
Inca (ĭng′kə) Indians, **34-37,** 39, 53, 62, **63**
Income, 640 (graph), 642, I 684-691, 744 (graph)
  See also Poverty, Prosperity

Indentured servants, 99, 112
Independence, Missouri, 278 (map), 279
Indiana
  In Civil War, 367 (map), 382
  Ku Klux Klan in, 623
  Negroes in, 413, 736
  In Revolution, 182
  Settlement of, 194 (map), 195, 196, 269, 275
  Transportation in, 314 (map), 445 (map)
  Treaty of Greenville, 266
  In U.S.: in 1853, 296 (map); in 1970, 794 (map)
  See also West
Indians
  Civilizations, 27-33, 61; Aztec, **38, 39;** Inca, **34-37,** 39, 53, 62, **63;** Mayan, **40-41,** 53; North American, **42-50,** I 128-129
  Cultural identity, I 23, 24, **738, 739,** I **774-775**
  Explorers and, **70,** 75, 150, **234, 235,** 275, 276
  In French and Indian War, **144-147,** 149
  Frontier wars with settlers, 150, 196, 237, **261, 266,** 272, 283, 284, 288, 293, 449
  Loss of territories, 209, 211, 448, 449, **450, 451,** I 523-525
  Negroes and, 79, 85, 95, 413
  Plains Indians, 274, 275, **448,** 449
  Reservations, 209, 211, 448 (map), 449
  Resettlement of, 270, **272, 273,** 307
  In Revolution, 179, 189
  See also specific tribes
Indigo, 99, 104 (map), 105, 270
Indochina, 702
  See also Vietnam War
Industrial Workers of the World (IWW), **500, 501,** 584, 625
Industry
  Automation in, 744
  Colonial, 104 (map), 108 (map), 109, **111,** 196
  Environment and, **742,** 743 (graph), I **774-777**
  Industrial Revolution, **306-319, 436-462;** North, 344, 347, 405, South, **270,** 271, 348, 405, **460, 461, 462;** West, 350, 351, **456,** 457, 459
  Mass production in, **316,** 317, **436,** 437, **440, 441,** 444, **446,** 447, **494,** 495, **588, 589,** I 695-697, 706, **707,** 709
  T.V.A. and, 652 (map), 653
  In World War I, **588,** 589
  In World War II, 706, **707,** 709, 718
  See also Business, Factories, Labor, Technology
Integration, I 422-429, **732, 733**
  See also Civil Rights, Segregation
International Brigades, 678, **679,** 680
International Court of Justice, 769
Interstate Commerce Commission, creation of, 503-504
Intrepid, **232**
Inventions
  Dependence on, 437, 464, 473, 486
  Electrical, 444, 617, 725
  Industrial processes, 442, 447
  Mechanical farm, **270,** 271, 336, **337, 452, 453**
  In transportation, **306,** 307,

312, 313, 377, **585,** 586, **587, 616, 617,** 618
  See also Industry, specific inventions, Technology
Iowa
  In Civil War, 367 (map)
  Exploration of, 235 (map), 278 (map)
  Settlement of, 195 (map), 348
  Transportation in, 445 (map)
  In U.S.: in 1853, 296 (map); in 1970, 794 (map)
  See also West
Iowa (ī′ə wə) Indians, **44, 45**
Irish-Americans, 114, 122, 309, I 330-331, **346,** 347, 382, **383,** 441
Iroquois (ĭr′ə kwoi′ *or* ĭr′ə kwoiz′) Indians, 26, 45, 46, 144
Isabella, Queen, 60
Isolationism, 594, 613, **660,** 661, 662, **680-682,** 699, 701
Italian-Americans, **440,** 441, 467, 625
Italy
  In Europe (1970), 752 (map)
  Medieval cities, 56, **57,** 60
  Rise of Mussolini, 661, 674, **675**
  U.S. diplomatic relations with, 560, 602, **666**
  In World War I, 583 (map), 592 **593,** 594
  In World War II, **675,** 678, 701, 702, **710,** 711 (map)
Iwo Jima (ē′ wō jē′ mə), battle of, 716 (map), 718

J

Jackson, Andrew, 239-240, **272,** 290, 322-**326,** 796
Jackson, Thomas J., 374, **384,** 385
James, King of England, 68-69
Jamestown, Virginia, 67, **68,** 68-69, 79
Japan
  In Asia, 677; (1970), 757 (map)
  Portuguese exploration in, 58, 59 (map), 60
  U.S. trade with, 531, 532; Perry in, 529, **530,** 531; Root-Takahira Agreement, 544; Gentlemen's Agreement, 548; investment in, 665
  At Washington Disarmament Conference, 662, **666**
  In World War II, 661, **676,** 678, **702,** 703, 716 (map), 717, 718, **720,** 721, 722, 754
Japanese-Americans
  Gentlemen's Agreement, 467, 548
  Life in U.S., **470,** 548
  In World War II, **704,** 705
Jay, John, 201, **222,** 223
Jazz, **620,** 621
Jefferson, Thomas, 102, 170, 180, 204-205, 222, **223,** 229-231, 232-234, 796
Jersey City, New Jersey, **346**
Jews, 114, 441, 623, 675, 678, 714
Jim Crow Laws, **410-411,** 418, I 423, 734
Jingoism, 539, 553, 559
Johnson, Andrew, 209, **210,** 398, 796
Johnson, Lyndon B., 733, 763, **765,** 796
Johnson, Tom, 492
Joliet (jō′lē ĕt′), Louis, 70, 74 (map), 75
Jones Act of 1917, 670
Judicial power
  Bill of Rights guaranties, 208

Constitution's policy on, 202–204
See also Supreme Court, System of Checks and Balances

K

Kansas
  "Bleeding Kansas," 359, 360, **361**
  Cattle industry in, 454, 455 (map)
  Economic relation to country, 642
  Exploration of, 74 (map), 75
  Integration and, 413, 733
  Ku Klux Klan, 623
  In U.S. (1970), 794 (map)
  See also West
Kansas-Nebraska Act, 359, 360, **361**
Kearny, Stephen W., 292 (map), 293
Keith, Minor, 567, 569
Kellogg, Frank, 667, 668
Kellogg-Briand Pact, **666**, 667
Kennedy, Cape, **724**
Kennedy, John F., I 518, 725, 759, **760, 761, 764**, 765–767, 796
Kennedy, Robert F., 725
Kentucky
  Alien and Sedition Acts, 230
  In Civil War, 367 (map), 378
  Settlement of, 257, 262 (map), 263, 347
  Transportation in, 314 (map), 315 (map)
  T.V.A. in, 652 (map)
  In U.S. (1970), 794 (map)
  In War of 1812, 239
Kernodle, Wayne, I 335–336
Key, Francis Scott, **239**
Khrushchev, Nikita
  China and, **755**
  Missile crisis, **760, 761**
  Peaceful coexistence and, 759
Killen, James O., I 132–134
King, Martin Luther, Jr., I 10, 725, 734, **735**
King George's War, 146, 157
Kiowa (kī′ō wä′ *or* kī′ə wə) Indians, 275
Knights of Labor, **496**
Korean War, **756, 757, 758**, 769
Kosciusko (kŏs′ē ŭs′kō), Thaddeus, 180, **180**
Kru, 80, 91
Ku Klux Klan, **402**, 403, **622**, 623, 624
Kuomintang (kwō′mĭn tăng′), 676, 754

L

Labor
  Child, **441, 494**, 495, 510
  Female, **317**–**319**, 441, 495, **588**, 707
  Immigrant, 439, **440, 441**, 547
  In Industrial Revolution, 307, **308**, 309, **356, 357**, I 512–514, 610, I 694–697
  National Labor Relations Act and Board, 654
  Sweatshops, **494–495**
  Unionization of, 320, 459, **495–501**, 654, 655, 656, 736, **737**
  See also Factories, Industry
Lafayette (lä′fē ĕt′ *or* lăf′ē ĕt′), Marquis de, 180, **181**
Lafitte (lä fēt′), Jean, 239–240

La Follette (lə fŏl′ĭt), Robert, **507**, 615
Land
  Homestead Act, **450, 451, 452**
  Limits on power of owners of, 205, 207, 213
  Mexican offers of grants in Texas, 284, **285**
  Ordinances of 1785 and 1787, 195, 196, 266
  Pioneers' search for, **256–280**
  Speculation: in Florida, I 608–611; in Panic of 1837, 324, 327
  See also Agriculture, Free-Soil Party, Ranches
Laos (lä′ŏs *or* lā′ŏs′), 757 (map), 763
La Salle, Robert de, **70**, 74 (map), 75
Latin America
  Alliance for Progress, **764**, 765
  Good Neighbor Policy, 670, **671**
  Investments in, 551 (map), 554, **555, 556, 557, 566**, 567, 569, 570, 655
  Military intervention in, **568**, 569, **570, 571**, 572, 668, **669**, **765**
  Peace Corps in, 766
Latrobe (lə trōb′), Benjamin, **226**, 227
La Vérendrye (lä vā rän drē′), Pierre de, 53, 74 (map), 76
Lawrence, James, 237
Leadville, Colorado, 457
League of Nations, 591, 592, 594, **594, 595**, 596, 662, **663**, 672, 677
Lee, Robert E., 294, 374, **375, 384**, 385, 390, **392**, 393
Legislative power. *See* System of Checks and Balances
Lend-lease, 701, 710
L'Enfant (län fän′), Pierre Charles, 224, **227**
Lenin, Vladimir Ilyich (Nikolai), 672, **673**, 674
Leshan, Eda J., I 690
Lewis, John L., 654
Lewis, Meriwether, **234**, 234, **235**
Lexington and Concord, battles of, **160–163**
Lilienthal, David, 654
Liliuokalani, Queen, 536, **537**
Lincoln, Abraham, 294, I 341, **362**, **363**, 366–368, 371, 378, **380, 381, 386**, 390, 398, 796
Lindbergh, Charles A., **632**, 634, **664**, 668
Little Big Horn, battle of, 449
Little Rock, Arkansas, 202, 445 (map), **732, 733**, 794 (map)
Livingston, Robert, 310
Lloyd George, David, **593**
Lodge, Henry Cabot, 594
Log cabins, **264**, 265, **269**
Lone Star Republic. *See* Texas
Los Angeles, California, 277 (map), 278 (map), 292 (map), 293, 445 (map), 704, **730**, 794 (map)
Louis, Joe, 634
Louisiana
  Agriculture in, 271 (map), **349**
  In Civil War, 367 (map), 372, 372 (map), 387 (map), 391 (map)
  Exploration of, 76, 233, **234, 235**
  Industrialization in, **306**, 310, 311, 314, 314 (map), 315 (map), 350, **351**, 445 (map), 460
  Ku Klux Klan in, 623
  Negro voter registration in, 736 (graph)

Reconstruction in, 404 (map), **404, 405**, 410, 422
In U.S.: in 1853, 296 (map); in 1970, 794 (map)
See also New Orleans, South
Louisiana Purchase, 233, **234**, 235 (map)
Louisville, Kentucky, 310
Loyalists, **678, 679**, 680
Lumber, 42, **47**, 67, 108 (map), 109, 377, 451, 460
See also Natural Resources
Lusitania (lōō′sĭ tā′nē ə), **580**, 581
Lynching, 298, **408**, 409

M

MacArthur, Douglas A., **647, 716, 717, 718, 756**, 758
Madison, James, 201, **233**, 237, 796
Mahan (mə hăn′), Alfred T., **538**, 539
Maine
  Admission as "Free State," 358 (map), 367 (map)
  Ku Klux Klan in, 623
  Railroads, 314 (map), 315 (map)
  Roosevelt, F. D., and, 657
  In U.S. (1970), 794 (map)
  See also North
Maine, sinking of, **558**, 559
Malaya (mə lā′ə), 665, 702, 716 (map), 717, 757 (map)
Malcolm X, I 424–425, **734**
Mali (mä′lē), 80, 81, 86
Manchuria, **676**, 677, 716 (map)
Mandan (măn′dăn) Indians, **30**
Manifest Destiny, **282, 283**, 291, 297, 298, 303, 526, 532, 554
Manila Bay, 540, **541**
Mann, Horace, 320
Mao Tse-tung (mou′tsĭ toong′), 676, **754**
Marbury v. Madison, 202
Mariana Islands, 716 (map), 718, 721
Marietta, Ohio, **194**
Marines, **568**, 569–570, 668, **669**
Marion, Francis, 184, 185
Marne (märn), battle of, 578, **579**
Marquette, Jacques, 70, 74 (map), 75
Marquis, Don, I 774–775
Marryat, Frederick, I 330
Marshall, George C., 754, 758
Marshall, John, 209, 211, 298, 324, **325**
Marshall, Thurgood, 733
Marshall Plan, 753
Maryland
  Agriculture in, 271 (map), 347
  In Civil War, 367 (map), 372 (map), 374, **375**, 378, 382, 385, 387 (map)
  Colonial, 99, 104 (map), 112, 113, 114, 124
  In Revolution, 179 (map), 185 (map)
  Transportation in, 313, 314 (map), 315 (map), 445 (map)
  In U.S.: in 1783, 188 (map); in 1970, 794 (map)
  In War of 1812, **236**, 237, **239**
  In Whiskey Rebellion, 225
Massachusetts
  Abolitionists in, 354, **355**, 356
  Brook Farm, 321
  Civil War in, 367 (map)
  Colonial, **69**, 70, 104 (map), 106, **107**, 108 (map), 109, **110, 111**, 124, 144, **145**, 152, **153**, 154, **155**, 158, **159**

Industrialization in, **312**, 317, 319, 347, I 432, I 433, 441, 498, **499**
Revolutionary War, **160**, 161, **162, 163, 164, 165,** 173, 179 (map)
Shays' Rebellion, **196, 197**
State government and, 213, 320
Transportation in, 314 (map), 315 (map), 445 (map)
In U.S.: in 1783, 188 (map); in 1970, 794 (map)
Mather, Richard, 106, **107**
Mayan (mä′yən) Indians, **40, 41**
McCarthy, Joseph, 758
McClellan, George B., 374, **375, 386,** 387
McCormick, Cyrus, 478
McKinley, William, **504,** 505, 508, 536, 540, 543, **558–560,** 796
Megalopolises, 726
Melting pot, I **330–331,** 470, 739
Memphis, Tennessee, 314 (map), 315 (map), 372, 372 (map), 387, 387 (map), 413, 445 (map), 794 (map)
Meredith, James, **732,** 733
Mexican-Americans, 704, 736, **737,** 739
Mexican War, 292 (map)
  Buena Vista, battle of, 293
  Expansionist debate over, 276, 279, 290, 291, I 332–334
  Guadalupe Hidalgo, Treaty of, 294, 296 (map), 297
  Mexico City, battle of, 294, **295**
  Palo Alto, battle of, 293
  San Pasqual, battle of, **292,** 293
  Santa Fe, battle of, 293
Mexico
  Adams-Onís Treaty and, 238 (map), 240
  Indian empires in, 39, **40,** 41
  Railroad from Central America to, 507, 569
  Settlers' conflict with, 276, 279, **555**
  Spanish conquest of, 62, **64,** 65
  Texas and, **284–289,** 291
  U.S. relations with, 551 (map), **570, 571,** 572, 668, 670, 765
  See also California, Latin America, Mexican War, Texas
Mexico, Gulf of, 66 (map), 70, 74 (map)
  Industrialization of area, **441,** 460
Michigan
  In Civil War, 367 (map), 377
  English possession of, 188 (map)
  Erie Canal in, I 330–331
  Exploration of, 262 (map)
  Industry in, **447,** 654, **655**
  Missouri Compromise, 358 (map)
  Settlement of, 195 (map), 195–196
  Transportation in, 314 (map), 315 (map), 445 (map)
  In U.S.: in 1853, 296 (map); in 1970, 794 (map)
  See also West
Middle class, 483, **483–486,** 486, 621, 728, **729**
Middle East, 655, 711 (map), 759
Midway Islands, 527 (map), 535, 716 (map), 718
Midwest. *See* West
Migrant workers, I 518, 519, **644,** 645, 653
Milwaukee, Wisconsin, 314 (map), 315 (map), 464
Mines, 257, 284, **440,** 442, **443, 445, 451, 456,** 457, 459, 460, **497,** 504
Minneapolis, Minnesota, 464, 794 (map)
Minnesota
  In Civil War, 360, 367 (map), 377
  Compromise of 1850, 358 (map)
  Indian reservations in, 448 (map)
  Industry in, 442, **443,** 464
  Settlement of, 348, 350
  As territory, 296 (map)
  Transportation in, 315 (map), 445 (map)
  In U.S. (1970), 794 (map)
Minutemen, **160–163**
Missile crisis, **760, 761**
Missionaries, 63–64, 532, **537,** 544
Mississippi
  In Civil War, 367 (map), 385, **386,** 387, 387 (map), 388
  Cotton frontier, 270
  Negroes in, 400, **401, 732,** 733, 736, 736 (graph), **737**
  Reconstruction in, 404 (map)
  Transportation in, 315 (map), 445 (map)
  T.V.A. in, 652 (map)
  In U.S.: in 1853, 296 (map); in 1970, 794 (map)
  See also South
Mississippi River, 70, 74 (map), 75, 146, 182 (map), 188 (map), 189, 234, 235 (map), 310, 350, **351,** 385, **386,** 387 (map), 388, 635
  See also Frontier
Missouri
  Agriculture in, 271 (map), 347
  And "Bleeding Kansas," 360
  In Civil War, 367 (map), 378, 382
  Frontier, 262 (map), 263, **278,** 279
  Industry in, 310, 350, **351,** 413, 454, 455 (map), 464
  Transportation in, 314 (map), 315 (map), 445 (map)
  In U.S.: in 1853, 296 (map); in 1970, 794 (map)
  See also South
Missouri Compromise, 357, 358, 358 (map)
Missouri River, 277 (map), 278 (map)
Mombasa (mŏm bä′sə), Kenya, 82
Monroe, James, 550, 553, 796
Monroe Doctrine, 550, 553, 569, 670
Montana
  In Depression of 1929, 645
  Exploration of, 75, 76
  Indian reservations in, 448 (map)
  Industry in, 457
  Transportation in, 445 (map)
  In U.S. (1970), 794 (map)
  See also West
Montcalm (mônt käm′), Marquis de, **148, 149**
Monte Cassino, battle of, 710
Monterrey, Mexico, capture of, 292 (map), 293
Montezuma (mŏn′tə zōō′mə) II, 38, 62
Montgomery, Alabama, 315 (map), 366, **734,** 794 (map)
Mormons, 279
Morocco, 710, 711 (map)
Morrill Act of 1862, 453
Morrow, Dwight W., 668

Mount Vernon, Virginia, 214
Muckrakers, **508, 509**
Muhlenberg (myōō′lən bûrg′), Frederick, 214
Murray, Harriet W., 398
Mussolini (mōōs′sō lē′ nē), Benito, 674, 675, 710

N

Nagasaki, (nä′gə sä′kē), Japan, 722
Napoleon, **96–97,** 99, 233–234
Nash, Roderick, I 695
Nast, Thomas, **392, 409, 490, 491**
National Association for the Advancement of Colored People (NAACP), 420, 733
National Civic Federation, 498
National Guard, **732,** 733
National Industrial Recovery Act (NIRA), 657
Nationalistic movements, 593, 594, I 604–605, 699, 717, 764
National Labor Relations Act (NLRA), 654
National Labor Relations Board, 654
National Park Service, 459
National Urban League, 413, I 425
Nativists, 470, 508, **622,** 623
Natural resources
  Colonial use of, **68, 69, 70, 71,** 75, 76, 104 (map), 105, 109, **112, 113,** 118, **119**
  Conservation and Ecology, 459, 743 (graph), I 772–777
  Frontier use of, 188 (map), 195, 234, I 252–255, 257, 259, **264, 265, 269,** 270, **271,** 271 (map), **276, 277,** 279, **284, 285, 298, 299,** I 330–331, I 335–336, **448–456**
  Indian use of, **30, 31, 32, 33, 34, 35, 36, 38, 39, 40,** 41, **42, 43, 46, 47,** 48, 49, 274, 275
  Industrial use of, I 12–13, **310, 311,** 437, **441, 442, 443,** 447, 449, **452–459, 534, 535,** 617, 618, **742, 743,** 743 (graph)
  See also Industry, Mines, Pollution, Technology
Navaho (năv′ə hō′ *or* nä′və hō′) Indians, 49
Navy, U.S., 182, 222, 223, **232,** 233, 237, 378, **379, 530,** 531, 536, **538–541,** 550, **558–560,** 562, 565, 570, 662, 701, 703, 711 (map), 718, **740, 741, 760, 761**
Nazis, 674, 675, 677, 678, 701, 714
  See also World War II
Nebraska
  Indian reservations in, 448 (map)
  Kansas-Nebraska Act, 359, 360
  Populists in, 488
  Settlement of, 278 (map), 377, **450**
  Transportation in, 445 (map)
  In U.S. (1970), 794 (map)
  See also West
Negroes
  African heritage, **82–87, 739**
  Civil rights movement, 725, **734, 735**
  In Civil War, 340, **341,** 342, 350, 351, 371, **380,** 381, 393
  Colleges, **414–418**
  On frontier, 75, 192, 196, 199, 200, 277, 454, **455**
  Housing and, **620,** 621, 726
  Industry and, **446,** 462, 467, **469,** 575, **589**

Integration and, I 424–429, **732**, 733
Legislation and: Civil Rights Acts, 399, **400**, 734; 14th and 15th amendments, **396**, 397, 399, 400; Jim Crow laws, **410**, 411, 418, 734; Voting Rights Act, 736
Militancy and, I 424–425, 734, 736
National Association for the Advancement of Colored People (NAACP), 420
Niagara Conference, **418**, **419**, 420
Politics and, 400, **401**, 404, **405**, 736, **737**
Presidential appointees, 227, 731, 733
Racial violence and, I 10, 382, **383**, **402**, 403, **408**, 409, 418, **622**, 623, 704, 725, 733
Reconstruction and, **396–420**
In Revolution, 152, 162, **164**, 170, 185
Rise of leadership, **414–420**
Segregation and, **406**, 407, **410**, **411**, 418, 733, **734**, 735
Slavery and, 59, 78, 79, 88–93, 108 (map), 109, **118–121**, I 130–134, **269–271**, 273, 287, 290, 307, **352–361**
In Spanish-American War, 562, **563**
Sports and, 632, **633**, 634
In War of 1812, 239, 240
In World Wars, 582, 704
See also Cities, Civil Rights, specific individuals
Neutrality Acts, 680, 682, 701
Nevada
  Exploration of, 277 (map), 278 (map)
  Indian reservations in, 445 (map)
  Mining in, 377, 457
  Transportation in, 445 (map)
  In U.S. (1970), 794 (map)
  See also West
New Deal, 647–657
New England
  Colonial, **106–111**
  Industry in, 279, **317–319**, 347
  See also North, Revolution
Newfoundland, 55, 66 (map)
New Hampshire
  In Civil War, 367 (map)
  Industry in, **312**, 313
  In U.S.: in 1783, 188 (map); in 1853, 296 (map); in 1970, 794 (map)
New Harmony, Indiana, **320**, 321
New Haven, Connecticut, **107**, 315 (map)
New Jersey
  In Civil War, 367 (map)
  Colonial, **112**, **113**
  Election of Washington, 214
  Exploration of, 72
  Industry in, **346**, 347
  Negroes in, 736
  In Revolution, **168**, **174**, 175
  Transportation in, 315 (map)
  In U.S.: in 1783, 188 (map); in 1970, 794 (map)
  See also North
New Mexico
  Atomic test site, **720**, 721
  Compromise of 1850, 358 (map), 359
  Exploration of, 276, 277 (map), 278 (map)
  Indians in, **48**, 448 (map)
  Pancho Villa in, 572

Santa Fe, battle of, 292 (map), 293
Transportation in, 445 (map)
In U.S.: in 1853, 296 (map); in 1970, 794 (map)
See also West
New Orleans, Louisiana, 188 (map), 189, 196, **238–240**, 306, 310, **311**, 314 (map), 315 (map), 350, **351**, 367 (map), 372 (map), 387 (map), 391 (map), 410, 413, 445 (map), 621, 794 (map)
New York
  In Civil War, 367 (map)
  Colonial, 67, 102, 104 (map), **112**, **113**, 114
  Constitution and, **201**, 213
  Erie Canal in, **308**, 309
  Industry in, 347
  In Revolution, **142**, 143, 150, 158, **172**, **173**, 179, 186
  Suffragette convention, 321
  Steamboat in, 310, **311**
  Transportation in, 314 (map), 315 (map), 445 (map)
  In U.S.: in 1783, 188 (map); in 1970, 794 (map)
  In War of 1812, 237
  See also New York City, North
New York City, 70, 72, **73**, 158, **172**, **173**, 179, 188 (map), 213, **214**, **215**, 300 (map), 301, 313, 314 (map), 315 (map), 346, 347, 382, **383**, 445 (map), **466–469**, **472**, 474–477, 482, 484, 490, 495, **580**, 640, 641, **643**, 767, **768**, 794 (map)
Niagara, Fort, 189
Niagara Conference, **418**, **419**, 420
Nicaragua, 301, 551 (map), 554, **555**, 568, 569, 570, 668, 669, 670
See also Latin America
Nicolet (nĭk′ə lā′), Jean, 70
Nisei (nē sā′ *or* nē′sā′), 704, **705**
Nixon, Richard M., 763, 796 (graph)
Normandy, invasion of, 711 (map), **712**, 713
Norris, Frank, I 598–599
North
  Civil War and, 365, 366, 367, (map), **376**, 377, 378, **380**, 381, 382, **383**, 387
  Colonial, 104 (map), **104–117**
  Exploration of, 66 (map), 67, **69**, 70, 71, 72, **73**, 74 (map)
  Industry and, 314, 314 (map), 315, 315 (map), I 343, 444
  Negroes and, **396–420**, **732**, 733, 736, **737**
  Sectionalism and, 344, **350–353**
  In Spanish-American War, 562, **563**
  See also Civil War, Industry, specific states
North Atlantic Treaty Organization (NATO), 759
North Carolina
  Agriculture in, 271 (map), 272
  Civil War in, 367 (map)
  Colonial, 104 (map)
  Constitution and, 201
  Exploration of, 75
  Frontier in, I 252–253, 262 (map), 263, 270
  Indians in, **43**, 272
  Industry in, 460
  Negro voter registration, 736 (graph)
  Reconstruction in, 404 (map)
  In Revolution, 175, 184, **185**, 185 (map)
  Transportation in, 314 (map), 315 (map), 445 (map)

T.V.A. in, 652 (map)
In U.S.: in 1783, 188 (map); in 1970, 794 (map)
See also Civil War, South
North Dakota
  Indians in, 448 (map), I 774–775
  Industry in, 453
  Pioneers in, **448**
  Transportation in, 445 (map)
  In U.S. (1970), 794 (map)
  See also West
Northwest Ordinance, 195, 195 (map), 196, 266
Northwest Passage, 66 (map), 67, 72, 74 (map)
Northwest Territory, 195, 195 (map), 196, 223, 266, 269, 348, 350, 363
Norway, 55, 682, 711 (map)
Noyes (noiz), John Humphrey, 321
Nuclear power, I 14–15, 741, 751, 758, 759, I 776
See also Atomic Bomb
Nueces (nōō ā′səs *or* nyōō ā′səs) River, 291
Nullification doctrine, 230
Nuremberg Trials, 714
Nye (nī), Gerald P., 680

O

Oceanic exploration, 740, **741**
Ogden, Peter Skene, 276, 277 (map)
Ohio
  In Civil War, 367 (map), 382
  Exploration of, 262 (map)
  Industry in, 310, **311**, 350, **351**, 438, **439**
  Negroes in, 736, **737**
  In Revolution, 180, 182, 182 (map)
  Settlement of, 195 (map), 196, 269
  Transportation in, 314 (map), 315 (map), 445 (map)
  Treaty of Greenville, 266
  In U.S.: in 1853, 296 (map); in 1970, 794 (map)
  See also West
Ohio River, 146, 180, 182 (map), 194, 195, 263, 310, **311**, 350, 653
Oil, 377, 437, **438**, 439, 442, 443, 617, 618, 665, 668, 710, 711 (map), **742**, 743 (graph)
See also Natural Resources
Okinawa (ō′kĭ nä′wə), 532, 716 (map), 718
Oklahoma
  Cattle and, 455, 455 (map)
  Dust Bowl, **644**, 645
  Indians and, 273, 448 (map), **450**, 451
  Ku Klux Klan in, 623
  Opening of, **450**, 451
  Transportation in, 445 (map)
  In U.S. (1970), 794 (map)
  See also West
Oklahoma City, Oklahoma, 450, 794 (map)
Olmsted (ōm′stĕd′ *or* ōm′stĭd), Frederick Law, 476, **477**
Olympics, 632, **633**
Omaha, Nebraska, 278 (map), 445 (map), 488, 744 (map)
Oneida colony, New York, 321
Open Door Policy, 543, 544, **545**, 662, 754
Ordinances of 1785 and 1787, 195, 266

Oregon
    In Civil War, 367 (map)
    In Depression of 1929, 645
    Indian reservations in, 448 (map)
    Trade, 528
    Transportation in, 445 (map)
    In U.S. (1970), 794 (map)
    See also Oregon Territory, West
Oregon Territory, 240, 257, 277, 278 (map), 279, 283, 290, 291, 296 (map), 297, 358 (map), 553
Organization of American States, 759, **760, 761**, 765
Orlando, Vittorio, **593**
Ostend Manifesto, 556
Owen, Robert, 321
Owens, Jesse, 632, **633**, 634
Oyo, 80, 81 (map)

P

Paine, Thomas, I 9, 155, 170, 174
Pakenham, Sir Edward, **238**
Palo Alto (păl′ō ăl′tō), battle of, 292 (map), 293
Panama, 62, 75, 300 (map), 301, 551 (map), 670
Panama Canal, 301, **564, 565**
Parker, John, 161
Parks, 459, 476, **477**
Patriots, **152-158**, 170, **171**, 175-176, **177**, 184, 185, 189
Pattie, Sylvester and James, 276, 277 (map)
Patton, George S., **712**
Peace Corps, **766**, 767
Peace-keeping forces (U.N.), 769
    See also Korean War
Peace movements, 581, **666**, 667
Pearl Harbor, 536, 702, **703**, 716 (map), 718
Penn, William, 114
Pennsylvania
    In Civil War, 367 (map), **384, 385**, 387 (map)
    Colonial, 104 (map), 112, **113, 114, 115, 116, 117**
    Constitution and, 146, 199, 201, 213
    Frontier life, **269**
    Industry in, 347, 464
    Natural resources, 377, **440, 494**
    In Revolution, 146, 150, 175, 176, **177**, 179
    Transportation in, 310, **311**, 314 (map), 315 (map), 445 (map)
    In U.S.: in 1783, 188 (map); in 1970, 794 (map)
    In Whiskey Rebellion, 223, **224**
    See also North, Philadelphia, Pittsburgh
Pennsylvania Dutch, 114
People's Party. *See* Populists
Perkins, Frances, 654, **655**
Perry, Matthew C., 529, **530, 531**, 532
Perry, Oliver Hazard, 237, **531**
Pershing (pûr′shĭng), John J., 562, **570**, 572, 582
Peru, conquest of, 62-63
Petersburg, siege of, 390, 391 (map), 393
Petroleum. *See* Oil
Philadelphia, Pennsylvania, 114, **116, 117**, 157, 158, 176, 179, 199, **200**, 214, **219**, 221, 228, **313**, 314 (map), 315 (map), 347, 437, 445 (map), 642, 794 (map)

Philippine (fĭl′ə pēn′) Islands
    American possession of, I 522-525, 527 (map), 540, **541**, **542, 543**, 562
    In World War II, 716 (map), **716**, 717, 718
Pickering, Timothy, I 243-244
Pickett (pĭk′ĭt), George, **384**, 385
Pilgrims, 69-70
Pingree, Hazen, **492**
Pioneers, **256-280**, I 330-331, I 335-336, **450**, 451, 452
    See also Frontier, West
Pitcairn (pĭt′kârn′), John, **160**, 161, 164
Pittsburgh, Pennsylvania, 104 (map), 146, 224, 263, 310, **311**, 314 (map), 315 (map), 445 (map), 464, 654, **655**, 794 (map)
Pizarro (pĭ zär′ō), Francisco, 62-63, **63**
Plains Indians, 42, 274-275, **448-449, 450, 451**
Platt, John, I 15
Platt Amendment, 562
Platte River, 277 (map), 278 (map)
Plessy v. Ferguson, 411, 733
Plymouth, Massachusetts, **69**, 70
Point Four program, I 601-602
Poland, 583 (map), 592, 665, 678, 681, 682, 711 (map), 752 (map), 753
Polish-Americans, **440**, 441, 467
Political parties
    Anti-Imperialists and, **542**, 543
    Minorities and, 736 (graph), **736, 737, 738, 739**
    Political machines, **490-493**, 623, 624
    Population growth and, 464
    Rise of, 202, **206**, 207, 228-230
    Sectionalism and, 350, 352, 353
    See also specific parties
Polk, James K., 290, **290**, 291, 294, 297, 298, 796 (graph)
Pollution, I 12-13, 18, **313**, I 691, 742, 743, I 774-777
Poor, Salem, **164**
Population, growth of, 199, 347, 353, 377, 413, 417, I 426, I 428-429, I 432-435, 453, 464, **465**, 467 (graph), 473, 490, I 603-604, I 696, 726, I 776
    See also Cities
Populists, 411, 488, **504-507**
Portland, Maine, 104 (map), 105
Portland, Oregon, 278 (map), 445 (map), 794 (map)
Portugal, 53, **58**, 59 (map), 60, 79, 91, **94**, 95, I 130-132, **666**
Post roads, 104 (map), 105, 218
Poverty
    Debate on responsibility for, I 10, I 16, I 18, I 512-519, I 601-604, I 686-689
    Industrial Revolution and, 478, **479**, 480, 481, 490-493, **494, 495**, 620, 621, 744, 745
    Minority movements and, I 422-428, 429 (table), **734, 744, 745**
    See also Cities, Depression, Prosperity
Powderly, Terence V., **496**
Powers, Johnny, 492, **493**
Prairie du Chien, Wisconsin, **273**
Prairies, 266, **267**, 275, I 330-331
Prescott, Samuel, **160**
President
    Choosing of, 205
    Powers of, 200, 204-205, 207, 209
Presidential electors, 205, 213
Princeton, battle of, 174, 179 (map)

Proclamation Line, 104 (map), 150
Proclamation of Neutrality, 222-223
Progressives, **507, 508, 509**, 510, 594, 615, 628, 631, 637, 656
Prohibition, I 609-611, 628, **629**, 631
Prosperity, I 428 (table), I 608-611, 613, 617, 621, **638**, 639, I 684-691, **708**, 709, 744, **745**
    See also Business, Poverty
Prussia, 553, 578, 583 (map)
Public Works Administration, 649, 650
Pueblo (pwĕb′lō) Indians, 45, **48**
Puerto Ricans, **738**, 739
Puerto Rico (pwĕr′tō rē′kō *or* pōr′tō rē′kō), I 522-525, 535, 551 (map), 562, 670
    See also Latin America
Pulitzer, Joseph, 559
Punch, John, 99
Puritans, 70, 106, **107**, 109, 114

Q

Quakers, 114, **115**, 122, **208, 209**, 213
Quebec, Canada, 67, **142**, 149
Queen Anne's War, 144

R

Railroads, 257, 283, 297, 313, 314 (map), 315 (map), I 330-331, I 334, 389, 441-444, 445 (map), 448, 449, 451, 454, 455 (map), 460, 498, 503, 504, 510, 554, 567, 569, 589
    See also Technology, Transportation
Ramsdell, Charles, I 342
Ranches, 65, 284, **285**, 350, 451, 454, 455 (map), 457
Raskob, John J., 639
Reconstruction
    Compromise of 1877, 403, **404, 405**
    Confederate states and, 398, 404 (map)
    Discrimination during: Black codes, 398, 399; Ku Klux Klan, **402**, 403
    Negro politicians in, I 24-25, 400, **401**, I 422
    See also Civil War, Negroes, South
Reform, 320, **488-510**
Religion
    African, 82, 84, 85, 87
    Attitudes today on, I 601-603, 667, 706
    Bill of Rights on, 204, 205, 208
    Colonial, **69**, 70, 72, 106, **107**, **114, 115**, 122, 207
    Conquest and, 63, 65, 75, I 129
    Expansion and, I 22-23, I 332-333, I 522-523, I 526
    Frontier and, **268**, 269, 279, 287
    Indians, I 23-24, 31-33, **34, 36, 37**, 38, **39, 40**, 41, 46, **47, 48**, 49, 50, 62, 63, 65
    As justification for: prejudice, 623; slavery, 79, 99, 101
    Negro, 413, 414, I 424-425, 734
    Scopes trial and, 626, **627**
Republicans
    "Black," I 342, 360, 365, 366, 382

Democratic, 218, **228–231**, 290
McKinley organization, **504, 505**
Radical, 399, 400, 404, 405, I 422
Resaca de la Palma, Texas, battle of, 293
Reston, Virginia, 726, **727**
Revels, Hiram R., 400, **401**
Revere, Paul, 111, **153**, **158**, **160**, 161
Revolution
    Background, **142–166**, I 138–141, I 254–255
    Bunker Hill, battle of, 164, **165**, 166
    English invade South, 182, **184**, 185
    European aid in, 180, **181**, 182, 183
    Leaders of, 169, **170**, 171
    Lexington and Concord, battles of, **160**, 161, **162**, 163
    New York, battle of, **172**, 173
    Saratoga, battle of, 180
    Tories in, 175, **176**, **177**
    Trenton, battle of, **168**, **174**, 175
    Valley Forge, battle of, 176, **178**, **179**, **181**
    Vincennes, battle at, 180, **181**
    War's end, 188 (map), 189
    Yorktown, battle of, **186**, **187**
    See also Colonies, Patriots
Rhode Island
    In Civil War, 367 (map)
    Colonial, 104 (map), 106, 109
    Constitution and, 199, 201
    Industry and, 317
    Transportation in, 315 (map)
    In U.S.: in 1783, 188 (map); in 1970, 794 (map)
    See also North
Rice, 99, 108 (map), 109, 270, 347
    See also Agriculture
Richmond, Virginia, 314 (map), 315 (map), 374, 387, 390, 391 (map), **392**, 393, 445 (map), 794 (map)
Rickenbacker, Eddie, 585
Riis (rēs), Jacob, 473, **479**
Rio Grande (rē'ō gränd) River, 278 (map), 291, 292 (map), 293
Roads, (1850), 315 (map); I 335–336
Rochambeau (rō shän bō'), Count, 186
Rockefeller (rŏk'ə fĕl'ər), John D., 438, **439**, 443
Rocky Mountains, 29, 53, 76, 234, 275, 276, 277 (map), 278 (map), 279, 291
Roebling (rōb'lĭng), John A. and Washington, 474
Rome, Italy, 710, 711 (map)
Rommel (rŏm'əl), Erwin, 710, 711 (map)
Roosevelt, Franklin D., I 516–517, I 600–601, 647, 648–655, **656**, **657**, 670, **680**, 682, 701, 702, 721, 796 (graph)
Roosevelt, Nicholas, 310
Roosevelt, Theodore, **416**, 459, **508**, **509**, 510, **538**, 539, 540, **552**, 560, **562**, 565, 569–570, I 773–774, 796 (graph)
Roosevelt Corollary, 569–570
Root-Takahira Agreement, 544
Roubaud, Joseph André, I 130–132
Rumania, 711 (map), 713, 752 (map)
Rush-Bagot Treaty, 240
Russia, Soviet Union
    Alaska and, 535
    In Cold War, **750**, 751, **752**, 753, **754**, 755, 756, 758, 759, **760**, **761**
    In Europe (1970), 752 (map)

Immigration to U.S., **440**, 441, 467
Oregon and, 553
In Pacific, 535, 543
Revolution in, I 245–246, **577**, 578, **672**, **673**, 674
In World War I, 577, 578, 583, (map)
In World War II, 681, 682, 701, **708**, 709, 710, 711 (map), 714, 722
See also Communism
Rustin, Bayard, 736
Ruth, George Herman (Babe), 632, **633**

S

Sacramento, California, 278 (map), 298, 445 (map), 794 (map)
Saigon (sī gŏn'), 760, **762**, 763
St. Clair, Arthur, 266
St. Lawrence River, 66 (map), 70, 104 (map), 146, 149
Saint Louis, Missouri, 234, 278 (map), 310, 314 (map), 315 (map), 350, **351**, 413, 445 (map), 464, 642, 794 (map)
Saint Mihiel (săn mē yĕl'), battle of, 582, 583 (map)
Salem, Peter, 164
Saltillo (säl tē'yō), Mexico, 293
Salt Lake City, Utah, 278 (map), 445 (map), 794 (map)
Samoan (sə mō'ən) Islands, 535, 536
San Diego, California, 276, 277 (map), 293, **595**, 741, 794 (map)
Sandino, Augusto, 668
Sandwich Islands. *See* Hawaii
San Francisco, California, 63, 276, 277, 278, 298, 300 (map), **302**, **303**, 445 (map), 469, 470, **471**, **546**, **738**, 739, 767, 794 (map)
San Jacinto (săn'jə sĭn'tō), battle of, 288, **289**, 292 (map)
San Pasqual, battle of, 292 (map), 293
Santa Anna (sän'tä ä'nä), Antonio de, 287, 288, **289**, 294
Santa Fe, 63, 276, 277 (map), 278 (map), 279, 292 (map), 293, 794 (map)
Santiago (sän tyä'gō), battle of, 551 (map), 560, **562**
Santo Domingo (sän'tō dō mĕng'gō), 96, 535
Saratoga, battle of, 176, **178**, **179**, 179 (map)
Savannah, Georgia, 104 (map), 185 (map), 314 (map), 315 (map), 387 (map), **388**, 445 (map), 474, **475**
Scandinavian-Americans, 347, 441
Scheeler, Charles, **664**
Schenck v. U.S., I 244–245
Schurz (shoŏrts), Carl, I 524–525
Science and Technology. *See* Technology
Scopes trial, 626, **627**
Scott, Dred, **360**
Scott, John Anthony, I 435
Scott, Winfield, 292 (map), 294
Scottish-Americans, 175, 347, 441
Secession, 357, 359, 365, **366**, **367**, 368
    See also Civil War
Security Council (U.N.), 769
Sedition Acts
    Of 1798, 208, 229, 230, I 242–244
    Of 1918, I 244–245, 584
Seeger (sē'gər), Pete, I 16, I 691

Segregation, 406, **407**, **410–411**, 418, I 691, 733, **734**, 735
    See also Civil Rights, Integration
Seminole (sĕm'ə nōl') Indians, 267, 272, 273
Senate
    Founding of, 199, 213
    17th Amendment and, 205, 501
    See also Constitution, Government of U.S., System of Checks and Balances
Serbia, 575, 577, 583 (map)
Sevareid, Eric, I 18
Seward, William H., 532, **534**, 535, 556
Shannon v. Chesapeake, sea battle, 237
Sharecroppers, 406, **407**
Shays' Rebellion, **196**, **197**
Sherman, William Tecumseh, **388**, **389**, 390
Sherman Antitrust Act, 503–504, 510
Shoberli, Frederic, 82, 83
Shoshone (shō shō'nē) Indians, 234
Sicily, 710, 711 (map)
Sierra Nevada (sē ĕr'ə nə vä'də *or* nə văd'ə), 276
Silberman, Charles E., I 10
Singapore, 716 (map), 717
Singleton, Otho Robards, I 341–342
Sioux (soō) Indians, I 23–24, 44, 275, I 774–775
Skyscrapers, 472, 473, 728, **729**
Slavery
    Abolitionists:
        rise of, 207, 320, 344, **354**, **355**, 356
    In Civil War, **364**, 365, 371, 378, 380, 381, 393–394
    Constitution on, 199, 200, 320
    Cotton and, 269–271, **271**, 287, 290, 352–353
    Debate over, I 340–343, **371**, **557**; defense of, **356**, **357**; Lincoln-Douglas debates, 362–363
    Dred Scott v. Sandford, **360**
    Emancipation Proclamation, 378, **380**, 381
    Jefferson and, 170
    Life, 94–102, **118**, **119**, **120**, 121
    Revolts, 92, 96, **97**, 99, 102
    In Revolution, 152, 162, 164, 185
    Territorial conflict over: I 340–343; Compromise of 1850, 358 (map), **359**; Kansas-Nebraska Act, 359, 360, **361**; Missouri Compromise, 357, 358, 358 (map); Northwest, 196; sectionalism and, 196, 287, 350, 352, 353, 554
    Texas and, 287
    Trade, 78, 79, **88–93**, 108 (map), 109, I 130, 200
    See also Civil War, Reconstruction
Smith, Alfred E., 623
Smith, Henry, **408**, 409
Smith, Jedediah, **256**, 257, 276, 277 (map)
Smith, John, 69
Snake River, 277 (map), 278 (map)
Social Security Act of 1935, 656
Socialists, 501, **506**, **507**, **508**, 584, 589, 645, 647, 667
Sockman, Ralph W., I 603–604
Somers, Richard, 232
Somme (sôm) offensive, 578, **586**
Songhai (sông'hī), 80, 81 (map)
Sons of Liberty, 155, 158
South
    Agriculture: cotton frontier,

813

269, 270, 271 (map); plantation economy, 104 (map), 118, **119, 120,** 121, **122, 123,** 347, 348, **349**
Attitude toward slaves, **98–102,** 207, I **340–343**
Civil War in, 367 (map), **371–394,** 372 (map), 387 (map), 391 (map)
Colonial: government, **124,** 125, 126; towns, 67, **68, 122, 123**
Exploration of, 70, 74 (map), 75
Frontier in, 122, 262 (map), **263,** I 335–336
Indians in, **42, 43**
Industry in, 460, **461,** 462
Negro life after Reconstruction, **406–420**
Reconstruction in, **396–405,** 404 (map)
In Revolution, 182, 183, 184, 185, 185 (map), **186, 187, 188** (map), 189
Secession of, 365, **366, 367,** 368
Tariff debate with North, 350, **352, 353**
Transportation in, 314, 314 (map), 315 (map), 350, **351,** 445 (map)
See also Civil War, Compromise of 1850, Integration, Kansas-Nebraska Act, Negroes, specific states

South Carolina
Agriculture in, 270 (map)
In Civil War, **366,** 367 (map), **367, 368,** 372 (map), 378, **379,** 387 (map), 388, **389,** 390, 391
Colonial, 102, 104 (map), 120, 122, **123**
Election of Washington, 213
Frontier in, 122, 262 (map)
Industry in, **460**
Negro voter registration in, 736 (graph)
Reconstruction in, 400, 404, 404 (map), I 422
In Revolution, 182, 184, 185 (map)
Tariff fight with Jackson, 322, 323
T.V.A. in, 652 (map)
Transportation in, 313, 314 (map), 315 (map), 445 (map)
In U.S.: in 1783, 188 (map); in 1853, 296 (map); in 1970, 794 (map)
See also South

South Dakota
Indian reservations in, 448 (map)
Mining in, **456,** 457
Pioneer life in, **448**
In U.S. (1970), 794 (map)
See also West

Southeast Asia Treaty Organization (SEATO), **759**

Southwest
Exploration of, 74 (map), 75, 275, 276, 277 (map), 278 (map)
Frontier in, 284
Indians in, **30,** 49, 50, **274,** 275, 448 (map)
In Mexican War, 292 (map), 293, 296 (map), 297
Ranches in, 454, **455,** 457
In World War II, 706
See also specific states

Soviet Union. See Russia

Space explorations, **724,** 725, 740, **741**

Spain
Adams-Onís Treaty, 238 (map), 240

Colonies in Latin America, 95, 96, 99, 550, 553
Conquest of Indians, 34, **38, 53,** 60, 61, 61 (map), **62–65,** I 130–132, 275
Exploration of New World, 74 (map), 75, 76, 105
Possessions in South and Southwest, **64,** 65, 188 (map), 189, 196, 233, 238 (map)
Spanish Civil War, **678, 679,** 680
Spanish-American War
Cuban revolt, 557
Philippines taken, **540, 541**
Preparations for war, 560
Santiago, battle of, 560, 562
Sinking of the *Maine,* **558,** 559
U.S. possessions gained by, I 522–525, 551 (map), 562
Springfield, Illinois, 315 (map), 794 (map)
Springfield, Massachusetts, **196, 197**
Stafford, Tom, **741**
Stalin (stä′lĭn), Joseph, 674, 681, 751
Stalingrad (stäl′ĭn gräd), battle of, **710,** 711 (map)
Stamp Act, **150, 151,** 155, 176, **177**
Stamp Act Congress, 150
Standard Oil Company, 438, 439, **502,** 503
Standing Bear, Chief, I 23–24
Stanton, Elizabeth Cady, **321**
States
Admission of, 195, 196
First election under Constitution, 212, 213
Rights, development of, 196, 197, 199, 200, 201, 202, 205, 208
Sectional problems, 352–353
See also Constitution
Statue of Liberty, 467, 625
Steamboat, **306,** 307, 310, **311,** 313, 314, **315**
Steel, 437, 442, **460,** 498, 617
See also Industry, Natural Resources
Stephens, Uriah, 496
Steuben, Baron Friedrich von, 180, **181**
Stevens, Thaddeus, **210**
Stimson, Henry L., 668, 670, 677, 681
Stock market, 640, **641,** 656
See also Business, Depression of 1929
Stockton, Robert F., 293, I 332
Stokes, Carl, 736, **737**
Stone, Chuck, I 24–25
Stowe, Harriet Beecher, **354**
Strikes, 320, 459, **496–501,** 655
See also Labor
Strong, Josiah, I 22–23
Stuyvesant (stī′və sənt), Peter, 72
Submarines
Fulton and, 310, **311**
Warfare, 581, 583, 586, 701, 718
Suburbs, 485, 613, 618, **619,** 726, **727, 730, 731**
See also Cities
Suez Canal, 710, 711 (map)
Suffragettes, 320, **321**
Sugar, 72, 79, **94,** 96, 104 (map), 108 (map), 109, 270, 271 (map), 347, 532, 536
Sumner, Charles, I 422
Sumter, Fort, 366, **367,** 368
Supreme Court
Powers of, 200, 202, 209, **210,** 211
See also specific cases, System of Checks and Balances

Sutter, John A., 298
System of Checks and Balances, 201, 204, 208–211
Szilard (sē′lärd′), Leo, 721

T

Taiwan (tī′wän′), 754, 757 (map)
Tallmadge Plan, 357, 358
Tammany Hall, 491
Taney (tô′nē), Roger B., **360**
Tanks, 586, **587,** 709, **710,** 711, **712,** 713
Tannenberg, battle of, 578, 583 (map)
Tariffs, 200, 322, 323, 352–353, 536, 557, 593, 594, 665, 670
Tarleton (tärl′tən), Banastre, **184**
Taxation
In Articles of Confederation, 196
Business and, 567, 615
On Colonies, **150, 151,** 152, 155
Constitution on, 199, 200, 202
Income tax, 504, 510
John Jay and, 223
In metropolitan areas, 731
Pollution and, I 777
On slaves, 199
In South, 348, 462
Taylor, Zachary, 292 (map), **293,** 294, 796
Technology
Agriculture and, 270, 271, **452–456,** 740
Colonial, 112, **113, 116,** 118, **119**
In communications, 283, 444, 725
Cultural change and, 745–748
Electrical, 422, 444, 464, 477, 486, 725
Environment and, I 11–18, I 688–691, I 694–697, 743 (graph)
Indian, 34–37, **38,** 39, 40, 41, 42, 43
Industrial Revolution and, 436–447, **457–459,** 460, **461, 462, 588,** 589, 699, 707, **708,** 718
Medieval European, 54–59
Military, **577–582, 585,** 586, **587, 588,** 589, 699, 707, **708,** 718, **720,** 721, 722
Poverty and, I 601–602, 744
Space, 724, 725, 740, **741**
In transportation, 300 (map), 301, **306,** 307, **308,** 309, **310,** 313, 314, 314 (map), 315 (map), 445 (map), 447, 564, 565, 617
Telegraph, 283, 444
Teller, Edward, 721
Teller Amendment, 560, 562
Temperance movement, 321
Tenements, I 432, 468, 472, 473, **479, 480, 481**
See also Ghettoes
Tennessee
In Civil War, 367 (map), 372, 372 (map), 387, 387 (map), 388
Negroes in, 413, 736 (graph)
Reconstruction in, 404 (map)
Scopes trial, 626, **627**
Settlement of, 257, 262 (map), 263, 288
Transportation in, 314 (map), 315 (map), 445 (map)
T.V.A. in, 652 (map)
In U.S.: in 1853, 296 (map); in 1970, 794 (map)
Tennessee Valley Authority (TVA), 652 (map), 653, 654

Territorial Expansion
Adams-Onis Treaty, 238 (map), 240
Alaska, purchase of, 535
Debate on, I 330–336
Frontier: across the Alleghenies, 262 (map), 263; across the West, 276, 277 (map), 278 (map); opening of territories, 195 (map), 196, 197, **450,** 451, 452
Gadsden Purchase, 296 (map), 297
Guadalupe Hidalgo, Treaty of, 294, 296 (map), 297
Hawaii, annexation of, 536
Louisiana Purchase, 233, 234, 235 (map)
Possessions gained in Spanish-American War, 562
Texas, 291
Texas
Annexation of, 290, 291, 296 (map), 297
Cattle ranches in, 454, 455 (map), 456
In Civil War, 367 (map)
Dust Bowl in, **644,** 645
Exploration of, 74 (map)
Ku Klux Klan in, 623
Oil strikes, **443**
Transportation in, 445 (map)
In U.S.: in 1845, 296 (map); in 1970, 794 (map)
Texas War for Independence
Alamo, battle of, 284, **286, 287**
Lone Star Republic, 288, **289**
San Jacinto, battle of, 288, **289,** 292 (map)
Textile Industry, 317, **318, 319,** 441, **460**
Third World, 764
Thoreau (**thôr**′ō *or* thə **ro**′), Henry David, 257, 365
Thornton, William, 227
Tilden, Samuel J., 404
Tilley, James, **110,** 111
Tillman, Ben, **410,** 411
Tobacco, 69, 79, 99, 104 (map), 105, 109, 118, **119, 120,** 121, 270, 347, **446,** 460
See also Industries, Plantations
Tobin, Richard L., I 247–248
Tojo (**tō**′jō), Hideki, **702**
Tom Thumb, **312,** 313
Tories, 175, 176, **177,** 182, **184, 185,** 189
Toussaint L'Ouverture (to͞o **săn**′ lo͞o vĕr **tür**′), Pierre, **96,** 234
Townshend Acts, 152, 155, 157
Tracy, Benjamin, 539
Trade
Clipper ships, 279, 300 (map), 301
Colonial, 70, **71, 72,** 104 (map), 118, 119, 122, 150, 157
Expansion and, I 522–525
In Latin America, **557,** 668
In Pacific, **528–533, 538–545,** 677
River, **306,** 307, 310, 350, **351**
Triangular, 108 (map), 109
World War I and, 581; post World War I, 662, **664,** 665, 665 (graph), 680
See also Business, Latin America, Slavery
Trade Agreements Act, 670
Trail of Tears, 273
Transportation
Automobile, **447,** 459, 616, 617, 618, 728
Canals, **308,** 309, 315 (map), I 330–331
City, 464, **465,** 474, **475**
Clipper ships, 300 (map), 301
Frontier, **260, 261,** 262 (map), 263, 276, 277 (map), 278 (map), 455 (map)
Railroads, **312,** 313, 314, 314 (map), 315 (map), I 334, 442, 444, 445, 445 (map)
Steamboats, 310, **311, 346,** 347, 350, **351**
See also Airplanes, Cities, Panama Canal, Railroads
Travis, William, 287
Treaty of Brest-Litovsk, 578, 583 (map)
Treaty of Ghent, 239
Treaty of Greenville, 266
Treaty of Guadalupe Hidalgo (gwä′*th*ä **lo͞o**′pā ē ***th*äl**′gō), 294, 297
Treaty of Paris, I 524
Treaty of Versailles (vər **sī**′ *or* vĕr **sī**′), 592–596, 661, 675, 678
Trenton, battle of, **168, 174,** 175, 179 (map)
Triangle Fire, 495
Triangular Trade, 108 (map), 109
Tripoli, war with, **232,** 233
Trotsky (**trŏt**′skē), Leon, 672
Truman, Harry S., **210,** I 601–602, 721, 722, **756,** 758, 796 (graph)
Truman Doctrine, **753,** 754
Trumbull, John, **164**
Trusts
Creation of, **502,** 503
Regulation of, 503, 504, **508, 509,** 510, 589, 615
Tubman, Harriet, 356
Tunisia, 710, 711 (map)
Turkey, 578, 583 (map), 752 (map), 753
Turner, Frederick Jackson, I 254–255
Turner, Nat, 356
Tuskegee (tŭs **kē**′gī) Institute, 414, **415, 416**
Twain, Mark, 307, 482, 543
Tweed, William Marcy (Boss) **490, 491**

U

Udall, Stewart, I 13
Uncle Tom's Cabin (Stowe), **354**
Unemployment
In Depression of 1929, **636,** 637, 640, 642, **643,** 645, **646, 647**
Minorities, 621, 738
New Deal programs and, 649, **650, 651**
Technology and, I 10, 744, **745**
See also Business, Industry, Poverty
Union of Soviet Socialist Republics, 673
See also Russia
United Auto Workers, 497, **654**
United Fruit Company, **566,** 567
United Nations, 756, 760, 767, **768, 769**
United Nations Educational, Scientific, and Cultural Organization (UNESCO), 769, 770
United States Housing Authority, 650, 653
Urban League, 413, I 425
Urban renewal, 728, **729**
Utah
Compromise of 1850, 358 (map), 359
Exploration of, 276, 277 (map)
Indians in, 448 (map)
Mormons in, 279
Transportation in, 445 (map)
In U.S. (1970), 794 (map)
See also West
Utopias, 321

V

Valley Forge, battle of, 176, **177,** 179 (map), 180
Van Buren, Martin, 290, 327, 796
Vanderbilt, Cornelius, 301, 554, **555**
Veblen, Thorstein, 482
Venezuela, 569
Veracruz (vĕr′ə **kro͞oz**′), battle of, 292 (map), 294
Vermont
In Civil War, 367 (map)
Roosevelt, F. D., and vote in, 657
Transportation in, 315 (map)
In U.S.: in 1853, 296 (map); in 1970, 794 (map)
See also Colonies, New England
Verrazano (vĕr′ə **zä**′nō), Giovanni da, 66 (map)
Versailles, Treaty of, 592–596, 661, 675, 678
Vespucci (vĕs **po͝ot**′chē), Amerigo, 60
Vetoes, 209, 322, 324, 547
Vicksburg, battle of, 372, 385, **386,** 387 (map), 388
Viet Cong, 760, **762,** 763
Vietnam War, I 604–605, **724,** 725, 760, **762,** 763, 765
Villa (**vē**′yä), Francisco ("Pancho"), **570, 571,** 572
Vincennes (vĭn **sĕnz**′), battle of, 180, **181,** 182 (map)
Virginia
In Civil War, 367 (map), 372, 372 (map), **373, 376, 384,** 385, 387 (map), 390, 391, 391 (map), **392,** 393
Colonial, **68,** 69, 79, 99, 102, 104 (map), 105, 118, **119, 120, 121, 122, 123,** 124, **125,** 126, 146, 150, 155
Frontier in, I 252–255, 263
Negro voter registration in, 736 (graph)
Ratification of Constitution, 201
Reconstruction in, 404 (map)
In Revolution, 180, 185 (map), **186, 187,** 188, (map)
State legislature, 207, 230
Transportation in, 314 (map), 315 (map), 445 (map)
TVA in, 652 (map)
In U.S. (1970), 794 (map)
See also South
Virginia City, Nevada, 457
Virgin Islands, 535, 551 (map)
Vote
Amendments: 14th and 15th, 399, 400; 19th, 631
Articles of Confederation on, 196
Constitution and, 205, 206
First election, 213
Lowered voting age, 748, 793
Reconstruction and southern states, 398, 400, 404 (map)
See also Civil Rights, Segregation, Voting Rights Act
Voting Rights Act, 736

W

Wagner Act, 654
Wake Island, I 522-523, 716 (map), 717, 756
Walker, David, 354, 356
Walker, Joe, 276, 277 (map)
Walker, William, 555
Wall Street, 508, 510
Waltham, Massachusetts, 319
War Industries Board, 589
War Labor Board, 584
Warner, Charles Dudley, 482
War of 1812, 236, 237, 238, 239, 240
Warren, Earl, 705
Washington, 445 (map), 448 (map), 452, 794 (map)
  See also Oregon Territory, West
Washington, Booker T., 397, 414-420
Washington, George, 164, 166, 168, 169, 172-180, 185-187, 198, 199, 203, 204, 205, 212, 213, 214, 215, 220-221, 229, 796
Washington, D.C., 8, 236, 237, 239, 314 (map), 315 (map), 358, 359, 372 (map), 374, 387 (map), 391 413,
Washington Disarmament Conference, 662, 666
Wayne, "Mad Anthony," 266
Weaver, Robert, 731
Webster, Daniel, 352, 353, 358, 359
Weir (wir), John, 436
West
  Acquisition of Texas, California, and Oregon, 282-304, 292 (map)
  Conservation in, 458, 459, 460
  Exploration of, 70, 74, 75, 76
  Frontier, I 252-255, 256-280, 262 (map), 277 (map) 278
  Income table, I 428
  Industry, 452-457, 459
  Louisiana Purchase, 233, 234, 235 (map)
  Opening of territories, 194, 195, 195 (map), 196, 450, 451, 452
  Sectionalism, 229, 344, 350, 351, 352, 353
  Transportation and, 307, 309, 314 (map), 315 (map), I 330-331, I 334, 445 (map), 455 (map)
  See also Natural Resources, specific states
West Virginia

622, 725, 734

Y

Yellowstone National Park, 459
Yorktown, battle of, 182 (map), 186, 187
Yoruba (yō'roo bä), 80, 85
Yosemite National Park, 459
Young, John, 741
Young, Whitney, I 425-427, 736
Youth movement, I 16, I 690-691, 746, 747
Yugoslavia, 701, 711 (map) (map), 752

Z

Zapata (sä pä'tä), Emiliano, 571
Zenger, John Peter, I 243
Zeppelin, Count Ferdinand von, 586
Zeppelins, 586

Armistice, 591
Argonne Forest, 582, 583 (map)
Allied Powers, 577, 583 (map)
World War I
World Health Organization (WHO), 769
Works Progress Administration (WPA), 630, 651
Worcester v. Georgia, 209
Woodstock Rock Festival, 746, 747
  In science, 741
  Reformers, 321
  In peace movements, 580, 666
  In 1920's, 612, 613, 630, 631, 632
  19th Amendment, 631
  In industry, 317, 318, 319, 496, 575, 584, 588, 706, 707
  In Cabinet, 654, 655
Women
Wolfe, James, 148, 149
  See also West
  In U.S.: in 1853, 296 (map); in 1970, 794 (map)
  Transportation in, 314 (map), 315 (map), 445 (map)
  Settlement of, 195, 195 (map), 196
  Reform in, 507
  Industry and, 350, 464
  Indians and, 273, 448 (map)
  Exploration of, 70
  In Civil War, 367 (map)
Wisconsin
Winthrop, John, 106
Williams, Roger, 106
Wilson, Woodrow, 510, I 513-514, 570-572, 581-582, 591-595, 596, I 599-600, 672, 796
Willamette (wĭl ăm'ĕt) River, 278 (map)
Wilkins, Roy, 736
Wilderness, battle of, 390, 391
Wigner, Eugene, 721
Whitney, Eli, 270, 271, 317
Whitman, Walt, 283, I 334, 347, 394, 437
Whitman, Marcus, 279
Whiskey Rebellion, 223, 224, 225, I 242
Wheat, 452-453
Weyler, Valeriano, 559
Whigs, 290, 294, 323, 327, 360, 531
  See also Virginia
Union occupies, 372
In U.S. (1970), 794 (map)
Strikes in, 497
  365
John Brown's raid in, 363, 364,
Daniel Boone in, 263

Central Powers, 577, 583 (map)
Espionage Acts in, I 244-245, 584
Germany defeated, 582, 591
New weapons, 579, 580, 581, 586, 587
Organizing for, 582, 584, 585
Production during, 588, 589
Treaty of Versailles, 592-596, 661, 675, 678
U.S. enters the war, 580, 581, 582
World War II
Allied invasion of Italy, 712, 713
Atomic bomb, 720, 721, 722
Axis victories, 700, 701
Background of, 672-682
Battle of the Bulge, 714
El Alamein, battle of, 710
In Europe, 710-716
Home front, 706, 707
Minorities during, 704, 705
Pacific war, 716 (map), 716-719
Pearl Harbor, 702, 703
Prosperity during, 708, 709
V-E Day, 715
Wright brothers, 586
Wyoming
  Exploration of, 276, 277 (map)
  Settlement of, 278, 279
  Transportation in, 445 (map)
  In U.S. (1970), 794 (map)
  See also West